# WASHINGTON MERRY-GO-ROUND

# WASHINGTON MERRY-GO-ROUND

## THE DREW PEARSON DIARIES, 1960–1969

### DREW PEARSON

Edited and with an introduction by Peter Hannaford

Foreword by Richard Norton Smith

POTOMAC BOOKS

*An imprint of the University of Nebraska Press*

∞

Library of Congress Cataloging-in-Publication Data

Pearson, Drew, 1897–1969.
Washington merry-go-round: the Drew Pearson
diaries, 1960–1969 / Drew Pearson; edited and with an
introduction by Peter Hannaford; foreword by Richard
Norton Smith.
pages   cm
ISBN 978-1-61234-693-9 (hardback: alk. paper)
ISBN 978-1-61234-742-4 (epub)
ISBN 978-1-61234-743-1 (mobi)
ISBN 978-1-61234-713-4 (pdf)
1. Pearson, Drew, 1897–1969—Diaries.
2. United States—Politics and government—1953–1961.
3. United States—Politics and government—1961–1963.
4. United States—Politics and government—1963–1969.
I. Hannaford, Peter, editor. II. Title.
PN4874.P38A3 2015
070.92—dc23
2015009042

Set in Lyon by M. Scheer.
Designed by Rachel Gould.

# CONTENTS

# ILLUSTRATIONS

# FOREWORD

*Richard Norton Smith*

His name is largely forgotten today, but for the middle third of the twentieth century, from Herbert Hoover and the Bonus Army to Richard Nixon's Silent Majority, Drew Pearson enjoyed unrivaled journalistic influence and visibility. As many as sixty million Americans began their day with his Washington Merry-Go-Round column, a readership far outstripping that of the Olympian Walter Lippmann or gossipy Walter Winchell. A one-man media conglomerate, Pearson spilled official secrets in best-selling books long before Bob Woodward was born. Though he gained no more than a foothold in the infant medium of television, he dominated the radio airwaves via the ABC network. And when Hollywood in 1951 needed an instantly recognizable face to combat the on-screen hysteria gripping Washington in the science fiction classic *The Day the Earth Stood Still*, the role inevitably went to Drew Pearson.

His casting made even more sense if the film is seen as a metaphor for the contemporary panic sweeping American politics, coming not from outer space but wherever Sen. Joseph R. McCarthy (R-WI) set up shop to peddle his highly personal brand of Cold War paranoia. That "Tail-Gunner Joe" should have Pearson for a nemesis was hardly surprising, given the columnist's left-of-center politics and open disdain for McCarthy's red-baiting allies on the House Un-American Activities Committee. Though himself a former Pearson source, McCarthy invited attacks from the powerful columnist after he went public with claims the State Department under Secretary Dean Acheson was riddled with Communist agents.

Here was one merry-go-round McCarthy was eager to get off, though not before settling scores with his journalistic tormentor. The opportunity presented itself the night of December 12, 1950, when the junior senator from Wisconsin encountered Pearson and his wife, Luvie, at Washington's posh Sulgrave Club. "How long are they going to let you stay out of jail?" Pearson goaded McCarthy, who did his talking with his knee, swiftly planted in Pearson's groin. For good measure he slapped the columnist to the ground. Adding to the surreality of the scene, it was at this juncture that then California senator Richard Nixon suddenly appeared in the self-professed role of Quaker peacemaker. Declaring McCarthy's fisticuffs "about as effective as his senatorial behavior," Pearson sued the pugnacious lawmaker. McCarthy took advantage of the legal immunity of the Senate floor to denounce Pearson as the "sugar-coated voice of Russia." For good measure he called for a boycott of Pearson's radio sponsor, the Adam Hat Company. The hatmaker promptly canceled its $5,000-a-week contract with Pearson, perfectly illustrating McCarthy's power to intimidate in the prevailing climate of fear stirred by his allegations.

It would take more than Joe McCarthy or a spineless radio sponsor to silence Drew Pearson. As a child, he had emulated his father, a professor of English and public speaking, who converted to the Society of Friends as a newly recruited faculty member at Swarthmore College. Pacifist by faith, in print Drew Pearson was every inch the Fighting Quaker—and thoroughly bipartisan in his willingness to challenge the most powerful figures in the land. Case in point: annoyed by Pearson's demands for an Allied second front in Europe to help alleviate pressure on Stalin's Red Army, Franklin Roosevelt called the offending columnist "a chronic liar." George Patton's reaction can be imagined after Pearson exposed the slap heard round the world and the temperamental general was forced to apologize for striking a shell-shocked soldier.

In the decided minority of Americans who didn't like Ike, Pearson repeatedly tried to make an issue out of the president's improvements to his Gettysburg farm with help from leading business luminaries. He had greater success in nailing White House chief of staff Sherman Adams over his friendship with a shady New England industrialist. The Kennedys sued Pearson over his assertion that JFK didn't write the Pulitzer Prize–winning *Profiles in Courage*. Even his own protégé and eventual successor, Jack Anderson, blamed Pearson for hounding Secretary of Defense James Forrestal into leaping to his death from the sixteenth floor of Bethesda Naval Hospital.

Half a century after these diary entries were penned, it is easy to portray Pearson as a forerunner of modern cable news, as thinly sourced, and just as blatantly partisan. When Lyndon Johnson's long-serving, long-suffering assistant Walter Jenkins was arrested in a Washington men's room by plainclothes police in October 1964, Pearson's immediate reaction was to suspect a setup by Republicans. His investigators quickly secured an affidavit to this effect, and Pearson himself prepared columns exposing other prominent homosexuals who had served in earlier administrations, only to have his flagship paper, the *Washington Post*, refuse to print them.

Privately, he grumbled that the fix was in. After all, hadn't FBI director J. Edgar Hoover ... *ahem* ... sent Jenkins a bouquet of flowers and sympathetic card? It is at just such moments that Pearson's unexpurgated diaries resemble nothing so much as raw FBI files—a well-spiced mulligan stew of whispered confidences, exaggerated claims, and irresistible gossip. His grudges did not end at the grave. Thirty years after he effectively blackmailed a litigious Gen. Douglas MacArthur into dropping a libel suit with some florid love letters the not-so-old soldier had written to his Eurasian mistress, Pearson observed MacArthur's passing with a series of columns exposing the general's alleged strategic blunders in Korea. (This was not so low a blow as it might appear, since it was Pearson who had first gained access to the same top secret intelligence about China's aggressive instincts that MacArthur had chosen to ignore.)

At his best Pearson displayed the fearlessness that is the cornerstone of journalistic credibility. At the same time he brought to his work a sense of history that is almost wholly missing from today's 24/7 news cycle. With good reason he saw himself as a whistle-blowing successor to the original muckrakers, those Progressive Era reformers whose dissatisfaction with the status quo helped fuel an expansion of economic and political democracy. For someone in the news business, he possessed a rare ability to step back from the headlines and to connect the historical dots. In the midst of the 1964 presidential campaign, putting aside the latest polls, the Jenkins scandal, the simultaneous overthrow of Soviet leader Nikita Khrushchev, a Labor Party victory in Britain, and the explosion of Red China's first nuclear device, Pearson rummaged through his cultural scrapbook for insight on a bitterly divided Middle East.

"I always remember what Harry Truman once told me about his talk with the late Ibn Saud, king of Saudi Arabia. Truman advised him, 'Why don't you get together with the Jews? After all, you're all related, even if the Jews do call you bastards.'

"Truman said that Saud laughed at this and replied, 'Yes, Abraham did kick us out into the desert.'"

Journalism is about nothing if not perspective. Unfortunately, much of what passes for Washington reporting in 2014 is more suited to the racetrack than the White House. In its preoccupation with the tawdry, the tactical, and the trivial, it rarely gazes beyond the sixty-nine square miles of the District of

Columbia. Pearson, his name synonymous with official Washington, refused to become a prisoner of the Beltway. As a youthful member of the American Friends Service Committee, he had firsthand experience of the war-ravaged Balkans. In the 1920s he supported himself by hitting the Australian lecture circuit and by syndicating his interviews with "Europe's Twelve Greatest Men." He reported from China and Cuba, from the Geneva Naval Conference and the Paris of Hemingway and Bricktop. His extensive travels gave his pronouncements an authority that was anything but parochial. They made him skeptical of "the semicolon men in the State Department" who were forever trying to frustrate presidential initiatives aimed at moving beyond Cold War suspicion. As early as 1965, he became convinced that the United States should withdraw its forces from South Vietnam. Meanwhile, his suspicions of the CIA foreshadow nothing so much as our own continuing debate over the national security state.

It seems a shame that Pearson, who died on September 1, 1969, should have been denied the revelations of Watergate. That scandal was to be entrusted to a much younger, more telegenic band of journalistic sleuths. It's harder still to imagine Pearson in a world without newspapers, though one suspects he would somehow find a substitute to spark watercooler debate while holding the privileged and powerful to account. In the meantime we have been gifted with this great, rich sampling of Washington crimes and capers, faithfully recorded by a connoisseur of official folly yet one who never surrendered to mere cynicism. The timing could not be better. Nor can I imagine a more suitable political and media climate in which to experience, if only vicariously, the gratifications of muckraking journalism as practiced by a loving critic and true patriot.

# ACKNOWLEDGMENTS

Foremost to be acknowledged is my friend of many years Tyler Abell, whose determination to complete the publication of this volume of the *Drew Pearson Diaries* made the project a reality. Tyler's growing-up years were in the household of his mother, Luvie Moore Abell Pearson, and stepfather, Drew Pearson. Many of the personages and names in the diaries were well known to him from childhood. As an adult, Tyler was no stranger to Washington politics and public service. He worked on Lyndon Johnson's campaigns in 1960 and 1964. He served as assistant postmaster general of the United States and in the Johnson White House as U.S. chief of protocol. He also had a successful law career. Upon Drew Pearson's death in 1969, Tyler began going over his diaries with an idea toward making them part of the public record. *Drew Pearson Diaries: 1949–1959* was published in 1974. Tyler intended to follow up soon with a volume of the diaries of Pearson's last decade, the sixties, but the demands of office and his career intervened. In late 2011 he asked me if I would edit those years, and I agreed.

My thanks go to my literary agent, Diane Nine, for her patience and professionalism; to the team at the University of Nebraska Press's Potomac Books, especially acquisitions editor Alicia Christensen; Marguerite Boyles, humanities editorial assistant; Joeth Zucco, senior project editor; and copyeditor Elizabeth Gratch. Finally, but not least, to my wife, Irene, for her constant encouragement, support, and love.

# EDITOR'S NOTE

As anyone who writes a journals or diary knows, each entry is not proofread, edited, or intended for publication. When someone is proxy to such compelling times and people as Drew Pearson, however, there comes a time when publication of personal experiences, opinions, and reflections is imperative to understanding our history. It should be noted in assembling this volume, I have edited Pearson's diary for felicity and present it in his wording—if not in all cases the precise capitalization, spelling, or punctuation he used—in the spirit, if not the exact letter, of the original. In doing so, it is my intention to allow the reader to appreciate the memorable and meaningful content.

# INTRODUCTION

From the 1940s until late 1969 there were two words no one involved in public life in Washington wanted to hear if they had anything to hide: *Drew Pearson*. For almost three decades Pearson was the most widely read, most listened to journalist in America. He chronicled the political and public policy news of the nation, but he did much more. Deeply dedicated to honest government, he was a tenacious digger of information to uncover corruption and self-dealing by those in influential positions in both business and government. He was practicing investigative journalism long before the term gained widespread usage following the Watergate revelations in 1974. Along with policy makers in the White House and Congress, he avidly promoted issues he believed would promote better government and world peace. Although not a pacifist, Pearson's Quaker background honed his desire to find peaceful solutions to problems. He became a back-channel conduit of important messages between international leaders of the day with the aim of supporting U.S. bilateral policies that he believed could help avoid the danger of a nuclear war.

Drew Pearson was a virtual perpetual motion machine. In his late sixties he maintained a daily schedule that would have impressed someone half his age. Pearson's daily newspaper column was the most widely published and read in the nation. He augmented his written work with regular radio and television broadcasts. He seemed to be constantly on the go, giving speeches far and wide. In the process he picked up useful information about the mood of the country. Pearson became a confidant of presidents—especially Lyndon Johnson—congressional leaders, media moguls, political insiders, and dozens of unsung sources of tips and rumors that led him to stories. In addition, he made numerous overseas trips to interview and exchange views with world leaders. He also made time to head the Washington chapter of Big Brothers, an organization whose purpose was to get local business and professional leaders to become mentors to urban boys headed for trouble.

Blessed with a near-perfect memory, he rarely took notes during his interviews but dictated complete conversations shortly afterward. While he minced no words in his columns about the wrongdoing he was uncovering, he saved his sharpest assessments of some public figures for his private diaries.

## BIOGRAPHICAL SUMMARY

Born December 13, 1897, in Evanston, Illinois, Andrew Russell Pearson was the first of four children of Paul M. and Edna Wolfe Pearson. In 1902 the family moved to Pennsylvania, where Paul had accepted a position as professor of public speaking at Swarthmore College.

In those days, before mass media, the Chautauqua circuit served as a kind of intellectual traveling circus. During the summers Paul ran a circuit on the Eastern Seaboard, featuring speakers and lantern slide shows. At fourteen Drew began helping his father. By the time he graduated from college, he was a lecturer himself. His Chautauqua experience sharpened his appetite for hard work and his showmanship abilities.

In 1915 Pearson graduated from Exeter Academy and entered Swarthmore. There he was a good student and was a member of Phi Beta Kappa. He was on the swimming, baseball, and lacrosse teams and served as managing editor of the campus newspaper. In 1919, as class valedictorian, he spoke to his fellow graduates about the need "to make the world safe for democracy." For him this statement was not just rhetorical; it became a guiding theme throughout his life.

The United States had entered World War I two years earlier. Despite his Quaker background, Pearson was keen to put into practice his belief in Wilsonian principles of democracy and enlisted in the student officer training program. But the armistice was signed before he could be called up. So, in late summer of 1919 he signed on with the American Friends Service Committee to do two years of relief work in war-torn Serbia. There he worked on rebuilding homes and villages destroyed by the war. He also began his first diary.

On his return he taught industrial geography at the University of Pennsylvania for two years, but he had an urge to travel and write. In 1923 he set out across the United States by train, often making stops to try to interest newspaper editors in buying articles he would write along his travels. In Seattle he signed on as a seaman on a ship going to Japan. From there he went to China, Siberia, Australia, New Zealand, and India—filing dispatches all the way. On his way home he received a wire from a news syndicate asking him to do a series of interviews with "Europe's Twelve Greatest Men."

Despite the recognition he gained from this work, his dispatches did not bring in enough money, so he became a lecturer in commercial geography at Columbia University. But the academic life, despite its security, could not hold him, and in 1925 he again turned to writing and roaming. He reported on anti-foreigner strikes in China, the 1927 Geneva Naval Conference, and the 1928 Pan-American conference in Havana, and he accompanied the U.S. Secretary of State Frank Kellogg to Paris to cover the signing of the Kellogg-Briand Pact in 1930.

On a trip home he visited Washington and was invited to the home of Eleanor "Cissy" Patterson, a well-known newspaper owner. There he met her daughter, Felicia. In 1925 Felicia and Drew were married. Two years later their daughter, Ellen, was born. Despite this happy event, the marriage declined and ended in divorce in 1928. In 1936 Drew married Luvie Moore Abell, and this marriage endured for the rest of his life.

Pearson moved to Washington and in 1929 was named Washington correspondent of the *Baltimore Sun*. He and Robert S. Allen coauthored *Washington Merry-Go-Round* and *More Merry-Go-Round*—both published anonymously. When the *Sun* learned he was a coauthor, he was dismissed by the newspaper. Based on the popularity of the books, Pearson secured a contract with United Features for Allen and himself to write a syndicated newspaper column beginning in 1932. It was to become the nation's most widely syndicated political reporting column and ran until Pearson's death in 1969 (after which his longtime associate Jack Anderson took up the column until his own retirement in 2004). At its peak the column was carried by nearly a thousand newspapers and had millions of readers. In 1940 he added a radio network commentary program and, in the mid-1950s, television.

In 1947 Pearson's deep belief in world peace and democracy led him to organize the Friendship Train as a people-to-people project to help the hungry citizens of postwar Italy and France. He envisioned a single train of a few cars collecting food from people coast to coast. Instead, it grew to ten trainloads that filled two ships. Pearson accomplished this act without government involvement. It was his proudest achievement.

In 1969, his seventy-second year, his health began to decline, and he died on Labor Day, several months shy of his birthday.

# WASHINGTON MERRY-GO-ROUND

# 1960

## ANNALS

John F. Kennedy was elected president over Richard Nixon. Both wanted to be the first of their generation to lead postwar America.

Kennedy captured the imagination of the media with his humor, charm, and attractive wife. Nixon, always appearing serious, had gained many enemies among American liberals after his allegations that the State Department's Alger Hiss was a Soviet spy (corroborated years later by Soviet documents made public). Liberals also resented what they considered unfair campaign tactics in his earlier House and Senate victories.

A central question in the Kennedy-Nixon campaign was could a Catholic be elected president? The contest ultimately turned on four televised presidential debates. This was the first election in which television became the primary resource for political news. (From 1950 to 1960 the number of households with televisions increased from 11 to 88 percent.)

The first debate was seen by more than seventy million viewers. The majority of radio listeners polled felt Nixon had won, but television viewers said it was Kennedy. Kennedy won the election by just over one hundred thousand votes—one of the closest in U.S. history. Nixon voters charged that there had been vote fraud in the Chicago area, but Nixon decided against making a formal complaint.

Fifteen American scientists were honored as *Time* magazine's Person of the Year. The United States was the primary beneficiary of a surge of European scientists arriving just before and during World War II. They and their students propelled the United States to the center of scientific innovation. From 1901 to 1939 the United States had won only thirteen Nobel Prizes in chemistry, physics, and medicine. From 1940 to 1960 it won forty-one.

In February, British prime minister Harold Macmillan said in a speech about

Africa: "The wind of change is blowing through this continent. Whether we like it or not, this growth of national consciousness is a political fact." Half of the thirty-two African nations that gained independence during the decade did so in 1960.

Iran, Iraq, Kuwait, Saudi Arabia, and Venezuela founded the Organization of Petroleum Exporting Countries (OPEC) in Baghdad. At that time most of the world's oil supply was controlled by the "Seven Sisters," Western oil companies, five of them American, that were instrumental in building the industry in much of the Middle East. As soon as these countries felt capable of running their own affairs, they nationalized their petroleum fields.

The summit meeting between President Eisenhower and Soviet leader Khrushchev collapsed over the U-2 spy plane incident. (In May an American U-2 was shot down over the Soviet Union while on a reconnaissance mission. The pilot, Francis Gary Powers, survived the crash and was captured.)

Later in the year Khrushchev banged his shoe on the table at the United Nations while denouncing Western colonialism. His speech was in response to the Philippine delegation's condemnation of Soviet domination in Central and Eastern Europe.

—Ed.

# THE DIARY

SUNDAY, JANUARY 3 | Late this afternoon associate Jack Anderson called with a tip that the steel strike was about to be settled. It came indirectly from Pat Hillings, who flew back with [Vice President Richard] Nixon from California this afternoon. There's a meeting at the Carlton Hotel between the steel industry and the workers. I tried all evening to get Arthur Goldberg or Dave McDonald on the phone. They were elusive. It's obvious, however, that the strike is being settled and that Nixon has had a lot to do with it.

MONDAY, JANUARY 4 | I started the New Year journalistically by calling on the chairman of the District of Columbia Commission, Bob McLaughlin. I wanted to worm out of him the inside story of Dewey's talk with Eisenhower regarding the 1964 World's Fair, which was suddenly switched to New York from Washington. My information was that Dewey, who represents some of the important New York businessmen who will make about half a billion dollars out of the fair, came to see Ike and persuaded him to make the switch.

Eisenhower during that talk is reported to have told Dewey that he wanted Rockefeller out of the race to give a clear field for Nixon. It was not so much that Ike loves Nixon but hates Rockefeller. This, of course, press secretary Jim Hagerty has denied.

FRIDAY, JANUARY 8 | The Yugoslav ambassador came to lunch. He is a young former university professor in Belgrade who has a sympathetic understanding of American-Yugoslav relations and some fears about Russia. He thinks the Soviets are reconciled to letting Yugoslavia alone but that some of the satellites are worried over the example Yugoslavia has shown as an independent Communist state.

WEDNESDAY, JANUARY 13 | Appointment with Lyndon Johnson. To keep him from monopolizing the conversation, I took a memorandum with me on confidential strategy to defeat Nixon. I started [by] telling him what was in the memo. I then urged that he read it.

If the Democrats want to win in November, I argued, they've got to do their main battling in the spring. When tempers get hot in the fall, people discount the charges. On the other hand, some quiet investigations into certain Republican operations without ballyhooing them as political investigations could strike some paydirt regarding Nixon.

THURSDAY, JANUARY 14 | To the Turkish embassy for dinner. Sat beside Mrs. Imbrie, whose husband, then vice consul, was killed by a Persian mob near Teheran some years ago, causing quite an incident. She has not improved with age.

FRIDAY, JANUARY 15 | NEW YORK—Lunched with Bob Kintner at NBC. He tells me Frank Stanton is so close to Lyndon that Stanton issued his statement on TV not from New Orleans, as publicly stated, but from Lyndon's ranch. Stanton expects to be secretary of defense in a Johnson administration. Returned on the midnight train to Washington.

SATURDAY, JANUARY 16 | Bill Benton came in immediately following a breakfast with Adlai Stevenson and Wayne Morse. Morse had told Adlai that he, Morse, had to get into the Oregon primary and some of the other primaries, but it would be a stopgap operation, and his delegates would be turned over to Adlai in the end. Wayne has been causing a lot of trouble among the liberals.

Benton is having a luncheon today for Adlai and a group of senators. I urged Benton to make a pitch to Magnuson to get some money for the investigation of the networks. He said he would. I called up Kefauver, Gruening, Neuberger, and [Eugene] McCarthy to try to get them to help out.

SUNDAY, JANUARY 17 | I telephoned Tom Hennings and told him that if he could filibuster for a day on his southern primaries amendment, I could probably pick up twenty-five votes for him. He said he would try to put off the amendment for a vote till Tuesday.

I then called [Senators] Neuberger, Joe Clark, and McNamara of Michigan (through his assistant) and urged them to do a little extra talking on Monday to tide the southern primary vote over until Tuesday.

MONDAY, JANUARY 18 | Lunched with the Czech ambassador at the Mayflower Hotel. This is almost revolutionary. A few years ago I called upon the then Czech ambassador at his embassy. He was secretive and unpleasant. This was during the Stalinist era. I asked whether we could send toys to the children of Czechoslovakia with the Tide of Toys Train. He did not like the idea.

Last year I lunched with the immediate predecessor of the present ambassador at a little restaurant on G Street. This time the Czechs invited me to the Mayflower ... [They] want me to go to Czechoslovakia this summer. I would like to go. I couldn't very well tell him this, but I would much rather go to Russia. There's a certain amount of jealousy between the satellite countries and Russia—which is healthy from our point of view.

TUESDAY, JANUARY 26 | Took California governor Pat Brown to lunch at the Russian embassy. En route he told me of his water troubles and the fact that the northern part of California is reneging on his program for supplying water to Southern California. He attended a White House conference yesterday with Eisenhower and Rockefeller and remarked that Rockefeller was critical of Eisenhower's do-nothing program regarding fallout and bomb shelters. Pat was also critical. "This administration just seems to be drifting," he told me. "There's no leadership. I hate to be critical because Eisenhower is such a nice fellow. He's so nice that you don't feel like leaving the White House and blasting him."

Pat told the ambassador he planned to go to Russia in April. The ambassador said he would arrange for his visit. I said that I would probably go at that time, too, and made another bid to interview Khrushchev.

[Ambassador] Menshikov complained that he couldn't go to San Francisco without special permission from the State Department. The governor countered that the Russians wouldn't allow American ambassadors to travel in Russia either. He told Menshikov he was trying to put across a water project in California to keep up with the great Siberian hydroelectric projects. He also discussed the fact that he is a Catholic and that many Catholics were against the USSR. He said that when he had welcomed Khrushchev in San Francisco, he received a letter from a Catholic bishop berating him for shaking the bloody hand of a dictator.

Brown left early to testify on the Hill. I then suggested to the ambassador the idea of a trailer caravan to Russia. He was noncommittal and suggested a Friendship Train instead. He didn't say so, but I gathered the roads in Russia would not be conducive to a friendship caravan. He also suggested that the idea would have to be reciprocal.

Tom Hennings called. The southern primary amendment passed. He reminded me that I promised to get twenty-five votes for him if he held the amendment over one day, and he said, "You got the twenty-five votes."

WEDNESDAY, JANUARY 27 | I saw Magnuson about getting some money for the Yarborough investigation. I outlined the same strategy I had given to Lyndon regarding investigations of Nixon—not aimed at him but which would culminate in some headlines. He liked the idea. He also volunteered that the money was coming up for Yarborough and he believed in starting at $50,000 and increasing the pot afterward. Maggie is a shrewd strategist.

FRIDAY, JANUARY 29 | Hubert Humphrey called to complain about my item last Sunday reporting how he had helped rescue Lyndon at the Democratic caucus from an immediate vote on whether members of the Policy Committee should be elected or not. Hubert was plaintive and said that this had hurt him in Wisconsin. Actually, I thought the column would help him because it showed he wasn't as much in the liberal corner as some people reported. He needs a little moderate and conservative strength. But Lyndon's name just doesn't set well in Wisconsin.

Dined at Tinnie Ansberry's. Joe Clark was there, together with Gale McGee and Styles Bridges. Bridges seemed surprised when I told him that I had no sympathy for Castro and thought Batista had done a pretty good job. Bridges had come from a closed-door session with Adm. Arleigh Burke over the danger of losing Guantánamo. He says that what Castro wants most is to get American intervention. Then he can scream about the imperialist USA cracking down on poor little Cuba.

**SUNDAY, JANUARY 31** | DETROIT—(After a speaking engagement.) Drove Gov. David Lawrence of Pennsylvania and Matt McCloskey, treasurer of the Democratic National Committee, to the airport.

Lawrence doesn't agree with the Marquis Childs column that Mayor Dilworth and Representative Green are going to swing Pennsylvania for Kennedy. Lawrence is for Symington. He thought Stuart made the best speech last night, with Lyndon Johnson's the poorest. Lawrence is sensitive about the difficulties of a Catholic running for high office. He pointed out that the newspapers, during his campaign, referred to the fact he would be the first Catholic governor in history, and he feels this lost him possibly 200,000 votes. Some Protestant rural counties were carried by Leader despite the fact that Leader ran far behind in the total vote.

I remarked to Lawrence that the Republicans were forging ahead partly because there was no scandal in this administration now. In '58, when he was running, there was the Sherman-Adams-Goldfine vicuna coat scandal. "The best campaign ammunition in the world is corruption," said the governor. "You can talk about everything under the sun, but there is one thing the voters understand—namely, when you point your finger at a man and call him a thief."

WASHINGTON DC—Went to a cocktail party in honor of Earle Clements. Quite a few of his old friends and Senate colleagues were there, including Lyndon. Lady Bird looked very pretty. Al Friendly remarked, "When Lyndon Johnson comes here for a cocktail party, you can be sure it's an election year."

**TUESDAY, FEBRUARY 1** | Had a long talk with Kefauver, who faces a reelection fight from Tip Taylor, former candidate for governor and an arch-segregationist. The big money in Tennessee is backing Taylor, also the big newspapers. They are trying to keep ex-governor Frank Clement out to divide opposition to Kefauver.

Estes received a phone call while I was there from someone in Tennessee wanting him to confirm the Republican nominee for U.S. marshal in Memphis. He declined to do so until he got a telegram of approval from the editor of the *Memphis Commercial Appeal*, who has been cutting his heart out editorially on the Negro issue. The editor was raised in Wisconsin but, like many Scripps-Howard papers, figures that "whipping the nigger" is a good circulation builder. The U.S. marshal is planning to appoint a Negro as his assistant, and Estes doesn't want to get murdered by the *Commercial Appeal* for approving the marshal's confirmation.

I talked to him about the proposed investigation of Justice and the Treasury regarding the Eisenhower scandals. I reported that Lyndon told me he had only two senators who could handle such a probe: Tom Hennings, who has trouble with sobriety; and Estes, who fumbles around but always comes up with the headlines and the heart of an investigation. Estes seemed surprised and pleased.

Matt McCloskey came up from Florida and is talking to some of the Gettysburg farm builders in Philadelphia to see what the facts are regarding the reportedly "free" construction of Ike's home. Tompkins, the builder, is one of the few people whose funeral Ike attended.

FRIDAY, MARCH 18 | Sen. Tom Hennings of Missouri had been absent almost a month during the civil rights debate on another of his benders and looked the worse for wear. I considered telling him that almost every senator had cursed him under his breath for his absence during the quorum calls and the filibuster—but I didn't.

I reminded Tom that about a year ago he told me that only three Democratic candidates for president had any courage: Lyndon Johnson, Hubert Humphrey, and Stevenson. I asked him whether he thought Kennedy had any courage now. The answer was a qualified affirmative. "Jack hadn't had too much experience in the past, but he's had a lot more now, and with experience you acquire confidence and courage. Jack now takes a position on some of the things you and I do which he ducked before."

I told Tom I had been in Lyndon's office when Lyndon telephoned him to tell him he wanted some important investigations made. Tom remembered the call and said he had never quite figured out what Lyndon wanted him to investigate. I told him I had been trying to get Lyndon to stage a real investigation of Republican finagling in the Justice Department and the Treasury and that Lyndon said he only had two good investigators, Kefauver and Hennings. I told Tom this election would be won not in October but right now, depending upon how the Democrats conducted themselves and especially how the Democrats bore in on Republican shenanigans.

We talked over some of his subcommittees of the Judiciary Committee to see which could handle an investigation. I said I thought he could get by Eastland with a proposal to investigate Adam Clayton Powell's operations with the Justice Department and cloak a complete investigation behind this entering wedge.

WEDNESDAY, APRIL 13 | Called on Senator Magnuson regarding the long-delayed investigation of the television networks regarding freedom of news. Before seeing him, I met with Sen. Mike Monroney, who said he would go along. This made eight votes. Mike was enthusiastic and pointed out that the networks were bombarding him and other members because he had introduced the "Adlai Stevenson Bill," requiring the network to set aside two periods each week during the election campaign for the two candidates to debate each other.

"Maggie" kept me waiting, which he doesn't usually do. Finally, I understood why. Sen. Ralph Yarborough was with him, arguing about the committee. I told Maggie that in view of the long delay he ought to give Ralph $75,000 instead of $49,000. He agreed. He said he would take the money out of his own committee funds, then go to Tom Hennings for more. He outlined to Yarborough a plan to call Truman, Stevenson, and Tom Dewey to testify on the debate proposal of Adlai.

Had a talk with Ernest Gruening. He thinks Hubert Humphrey is by all odds the best candidate and is hopeful that there will be a deadlock, which can swing votes to him. He thinks Kennedy will be knocked off, first in West Virginia and later in the convention. He thinks Lyndon can't possibly win and . . . will throw his weight to Humphrey.

I told him not to discount the power of Truman, Pauley, Dave Lawrence of Pennsylvania, and the other old pros. They are strong for Symington. We discussed Adlai, who just made a rip-roaring speech at the University of Virginia which indicated he's still in the running.

Lunched with Tom Hennings. He showed me some clippings from the *St. Louis Post-Dispatch* in which Pete Brandt took some caustic pokes at Symington as a man who doesn't make decisions and doesn't have the respect of his colleagues. Tom thinks that the *P-D* will come out against Symington. This would be a body blow.

I reviewed with Tom the idea I've been harping at—both with him and Lyndon—for a real investigation of the Justice Department and its failure to prosecute Republicans while cracking down on Democrats. Tom listened, but I made no headway. As chairman of the Rules Committee, he has not even appointed an election subcommittee to keep an eye on campaign contributions.

Tom doesn't think much of the Civil Rights Bill [of 1960]. He quoted a statement made in the Judiciary Committee and later aired on the floor when Senator Hart asked Deputy Attorney General Walsh whether the referee plan would mean that many Negroes could vote. "I'll answer that question for you," interrupted Eastman of Mississippi. "Damn few."

**THURSDAY, APRIL 14** | Magnuson wrote me that he hadn't read the column before he went into committee meeting yesterday, not realizing why the Republicans did not oppose the resolution to investigate fairness on the airways. The resolution, he said, breezed through. The column to which he referred told how the Republicans were investigating certain Democratic senators who owned TV stations and were trying to use this as blackmail to stop the Yarborough investigation.

**SUNDAY, APRIL 17** | Ernest and Margaret Cuneo came to dinner. We discussed the hopes and problems of the [Geneva] Summit Conference and whether we should go. Ernest, Margaret, Luvie, and I went to the Paris Peace Conference in 1946. Ernest, Luvie, and I went to the Geneva Summit Conference in 1955. I expect I will have to go in May, though.

The battle is going to be between the British on one side and the French and Germans on the other. Ernest thinks that if Dulles were handling things, he would side with the Germans immediately and put the British in their place. He's right. Dulles, after all, was the attorney for the bankers who put so much money into Germany prior to Hitler. Herter is more pro-British.

Behind the summit conference is the British battle to keep its prestige and superiority in Europe. The battle is being lost. Ever since the Suez war the British have been coasting downhill. They are losing Cyprus. They are losing Africa. And now they are losing Europe. Actually, the British have become an American satellite. We are not only defending the British Isles with bomber crews, but the amount of money spent by those crews is a very important support to the British economy. Last week's British abandonment of its own missile was the final admission that Britain has become an American satellite.

**TUESDAY, APRIL 19** | Cuneo called from New York to say that Sen. Prescott Bush of Connecticut wants to deny my column of last week that said he is opposed to the reappointment of William Connole, the consumer champion who opposed gas rate increases. Bush's son George is head of one of the gas companies operating in the Gulf of Mexico. Subsequently, the White House let it be known that Connole was not being reappointed.

Baron Shacklette, now an investigator for Representative Bellino, is having trouble with the investigation of highway scandals. Carmen Blatnik has taken over the Bob Kennedy investigative unit from the McClellan committee. They are a Kennedy cell and apparently intent on investigating possible opponents of Sen. Jack Kennedy for president. Shacklette went to Trenton to probe the New Jersey Highway Commission and found it to be doing an excellent job. It's under my old critic Dwight Palmer, now retired from American Cable. Shacklette reported that he could find no dishonesty, but that didn't satisfy Bellino. He has now sent for all the income tax returns of Palmer et al., apparently is determined to smear him. Shacklette says one reason is that Palmer is a friend of Drew Pearson.

Ironically, Palmer once circulated a devastating story against me saying I had received $25,000 from Clendenin Ryan for agreeing to suppress some information regarding the late James Forrestal.

Bellino is also out to get Governor Lawrence in Pennsylvania and is investigating Pat Brown in California. These two happen to be anti-Kennedy and, incidentally, both Catholics. This is the type of blackmail politics that I have suspected Kennedy of but couldn't hitherto prove.

Dined at Walter Ridder's. Met Rep. Craig Hosmer of Long Beach, a Republican who says I once defamed him. He was reasonably pleasant about it. Also met a representative of Douglas Aircraft named Tollefson, who chided me gently about being down on Douglas. I told him that whenever a newspaperman is called a liar, he is dead set to prove himself not a liar. In 1939 Douglas had called me a liar when I reported that it had sold the blueprints of the DC-4 to Japan for $1 million. Douglas had pressured the United Features syndicate into killing the column as well. Therefore, when a Senate committee showed that the DC-4 was sold by Douglas to Japan, I rubbed it in. Tollefson admitted that the DC-4 blueprints had been sold and said he didn't blame me.

Rep. Chet Holifield figures that Eisenhower will pull a "Munich" at Paris. He has to set the stage for Nixon to run on a platform of peace. "If he does what he did in Korea, it will be disastrous. He gave into the Communists in Korea without requiring the return of American war prisoners or a ban against bases in North Korea. Truman could have gotten this kind of peace any time," said Holifield.

Holifield has been pressured by Marquis Childs and Tris Coffin against going ahead with the hearing on seismographic tests for discovering A-bomb explosions. They think he is too belligerent and may upset the Geneva disarmament talks. Chet is going ahead anyway.

FRIDAY, APRIL 22 | I spent the morning interviewing Hubert Humphrey. Jack [Anderson] and I asked him some tough questions similar to those I asked Kennedy. Hubert answered them well. He looks tired, says he works until 3:00 to 4:00 a.m. writing speeches and hasn't any money to speak of. He's been scraping around trying to find enough to carry on the balance of his West Virginia campaign. When he was told he would need $75,000 to run his headquarters at the Los Angeles convention, he threw up his hands and was almost ready to quit.

We asked him about a talk with Sen. Bob Kerr. He admitted he had asked Kerr for money to help the campaign. Hubert, in turn, asked our advice as to whether he should accept it. I told him to go ahead, though Kerr is a strong Lyndon Johnson man. I told Hubert about the Bobby Kennedy cell working under Representative Blatnik and the attempt to investigate Kennedy opponents. Hubert said he would talk to Blatnik about it.

Many people have been in to see Humphrey to urge him to get out of the race, including Arthur Goldberg of the Steelworkers and Alex Rose of the Hatmakers Union.

Eric Johnston came to lunch. He's still working on peace in the Near East through his Jordan River irrigation plan. He seems to think there is a chance to get it accepted. King Hussein had dinner with him twice on his trip through the United States, and Eric thinks Jordan would come into the pact more easily than any other country except Lebanon, which is also amenable.

I told Eric that in talking to some of the Iron Curtain diplomats I discovered they figure they have two "secret weapons" at the coming summit conference: the British who demand some kind of an agreement and Nixon who must run on a platform of peace.

Eric claimed we had a couple of "secret weapons" just as potent as Khrushchev's. One is the Chinese, the other the fact Khrushchev doesn't want to strengthen East Germany. He's afraid of Germany.

On the second, he said his intelligence indicated Russia was having trouble with China and also countries around China. It was such that Moscow was dealing direct[ly] with the Communist parties in Burma, Vietnam, and other areas, which meant that it does not trust the Chinese Reds. Normally, it would work through them.

On that point the last thing Khrushchev wants is a united Germany. We don't want it. De Gaulle doesn't want it, and many Germans don't want it. Part of Eric's information comes from Central Intelligence but some from his own motion picture people around the world.

**SATURDAY, APRIL 23** | We went to the de Gaulle reception. We arrived right on the button, four thirty, and were ushered in with almost no delay. I was surprised when de Gaulle recognized my name and shook hands very cordially. "I remember you," he said. "I know you. I've heard a great deal about you." I said, "Good luck to you on your mission here." He replied, "Good luck to you."

I was a little surprised because the last experience I had with de Gaulle was in Paris in 1953, when I had asked for an interview and was told that I could see him but not for quotation. I then asked if I could have a photographer present to take our picture together. The answer was no. I then told his aide that there was no use in my wasting his time. However, at five fifteen, about fifteen minutes after the appointed time for the interview, his aide called and said, "Mr. Pearson, where are you?" I replied, "I told you that since the general didn't want to be quoted nor to have his picture taken, there was no use in my wasting his time."

Later some of my French newspaper friends heard about the story, and the Paris press the next day carried big headlines, "Pearson Refuses to See de Gaulle." De Gaulle, however, either didn't remember the incident or was bending over backward to be cordial. He looked well and has a gracious and charming personality.

I thought back to the war days, when every one was jumping on him, including Roosevelt, Churchill, and Cordell Hull. I was among the few then who stood up for him consistently and vigorously. I have been somewhat critical in recent years, but to look back over the long record of his courage and foresight, he is truly one of the great men of this time.

**FRIDAY, MAY 6** | I have been unable to write anything intelligent regarding the American plane which Khrushchev says was shot down over Russia. I asked Jack Anderson to talk to the Pentagon about it to try to get an inside story. As a result, I sent out an "immediate release" this afternoon stating that the plane was on a weather reconnaissance flight to test the jet stream in the higher altitudes and that high air force officials didn't believe the plane was shot down but had to land of its own accord because of engine or oxygen trouble.

**SATURDAY, MAY 7** | Khrushchev has now announced to the Supreme Soviet that he has captured the pilot of the "spy" plane, an ex–air force lieutenant, Francis Gary Powers, from Georgia. He has confessed he was instructed to fly from Pakistan to Norway. He was equipped with all the paraphernalia of espionage, including photographs; camera equipment; a poison needle for suicide; gold francs, which Khrushchev described as wrapped in cellophane according to the "cultured American way"; seven ladies' rings, which Khrushchev speculated were to lead Martian ladies astray. There's no doubt from the detailed description given by Khrushchev that he has the pilot of the plane. This makes my immediate release story giving the air force's alibi look pretty bad.

**SUNDAY, MAY 8** | Sent out a special column on the U-2 plane trying to catch up with the "immediate release." The new one said that Central Intelligence had been in charge of these spy operations and that very few people knew about them—even inside the government. I questioned whether Secretary of State Herter or even Eisenhower knew about this flight just before the conference, for it was bound to cause trouble when Eisenhower got to Paris. Khrushchev had said in talking to the Supreme Soviet that he was sure Eisenhower had not known of this flight. Knowing Eisenhower and his refusal to pay much attention to the functioning of government, I think Khrushchev was right.

(Flight delayed from New York to Berlin due to rain.)

We left early the next morning on Pan American for London and Düsseldorf, arriving at 1:00 a.m., after an all-day flight. No hotel rooms and no reservation on to Berlin early in the morning. We finally drove out to Duisburg and got rooms in a clean, old-fashioned German hotel, without baths. The next morning through good luck we got on the 7:30 a.m. plane to Berlin, arriving there only about twenty hours late. I found that Mayor Willy Brandt had been looking for me the day before because of a cable received from the German embassy in Washington. I saw him that night at a buffet supper given by Charles Blackman, information officer of the U.S. embassy.

Brandt said he was willing to run for chancellor to replace Adenauer. He belongs to the opposition Socialist Party, though his general views are about the same as Adenauer's. He said he would run if urged—under certain conditions. The election is about a year from now, but it has already started with a bang in Germany.

I asked Brandt why the East German government was pushing farm collectivization just before the summit meeting and thereby causing so many refugees to flee to West Berlin. Brandt's answer was that Ulbricht, the top man in East Germany, is a stern Stalinist and wants to purge anyone who is not a good Communist. He wants to demonstrate that he can out-Stalin Khrushchev, who has gone soft on capitalism. Brandt added that the East Germans wanted to please China.

I called Brandt's attention to a press conference statement by Eisenhower that he wasn't worried about a blockade of Berlin because there was so much trade between West Berlin and East Germany. Brandt said he was puzzled by this because there was practically no trade with East Germany. Housewives come over occasionally to shop, but there's little more than that.

He said he wasn't as much worried about a blockade as in '49 because Khrushchev is smart at public relations and knows the story of a city that is starving is one that won't help Russia. It would arouse sympathy throughout the world. Brandt also said: "We are much better prepared than we were before. We have enough gasoline and coal and other staples to last us some time. It is now eight o'clock," he said, looking at his watch, "and if we should be blockaded right now, at 8:30 p.m. our gas stations would close down, and two days from now we would go on gasoline rationing."

"Are your ration tickets printed?" I asked, remembering that it would take about a month to print ration tickets in the United States. "Yes, they are printed and ready," replied the mayor. "What Khrushchev wants, I think, is some kind of a limited blockade in order to get recognition of East Germany." He noted that East Germany is the only country in the world today which is losing population.

Harry Golden, author of *It Could Only Happen in America*, is in Berlin studying anti-Semitism. He told me that the young Germans are burning in their desire to make up for what their fathers did persecuting the Jews. They realize the crime of killing six million Jews and are determined to atone for it. Older Germans, he said, are more complacent. "There are only thirty thousand Jews in Germany today," Golden told me, "and it's difficult for a Jew to live here. As he goes down the street and passes an officer, he can't help thinking to himself, 'Is that one of the Nazis who murdered my relatives?'"

At the suggestion of the Soviet embassy in Washington, I had telegraphed the East German foreign minister asking for permission to travel through East Germany. When I called at the East German Foreign Office, a young bureaucrat gave me a flat turn-down. He said they didn't have enough notice and that they wanted to set up a tour. These carefully prepared tours are the last thing I want.

WEDNESDAY, MAY 11 | I found East Berlin vastly changed from 1951, when it was rubble, and considerably changed from 1953, when a few small apartment houses had been built along Stalinallee. Today Stalinallee is quite a boulevard, with a row of impressive apartments, modern shops, and office buildings. The elevated train functions efficiently to West Berlin and goes by the rear of our hotel every five minutes or so. The subway is clean and up-to-date. There is complete freedom of transportation between East and West Berlin.

From Mr. Trinnors, the U.S. embassy's expert on East Germany, I learned that the country is booming. It is now Soviet Russia's biggest customer and ranks ahead of Italy in industrial output. Only the United Kingdom, West Germany, and France are ahead of it.

The question often comes up, however, whether the two Germanies would once again become the aggressor of Europe and cause war. Berlin and the two Germanies were the key to the 1955 summit meeting in Geneva. It will be the key to the 1960 meeting in Paris next week. The question of peace or war has hinged on Germany ever since 1870.

I came to Berlin for the first time in 1923. It was a pathetic city. It cost a million marks to buy a copy of the *London Times* and about five million marks to get a cup of coffee. Children looked gaunt and forlorn.

In 1936 I came back briefly. Hitler had just marched into the Ruhr and the Rhineland, and Germany was on its way to new conquests. When I tried to call Baron von Prittwitz, the former German ambassador in Washington, he was very cagey and would not talk on the phone. Obviously, he was afraid his wires were tapped.

In summer 1951 Tyler and I flew to Germany to launch our Freedom balloons across the Iron Curtain. In February 1953, a month after Ike took office, I flew to Berlin for a few days to look over the refugee situation.

The chief mistake we made during the post–World War I era was to pump money into Germany on short-term credits, then yank it out suddenly when we faced a depression in the United States. That sudden withdrawal of capital, plus heavy reparations payments Germany was making to France and the other Allies, made a social revolution and Hitler almost inevitable.

Today we are doing things differently. We are not giving Germany short-term credits but outright grants that don't have to be returned. We ourselves did most to build up Germany. Significantly, it was Jack McCloy, now head of the Chase Bank, former high commissioner to Germany, who put this policy into effect. The Chase Bank was the biggest and most guilty party in yanking short-term credits out of Germany in 1927 and '28. Also Clarence Dillon, former head of Dillon, Reed, was the biggest underwriter [of] loans to Germany in the post–World War I period; now he is undersecretary of state in charge of policy about Germany. And it was John Foster Dulles, who made so many mistakes in the loaning of money to Germany in World War I, who, as secretary of state, battled for German unification.

THURSDAY, MAY 12 | I caught an early plane to Bonn for an interview with Chancellor Adenauer. They wanted me there by eleven. I got there about nine thirty, then waited all day until five fifteen. The chancellor had a lot of engagements, and I was told to keep by the telephone. It was not unpleasant, however, because the hotel looks out on the Rhine, where an unending stream of barges carry the prosperous trade of West Germany back and forth.

Bonn is a beautiful old university town, rather sleepy. Diplomats complain about being here. It isn't as lively as Berlin, but the West Germans cherish the ambition that their capital once again will be in Berlin, so they don't want to make permanent plans for a capital in Bonn.

Chancellor Adenauer's office looks out over the Rhine. He received me promptly at five fifteen. The interview was handled with German efficiency. The interpreter was excellent. A male stenographer took down questions and answers.

Adenauer does not look eighty-four. He has very sharp eyes that look at you piercingly as you talk and as the interpreter translates. I had prepared some questions, which I rehearsed very carefully in my own mind, but I never got a chance to ask them in sequence. He took the initiative by asking me what I was doing in Germany. And when I told him that I was spending a week in Germany and a week in Paris, he asked me why I was spending so long in Germany.

"Because I think that Germany is the heart of the problem at the summit conference," I replied. He disagreed somewhat with this and went on to emphasize the importance of disarmament and the fact that it should be the most important question to be discussed in Paris. This, of course, was the line which Adenauer sold to de Gaulle and de Gaulle in turn sold to Eisenhower; however, it has not yet been accepted by Khrushchev. The Western leaders want to divert the conversation at Paris away from Berlin and figure that Khrushchev is chiefly interested in disarmament. I'm not sure they are right.

"In November '58," Adenauer told me, "Khrushchev started talking about Berlin. It is now May 1960. A long time has passed since then, and Berlin is not so hot anymore. Much hotter has become the question of disarmament, and if the West in Paris will proceed cleverly—and I hope it will—then the West will succeed in talking Khrushchev into disarmament. Khrushchev himself has decided that disarmament is the most important question."

When I asked Adenauer what would happen if Khrushchev refused to be diverted and insisted on making an issue of Berlin, he replied, "If the Western powers give in on Berlin, then America will lose face. It would be a definite defeat. It would have an effect around the world, especially in Asia.

He said emphatically that the spy plane over Russia should not be important because Russia has been spying on the United States and the West for years. "There are one thousand Russian spies in West Germany right now," Adenauer said. Later the American embassy told me that an official statement put out by the West German government showed twelve thousand agents and spies in West Germany and Berlin.

FRIDAY, MAY 13 | I called to pay my respects to Ambassador Walter Dowling, a career diplomat whom I had not met before. He impressed me as able. He said that the trouble regarding Berlin and the failure to have an access corridor was not that the Allies would have difficulty reaching Berlin but that the Federal Republic (West Germany) would. He said he had told Adenauer that he will have to become reconciled to the recognition of East Germany but that Adenauer and the other West German leaders just can't see it. They still dream of the unification of Germany. They recognize that unification is a long way off but are certain it will come.

The danger of Soviet recognition is that other countries will follow suit. If

India recognizes East Germany, then the Hallstein doctrine can't very well be enforced. The Hallstein doctrine calls for the severance of diplomatic relations with any country that recognizes East Germany, and it would be impossible for West Germany to sever relations with India. India's lead would mean that a lot of Asian and African nations would follow.

I also called on Gen. Herbert Thatcher, commander of MAG [Marine Aircraft Group], a U.S. military mission to Germany. He discussed the problems of organizing the German army, including the controversial matter of German bases in Spain, which caused a furor in England and the United States.

Germany is full of Allied military installations and has no place to maneuver: no bombing range and not enough airfields. In addition, the German army needs a ninety-day supply of oil and other munitions in case of attack. It can only store about a fifteen-day supply in Germany because that supply would either be bombed by the enemy or overrun in a short time.

Franz Joseph Strauss, the genial minister of defense, with whom I dined on Long Island last year, proposed that these bases be in Spain. This move was really in order to dramatize Germany's need. Spain was going to charge a very high rental.

In the end France has now given its okay for these bases, and German pilots in addition can use French military airports but cannot go into town from those bases. In other words, they can't mingle with the French people.

Germany has purchased $1.4 billion worth of military supplies from the U.S. government, plus another $1 billion from American private contractors. Germany has been declared ineligible for foreign aid and is paying for these supplies in cash. Significantly, German factories don't want to take munitions orders. They've been too busy making civilian goods.

SATURDAY, MAY 14 | (Traveled to Paris; witnessed Khrushchev's arrival at Orly Airport.) Secretary Herter had a background press conference with us in the library of the U.S. embassy at 8:00 p.m., saying he did not have high hopes for the conference; that he didn't know how the Soviet attitude would be affected by the U-2 incident. He was peppered with questions.

He was asked whether he had meant to say that spy flights would continue over Russia. When he was pinned down by the press whether we would continue flights over Russia, he replied, "I'm not going to predict what we are going to do."

He was evasive over the question whether our arrangements permit us to land planes in Norway. He was more definite regarding Germany. As long as Germany remains divided, he said, it's a threat to peace. Germany must be united. Significantly, Herter dropped hints that Khrushchev was having a hard time with his own military people and indicated this was the reason why the U-2 incident had been played up as a diversion. Herter said that cutting down the Red Army has caused a lot of opposition from Soviet military people. He hinted that the Chinese were also opposed to relaxing the Cold War. Asked whether the United States would tell Russia whether the flights will continue, Herter said, "I don't know."

He said Russian spy flights had gone over Alaska but not over the Lower 48 states. Foreign Minister Gromyko, Herter said, had never gone as far as Khrushchev in demanding as he did at Baku that all troops be removed from Berlin.

(Sightseeing trip to Fontaineblew.) Back to Paris in time for another briefing, this time by Jim Hagerty. I have not seen him handle a press conference for a long time, and I must say he is adept and agile. Eisenhower had arrived that morning but had not yet seen Khrushchev. The newsmen began to smell a rat. They were curious as to whether Ike had tried to see Khrushchev and whether Khrushchev had been boycotting the president. Khrushchev had seen de Gaulle and Macmillan for lengthy conferences but not Eisenhower. One question was whether Ike would try to see him tonight. The answer was that Ike would have dinner at the embassy with Ambassador Houghton and his wife, Secretary Herter, and Maj. John and Barbara Eisenhower. On the surface he doesn't seem worried about the obvious cloud hanging over Paris.

Walter Kerr makes the point that Hagerty is the worst enemy of a free press we have ever seen around the White House. He's not only efficient, but the press corps which travels with the president is in the habit of depending upon Hagerty for everything. He has their baggage properly checked to the plane. He has their baggage sent to the hotel. He gets the hotel reservations for them. And they know that if they play ball with Hagerty, he will protect them. They won't get scooped—but this leaves nothing for any investigative journalism. Nobody digs behind the scenes. Nobody criticizes Ike.

**MONDAY, MAY 16** | This is the day the conference is supposed to open; however, it didn't, and in my opinion it won't. I began to detect signs of conference failure about noon. Sometimes you can smell diplomatic failure in the wind before it becomes apparent. I suppose it's because I've been to a lot of international conferences. It used to be that I got irked at old-timers such as Frank Simonds who would predict at the start of an international gathering that it would fail. With so much hanging on these meetings, it seemed to me blasé to make such predictions. Simonds and the others had one factor on their side: human nature, consisting of the refusal of diplomats to agree, insistence of countries on their national sovereignty and their big military establishments.

I began to realize that this conference was doomed to failure when around 1:00 p.m. word trickled back from the Elysée Palace that Khrushchev had refused to sit with Eisenhower in a meeting of the Big Three only. He finally consented to meet only in a plenary session. In other words, with the foreign ministers and the staff present. Thus, the Big Four did not meet at ten, as scheduled, but at around eleven, when everyone was present except for the public. The word is that Khrushchev refused to shake hands with Ike or meet with him because of the U-2 incident and Ike's statement that he had authorized the flight, plus the intimation that these would continue.

I was to file a column to New York about 2:00 p.m. but held up pending the Russian briefing. It was delayed but finally came at about two. The Russian spokesman read the Khrushchev statement which he had delivered to Ike and the other heads of government this morning. It was a lulu and unfortunately bears out my prediction that the conference was over.

Khrushchev flatly refused to meet with Eisenhower unless he received an apology and assurance that there would be no more spy flights over Russia. The statement fairly bristled with animosity against the man whom Khrushchev has been praising as his personal friend.

Late this evening Hagerty held a press conference. He made the best of a humiliating experience. He said that Eisenhower was under no illusion regarding the probability of success. Eisenhower had been informed prior to this morning's meeting by de Gaulle and Macmillan that Khrushchev would issue a blast and had prepared his reply. It was to the effect that the United States had no aggressive intent and that the United States and the free world and most other countries are targets of elaborate and systematic Soviet espionage. Eisenhower told Khrushchev that these flights have been suspended and will not be resumed. He said he had come to Paris to get rid of all forms of espionage, including overflights; that he was planning to place the matter before the United Nations.

Hagerty said both de Gaulle and Macmillan had argued with Khrushchev the day before, urging him to be less violent and in any event not to make his statement public. After publication of the statement, they said, it would be impossible to continue the conference. Hagerty was questioned as to when Eisenhower had ordered the end of the overflights over Russia. The reply was "Last Thursday (May 12) in an order to Secretary of Defense Gates and the chairman of the Joint Chiefs of Staff [JCS] General Twining."

Later it occurred to me that this was a faux pas, inasmuch as Twining and Gates are military men and Eisenhower had previously stated publicly that these were civilian flights having no connection with the military.

Chip Bohlen, who was present with Hagerty, told some details of the morning's meeting. He said that when Eisenhower had accused Russia of espionage, Khrushchev had raised his hands over his head and said, "As God is my witness, my hands are clean, and my soul is pure."

**TUESDAY, MAY 17** | The tragedy of this conference is its effect on the next generation. It may be the beginning of a toboggan toward war. The second tragedy is a personal one: its effect on Eisenhower.

Eisenhower was hoping to end his career as a man of peace. Now he is not seen as a man of peace. His greatest triumph perhaps in his entire career was retaking Paris toward the end of the war. His greatest defeat is also suffered in Paris—the blow-up of the summit conference.

Eisenhower's luck has been phenomenal. He was picked by George Marshall when he was a lieutenant colonel, promoted in a year to be a lieutenant general, and made commander of the biggest expeditionary force in history. Churchill and Roosevelt, with Marshall, actually made the major decisions. Eisenhower got all the good publicity. Churchill and Roosevelt sometimes got brickbats but Eisenhower never.

During the war Ike played bridge and relaxed, much as he has as president. Kay Summersby tells all this in great detail in her book, *Eisenhower Was My Boss*. The great achievements of the war, plus censorship, cover this up. Eisenhower's luck continued when he ran for president. Everybody was tired of the Democrats.

Now Ike's luck suddenly has changed. It has been with him all through life, but a U-2 pilot flying slowly over Russia on May 1 blew up Ike's luck.

Alibis are in the wind regarding what caused the summit conference failure. There is the story of the Red Army, which is supposed to be bucking against Khrushchev. There is the story of the Chinese, who unquestionably are somewhat down on Khrushchev. And there is the reported influence of the Stalinists, who don't want relaxation of the Cold War; however, the crucial fact is that there would have been a summit conference, and although it might not have accomplished very much, it would have patched things up and paved the way for Eisenhower's visit to Russia, which would have been a triumph. Furthermore, it would have helped American-Russian relations as no other event in recent years. Now that has gone glimmering.

I went to the Palais de Chaillot to compare notes with some of the newspapermen. It was dreary. Most of them are staying on for a while. Eisenhower, de Gaulle, and Macmillan are holding a NATO [North Atlantic Treaty Organization] conference to cement relations between the Western leaders, but it is largely a face-saving device. They have very little to talk about except their own gloomy thoughts.

**WEDNESDAY, MAY 18** | Khrushchev made his first tactical error. So far he had played his cards with skill, but now he held a four-hour press conference at which he berated Eisenhower and the United States. He did it in such vituperative language that the pendulum swung back to sympathy for Ike.

Actually, his press conference was not as bitter or vindictive as the headlines indicated, but the public reads the headlines. It was quite an amazing performance. Neither Eisenhower nor de Gaulle or Macmillan even met the press. Khrushchev, however, dared stand up before about two thousand newspapermen, some of them exiles from Hungary, Poland, and Czechoslovakia who hate him, and answered questions from all comers.

**THURSDAY, MAY 19** | There are many alibis and explanations for the Paris failure. The most important question and the most difficult to answer is who sold Eisenhower on the idea of taking responsibility for the U-2 flights? This was really what got under Khrushchev's skin. Prior to that he had given Eisenhower an out and told the Supreme Soviet that Eisenhower was not responsible. Jack [Anderson] has picked up a story at the State Department that Eisenhower himself told Herter, "I can't face Khrushchev at Paris unless I make a clean breast of it." This sounds rather like Eisenhower. He has excellent intentions but is naive. When he takes a stand like this, the people around him don't argue. They take the position that the boss is right.

It now appears that the U-2s were not grounded on May 12, as Hagerty announced in Paris, but only on Sunday, after de Gaulle and Macmillan stormed at Eisenhower that the flights must be stopped. Significantly, Nixon in his television program Sunday, May 15, talked about the continuing flights, when, according to Hagerty, they were stopped May 12. Nixon is not dumb. He doesn't go out on a limb unless he has the right word. At Syracuse University one day later he hastily contradicted his previous position and said the flights had been stopped.

**FRIDAY, MAY 20** | Eisenhower has gone to Portugal, received a great welcome, and is coming back to Washington to be received as a hero. Yet he has just perpetrated one of the worst blunders in modern times. The interesting question to me will be whether Madison Avenue is able to depict Eisenhower's defeat as a triumph. Sam Rayburn and Lyndon Johnson are helping. They have taken their old Democrats-behind-the-president stand, as in the past.

**WEDNESDAY, JUNE 8** | Rockefeller had breakfast with Eisenhower; came out of the White House to indicate that he was against Nixon and had told Eisenhower this. Then he went to New York and held a special press conference, issuing a carefully prepared statement criticizing the administration for lagging behind Russia and indicating why he was against Nixon. The statement carried some personal words of praise for Eisenhower at the same time he blasted his administration. This illustrates the difficult position Rockefeller is in. He either can't or doesn't want to break with Ike, though Ike is obviously boiling at him.

**THURSDAY, JUNE 9** | Nixon held a press conference in Camden, New Jersey, before a speech there. It was a masterful job, and on the whole he came out ahead of Rockefeller. He gave the appearance of answering a lot of questions fully and sincerely, though anyone knowing the facts could see that he was fooling the public. The Republican press, however, is not going to diagnose the facts nor dig beneath the surface. Nixon even went out of his way to praise Rockefeller and his right to make any statement he wished. This man will be a remarkable vote getter.

Michael Arnon, of the Israeli embassy, has been putting out remarks derogatory of Tuvia Friedmann (and his role in capturing Nazi Adolf Eichmann). I told the ambassador these remarks should stop. The Argentine government has cooperated in helping to put across the Friedmann story. They are demanding the return of Eichmann and indemnity from Israel. Eichmann's capture has become an international incident.

**FRIDAY, JUNE 10** | Lunched with Leonard Marks. He thinks Lyndon can be nominated. I doubt it, but the enthusiasm of the Lyndon crowd can be contagious (especially when Bess and Tyler are so enthusiastic).

The riots in Tokyo against Eisenhower are becoming more ferocious. He still claims he is going to Japan. The State Department confidentially says that to back down now would be a blow to American prestige and would mean the fall of the Kishi government.

I have been telling my family, facetiously, that I put the hex on Kishi when I was in Tokyo. He was the only prime minister or potentate who refused to grant me an interview.

Lyndon Johnson has written me a long letter outlining the reasons why he has had to go along with Eisenhower when Ike made each miserable mistake in foreign policy. It was a flag-waving letter. It ends with the statement: "It's my country."

**SUNDAY, JUNE 12** | Spent a day with the Friedmanns. It is not going to be easy. He speaks Polish, Yiddish, and German but rather broken English. She is an eye surgeon, intelligent, attractive, and speaks excellent English; however, he's never satisfied with her translations. We spent the day exploring their story, ending with a dinner at the Chinese Oriental Restaurant. I tried to introduce them to the use of chopsticks.

Jim Hagerty, arriving in Tokyo, was mobbed at the airport. He was not injured. The mob shook his car for an hour, teetered it back and forth. Jim spent the time taking photographs of the crowd.

Nelson Rockefeller laid an egg on television. When his ghostwriter isn't around, he doesn't come off anywhere nearly as well as Nixon.

**TUESDAY, JUNE 14** | Apparently, Israel's top Defense Department man is down on Friedmann, and I'm beginning to understand why. Arthur [name omitted], who was undersecretary of defense, was the head of the Haganah, Jewish underground in Vienna, between the end of the war in 1946 and the beginning of Israel as a state in 1948. Friedmann worked for him. They collaborated for a time on trying to find Eichmann. Then Arthur moved on to other things in Israel. Friedmann remained behind in Vienna, eventually married the young student who has supported him for a good many years and became more and more disagreeable in hounding the Israeli government.

As the story unfolds, I begin to see that Friedmann actually did not play much of a part in finding Eichmann, except from one point of view. He was a persevering gadfly. He had studied all the records on Eichmann, collected many documents, which he has shown me (most of which figured in the Nuremberg trials). He actually had no scouts out looking for Eichmann. He merely corresponded with people.

The secret of Eichmann's final discovery was a letter received from Eichmann's neighbor in Buenos Aires to Friedmann, squealing on Eichmann. The neighbor wanted a $10,000 reward and, now that Eichmann has been captured, has written to Friedmann demanding the $10,000.

Friedmann received the tip in September 1959 but got nowhere with the Israeli government. He kept badgering them until finally he was able to appear on the same platform with Ben-Gurion during a political rally in Haifa. This was in early December 1959, when Ben-Gurion was running for reelection. Friedmann made a speech to the 250,000 former occupants of Nazi concentration camps, saying in brief, "I belong to no political party; I belong to the vast number of Jews who suffered in Hitler's concentration camps, and we demand the capture of Adolf Eichmann."

Friedmann got such a reaction from the crowd that Ben-Gurion promised to go after Eichmann. That was the beginning of the subsequent expedition by which a group of very tough Jewish security men, all of whom had served in concentration camps, went to Buenos Aires and put a sack over Eichmann's head as he was returning from work to his home in the suburbs.

Friedmann was not along on the trip and knew nothing about it until he read it in the papers; however, he does deserve some credit for being so persistent.

**THURSDAY, JUNE 16** | Premier Kishi has canceled Eisenhower's visit to Japan. It was probably the most humiliating blow Eisenhower has received. He had hoped to make up for the failure in Paris by a triumphal tour through the Far East; however, it has been obvious for some time that Eisenhower could not go to Tokyo with safety. Ironically, Eisenhower was in the Philippines, which at first he had refused to visit, when word came to him that he was not wanted in Japan.

I had written several columns some weeks ago urging that Eisenhower visit Manila, where he could be received royally by the best friends we have in Asia; however, he consistently said he would not go to Manila—until the failure at Paris. Then he had to go to someplace where he would get the plaudits of the multitude.

**FRIDAY, JUNE 17** | I am convinced that Ambassador Douglas MacArthur is chiefly to blame for the snafu over Ike's visit. He wanted Ike to come there for his own personal kudos. I could tell this by my conversation with him in Tokyo last December. Doug is a vain, small-bore man, much more intent on his own personal aggrandizement than the welfare of his country.

He put me through two hours of briefing on elementary classroom subjects that I already knew or could have read in the tourist guides. Of course, I may be prejudiced because MacArthur didn't lift a finger to arrange an appointment for me with Kishi or with the emperor.

Lyndon Johnson, as usual, has rallied to the side of Eisenhower and denounced the Communist Japanese for snubbing him. What Lyndon doesn't realize is that the minute Eisenhower took responsibility for the U-2 flight over Russia, thereby ending any chance of a summit conference, Khrushchev was going to pull the plug on Ike's visits to Japan and elsewhere. It was through the courtesy of Khrushchev that the Italian Communists waved American flags and yelled, "I like Ike," when he visited Rome last fall. That U-2 flight and Ike's statement admitting responsibility for it set off a chain reaction which is going to hurt our foreign affairs for a long time to come.

**SATURDAY, JUNE 18** | Eisenhower, I now learn, is sore as blazes at MacArthur and would like to have him fired. He blames MacArthur quite rightly for faulty intelligence and for not warning him regarding the seriousness of the Japanese riots.

**TUESDAY, JUNE 21** | The Friedmanns left for New York. I have had Milton Friedman of the Jewish Telegraph Agency doing the ghostwriting for them, such as it is. The Argentine government is keeping the matter hot by the debate in the UN. I talked with Victor Andrade, the Bolivian ambassador, about this. He is close to the Argentines. There is some thought that the Argentine government might demand the surrender of Friedmann as compensation for the kidnapping of Eichmann. The Israeli ambassador told me this had been suggested to him by Undersecretary of State Douglas Dillon as a way out. I told Andrade that it would be a wonderful piece of promotion for Friedmann's book and suggested he might encourage the Argentine ambassador. I'm quite sure we would not have to surrender Friedmann.

**FRIDAY, JUNE 24** | Lyndon Johnson wanted to see me. He has been irked at some of the sideswipes regarding him in the column by Jack [Anderson] and me. He made no mention of this, however, or of the letter I had written calling a spade a spade regarding his constant defense of Eisenhower. He has been excoriating Jack Kennedy for Kennedy's impolitic but nevertheless accurate remark that if he had been Eisenhower he would have "expressed regret" for the U-2 incident in order to save the summit conference.

SATURDAY, JUNE 25 | I have now received the translation of Friedmann's manuscript regarding his days in Nazi concentration camps during the war. It is fascinating reading. One of the most amazing parts is his description of how Jews were entrusted with the job of gassing other Jews. The job of stripping Jewish victims of their jewelry and clothes and then herding them into the gas chambers was done entirely by Jewish camp attendants. They were, of course, under the command of the Nazis.

One significant document I've had translated is a report by a high Nazi official that he had gone to one camp because of a report that Jewish inmates had held a wedding and a very ornate and extravagant ceremony. He found the report was true. The Jews who were in charge of gassing and burning other Jews had collected their jewelry and were becoming wealthy. They had saved the ornaments, clothing, and jewelry and had staged a wedding of a Jewish couple, which was the talk of that part of Poland.

This might be discounted as anti-Jewish propaganda were it not for the fact that the report was given in such minute detail and for the further fact that Friedmann himself tells how Jews persecuted their own kind, both in the camps and in the villages which sent the victims to the camps.

MONDAY, JUNE 27 | Leon Wollenberg, who entertained me in Rome, came to lunch with Pete Lisagor of the *Chicago Daily News* and Elie Abel of the *Detroit News*. Pete was just back from Asia, where, he said, it was nearly impossible to protect Eisenhower's life even in such friendly places as Manila and Korea. In one parade in Manila two American photographers pulled two Filipinos off the rear of Ike's car. The Secret Service was not around. More trouble is expected in South Korea.

Milt Friedman confided after lunch that Nixon had been on the telephone to Henry Cabot Lodge in New York and got him to tone down the Argentine resolution against Israel. Nixon had been coked up by some wealthy Zionists who promised healthy campaign contributions. Lodge, who had been rather tough the night before, got hold of the Argentines, and they omitted the demand that Eichmann be returned to Argentina.

**TUESDAY, JUNE 28** | Lunch with Teddy Wiental, who confirmed my belief that Hagerty is dominating Eisenhower and interfering with foreign policy. Herter isn't strong enough to stand up to Hagerty as Dulles did. Ike has no great respect for Herter, and between Hagerty and Ike, Herter plays second fiddle on foreign policy. Immediately after the first phony explanation of the U-2 incident, which at least had the value of not saying much, Hagerty instructed Herter to come out with a statement in which the White House took complete responsibility. The earlier statement had made it appear Eisenhower didn't know what was going on. Hagerty always believes that the president must know exactly what's going on everywhere.

Wiental, who writes for a conservative Republican magazine, said that he had never known an administration in Washington so specialized in lying. In the old days State Department officials at least refused to comment— they wouldn't lie—but this administration lies deliberately, brazenly, on any occasion.

**WEDNESDAY, JUNE 29** | Frederick Eaton of Monsanto has come back from Geneva for instructions from the State Department regarding new disarmament policy. He returned because the French and the British were so fed up with American intransigence on disarmament that they threatened to accept the Russian proposals. Just as Eaton was about to arrive back in Geneva, however, the Russians broke off talks until a new president is elected here. Actually, the Russians had come rather close to the French proposal of abolishing all means of delivering the atom bomb (namely, the Polaris submarine and the B-47). We didn't like this. I can't understand why the Russians broke off the talks at this time, unless it was to show their disdain for Eisenhower—and the fact they don't want to have anything to do with Nixon.

This afternoon Harry Truman announced he was not going to the Democratic convention as a delegate. This has thrown the Democrats into a tizzy, especially Stuart Symington. Clayton Fritchey came to dinner. He is now masterminding press relations for Symington and says Stuart telephoned Truman in Independence this afternoon to ask, "Is there anything I have done wrong, boss?" "No," replied Truman, "I'm holding a press conference on Saturday." I suspect Lyndon Johnson had something to do with Truman's withdrawal.

**SATURDAY, JULY 2** | Tyler confided to me that the Justice Department had received a report on Kennedy's vote buying in West Virginia, which looked very bad. They will spring it after Kennedy is nominated. He also sat in on a conference Tuesday night with Lyndon, Earle Clements, Bobby Baker, and Hubert Humphrey, in which they tried to persuade Humphrey to swing the Minnesota delegation to Lyndon. Humphrey proposed Eugene McCarthy as vice president on Lyndon's ticket and said that he, Humphrey, had told Orville Freeman, governor of Minnesota, that if he wanted to run for vice president, he, Humphrey, would have to oppose him. Orville told him that he had been approached by Kennedy to be his vice presidential running mate and that he was considering it.

Truman held his press conference. He blasted the rigged convention in Los Angeles and told Kennedy he should be patient about becoming president. I suspect that it will hurt Kennedy somewhat, though it may not stop him.

SUNDAY, JULY 3 | (Dined the previous evening with Florence Mahoney, the George Dixons, and the Chinese ambassador [Taiwan], George Yeh, recently returned from meeting with General MacArthur in New York.) Yeh said MacArthur thought Johnson and Symington were best qualified to be president. "I remember Kennedy when he was a PT boat commander in the Pacific," MacArthur said. When Yeh remarked that Kennedy had a great record, MacArthur grumbled: "He should have been court-martialed. Those PT boats carried only one torpedo. They were under orders to fire it and then get out. They were defenseless and shouldn't be anywhere in the vicinity of a Japanese vessel after they had fired their torpedo. Kennedy, however, hung around and waited. He should have been court-martialed for letting his boat get run over by the Japanese destroyer."

I reported on the radio this week that the Joint Chiefs of Staff had recommended U.S. military intervention in Cuba. They want Eisenhower to act before Raúl Castro signs a military defense pact with Russia.

Jack [Anderson] is leaving for West Virginia today to see exactly what's happened regarding Kennedy's vote buying.

Hubert Humphrey called today and denied that he told Johnson he would try to keep Orville Freeman out of the vice presidential race. Obviously, Humphrey was lying. Tyler is too good a reporter to go wrong. Humphrey confided that what he was trying to do was to keep his Minnesota delegation from bolting to anyone on the first or second ballot. He wants to keep them split up into small groups for different candidates. "Then if the convention gets stuck on the third ballot," Humphrey told me, "maybe I'll re-declare for president."

**SATURDAY, JULY 9** | LOS ANGELES—The strategy of the Stevenson leaders is to bring about a deadlock between Johnson and Kennedy. It's also the strategy of the Symington group. The Lyndon Johnson leaders hope they can stop Kennedy on the first ballot. The "favorite sons" have been talking to Kennedy and are preparing to withdraw. If they don't withdraw, Kennedy can be stopped.

I went to see Pat Brown, one of the favorite sons. He is very wobbly. He explained that last December, even before Mike DiSalle had come out for Kennedy, he, Brown, had told Kennedy that he would be for him if Kennedy did not come into the California primary and stir up the Democratic Party and provided that Kennedy was able to win in such difficult states as West Virginia and Wisconsin. After Kennedy won in those states, he called Pat and asked him to come out for him. Pat said he probably would. The next day the story appeared in the *New York Times*, though Pat said he thought he was talking privately.

Last week Bobby Kennedy telephoned him and said it would be very helpful if he, Brown, would announce now. Pat hesitated. The next day Bobby held a press conference and announced that Pat Brown was coming out for Kennedy. The whole series of Kennedy publicity announcements has made it appear that Pat couldn't make up his mind. I told him he ought to give an ultimatum to the Kennedy forces that either they keep quiet or he would come out for someone else.

I talked to Henry Leader, brother of the ex-governor of Pennsylvania, who said: "You walk around here and talk to other delegates and think there isn't a chance of doing anything for anyone except Kennedy. You feel as if this was not a real convention." Henry, however, stood up in the Pennsylvania caucus and announced, "I'm not with big brother George. I'm for Adlai Stevenson." He said that if he had known how strong Stevenson was inside the California delegation, he could have got a lot more Pennsylvania delegates to hold back from Kennedy, but with the Republican press apparently determined to nominate Kennedy, only eight Pennsylvania delegates stuck with Stevenson.

**TUESDAY, JULY 12** | Lunched at the California Club with George Arnold, Tyler, and Leonard Marks. Leonard proposed I take out a full-page ad in one of the Los Angeles papers telling about being barred from the air last night, then giving the text of what I would have said—namely, that the Los Angeles press and radio had been covering up the facts of this convention. I was not sure the idea was a good one, but with three eminent young lawyers, all friendly to me, advising me to go ahead, I acquiesced. Tyler got the rate on a full-page ad and a deadline of two hours to get publication tomorrow morning. We drafted part of the ad at the lunch table, then went to George's office and typed it up. I took it over to the *Mirror News* before the deadline.

The drive is on to block Kennedy on the first ballot. Tyler tells me he has talked to the Maryland delegation and they will switch away from Kennedy on the second ballot. The same is true of Indiana. Kennedy has very little reserve strength. All his forces are in the first ballot, and if he loses then, he is probably cooked.

WEDNESDAY, JULY 13 | The balloting began tonight. All day the Kennedy forces were worried. It looked as if the blitz might have backfired. Too many delegates have become aware of the fact that Kennedy has been operating the smartest public relations campaign since the heyday of Jim Hagerty. Kennedy has been trying to pick up delegates in ones or twos, which means he isn't sure of winning on the first ballot.

My newspaper ad was reprinted to the tune of $16,000 and distributed to every delegate. Also, my column for Monday giving Joe Kennedy's record with the German ambassador in London has been reprinted and apparently has had some impact.

I went to the convention hall for the first time. Stevenson's loyal cohorts staged what was described as "the greatest demonstration in history." The delegates, however, sat on their hands. I doubt if the convention changed a single vote.

The rumor is that the Irish big city bosses of northern New Jersey have served an ultimatum to Governor Meyner that he must withdraw his name. In this case Kennedy has it on the first ballot. Charlie Engelhard, however, tells me that Meyner will stand pat unless Kennedy is within thirty votes of winning, then he will have to yield. The Catholic leaders of New Jersey have made things too tough for him. I saw Meyner. He was adamant that he was not going to withdraw his name.

Under the platform Tom Finletter paced the floor waiting to second Adlai's nomination. The liberal forces of New York are on the verge of defeating Carmine DeSapio, but they can hardly scrape up a handful of votes for Stevenson. It shows that you can't stage a draft with a few well-meaning people, such as Mrs. Roosevelt, Agnes Meyer, and Herbert Lehman.

On the floor of the convention I saw Newton Brewer, a Maryland delegate who guaranteed that Maryland would go for Johnson on the second ballot. They are tied to Kennedy on the first. Tommy D'Alesandro, who put across the Kennedy blitz in Maryland, was his usual backslapping self.

The Iowa delegation broke ranks and voted largely for Kennedy. The Kansas delegation passed—still huddled in caucus. New Jersey stood pat; however, other smaller states began to wobble that were not originally in the Kennedy column. He made it on the first ballot. Missouri moved to nominate Kennedy by acclamation.

That was that. Symington is now supposed to get the vice presidency. During the turmoil of the convention, we served notice on Bart Lytton in my suit against him for breach of contract.

THURSDAY, JULY 14 | Worked most of the day on the radio program. Just before I was to go on the air, I called Earle Clements regarding the rumors that Lyndon Johnson would take the vice presidency. Earle confirmed it. I never thought Lyndon would do it. The majority leadership is too important.

Walter Reuther, Joe Keenan of the Electrical Workers, and Jim McDevitt had been working to persuade Kennedy not to take Lyndon. Arthur Goldsborough of the Steelworkers, however, finally smoothed things over and got labor back into line.

SATURDAY, JULY 16 | Kennedy made a great acceptance speech last night. He begins to look good. Even those who opposed him are getting enthusiastic over the Kennedy-Johnson ticket.

SATURDAY, JULY 23 | Nixon flew to New York last night for a private conference with Rockefeller, thereby turning a drab [Republican] convention into one with at least one flurry of excitement. They conferred for six hours, until three o'clock in the morning, drafting a new Republican platform which goes all out on civil rights and national defense and is just about as liberal as the Democratic platform.

Nixon made the trip to New York because he recognized he had to have Rockefeller with him in order to win. Conservative Republicans are fit to be tied. The platform committee, which had just about completed its draft, is especially sore. Three members wept when they heard the announcement of the new platform written behind their backs by only two men.

SUNDAY, JULY 24 | CHICAGO—Had breakfast with Tom Pappas of Boston, a member of the Republican finance committee. He confirmed John Hamilton's report of dissension over the Rockefeller-Nixon platform. The finance committee still has about $4 million to raise, and Tom thinks it will be difficult to raise between now and November.

We picked up Eric Johnston, the movie mogul, and drove out to a Negro Baptist church where Nelson was to speak. The place was hot and crowded. We sat on the platform.

Poor old Harold Stassen, who has been ignored by most Republicans as if he were the plague, came in the front entrance and straggled down the front aisle to the platform. He is for Rockefeller, which is bad luck.

Nelson made a poor speech. It was too long, full of bombast, and not entirely accurate. He paid tribute to the Eisenhower administration as winning more for Negroes than at any time since the day of Abraham Lincoln.

We dined with Dave Karr at the Pump Room in the Ambassador East Hotel. Dave flies out to Chicago for part of each week in his private plane, bringing his valet-secretary along. The Pump Room is impossible. The food is bad and the noise terrific. Alice Roosevelt Longworth was there and most everybody else who counts.

MONDAY, JULY 25 | The convention opened today. Nixon and Rockefeller are working together closely on the platform, and both have given a virtual ultimatum that their platform must be adopted. They've even threatened to go before the convention and make a floor fight if it isn't.

Eisenhower is sore about the defense plank, which proposes unlimited spending and insinuates that he let the nation down on national defense. Nixon is willing to modify the platform somewhat to appease Ike.

Luvie telephoned Mary Rockefeller, who makes no secret that she doesn't like Nelson's new liaison with Nixon. "Nelson has just come into the room wearing a big Nixon button," she said, "and I could throw up."

Terrific sentiment continues here for Goldwater—at least on the surface. Rockefeller now has a band and a sound truck, but it's obvious that none of the Rockefeller economic empire has been tapped to put him across for president. He has been insistent that he will not run for vice president.

The Republican convention is dull and orderly compared with the Democrats. Word has been passed that the delegates are to be models of good behavior. There are no parades and no delegates whispering and backslapping in the aisles. I left the San Francisco convention on its first day four years ago for Israel. I have no excuse for leaving this one early despite its drabness.

**TUESDAY, JULY 26** | Nixon is taking Rockefeller at his word that he doesn't want to run for vice president. In addition, Nixon wants to set himself up as a poor boy running against the son of a wealthy liquor dealer and stockbroker, Joe Kennedy. Nixon is now veering toward Henry Cabot Lodge. He realizes that foreign affairs will be all-important.

Lunched with Jean Beliard, French consul general, in Chicago. He is worried de Gaulle may be assassinated; has very little security around him, takes many chances, and the military are up in arms against him. The attack on white residents in the Congo will make it more difficult for de Gaulle to solve the Algerian question. The one million French residents of Algeria now figure they, too, will be assaulted.

There is no one in France to take de Gaulle's place, and if he should die, France would probably become a Fascist state. De Gaulle drives back and forth to his country place at a speed of about 100 miles an hour. He refuses to take a helicopter because it would attract too much attention. (How unlike Eisenhower.)

**FRIDAY, AUGUST 5** | Kefauver ran two-to-one against his opponent, even rolling up a big vote in western Tennessee, which is segregated and vigorously anti-Negro.

Estes stood up for the things that he believed in regardless of sentiment back home. He was the only senator to vote against outlawing the Communist Party because, as he told me, you can't set a precedent for outlawing any political party in this country.

**TUESDAY, AUGUST 9** | Went to see Senator Magnuson to get more money for the TV watchdog committee. He promised it. I mentioned $150,000.

**WEDNESDAY, AUGUST 10** | Had breakfast with Lyndon Johnson at his home. He was full of praise for Tyler and said he had read over my recommendations passed on through Tyler. I doubt, however, whether he accepts any of them. He is too much concerned with the congressional session. Lyndon has a habit of getting so embroiled in the job of the Senate leadership that he forgets the major strategy of a campaign for the nation.

I tried to sell him on the idea of getting more money for the TV watchdog committee, and he agreed—at least theoretically. I also suggested a small group of backstage experts to work for Kennedy and Johnson who could trump the Republican statement makers; however, Lyndon was too busy thinking about his own legislative problems to give either idea much thought.

He tells me he gets along well with Kennedy; that Kennedy knows what he wants; makes decisions in a hurry and gives directions clearly. Lyndon was anxious to have something written regarding Ike's phony position on withholding military funds. Eisenhower has put across a lot of hoopla that he has always favored adequate defense, when the real fact is he's held back funds previously voted by Congress.

FRIDAY, AUGUST 12 | Wayne Morse came to breakfast. I tried to persuade him to start an investigation of administration mistakes in Cuba. He was lukewarm. Obviously, he doesn't want to get into this election battle. He talked about his duties at the UN delegation.

I wanted him to dig into the terrible errors we have made in appointing ambassadors to Cuba, in sending Ike's brother-in-law and Dulles's son-in-law to the Dominican Republic to lobby on sugar contracts, and the weird position Nixon has put himself in by writing the ambassador in Havana to intervene in a gambling debt for the man who collected Nixon's $18,000 expense fund—but Wayne was listless.

The Soviet ambassador invited me to lunch. He is just back from Moscow. It is no longer popular to go to the Soviet embassy, but I went. I suppose some future Joe McCarthy will throw this up at me because the FBI takes photos of everyone who goes in or out of the Soviet embassy. Their camera is located just across the street. Nevertheless, as a newspaperman, I think it's important to keep in contact with what the other side is doing.

The first question the ambassador asked was, "How many wealthy men are lined up behind Kennedy?" I told him I thought Kennedy had a few more wealthy supporters than most Democratic candidates but not many. Picking the figures out of the blue, I said he might have 10 percent of the wealthy backers. The counselor of the embassy was also present, and from their questions I gradually began to conclude that they were genuinely interested in knowing which candidate had the backing of big business and those whom the Russians believe want to continue munitions output. It has been Moscow's theory for a long time that there will be no disarmament as long as American business wants to continue munitions production.

I also asked the ambassador about the AP [Associated Press] report of increased friction between the Chinese and the Russians at a recent labor conference. He pooh-poohed this but emphasized that Khrushchev is for peace.

**TUESDAY, AUGUST 23** | Lunched with Pierre Salinger, Kennedy's public relations man. Tyler joined us. Salinger said that Kennedy had asked him to talk to me because of the column I wrote on the first day of the Democratic convention regarding old man Kennedy's conversations with Hitler's ambassador in London. It had hurt very deeply. He said mail was still coming in.

I told Salinger that Kennedy had not been my favorite Democratic candidate because I didn't think he could win, and I was afraid some of the pessimism was now becoming justified and that in my opinion his campaign had bogged down.

Salinger offered to make some news available. I told him he could give me the inside story on Kennedy's talks with Sen. Harry Byrd of Virginia. I doubt whether anything will come of this.

**WEDNESDAY, AUGUST 24** | (Conversation with Lyndon Johnson regarding Bicks's confirmation as head of the Justice Department's Antitrust Division; conversation with Estes Kefauver about same; suggested investigation into Eisenhower connections with Dominican dictator.)

**FRIDAY, AUGUST 26** | Luvie had lunch with some close friends of Jack Kennedy. They report Bobby has aged because of worry over the Gallup poll and Jack's slow start. At Los Angeles, Stewart Alsop had dinner with Otsie Leiter and Flo Flo [Florence Pritchett] Smith, wife of Earl Smith, our ambassador to Cuba. Flo Flo made no secret of the fact that she was and still is Jack Kennedy's girl. "We are so close," she kept saying. "I see him all the time." Alsop finally asked her what about her husband, and she replied, "I don't give a damn for that old bore."

This apparently was the woman Kennedy took down the hotel fire escape on a date at the time in Los Angeles that he said he was going to see his father. There was a front-page story in the *New York Times*.

The gossip is that Jackie Kennedy is not pregnant but wants this as an excuse to keep out of public appearances, which she hates. The further gossip is that she has ordered clothes to be delivered in November of exactly the same size as her pre-pregnancy status; also that she will get a divorce if Jack loses. There is no question they have been unhappy—or at least she has—for some years.

**SATURDAY, AUGUST 27** | Clint Anderson says the most important thing Kennedy was doing was to register about 40 million voters who don't vote. I asked how he was doing it. The reply was, "He's paying for it." Already about 100,000 voters in Baltimore have been registered, most of them Democrats.

**TUESDAY, AUGUST 30** | The Democrats have a golden opportunity to embarrass Eisenhower by showing that Ike's brother-in-law, Dulles's son-in-law, and Ike's former assistant secretary of state for Latin America were paid by Trujillo. Instead, the Democrats have become defenders of Trujillo in the House of Representatives, making speeches to protect Trujillo's sugar quota (which Eisenhower wants to cut). Those defending Trujillo are the same congressmen who accepted free joyrides to the Dominican Republic. In the Senate, Ellender (LA) and Eastland (MS) have made speeches praising Trujillo. You can imagine the effect of these speeches in Latin America just after the Pan-American nations have unanimously voted to sever relations with Trujillo.

**THURSDAY, SEPTEMBER 1** | Hugo Black and Dick Sanger came to dinner. Sanger is just back from the Congo. He says Lumumba got his start by attending a meeting of Congolese independence leaders against Belgium at which a manifesto was drawn up. The question arose as to where the manifesto should be printed. Lumumba said he knew of a printer who would do it for nothing. When the manifesto returned from the printer, it was signed, "Lumumba, President." This is how he became prime minister of the new Republic of the Congo.

Andrée Blouin, the French Negress who once worked at a news counter in an African hotel, is now a chief influence in Lumumba's life. She first became the mistress of the prime minister of Guinea, then mistress of the Congolese minister of the interior, and now Lumumba's. Most of the cabinet have been in bed with her at one time or another. She has strong leftist leanings.

The American ambassador, Timberlake, who is an able man, sees Lumumba perhaps three hours a week. Lumumba's leftist advisors see him perhaps eighteen hours a day.

Ralph Bunche of the United Nations was a flop in the Congo because he expected that, as a Negro, he would be welcomed as one who is helping his fellow Negroes. Instead, they gave him the back of the hand, treated him as an enemy. Bunche returned to New York disillusioned.

**WEDNESDAY, SEPTEMBER 7** | Norman Vincent Peale and a group of Protestant clergyman met in Washington. They issued a declaration that religion must be an election issue because of the influence of the Catholic Church over its members. This has thrown a hook into the Kennedy camp.

The influence of the Catholic Church is not merely religious but political and economic. It's when the church gets into the political and economic fields that it is powerful. Franklin Roosevelt bowed to the Catholic Church probably more than Kennedy would. Roosevelt was surrounded by Catholics, from Missy LeHand to Tom Corcoran. I remember Corcoran telling me when I argued with him about the Roosevelt policy toward Franco, "We'll have to talk to Cardinal Mundelein about that." Chicago's Cardinal Mundelein was a relatively enlightened clergyman. Nevertheless, he was against any republican form of government in Spain because under it the church would not be supreme. Under Franco the church is supreme, and no Protestant president has really dared tangle with that position, despite the fact that we have been subsidizing Franco with defense money for approximately ten years.

**THURSDAY, SEPTEMBER 8** | I haven't yet found a good reason why Khrushchev is coming to New York with a battery of satellite leaders. There is a feeling that he wants to interpose his position with the West to offset Red China's militarism. There is also the feeling that he wants to make this a propaganda visit to appeal to the uncommitted and neutral countries. Certainly, a few years ago no one would have dreamed that the dictator of Soviet Russia would come to New York uninvited and bring his entire satellite entourage with him.

**FRIDAY, SEPTEMBER 9** | Things are getting worse in the Congo. Premier Lumumba—whom I call Premier Lumbago because he's a pain to everyone— now demands that the UN get out.

**TUESDAY, SEPTEMBER 13** | NEW YORK—Breakfast with the Romanian ambassador to the UN, Silviu Brucan. I have found him the frankest of the Iron Curtain ambassadors, and I was anxious to find out what Khrushchev was up to. I am not sure that I did. Brucan was vitriolic against Dag Hammarskjöld and his conduct of UN forces in the Congo. He claimed Hammarskjöld was pulling the West's chestnuts out of the fire in the Congo and had been completely unfair to Lumumba. My information is just the contrary, but I was unable to make any headway in arguing with Brucan.

He said that the state of the world was so precarious and the danger of an accident which might cause war so serious that Khrushchev could not wait for the new president. He felt something must be done immediately to ease tensions.

Brucan was frank regarding Red China. The last time I talked to him, he pooh-poohed my columns that Red China had increasing friction with Khrushchev. Today he admitted there was friction, though he minimized it as not too serious. He was also frank about Molotov. I asked why Molotov had been transferred to Vienna to be a member of the Atomic International body. He replied it was because Khrushchev wanted to show that he was unlike Stalin and did not believe in purging his enemies, yet could not find an acceptable post for Molotov. Brucan recalled that *Agrément* [diplomatic term for the foreign government's approval] had been asked for Molotov to be ambassador to the Netherlands but was turned down. *Agrément* was not necessary for his appointment to the Atomic International Committee in Vienna.

**SATURDAY, SEPTEMBER 17** | MEXICO CITY—The U.S. press went to the president's palace, where we all met Adolpho Lopez Mateos. This is my third meeting with him. He was cordial and wanted me to stay and have a talk with him after the festivities are over. I explained that I had to go back to cover Khrushchev in New York.

We went to a small-scale bullfight, but I left early to have lunch with four members of the U.S. embassy staff, who filled me in on Mexican political developments. They do not feel that Mexico is drifting away from the United States but, rather, is following the natural course of the revolution: land reform and nationalization of Mexican industries are a part of the basic platform of the PRI (Party of the Revolutionary Institutions). The Mexican government has just purchased the Mexican Light and Power Company, a Canadian corporation, and American and Foreign Power [Company]; however, it purchased the stock on the open market and did not seize the companies, as did Castro.

I lunched with Ambassador Hill, who said he was concerned over the anti-Americanism of the Mexican University students and faculty. The riots against the United States were so severe that the police were called out three times. The university was finally suspended for the summer. Part of the demonstration toward the end was against President Lopez Mateos.

**MONDAY, SEPTEMBER 19** | WASHINGTON DC—We watched Khrushchev's arrival on television. The day was wet and uncomfortable. His reception was cool in more ways than one. Not a single American was there to greet him. He landed at a decrepit East River pier, with its leaky roof. Nevertheless, he delivered a conciliatory statement to the American people. Considering the demonstration against him, including the longshoremen who hired a special boat to meet him with "Drop dead, you bum," I thought he handled himself with dignity.

I still can't figure out why he is here. He is subjecting himself to abuse and physical danger. Yet he has mobilized all the leaders of the Communist world and has also induced Nasser, Tito, Sukarno of Indonesia, and even Castro to come to New York. Nehru and Macmillan are coming too. All these despite the fact that the United States doesn't want them and we have purposely tried to discourage some of them. So far, Chancellor Adenauer has made no plans to come, though he has urged the State Department to let him come and debate Khrushchev. De Gaulle is remaining in Paris.

Aside from this, the greatest conglomeration of heads of state ever to be in one city is now in New York. And Khrushchev is calling the tune. He has even forced Eisenhower to come to New York to speak on Thursday, although Ike did not want to come.

Fidel Castro moved from the Sherbourne Hotel in downtown New York to the Teresa Hotel in Harlem. It was a smart move, calculated to win Negro support.

**TUESDAY, SEPTEMBER 20** | Went to the opening of the UN. Khrushchev was the focal point. Many delegations from Africa and Asia came over to shake hands and be photographed with him.

Finally, a public relations man for Castro came over and persuaded Khrushchev to walk halfway around the large assembly hall to Castro's seat, where they were photographed in fond embrace.

When the time came to ballot for a new president of the General Assembly, most heads of delegations had their No. 2 men carry the ballot up to the ballot box at the front of the hall. Not so Khrushchev. He took his ballot in his hand and walked the full length of the hall to the ballot box. He then turned around and made a motion to the assembly, pointing his finger down into the box. Khrushchev is not missing a trick. He's something of a clown, and all the world likes a clown. Obviously, though, the American delegation doesn't like this clown.

**THURSDAY, SEPTEMBER 22** | Eisenhower delivered his speech at the UN—on the whole a good speech, though not one to win friends behind the Iron Curtain. It was geared more to help Nixon, being studded with sideswipes at Khrushchev. Ike twisted the knife regarding the RB-47 incident but did not mention the U-2 incident. I doubt whether this speech is going to help bridge the gap between Russia and the United States.

I finished the radio broadcast and dropped in at a reception for UN delegates given by the president of the new Republic of Togo. Khrushchev was present. He stayed for an hour, patiently answering questions and talking to anyone who wanted to talk to him. Eisenhower did not come, nor did any important American. I finally got close enough to Khrushchev to ask him the question which has interested me since the Paris summit conference—namely, whether he was willing to meet with Eisenhower, as reportedly suggested by Prime Minister Macmillan. I had written this, but the State Department denied it. Khrushchev's reply was: "Of course, I was willing to meet with Eisenhower. I discussed this twice with Macmillan."

**FRIDAY, SEPTEMBER 23** | I sat in the UN assembly for two and a half hours listening to Khrushchev's speech. It had some conciliatory passages but on the whole was calculated to antagonize the United States. Khrushchev's worst attack was on Hammarskjöld and the UN operation in the Congo. Khrushchev is not going to win many friends in the West, or perhaps even in Africa, with his diatribe because the African states had just voted overwhelmingly to support Hammarskjöld.

He bored in hard on the U-2 incident and demanded that the UN investigate the violation of Russian territory. He also demanded the UN be moved from New York City.

Lyndon Johnson called from Kansas City during the afternoon about Earle Clements's tax difficulties. He is concerned. He's issuing a statement which is a little mild but reasonably good. He put Harry Truman on the telephone, and Truman reported he had been out campaigning at the supermarkets for Lyndon and that Missouri looked good. I asked Truman whether he was going to campaign in Kansas, where things do not look so good. He said he was making a couple of speeches there. I suggested he ought to whistle-stop. His reply was: "That's up to Kennedy; he's the boss. I'll do whatever they want me to."

I reminded him that the last time he had whistle-stopped, I had traveled with him—in 1952. "Yes," he said, "but then we had a candidate we couldn't do anything with." Of course, Harry had felt the same way about Kennedy before the nomination as he now feels about Stevenson. Alas, Harry Truman will always be Harry Truman.

**WEDNESDAY, SEPTEMBER 28** | CLEVELAND—Lunch with Mayor Anthony Celebrezze, who told me how he had to persuade Sen. Frank Lausche to join the Kennedy entourage yesterday in the suburbs of Cleveland. Frank did not want to come. Kennedy had asked him to come. Frank hung back. Finally, he came with the idea of only remaining for breakfast. When he saw the crowds, you couldn't pull him away. I asked Celebrezze if there had been much organization work necessary to get the crowds; the answer was no.

Ray Miller, the boss of Cleveland, was also present. Ray has battled against Mike DiSalle, the governor, and Lausche for some time, but they worked out an alliance of convenience.

**THURSDAY, SEPTEMBER 29** | Khrushchev lost his temper on the General Assembly floor while Macmillan was speaking. He interrupted, pounding on the desk, shouting at Macmillan, "Quit sending U-2 spy planes over Russia." It played into the hands of the preventive-war mongers in the United States and elsewhere. After the fireworks, however, Macmillan and Khrushchev did sit down to confer.

**WEDNESDAY, OCTOBER 12** | Kennedy and Nixon argued over Quemoy and Matsu in their final television debate. Nixon is proceeding to hit Kennedy with the idea that he, Kennedy, would withdraw American support for the defense of these two islands. Nixon is calling Kennedy an appeaser and soft on communism. He piles this on top of [Kennedy's] statement that he would have "expressed regret" to Khrushchev over the U-2 flight. What the American public doesn't know is that Chris Herter, when undersecretary of state, had persuaded Dulles that we should withdraw from Quemoy and Matsu and since he has become secretary of state has urged it on the Joint Chiefs of Staff. The JCS have opposed chiefly because of the blow to Chiang Kai-shek's "face" if there were a withdrawal.

**THURSDAY, OCTOBER 13** | I dug up some facts regarding the China lobby and the contribution Louie Kung made to Nixon's campaign in 1950. Leo Casey, who gave me this information, was then working for the Bank of China and David Charney. Leo is now dead, but I called Charney, who told me that Nixon once had dinner with Dr. Kung at his Riverdale residence and had several meetings at the Mayflower with Kung and Alfred Kohlberg, then head of the China lobby.

Charney is a close friend of Sen. Styles Bridges. On one occasion, according to Colonel Hsiang, $500,000 in cash was carried by the Chiang Kai-shek people up to Concord, New Hampshire. It was used [by Bridges] for the campaign expenses of various Republican senators. It's hard to document this, but Hsiang was in on these things and in the past has told us the truth.

**MONDAY, OCTOBER 17** | My column on Nixon's contributions from the China lobby was not used in St. Paul, Chicago, or Cedar Rapids. It was also not used in New York. This illustrates the difficulty in trying to tell the truth about the Republicans when 80 percent of the newspapers are pro-Republican.

Creekmore Fath came for lunch. We have been helping him track down a story on U.S. Steel which has suddenly blossomed with some peculiar commercials parroting exactly what Nixon has been saying in his speeches, that the United States is higher than ever in its prestige and that business is booming. The advertising agency for U.S. Steel is BBD&O, the same agency which handles the Republican National Committee and the White House. I called Senator Magnuson in Seattle to get some subpoenas issued so that Fath could swoop down on the BBD&O offices in New York. We now find, however, that the Democratic National committee alerted both CBS and BBD&O rather stupidly by lodging a complaint. If there are any incriminating documents, I'm sure they have been destroyed.

**THURSDAY, OCTOBER 20** | Jim McInerney, former assistant attorney general under Howard McGrath, told me George Allen had deducted from his income taxes the cost of Ike's farm to the tune of from $40,000 to $60,000 a year. You can't deduct farm expenses if you're running it as a hobby. I also got wind of a $205,000 loan made by Howard Hughes to Nixon's brother Don, through Nixon's mother.

**FRIDAY, OCTOBER 28** | The ironic part of the Hughes story is that Hughes was instrumental in sending a lot of dough to Maine to help defeat Senator Brewster, who had tapped Hughes's wire at the Mayflower Hotel and showed up some of his philandering and lobbying in Washington. Brewster was motivated by Pan American Airways, which wanted to get even with Hughes and Trans World Airways [TWA].

**SATURDAY, OCTOBER 29** | Jack Anderson has talked to Bobby Kennedy's office. They are not anxious to get mixed up in the loan story. I suspect they are afraid the Nixon camp may pull something on Jack's sex life.

**TUESDAY, NOVEMBER 1** | Ike has now realized that his prestige is at stake and has jumped into the campaign.

I telephoned Rep. Jack Brooks of Texas from Miami to ask him to investigate the TWA benefits that were received from the CAB (Civil Aeronautics Board) after the $205,000 loan. He was mildly interested. I then got Rep. Bob Jones of Alabama, who promised to phone him and increase the enthusiasm. Bob is a member of the committee. Meanwhile, Jack Anderson had called Rep. John Moss in Sacramento.

Phillip Reiner in New York has given an interview to the *New York Post* stating that Nixon did know about the Howard Hughes loan and was kept advised. His interview was carried by the AP and hit the front pages in Miami this afternoon. This now supports nearly every part of the story previously denied.

**WEDNESDAY, NOVEMBER 2** | Arrived home from Miami at 6:30 a.m. Discovered Reiner has a criminal record—not very important but enough to upset things a bit. He came to see me with the idea of possibly holding a press conference, which I favored but which he and his attorney vetoed.

Phil Graham of the *Washington Post* has asked Bobby Kennedy to play down the story. This explains why I have had no cooperation from the *Post*, which refused to run the story.

Oscar Chapman came to lunch with some data regarding Joe Kennedy and the manner in which he helped Jews to migrate from Germany to Palestine and other places around 1939. If I use it, I will be accused of currying favor with Kennedy to escape his revenge list; however, I'll probably use it.

**THURSDAY, NOVEMBER 3** | Ike and Nixon have been in New York. Nixon is leaning heavily on Eisenhower, but I believe the public is seeing through it. I'm still convinced Nixon will lose all the northern industrial states and that Kennedy may win by a landslide.

I telephoned Rep. Henry Reuss in Milwaukee to put pressure on Rep. Jack Brooks in Texas to issue that statement for an investigation of the Don Nixon loan and the effect on the CAB for TWA. Brooks issued the statement this afternoon.

**SATURDAY, NOVEMBER 5** | There is a woman parading in front of the White House with a picture of Kennedy taken as he left his girlfriend's house with his hands up over his face to keep from being photographed. This is the picture which Jack Anderson mentioned to Kennedy when he and I had breakfast with him last March. Unquestionably, it is bona fide. The woman in question, known as a "Miss Cantor," has been parading in front of theaters and other places to embarrass Kennedy, but apparently it hasn't hurt. Judging from the women who are eager to touch his hand and kiss him, it may even help him.

Someone called to say that the Kennedy family had pulled out of the dedication of St. Paul's Chapel honoring the war dead in England in 1958. The navy had chosen the Kennedys to be their official representatives, but the Kennedys backed out at such a late hour the navy didn't have time to replace Jack, so that no one was present to represent the navy. The situation appears to be similar to Kennedy's refusal to participate in the dedication of the Three Chaplains Chapel in Philadelphia some years ago because the cardinal of Philadelphia asked him to abstain.

The telephone has been ringing regarding new angles on the Howard Hughes loan story. I got a tip later this afternoon from Bob Strauss in Los Angeles, who claimed that the attorney general of California had additional information on a Nixon loan—this one involving Central California Airlines and a route to San Diego. The dope is that the Chandler newspapers found out about this loan and are so worried about Nixon that they almost hope he'll be defeated. They decided, however, not to use any more information which might hurt him.

I discovered today that Jack Kennedy has given orders to play down all personal matters, including the Hughes loan. Phil Graham advised against doing anything with the Hughes story. Apparently, Kennedy is following his advice.

I received a letter late today from a John Wells indirectly threatening a libel suit unless I retracted the Howard Hughes loan story.

**SUNDAY, NOVEMBER 6** | I finally got the attorney general of California on the telephone regarding the new Nixon loan fund. He doesn't know any more about it than did Bob Strauss. We did find in our files some significant data showing that California Central Airlines had hired Thomas Bewley, Nixon's law partner, and Murray Chotiner to try to get the route to San Diego after their regular lawyer told them it was impossible. There were some conferences with Nixon, but they failed to get the route.

**TUESDAY, NOVEMBER 8** | Election Day. We had a few friends in to dinner to listen to the election returns. At 7:00 p.m. the United Press total count showed Nixon ahead. Kennedy, however, pulled ahead shortly in Connecticut, New York, New Jersey, and Pennsylvania and then kept a slight lead over Nixon all night. Kennedy did lose Ohio, which surprised me, also New Hampshire, together with Kentucky and Tennessee, where the religious issue was very strong. Earle Clements was quoted as saying, "This was a Democratic year, and yet they had to nominate a Catholic." Later he denied saying this, but I'm sure he did. He was always worried about carrying Kentucky for Kennedy. I went to bed at 4:00 a.m. still not quite sure Kennedy was elected. His popular margin is only 300,000; several states are still undecided.

**THURSDAY, NOVEMBER 10** | The close vote may be a good thing after all. There is a lot of arrogance in the Kennedy family, and this may dampen it. Bobby Kennedy, in a press conference, outlined the Hughes story as one of the reasons for the victory. He placed it second to the TV debates as an important factor.

Jim McInerney telephoned to say that the reason Los Angeles County went for Kennedy was the Hughes story and my press conference out there. Bill Hart also telephoned from Morgantown, West Virginia, to say the Hughes story had turned a lot of votes.

Lyndon Johnson also called from Johnson City to thank me.

It looks to me as if Nelson Rockefeller is washed up. He didn't deliver New York State for Nixon, though he tried hard. New York went for Kennedy by an overwhelming margin. Rockefeller now has the enmity of both the right-wing Republicans and all the Democrats. He got in the middle, and it never pays to be in the middle.

Khrushchev has sent a fulsome message to Kennedy. It looks as if my hunch that things would improve with the Kennedy election was correct.

**THURSDAY, NOVEMBER 17** | Bill Walton came to supper before I caught a train to Cleveland. Bill spent election night in Hyannis Port with the Kennedys. Next morning he said old man Joe made a speech at the breakfast table, avowing that he would get even with the one-sided press and TV if it was the last thing he did. Joe also vowed to get even with Cardinal Spellman for the way he had helped Nixon, despite long years of friendship between Joe and the cardinal. I gather that Spellman was blamed for getting those Puerto Rican archbishops to inject the church-and-state issue at the last minute. Jack Kennedy apparently has a sense of humor. Looking over the electoral map and the manner in which the Middle West went for Nixon, he said: "That solves one cabinet problem. The farmers want to keep Ezra Taft Benson."

**FRIDAY, NOVEMBER 18** | CLEVELAND—Governor DiSalle came in late for dinner, and we sat together. He was a little irritated over the story I had written that he had met with Bobby Kennedy at a Pittsburgh motel around the first of the year to arrange that Ohio should be pledged to Kennedy at the Democratic convention. Mike denied it. "You called me regarding a contribution from the Teamsters," he added. "They hate me. They want to put me out of business. Why should I do any business with the Teamsters?"

On the whole, however, Mike was his usual self. I asked him why he had issued a statement taking the blame for the Ohio defeat. "I knew they'd blame me anyway, so I beat 'em to it," he replied. "I've had wonderful mail in response."

"Why didn't the Catholic issue hurt you when you were running for governor?" I asked. "Because they didn't denounce me from the pulpits," he said.

**SUNDAY, NOVEMBER 20** | Lyndon Johnson, now in Paris, made a speech praising Eisenhower and promising that the United States would continue Eisenhower's policies for NATO. This is just what I have urged Lyndon not to do. It was originally Truman who founded NATO, not Eisenhower. Also, Ike has let NATO reach the lowest depth of strength in its history.

It looks as if George Smathers is going to be Kennedy's right-hand man. They are already hobnobbing together in Palm Beach. The Kennedy family put up some of the money to defeat Claude Pepper, and Smathers has been one of the "companions" for Kennedy in Washington and Miami. When Kennedy wants a girl in Miami, Smathers produces her.

Clark Clifford is another member of the "companionship" club who is strong on women and scant on principles. He has been appointed by Kennedy to arrange the transition from the Eisenhower to the Kennedy administrations.

**TUESDAY, NOVEMBER 22** | The report is that Khrushchev is going to make Kennedy a present of the release of the RB-47 flyers now in jail in Moscow in an effort to get American-Russian relations off to a good start.

**WEDNESDAY, NOVEMBER 23** | Eisenhower has decided to call American servicemen's dependents home in order to stem the flow of dollars abroad;

also Secretary Anderson has gone to Bonn to try to persuade the Germans to pay for the cost of the American troops stationed in West Germany.

**THURSDAY, NOVEMBER 24** | The Republicans are trying to make up their minds whether to go all out in an investigation of alleged Democratic vote frauds in Chicago and Texas in order to upset the election. Ike has been goading them on, though Nixon, as far as we can find out, has been quite statesmanlike (for a change) and says he doesn't want to win by default. Kennedy is privately scared to death as to what may happen. It's one reason he's been slow in picking his cabinet.

**FRIDAY, NOVEMBER 25** | Lunched with the Czech ambassador . . . He expressed the opinion that the West underestimated China, considered the Chinese illiterate and uninformed, but pointed out that since 1945 the Chinese did not need to read. They could hear and look. Television has speeded up the world outlook of the Chinese masses, likewise with Africa. European jealousies have been transferred to Africa, as in the battle between Tunisia and Morocco over Mauretania.

**MONDAY, NOVEMBER 28** | Lyndon Johnson called from Texas to talk about his trip to Europe. He was bubbling with enthusiasm regarding the way world statesmen had treated him. It was unusual to have the top senators in Europe just after an American election: Johnson, Fulbright, Kefauver, and several others of lesser stature. I asked Lyndon about Fulbright as secretary of state and pointed out that it was bound to bring resentment from Jewish groups.

"Fulbright would be absolutely fair if he were secretary of state," Lyndon argued and said: "I don't owe him anything—not as much as I do you. You had a party at your house when Fulbright was there, and you plotted to try to keep me from being Senate majority leader back in 1952."

"Your intelligence is awfully good," I interrupted to say.

**WEDNESDAY, NOVEMBER 30** | Kennedy is now three weeks behind in appointing his cabinet. He's doing everything himself and concentrating chiefly on foreign affairs. His father is worried about the spreading depression. I asked three days ago to see Bobby Kennedy—so far no reply. He seems to be following the usual Kennedy course of forgetting those who helped them.

**THURSDAY, DECEMBER 1** | [G. Mennen] "Soapy" Williams has been persuaded to become assistant secretary of state. This is quite a comedown for

Williams, a man who was six times governor of Michigan and is probably the most outstanding Democratic governor in the United States.

Abe Ribicoff, governor of Connecticut, was named secretary of health, education, and welfare. This aroused Protestant hackles. Ribicoff was very pro-Catholic as governor of Connecticut, signed the school bus bill for state funds to Catholic schools. Now he will be in charge of allocating funds to the schools of the nation through the aid-to-education bill, if passed by the Kennedy administration.

Last night Rep. George McGovern came to dinner. After his defeat in South Dakota, he wants to be secretary of agriculture. He thinks he has a chance, but in his conversation with Kennedy he was told that if he wanted to run for the Senate, being secretary of agriculture would hurt him politically, since it was one of the toughest jobs in the cabinet. Kennedy also expressed doubt as to whether he should take on a cabinet member for a short term, since McGovern might run for the Senate again in two years. He tried to get McGovern to take a job as assistant secretary of state. Both he and Bobby are peddling these assistant secretaryships, emphasizing that they are all-important jobs with the peace of the world at stake.

During the conversation McGovern told Kennedy that it didn't hurt Henry Wallace, who became vice president after serving as secretary of agriculture; nor did it hurt Clinton Anderson, who ran for the Senate after being secretary of agriculture. The question of the appointment was left up in the air.

When I mentioned to McGovern the manner in which J. Edgar Hoover had helped to cut his throat politically by backing Mundt, McGovern agreed but said he did not want to mention the matter to Kennedy since Kennedy had already reappointed J. Edgar Hoover.

**FRIDAY, DECEMBER 2** | Eisenhower has become sentimental over the dollar crisis. When he and Secretary Anderson conferred in Augusta in the little office over the golf pro shop, Dr. Snyder, Ike's personal physician, said that both Ike and Anderson had tears in their eyes when they decided that Anderson should go to Bonn to protect the dollar. The State Department, however, didn't know anything about it until the last minute. They were skeptical, and it was finally decided that Dillon would go along, so as to keep Anderson from making an ass of himself. Dillon did but apparently did not succeed. Anderson got nowhere and did make himself—and the United States —look foolish.

Wall Street is spreading the same kind of rumors they did about Roosevelt—namely, that Kennedy will nationalize industry and that we will go off the dollar.

**SATURDAY, DECEMBER 3** | Conferences have been going on all week between Kennedy and advisors over the question of Berlin. Berlin is probably not being mentioned, but what happens in Kennedy's house on N Street will probably decide the future of it. Dean Acheson wants a tough secretary of state who will not yield an inch on Berlin. He particularly wants David K. E. Bruce, former ambassador to Bonn. Acheson says that Adlai Stevenson would be catastrophic as secretary of state. Kennedy wants Acheson to be head of NATO. NATO is falling apart and needs bolstering, but Acheson wants to know who will be secretary of state before he accepts the NATO position.

Meanwhile, the word from Moscow is that the Chinese and the Russians have arrived at a six-month truce. The Chinese have accepted Khrushchev's theory that war is not inevitable and will let him work at it. If at the end of six months he is not able to work out an agreement with Kennedy over Berlin, then Khrushchev will yield to the Chinese and follow their leadership regarding Quemoy, Matsu, and Taiwan. So, Kennedy will have one of the worst crises of modern times on his hands come next June.

**MONDAY, DECEMBER 5** | Kennedy is flying to New York for conferences, including breakfast with the UN's Dag Hammarskjöld. Wayne Morse tells me he did his best to persuade Kennedy to come to the UN later after appointing his secretary of state and UN ambassador. Then all three could meet every UN delegate with Secretary Herter beside them, thus giving every delegate a chance to go home and say he had met with the new president of the United States; and also an opportunity to say that the outgoing and the incoming administrations stood side by side together. Apparently, however, Morse's proposal was turned down.

**TUESDAY, DECEMBER 6** | Flew to Washington in time to have dinner with Florence Mahoney, Ribicoff, and Sen. Clair Engle of California. Ribicoff ribbed Engle regarding his pre-convention position for Symington. "Just who were you for?" Ribicoff asked when Clair was telling about his needling of Pat Brown not to come out too early for Kennedy. Clair explained that Pat would have lost the allegiance of most of his delegation, which was for Stevenson, so that he, Clair, did his best to keep the governor from coming out too early for Kennedy.

**WEDNESDAY, DECEMBER 7** | Kennedy spent two hours with a mysterious friend in the Waldorf Tower—probably a woman. When the Press Associations inquired of Pierre Salinger regarding this, the answer was, "It's purely personal." Hoover and MacArthur both live in the Waldorf Tower, but apparently Kennedy did not see them. He did spend some time with Flo Flo Smith and her husband [Earl T. Smith], going to the theater the night before.

His conference with Eisenhower was full of folderol, military pomp, and cordiality. It was just the opposite of Ike's bitter and snide remarks against Kennedy. Ike spent about two hours with Kennedy alone, talking in large part about the monetary crisis and urging Kennedy to act swiftly to stop the flow of the dollar.

When [Herbert] Hoover invited FDR to confer with him at almost the same week twenty-eight years ago, Hoover was anxious for FDR's cooperation. In this case, however, Eisenhower made it clear that he would carry on without any Kennedy cooperation to the last minute of January 20.

Roosevelt obviously wanted to stay away from Hoover. Even that early, his attitude was that Hoover was tainted with political typhoid fever.

The New Dealers are swooping down on Kennedy (pushing the case for various appointees). Kennedy doesn't know what to do.

**THURSDAY, DECEMBER 8** | Bill Douglas, the Kefauvers, Senator Yarborough, and Pat Brown came to dinner. Pat and Senator Engle had just seen Kennedy late in the afternoon and put in a plug for George Killion or Jessie Tapp of the Bank of America to be secretary of the treasury. I gather that Pat really plugged harder for Tapp than for Killion. They got the impression that Kennedy was for Douglas Dillon, though he said he would like to have Killion in his administration.

Bill Douglas pointed out that if you control the presentation of facts, you control American foreign policy. With Allen Dulles in charge of Central Intelligence Agency, he will run Kennedy's foreign affairs. Bill was bitter, pointing out that Dulles had been wrong in picking Castro, had been wrong in betting all our chips on Nouri Said in Iraq, and had pulled a lot of other lulus the public didn't know about. Bill described Smathers as a good-time boy who had a bad influence on Kennedy and was only worth something when you wanted to get a girl in Miami.

**FRIDAY, DECEMBER 9** | I had a long hassle with Ralph Yarborough and Fath. Yarborough had asked Kennedy the night before to make Fath assistant secretary of the interior in charge of oil and gas. He wanted to strike back at his Texas enemies that way. Kennedy replied that any appointment would have to be okayed by Lyndon.

I talked tough to Yarborough. He is a real liberal but fuzzy-minded. He is so inefficient that you simply can't get any action out of him unless it's speech-making. When you try to pin him down, it's like wrestling with a big balloon.

**MONDAY, DECEMBER 12** | Someone has been calling me about Kennedy's romance with Inga Arvid, who used to be a photographer for the *Washington Times-Herald*. She was a Dane or a Swede, and I remember her vaguely as being statuesque and sexy. Kennedy was stationed in Washington and took her to Fort Sumter, South Carolina, for several weekends in February 1942, shortly after Pearl Harbor. ONI [Office of Naval Intelligence] tagged along and investigated Kennedy because Inga was married to Paul Fejos, who was suspected of Axis connections in New York. The FBI finally became involved because Inga was supposed to be a security risk.

The navy finally transferred Kennedy to the South Pacific in order to break up the romance. Luvie, who remembers Inga better than I, recalls it was old Joe Kennedy who arranged the transfer. Luvie also recalls that it was Jackie Kennedy (then Jackie Bouvier) who replaced Inga as a photographer at the *Times-Herald* and whom Jack finally married.

**TUESDAY, DECEMBER 13** | Bobby Kennedy telephoned to thank me for my letter advising him not to become attorney general. He remarked that obviously I had given it considerable thought—which was true. It has now been about ten days since I requested an appointment to see him.

**THURSDAY, DECEMBER 15** | Phil Graham has been giving Bobby Kennedy the opposite of my advice—namely, that he should become attorney general. He said Bobby remarked that he had received "a very thoughtful letter from Drew Pearson." Phil said he seemed surprised and pleased. Phil even went to Felix Frankfurter for advice as to whether Bobby should become attorney general. Frankfurter—in my opinion the worst judge in the world—advised: "Every president has a right to have his own man in a key post as his special prime minister. There's no reason why Kennedy's brother should not be AG."

Phil confirmed what I had suspected: that he was the man who put the kibosh on more use of the Howard Hughes–Don Nixon story. His alibi was that Nixon would go on television with his mother, Hannah, sitting in a rocking chair talking about the family fortunes, and this would turn sentiment in favor of Nixon. I didn't argue with him. The election is over, and the story has been pretty well circulated anyway. One trouble with the Kennedy campaign was too much amateur advice of this type. If Nixon had tried to repeat on television what he did with the little dog story in 1952, he would have been murdered. You can't repeat that kind of showmanship.

I have just learned that Jim McInerney is chiefly retained by old Joe to handle Jack's girls when they want to be paid off.

**THURSDAY, DECEMBER 22** | I heard that McNamara, the new secretary of defense, had vetoed Franklin D. Roosevelt Jr. to be secretary of the navy. I called FDR Jr., who revealed that McNamara had come to see him. He wanted to know how Franklin felt about unification. Franklin replied that he agreed with General Motors that competition was essential within an organization. I gather he didn't make a very good impression. Franklin asked me not to write anything for the time being since it might scare McNamara away. I agreed not to do so. Obviously, Franklin wants the job.

Remembering all he did for Kennedy, I would say he deserves it. He even launched that smear against Hubert Humphrey in West Virginia about Hubert's draft record, which really hurt. I have a strong hunch, however, that Franklin will not get it, even though Kennedy told me last April that he thought Franklin would be a natural for the Navy Department.

**CHRISTMAS DAY** | Lyndon continued talking about the qualities of Fulbright, most of which I agreed with. Nevertheless, I still believe it would be a mistake to make him secretary of state, and I've written an article which Bill is not going to like. The reaction of African leaders would perhaps be worse than that of the Jewish leaders.

# 1961

## ANNALS

At forty-three John F. Kennedy was the youngest president ever elected. His inaugural address on January 20 was widely praised. Its most quoted line was "Ask not what your country can do for you; ask what you can do for your country."

Initially, the Kennedy administration was focused on the Cold War more than domestic issues. The civil rights movement soon rose in importance. In December the Supreme Court ruled that segregation at bus terminals was unconstitutional.

In response to the Soviet space challenge, President Kennedy, addressing a joint session of Congress, said, "I believe that this nation should commit itself to achieving the goal, before this decade is out, of landing a man on the moon and returning him safely to the earth." This speech galvanized the nation's determination and resources.

The Bay of Pigs invasion of Cuba in spring was a failure. Before Kennedy's election the Eisenhower administration had authorized a plan to train Cuban exiles for the purpose of overthrowing Fidel Castro's regime. Kennedy gave it the green light. More than one hundred invaders were killed and nearly twelve hundred captured.

In early December Castro declared himself a Marxist and nationalized much of the remaining private property in Cuba. With the death of Ernest Hemingway that summer, the Cuban government seized Finca Vigia (Lookout Farm), which had been the author's home for twenty years.

Meanwhile, the Communist leaders of East Germany and the Kremlin were alarmed by the flow of residents to West Berlin—more than 3.5 million since the end of World War II. In August the East German authorities suddenly erected a wall between East and West Berlin to prevent more defections.

In the Soviet Union, Nikita Khrushchev's de-Stalinization program continued. By the end of the year Stalin's body was removed from the Lenin Mausoleum, while many cities and monuments named after Stalin reverted to their old names. De-Stalinization helped create a split between the USSR and Communist China. China's leaders were worried that widespread criticism of Stalin's crimes in the USSR could legitimize opposition to their own system. When Khrushchev criticized Albania's Stalinist regime at the Twenty-Second Congress of the Communist Party in Moscow, China's delegation walked out.

June's Kennedy-Khrushchev Summit in Vienna was seen as a failure. Their discussions centered on Berlin. Khrushchev considered Kennedy naive. Nothing substantive was accomplished. Nevertheless, Kennedy's approval was in the low eighties by the end of the year.

Roger Maris beat Babe Ruth's single season home run record in 1961.

Some basic facts in 1961:

World population: 3,083,508,955

U.S. population: 183,691,481

U.S. gross domestic product: $544.8 billion

Makeup of U.S. Congress (based on 1960 election):

Senate: Democrat 64, Republican 36

House of Representatives: Democrat 262, Republican 175

Number of women in the Senate: 2 (2.2%), House 18 (4.1%)

—Ed.

## THE DIARY

**TUESDAY, JANUARY 3** | Lunched with Arthur Goldberg, the new secretary of labor. He is making a clean break with the past, even selling his stock in the Conandogo Hotel in San Juan, because he has to administer the minimum wage act in Puerto Rico. He is convinced the minimum wage increase to $1.25 will help the economy by boosting spending power. The Kennedy advisors even want to get rid of the withholding tax for the time being in order to give the economy more spending power. They claim that once the take-home pay is increased, it goes immediately into the economy.

Arthur talked at length about the manner in which the Communist world was winning the war for men's minds by clever propaganda among working people. This is something the United States has almost completely neglected. He has labor attachés in different parts of the world, but they function largely under the State Department.

After the steel strike the Communist labor organization in Vienna circulated widely a clever pamphlet claiming that the steelworkers of the United States had been suppressed during the steel strike which (ended one year ago tomorrow). Arthur circulated a counter-statement with these points: (1) U.S. steelworkers were permitted to strike, which wouldn't have happened for even one day in Communist countries; (2) they were permitted to go to court, and in the circuit court of appeals one-half [of] the judges voted for them, which would happen in no country behind the Iron Curtain.

Talked to Bill Rogers, first about the Hoffa alliance with Nixon and the delay of the Florida indictment of Hoffa. Bill claimed he knew nothing about this, that the delay in indicting Hoffa was due to the fact they wanted a stronger case, were waiting until after the election.

Bill talked about the job he is doing in the Justice Department. He obviously resented some of the things I have written about Lamar Caudle's case and the charge that there are two brands of justice being ladled out, one for Republicans, one for Democrats. He cited cases to show that he has been evenhanded in his judicial outlook. Certainly, he has done a terrific job on the antitrust cases and, of late, the civil rights cases, though he was slow getting started. He argued that he could not very well bring a bill of information against the Mississippi mob which lynched Mack Parker because he could only bring a misdemeanor charge against them, because they had already been exonerated by a grand jury. Obviously, he said no judge or jury would convict, so why bother with a mere misdemeanor charge? I was inclined to agree.

Bill said he had told Bobby Kennedy he would have his men stay on at the Justice Department to help try the Hoffa indictment or do anything else within reason to cooperate. He said he was determined to get Hoffa but that some of the other cases against him had been weak. He seemed to think the Orlando case was a good one. I have heard the opposite.

I found the liberals burned up at Lyndon Johnson, who now has himself a job as "guest chairman" of the Democratic caucus. The liberals were looking forward to the day when they would get rid of Lyndon and have a liberal leadership. Mansfield, the new leader, virtually abdicated this leadership by demanding that Lyndon have the right to preside from time to time at Mansfield's request. According to Senator Gore of Tennessee, "This smells of oil." Estes Kefauver, who had fought shoulder to shoulder with Lyndon during the campaign, told me that he had to oppose Lyndon on this role. The constitutional division of the executive and legislative branches of the government is at stake.

THURSDAY, JANUARY 19 | Have had some important research done on [John] Connally. The *Washington Post*'s Phil Graham dropped my Wednesday column on the argument that Connally had not lobbied for the natural gas bill in 1956. I dug up the Senate hearings showing that he was listed as a member of the steering committee and that it is charged with putting into effect the natural gas legislation of the general committee, namely the Natural Gas Act. I also dug up some vigorous editorials written by the *Post* opposing Ed Pauley for exactly the reasons I am opposing Connally. I had them mimeographed and sent them to about half the Senate. The town, however, is full of visiting Democrats, and I doubt many senators read much of anything.

I talked with Eugene McCarthy of Minnesota again. He remarked that he thought oil had become rather respectable. Paul Douglas tells me that McCarthy made a deal to get on the Senate Finance Committee and has voted with the oilmen on the depletion allowance. Paul doesn't want to oppose Connally's confirmation [to be secretary of the navy]. I have told him, Joe Clark, and others that they always wait until the end of Congress to make a fight on the tax loopholes but that the time to wage tax oil battles is the beginning of the session. Every time oil comes up, they should knock it on the head—beginning right now with the Connally appointment. John Carroll of Colorado argued that the oil companies were going to pour money into Colorado to defeat him and he had to be careful. He doesn't like to oppose a Kennedy appointment at the very start. Sympathy for Kennedy is high in Colorado.

I'm not sure I'm going to make much headway in this fight, but Proxmire's working hard on a speech and apparently is going to stand firm.

It started snowing in midafternoon, took me one hour to drive one mile to the radio studio. It then took one hour to drive from the studio to Phil Graham's house in Georgetown, where he was giving a reception for Kennedy and Johnson. Neither showed.

We had tickets to the $100 gala at the Armory, staged by Frank Sinatra, but the snow was too heavy. Tyler got there, but we stayed home. The city is paralyzed. It will be a miracle if there is an inaugural parade tomorrow.

FRIDAY, JANUARY 20 | The snow plows and the army worked all night and cleared Pennsylvania Avenue. The temperature was down to about twenty, but Kennedy stood without an overcoat to take the oath and deliver his inaugural speech. He took the oath fifty minutes late, so that for almost an hour the United States was without a president. Before he spoke and while Cardinal Cushing was haranguing the multitudes with the longest and most raucous benediction I've ever heard, a motor started smoking underneath the speaker's stand—as if somebody had set off a time bomb.

Kennedy delivered an excellent address, which opened the way for negotiations with Russia without, however, doing any appeasing. Eisenhower watched rather critically as Kennedy referred to the dangerous position in which the United States found itself. Just a few days before, Eisenhower had been assuring Congress that everything was hunky-dory. The most interesting face of all was that of Richard Nixon. He sat watching Kennedy's every move. The television camera has a way of detecting character, and you could see a note of bitterness mixed with envy in Nixon's face.

We had a buffet supper attended by a few stalwarts who braved the snow and then went on to the Sheraton Park Hotel for an inaugural ball, where Luvie was a hostess. It was jammed. Women fainted and were carried out to the room where the cabinet lined up to march in and greet the dancers. Kennedy finally turned up at 1:30 a.m. He made all five of the balls and ended up at Joe Alsop's down the street from us at about two thirty, where he stayed until three thirty.

I had written a column for publication today that after the parade was over Kennedy would doubtless go up to the Lincoln Study and look out over the troubled panorama of the world to study the problems he had inherited. Instead, he celebrated at Joe Alsop's.

SUNDAY, JANUARY 22 | Lyndon Johnson arrived [probably at Walter and Marie Ridder's] while I was talking to Hale Boggs. Hale remarked, "I'll have to take another drink." He then rushed out to keep Lyndon in another room, since Johnson was Connally's main backer. I managed to get away without causing any embarrassment. Yet it was only a few weeks ago that Lyndon was calling me from Texas to consult about this and that and putting Harry Truman on the phone to consult further. The trouble with a newspaperman's life is that you can't have any permanent friends in politics.

| I telephoned Proxmire early in the morning to report that Hubert Humphrey was planning to ask Mansfield to hold Connally's name over until Tuesday. At noon Proxmire called me. He'd been summoned to Humphrey's office and found Connally sitting there. Humphrey told him, "I'm planning to vote for Connally, and I shall tell my friends to do likewise. I want you to talk to Connally, and I believe you will change your mind."

Proxmire said he was flabbergasted but did talk with Connally, who of course denies that he had anything to do with the natural gas lobby—a lie. He was the leader of the lobby, as I have frequently reported without any protest or denial from him. I telephoned Humphrey, who said that he had decided to call Connally in. "He made a fine impression on me," Hubert said, "and I decided that instead of opposing him, I would help him."

By this time I had secured from Allan Witwer an interesting affidavit to the effect that in 1955 Sid Richardson, Connally's boss, had been at the La Jolla Beach Hotel, of which Witwer was manager, and left a large envelope on the breakfast table by the swimming pool. The envelope was open. Inside Witwer found a report from Perry Bass, Richardson's nephew, giving an account of the oil sales to the navy during the previous year.

Witwer had written me from San Francisco that he had further information regarding the oil connections with Eisenhower's Gettysburg farm, and I asked him to come to Washington at my expense. He had some amazing and colorful information regarding J. Edgar Hoover and the fact that about $20,000 worth of hotel bills had been charged up to the Taylor-Delhi Oil Company during the racing season at Del Mar. I persuaded him to give me an affidavit regarding Richardson's envelope. This was important because Connally had testified before the Senate Armed Services Committee on January 18 that the Richardson estate sold no oil to the navy.

When I told this to Senator Humphrey, however, he was unimpressed. He was hell-bent for confirming Connally, and nothing was going to stop him. I heard earlier this morning that the administration was beginning to apply the heat. Obviously, the heat had reached Hubert.

Tyler came to lunch. I had hoped to be alone with him so I could explain my position about Connally. I feel badly about the embarrassing position I have put Tyler in. He began work today at his new job at the Post Office Department; however, I had to have Witwer at lunch, so I didn't get a chance to talk.

Went to the Italian embassy for dinner in honor of Stanley Marcus, of the Neiman Marcus department store in Dallas. Who should turn up but

Connally. Proxmire stuck it out this afternoon and delivered his speech. He didn't do well in the debate with Senator Russell. None of the senators I had talked with stood up or even inserted one question to help Proxmire. It was a lone battle, Morse being away. In the end there was only one vote—Proxmire's—cast against Connally.

Who should also turn up at the Italian party but the new vice president and Lady Bird. We shook hands—a bit restrained but smiling. After the dinner Connally came up to shake hands, and I congratulated him. As we left, he admired my Russian lambskin hat, and I promised to send him one. That is the end of that chapter.

**WEDNESDAY, JANUARY 25** | Kennedy held his first press conference and staged it on live television. I had planned a question about the Free University of Cuba but couldn't get hold of Salinger to coach Kennedy in advance. The press conference went pretty well, though it bogged down at times. Kennedy was careful, didn't talk with the same alacrity that he did in the Nixon debates.

He announced the release of the RB-47 flyers held prisoner in Russia since last July. I had predicted this on the radio, and it was not exactly news but made tremendous headlines and started speculation as to whether Kennedy made any kind of a deal in return. The only deal I can find was that we agreed not to have the flyers talk and become propaganda springboards against the Soviets.

**THURSDAY, JANUARY 26** | Good repercussions from the Kennedy press conference. He plans to use these, instead of Roosevelt's fireside chats, in order to mobilize public opinion against Congress when necessary. Kennedy has set a tough standard for other presidents to follow. Future presidents will have to have a touch of John Barrymore about them and be gifted debaters.

**SATURDAY, FEBRUARY 18** | CARACAS, VENEZUELA—The president rents a rambling old Spanish house with thick walls, open windows, and open doors. There seem to be no mosquitoes or flies in Caracas and no screens on windows or doors.

We sat on a hammock on the veranda listening to parrots chatter in Spanish. In about three minutes President Betancourt arrived—a swarthy, pleasant man with horned-rim glasses, a pipe, and hands from which the skin had been peeled off. I did not know at first what the trouble was, but later when the mention of Dictator Trujillo came up, the president exhibited his hands and remarked, "This is what Trujillo did to me." I remembered then how Trujillo had tried to assassinate him last July, and one of the guests explained that Betancourt had been trapped inside his limousine when the bomb exploded, and a terrific fire had severely burnt his face and hands. One of the aides who rescued him said that he never expected the president to live. An aide in the front seat was killed, and the minister of defense, who sat beside Betancourt, was permanently deafened.

We drank planter's punch and munched on some tortillas before going into lunch. The luncheon was almost my undoing. It began with soup, then a large piece of cornmeal cooked in a banana leaf, then raw fish, then steak, followed by a native dessert, then fruit.

Luvie sat between the president and the vice president of Congress, Garcia Cordela, who probably will be the next president. Betancourt cannot succeed himself, and his term expires in about three years. No other president in the 150 years of Venezuelan history has served two terms. Every other elected one has been kicked out. Dictators, of course, have served much longer.

I first became interested in Venezuela when I was working for the *Baltimore Sun* around 1929 and helped to stage a demonstration in front of the White House of a "Gomez Iron," an anklet with a large chain and heavy ball which prisoners wore in Gomez's jails. Gomez was a dictator of Venezuela for twenty-seven years. During many of those years' time I wrote critical pieces about him. He finally died in 1936.

I learned that Betancourt is going out of his way to talk to his opponents and let bygones be bygones as far as political hatreds are concerned. Vice President Cordela remarked to me that Kennedy had supposedly set the standard for making friends with his political enemy by flying to see Nixon in Palm Beach last November. "But," said Caldera, "actually it was President Betancourt who set the precedent by coming to see Admiral Laraziball and me after he defeated us in 1958." Cordela had been a candidate for president against Betancourt in '58.

SUNDAY, FEBRUARY 19 | Enrique Tejera París, former governor of Sucre Province, drove us down to the beach, where we lunched with Minister of Foreign Affairs [Marcos] Falcón Briceño at a beautiful beach apartment owned by the former ambassador to Mexico. The foreign minister, Luvie, and I swam. The water was quite chilly.

The foreign minister told me that the foreign minister of Ecuador, en route home from Washington, had stopped off and told him that the United States was calling a meeting of the foreign ministers of the Pan-American countries shortly, in order to try to take concerted action against Castro in Cuba. I expressed doubt whether the move would get far. Mexico, Bolivia, and Brazil are certain to object.

MONDAY, FEBRUARY 20 | The Venezuelans lined up quite a day for me, beginning at 9:00 a.m. with the American ambassador and appointments every hour with cabinet ministers. Ambassador Eddie Sparks showed up half an hour late for a nine o'clock appointment. I had known Sparks in Bolivia, where he had done a good job, though he is not very alert politically.

Sparks was one of the few career ambassadors who has had his resignation accepted by Kennedy and seems to feel blue about it. Probably the reason for his exit from diplomacy is the attempt on Nixon's life in Venezuela in May 1958. I asked him about it and whether he had properly warned Nixon. The Municipal Council of Caracas had passed a resolution urging Nixon not to come, but Sparks said that the vice president of the United States could not put his tail between his legs and run. I also asked Sparks if he had been responsible for dispatching the U.S. Marines to Puerto Rico during the Nixon crisis. Sparks was cagey about this but said that no one in Caracas had telephoned the White House asking for the marines. Apparently, this puts the blame on Eisenhower. At any rate the dispatching of the marines set us back in Latin America.

I learned from members of the embassy staff that Nixon had not been as heroic as described in his memoirs. Jack Cates, security officer of the embassy, told me Nixon had requested an open car, but when he saw the crowd at the airport, he, Cates, had asked Nixon, "Do you still want an open car, Mr. Vice President?" and Nixon replied, "No."

Part of the trouble lay in the fact that Nixon had insisted that photographers drive ahead of him in order to film his advance through the crowd. The truck made a speed of twenty-five miles an hour, and when it got to the crest of one hill, it slowed down to the point where the crowds were able to come out and surround Nixon's car. Had it not been for the truck, the incident would never have happened.

Lozada said that President Betancourt was caught between the army on one side and Venezuelan business on the other. If Betancourt increases taxes sufficiently to put across a truly democratic social reform administration, business will conspire with the army to throw him out. Or if he cuts the military budget in order to pay for his social reforms, the military will conspire to throw him out. This, incidentally, is the problem which most democratic leaders face in Latin American nations.

TUESDAY, FEBRUARY 21 | Early breakfast with the former Venezuelan ambassador to the United States, Hector Santaella. He loaned me his Cadillac to drive to an appointment I had at 10:00 a.m. with some labor leaders at the Casa Syndical (labor headquarters). The chauffeur drove me past a military car loaded with troops on one side of a bridge, then across the bridge, and stopped in front of the Casa Syndical. A crowd of workers let out a roar at my swank car, as if they were planning to do to me what they did to Nixon. The chauffeur looked frightened. I confess I was too, but there wasn't anything for me to do but get out of the car and act as if nothing was happening.

This I did as nonchalantly as possible, walking past about five hundred loitering workmen who had come to the Casa Syndical either to demonstrate or find jobs—I never could tell which. I went inside the building, poking my head into various offices and trying to find someone who could speak English. No luck. The building was swarming with union members. Finally, I located a telephone and called one of the cabinet members who spoke English, and he got a man to the telephone who tried to locate the gentleman with whom I was supposed to confer. After hanging around an hour, I decided to leave. I was a little worried about passing through that crowd of angry demonstrators, and I didn't know whether I would be able to get a taxi anywhere in the vicinity.

I set out on foot. The demonstrators were still demonstrating, and across a bridge I saw the troops still stopping anyone who crossed it. They seemed bent on keeping the workers on this side of the bridge. I walked across the bridge, a sort of no-man's-land, to the side occupied by the troops. I wasn't sure what was going to happen, but the troops didn't bother me, and I walked on.

WEDNESDAY, FEBRUARY 22 | We left about one o'clock on a military plane for the iron ore region, enjoyed a good lunch on the plane, and flew over the famous iron ore mountain which is being mined by U.S. Steel.

It is almost pure iron and has the advantage of having the ore at the top. Thus, the bulldozers can scrape the iron ore off and work their way down. They don't have to dig and lift the ore up. The chief problem is with the brakes on the dump trucks and on the trains which carry the ore ninety miles down the mountainside to the Orinoco River. Already two hundred feet of the mountain have been taken off; however, it has four hundred million tons of ore, and it will take fifty years to eat it down to the ground. Most of the ore sails up the Delaware River to Trenton and the Fairless plant.

Landing at Puerto Odaz, I was taken immediately to an immense steel plant between the Orinoco and Caroni Rivers. This plant is four hundred miles from the equator and was constructed by an Italian firm. It will manufacture, when completed, seamless tubing for oil pipelines. It has already cost $250 million and will cost $150 million more. I'm not sure that it is practical, but it certainly it beautiful.

In typical Italian and Venezuelan manner, however, the offices were finished first—with Coca-Cola fountains, executive dining rooms, and glass-enclosed balconies high over the tropical one-time jungle. The more important parts of the plant have not yet been finished. I was entertained at the guesthouse of the Orinoco Mining Company, which is a subsidiary of U.S. Steel. The officials were cordial. Possibly they had forgotten how I once tried to block a congressional appropriation of $90 million to dredge the Delaware River up as far as Trenton and the Fairless plant. I pointed out that Ben Fairless, head of U.S. Steel, had bribed Rep. Mike Kirwan of Youngstown, who had been opposed to the appropriation, by giving his son, young Mike, a job with U.S. Steel in Pittsburgh. I also pointed out that the steel company in Venezuela was forced to dredge the Orinoco at its own expense.

After a dinner with about thirty employees and executives of U.S. Steel, we went down to the river's edge, where I witnessed the amazing operation of unloading iron ore, crushing it, and loading it on ships, with only about two men operating the intricate machinery.

THURSDAY, FEBRUARY 23 | (Awoke at 5:30 a.m. for boat trip to Tennessee Valley project on the Caroni River; visited housing projects, tropical jungle and waterfalls, giant dam and hydroelectric project; hair-raising flight back to Caracas, detouring to view Angel Falls; lunch meeting with minister of defense; flew on to Maracay, inspected agricultural and housing projects; spent the night.)

FRIDAY, FEBRUARY 24 | Arose at 5:00 a.m. and flew two hours to Maracaibo, the famous oil lake. The pilot of our military plane flew low over the lake so that we could see the forest of derricks jutting into it, with little tender boats cruising in between to check on the oil pumps which send several million barrels of oil weekly to the United States.

CARACAS—At the airport we were informed that we could not fly because we had no visa to stop in Havana. This was the first word I had of the plane stopping in Havana or that Americans were barred from going through the airport. I finally got the American consul, Don Lewis, on the phone. At first he flatly refused to give us a transit visa and attempted to call the ambassador in Caracas. Finally, he relented, scurried down to the airport, and issued the visas.

The plane was an island-hopper. It stopped on Aruba, then Kingston, Jamaica, and finally Havana, before we got to Miami. On the plane were thirty Russians en route from Moscow via Amsterdam and the Dutch West Indies. They had come this way because they didn't want to stop in New York. The Dutch stewardess told me that about six hundred Russians had been carried by KLM [Koninklijke Luchtvaart Maatschappij, or Dutch Royal Airlines] in the last two months.

At the Kingston airport the British customs official came aboard and announced, "No Iron Curtain passengers will be allowed to debark." After inspecting the down-at-the-heel Kingston airport, I wondered whether it was because the British were ashamed of their facilities or whether they wanted to retaliate against the Russians.

The Russians traveled economy, whereas most American government servants insist on going first-class. The Russians were quiet, well behaved, and spent their time playing cards.

When we got to Havana, the Russians were given special treatment. They were admitted through the passport line ahead of everyone else.

There were also three Cuban musicians to meet the plane, a formality which I understand Castro gives to every incoming plane. The airport looked just about the way it did when I was here during the Batista regime circa 1955. The American ticket counters were closed, but other lines were busy. The airport was plastered with signs exhorting the Cuban people, "For the country, not for yourselves," together with explanations of the "back-to-the-farm movement," whereby Che Guevara is trying to get the people out to cut sugarcane. The security in the Havana airport was nil. Nobody seemed to care whether an American was wandering around loose except the shoeshine boy, who complained that business was bad and appreciated the extra tip.

Our plane was delayed about two hours because so many Cuban refugees were anxious to leave the country that they overloaded the plane. The Cuban authorities inspected all the baggage. Apparently, they were looking for needles, soap, and cash. We finally got aloft. It was hot, sticky, and the airport in Miami is particularly loaded with red tape.

**THURSDAY, MARCH 2** | WASHINGTON DC—Last night I had dinner with the Clementses. Earle talked about Lyndon. He wants us to get together at a dinner fairly soon and make up. Lyndon, according to Earle, has high respect for me. I told Earle that I had always liked Lyndon but that whenever I try to go to bat for him, as I had done with Wayne Morse, Proxmire, and Joe Clark to win them around to Lyndon's side, Lyndon pulled the rug out from under me by putting across high-handed operations, such as his desire to preside over Democratic caucuses.

Anyway, I agreed to have dinner with Lyndon, though I'm not so sure it's a good idea to get together at a social function. Lyndon does all the talking and ends up thinking he's won you over, when actually all he's done is to convince himself.

**SATURDAY, MARCH 4** | Kay Denckla's doctor says that there is no question but that Kennedy is taking cortisone and that it has the following side effects: (1) retention of salt and water, which makes the face get round; (2) great energy and a sort of euphoria which makes you think you are on top of the world and accomplishing great things; (3) increases in appetite; (4) increases the sex desire.

The doctor said that some people can stop for a time, but some people can't. If they are taken off, three weeks are required to clear the body of aftereffects. Cortisone is a new drug, and nobody knows the final effect. It's only been in operation for about fifteen years, but if the proper doses are taken, you can go on for about ten or fifteen years with no aftereffects.

Kennedy needs something for his adrenal glands. His back ailment, plus malaria during the war, were too much for his glands. Kennedy does not have Addison's disease, however, which is the complete absence of adrenal glands. If he had this, he would be a gone goose. He did have hepatitis in the navy, which makes his skin sallow. The doctor is excellent, according to Kay's doctor, and she has advice on these matters from Dr. Eugene Cohen in New York, an expert on adrenal problems.

The Cuneos came to dinner. We spent most of the evening discussing the favorite topic of conversation: the sex life of the president of the United States. Jackie Kennedy has just left her husband for Palm Beach. She walked out after the last Saturday night's dinner given by the White House Correspondents'

Association. Kennedy shacked up with the female singer who had entertained the group. He had never met her before but sent for her.

Mrs. Kennedy was in Middleburg [Virginia] but came back to find out about it. Possibly, the woman was still in the White House. Anyway, Jackie walked out.

Joe Kennedy has remonstrated with Jack, to which Jack replied, "Look who's talking." Of course, the old man led the most flagrantly unfaithful sex life of anyone I know. He kept Gloria Swanson for years and incidentally charged up the cost of her gifts, which he supposedly paid for, to her motion picture production company. In the end Gloria made quite a bit of dough for old Joe.

Ernie used to know Florence Pritchett Smith, wife of Ambassador Earl Smith, when she was a "girl about town." Flo Flo lived with her mother as a sort of cover, did some TV shows, and finally married Earl Smith, had a baby by him, and then proceeded to revert to type.

Apparently, it's Jackie Kennedy who wants Earl Smith and Flo Flo appointed to another ambassadorial post. She wants them out of the country. Kennedy, having Smith turned down for Switzerland, has asked Dean Rusk to find another post—which is not going to be easy.

**MONDAY, MARCH 6** | Continued the lobbying battle against [Charles M.] Meriwether [nominated to be director of the Export-Import Bank]. Over the weekend I have been trying to get the police record on Meriwether, which reportedly was removed from the Birmingham police files but which showed he was arrested in 1947 for passing bad checks and driving a car which did not belong to him. Various calls to both Birmingham and Memphis, where Meriwether once worked for Boss Crump, failed to track this down. Wayne Morse, however, wrote a letter to J. Edgar Hoover asking whether these facts were correct; also sent a telegram to Meriwether asking him for a reply regarding the facts; finally, wrote a letter to Kennedy asking him for the facts regarding the alleged arrest.

Later in the day Ed Reid called from Alabama to say that sentiment had switched rather critically on Meriwether. Previously, it had been favorable. Now the feeling was that he had testified in a manner which did not bring pride to the State of Alabama. His answers, as published in the *Birmingham News*, were evasive. In addition, the Alabama legislature's executive committee had just published a report asking for a budget director of its own because of Meriwether's incompetence in making budget estimates; also, recommending legislation to prevent the sale of surplus commodities by the state without competitive bidding. Meriwether had sold a lot of surplus to Governor [John] Patterson's political friends at very low prices.

I talked to Senator Capehart of Indiana, a member of the Banking and Currency Committee, about opposing Meriwether. He was undecided. I also talked to Sen. Clint Anderson of New Mexico.

The Kennedy forces are throwing everything they have into the battle. During the weekend, however, I was on the telephone to groups in New England and Illinois to try to put the heat on Muskie of Maine and Paul Douglas of Illinois. They are members of the Banking and Currency Committee who did not vote. If they can be persuaded to get up on the floor when the debate opens tomorrow and say they've changed their minds and will vote against Meriwether, it will have a terrific impact. Both, however, are hard to move.

**TUESDAY, MARCH 7** | Morse got a visit yesterday from a White House aide, Mike Manitos, who brought up some excerpts from the FBI report, which did not, however, answer the question Morse gave the president—namely, whether Meriwether had a police record. In the interim I learned from Ed Reid that Meriwether himself had gone to the house of Grover Hall, editor of the *Montgomery Advertiser*, after Patterson's 1958 election and told him: "You boys were working awfully hard to get something on me, and at times you came close, but you missed. What you missed was the time when I got drunk and stayed in a hotel for a week. My boss came up to get me out; we got into an argument, and I hit him. He then had me arrested for driving his car. I swore off liquor after that."

Morse is preparing to filibuster unless the Senate will consent to a roll call vote. He asked me to get him more material for a long speech.

Earle Clements has invited us to dine with Lyndon tonight, and I asked Earle to pass the word to Lyndon that at least we should have a roll call vote. We are going to lose, but the senators are already maneuvering around to duck a roll call.

When the debate opened this afternoon, Javits made a good speech, but nobody was listening. Sparkman of Alabama and Robertson of Virginia defended Meriwether. Then Douglas killed the fight by saying that he would vote for Meriwether, chiefly because there was an anonymous report against him by a "faceless" informer: "For years we fought against these faceless informers during the McCarthy era, and we cannot listen to one now merely because he's on the other side."

This just about ends the debate. It was agreed by Mansfield that the vote would be taken at 2:00 p.m. Wednesday and that it would be a roll call vote. In the interim I had been on the telephone to various others, including newspaper editor Hank Greenspun of Las Vegas, who in turn called both Senators Bible and Cannon. Hank told Cannon, "Did you see Drew Pearson's column yesterday on Meriwether?" "Yes," replied Cannon, "but Meriwether has denied it under oath, and Pearson wasn't under oath."

This illustrates what you're up against in a Senate debate. Cannon didn't bother to read the record and to note that Meriwether was never put under oath. Cannon said, incidentally, that Kennedy had telephoned him at noon, urging him to vote for Meriwether. If this is true, Kennedy is using up his blue chips awfully fast on a very bad appointee.

**WEDNESDAY, MARCH 8** | Dined last night with the vice president and Lady Bird at the Earle Clementses'. Lyndon looked very thin and very well. Before dinner he pulled a doctor's report out of his pocket and read it with considerable pride. It showed a blood count of 116 over 72 and a cholesterol count of 265 as against something like 400 at the time of his heart attack. His weight is down to 183, though the doctor wants it to come to 180. He's eating Metrecal (a food supplement for weight loss) during the day but was obviously so famished that he ate more than anyone else at dinner.

Lyndon was enthusiastic over the executive order issued the day previously by which he takes over racial discrimination in the government and government contractors. "Abe Fortas worked a month drawing up that executive order, and there wasn't anything he didn't think of. It gives me all the powers there are in government to enforce racial equality. Nixon brought two Negroes into the government in eight years when he was handling the job. I've already brought in two hundred."

Johnson told of calling up Secretary of Defense McNamara at 7:30 a.m. to discuss race bias in the armed forces. The secretaries of the navy, the air force, and the army were on Lyndon's committee, and he thought that was probably enough, that it wasn't necessary to bother the secretary of defense. McNamara said, "I've got my secretaries on your committee, but I think I'd just as well be on there myself and see how things go."

Lyndon told him that he wanted to get after the big airplane companies, such as Lockheed, Douglas, North American, and make sure they were practicing no discrimination. McNamara said, "Within a couple of days I'll give you a list of the one hundred biggest contractors with the Defense Department."

Lyndon talked enthusiastically about McNamara and his behavior in cabinet meetings. He said McNamara was a slow starter and began at first talking like a Harvard professor but then waxed eloquent and was a great enthusiast. He rated Rusk and McNamara as perhaps the most effective members of the cabinet, with Arthur Goldberg right behind them. Dillon was rather quiet and mumbled his reports to the cabinet in a halting manner. Luther Hodges was described as a Chesterfieldian gentleman, far more liberal than people realized and with very liberal policies in the Commerce Department.

The attorney general, Bobby Kennedy, seldom said anything, but when he did, he was to the point. I asked Lyndon whether Bobby ever had a tendency to talk back to his brother. Lyndon replied that there was never any trace of resentment; that Bobby had not been for him [Johnson] in Los Angeles for vice president and gave in detail the story of what happened there, after Jack Kennedy had first invited him to be vice president. Bobby told him that there was opposition from labor circles. "Which labor circles?" Lyndon asked. "From Chicago and New York" was the reply.

Bobby indicated they had planned to talk to Governor Freeman of Minnesota and Senator Jackson about running for vice president; however, since Lyndon had already indicated he was willing to accept, he stood pat, and in a short time Jack Kennedy called him on the telephone, read a statement he had drafted, and a few minutes later went on television to announce that he had picked Johnson.

After dinner Lyndon told me privately: "You know there was only one reason why I am playing second fiddle and why Lady Bird is playing second fiddle and why I am not running the Senate anymore. It's because I didn't want Nixon to win. If I hadn't taken second place on this ticket, Nixon would have won."

Lyndon described Kennedy as patient, listening to the briefings by others and quick in making up his mind. The problems of Laos, the Congo, and Berlin are something "to make your hair stand on end," Lyndon said. While discussing Berlin and the National Security Council, General Lemnitzer, the chairman of the Joint Chiefs of Staff, was asked how much food West Berlin had on hand. Lemnitzer fumbled around, didn't have the answer. Finally, Secretary McNamara broke in, "You know, General, its six months'."

Lyndon talked about his problems with the liberals. I pointed out that they had chafed at his leadership for a good many years and that, when he became vice president, they expected him to be on the sidelines. Then, when he came in to preside over caucuses, there was resentment.

Lyndon summarized the conversation by saying: "You've always been with me when I needed help. If it hadn't been for you, I wouldn't be in the Senate. You were for me when I wanted to be president. You were for me when I ran for vice president. In between, when I haven't needed you, you've sometimes been against me. Naturally, I get mad, but I know that when the chips are down, you'll be with me again."

I agreed. I also pointed out that editors were prone to expect criticism of those in office and just in the last two days I had received two letters from editors wanting to know about Johnson and his private plane, which they compared to some of Nixon's help from private individuals. Johnson went into a lengthy explanation of his plane, which really missed the point, but I didn't press. The point is that he has some secret partners paying the expenses of the plane, just as Nixon had some secret contributors to his personal expense fund.

**THURSDAY, MARCH 9** | Continued lobbying against Meriwether with Senators Proxmire, Capehart, and Muskie. The attitude of most senators is: "Kennedy wants this appointee. He's a bad appointee, but since Kennedy wants him, we'll have to vote for him."

That was the way it worked out. The great majority of Democrats did vote for him. The Republicans split about fifty-fifty.

One of Kennedy's assistants, Mike Feldman, told Jack [Anderson] that Kennedy had decided to withdraw Meriwether's name. He was shocked at the information regarding his record. Then he slept on it overnight and the next day told his staff that the appointment was not a very important one and that if the name was withdrawn, it would be a sign of weakness. Coming on top of the withdrawal of Earl Smith as ambassador to Switzerland, Kennedy thought it would be bad policy to withdraw, so he gave the word for a showdown vote. This is the first time in the Kennedy administration that there has been a roll call on anything. Though we lost, most of the senators admitted they had held their nose when they voted for Meriwether.

**SATURDAY, MARCH 11** | Phil Graham has just purchased *Newsweek* magazine and added it to his publishing empire. During the course of the afternoon he telephoned me that his wife, Kay, had a tuberculosis examination and might have TB. He was upset and asked Luvie to drive down. Luvie departed. She seemed to think that Phil was going to go off the deep end, which I doubt.

WEDNESDAY, MARCH 15 | Kennedy faces a serious showdown over Laos. His letter to Khrushchev, delivered by Ambassador Thompson asking for cooperation to make Laos a neutral state, didn't get anywhere. Khrushchev knows that we are up against it when it comes to fighting a war eight thousand miles away. He has thrown supplies into Laos. Now Kennedy either has to put up or shut up. He has started to send more American supplies, but I don't see how he can risk war.

At the press conference today Kennedy asked the public to discuss the church-and-state issue in regard to schools with "reason." He now finds himself with the Baptists supporting him and the Catholics criticizing him.

FRIDAY, MARCH 31 | No word yet received from the Russians on Laos. The Red bloc has been meeting in Moscow and issued a statement warning of militarism and the menace of Western Germany. There was not a word about the Far East and Laos. The reports coming from Moscow indicate that the Russians are going to be reasonable. Gromyko had a session with Kennedy at the White House during midweek. Nothing is leaking out. It used to be that memos were sent to the Joint Chiefs of Staff for their information, not now.

One interesting angle to the Gromyko-Kennedy conference, however, was that after talking about forty-five minutes with others present in his office, Kennedy took Gromyko out into the garden for about fifteen minutes, alone. Jackie Kennedy came up to say good-bye en route to Palm Beach. During this private session it is speculated that Kennedy told Gromyko: (1) that he was up against some pressures here at home; (2) that he would cooperate with Khrushchev; but (3) that he meant business, and there must be a cease-fire in Laos.

SATURDAY, APRIL 1 | The Russian note was delivered today to the British ambassador in Moscow and immediately conveyed to Palm Beach, where Kennedy is spending Easter. It reverses Kennedy's demands by agreeing, first, to an international conference; second, to the reinstatement of the neutral commission to supervise hostilities; and third, to use its influence to bring about a cease-fire. This insinuates the fear previously expressed by the French ambassador to me, that if a fourteen-nation conference were called, the fighting would continue during the deliberations until all of Laos became Communist—leaving nothing to talk about.

The Russian reply is clever because it puts the onus on Kennedy. It also puts the Russians in a position of favoring peace. Kennedy can't reject the note without appearing to be for war. His reply, issued in a brief public statement, was therefore cautious.

**WEDNESDAY, APRIL 12** | There are rumors that Russia was putting a man into space, had in fact done so last Friday. I predicted on the air Sunday that Russia would put a man into space around May 1.

This morning there was an official announcement by TASS that a Russian, Yuri Gagarin, had orbited the earth in one hour and twenty minutes and landed safely "somewhere in the Soviet Union." There were no details as to how he landed. Apparently, our tracking stations caught his satellite as it spun around the earth, and thus the first man in history to travel through outer space has notched a position for himself in the history books, alongside Christopher Columbus.

I wrote a column for immediate release which I suspect few newspapers will publish. I said two men were responsible for Russia's triumph: Khrushchev and Dwight D. Eisenhower. It may be that I overemphasized Khrushchev's part in this space achievement, but I did not overemphasize Eisenhower's part. We are now so far behind Russia that it's doubtful we can catch up within my lifetime.

I was in Huntsville, Alabama, two years ago, talking with the commander of Redstone Arsenal as to why we had not built a rocket launcher with the same power as Russia's. He said we were now producing one. That was two years ago. Actually, it was not until two weeks ago that Kennedy sent a real appropriation to Congress which would help to close the gap.

**THURSDAY, APRIL 13** | Pierre Salinger telephoned to volunteer a story. He said Kennedy was in the process of desegregating the White House Photographers Association, which hitherto had not accepted Negroes. Kennedy is not going to the May 19 White House Photographers Dinner unless they desegregate before that time.

Lyndon Johnson has arrived back from Africa and Geneva, just in time for the hullabaloo over Russia's man in space. I wonder where this leaves him as the new general advisor in charge of space. Actually, he is not responsible.

Furthermore, he told me two weeks ago how he was insisting on more money for a rocket launcher and had persuaded Kennedy to put more money in the budget for such a launcher; however, our failures in space are bound to hurt him, unless we can make a dramatic recovery, which is doubtful.

FRIDAY, APRIL 14 | Called on the president today to invite him to the Ed Foley Big Brothers Dinner. Although I'd had some private conferences with Roosevelt and once had a memorable scene with Harry Truman when he bawled me out after a press conference . . . I never called formally on a president of the United States before. Once I called on Calvin Coolidge by regular appointment, but I don't believe it was scheduled on his calendar.

It is indicative of the power and prestige which surrounds the White House and any president that every one of us who called on Kennedy this morning—and most of us have known him fairly well—greeted him as "Mr. President" and acted as if we had scarcely known him before. I, for one, am quite frank in admitting that I kept waking up at night rehearsing some of the things I was going to say to him. And I am supposed to be a hard-boiled newspaper reporter who makes or breaks presidents. (If the public only knew!)

At any rate I had breakfast at the Carlton at eight fifteen with Judge Luther Youngdahl, former governor of Minnesota and himself a Big Brother there; Judge David Bazelon, of the circuit court of appeals; Jiggs Donohue, former commissioner of the District of Columbia; and Arthur Clarendon Smith, seventy-eight and famous for his moving company's motto ["Don't make a move—without calling Smith"]. After[ward] we rehearsed our strategy. It was decided that I should make the opening pitch, then let the judges talk about juvenile delinquency.

It was so long since I had been in the Executive Offices that I was a little confused as we were ushered into the president's office and almost stopped in his outer room, which was filled with secretaries. He was standing behind his big desk and came over to greet me. I called him "Mr. President." He called me "Drew." I told him it was wonderful to see him here. He greeted the others without any introductions. Jiggs remarked on how well Kennedy looked. Kennedy said something about the fact that any work was easier than the strain of last fall's campaign.

The Oval Office had been repainted an olive green instead of the old white in Roosevelt's and Truman's days, and the etchings which were so famous in FDR's day were gone. I was so busy concentrating on the subject at hand that I didn't get a chance to look at the room carefully. The desk, which used to be cluttered with donkeys in FDR's day, was neat and clean, as it was also in Truman's time. We sat in front of the fireplace on two white sofas. The president sat in a rocking chair at the head of the sofas. I opened by remarking, "I've just written a story about you," and then I paused very briefly, "that you prefer peanut butter sandwiches to official dinners; however, despite that, we are now inviting you to a dinner."

Kennedy said briefly that when prime ministers or presidents came to see him, he had to give them a dinner, then they had to give him a dinner. I explained that this dinner was in honor of Ed Foley, who did such a good job as chairman of Inaugural Week and was for the purpose of emphasizing the remedies for juvenile delinquency (Ed Foley being one of the pioneers in the Big Brother organization).

"The judges have been holding our feet to the fire about the problem of juvenile delinquency," I said. "We haven't been doing enough about it, but we've been trying. Judge Youngdahl was telling us this morning that he had been up until midnight last night reading seven presentencing reports regarding criminals he must sentence this morning."

Youngdahl pointed out that in each case the story was the same—broken home, illegitimacy, no parents, no education, no chance. If they had been helped early in life, none of these men would have ended in jail. Now they are repeaters and hopeless. "It makes you sick when you come up against this hopelessness," Youngdahl said. "There isn't anything you can do about it when you catch them late in life. What you have to do is to catch them early. It makes my blood boil when they accuse the Negro population of running up the crime rate. Of course, it's true that 53 percent of the DC population is Negro and a much larger percent of the criminals, but when they haven't been to school, haven't any father or mother, what can you expect? We have the highest percentage of illegitimacy of any city in the United States. Also, the highest percentage of syphilis and gonorrhea."

We also mentioned that the president's brother had spoken eloquently about the problem of juvenile crime at his recent press conference. He wanted to know more about Big Brothers, and Judge Youngdahl, who had been governor of Minnesota and a Big Brother himself, explained. Kennedy wanted to know how many Big Brothers there were in the District, and I had to tell him that we only had a hundred. Actually, this was stretching it a bit, as I found later. Our chief problem is to get older men to help us out, and

I explained to the president that we were new in the District of Columbia, having just revived the organization.

He came to the point by saying: "These dinners get to be rather wearing. Would it be all right if I came in a little after the dinner to speak?" We replied that this would be wonderful, whereupon he got up, went into the next room, and came back with his calendar. Looking over his calendar, he settled on June 7.

As we arose to go, Arthur Smith asked about a photograph and said he had his own photographer present. The president readily assented and went over to a door to the left of the fireplace and opened it. Out burst not one photographer but twenty. They even had their own klieg light along and proceeded to shoot us from all angles, both by still and motion picture. The president came out to the little hallway to open the door for us. Everyone was impressed with his charm and cordiality. Also, he looked very well. He has put on a little weight around his face but otherwise looks trim and fit.

Outside the office in the White House corridor we gave the story to the newspapermen. I have interviewed a lot of people myself in the White House lobby but have never been interviewed. In this case I had prompted Judges Bazelon and Youngdahl to emphasize the problem of juvenile delinquency, which they did.

I wrote a column on the problem of building a high-powered rocket launcher to launch satellites and Kennedy's tough job of deciding between the solid fuel launcher and the liquid fuel launcher. He could find himself in the same box Eisenhower did by concentrating on the wrong launcher. The Atlas, which is liquid fuel, has about run its course. The Polaris and Minuteman, which are solid fuel, are taking over. Yet we are still concentrating on the liquid fuel Saturn as a booster.

MONDAY, APRIL 17 | ST. PETERSBURG FL—The Cuban situation is getting hotter. The bombing of Havana by three Cuban pilots over the weekend has marked the signal for an invasion. Actually, it looks as if the pilots were exiles, not defectors from the Cuban air force, as announced.

There is no question that this is the CIA-organized invasion, though Kennedy has stated—and so has Rusk in a press conference this morning—that the United States had nothing to do with it.

I was met at the airport and interviewed on the subject, especially whether the invasion would be a success. I took the optimistic view, though I doubt if it is justified.

**THURSDAY, APRIL 20** | WASHINGTON DC—Kennedy spoke before the [American Society of Newspaper] editors at 2:00 p.m. and outlined a vigorous position regarding Cuba in which he virtually put the United States and the world on record that we would intervene unilaterally in Cuba if the Pan-American Union did not support us. I fear the speech was more courageous than wise. Kennedy is not going to be able to intervene in Cuba unilaterally without getting the entire hemisphere against him.

I remember another speech which Vice President Nixon made before the same Association of Newspaper Editors in April 1954, which also made history—in reverse. Nixon told them the United States would land troops in French Indochina. The reaction was such that Eisenhower very quickly made it known that we would not land troops. While Kennedy did not go this far, nevertheless the reaction in Latin America is going to be similar. He will probably have to backtrack.

**FRIDAY, APRIL 21** | Lyndon Johnson telephoned this morning to say that the crisis in regard to Cuba and the world, including Laos, was much more serious than anyone realized, much more serious than he realized before he got into the administration.

Wrote a column on the CIA's poor handling not merely of the Cuban invasion but also of the U-2 incident and other things. The column was long overdue, as is an investigation of CIA.

The Cuba invasion has now folded into a real tragedy. The so-called Freedom Fighters are now being shown in humiliating captivity on television by Castro.

**SATURDAY, APRIL 22** | Kennedy conferred today with Ike at Camp David. This is a sign of weakness. And I'm afraid it will be so interpreted by the country. During the week he also conferred with Nixon. Obviously, Kennedy is looking for support, and he will need it.

Kennedy has now got himself boxed in. My information is that he will chart an embargo or blockade of Cuba to keep out all arms shipments. It now develops that some thirteen ships were unloading in Havana harbor with arms—at the very moment of the invasion.

Keeping Soviet ships out of Havana means boarding them on the high seas, and this is what brought on the War of 1812, when the British did it to us. Bobby Kennedy is now studying the law books to see what justification he can find for a blockade of Cuba.

**MONDAY, APRIL 24** | Salinger came to lunch. He volunteered that the president was sore at his secretary of the interior, Stewart Udall, for making a remark on TV yesterday that the Republicans had handed Kennedy a bad mess in regard to Cuba. Salinger pointed out that this had come just after Kennedy had invited Ike to luncheon at Camp David and secured Ike's complete cooperation. He said that Kennedy was taking the blame for the Cuban fiasco and that no one else was going to be blamed.

I said that while I was for Kennedy on most things and hoped very much he would succeed, that I couldn't possibly refrain from criticism. I suggested that when the going got tough and I got too much hell from Republican editors, I would ask Kennedy a favor—namely, that he do to me what Harry Truman did: blast me. This would really set me up with the press. Salinger said that when the time was desperate to call on him.

**MONDAY, MAY 1** | For some time Jack has been trying to get a couple of the Cuban Freedom Fighters to come from Miami to Washington. Today they finally turned up. I made a date for them to see Wayne Morse, who is chairman of the Senate Foreign Affairs subcommittee on Latin America. They told a shocking story of mismanagement in organizing the rebel invasion. At the last minute, when Kennedy approved the entry of U.S. combat planes into the battle, the navy planes, based on an aircraft carrier offshore, proceeded to bomb one rebel B-26. This was the help which American planes gave the Freedom Fighters.

All the aviation gas, tanks, shells, and antitank guns were loaded on the slow-moving *Escondido*, which had to proceed at four knots an hour ahead of the rest of the flotilla. When she arrived off the Bay of Pigs, Castro, either by luck or otherwise, proceeded to bomb her and knocked her out.

Judging by some of the questions from my audience, the American people are stunned and bewildered over the Cuban fiasco. I would say that if Kennedy were running for reelection today, he would lose overwhelmingly. I also suspect that when the congressional elections come along next year, he may lose the House of Representatives. People still seem to enjoy those bromides by Eisenhower that all was right with the world, and they believe that when Kennedy went to see Eisenhower, he went for advice. They don't grasp the fact that Kennedy's frantic moves to confer with . . . Ike, Nixon, MacArthur, and Hoover were in order to kill Republican criticism, not ask advice.

**WEDNESDAY, MAY 3** | I said in my speech in Jeffersonville yesterday that Kennedy resembled a young boxer who had all the right footwork and all the right passes, but then suddenly, as he waves to the crowd, someone clips him in the jaw and knocks him out—in this case Fidel Castro. Kennedy is still going through the motions of the young boxer. He received a degree today from George Washington University and made a speech on liberty. The Senate Foreign Relations Committee has been meeting meanwhile to fix the blame. Bill Fulbright has made a statement that the invasion should never have been undertaken. The Republican press has tried to put the blame on Adlai, Chester Bowles, and Rusk for not permitting the use of American planes. Nixon held a breakfast (off the record) with newspapermen in which he was bitter against the Democrats for the same reason. He claimed American planes should have gone in and mopped up.

**THURSDAY, MAY 4** | The two Cubans who gave information to Wayne Morse went back to Florida. This morning I got a call that they were in some difficulty. Morse had told them to go back and collect their papers. Central Intelligence was either tapping the telephone or got wind of what was up because a man named Felix Gutierrez, a flunky for the CIA, turned up at Mirro Cardona's in Coral Gables and demanded the files. The lease for the house was in Gutierrez's name, and when the files were not forthcoming, he went to the police for nonpayment of rent. The police then moved in and sealed the house with the files inside until Monday.

I asked Morse to try to get action from the Senate Foreign Relations Committee, preferably a subpoena for the files. He was busy all day with an education bill, plus other hearings on Cuba, but tried belatedly to get a subpoena. I have written two stories about the bungling of the invasion.

The United States finally put a man into outer space. He was sent up from Cape Canaveral about 150 miles and landed downrange near the Bahamas. This was like a bunt after a Russian home run. Nevertheless, it was received with great acclaim. Most people didn't realize that the Russians had sent a man in orbit around the world.

Alicia Patterson, cousin of Felicia [Pearson's first wife] and now publisher of *Newsday* on Long Island, came out with a front-page letter to Kennedy wanting to know what the American people should do to combat communism.

She reminded him that he had several times told the people that they must work and sacrifice, so now she wanted to know just what they should do.

This really puts him on the spot because there isn't very much the American people can do besides pay higher taxes—and this is the last thing they want to do and the last thing Kennedy wants to ask for right now.

Yesterday at the Bourgiba reception I bumped into Russian ambassador Menshikov. He said, "I hope you didn't mind my referring to you the other day as a friend." He made a statement published in the *Washington Post* society columns that I was his friend. I told the ambassador that I didn't mind. He went on to say, "Of course, they might call you up before the Un-American Activities Committee and investigate you." While this will not happen, I'm sure the John Birch Society will make hay with his statement.

**THURSDAY, MAY 18** | Kennedy is in Canada. Jackie went along and is making a hit with the French Canadians because of her use of their language. She and Jack seem to be getting along better. I suspect that the old man's warning to his son to start sleeping with his wife for a change finally sunk home. Also, I suspect that Jackie had something to do with it. She was in a position to make her husband a one-term president, and she's tough enough to lay down the law. Although sympathy would have been very much on her side, actually she's pretty tough and conceited, without much consideration for other people.

Before Kennedy went to Canada, he wrote a letter to Alicia Patterson, who had asked him to specify what people should do for their country. He specified higher taxes, a long-range foreign aid program, farm controls, price-and-wage levels to meet competition, avoiding work stoppages on vital defense jobs, and more local effort on school programs, plus the end of racial discrimination. He is right, but this program isn't going to satisfy a lot of people. He's already mentioned these things in various speeches, and they want to be told in more detail what they should do.

Lyndon Johnson is now in Thailand. Rusk is in Geneva. Thus, about three months after Kennedy assumed office, he is engaging in personalized diplomacy just as avidly as did Eisenhower and Nixon.

**FRIDAY, MAY 19** | In the South the screwballs and rascals supported Kennedy because it wasn't very popular to support a Catholic; the more staid Democrats supported Lyndon Johnson, and the real reactionaries voted for

Nixon. Kennedy is now stuck with the rabble-rousers, such as Patterson and Meriwether, who in fact have nothing in common with him.

SUNDAY, MAY 21 | All week there's been trouble in Alabama. Negro Freedom Riders, seeking to test their right to travel in interstate commerce unsegregated, first went to Birmingham and yesterday to Montgomery, where there were riots, and several were nearly killed. The Ku Klux Klan and Bobby Shelton, its Grand Dragon (about whom I have written frequently), led the attacks, and the police were a minus quantity. I wrote a column putting the bee on Bobby Kennedy and his determination to confirm Charles Meriwether, despite our evidence that Meriwether was a friend of the Klan and that Patterson had been elected with Klan support.

MONDAY, MAY 22 | (Speaking engagement: Pennsylvania Association of Broadcasters.) Sen. Hugh Scott spoke before the broadcasters the night before I did and excoriated Kennedy as running the government by leaks and Harvard boys. He is certainly right about the government by leaks.

In my talk I denied government by Harvard boys and pointed to the part which the Joint Chiefs of Staff played in the Cuban fiasco. I laid it on the line regarding the TV networks and the part they had played in adding to the complacency of the American people. I don't think my speech went down well.

In Alabama last night there was the worst riot of all. Bobby Kennedy sent U.S. marshals just in time to protect Negroes. A white mob nearly burned down the First Baptist Church, in which Dr. Martin Luther King was speaking. The automobile of Cliff Burr, brother-in-law of [Supreme Court justice] Hugo Black, was burned outside the church. He had loaned it to an English lady reporter.

MONDAY, MAY 29 | Lyndon telephoned. He didn't like the story I had in the column today that he was down on Emperor Diem of South Vietnam and thought the United States could not support him. On the contrary, Lyndon said, Diem was putting across some excellent land reforms and reorganizing the country in the same way the British did the Malays. Lyndon was quite vigorous about these. He also took issue with the story that Mme Chiang Kai-shek had been neglectful of Lady Bird and the president's sister, Mrs. Smith. "After all, the head of a state's wife doesn't receive the vice president's wife," Lyndon said. He was impressed by the social reforms put across on Formosa [Taiwan], and I agreed with him.

(Lunched with Tom Corcoran.) Our discussion was aroused by the election of John G. Tower as the first Republican senator from Texas in a hundred years. He is even more reactionary than Goldwater. Tom reminded me that Texas has the right, under the treaty which admitted it to the Union, to split into five states whenever it wishes. This would give it ten senators, all of whom could be a replica of John G. Tower. This in turn would mean that Texas would dominate the Senate and could start a move by New York, California, Pennsylvania, to increase their number of senators.

Of course, these states would have to get an amendment to the Constitution to increase their senators, while Texas would not. Tom is worried as to what will happen in Congress when Sam Rayburn goes. Sam, more than the northern liberals, has put across the great reforms of the New Deal. He commands great loyalty and can crack the whip. Without him the liberal bloc in Congress will have no real leaders.

**WEDNESDAY, MAY 31** | Jackie Kennedy is giving a big reception in Paris. The president, meanwhile, agreed with de Gaulle during their first thirty-five minutes of discussion to stand firm on Berlin. Yet just prior to his departure Kennedy received a memorandum from the Joint Chiefs of Staff that it would be impossible to stand firm on Berlin without nuclear war. The Joint Chiefs went into detail to show how the conventional forces of the United States had deteriorated so badly that we couldn't possibly force our way through East Germany to reach Berlin nor conduct a Berlin airlift. Therefore, our only recourse, if we are going to hold Berlin, would be nuclear war. Kennedy's decision in Paris, therefore, means that either he is prepared to go to war or doesn't intend to live up to his commitment with de Gaulle.

**THURSDAY, JUNE 1** | Generalissimo Trujillo was assassinated in the Dominican Republic yesterday. He was driving for a rendezvous with his mistress, Moni Sanchez, when the car was ambushed.

I recall it was Angel Morales, the vice president of the Dominican Republic, then in exile, who first put me wise to Trujillo, back in 1930 or '31. Morales had been shaving in his apartment in New York City when suddenly he looked in the mirror and saw a man approaching behind him. He ducked. Fortunately, the shot went wild. This was the first of Trujillo's attempts to assassinate his enemies, and I am surprised now that I look back on it that he dealt with me so generously when I went through the Dominican Republic in 1931 and again in 1959.

It was at the old Faustus Hotel in Santo Domingo. He sipped warm champagne with me, just after I had written a series of articles about him, calling him a cattle thief and an embezzler.

Dean Rusk has delayed his trip to Paris because of the assassination. Apparently, the State Department expects trouble in the Dominican Republic.

**FRIDAY, JUNE 2** | The Kennedys are taking Paris by storm. Jack has done all right, but Jackie is the toast of Paris.

This is a cold gal who deep down doesn't have much sympathy for the aims of her husband and wouldn't know a social reform when she saw one. I have found that a lot of Americans, with people unemployed, resent her hoity-toity manner and her riding to the hounds in Middleburg; however, there's no question that she is a terrific asset to her husband on this trip. For the first time she has come into her own.

**SATURDAY, JUNE 3** | Kennedy is in Vienna. Before leaving Paris, he held a press conference which was excellent. He told what he would do if he were Khrushchev and, among other things, pointed to the disunity between American leaders but warned Khrushchev that this was not serious. This in turn gave him a chance to comment on the disunity between Khrushchev and the Chinese Communists and Albania. He's handling himself well.

**SUNDAY, JUNE 4** | Dined with the Thurman Arnolds, Hugo Blacks, Florence Mahoney, George Killion, and the Senator Monroneys of Oklahoma. Larry O'Brien, the White House secretary for congressional affairs, was also present. The conversation turned to whether Nixon would run for governor of California and whether Pat Brown could beat him. It was Killion's belief that if the election were held today, Nixon would win. I suggested a fairly simple way to help turn the tide in the opposite direction—namely, to release, or rather leak, the text of the Khrushchev-Nixon debate held inside the Kremlin. This shows Nixon apologizing to Khrushchev for the Captive Nations Week resolution passed by Congress.

**WEDNESDAY, JUNE 14** | Talked with Lyndon Johnson. He's enthusiastic over his trip to Southeast Asia and wants me to rally behind his move to bring over a Pakistani camel driver (whom he invited here). Though Lyndon is always enthusiastic about his trips, I have the feeling not merely from him but from others that he did a very good job.

He invited me to go on a brief yachting cruise down the Potomac with the secretary of state of South Vietnam. We were the guests of the secretary of the navy, John Connally, whom I tried to defeat for confirmation. On board were the former ambassador to Thailand, Johnson, whom I met in Bangkok a year and a half ago, together with the new ambassador to Thailand and various State Department Asia experts.

Sen. Hubert Humphrey pulled me aside to express his concern about the way the administration was heading. He believes Kennedy is making too many speeches, too much general talk, and not enough action. He pointed out that Kennedy had not talked with Adlai Stevenson, Mrs. Roosevelt, HHH, or any of those who had talked to Khrushchev before he went to Vienna.

Had a long talk with Walt Rostow, Kennedy's personal advisor, who expressed the opposite view. He was concerned that the story was getting abroad that Kennedy ignored advice and, due to the failure to hold cabinet meetings, did not operate efficiently. He said that afternoon there had been a meeting of the National Security Council for two hours, but when you have top officials with staff assistants driving up in limousines and holding a full-dress debate, you don't get things accomplished in the same way as when you have a handful of intimate advisors talking to the president.

Rostow said he'd had dinner with four of Eisenhower's former assistants, including Arthur Krock, and they were critical that Kennedy was being run by a bunch of professors. They particularly jumped on Rostow, who argued that the White House is well organized and a little group of advisors get together frequently and quickly to handle important problems.

He emphasized the esprit de corps around the White House; told how, after the Cuban crisis, both Rusk and McNamara rallied round and tried to take the blame. Kennedy's position was to avoid the split internally which occurred in England after the Suez crisis. He moved to take the blame himself and to confer immediately with Eisenhower, Nixon, Hoover, and MacArthur, in order to avoid dissension.

Rostow's opinion on Berlin was identical with that Kennedy expressed to me at the Big Brothers Dinner. In some respects it's alarming. He said Kennedy had made the decision before he took the oath of office that he would face war if necessary. He took this decision despite the fact the Democrats have been branded as the war party and despite the fact that war might keep them out of office for twenty years. Kennedy felt that the real showdown regarding war would take place over Berlin. He believes Khrushchev is banking on American retreat and dissension among our allies. In this he will be disappointed. Actually, de Gaulle is pretty firm, though he has no troops to fight with; the British are not firm but will be in on our side in a showdown. The West Germans are what Khrushchev really fears.

Rostow talked as if war had better than a fifty-fifty chance this fall. I can understand where Kennedy is getting much of his advice. In retrospect it may be that this position was expressed to me for the purpose of helping to consolidate public opinion. I do not know, but I do know that he plays a very important role in the White House.

**THURSDAY, JUNE 15** | To New York to attend dinner for Italian premier Amintore Fanfani. The dinner was dull, including the speeches of Fanfani and Vice President Johnson, but had a good time meeting old Italian friends, including Ferd Pecora, who is now eighty years old but still dapper. He recalled how he had represented me when General MacArthur sued us for $1,750,000.

**SATURDAY, JUNE 17** | Kennedy has just warned the Soviets that we will resume testing of hydrogen and atomic bombs if they don't get an agreement in Geneva.

**WEDNESDAY, JUNE 21** | The Venezuelan minister of mines, Perez Alfonso, came to see me. He said the oil companies are now behaving much better in Venezuela; had put full confidence behind the Betancourt government and were trying to encourage other businesses to extend credit.

I told him about my conference with David Rockefeller after my return from Venezuela and how I had urged him to relax credit in favor of Betancourt. I had forgotten to tell any of my Venezuelan friends in Caracas about this.

**THURSDAY, JUNE 22** | Kennedy came down with strep throat last night. His doctor shot 2.5 million units of penicillin into him—far more than the dose given to the average person. Apparently, his adrenal insufficiency makes him susceptible to contagion. He is still on crutches but just beginning to get off. It has been a source of concern to the country that Kennedy should remain on crutches for two weeks, merely from planting a tree in Canada a month ago.

**SATURDAY, JUNE 24** | The Thurman Arnolds brought Mr. and Mrs. Sifton of Canada to dinner. He is publisher of the Regina and Saskatoon, Saskatchewan, papers. Larry O'Brien backed out at the last minute—his wife's sister had died. John Blatnik, congressman from Minnesota, whom I was getting ready to needle on his failure to probe the Massachusetts highway scandals (because he's protecting Rep. John McCormack [Boston]), also did not show. The Arthur Goldbergs did, however, and we had a most enjoyable evening.

Arthur, I suspect, is discouraged by events in the Kennedy cabinet. He agrees with me that Kennedy's illness is due in part to the realization of the tremendous problems facing him and the fact that he may fail. He had complete confidence in himself, now realizes that solving the world's problems is by no means easy.

Kennedy is not intimate with any of his cabinet. The only man he lets his hair down with is his brother, Bobby. Perhaps he is closest to Douglas Dillon, the secretary of the treasury, because of a social affinity. Both have been in the same social whirl, and their wives come from the same general social stratum. Rusk, whom I always thought was an influence in the cabinet, has a civil service attitude. Apparently, he gives Kennedy the various alternatives in regard to policy but doesn't make decisions or even vigorous recommendations. Arthur believes that Kennedy is not even close to Ribicoff, the first governor to come out for him.

I suspect that Arthur feels the lack of cabinet meetings. Actually, the cabinet members could contribute a lot. Arthur was one of the experts on the OAS [Organization of American States] and remarked that the experience taught him that there could be no revolution in Cuba, that revolution had never taken place under any dictatorship.

Kennedy is devoting all his time to foreign affairs, despite the fact that his past experience has been on the domestic front. He has been paying almost no attention to the latter. Since the vice president is also concentrating on foreign affairs, domestic problems now run themselves. I remarked that perhaps it was just as well to let Lyndon work on foreign problems.

Arthur says that Kennedy is searching for a way out of the Berlin crisis but is stuck with his current position. He got stuck in talking to Khrushchev and later reporting to the nation. Yet we simply can't afford to be committed to war over Berlin. It's an impossible situation, and we can't defend it short of nuclear war.

Arthur had just come from prolonged sessions over the maritime strike, which has shut down every American vessel on the East, West, and Gulf Coasts. He says the Taft-Hartley Act will have to be invoked.

Arthur is reconciled to losing his labor friends, in fact announced when he took office that he would not go back to labor practice afterward. He said he has seen too many lawyers who, as commissioners before the Power

Commission or the FCC [Federal Communications Commission], figure they had to go back to practice law in that field and therefore kowtowed to industry. He doesn't want to be in the position of kowtowing to labor as secretary of labor. Some of his old clients, especially the United Steelworkers, were miffed at this.

Unfortunately, there is no top labor leader today who can knock union heads together. Arthur wishes there were. John L. Lewis used to do it; so did Phil Murray. The present maritime strike is one in which the unions are pricing themselves out of the market. There are now only nine hundred American ships as against four thousand in 1948. I recall that as an ordinary seaman in 1922, I was paid $45 a month. Today a seaman gets $400 a month, plus a lot of fringe benefits. He also now demands one man per stateroom. I slept in the fo'c's'le in an upper berth with about forty men.

Arthur wanted to know how they treated us at that time, and I told him fine. The food was excellent, we worked only eight hours, and my chief complaint was that we didn't have enough to do. I can't understand how an able-bodied seaman could earn $400 a month. There's practically nothing to do aboard ship between ports except a little scrubbing, sweeping, and painting.

One of the administration's mistakes, according to Arthur, is the feeling that it must be popular. The president has talked a lot about sacrifice and danger, but his administration still talks about easing taxes and the soft approach. You can't talk about danger and yet act as if there were none. When Arthur told the president there was no easy way out of the maritime strike and that the administration would have to receive some brickbats, Kennedy was not happy.

MONDAY, JULY 3 | Washington is almost empty. The president is in Hyannis Port, and everyone who can is vacationing from the government.

I went to see Walt Rostow. He gave me a long explanation as to why Kennedy had set up separate advisors in the White House on foreign policy and the military, namely himself and McGeorge Bundy, the first from MIT [Massachusetts Institute of Technology], the second from Harvard. He said Kennedy did not trust the hard core in the State Department or in the military. He felt they were bogged down with red tape, and he wanted someone who could give him an independent view.

The goal of the White House advisors on these matters, he said, is to look ahead. The Eisenhower administration had always been playing catch-up to

Russia in crises for which it was not prepared. Kennedy has been the same way regarding Cuba and Berlin but wants to look ahead on other problems.

Rostow described four areas facing Kennedy where Khrushchev had penetrated the free world: the Congo, Laos, Cuba, and Vietnam. Vietnam will be the big test of the future. He thinks Khrushchev will turn the heat on in Vietnam at the same time he turns it on in Berlin. The Communist guerrillas in Vietnam have been increased from two thousand to ten thousand. To offset this, counter-guerrilla training and subversive tactics have been made one of the big agendas on the Kennedy program for the White House task force.

Rostow said one immediate objective was to prepare for the visit of President Ayub of Pakistan. They have to repair the fences damaged in Pakistan. He referred to Pakistan's jealousy toward India and the fact that we have given a very large loan to India. He referred to the Ayub trip as on a par with that of the Japanese Premier Ikeda and Kennedy's trip to see de Gaulle. In both of these, he said, Kennedy scored big.

The president has a knack of asking these heads of states what their problems are, thus getting them to talk about their troubles. He then talks about his and thereby breaks down their reserve.

Rostow described the world today as similar to that in 1947, when the Communists were on the march: general strikes in France and Italy, guerrilla fighting in Indonesia, and the Kremlin determined to break down the Western world. I recall that this was the year when I organized the Friendship Train to France and Italy just because of the general strikes and the breakdown in collecting food.

**TUESDAY, JULY 4** | Wayne Morse came to dinner, together with Russian ambassador Menshikov and Robert C. Weaver, head of the Federal Housing Administration. Weaver used to work with my father when he came back from the Virgin Islands to start the first public housing unit of the Public Works Administration. He impressed me as a very able citizen.

Vasso Vournas brought some fireworks, and we had a good time after dinner celebrating the Fourth of July. The Russian ambassador joined in with dignified gusto and waved the sparklers in honor of American independence. Menshikov and I got into a long argument about the question of trust. I pointed out that you couldn't have peace until you had trust and that we had given various opportunities to arrive at trust with the Soviet Union without success. One of them was the testing of nuclear bombs.

Menshikov also gave the Congo as an excuse for refusal to cooperate in regard to nuclear bomb testing. He pointed out that the United Nations could not be trusted regarding cooperation and inspection. This was too complicated for me to argue about; besides, I knew I wouldn't get anywhere.

We did discuss the question of Berlin. The ambassador kept saying, "There will be a peace treaty." He set the time as November. He pointed out that fifteen years have passed since the end of the war and there must be a peace treaty. "All will be invited to sign," he said. "We must have peace." He also made the statement that access to Berlin for the Allies would be guaranteed. This was important because it conflicts with the statement made by Kennedy at his last press conference.

I made a pitch for an interview with Khrushchev in Moscow in late August. Menshikov sidestepped. Wayne Morse put in a plug by pointing out that an interview with Pearson was far more important than an interview with Lippmann. The ambassador took it under advisement.

**THURSDAY, JULY 6** | Jack came up with information from the Pentagon that Khrushchev will sign a peace treaty with East Germany on August [the date is not legible on editor's copy].

Talked to Marquis Childs earlier in the day. He made the point that Dean Acheson is trying to take Kennedy into a war in order to vindicate his own past policies.

**FRIDAY, JULY 7** | The head of Putnam Publishing came to Washington to lunch with Jack and me regarding the writing of another book. He wants a "Washington Merry-Go-Round." I suspect he also wants us to blast Kennedy. We may do it.

East Germans have begun a war of nerves. They are demanding that East Berliners who work in West Berlin get permits to cross every day. The Russians have rejected the latest American offer on banning nuclear weapons. It looks as if the crisis is approaching even more rapidly than the Pentagon anticipates.

**SATURDAY, JULY 8** | Dined at Senator Javits's home. His wife has moved to Washington for six weeks. She's a vivacious liberal who needles her husband to keep away from die-hard Republican policies. Otto Preminger was there, together with his young wife. He is working on *Advice and Consent* as a movie. Clark Foreman was also there. He produced *The Guns of Navarone*.

Cliff Case, the senator from New Jersey whom I have tried to help, was also there. I had not seen him for many months.

Mrs. Javits described Kennedy as a compromiser and not willing to stand up for his principles. She recalled how he walked out on the McCarthy battle. I have the feeling that after Kennedy has compromised on a lot of domestic problems, he will stand up on the question of war and, as a result, get the nation into war.

I did not tell Senator Javits that I had a memorandum regarding the fact he had helped to kill the SEC [Securities and Exchange Commission] reorganization plan proposed by Kennedy because the SEC is about to investigate the part Javits's brother played in the Canadian Javelin Company.

**SUNDAY, JULY 9** | Khrushchev announced last night that the Red Army would no longer be cut back and defense cuts restored. It looks as if Khrushchev has been reading the American papers as to what Kennedy was thinking of doing but has not yet done.

The newspapers are full of vacation plans for Washington society. Kennedy is away at Hyannis Port again. The beaches are crowded.

**MONDAY, JULY 10** | Ted Sorensen phoned from the White House to, as he put it, "ask a favor. We've done some favors for you." The favor was a relatively simple one. He wanted a story written about Senator Smathers of Florida and the manner in which he had accepted Kennedy's hospitality, then opposed him on the Senate floor and in speeches in Florida. Sorensen promised to send me a clipping of the latest opposition. "I wish he could read your column just before he comes to breakfast tomorrow morning," said Sorensen.

Smathers has been knifing me for some time by sending editors letters whenever I even mentioned his name. This may be the opportunity I've been looking for.

**FRIDAY, JULY 14** | (Lunched with Sen. Estes Kefauver.) I left the lunch early to go to the Russian embassy for lunch with Ambassador Menshikov. He is leaving in a couple of days, and I've been trying to get him to set up an interview for me with Khrushchev. We had the usual indecision as to whether we were to drink vodka or sherry. I finally said, "This is just as difficult as what to do about Berlin, but I decide for vodka."

"Since you have raised the question of Berlin," said the ambassador, "what about it? What is your opinion?" I started to express my personal opinion, but he interrupted to ask the opinion of the government. I told him I couldn't speak for the government but that I would give him some history and compared the present bitterness and unwillingness to budge on either side to the Reformation Era of Europe, when it was impossible for a leader to say anything good about the other side. I pointed today to the John Birch Society and right-wing groups in the United States, which made it difficult for Kennedy to say anything good about Russia—"and there are some good things about Russia," I added.

"You don't hear very many of them in this country," he said. He wanted to know more about the John Birch Society and who was behind it. He particularly wanted to know whether Wall Street was supporting it. I answered in the negative and said I thought it was supported chiefly by midwestern industrialists, with some tacit support from the Republican Party. I pointed out that crackpots and isolationists were beginning to mold opinion in some parts of the country, and this made it difficult for Kennedy to compromise over Berlin. The Republicans, I pointed out, have always accused the Democrats of being the party which takes the country into war, yet at the same time the Republicans have been demanding that Kennedy stand firm on Berlin.

I made the point that Khrushchev was in the same position, thanks to the opposition of the Red Chinese and others. The ambassador disagreed. He said there was no difference between the Red Chinese and the Soviets, that they have never been closer, that the *London Times* letter indicating bitterness between Khrushchev and Mao Tse-tung was a forgery, and that Khrushchev was a free agent with complete support inside Russia. He added, "Not only Russia but with the entire group of Communist nations." This impressed me as the usual Communist line.

I described Kennedy as a man with a *dobro certzi*—good heart—who very much wanted to have peace and had wanted to cooperate with the Soviet Union. "I agree with you that Kennedy is a man with a *dobro certzi*," the ambassador replied, "and I told my government before his election that he would be much easier to get along with, and more friendly, than the previous administration."

He then went into detail regarding Khrushchev's position on Berlin. He added that he had been in the Kremlin when this position was decided. He said that Khrushchev was not proposing anything belligerent or extreme but namely a peace treaty with East Germany which he hoped the other allied countries would sign. If not, Russia would sign on its own, and he said the date would not be August 1, as the Pentagon believes, but some time in November after the Communist Party conference.

He said this treaty would mean Berlin would continue as it is but without troops occupying it; with no army by the West Germans other than a police force; and no subversive attempts against East Berlin (this referred to the RIAS [Rundfunk im amerikanischen Sektor] radio station).

I said this would not be too hard to take on the face of it if both sides had not got dug in and if there was a feeling of trust on both sides. I pointed out, however, the complications are Adenauer, de Gaulle, and trust. I made the point I had made to him before, that when Kennedy at Geneva found the Russians were not willing to go as far as they had in the past regarding atomic bomb testing and wanted a veto over the right to inspect—this had set back all of Kennedy's hopes for cooperation. Menshikov interrupted to explain that Russia had been rebuffed over the Congo and no longer trusted an international group such as the United Nations.

I then suggested that if the Soviet would make some concession, such as nuclear testing, Kennedy might well make a concession regarding Berlin. Some move would have to be made to reestablish confidence, such as cooperation regarding nuclear bomb tests.

Menshikov indicated Khrushchev would not budge on this and said, "You always asked us to make a goodwill gesture." I then suggested they might do so by getting out of Cuba or keeping hands off. "We don't interfere with the internal affairs of another nation," said Menshikov. "We could not possibly do that."

"Only in Hungary," I remarked.

The ambassador let this go by. He had quite a bit to say about the days when Franklin Roosevelt was in office and relations were much better with the Soviet Union. I could have pointed out that some of our troubles today resulted from the fact that Roosevelt was perhaps too trusting and too anxious to cooperate, but I instead pointed to the real difference between the political situation in the United States today and Roosevelt's day. Roosevelt, I said, was elected by a large majority and then reelected by a bigger one, then had the wartime popular support of the country behind him. Kennedy, instead, was elected by a very slender margin and feels a political inferiority complex so that he confers repeatedly with Eisenhower or Nixon and Herbert Hoover. This feeling of political insecurity is why it's impossible for him to make any retreats or concessions regarding Berlin and why any concessions will have to come from Moscow.

The ambassador seemed impressed with this, and I have the feeling he will make a report on it when he gets back to Moscow next week.

Our discussion lasted such a long time that I was late getting back to write a column. I hope, however, that this may have contributed a little to an understanding on the part of the Russians that Kennedy is not likely to retreat and that we are heading toward a possible war.

[The pages for July 15 through August 12 are missing. During this time Pearson's request to meet with Khrushchev was granted, and he spent time preparing for the journey to Moscow. His wife, Luvie, kept daily notes during the trip. Excerpts follow.]

MONDAY, AUGUST 14 | MOSCOW—Hard time getting breakfast: no fruit, no juice. Big crush around Intourist Bureau desk. Guide Tanya found us. Peroxide blonde with chip on shoulder. Took drive to university, then old church nearby. Memorial service going on with about twenty old people.

Went to fair. Shoddy goods, long queues. Back to hotel for lunch. Put at table with a Mr. Vickers and a Ghanaian and an Ethiopian. Went to Pushkin Art Museum. Place seems dead, the people unattractive and lethargic. It does not seem possible we are in such a state over the Russians. Weather cooler than expected. Cloudy, gusty. Went down to dinner. Long queue. Waited and waited. Finally, a waiter came up and said if we went to our room he'd bring dinner right away.

TUESDAY, AUGUST 15 | Maid awoke us with breakfast. Apologized for no jam, fruit juice; proud of two apples the size of big cherries.

Intourist's Tanya is improving. Went to opening of French exhibition. Long speeches; band standing at attention playing "Le Marseilles." Tanya carried away by French consumer goods; said exhibit much better than British or American. Great collection of pictures.

Back at hotel maid and waiter said eating in room is a "must." Out to Kremlin Museum—fantastic things. Tea in room. Out to a variety show, mostly jazz. Not good.

FRIDAY, AUGUST 18 | Newspapermen called to invite us to lunch tomorrow at [the] Prague Restaurant. Went to state farm in morning. Pigs very clean and healthy, cows, acres of vegetables in greenhouses. Farm manager, a delightful man who loves his work, pressed masses of fruit on us. Lunch in hotel. Drew called Helsinki. Back to French exhibition with Tanya in p.m. Such crowds, especially around fashion show, beauty parlor, consumer goods. Industrial exhibit drew many less. Dinner at hotel with interesting French couple. He has an exhibit at the fair.

SATURDAY, AUGUST 19 | Much excitement: Drew might get to see Khrushchev. Told to stand by, check in every hour. Tanya took me to Tolstoy's home. Then to Lenin and Stalin tombs. Many people in line all day, every day. Lunch with the journalists was fun but too much to eat and drink. Went to movie on reindeer raising.

SUNDAY, AUGUST 20 | Sick all day. Rainy. We just read and waited [for] phone call about Mr. K., which never came.

MONDAY, AUGUST 21 | Recovered. No call in morning. Went to Achievement Park with Tanya. She called her office and found Zhukov was trying to reach Drew. All jumped in car and dashed to his office. Got word Mr. K. will see Drew on Thursday. Afternoon spent sending cables, changing plans and tickets. Decided to take night train to Leningrad to spend a day there seeing sights. Dinner at hotel with Seymour Topping and Hull of *New York Times*. Seems they knew of Thursday meeting with K.

WEDNESDAY, AUGUST 23 | Up at six to meet Zhukov and Tovarich Kelly (she will type); on plane at eight. Kelly is an American who came here in 1928 with her father, an engineer. She has one son and a sister and talks in English but looks Russian—with gold teeth. Arrived at Black Sea. Air like Florida but with hills and small mountains. People had a sunburned, beachy look. Many wore big white straw hats. Met by interpreter and his wife. Drove along coast. Sea calm, rocky beaches. Hills looked much like Los Angeles. Eucalyptus trees. Waited for room to be ready in town about an hour from K.'s dacha. We were told we had an hour to eat or rest before leaving for K.'s.

Car came for us at three thirty. Had an hour's drive, ending at tall concrete wall and big iron gates. Driver blew horn; gates opened. Drove down a lane lined with pine trees. There in the middle of road was Mr. K. and a chum. We got out of the car and shook hands. K. has the sharpest, twinkliest eyes I've ever seen. He had on a hat, a tan tropical suit, and Ukrainian blouse.

We walked to the swimming pool, which is indoor or outdoor, depending on glass panels which work with a push-button. Pool house is large, with rooms to entertain and to change. All right near the sea. There were two small Formica-topped tables and eight small chairs. Drew and I sat on one side, with Mr. Zhukov next to me. Opposite sat Victor, the interpreter, Mr. K., and a stenographer. At one end sat the chum who took still photos and movie footage. He broke the ice at Mr. K.'s suggestion and showed us pictures he had taken of the McCloys.

So, it finally began. Much impressed with Mr. K.'s sincere desire for peace. I was allowed to ask questions and asked why, if his system was so great, did the East Germans stream into West Germany? He said consumer goods were so scarce in East Germany because they had to pay reparations and didn't have all the help we gave the West.

Around seven thirty he suggested we swim. He sent for our bags and said it was better this time of year to swim in the sea and if we could not swim he could give us a rubber tube which he used, as he was not a very good swimmer. He called for his daughter, who took me to a beach cabana to change, while he took the men to another one. The beach is small and rocky, so we went out to a pier with stairs on one side for swimmers, the other side for boats. The water was warm. We swam and talked for quite a time. Mr. K. said, "I will show you that I can swim without this rubber tire, even though I cannot swim very far." He went up the stairs, made a frog dive into the water, and dog-paddled for a few minutes.

Then we went to dinner in the main house. On a large balcony Mr. K. motioned me to sit to his right, Drew to his left. On my right was one of his daughters, about thirty-five. At each place was mineral water, cold cuts, caviar, tomatoes, and a jar of yogurt. Different dishes came and went.

Victor can interpret like lightning so that the conversation seemed like any other. We did not get to our room until after 11:00 p.m.

THURSDAY, AUGUST 24 | Victor appeared and said, "Hurry, Mr. K. is waiting for you." All went to his house for breakfast. We were at the table a full two hours. Afterward I got pictures with the Brownie camera and a movie of Mr. K. hugging Drew. I went down to the beach with Victor's wife, Inya, and Tovarich Kelly. At 2:00 p.m. it was lunch/dinner time. Many delicious courses. Mr. Mikoyan called during lunch. Mr. K. went out to speak with him; returned to say what a success his trip to Japan had been.

We have a big room and huge bathroom. Ghastly late Victorian furniture.

Beautiful flowers on the grounds. Gravel walk along the sea through the pines. What is outstanding is the sense of peace and quiet; no visible security inside the wall. No one seems the slightest rushed except Drew and Mr. Zhukov, certainly not Mr. K.

FRIDAY, AUGUST 25 | Mr. Zhukov said breakfast would be at eight and that we would go to Sochi to spend the night, interview people, and on to Moscow on Saturday a.m. Drew upset to miss Saturday morning plane to Copenhagen. I took it up with Mr. K.'s chum, who swam with us in early a.m. before breakfast. He is a government official who, with his wife, was enjoying his vacation in the dacha we'd moved into.

We went to breakfast but found Mr. K. was swimming. Finally started around nine thirty. Same big feast. Got off around eleven; drove to Gagara. Walked through nice park. Lots of people, all Florida-looking, taking pictures. Asked Mr. K. if Russians had Brownies. He said Russians don't like cheap things. Drove on to Sochi. Chauffeur never went under forty, both horns blowing. Went to town hall, met mayor. Just like mayor in any small town. Went to Metelar Girls' Sanatorium. Beautiful place with marvelous view of the sea. Ended tour in library, where Drew had press conference. After lunch went to sulfur baths, then airport. Weather perfect. Arrived Moscow in terrible storm. Tanya met us. Arrived hotel to our old room. Maids so friendly, felt like home. [This ends the diary notes made by Luvie Pearson.]

WEDNESDAY, AUGUST 30 | WASHINGTON DC—Had an appointment at 5:00 p.m. with President Kennedy via the East Wing of the White House, which means that there is to be no publicity. I arrived a little early and was met by a young man from Massachusetts, who said the president would be a bit late. I was taken up in the elevator to a sitting room in the residential part of the White House—books and magazines spread out on tables and a small bar in one corner featuring Beefeater Gin. I sat there for a few minutes and was glad to get a chance to compose my thoughts, but the young man came back and took me upstairs to the "Yalta Room." This overlooks the south grounds of the White House, a beautiful fountain, Easter ducklings that someone gave to Caroline Kennedy, and immediately outside the room is Harry Truman's famous balcony, or "back porch."

Actually, I can see why Harry wanted the back porch. It's a very nice place to sit and has a beautiful view of the Washington Monument toward the Potomac [River]. Harry didn't take quite as many weekends away from

Washington as either Eisenhower or Kennedy, so he liked to have his friends around on the back porch.

The White House, as far as I could see, was completely empty. Jackie was up at Hyannis Port with the children, and the president was apparently not expecting anyone for dinner. I waited. When he finally arrived, he explained that an intercepted message had just come in saying that the Russians were about to resume nuclear testing. Kennedy was quite upset. He said he didn't know whether the report was true or not but they had to be ready for it. While we were talking, he got a telephone call and directed the person on the other line to prepare a statement for him to issue in case the announcement was bona fide.

I had prepared to give the president a report on my visit with Khrushchev, but the sequence was more or less knocked out by his own perturbation. I did gave him a brief report, during which I said they had talked to me about having Bobby Kennedy come over and also Joseph P. Kennedy. I said that I had advised them not to invite Joseph P. Kennedy but that Bobby Kennedy might be a good idea.

"We don't want to send Joseph P. Kennedy," interrupted the president, "he's a pacifist. He'd give everything away."

Kennedy summarized his views on Berlin, and it seemed to me they were more than reasonable. He said: "I'd give on Berlin; we have several points that we could give. There's the Oder-Neisse line, which should be fixed definitely. I would also recognize East Germany. It's a fact, and we might as well recognize it as a fact. RIAS is not too important, and I'd be willing to give on that, but we can't sacrifice Berlin. If we do, the entire structure of NATO comes down, and that's the only real alliance we have. We can't afford to weaken it."

I said Khrushchev was willing to guarantee Berlin and even put his own troops in Berlin with allied troops as a guarantee. Kennedy didn't like that idea. He said something about Russian troops causing friction and trouble. I also pointed out that K. was willing to guarantee the access between West Berlin and West Germany and volunteered the statement to me that West Germany was entitled to all diplomatic relations and contacts with West Berlin.

I said that what it really came down to was a matter of trust, and I told him how I had talked to Khrushchev at some length about this point and about him, Kennedy. I said, "I told him about you having a *dobro certzi* (good heart) and about your sense of humor."

I also told him what I had told Khrushchev about the importance of emphasizing some of the constructive things which had taken place between the two countries, such as the Pribilof seals convention [North Pacific Fur Seal Convention], the Antarctic Treaty, and the cooperation to prevent opium smuggling. I suggested a thirty-day cooling off period but didn't press it hard because I could see that he was not in the mood and that he was terribly upset by the announcement of the resumption of nuclear testing.

I suggested that Averell Harriman go to Moscow as a special envoy and that it was a mistake to have Tommy Thompson away from Moscow at this time, on vacation. Kennedy agreed. He said, however, that Averell had to go back to Geneva to handle Laos and that Tommy was on his way back to Moscow immediately with instructions to sound them out regarding the question of talks to begin at New York at the UN either with Gromyko or Khrushchev.

"I was delighted to meet Khrushchev at Vienna," Kennedy told me, "but when he handed me that aide-mémoire and began talking tough, well I . . . He certainly can be tough!" And Kennedy talked as if Khrushchev had given him a really bad time. "We'll give him Laos. He's got British Guiana. He's more or less got Cuba, but we'll not give him Berlin," he said. "How can we guarantee that he won't strangle Berlin? He wants to put Soviet troops in there. How do we know he won't use harassing tactics later?"

Kennedy mentioned the January 6 speech of Khrushchev, in which he was even tougher than previously. I told the president I was seeing him partly at the request of Khrushchev, though I would have wanted to report to him anyway. I asked him whether he had any message he wanted me to send back to Khrushchev because, obviously, Khrushchev would be expecting one.

"Have you written to Khrushchev to thank him for his hospitality?" Kennedy asked. When I replied in the negative, he suggested, "Why not write that if we can get Laos straightened out, then we can go on to other things?" Kennedy added. "The rainy season is going to be over in a couple of weeks, and if we don't get that straightened out, all hell will break loose there pretty soon."

Kennedy talked in a very discouraging mood about Berlin. "The closing down of the Berlin border wasn't so bad," he told me. "They had the right to do that. And they had to stop the hemorrhaging. I was surprised they didn't close it down before. The West Germans, of course, made the mistake of playing it up too much, which was very embarrassing to us, but when he (Khrushchev) comes along later with this note on air access for West Germans to West Berlin, well, that's something else. That's something we can't take."

I could see that the president was rather restless, and I moved to terminate the conversation, which already had lasted about fifty minutes. He served me some tea and toast and drank some tea himself. As we went out in the hall, he said: "Hope to God they don't start testing again . . . The Lord knows the last thing I want is for history to record that Kennedy and Khrushchev started atomic war."

**THURSDAY, AUGUST 31** | Telephoned Averell Harriman in New York that I had not been able to persuade the president to send him back to Moscow, that Tommy Thompson was going instead. Averell said he was en route back to Geneva very soon to try to get an agreement on Laos.

**FRIDAY, SEPTEMBER 1** | Long talk with Senator Fulbright. Yesterday the congressional leaders went to see Kennedy at his request, to get a briefing on the resumption of Soviet nuclear tests. Jack McCloy was there and said he was taken by surprise and had no explanation for the resumption. Kennedy went around the room asking opinions. He didn't seem to have a clear opinion of his own. Fulbright was disappointed at his failure to lead. While Bill thought Dulles went too far in telling Eisenhower just what he should do, he felt that Rusk didn't advise Kennedy vigorously enough.

Fulbright said that a long time ago he and Mansfield both urged Kennedy to take the initiative in regard to Berlin and say that the situation does need changing. Then it would look like the negotiations were held on our move, not the Russians; however, Dean Acheson told Kennedy to sit tight, and Dean's policy prevailed.

This is not what Kennedy advertised to the nation during the campaign. Rather, that he would make some new starts for peace. Instead, he picked Allen Dulles, J. Edgar Hoover, and put Dean Acheson in the position of trust as his top advisor on West Germany. Fulbright, who was rather pessimistic during the McCarthy era, was even more pessimistic. He said that McCarthyism was increasing, that Strom Thurmond and Barry Goldwater now want to investigate Fulbright because he, Fulbright, wrote a letter to the secretary of defense demanding that generals keep out of politics and particularly keep out of their hitherto close alignments with big defense contractors who are playing politics. This was a red flag to the China lobby crowd.

Tom Dodd of Connecticut makes a speech at the drop of a hat according to Fulbright. Even Keating, Kuchel, and Scott of Pennsylvania got into the act over Soviet atomic testing. "We are running the government from Congress," said Bill, "and the president is losing his leadership."

Fulbright told me he went to Palm Beach with Kennedy and talked to him at that time about the foolishness of the Cuban invasion. Bill said he and Betty were going there to visit some friends, and at the last minute Kennedy invited them both to go on his plane. On the plane Fulbright talked about Cuba and handed the president a memo. They talked most of the way to Palm Beach. After the weekend, and at the last minute, Kennedy invited Bill and Betty to ride back to Washington, and at the end of the trip he said there was a meeting on Cuba and invited him to come. At the meeting Kennedy called on Fulbright to express his views. Apparently, what Bill had said in his memo and on the trip to Florida had made an impression; however, Admiral Burke and Adolf Berle argued vigorously the other way. Kennedy listened carefully and decided with them. [Arthur] Schlesinger was present but kept quiet, according to Bill. Schlesinger has protested to me that he opposed the Cuban operation.

Kennedy has made a good statement regarding atomic testing. He said the United States had plenty of atomic arms and that there would be no new tests for the time being. Yesterday he called the Soviet tests "Atomic Blackmail."

This afternoon I asked the chargé d'affaires of the Russian embassy to drop around. I handed him a copy of my letter to Khrushchev and also a letter to Zhukov which went into more detail about my talk with Kennedy. I also emphasized the importance of Laos and quoted the president on this point. The chargé said he had been in Geneva for some weeks negotiating on Laos and the main trouble was our insistence that the neutral commission guarantee no change in government. "How can you prevent social changes in a country," he asked. "You won't agree not to have social changes even in the United States," he argued.

TUESDAY, SEPTEMBER 5 | Lunched with secretary of the air force, Gene Zuckert, at the Pentagon. Gen. Arno Lehmann and Ed Trapnell, a former public relations officer for the Atomic Energy Commission, were also present. Zuckert was pessimistic about the state of the world; felt there was no use in trying to negotiate with the Kremlin. I told them about my talks with Khrushchev, which they said did not increase their optimism. I tried to give Zuckert the idea that both Kennedy and Khrushchev were very close on the question of Berlin and that the chief problem was to get some trust on both sides. I also gave them the argument advanced to me by Stevenson and Fulbright (without quoting either) that if we had taken the initiative in regard to Berlin, we could have come off with high honors. Now we are fighting a rear-guard action.

Zuckert didn't buy this. He seemed to think we needed a showdown over Berlin and make it plain we meant business. There must be no retreat. I argued that Kennedy was not in a position to bargain from strength. Zuckert argued that the Strategic Air Command was stronger than you think. When I told them the story of how Henry L. Stimson had argued, at his last meeting of the Truman cabinet in October 1945, that we should give the secret of the atom bomb to the Russians because they would get it anyway, Zuckert said he had always argued with Adm. Lewis Strauss on the AEC that the Russians had the secret of the A-bomb just as soon as we did but hadn't been able to work out its know-how. "I told Lewis that Fuchs never really gave the Russians the secret. All he did was to give them the know-how with which to make it more quickly. They had the basic facts even before the war, and so did the Germans. It was only luck which prevented the Nazis from developing the A-bomb during the war."

After lunch General Lehmann gave me a briefing on U.S. missile strength. It certainly doesn't look good. We are in effect caught with our missiles down and will be this way for the next two years.

Late this afternoon Kennedy announced the resumption of U.S. nuclear testing underground and in the laboratory. Once again, he bowed to Republican criticism and some of his timid advisors. If he had waited until after the first session of the UN assembly, when he could have made another appeal to the Soviet Union, his hand would have been far stronger.

**MONDAY, SEPTEMBER 11** | Went to see Attorney General Bobby Kennedy. He's a gimlet-eyed, cold young man who sits in his shirtsleeves with his tie undone, looking at you in a much more fierce manner than Khrushchev does. As I went in, a small girl scampered out. I asked him which daughter this was, and he said it was his eldest, Kathleen, aged ten.

I had not seen him he since he became attorney general. I've talked to him on the phone several times during the hectic days of the transition before the inauguration, but he apparently has ducked seeing me in person.

I said I understood the Federal Communications Commission was about to reissue TV and radio licenses to General Electric and Westinghouse, despite their record of criminal activities. I went into detail as to how they monopolize the airwaves and, because of their defense contracts, never permitted any criticism of the Defense Department and that the Kennedy administration was now paying the penalty for eight years of lagging defense. Bobby looked interested and said he would talk to the FCC chairman Newton Minow.

I told him about my talk with Khrushchev and the fact that some of the Russian leaders explored the idea that Joseph P. Kennedy and he should be invited to Moscow. Bobby seemed very much interested in this and asked me several questions. I pointed out that this was an indication they definitely wanted peace, not war. I told of Khrushchev's remark that since Kennedy's election margin was very close, he considered that he probably elected Kennedy and how the Russians had censored this out of my column. "I think they were probably smart," I said, "because right now some of the Republicans want to investigate Averell Harriman and me because Averell told the Russians not to criticize Nixon without criticizing Kennedy too."

Bobby wanted to know, "What did he think of the president?" I replied that he thought the president was a bit young and, while he liked him, felt that he was surrounded by the wrong advisors and somewhat a prisoner of them. I said I had been planning to tell the president—"because he could take it"—the story that Khrushchev told me of how Molotov almost defeated him and how Kennedy should realize that, despite the closeness of his margin, he was the president and should lead, instead of looking to the right and the left. Bobby made no comment about this.

The attorney general was quite interested in my description of Khrushchev's views on Nixon and the fact that Nixon had apologized to Khrushchev for the Captive Nations Week resolution. As I left, Kathleen came back in the room and asked, "Daddy, are you going home for lunch?"

One interesting point regarding the Kennedy family: Bobby never refers to "my brother." It's always "the President."

I am getting invitations from Iron Curtain diplomats, and I don't consider it much of a compliment. The Polish press attaché has been wanting to lunch with me, and I finally had him to the house for lunch today. He wanted to know all about Khrushchev. I told him I considered the Russians very unwise in antagonizing American public opinion. They had put Kennedy in the hole and made it more difficult for him to agree on Berlin. Public opinion, I pointed out, was something the Russians didn't understand too well because they don't have to worry about it, but an American president does. My guest seemed surprised when I said that Kennedy would agree to the recognition of East Germany. He said that Gomułka is quite pro–United States, that he has a sister living in Chicago and came close to being born in the United States himself.

At 3:00 p.m. I went to the CIA to brief their top experts on Khrushchev. General Caball was acting director in place of Allen Dulles. He received me cordially, despite the fact I have been panning the CIA for years. In introducing me to the roundtable of Russian experts, he said: "You have had an experience which all these gentlemen would like to have had: that of spending some time with Khrushchev. You are a trained and expert observer. They've all read your column. Just give us your impressions, and you can save your time by not duplicating what you've already written." This was a little difficult because I've written so much. In general the discussion centered on the question of whether Khrushchev was really running the Soviet government. I pointed out that he had no stenographers around; they got only one telephone call while he was with me and that he seemed so lackadaisical that he took a trip to see some Ukrainians after we departed.

They were also interested in whether Khrushchev wanted war. I said he explored the question of inviting the Kennedy family to Moscow, that he emphasized that he wanted me to report to the president, and that Zukhov had told me that wars hang on very little things and that they considered my interview very important. My impression was that Khrushchev did not want war. I emphasized, however, that he would practice what Mr. Dulles did and go right up to the brink.

They wanted to know why he had become an admirer of Dulles. "Because," I replied, "he knew where Dulles stood and that he would not go to war. He doesn't know where Kennedy stands, and it worries him."

I reported that Khrushchev had a pretty good understanding of Kennedy's advisors; that he knew that Acheson, Rostow, and Bundy were very hostile and considered them warmongers. I said I thought Khrushchev had started to loosen up with me after we began discussing farming, and I recommended sorghum instead of corn for the more arid areas of the Soviet Union.

WEDNESDAY, SEPTEMBER 13 | Lunched with Ambassador Menshikov, who reported that Khrushchev had sent his special regards to Mrs. P. and me. Menshikov added that he, personally, had recommended that Khrushchev grant the interview. I doubt whether this is true. When I got to Moscow, I couldn't find any trace of any Menshikov recommendation.

I pulled a couple of telegrams from my pocket to show the reaction I had from some readers—one from Jacksonville, the other from San Francisco, excoriating me for "being taken in" by Khrushchev. These were just a few illustrations of the critical mail I've been getting.

For the first time Menshikov seemed to be really worried about war. He emphasized that the time was getting very short, that there were only about three weeks left in which to negotiate. For the first time also, he admitted that Khrushchev had some opposition. "These decisions are made by council, not by Khrushchev alone," he said. This fits with the feeling I've had for some time that Khrushchev is not as powerful within Soviet councils as is generally believed. I told Menshikov about Khrushchev's description of his battle with Molotov and the vote inside the Central Committee of the Communist Party. "I was there when the vote was taken," remarked Menshikov. "Was it unanimous?" I asked. Menshikov indicated that it was either unanimous or overwhelming.

Menshikov obviously had invited me to lunch one day after he returned to Washington in order to get the lay of the land. He asked for suggestions on how to break the current negotiation deadlock. I made two. One was to let Eisenhower go to Moscow and handle the negotiations. The ambassador suggested that Kennedy would not like this, which is probably true. I said that Kennedy had continually consulted Eisenhower, was anxious to curry favor with the Republicans, and Eisenhower was in a position to get him off the hook with the Republicans in case he wanted to make concessions regarding Berlin (such concessions were almost essential). I said that Kennedy and Khrushchev were nearly together regarding Berlin, but it would take some catalytic agent or personal emissary, such as Eisenhower, to tie up the package.

The second suggestion I made was for a package deal in which the Kremlin would prove its desire to get along with the United States. I noted there had been no agreement regarding Laos, even though Kennedy and Khrushchev let it be known after Vienna that there would be an agreement. I said Kennedy was irritated over this and that this was one reason why he figured he couldn't entirely trust the Soviets. Khrushchev had said one thing in Vienna, and his emissaries had done the opposite in Laos.

I also suggested there might be a further sweetening for the package, such as the purchase of U.S. surplus grain. I suggested the need of winning the support of a large segment of the American population, such as the farmers, and that inasmuch as the Soviets had not done anywhere near as good a job agriculturally as American farmers, they could pay a little tribute to the farmers by buying surplus grain. I am sure this suggestion did not go down very well.

I reemphasized that in order to make a Berlin settlement palatable to the American public, some "sweeteners" would have to be put in the package in the same manner Roosevelt used to work out package deals.

I drove out to the farm for a swim with [nephew] Drew. He is going to the [Thurman] Arnolds' and then to school tomorrow. I feel very discouraged.

FRIDAY, SEPTEMBER 15 | Lunched with the Yugoslav ambassador; told him that the State Department had received a cable from George Kennan in Belgrade regarding a conversation with Marshal Tito, who reported that Khrushchev was in some difficulty with Red Army leaders and the Stalinist crowd; that if he didn't follow their ideas, he was likely to be bounced.

The ambassador replied that he had no information regarding the conversation, but it was only natural that Khrushchev would be under some military pressure. "After all," he said, "you have a division of opinion between the military and the civilians in your country, so why should it not exist in the Soviet?" He asked whether the Tito conversation was in connection with U.S. reaction to the recent conference of neutrals and added that he had been called in by Assistant Secretary of State [Harlan] Cleveland and Undersecretary George Ball and made to understand that the United States was very unhappy.

I told him that President Kennedy was not only unhappy but quite irritated and that he had moved to cancel tentative plans for Tito's visit to the United States as well as to cut off aid to Yugoslavia. The ambassador said this probably had been taken up in Belgrade with Tito.

I said that Kennedy had been disappointed over [the] neutral reaction to the Soviet nuclear test resumption. I said that I'd seen Kennedy immediately after the Soviets announced resumption and that I knew he was expecting some reaction from the neutrals. It didn't come.

The ambassador explained the lack of reaction this way: "We had generally expected that the United States would resume testing. There had been so much in the American press that testing would be resumed, and there can't be that much published without the Kennedy administration being for it. So, we figured that American testing was inevitable and that Russia merely got the jump. The United States, it was obvious, had been preparing for testing all along."

I asked why the neutrals hadn't taken a stronger stand in Belgrade when they knew the United States had not only been a great aid to undeveloped countries but had no political or military designs on them. The ambassador said the United States was always lining up with the "older countries," and the older countries have been too long champions of colonialism. "The Soviet," he said, "has been the champion of the newer nations; you have been the defenders, at least indirectly, of colonialism." The ambassador also expressed his fear that the United States was much more likely to go to war than the USSR. The temper of the American people, he said, is for war. I couldn't help but agree with him.

Henry Wallace telephoned me from South Salem, New York. He said *Newsweek* had queried him about one of my columns, in which I reported he had voted with Henry L. Stimson to give the secret of the A-bomb to Russia in the fall of 1945. Henry read from his testimony before the House Un-American Activities Committee in 1948, in which he said that Stimson had proposed giving the secret of atomic energy to the Russians because scientists in the Pentagon had reported it would be impossible to retain the secret; also because in the competition to build bombs they would become more destructive.

I asked Wallace whether there was any real difference between the secret of atomic energy and the secret of the atomic bomb. He maintained there was. The most important part of our conversation was his lineup of the vote with Stimson. Fred Vinson, who had told me about the vote shortly before he died, had said that Jimmy Byrnes voted with Stimson. This turned out to be erroneous. Dean Acheson was there acting for Byrnes. Vinson's memory was that only Acheson and Wallace had supported Stimson, but Henry read me his own notes, which show that Bobby Hannegan had spoken briefly for Stimson's proposal and that the others who supported it were John Snyder, then head of RCA, later secretary of the treasury; Law Schwallenbach, secretary of labor; Abe Fortas, acting for Harold Ickes as secretary of the interior; and General Fleming, head of war controls. Those who opposed were Fred Vinson, then secretary of the treasury; Clinton Anderson, secretary of agriculture; and Tom Clark, attorney general; with Forrestal, secretary of the navy. Henry said that you couldn't trust people's memories; that some time ago he had talked to Abe Fortas, who couldn't even remember that the matter came up. Obviously, Henry had taken careful notes immediately after the cabinet meeting.

**WEDNESDAY, OCTOBER 4** | Joan Hill, Luvie's cousin, who has been in the real estate business, entertained us, telling how she took Bobby Kennedy and his wife to look at houses when they first arrived in Washington last winter. Bobby carried with him a football marked "The Kennedy Tigers," and as they drove up in front of houses, he proceeded to pass the ball back and forth to his wife and sometimes knock her in the back of the neck. He thought it was very funny. He also carried four dogs in the car, and on one occasion, when his wife was opening the front door of a house, a dog grabbed her hand. She called for help, but the future attorney general replied, "Take care of yourself, pal."

**FRIDAY, OCTOBER 6** | Eric Johnston came to lunch. He told about the luncheon with . . . Madame Furtseva, in Paris. She is minister of culture—tall, rather thin, a woman of about fifty. Eric said she opened the luncheon by downing a large cup of vodka and insisting he do the same. He did so, then threw the goblet against the wall, breaking it. She did likewise, threw her arms around him, and kissed him.

Mme Furtseva rounded up members of the Central Committee of the Communist Party when Khrushchev was defeated by Molotov on that test vote in the Politburo, of which she is a member. Khrushchev told me about this battle when we talked to him but didn't mention Mme Furtseva—and I don't think the omission was prompted by the fact that I had already written about it in the column.

Gromyko met with Kennedy at the White House for two hours and fifteen minutes, discussing Berlin. The news reports of the meeting were pessimistic. [Secretary of State Dean] Rusk was noncommittal, though not pessimistic. I have already gone out on a limb, based upon information previously obtained at the Pentagon, that the two sides are very near an agreement over Berlin. I am convinced that despite the pessimism of the press, they will have to get together and are now in the process of doing so.

**SUNDAY, OCTOBER 15** | Spent the weekend at Mount Kisco with Agnes Meyer. She had quite an array of guests, including the top editors of *Newsweek*, which is now owned by her son-in-law, Phil Graham. Luvie and I found, much to our surprise, that they agreed with us completely regarding Khrushchev. The editorial policy of the magazine is just the opposite—doubtless because of Phil.

**TUESDAY, OCTOBER 17** | At the Twenty-Second Communist Party Conference in Moscow, Khrushchev blasted Albania. [China's] Chou En-lai sat on his hands. Significantly, the foreign press was admitted. It was only a few days ago that Chip Bohlen gave Jack Anderson a story that there would be complete harmony between the Red Chinese and Khrushchev, that he had nothing to worry about. I did not use it. I've had a strong hunch that for some time Chip Bohlen didn't know what he was talking about regarding Russia. The Red Chinese have been supporting Albania, have sent various advisors to Albania, and this looks like a real split in the Communist world.

**THURSDAY, OCTOBER 19** | Attacks on Molotov and the Stalinist crowd are continuing at the Communist Party Congress. The rift seems to be deeper than I suspected when I talked to Khrushchev last August. Shepelov, former foreign minister, got the oratorical meat ax today. The amazing thing is that Voroshilov was sitting on the floor of the Congress, together with Bulganin, when he was blasted by Khrushchev. Later Voroshilov was elected to the Presidium.

All this confirms what I've been writing, that there's a new democratic spirit of criticism, not assassination, in effect in Russia. The American public probably won't understand this because most newspapermen won't put it out; however, I maintain that Lippmann, Eisenhower, Stevenson, Humphrey, and Kefauver cannot all be wrong regarding Khrushchev. He is a straight-from-the-shoulder man.

**SUNDAY, OCTOBER 22** | Arthur Goldberg urged that I see Kennedy and talk to him again about a meeting with Khrushchev. Arthur thinks Kennedy saw Khrushchev too early, when he was not sufficiently prepared, and that enough water has now gone over the dam for the two men to reach an agreement.

I'm doubtful whether I'd have much influence with Kennedy, but I didn't tell Arthur this. Arthur told how Secretary of State Rusk does not have any ability to make up his mind, even on small matters, let alone Berlin. When Arthur was in Oslo, he got a cable from Chancellor Adenauer asking him to come to Berlin to see him on Monday. The cable was received on a Friday.

Arthur had been traveling all over the Scandinavian countries and had an itinerary arranged which could not be easily changed; however, he cabled Rusk, saying he had been invited to Berlin and would go if the State Department so desired, but it would take some rearranging. He asked for a specific recommendation from Rusk. Rusk cabled back evasively for Arthur to use his judgment. Later, when Arthur came home (without going to Berlin), Rusk bumped into him and said, "Thank you for being willing to go to Berlin."

**TUESDAY, OCTOBER 24** | China's Chou En-lai has now bolted the Moscow Congress and gone back to Peking. This is significant. It bears out everything I've been writing for the past year regarding the division between the Red Chinese and Khrushchev. Dined last night with Clayton Fritchey. He says the Russians are softening their position regarding Hammarskjöld's successor, and that Adlai will win everything he wanted. The State Department has been impatient with Adlai [Stevenson], claims he's too soft. Adlai has replied: "What do you want? An agreement or headlines?" He could have made headlines, as did Henry Cabot Lodge, but instead he's going to get an agreement.

Clayton also says the talks between Rusk and Gromyko went well, and there is a much better atmosphere, despite newspaper reports to the contrary. We discussed the fact Dean Acheson and Chip Bohlen have never gotten over the attacks by Joe McCarthy. As a result, they have been leaning over backward to prove they are anti-Communist.

**WEDNESDAY, OCTOBER 25** | Gromyko spoke before the Communist Congress, in which he paraphrased what Kennedy had told me—namely, that he "didn't want historians to record that Kennedy and Khrushchev set the world on fire with atomic war." Gromyko said this statement had been given to him by Rusk, and he, Gromyko, said he shared this view. Gromyko told the Communist Congress that Kennedy was of the same political party as FDR, with whom Russia had had excellent relations. It was one of the most hopeful speeches I have heard in recent months.

**THURSDAY, OCTOBER 26** | MIAMI—Pickets appeared outside my hotel, demanding that I go back to Russia. Some of the signs coupled me with Eleanor Roosevelt and the *Miami Herald*—which is not bad company. This is the second time in my life I have been picketed, the other having been by George Lincoln Rockwell, head of the Nazi Party of America.

I spoke before the Outdoor Advertising Association, which I suspect was not too happy about the pickets or my presence. Gromyko's speech was played down by Miami papers, while friction over East Berlin was played up.

Jack Gordon of Washington Federal Savings & Loan says that bigotry is increasing in Miami. The Miami school board has even voted to study the question of whether or not United Nations materials should be used in Miami schools. The motion was made by Douglas Voorhees, the same guy who picketed me. Later in the day he picketed Mrs. Roosevelt and also marched pickets in front of a meeting of Sigma Delta Chi editors, demanding they cancel my column.

Another development at the Moscow congress: Molotov has written a letter to the editor of *Pravda* stating that "there can be no progress, no advance, of communism without war." This is the frankest admission I've ever seen made by any of the Stalinist group publicly. It shows what the real issue is between Khrushchev and Molotov and perhaps explains why Khrushchev was so frank in telling me of his rows with Molotov.

**TUESDAY, NOVEMBER 28** | Chester Bowles was fired last weekend as undersecretary of state. Averell Harriman was made assistant secretary of state for the Far East. This is quite a kick in the pants for Bowles. He came out for Kennedy very early and did an excellent job of picking new ambassadors but made the great mistake of neglecting his relations with Congress and with newspapermen. Kennedy watches his politics very carefully; Bowles didn't.

[Dined with the Johnny Walkers.] Johnny, who's in charge of the National Gallery of Art, says the big foundations and the wills of wealthy people are now written to encourage the acquisition of Old Masters. As a result, some museums can't pay the janitors' expenses. They have millions to spend on buying new paintings but little for upkeep. He speculated that the Russians could easily have outbid us on the purchase of the Rembrandt which sold in New York the other day for $2.3 million. Erickson, of McCann-Erickson Advertising, had bought the Rembrandt before the war for $500,000 and was continuing payments on the installment plan to Devine, the New York art collector. During the war he couldn't meet his payments and gave the portrait back to Devine. Then he reorganized after the war and went back to Devine for the Rembrandt. "Okay," said Devine, "but it will cost you $750,000 now." It sold for $2.3 million the other day, out of which Uncle Sam will get a tax bite of $1.7 million.

**SUNDAY, DECEMBER 3** | BINGHAMPTON NY—As I visit some of these thriving communities, I feel we have nothing to worry about regarding Russia, except complacency and fear. We are so far ahead of Russia in material things that we put them in the shade. Recently, we have stopped being complacent, but we have switched from complacency to fear.

**THURSDAY, DECEMBER 7** | Have just learned that Khrushchev has put out a feeler through the American embassy in Moscow to have Kennedy visit in June. This is significant. It's along the lines of what I suggested to Khrushchev in August and comes on the heels of a peace settlement in Laos, the interview between Kennedy and [Aleksei] Adzhubei, and the easing of the Berlin deadline beyond December.

Bobby Kennedy today announced the indictment of Judge Vincent Keogh, brother of the congressman, for accepting part of a $35,000 bribe in a fixer case in New York. This is the story which we broke in the column on October 29. I was getting worried for fear Bobby was going to hush the whole business. He went out of his way to say that Representative Keogh was not involved. He did not add, of course, that Keogh was the man who rallied the delegates for Kennedy at the Los Angeles convention and has been Kennedy's main bulwark in the Rules Committee since that time. This scandal began to break last spring, and I suspect that the more evidence that piled up, the more Representative Keogh worked to put across the Kennedy program.

**SUNDAY, DECEMBER 10** | SAVANNAH GA—I spoke before a Jewish group and was amazed to discover the extent to which the John Birchites and the hate-mongers have taken over this part of the South. Several books have been banned from the public and high school libraries because they touched on the race question. Negroes are now alleged to be Communists because of their battle for equality. It has become dangerous to speak out. One member of the *Savannah News* staff says the newspaper has become so intimidated it doesn't try to print anything which the city council doesn't want printed.

**MONDAY, DECEMBER 11** | WASHINGTON DC—Lunched with the Pakistani and Iranian ambassadors at the Iran embassy. The Pakistani has been angling for a luncheon date ever since I was critical of his boss, President Ayub. I did not tell him that I was just mean enough to resent the fact that Ayub was the only head of state on the entire trip I took around the world who had refused to see me. No, there was one other, the prime minister of Japan.

We talked at luncheon about Kennedy neglecting the Middle East and South Asia in favor of European allies. I explained that Kennedy had problems all over the world and was going to Latin America because of pressing problems there. They agreed but pointed out that Pakistan and Iran had been 100 percent in the United States' corner from the start. They were sad that Kennedy mentioned European allies in his inauguration address while leaving out any mention of Near Eastern allies.

**THURSDAY, DECEMBER 14** | The Venezuelan government has invited me to come to Venezuela ahead of President Kennedy and stay during his visit. I inquired whether this was part of a newspaper junket and was informed by the ambassador that I was the only American being invited aside from Kennedy. This flattered my ego considerably, and I accepted.

CARACAS, VENEZUELA—It's only a three-hour-and-forty-five-minute flight to Caracas. It was cold in Washington, but the night in Caracas was tropical and beautiful. I wish Luvie had come along. Eric Carlson met me, and we went to see the deputy undersecretary of the interior immediately. He is in charge of security for Kennedy's visit. Bombing attempts have increased to a point where two Molotov cocktails were thrown at the printing presses of the English-language newspaper, the *Daily Journal*. There have been so many bombs touched off in the Sears, Roebuck store that the store keeps wet sand in buckets on every floor.

**FRIDAY, DECEMBER 15** | Breakfasted with Hal Horan. It's been a long time since he was fired by Hearst and lived with me on Dumbarton Street. I was fired about the same time by the *Baltimore Sun*. Called on Everett Baughman of the Creole Oil Company. He told me with pride that Creole had put up a $10 million revolving fund to lend money to local companies. I did not tell him that after my last trip to Venezuela, I called on David Rockefeller, head of the Chase Manhattan Bank, the biggest stockholder in Creole, to urge that the oil companies get busy and loosen credit for Venezuela; otherwise, the Betancourt government might go under, and they would have Castroism.

Called on Dr. Gabaldon, the minister of health, who was bubbling over the Kennedy visit. Kennedy will dedicate one of Gabaldon's housing projects. He got into housing because it was necessary to clean up malaria and health conditions in rural areas. Part of this cleanup consisted of building better housing.

I also called on Perez Guerrero, minister of planning, who, together with Eric Carlson, worked out the whole housing rural agrarian reform program and, I suspect, was largely responsible for inviting me. He has served about twenty-five years with the League of Nations and the United Nations and is typical of the enterprising men Betancourt has around him.

Lunched with William Hinkle, president of the American Chamber of Commerce, and Jules Waldman, publisher of the *Daily Journal*, whose presses were the object of Castroism last night. They were not severely damaged, and the paper was published despite the Molotov cocktails. Significantly, Hinkle and the American business group are now very pro-Betancourt. When I was here last February, they were not. They were irked, however, when I reported this in the column, and I suspect that my critical reporting may have helped to steer them around a bit.

Called on Miguel Otero Silva, publisher of *El Nación*, which has long published my column. Otero is probably still a Communist. Most of the liberals in this country were Communists at one time. His paper has been the subject of a boycott by American business groups because he still has some definite Communists on his staff and has followed a semi-Castro line; however, he has given a big welcome to Kennedy and still has the largest circulation in Caracas.

Communism here started long before Castroism and probably in large part as a result of the succession of military dictators. As in Mexico, it had little to do with Soviet Russia. The revolution began in Mexico in 1910, seven years ahead of the Russian Revolution, and some of these Venezuelans started revolting against the established order, particularly that of Dictator Gomez, who ruled Venezuela for about twenty-five years.

Called on Eugenio Mendoza, the biggest businessman in Caracas, who is working on [a] slum clearance program completely on his own. This is unusual in Latin America. He has spent his own money and has been so successful that he recently got an $8 million loan from the U.S. Development Fund.

I called on the minister of foreign affairs, Falcón Briceño, who is living at my hotel. The governor of Caracas was also present and told me about his ambition to clean up Caracas's slums. They exist, unfortunately, around every Latin American city, but they are more noticeable in Caracas because they are on the hillside in plain view.

Falcón said that the Communist activity against Kennedy was largely of the Red Chinese type and probably Chinese inspired. He doubted that the Russians had anything to do with it. He based this diagnosis on the fact that the attempted killings are of a brutal, savage nature. Almost every night one or two policemen are killed. Falcón indicated that Venezuela would go along with a boycott of Castro if the OAS wanted to vote it.

SATURDAY, DECEMBER 16 | I've worried whether there would be helicopter space to travel around with Kennedy. About 1:00 a.m. last night, however, a gentleman named Soler arrived with letters from the minister of the interior admitting me to the small airport for the helicopter takeoff. He advised me not to go to the main airport to welcome Kennedy.

Earlier I had received a call that a Mr. Soler would arrive at 7:00 a.m. to take me to the main airport to meet Kennedy. So, I went to bed at one thirty. At six fifteen, however, I was awakened to learn that Mr. Soler was in the lobby waiting for me to take me to the main airport. I was a long way from being ready; however, I then found that there were two Solers, the latter being chief of protocol and having been sent by the minister of foreign affairs to be my personal escort. I dressed and shaved in a hurry, and we got to the airport in ample time. In fact, we had to wait about two hours. Soler was the first man to go aboard Kennedy's plane to greet him, and after the greeting, it began to rain. It rained steadily while Kennedy made his speech and President Betancourt made his response.

I lost my car in the shuffle at the airport, but the minister of agriculture very kindly picked me up in his limousine and drove me to the helicopter airport, where there was a big scramble for helicopters. I was slated to go in the helicopter of Minister Perez Guerrero; however, so many American embassy personnel were shunted into other helicopters that our group was left out. We finally took a small plane to the Maracay Air Base and then a Venezuelan helicopter from there to La Morita, where Kennedy made his chief speech, dedicating a small housing project.

Kennedy made an almost revolutionary speech. Eisenhower and John Foster Dulles certainly would have considered it so. Kennedy pledged American aid for agrarian reform, social reform, and the eradication of poverty. Certainly, Nikita Khrushchev could have found nothing wrong with what he said. The interesting fact is that the Kennedy administration has edged more and more toward some of the Khrushchev proposals in his twenty-year plan, while Khrushchev has edged more and more toward a moderate program.

Jackie Kennedy made a nice little speech in Spanish, which brought down the house. She merely told the assembled farmers how deeply her husband felt regarding the eradication of poverty. The fact she said it in Spanish gave her speech more impact than his.

I boarded another helicopter with the Venezuelan commander and got to the Hotel Maracay for lunch in five minutes. It was the first time I ever traveled in a helicopter with the door open. The day was hot, however, and the air felt good. The hotel is one of the most beautiful I have ever visited, built by dictator Perez Jiminez, and almost empty. I sat some distance from Kennedy at lunch but noticed during the lunch that he kept looking my way. Later that evening, at the presidential reception, when I shook hands with Kennedy, he said: "What are you doing here? I thought I saw you at lunch, and I asked him (Betancourt) whether that was you. He remarked, 'It does look like Drew Pearson.'"

Jackie Kennedy, whom I congratulated for her speech, took a moment to recover from the shock of seeing me and finally said, "You look much more benign down here."

The Venezuelan government had much security. There were thirty thousand troops along the streets. The crowds were not too friendly and not too big, but on the whole things went off well.

SUNDAY, DECEMBER 17 | Eric Carlson called for me at seven, and we went first to the tomb of Simón Bolívar, where Nixon had been supposed to lay a wreath but didn't because of hostile crowds. The tomb is located in a working-class district. It was well protected, however, and Kennedy performed the ceremony without difficulty. Eric and I finally got to the presidential palace, Miraflores, ahead of Kennedy, where he had to sign the final papers on a loan deal. We ducked in and out just as Kennedy was arriving.

We raced for the plane and got there just as the president was arriving. It's amazing how many bureaucrats it takes to operate one of these press planes. Pierre Salinger rides with Kennedy, not with the press. Andy Hatcher, who smokes a big cigar and looks like a ward heeler, rides with the press but does nothing except peddle a few handouts. Andy is a Negro, the first of his race ever to hold this job. Then there are three transportation officers who actually run the press plane, plus a transportation officer from the State Department. Actually, if it wasn't for Hatcher's race, the newspapermen would make it rough for him. Salinger is not as vindictive as Jim Hagerty but not as efficient.

BOGOTÁ, COLOMBIA—Immediately upon arrival, we got through the usual airport ceremonies and then drove to the Techo Housing Project, which Kennedy was to dedicate. The crowds were much bigger and more enthusiastic. Three buses were supplied for the newspapermen. I feel a little awkward since this is the first presidential trip I have taken [overseas] since Calvin Coolidge went to Havana in 1926. Frankly, I do not know many of the newspapermen on this trip—which shows I'm getting old.

I went on Eisenhower's campaign trip briefly in '52 and on Truman's campaign trip in '52, when he was helping Adlai Stevenson. I also took a trip with Sumner Welles to Rio de Janeiro in '42. Aside, though, from the Friendship Train and trips with several South American presidents, I haven't been on many junkets. Usually, I travel by myself. You can go faster and actually get more news.

Kennedy went to Mass and conferred with President Lleras until the evening when he had a state dinner to attend. Caught the plane at about midnight for Palm Beach and Washington.

Salinger was ecstatic over the crowd. He estimated it at one million and said it was bigger than any crowd Kennedy ever had, even in New York or Chicago. This, frankly, is a triumph. It was only a few years ago that Colombian crowds stoned the American embassy on every Fourth of July as a reminder of Teddy Roosevelt's seizure of Panama.

**TUESDAY, DECEMBER 19** | MIAMI—It is a four-hour hop from Bogotá to Miami, but our plane was a bit late. Besides, all planes were canceled in New York and Baltimore, so I had to sit around the Miami airport for a couple of hours. There I saw Claude Pepper and Jimmy Hoffa—though not together. Hoffa told me that there's only one thing the American people want: "More." Then he added: "For less. They want more money, and they want to work less," he said. I can understand, after talking to Hoffa, why George Meany, slow and dumb as he is, doesn't want him around. Hoffa is ready to do his best to undercut Kennedy's appeal for less wage boosts and says that Kennedy's trip to Latin America was pure hokum. "You can't get anywhere down there just talking to the leaders," according to Hoffa.

I tried to point out that Kennedy was spurring on some important agrarian reform plans and new housing. Hoffa went on like a stuck record that it was a waste of time. He says he is renegotiating all his contracts to expire simultaneously in 1964. Then his union will not have to cross any picket lines. He wants all unions to have their contracts come up for negotiation simultaneously. Otherwise, under the Landrum-Griffin Act they'll have to cross each other's picket lines. He claims Kennedy lied about this phase of the Landrum-Griffin Act.

A group of Negro shoeshine boys came in to ask him to organize them because the Cuban refugees were taking their jobs away. Hoffa refused. "It's martial stuff," he told me, "not worth bothering about." On the other hand, he is starting to organize the white-collar workers in the Miami airport. They are not martial and will bring in some real money to the union. He told me: "I'll spend a million dollars in our Birmingham strike. Our men are now out, striking against Bowman. We'll break him."

"How?" I asked.

"We'll discourage the strikebreakers," he said, with a knowing look.

Hoffa has now organized the women workers at the Minute Maid Orange Juice canning plant in Lakeland, Florida, and says he will soon organize the oil workers in Baton Rouge. You don't have to be a truck driver to belong to Jimmy's union. "Some of my men get $30,000 a year," he said. "They work fifty-two hours a week and earn it. I don't let my men waste any time hanging around. The minute they appear on the job their pay begins. These pilots have to wait around the airports for several hours before they start work and aren't paid for it. I wouldn't stand for that as far as my truck drivers are concerned."

**WEDNESDAY, DECEMBER 20** | WASHINGTON DC—Joe Kennedy has suffered a stroke. He is seventy-three years old. It's a wonder he hasn't suffered one before this. It's also lucky that he was stricken on a golf course and not in a lady's bed.

I looked over my file on him and was surprised to see how many letters Joe had written me when he was ambassador in London. All of his letters were completely wrong on the subject of Hitler and Mussolini. As ambassador, he just didn't seem to know what was going on so far as the dictators were concerned. There was an interesting paragraph in one letter in which he squawked over something he'd said in praise of Franco, which I had published.

The world seems to be on fire at this Christmas season and depressingly so. Prime Minister Nehru, the great disciple of peace, has sent Indian troops into Goa. Herbert Hoover has issued a statement supporting Katanga, and Sen. Tom Dodd, one against the United Nations. Of course, Hoover was always an isolationist, always against the League of Nations, and helped to undercut the basic efforts for peace made by his own secretary of state, Henry Stimson.

**FRIDAY, DECEMBER 22** | Talked to Acting Secretary of State George Ball. He dropped a hint that Katanga had tried to bribe one Latin American country to vote for it at the UN. I deduced that it was Costa Rica.

Ball said that Katanga has been flooding the newspapers with propaganda, even paid $150,000 rent for their information office in New York. Tshombe gets $85 million a year in royalties from the British and French mining interests and has spread his money all over the place. The Belgians, however, according to George, realize that if they don't stabilize the Congo, the Russians will move in and are now backing the United Nations. The French and British are not.

I told George the right wing was preparing to attack him because his law firm had represented the European market, while the left wing was preparing to attack him because his firm had represented Cuban sugar interests. I am planning to publish something about this.

Talking to Ball, I can understand why Kennedy eased Chester Bowles out of the job as undersecretary of state. Ball is concise and to the point. He knows what he's talking about and makes decisions. Chet Bowles is a wonderful guy but palavers all over the place. I have been trying to see Bowles for about nine months. I never did see him except when I got back from seeing Khrushchev and he wanted to have lunch with me. George Ball made the appointment within a couple of hours. Of course, the picking of an undersecretary of state should not depend upon whether he sees Pearson, but it should depend upon quick action and decisions. George Ball apparently makes them.

His explanation for Nehru's advance into Goa was that he had to help get Krishna Menon reelected. Menon can't speak any native language—only English. And he was in a bad way for reelection from Bombay. Goa is just north of Bombay, and this military invasion really was popular with Krishna Menon's constituents.

**THURSDAY, DECEMBER 28** | (Hosted dinner for fifty-five people prior to debutante party of Lally Graham, daughter of *Washington Post* publisher Phil Graham and his wife, Katherine.) The Meyer home on Crescent Place was decked out as never before for the debutante party. A huge tent was on the lawn. Every stick of furniture was moved out of the building into a storehouse. Tables were set for supper. Not even the debutante party of Florence Meyer, eldest daughter of Agnes and Eugene, could equal this one.

Finally got the Costa Rica ambassador to the UN on the telephone. He reluctantly confirmed the story of the million-dollar bribe offered to his government by Katanga if Costa Rica would recognize Katanga as the real government of the Congo. I have sent out an immediate release.

President Kennedy couldn't believe at first that Nelson Rockefeller wanted a divorce. He labored under the impression that it was Mrs. R. who had taken the initiative. He remarked to Kay Graham: "I don't believe it. No man would ever love love more than he loves politics."

FRIDAY, DECEMBER 29 | Mrs. Woodrow Wilson died last night. There were glowing obituaries in the newspapers today. The real fact, in my opinion, is that she caused more pain in this country than any other woman. Probably she paved the way for Word War II. I have been in Wytheville, Virginia, and seen the grocery store over which she lived. She came up to Washington at about the age of sixteen and married the jeweler Galt, who used to have his store next to the old *Evening Star*. When her husband died, she set out to catch Woodrow Wilson, then a widower. (It's possible she set out to catch him even before he became a widower because Wilson had a wavering eye.)

Like a lot of small-town girls in big cities and in high places, she became most possessive. She was jealous of those around Wilson and ostracized loyal Joe Tumulty. Joe used to tell me with tears in his eyes how she had refused to have him at Wilson's funeral. Joe had urged her to let the Republicans come in and see the president when he was ill in order to dispel their opposition to the League of Nations. She refused. I am sure that if she had not been so possessive, Wilson would not have suffered a stroke in the first place and would not have been so isolated from the Senate. The Versailles Treaty would have been ratified.

# 1962

## ANNALS

China and India ended a brief border war. The French ended their eight-year war against Algeria and recognized its independence. The United States and the USSR came close to war over the Cuban missile crisis.

In 1962 the first live transatlantic transmission through television was made via the Telestar satellite. Audiocassettes were also invented this year. Walmart, Target, and Kmart opened their first stores.

Eleanor Roosevelt died. She lived long enough to know that Dr. Albert Sabin had licensed his oral vaccine for polio, which had confined her husband to a wheelchair.

Adolf Eichmann, one of the organizers of the Holocaust, was executed in Israel. (This was the only time in Israel's history in which the death penalty was used.)

The U.S. Supreme Court decided *Baker v. Carr* and *Engel v. Vitale*. In the first case the Court decided that federal courts can force state legislatures to reapportion their seats. This decision led to the principle of "one man, one vote" in 1964's *Reynolds v. Sims*. In *Engel v. Vitale* the Court ruled that mandatory school prayer violated the Constitution.

In October, James Meredith became the first African American student to successfully enroll at the University of Mississippi. Despite Governor Ross Barnett's opposition, the Kennedy administration sent federal forces to quell riots so that Meredith could register.

That month Kennedy's most difficult crisis began when a reconnaissance plane confirmed that the Soviets were building missile bases in Cuba. Kennedy ordered a naval quarantine designed to prevent further Soviet ships from docking in Cuba. For thirteen days the world was at the brink of nuclear war.

With intense diplomacy between U.S. attorney general Robert Kennedy and Soviet ambassador Anatoly Dobrynin, the United States agreed not to invade Cuba as well as to remove Jupiter missiles in Turkey. In exchange the Soviets removed missiles from Cuba.

By the end of the year Cuba had released the survivors of the failed Bay of Pigs invasion, in exchange for food and medicine worth $53 million. The Cuban missile crisis also led to the creation of a "hotline" between the United States and the USSR to communicate directly in order to prevent a nuclear war.

—Ed.

# THE DIARY

**WEDNESDAY, JANUARY 3** | Averell Harriman came to lunch. He is now assistant secretary of state for Far Eastern affairs and seems to love it. He wanted to know if I had any suggestions about new starts for peace over Berlin. I had none. Some weeks ago the Russian embassy asked me whether the Kennedy administration would go along with the idea of having Eisenhower go to Moscow. I had sounded out Ted Sorensen, who frowned on the idea. Averell and I agreed it would help Kennedy considerably if Ike took the trip. This would take the heat of the right wing off Kennedy and pave the way for Kennedy himself; however, it would make Ike something of a hero, and a lot of people around Kennedy don't want to see this happen.

Long talk with Senator Fulbright, just back from Arkansas. He is concerned over the poor quality of men being appointed to U.S. ambassadorial jobs. It's too much of a closed shop. The new man to Argentina is McClintock, who was in Lebanon. John Cabot, whom Fulbright described as nice but dumb, is also being rewarded.

Dined at Florence Mahoney's. Abe Ribicoff was there and apparently not irked at the skeptical column I wrote about him last week. Ribicoff was quite eloquent about his work and his future. He said he wanted to get into the Senate, where he could say anything he wants. "Where I am now, I can't tell the teachers or the teachers' colleges what I think of them."

Ribicoff is distressed that thirty-five thousand people a week are being replaced by automation. Today we have relatively high prosperity at the top and near starvation at the bottom. This chasm is not one which produces democracy.

Ribicoff talked at length about his welfare program. He pointed out that the present plan had been on the books for twenty years, had never been revamped, and needs drastic overhauling. "We've got to train people to get them back to work," he said, "not leave them on relief the rest of their lives."

The Walter Lippmanns came to tea for Harriett Welles, together with Senator and Mrs. Fulbright, George Killion, Carlo Perrone, and my nephew Drew. Drew has just come back from Africa, where he crossed the lines from the Katanga side to the UN side without being shot. He says there was quite a bit of firing in his direction from time to time, but one got used to it. His sympathies seem to lie with Katanga and President Tshombe, but the main point he makes is that the Congo is far from ready for self-government. What it needs is a reinstatement of colonialism, though under a different name.

**TUESDAY, JANUARY 23** | Bobby Kennedy has been invited to go to Moscow. This is apparently a follow-up on the suggestion I gave Khrushchev last summer. When he and Zhukov wanted to know whether they should invite Joseph P. Kennedy to Moscow, I said, "No. The president doesn't like to have it appear that he's taking advice from his father. On the other hand, Bobby Kennedy is very close to the president and could do more good in improving relations."

**THURSDAY, JANUARY 25** | [The Big Brothers'] . . . dinner last night was a knockout. We were worried because this was the first integrated dinner on a large scale in the history of Washington. It was in honor of John Duncan, the first Negro commissioner in history, and was attended by about one-third of the cabinet, most of the top senate leaders and Vice President Johnson. About one-half the audience was Negro. At first we had a hard time selling tickets, but after it became known that Floyd Patterson would be there, the Negro attendance zoomed. Floyd arrived—a little late—and made quite a speech after he received the A citation from Bobby Kennedy as a Big Brother of 1962. The speech read, "Ladies and Gentlemen, Mr. Toastmaster—Thank you very much."

Bobby Kennedy also made an excellent talk. I introduced him by saying, "No meeting of the Big Brothers would be complete without having present the most famous Little Brother in America." He replied: "The reason I'm here is because my big brother told me to be here. He was here last year, and he felt that a meeting of the Big Brothers should have a Kennedy present."

He then proceeded to tell about what the Justice Department was doing about juvenile delinquency, particularly the halfway houses to help boys just out of institutions. This is the kind of thing Patterson is doing in New York.

Lyndon also made a good speech (perhaps I'm prejudiced because I wrote it for him).

**SATURDAY, JANUARY 27** | General [Arthur] Trudeau is now being discussed as No. 2 man for McCone at CIA. Trudeau is one of the active preventive-war clique which wants to put the military ahead of the State Department in deciding foreign policy. This clique has been trying to undermine Fulbright and inspired the present hearings on civilian censorship of the brass hats.

Kennedy, however, made a firm statement at his press conference that he would continue censorship. He really has guts when the chips are down on most of these things. Stennis of Mississippi and Saltonstall of Massachusetts became so worried about public opinion supporting the brass hats that they went to see Eisenhower at Gettysburg and persuaded him to issue a statement which was supposed to mollify the military and public opinion. While it was a moderate statement, Ike went back on his own policies as president, in which he enforced very rigorous censorship. Kennedy has actually taken over the system he inherited from Ike.

I have prepared a memo on Arabian Oil in the Near East and the part played by Central Intelligence and distributed it to several senators. I've also prepared a memo on erroneous aspects of McCone's testimony before the Armed Services Committee. I don't know that this will do any good, but several senators are steamed up.

**MONDAY, JANUARY 29** | Senator Mansfield has postponed the vote on McCone until Wednesday, at the urging of Wayne Morse. Apparently, my cables to Wayne paid off.

**WEDNESDAY, JANUARY 31** | Talked with Bill Fulbright just before the McCone vote and urged him to make a statement. He did. It was brief but effective. The vote went against us, as I expected, but we polled twelve. And when you consider that three members of the Senate Armed Services Committee were against McCone, plus the chairman of the Senate Foreign Relations Committee, Fulbright, this is a significant defeat. Senator Case of South Dakota switched his vote and opposed McCone. This means that I will have to support him for reelection in South Dakota.

Clint Anderson and Stuart Symington did the floor lobbying for McCone.

Javits did not produce. Neither did Keating; however, Ev Dirksen did exactly as he promised. He made quite a speech, saying that "Mr. Pearson's columns have aroused considerable doubt in my mind. This matter of conflict of interest should be examined carefully."

**THURSDAY, FEBRUARY 1** | The lineup against McCone was such that I think he will watch his step very carefully. The *New York Times* played up the fact that Fulbright was against him. It commented that he would not have the confidence of the chairman of the Foreign Relations Committee. I had told Fulbright [that] McCone was considering the appointment of General Trudeau as his No. 2 man—to make sure Fulbright voted the way he did. He was already wavering, but when I pointed out that news stories speculated that the leading preventive-war general in the Pentagon might be McCone's assistant, this clinched Bill's vote.

Hubert Humphrey, as I suspected, paired for McCone. Some very good friends of mine, such as Kefauver, McNamara of Michigan, and John Carroll of Colorado, voted for McCone.

The meeting of the OAS foreign ministers ended with a fourteen-to-six vote to oust Cuba from the OAS. It was a long, difficult siege.

Kennedy, at his press conference yesterday, raised Cain about the tremendous stockpiling of strategic material. This is going to reflect more on Stuart Symington and the Democrats than on the Republicans, I suspect.

**FRIDAY, FEBRUARY 2** | Talked to Salinger about his visits with Adzhubei, Khrushchev's son-in-law. Salinger is about as communicative as an overgrown beet, which he somewhat resembles. He said that the only stories he could tell me about Adzhubei were not printable and then proceeded to tell one which he thought might be printable, but he said he didn't want it printed anyway. Salinger said that Kennedy and Adzhubei had delayed their White House luncheon one hour while they talked about major problems. Mrs. Kennedy had come in twice to say that luncheon was ready, but the president had given the high sign to hold things up. I asked what they were talking about but got nowhere.

**SUNDAY, FEBRUARY 4** | Mary Rockefeller has now arrived in Reno for her divorce. Nelson castigated Kennedy this week in Des Moines for setting up a Department of Urban Affairs with a Negro in charge. Bob Weaver, who will be in charge, called me day before yesterday to say that he had placed a newspaperman, whom I had recommended, who was fired from the *Boston American* when it folded. Weaver recalled that he had known Rockefeller fairly well in New York and that Rockefeller once had proposed a department of urban affairs.

Yesterday I asked Pierre Salinger whether he was still convinced that the Genealogical Tree which is published in great detail in the Library of Congress, regarding Kennedy's alleged first marriage, was inaccurate. Salinger swore that it was. I thought he would be amused by the fact that Senator Tower of Texas was steering an army of Republicans up to the library to look at the book. Salinger was not amused.

Old Joe Kennedy seems to be recuperating slowly, but he will never be the same. Ernest reported the other evening that he had been subject to violent fits of temper of late, some of them aimed against me, Arthur Krock, and Scotty Reston. If we so much as chided his son, old Joe considered it treason.

SUNDAY, FEBRUARY 5 | Arthur and Dorothy Goldberg came to lunch. I suspect Arthur is getting a bit antilabor—or rather, getting to know the problems of industry better. I told him labor was gradually wiping out the newspapers of the United States. The *New York Post* is now up for sale, and David Karr is trying to buy it. If, however, the technical unions and the guild insist on a wage hike, the *Post* will be out of business. "In the days of Dubinsky and Sidney Hillman," said Arthur, "they would be around to help the industry and not put it out of business."

He noted the irresponsibility of many local leaders and the fact that labor union members never attend meetings. This puts control of the union in the hands of a few local politicians. He said that Egburt, the head of Studebaker, had telephoned him to help settle the Studebaker strike. "Egburt's car was stopped by a picket, and he got out and threatened to beat up the picket. I don't blame him," said Arthur. "I telephoned Reuther, and he got together with the Studebaker people and helped to work out a compromise. Studebaker had been giving its men a thirty-nine-minute wash-up period, as compared with twenty-four minutes for General Motors. That fifteen-minute difference multiplied by several thousand men would mean a lot of money in the cost of producing cars, and Studebaker has to worry about General Motors competition."

"Yet," said Arthur, "with eleven thousand people already unemployed in South Bend, the union was holding out for that extra fifteen minutes. The strike lasted six weeks. Finally, Reuther worked out a compromise whereby five minutes was dropped from the wash-up time. Yet the local union was about ready to put Studebaker out of business."

I told Arthur about my visit with George Romney in Detroit. He remarked that Kennedy felt Romney was going too far by publicizing God and his communion with God as to whether he should run for governor of Michigan.

I expressed the belief that Kennedy was going to be judged on whether or not he carried out his campaign pledge of making "fresh new starts for peace" and whether he finally achieved it. He has been making no fresh new starts. Arthur agreed. He finds the president alert, intelligent, and dominating on domestic policy but not sure of himself on foreign policy. At the recent luncheon for Hugh Gaitskell, the British Labour Party leader, Kennedy went far in regard to West Germany and put himself emphatically in the position of opposing nuclear arms for the West German army. This is the British position. "One thing the Russians have a legitimate reason to worry about is Germany," Arthur said, "and Kennedy recognizes this. He is also worried about the danger of German science getting together with the progress France has already made with the A-bomb and combining to build up a real nuclear force."

He agreed that Kennedy is surrounded by poor Russia advisors. Bohlen is warped and out-of-date, probably because he's been so anxious to disprove McCarthy's charge that he was soft on communism. Walt Rostow is superficial and talks for the sake of hearing himself talk. McGeorge Bundy, whom I do not know, does not rate with Arthur. He's inclined to be snobbish, and Arthur pointed out that any man who joined the Metropolitan Club at the same time Bobby Kennedy was resigning shouldn't rate with the Kennedy administration. Bundy is the brother of Dean Acheson's son-in-law and represents Dean's thinking inside the administration. Dean is still trying to prove the points he made as secretary of state, but nine years have passed, and a lot of his ideas are out-of-date.

I expressed the view that the man Kennedy should have as his Russia advisor is George Kennan, now ambassador to Yugoslavia, but the career clique doesn't like him. "Kennedy should not let Khrushchev continually take the initiative regarding a summit conference," Arthur said. It looks as if he were dragging his feet regarding peace and disarmament. He should have told Khrushchev that a summit conference in Geneva was too cumbersome, but "I'd like to come and see you personally to talk over the problems of the world." This is the kind of initiative which would have captured world imagination. Instead, the president has been put in the position of constantly quibbling.

The Kennedys use three tables to get around the problem of who should sit where at dinner. At the big dinner for his cabinet, the Supreme Court, and the leaders of Congress, Speaker John McCormack was rated ahead of the chief justice. Kennedy did this in deference to Sam Rayburn but probably is now sorry. After the dinner was over and the guests were about to depart, Arthur saw Jackie standing by the elevator looking rather wistful. She said, "Oh, Arthur, wouldn't it be nice to just dance?"

What most people don't realize is that a girl of thirty-one has different ideas about entertainment than senators and cabinet members twice her age.

**WEDNESDAY, MARCH 14** | Lunched with Kmeicik, first secretary of the Polish embassy. He admits Khrushchev has problems at home and that Red China is one of them. This is one reason Kmeicik thinks we will not have disarmament. He didn't elaborate, but I gather that both the Red Army and Red China are too powerful.

The Poles are peeved at Kennedy for deserting his old idea on wheat for Poland. When he was in the Senate, he sponsored this. Now, as president, he is only permitting a niggardly amount of wheat. This has played into the hands of the anti-Americans in Poland. The Poles have an important arrange-ment with the Czechs for the exchange of materials. The Poles have agreed not to make tractors but to buy them from Czechoslovakia. Poland in turn sells a lot of other stuff to Czechoslovakia.

**THURSDAY, MARCH 15** | Dined with the Thurman Arnolds. Hugo Black Jr. was there and is leaving Birmingham, Alabama, for good, to practice law in Miami. It's impossible, apparently, to live happily in Birmingham if you are the son of a Supreme Court justice who ruled for integration. The parks and tennis courts have been closed down, and there's no place for young people's recreation.

Winifred Reed was quite vitriolic about Frankfurter. She told me that Philip Graham had been a clerk for Stanley Reed at the R F C [Reconstruction Finance Corporation] and had advanced him in government, when Felix Frankfurter gave Phil a job as his law clerk. Felix was interested in Kay Meyer and helped to arrange the match between Kay and Phil.

Everyone on the Court hates Felix, according to Winifred, and is looking forward to the day when he will retire. Someone was talking to him about when an elderly justice would retire. Felix naively speculated, "Who could that be?"

**WEDNESDAY, MARCH 28** | Teddy Kennedy has admitted to the *Boston Globe* that he hired someone to take an examination for him at Harvard and was kicked out as a result. After the war he was permitted to come back and take his diploma. Of course, no one except a Kennedy or someone who had given bountifully to Harvard could get away with this. It will be interesting to see what effect this has on the Senate election. In my opinion neither Teddy Kennedy nor Ed McCormack deserves to win. George Lodge, a very decent young Republican, would make a far better senator.

**THURSDAY, MARCH 29** | Bill Neel proposes a series of columns to combat the idea that I am a friend of Khrushchev and am soft on communism. Jack Anderson and Bill are both worried about this.

**SATURDAY, MARCH 31** | CLEVELAND—I made my speech at the City Club, and apparently it went over well. I talked about press monopoly and the big newspaper empire built up by the Scripps-Howard papers but gave credit to Louis [Seltzer] as a great editor. I confess I did this a bit with tongue in cheek. The broadcast was carried for an hour over the radio.

Afterward one man from the audience asked me, "Why don't you answer your mail, and second, isn't it true that all the information you get comes from skunks?" I replied: "It's true I don't answer all of my mail, even though I try hard. I just have too much. And some letters are like the second part of that question. They don't deserve a reply."

Ches [Kemp], Luvie Pearson's sister-in-law, had a cocktail party for me. Mayor Celebrezze came, together with Mayor Celeste of Lakewood. They say that Governor Mike DiSalle, running for reelection, is going to have a tough time. He had planned not to run, but Kennedy came out to a big Democratic dinner in midwinter and told him to run. DiSalle has figured on a cabinet post, probably replacing Abe Ribicoff. After all, it was DiSalle who came out for Kennedy very, very early and at a crucial time in the preprimary campaign. Mike, however, is being a faithful friend and is doing what Kennedy tells him to do—running again, even though he will probably be defeated.

**MONDAY, APRIL 2** | Called on Chief Justice Earl Warren. Jack Gordon in Miami wanted him to speak before the American Jewish Congress on the Bill of Rights, but the chief declined. He says he can't stick his neck out before liberal groups at the same time he is writing opinions of the Court. He didn't say so, but obviously he is doing far more for the liberal groups where he is than making speeches before one or two organizations.

He reminisced about Nixon in California and what a mistake he had made by branding Kennedy a "carpetbagger." I reminded him that I had lunched with him in Sacramento, just as he was going to meet Harry Truman, then president, during the '52 campaign and welcome him into the state of California. Warren said that the other day in Kansas City he was attending the Truman Library trustees' meeting when he and Truman discussed the fact that in 1948, when Earl was running for vice president on the Dewey ticket, he had gone to meet Truman, who was campaigning for reelection. He did not consider him a carpetbagger.

WEDNESDAY, APRIL 4 | Luvie's piece appeared in the *Saturday Evening Post* yesterday. The reaction has been good. I had expected all hell to break loose from the radical right wing. It still may come.

The chief hell today came from an editorial published by Louis Seltzer in the *Cleveland Press* denying categorically that Roy Howard had ordered the cancellation of my column. Louis is lying, but it puts me in an awkward spot—after all the praise I gave him.

Rep. Dante Fascell, hitherto a stalwart supporter of Kennedy and a liberal congressman, has begun to backtrack. The right wing is too strong for him. Kennedy went to Miami and endorsed him publicly at a big hundred-dollar-a-plate dinner, but the other evening on the radio Fascell practically apologized for being a "Kennedy lackey."

Kennedy is going to lose more and more of his liberal members of Congress if he doesn't help them out against the right wing. Already, scores of congressmen have evaporated on crucial votes, such as foreign aid. Kennedy must stand up and be counted, the same way Franklin Roosevelt did during the period when Hitler had a lot of people bamboozled before Pearl Harbor.

Radio Moscow has taken a crack at me—thank God. They broadcast a repetition of my column that five Russian astronauts had disappeared prior to Gagarin's successful flight. I remember that when lunching with Adzhubei, Khrushchev's son-in-law, he promised that he would write some critical stories about Pearson if I got too much criticism at home for trying to tell the truth about the Soviets. I doubt whether Adzhubei had anything to do with Radio Moscow's blast; however, it was helpful.

**FRIDAY, APRIL 6** | Kennedy won his vote for the UN bond issue by an overwhelming majority. This country is not as isolationist after all as some people would have you think.

**SATURDAY, APRIL 14** | Mary Rockefeller refused to go to the Ernest Gruenings' for dinner. I went alone and was quite late arriving because, believe it or not, I got lost in Rock Creek between Connecticut Avenue and Sixteenth Street. Mrs. Orville Freeman said she was delighted because they were late too. Orville had just flown in from California to find that yesterday, Friday the thirteenth, both Agriculture Committees of Congress had meat-axed his farm bill. He told me at great length how he had counted noses and hoped to get the farm bill passed in both committees. Ellender of Louisiana had been a tower of strength—thanks largely because Orville had courted him on almost every move he made. He has also gone up to see every representative and senator in one of the most efficient selling jobs performed by any cabinet member. Proxmire of Wisconsin walked out of the Senate committee yesterday for what Orville described as "unprintable" reasons. This left the majority nine to eight against the administration. Owen Johnson also deserted on one vote, having been pushed away by Eastland. Milt Young of North Dakota had also promised to back up the administration as a result of Farm Union persuasion, but when the feed grain provision in the bill was modified, he voted against the whole bill, thereby lining up with the Farm Bureau.

Mrs. Freeman remarked: "You'd think before you come to Washington that congressmen vote their convictions, but they don't. They vote according to personal prejudice and pressure."

Ernest Gruening, at the age of about seventy-six, is still going strong. I have known him ever since he was editor of the *Nation* and editor of the *Portland (ME) Express*. He doesn't really know that I helped to bring him to Washington by persuading Harold Ickes he should set up a Department of Insular Affairs and make Ernest director.

He's up for reelection to the Senate this year and makes long weekend trips to Alaska. His energy is boundless. I learned for the first time tonight that he had persuaded Muñoz Marín to give up a life of poetry and Greenwich Village and return to Puerto Rico to run for governor. This really changed history in the Caribbean.

**SUNDAY, APRIL 15** | I spent part of the weekend putting together an immediate release story on the background of what happened in the steel crackdown. I couldn't persuade Arthur Goldberg to talk about his session with Blough. This was taking place when Bethlehem Steel capitulated on Friday, April 13, thereby causing U.S. Steel to capitulate too. One of the most interesting telephone calls was made by Douglas Dillon, secretary of the treasury, to Henry Alexander, head of J. P. Morgan and the banker for U.S. Steel.

While I was talking with Goldberg on the telephone, he interrupted to say that the president was calling on his other line. The president yesterday was on an aircraft carrier off Norfolk but was keeping his eye on all the steel minutiae. I wonder, however, what would have happened if Blough had made his announcement of a price increase on Friday afternoon while Kennedy was in the air en route to Norfolk, instead of making it on Tuesday, April 10, just before Kennedy's Wednesday press conference. The steel people hire plenty of smart public relations men. The trouble is they just don't give a damn about public opinion. This time they learned better.

**TUESDAY, APRIL 17** | Dined with Bill Walton. Averell Harriman came late. He's looking for a good ambassador for Formosa [Taiwan], someone who will stand up to Chiang Kai-shek. I suggested Col. James McHugh, who has written a textbook in Chinese as a minister counselor. Averell suggested Gen. Russell Dean, his former aide in Moscow, or General Anderson. We discussed Gen. Omar Bradley, who is probably too old and too anti-Chiang; also Gen. Matt Ridgeway, who did a great job in Korea but Averell thought was too dumb. I agreed. The one man we all were unanimous on was Walton—except Walton.

I suggested Senator Ellender as ambassador to Russia to replace Tommy Thompson but got no takers. I was also ribbed for suggesting Anfuso as ambassador to Rome. There was general agreement, however, that career men reach a point where they don't make good ambassadors. They are too riveted to the routine. Freddie Reinhardt in Rome is afraid to get his feet in Italian political waters, and an ambassador to Italy must get mixed up in politics.

Averell had an interesting session with the new Russian ambassador, Anatoly Dobrynin, whom he asked to help out with Souvanna Phouma, the neutral in Laos. He and Averell got to kidding each other about doing the Twist, and the ambassador took his coat, put it around his fanny, and did an imitation American Twist with a couple of steps thrown in.

Averell thinks Kennedy is now coming around to the position which Averell and I held some time ago—namely, that the Russians are ready for a settlement of Berlin, with a little give-and-take. The greatest tragedy was when Kennedy turned to Dean Acheson after he took the inaugural oath in January 1961, at which time Dean advised: "Don't do business with Khrushchev. You can't trust him." It was the general consensus that Dean is trying to live down the days when Joe McCarthy called him pro-Communist, therefore leans in the other direction.

At lunch with George McGovern, Howard Chernoff, and Bob Allen, McGovern expressed the view that if a direct approach was made by Communist China to Kennedy for food, it would be given. No approach has yet been made. Alf Landon, the ex-GOP candidate for president, has come out for food to China, and Sen. Frank Carlson of Kansas has also indicated that he would favor it in talks with Mrs. Menninger in Topeka. At present there is no surplus wheat any place in the world except here. Canada has sold all its surplus crop, and so has Australia.

Averell reports that John McCone is doing a lousy job at Central Intelligence. Neither he nor Bill could figure out why Kennedy appointed him. It's suspected that Bobby Kennedy made the real decision. McCone's name came up when Averell pointed out that the trouble with the American embassy to Rome is a guy named Outerbridge Horsey, the counselor, whom he described as the same kind of a Catholic as McCone. He is such a right-wing Catholic that he hasn't permitted any merger of the Nenni Socialists with the Christian Democratic Party for years. This should have come about long ago but only occurred this winter.

WEDNESDAY, APRIL 18 | The American delegation to Geneva has put forward a sweeping disarmament proposal. It's the most comprehensive disarmament plan this country has ever made and has the ring of sincerity about it. Of course, it requires inspection, and this is the stumbling block which the Russians will not accept. I recall Khrushchev telling me that if there was real disarmament, then he would go for inspection. What he claims to be opposed to is inspection during partial disarmament, which would give so-called spies an opportunity to spy on Soviet arms. I think, in part, he is telling the truth about this. There is a deeply ingrained suspicion on the part of the Soviet military and others against the American military and its preventive war group. I don't see how either side can get ahead unless there's some kind of inspection. On the whole Kennedy has been much more amenable on this point than Eisenhower was.

THURSDAY, APRIL 19 | Perez Alfonso, the Venezuelan minister of mines and petroleum, came to lunch. He told me of a session he had with David Rockefeller of the Chase Bank, pointing out that the oil companies were taking 30 percent profits out of Venezuela and putting no money back. Perez Alfonso showed me a report from Sinclair Oil proving what he had told me in Venezuela some months before, that the oil companies had deliberately stopped exploration and development after the Betancourt government came into power. Betancourt has now lost his majority in the Venezuelan congress to the Castroites. Perez Alfonso doesn't seem to be alarmed about this and says it was probably a good thing to get the screwballs and dissidents out of the government. Nevertheless, if Betancourt doesn't get the cooperation of the oil companies, he could have serious trouble from higher taxes, which could amount to expropriation. I had the feeling that Perez Alfonso is a real asset to the oil companies, even though they don't realize it and even though it would be suicide to have this mentioned in Venezuela.

Dined at the Eugene Meyers' in honor of the Goldbergs. Arthur admitted to me very briefly that Jack Kennedy had to be "talked into a tough stand against the steel industry." Arthur added, "If he hadn't adopted that policy, I would have had to resign." The steel toughness is beginning to pay off already, however.

Just before dinner Walter Ridder called, incensed over the ruling of the Arlington Zoning Board, whereby three seventeen-story apartments will be built on the banks of the Potomac on the property owned by Hugh Auchincloss, stepfather of Jackie Kennedy. Walter claims there must have been a fix. At dinner Wendy Morgan, who lives in that neighborhood, was also incensed. They all want me to write a story. It just so happens that the builder of these apartments is Magazine, with whom I have been working to get a bid on a downtown tract of property. Whenever I get in the position to make a little money on real estate or oil, I always have to write something. And it goes glimmering. I suppose I could pass this one up.

FRIDAY, APRIL 20 | Leo Wallenberg came to breakfast. He has been talking to the State Department career boys about the new Fanfani government in Italy. They have been trying to sabotage it, probably because they predicted that it would not succeed, and now they have to prove they were right. The only way they can do this is by sabotage.

I wrote a column on Sunday proposing Rep. Victor Anfuso, from Brooklyn, as the new ambassador because our career diplomat, Freddy Reinhardt, is not doing well. This also rubbed the career boys the wrong way. It seems to me we have a great opportunity in Italy. First, we've done a great job in Italy, and it has become a vigorous, prosperous country. Second, there is a Catholic party in Italy which is reasonably progressive and which can be used all over the world to fight communism, not by force of arms but by example. The new government, for instance, has just provided free schoolbooks, which has never been done in two thousand years of Italian history. Third, they have just abolished the old Fascist censorship, which no other republican government in Italy has done. Fourth, they have increased old-age pensions. Yet the State Department remains aloof and critical.

The Russian delegate to Geneva, Zorin, has accepted the neutrals' proposal for abandoning nuclear tests. Arthur Dean, the U.S. delegate, has categorically said no. The only issue is that of inspection, and in the case of nuclear tests, any test can be spotted without inspection. The question is whether an on-site inspection should follow a nuclear explosion. It seems to me we are being rather sticky on this point.

SATURDAY, APRIL 21  |  Estes Kefauver was at the [Mrs. Silliman] Evans's party. I told him that Kennedy owed him more than any other one man in the United States. If Kefauver hadn't blocked Kennedy's nomination for vice president in 1956, JFK would be just another defeated vice presidential candidate. There's a bit of resentment on the part of the Kennedy family against Jiggs Donohue and Kefauver because they did block Jack for the vice presidency in '56. It should be the other way around, but the Kennedy family, particularly Bobby, believes in revenge.

Estes complained that only two other senators would go along with him in trying to block the American Telephone and Telegraph satellite giveaway. Ed Welsh, counsel for the space agency, confirmed this. Privately, he is with Kefauver and opposed to his own committee in believing that the present bill is an outlandish giveaway to the biggest corporation in the world. Nevertheless, Bob Kerr is adamant that AT&T must get the concession, and Representative Harris of Arkansas rushed the House bill through his committee last week so there could be no excuse for stalling in the Senate. Welch describes Kerr as the most potent and effective senator, that none dare tangle with him except Morse of Oregon and Mrs. Neuberger. Kerr says he'll marry Mrs. Neuberger to prevent her opposition, but he can't deal with Morse's brilliant debate.

I ribbed Estes gently about being for confirmation of any man Kennedy sends to the Hill, having reference to John McCone, CIA chief. Estes replied: "For a long time I wasn't able to look old Drew in the face about John McCone, but when I went to the White House to stop the appointment of Woods of the First Boston Bank to be head of Foreign Aid, Kennedy told me about his problem in getting good men. 'They talk about getting more good men in government,' he said, 'but every time you bring a bunch of businessmen in here and ask them to serve their government, they refuse to leave their jobs.'"

TUESDAY, MAY 22 | Lyndon Johnson telephoned to complain that I had not been checking in with him. "You let people get at me through you," he said, and went on to explain that he had never put in a word for Brown & Root to get any space contracts—they were entirely in the hands of the army engineers. "Besides," he said, "Brown went to school with Albert Thomas, who is chairman of the Appropriations Subcommittee, and that, together with Rice Institute, is enough to get the space agency in Houston."

Jack had just picked up a story that Billie Sol Estes had landed his plane at Lyndon's airport in Johnson City twenty to thirty times and that Lyndon had intervened with the Agriculture Department to get Estes back on the Cotton Advisory Board; further, that Charlie Murphy had cleaned out the files so this would not show. I asked Lyndon about it, though I didn't tell him I'd already asked Orville Freeman, who denied it. Orville even said that Lyndon had telephoned to complain over the fact that Estes had been put on the Cotton Advisory Committee. He said all Texas appointments had to be cleared with him. Lyndon was positive that Estes's plane had never landed at his airport and had never been in his home in Texas. "He was in my home once in Washington just before the January 20 dinner, when all Texans came to see me, and I only shook hands with him once as he came through the reception line." I am pretty sure Lyndon was telling the truth.

Orville Freeman wrote to me about a year and a half ago complaining about a story I wrote (during the Los Angeles convention) of a battle between him and Hubert Humphrey. He thought the story was unfair. I told him that when the time was right, I would rectify it. So, I went to see him today. He has done an excellent job and was on the verge of really bringing order out of the chaos he inherited from Benson. He looked distraught. He said, among other things, that Charlie Murphy was terribly upset over the whole business. It was Charlie who put Billie Sol Estes back on the Cotton Advisory Board after he had been kicked off because of cotton finagling. That was an error in judgment but not an uncommon one when members of Congress go to bat for their friends, as both Yarborough and Rutherford did for Estes.

WEDNESDAY, MAY 23 | Lyndon is beside himself over Mary Margaret Wiley's marriage to a wealthy Houston oilman on June 1. Lyndon is so upset that the children notice his behavior. He came home late the other night and woke up his eldest daughter, kissed her, and told her how much he loved her. The next morning she was worried and got up to see how her father was. He had not been in bed all night.

Lady Bird, who is back in Texas, is taking it philosophically. Obviously, she has known what's been going on with Mary Margaret for a couple of years, but she remarked, "What does Mary Margaret mean by leaving without breaking in someone to take her place?" This is the luckiest break Lyndon has had in a long time. Mary Margaret was about to ruin him and his family and his political career. His attentions to her had been so noticeable at diplomatic functions that the society writers scarcely refrained from mentioning it.

Kennedy called Arthur Goldberg just before he appointed Whizzer White to the Supreme Court and told him, "You should be the first on the Court, but I can't spare you." Arthur said that Juan Trippe had come to see him the other day to thank him for the arbitration of the Pan American pilots' strike and sang the praises of the Kennedy administration. Arthur asked him, "Do you stand up in business meetings with the U.S. Chamber of Commerce, where they're berating Kennedy, and tell them what you've told me?" Trippe was evasive.

Luther Hodges says that Kennedy is worried over the stock market decline. Agnes Meyer had dinner yesterday with Mrs. Roosevelt, who was her houseguest. Mrs. R. was kept waiting in the hot sun over the weekend by Kennedy. She remarked, "You know I'm not frail, but two hours in the hot sun is a little long."

FRIDAY, MAY 25 | I saw something I had never expected to see before in the District of Columbia. I called on John Duncan, the first Negro commissioner of the District, and as I left, he asked me to come in to meet twenty-five doctors who were trying to find a new public health officer for the District. All of them were white, and as Duncan and I entered, all of them rose in deference to him.

**SATURDAY, MAY 26** | Clayton Fritchey came from New York for the Fortas dinner, and I asked him whether Adlai was under instructions from the State Department when he introduced the resolution of censure against Israel in the Syrian–Sea of Galilee incident. He was. Clayton added that Adlai would have introduced it without instructions. "Adlai's biggest supporters have been wealthy Jews," Clayton explained, "but he has that independent streak in him which demands that he act regardless of friends and supporters."

In 1956, when he was running for president, he made it clear that he was not going to kowtow to his Jewish friends regarding Israel. And when Ben-Gurion came here some months ago, he had a happy visit with Kennedy but an unhappy one with Adlai. Kennedy didn't tell him the real facts of life, but Adlai did. He warned Ben-Gurion not to stir up any trouble along the border or the United States would have to take a stand against Israel. Ben-Gurion later complained to Jewish leaders in New York about Adlai. "Adlai's position is that we are for Israel, Israel couldn't exist without us, but Israel should not make it tough politically."

**MONDAY, MAY 28** | The new Russian ambassador, Dobrynin, came to lunch. He is charming and more intelligent than Menshikov. I had invited him with the idea of having George McGovern present. George had been trying to arrange for the shipment of surplus food to Red China. Once before, he asked me to get him together with Menshikov, and then my flight was late en route from Dayton, and the luncheon fizzled. Kennedy has now decided that if China makes a direct approach to the United States, surplus food will be given.

I explained to Dobrynin that McGovern had to go back to South Dakota but that, as head of the Food for Peace Committee, he was interested in talking on an informal, confidential basis about the possibility of food for China, provided a direct approach was made or even an approach through a third party.

Dobrynin's reaction was immediate and significant. "I would think that the way to handle that is through your own ambassador in Warsaw," he said. "You have direct contact with the Chinese all the time, and I would think that is the most efficient way to handle it." Either the Russians are not on sufficiently good terms with the Chinese to handle this, or it's too delicate a matter politically. The Chinese hitherto have rebuffed any idea of food from the United States, hinting that they would rather have Formosa [Taiwan] back.

The other significant part of our luncheon conversation pertained to Laos. The ambassador made the point that the United States and Russia long ago agreed that Laos was to be neutral. It was first agreed by Kennedy and Khrushchev in Vienna, he recalled. "We cooperated with you to get a neutral government," Dobrynin said, "and we can't understand why you are not able to bring your man around to participate in this neutral government. It is very difficult for us to understand why President Kennedy, with his power in this part of the world and the money he has been giving Laos and the military direction, cannot prevail upon the royalist government to participate. We try to understand your problems, but this is one question we simply cannot understand."

This had me stumped. I recalled that Kennedy had cut off the $3 million a month foreign aid to Phoumi Nosavan in February. The ambassador said that Rusk had told him about this. I recalled that both Kennedy and Averell Harriman had told me how they favored a neutralist government, but I could not explain why Kennedy had not been able to bring Phouma around to neutral participation, unless it was the possibility that American military men were undercutting the president. I strongly suspect that military reports exaggerated the Communist attack in Laos and got Kennedy into a trap in sending U.S. troops to Thailand. The ambassador remarked that now the American troops were in Thailand, he could understand how it was difficult to get them out.

I remarked that Kennedy had been sore at Phouma Nosavan when he learned that the attack in north Laos was a put-up job and that Averell had remarked to me, "I wish we could forget about Laos." I recalled that Kennedy had asked me to write to Khrushchev when I came back from Moscow, emphasizing the importance of settling Laos, and that I had written such a letter. Now, one year after Vienna, we are still at odds on Laos.

Ambassador Dobrynin paid high tribute to Tommy Thompson as a quiet, effective ambassador. He said, "He never gets excited." He explained: "He listens carefully and explains, 'This is the position of my government.' We respect him, and we like him."

I asked him who he thought would be a good man to take Thompson's place. He replied, "This is a question not for us." Nevertheless, we discussed some possibilities, among them Averell Harriman, who very much wants the job, and George Kennan, who was once declared persona non grata and forced to leave as ambassador. I tried to find out whether Kennan would be welcomed back but got no clear reply.

I told him Salinger and Harriman had lunch with me last week. He wanted to know what Salinger thought of Khrushchev. I told him that he had liked Khrushchev very much, had thought there was room for greater exchange of cultural activities, but that there were real problems still to be worked out over Berlin. The ambassador agreed that Berlin remained difficult.

I told him that reaction to my articles on Khrushchev had been very critical, but the reaction to my wife's piece in the *Saturday Evening Post* had been about 90 percent favorable.

Previously, he served in the Russian embassy here when Zaroubin was ambassador. I remarked that I had once done Zaroubin an injustice in that I had reported he was anti-American. Later, after he died, I learned how he had once reminded his staff that during the war the United States had permitted Russia to establish its own radio communications center inside the Pentagon, guarded by Russian soldiers, and into which no American was permitted to enter. Dobrynin had not known this.

He asked me how my Khrushchev peas were getting along. I told him they were planted alongside some American peas to illustrate the fact that there can be coexistence. I also told him I was sending Khrushchev some sorgo seed but that I had found there was a law passed by Congress in 1950 which stated that if you gave a present to a Communist, you thereby became affiliated with a Communist.

**TUESDAY, MAY 29** | The stock market, which took the lowest drop yesterday since 1929, bounced back again today about 27 points. Privately, the Kennedy administration is still panic-stricken.

Today Kennedy sent to Congress a proposal to raise money for campaigns by permitting tax exemption on contributions up to $750. It was in 1956 that Sen. Tom Hennings did his best to pass a clean elections bill but got no support from Lyndon Johnson, who has always had the benefit of a lot of Texas oil money and wants to keep it that way. Tom died with his clean elections bill also dead. Now Kennedy has revived it, thanks in large part to the scandal over Billie Sol Estes and the tremendous amount of money he passed around to Democrat candidates.

**FRIDAY, JUNE 8** | This is the queen's birthday, and the British embassy gave its annual garden party. It was the first time I'd met Ambassador Ormsby-Gore, who turns out to be a very young and attractive diplomat. He is speaking before the Women's Democratic Club on Monday, and this is the first luncheon of the year when no member can bring a guest. There is standing room only. All of which, plus the garden party, shows that the British still know how to do things right and still rate tops in this country. There was a day when an invitation to dinner at the British embassy was more coveted than one to the White House. I don't think this is true anymore, but the reception as usual was very well done, with handsome military aides escorting the ladies up to the receiving line and large trays of huge strawberries served with ice cream and champagne.

(Attended Women's Press Club Dinner.) Sargent Shriver, plus most of the Kennedy family, was at the dinner. The president himself was not there nor his younger brother, Teddy, who was fighting it out for the nomination to the Senate in Massachusetts (at about midnight he won).

Lyndon was the guest of honor and did a reasonably good job of making an ineffectual speech. I sat beside Mrs. Klotz, assistant to Luther Hodges, who lives across from the Bobby Kennedys in McLean, Virginia. She told how Bobby rides with his eight-year-old daughter, Kathleen, almost every morning, even when the weather is about eight degrees above zero. The first morning after he came back from his round-the-world tour last winter, he was out on horseback at seven thirty riding with Kathleen. One of the most interesting spectacles of the neighborhood is to see the entire Kennedy family, the parents ahead on horses, the other children on ponies, and the two-and-a-half-year-old baby bringing up the rear in a donkey cart.

SUNDAY, JUNE 10 | Russian ambassador Dobrynin, together with his counselor, Kornienko, and his agricultural attaché, Emilianov, and their wives came for lunch and a swim. I wanted them to see the Khrushchev peas, which are planted in a two-acre strip as part of a twenty-five-acre pea patch. The Khrushchev peas are much taller than the American Pride, but Madame Dobrynin pointed out that the Prides had more pods on them. And of course, this is what counts.

In proposing a toast at lunch, I quoted Mr. Taylor, the farm manager, that even if I combined the Russian peas and stored them for next year, the bees would not permit the next crop to be truly Russian. When you have an American crop and a Russian crop side by side, the bees, who believe in coexistence, will make sure that they mix. "Perhaps we should follow the advice of the bees rather than the diplomats," I said. The ambassador replied with a toast, "Here's to more beehives in the State Department," while Madame Dobrynin made up a little rhyme about peas, bees, and peace.

I talked to Averell Harriman the other day about the next ambassador to Russia. He made it clear that he didn't want to go himself for a long and protracted period, though he was not averse to going as a special ambassador. Apparently, the president has asked him to make recommendations.

**THURSDAY, JUNE 21** | BOZEMAN MT—Montana State College [is] the biggest in the state. I lunched with Dr. Renee, president, and several faculty. Renee is a courageous educator who has refused to fire twenty-two teachers because, allegedly, they were Communists. Significantly, the head of the radio station, who is supposed to use my program but doesn't, started a campaign to get these teachers fired. "They're among my best teachers," President Renee told me, "and I refuse to fire them. They are no more Communist than I am. They inspire their classes and challenge them. One teacher had taught the idea that some of the Scandinavian countries, which adopted labor-socialist governments, had helped to offset communism, and as a result, he had people peeking over his transom to see what he was teaching. They hounded him so that he is going to leave."

You can hardly believe the strength of the right wing and the John Birchites in the Northwest. This is a state which produced a Tom Walsh, a Burton Wheeler, H. M. Murray, who founded Social Security, and two fine senators today. Yet to read the papers and listen to the radio, you'd never guess there was any liberal sentiment in the state.

**FRIDAY, JUNE 22** | SPOKANE—Spoke before the International Consumer Credit Conference with the line I've given elsewhere, that we can do business with Khrushchev and that he is our best friend inside the Communist world. After I finished, I heard Governor Handley of Indiana haranguing against coexistence. I had to rush out to catch a plane, but it would be interesting to know whom the audience believed, Handley or me.

**SATURDAY, JUNE 23** | WASHINGTON DC—The big talk . . . is about the Bobby Kennedys' swimming pool party, at which several people got dunked. This kid stuff hurt the president, and this particular party helped switch some votes against him on the farm bill fight.

**SUNDAY, JUNE 24** | POUGHKEEPSIE NY—A bond dinner. Gore Vidal, the playwright, was toastmaster. He's the grandson of Senator Gore of Oklahoma, who used to lecture on the Chautauqua circuit, and the son of Gene Vidal, the first Civil Aeronautics Board chairman under Roosevelt. He and Ellen used to go out together when they were children.

Vidal has now become one of the most successful playwrights on Broadway. In one of his plays, *Story of a Small Planet*, he characterized a newspaperman (who many thought was me) most unfavorably. At dinner we talked about the Kennedys. Gore has not been to the White House since last February. At a White House dinner then he got into a fight with Bobby and told him to "go f— himself." Bobby has a long memory, and I can understand why Gore has not been invited back. Gore described Bobby as vindictive, conceited, half-educated, and intent on playing up J. Edgar Hoover as a great patriot. He described the president as a man of far more compassion and understanding, though he wished he had Bobby's energy and guts on some fronts.

I must say that the young man who used to squire my daughter has developed a considerable understanding of people, politics, and Washington. Gore ran for Congress in his district, a tough Republican area which not even FDR carried, and did amazingly well. He carried the city of Poughkeepsie, though lost the surrounding rural areas. He is discouraged and will not run again.

**MONDAY, JUNE 25** | The Supreme Court this morning handed down a historic decision banning prayer in the public. This will make it more difficult for parochial schools to get federal money and will widen the division between church and state. It's a courageous and historic opinion.

**THURSDAY, JUNE 28** | All week the Red Chinese have been concentrating troops opposite Formosa [Taiwan]. CIA reports are that this is a diversionary tactic to take the Chinese people's attention away from food shortages. Mao Tse-tung apparently drafted a shrill denunciation of the West and claimed that Chiang Kai-shek was threatening to land. It is true that Chiang has asked us for permission to land, but Kennedy has been firm against it. The Russians apparently have been firm in trying to discourage their Chinese allies from any rash moves.

Rep. Charlie Halleck has really been cracking down on the Republicans and has done an amazingly successful job. Some of them are getting irate about it and are threatening to bolt. Today they did. Kennedy won approval of the trade bill by an overwhelming margin, thanks to the bolt and thanks to the fact that Eisenhower supported him.

[From July 25 through August 24 Pearson traveled with a large party of friends and acquaintances along the Adriatic coast. Members of the party included Pearson and his wife, Luvie, Agnes Meyer and her granddaughter Elizabeth (Lally) Graham, Alicia Patterson, Sally Hooker, Clayton Fritchey, Bill and Simone Attwood, and others.]

**WEDNESDAY, AUGUST 29** | WASHINGTON DC—Arthur Goldberg was appointed to the Supreme Court. I talked to Dorothy Goldberg on the phone. She was ecstatic. I am wondering, however, what Kennedy will do without Arthur in his cabinet to handle labor problems. Arthur is in Chicago trying to settle the Chicago & Northwestern railroad strike.

I received a cable from Thayer Waldo in the Dominican Republic that Russia had shipped atomic weapons to Cuba. Went to see Dick Goodwin in the State Department for a reaction. He could not conceive that Russia had sent any atomic weapons outside its own borders and said it had never even sent them to Red China. Obviously, he was worried, however, that this idea would get abroad. He said when Kennedy was campaigning for president, he, Goodwin, had screened the questions asked in television debates and found that questions on Cuba predominated. "We have not neglected the possibility that the shipment of arms and material to Cuba may not be a squeeze on us in Berlin," he said, "but the general consensus is that this is a buildup to make Cuba an economic showplace as an example to the rest of Latin America."

Dined with George Baker at the Walter Ridders' home, which he's occupying for part of the summer. The Ridders were upset over my column telling how Jackie Kennedy had refused to attend the Angier Biddle Duke wedding unless it was moved out of the Ridders' home. The reception was moved across the river to the Pells' home. Walter and Marie discussed the effect the story would have on them and feared that, vindictiveness being what it is around the White House these days, all news sources would be closed. Walter said, however, that it would be a mistake to try to kill the column and that any kill in the Ridders' own newspapers would merely reflect on them. The *Washington Post*, however, stripped the column to ribbons, publishing only the bare essentials.

Kay Graham, while in Venice, told Luvie and me she was going to run Marie Ridder out of town. Apparently, it was partly because the Kennedys are sore at the Ridders, partly because Kay says Marie has been trying to steal Tracy Barnes away from his wife. It's still a great life in Washington.

**THURSDAY, AUGUST 30** | Dined at Scottie Lanahan's. Arthur Schlesinger was there. Told him I had heard in Venice that the president had remarked,

"How can they endure Drew on the yacht?" Arthur confirmed the story and said that Kennedy was sore over something I had written about Jackie. Arthur told him that it must have been written by Jack Anderson after I left, but Kennedy pointed out that I had put the same item in a broadcast. "Not one sparrow falls," remarked Arthur, "but that he (Kennedy) doesn't know about it." The question had come up when the president asked Arthur, "What's Adlai Stevenson doing cruising on the Adriatic with Drew Pearson?" "You don't know the half of it," Arthur replied and then gave him the guest list.

I suggested to Arthur the president would have to get over his sensitivity and that Jackie's conduct in Europe was the talk of sophisticated people all over Europe, ranking second only to the death of Marilyn Monroe. Arthur was inclined to agree.

I can tell, however, that I am going to be in the same box with Kennedy that I was with Truman when it comes to any comment on their wives.

Charlie Bartlett, who was very cordial to Luvie in the Adirondacks last month, was as cool as a cucumber, also his wife. This is an administration where the close friends of the president take it out on the wives of newspapermen.

I sat beside Lindy Boggs. Her husband has just won renomination in Louisiana after a tough battle from the right-wingers. She confirms that Kennedy and most northerners have no idea of the intensity of the feeling stirred up by the right wing. Lindy bears out my contention that this continued pounding by a rabid minority is going to do Kennedy more harm than almost any other development in the United States.

SATURDAY, SEPTEMBER 1 | Bobby Kennedy swung the decision inside the White House to have Arthur [Goldberg] appointed to fill the Frankfurter vacancy. Frankfurter had proposed Paul Freund, Judge Henry Friendly, or Judge Bill Hastie. In mulling this over among the close coterie with whom Kennedy consults, Bobby remarked, "What have they ever done for us?" Arthur had done a great deal, and he got the nod. Kennedy called Arthur to the White House on Tuesday night just before Arthur was to go to Chicago and said rather diffidently: "Frankfurter has resigned. I'm going to offer this to you. I hate to have you go, but I think you've earned it."

Arthur said that if Kennedy had come out in a firm manner and told him that though he deserved the job, he needed him in the cabinet, he, Arthur, would have turned it down and taken his chance on a future opening. Instead, the president spoke in a halfhearted manner, fumbling for words.

Furthermore, Arthur has never been brought into intimate discussions in the White House. He has a very small group around him in the evening—usually Bill Walton, Charlie Bartlett, and close friends—but never members of the cabinet. Not once has Arthur been invited to one of these gatherings, nor has he conferred with Kennedy on intimate problems.

Arthur felt so badly about leaving his department that during a champagne party at the Labor Department when everyone was celebrating, he told a friend, who also was a close friend of Kennedy's, "Never during nineteen months have I been invited over and told, 'Thanks for doing a good job.' Never have I been invited over in the evening with the president's close friends. Of course, being offered the Supreme Court is the equivalent of a very important and official 'thank you,' but if there had been some thanks along the way, I wouldn't have taken this job."

The friend went to see Kennedy and reported later that Kennedy had tears in his eyes when he got this message from Goldberg.

After I had lunched with the Goldbergs at Camp David last July in honor of George Brown, the British Labour [Party] deputy leader, Arthur called me to say he had spoken to Kennedy about seeing me and that Kennedy had replied that he didn't know I had asked for an appointment. Arthur added at the time that Kennedy seemed peeved over a story I'd written that day on Kennedy's business luncheons and his futile attempts to appease executives.

Arthur confided tonight that he hadn't told me the whole story. After he had submitted the guest list for his Camp David luncheon, he got a call from Adm. Tazewell Shepard, the White House naval aide, asking: "Is it true you've invited Drew Pearson to Camp David? He's been trying to work his way into Camp David for ten years." Arthur explained that he was having a luncheon for George Brown, that I had known George Brown, and this was a private luncheon, not a newspaper gathering. Tazewell was still quite negative. Whereupon Arthur got a little huffy and said, "He's my guest, and if you don't want him, I'll just look for another place to hold this party." Tazewell then acquiesced.

The following Monday morning Arthur marched in to see Kennedy and asked that Tazewell be present. In front of Tazewell he said, "I want to know whether your naval aide is to censor the people I invite to a luncheon." He told Kennedy what had happened. "Incidentally," said Arthur, "I understand that Drew has been trying to get an interview with you and hasn't been able to get it." "That's the first I have heard about it," Kennedy replied. Arthur ded to me tonight, "And then right after this, you go and write about Jackie's staying out until 4:00 a.m. in Italy."

My request to see Kennedy at that time was in order to report to him on what was happening in the Northwest, where the Hargis and Birch crowd are eating away at his policies and his congressional supporters. I had asked for the appointment at the suggestion of Lyndon Johnson. Arthur told me I should renew the request in order to report on Tito; however, I don't believe I shall do so.

**SUNDAY, SEPTEMBER 2** | The newspapers have been playing up the Russian shipments of arms to Cuba. The Scripps-Howard papers have been criticizing Kennedy for lack of action. Goldberg says Kennedy's knowledge of foreign affairs is terrific. I argued with him on the point and thought that, as of last year, they were immature. Arthur says he has grown.

**TUESDAY, SEPTEMBER 4** | Wrote what I thought was a good column on Khrushchev's new policy in Cuba—namely, to contain the United States in Cuba as we have done in Turkey and West Berlin; second, to build a Soviet showcase in Cuba as we have done in West Berlin. I got a call from Jack Wheeler in New York urging that the column be modified or killed. I don't often get calls from him except regarding his personal friends, such as Pete Jones of Cities Service [Corp.]. His argument was that I was already in hot water with editors over the Khrushchev columns of last year and we would get more cancellations.

The column was rewritten. Congressional leaders of both parties were called to the White House late this afternoon to explain the buildup of Russian arms in Cuba. Kennedy emphasized what Dick Goodwin had already emphasized to me, that there were no atomic weapons and no long-range missiles. The Kennedy administration is worried for fear Cuba will get into politics.

**SUNDAY, SEPTEMBER 9** | (Dined with the Earle Clementses and [my] daughter-in-law Bess, who had just returned from touring the Near East with Lyndon Johnson.) Earle expressed some critical views on Kennedy and his being pushed around by Congress and others. He points out that the speeches by Republican senators, particularly Capehart of Indiana, saying that Kennedy would call out the reserves after the election is what is really guiding Kennedy's policy toward Cuba.

Mary Margaret and Lyndon seem to have come to a parting of the ways. She went on this trip, but during the middle of the trip he gave her a roommate, namely his daughter, Lynda Bird, which was the signal that their long romance was over.

Mary Margaret now says she's had it, that she's going back to Texas and will stay there. After all, she now has a husband and a new house to do over, which will probably keep her occupied. Mary Margaret's job on the trip through the Near East was to carry a tape recorder and make sure that everything Lyndon said was recorded.

Just before the party left Washington, Bess prepared a postcard list for Lady Bird to send back to some of her intimate friends. Lyndon saw it and immediately wanted a list for himself. His staff struggled to get one together at the last minute but came up with an old campaign list, on which some of the people were dead. During the trip some postcards were written carrying exactly the same message, "Regards from Greece from Lady Bird and Lyndon." Since some of them went to members of the same family and members of the same law firm, who would obviously compare the messages, Bess, when given the postcards to mail, destroyed them.

THURSDAY, OCTOBER 25 | The first Russian ship to pass the U.S. blockade to Cuba was a tanker. She was not boarded; the navy allowed her to proceed. Obviously, Kennedy is being very careful. U Thant has proposed a suspension of the blockade during talks. Khrushchev accepted; Kennedy did not.

Adlai Stevenson got really tough with [Soviet ambassador] Zorin in the UN. He really cracked down for an answer from Zorin as to whether there were missile bases on Cuba or not. When Zorin refused to answer, Adlai showed enlarged photographs of them in the UN lobby.

FRIDAY, OCTOBER 26 | A Soviet vessel was stopped and found to have no offensive weapons, then permitted to pass. Khrushchev has sent Kennedy a private message accepting the plan to remove bases from Cuba but also proposing the United States remove its bases from Turkey.

SUNDAY, OCTOBER 28 | Apparently, Khrushchev is going to knuckle under to Kennedy. I never really expected it. I have long been convinced that Khrushchev did not want war and was quite serious in telling me this one year ago. Nevertheless, I thought he would reciprocate against Kennedy with a Berlin blockade or some other kind of operation closer to the Soviet Union.

**MONDAY, OCTOBER 29** | Khrushchev's backing down continues to astound me. He offered to let the UN inspect missile bases in Cuba to make sure they had been removed, and he also proposed a meeting with Kennedy. Kennedy has accepted with a pledge of no invasion. All this is what I had hoped for but never expected. Castro came in with a demand that the United States give up Guantánamo, but the Russians apparently are not buying it.

**THURSDAY, NOVEMBER 8** | The election came out just about as I predicted, with Kennedy picking up apparently five Senate seats and losing about four House seats. Obviously, the Cuban crisis helped him.

Last Monday in Los Angeles I had lunch with Jimmy Roosevelt, who told me that his mother was not expected to live more than a week. He thinks she has cancer. This afternoon she died. I tried to write an adequate column in tribute to her but not sure I succeeded. I left out the occasion when Steve Early kicked the Negro policeman in Pennsylvania Station in New York and almost lost the Negro vote for FDR. Steve telephoned me that night and asked me to get Mrs. Roosevelt to help out. He knew she was the only one who could sway the Negro vote. I telephoned Mrs. Roosevelt and found her visiting the Deerfield School and Diana Hopkins, daughter of Harry. Mrs. Roosevelt remarked, "Oh, why does Steve do these things?" She agreed, however, to visit the policeman in his hospital in New York. It switched the vote back into line.

**FRIDAY, NOVEMBER 9** | Yesterday the first Russian missiles were inspected aboard Soviet ships on the high seas. The tarpaulins were removed by the Russian crews and lifted so that U.S. vessels could inspect the missiles. This in itself was an amazing operation. I never thought the Russians would permit it; however, some die-hards in the United States are still griping over the fact that Kennedy did not invade nor insist on inspection of Russian missiles on Cuban soil.

Secretary Rusk remarked in one White House meeting that the Russians were having as much trouble with Khrushchev as we. John McCone, however, who seems to be dominating Kennedy's policies, remarked that Khrushchev could get what he wanted out of Castro simply by "turning the nut."

The Chinese are needling the Russians as appeasers over Cuba. There's been no time when the row between China and Russia has been worse. Yet many Americans still think this is a sham performance.

**SUNDAY, NOVEMBER 11** | The Chinese have continued their advance into India, despite an airlift of arms from the United States and millions of words of encouragement. The Indians are just not fighters. The Chinese are. The Chinese have one secret weapon—the one they used in Korea—the cheapness of life. They don't care how many lives they lose. Khrushchev is reported to be in a quandary as to what to do. Originally, the Russian ambassador had secured helicopters for Nehru to transport Indian troops into the mountains. Now the ambassador has advised Nehru to come to terms. Nehru has refused. He is officially a pacifist, but anger is running at such a white heat in India that he must keep on fighting.

**MONDAY, NOVEMBER 12** | I went to see Bill Foster, chief of disarmament and formerly vice president of Olin Mathieson [Corp.]. I once wrote a line indicating criticism of Kennedy for appointing top Republicans such as Bill to high positions, but in retrospect I think Kennedy was wise. Bill is a dedicated public servant, and it strengthens Kennedy's hand to have a Republican in this post.

Bill is hopeful about an agreement on nuclear testing. The United States has already stopped testing, and Russia will stop November 20. The two countries are only about an inch apart—namely, the question of having ten inspectors or twelve on Soviet soil.

I have believed and written that with better relations over Cuba, the two countries could come to an agreement. If some of the nagging right-wingers would cut out their nagging, and if Kennedy wasn't too worried over his political opposition, I believe the United States and Russia could begin a great new era for peace. I am called an appeaser for so writing.

**THURSDAY, NOVEMBER 15** | PHILADELPHIA—Spent the day . . . doing a broadcast and speaking at the 32 Carat Club. Jack sent me an interesting report, which I used on radio, that Khrushchev had put his military leaders in the background and increased the power of his moderate leaders in a major upheaval inside the Kremlin. This was the report cabled to Washington by Ambassador Foy Kohler.

On Tuesday I had a long talk with Tommy Thompson, who came back from Moscow as ambassador because of ulcers. I recalled Khrushchev telling me how much he liked Tommy and asked Tommy, in turn, whether Khrushchev could be trusted. I told him that I gained the impression that K. sincerely wanted peace but that I was somewhat shaken by his placing of missiles in

Cuba and having Gromyko lie about them. Tommy said that unquestionably there had been deliberate deception. He said he was convinced that Khrushchev did want peace and that he had been reluctant about resuming nuclear testing. He yielded to his military men on this point and also apparently went along with their plans for missiles in Cuba.

He thinks the rift between China and Russia is deep and went into some detail to point to the rapidly increasing Chinese population, which in ten years will increase by the same amount as the present population of the United States, or about two hundred million.

**TUESDAY, NOVEMBER 20** | NASHVILLE—The Hoffa trial is taking place. I talked to James Stahlman, publisher of the *Banner*, about his telephone conversation with Bobby Kennedy. He confirmed what happened. I also talked to Chon Hooker Jr., the man who invited presiding Judge Miller and Bobby Kennedy to lunch. Hooker said there were about fifteen or sixteen people present, not thirty, as Bobby had told me, and that Bobby sat beside the judge. Bobby had said that several judges were present, but Hooker said there were only two. The luncheon took place on June 29, after Hoffa was indicted and after the judge was sitting on the preliminary stages of the case.

The trial itself was boring. Toward the end of the morning I caught a plane back to Washington. Hoffa came up to me in the corridor and told me I was looking pale. He recalled that the last time we had met was in the airport in Miami when I was en route from Venezuela. Our chief conversation was not about the trial but the Indian-Chinese war. The Chinese are now fifty-eight miles from the fertile plains of Assam, one of the greatest tea-growing areas in the world and the source of British breakfast for most of the empire. I don't believe the Chinese are going to stop.

**WEDNESDAY, NOVEMBER 21** | Kennedy, at his press conference last night, announced that Khrushchev had promised to remove the Ilyushin bombers, which the cabinet [members] don't consider important, but Kennedy does. This is a real victory for JFK, though personally I think an unnecessary one and one induced almost entirely by the political yammering of Goldwater, Keating, and the Scripps-Howard papers. Khrushchev arranged (apparently through Mikoyan) to have Castro come out ahead of the press conference and say that he was surrendering the bombers. This saved face for Castro.

Jack tells me that Kennedy won the victory largely by ordering the First Marines through the Panama Canal and by intensive military activity along the Florida coast, which obviously got back to the Russians. In other words Kennedy was making "invasion" noises. He also called the British ambassador down to his Virginia estate about two weeks ago and told him the United States was ready to invade. The British are excellent leakers, and obviously this got back to the Russians via London. This is probably what Kennedy had in mind. The Chinese have announced a truce for midnight tomorrow, but nobody seems to take them seriously—certainly not Nehru.

**FRIDAY, DECEMBER 7** | Lunched with Clayton Fritchey. He says he first heard of the *Saturday Evening Post* article on Saturday and immediately canceled all weekend plans. The *Post* sent out an advance publicity letter calling Stevenson's actions "Neville Chamberlain diplomacy," which letter was later withdrawn. Chalmers Roberts of the *Washington Post* was breaking the story on Monday, one day ahead of the release date, on the grounds that it was a local story. Stewart Alsop had called Clayton some weeks ago and told him he was going to do this story. They had lunch in Washington and Clayton gave him Adlai's point of view and account of Adlai's operations. Stewart apparently disregarded everything Clayton said.

Acheson is the culprit, according to Clayton. Dean began disliking Adlai during the 1952 campaign, when he was not called upon for advice on foreign affairs. Bundy, who is related to Acheson, was completely wrong on the Bay of Pigs operation and, during the recent discussions on Cuba, was for the invasion of Cuba. Adlai was just as vigorously opposed. I showed Clayton the item I'd used on the radio about the fact that the Joint Chiefs of Staff had favored withdrawal of American missiles from Italy, Turkey, and England long before the Cuban crisis. I pointed out that Adlai was merely in favor of bargaining with something that we wanted to get rid of anyway. Clayton said Adlai was willing to bargain only after Khrushchev had agreed to withdraw Russian missiles from Cuba.

**SATURDAY, DECEMBER 8** | NEW YORK—Last night Luvie and I had dinner with Alicia Patterson and her husband, Harry Guggenheim. I had not seen him since he was ambassador to Cuba.

Before dinner I stopped to see Adlai at his apartment in the Waldorf Towers. He spoke frankly about his position inside the National Security Council. He said he could not talk about anyone else's position. First, he said he had not read my column of Wednesday until today and wanted to correct some points in it. The most important was that he had not been in favor of trading our missile bases in Turkey and Italy until after Khrushchev had agreed to remove Russian bases from Cuba. He said that the U.S. missiles in England had never come up. (Six of these Thor missiles are already being removed from England, though he apparently did not know it.)

He also remarked that although I had reported Dean Rusk as being against any drastic action toward Cuba because he argued that the Russian submarines were just as important as intermediate-range missiles, actually Rusk had not taken this position and had not been vigorous in opposing drastic action. This is interesting because it is exactly the opposite of what Jack Anderson reported from the Pentagon. The *Saturday Evening Post* authors, however, also report that Dean Rusk did not take a firm position, and in view of what Adlai now tells me, this must be right.

Adlai said he had been lunching with Kennedy on Tuesday, October 16, two days after Kennedy received the clear-cut photos of Russian missiles in Cuba. Kennedy reported on this alarming development and asked Adlai to remain in Washington. "We'll need you here for a few days," he said. Adlai said he had just come down for the day, but Kennedy told him to send up to New York for some clothes and remain. This part of the conversation apparently took place upstairs in the White House after the luncheon. Adlai did remain, except that on Thursday he went back to the UN to argue against the admission of Red China.

During the internal debates Adlai took a vigorous stand against an air strike, which he said would only mean an invasion. An air strike would be a sneak Pearl Harbor and would have to be followed up with a landing operation. Once American troops were in Cuba, they couldn't be withdrawn for years. "It took fourteen years to get our troops out of Haiti," he said.

He also said it would look terrible for the United States to bypass the OAS, which we had helped organize, and the UN, which we had inspired. I gather that Adlai was eloquent and persistent in his argument and at first he said almost no one was with him. Almost everyone else was on the other side—in favor of an air strike. Bobby Kennedy, however, swung the argument his way, and eventually they compromised at a blockade or quarantine.

Acheson was not present at the discussions, despite the *Post*'s report to the contrary. Apparently, he was out of the country, but they got in touch with him to present the matter to the NATO nations, where he did a good job. I asked Adlai why Dean had been gunning for him over the years. Adlai had no explanation except that when he was running for president in 1952, Alice

Acheson [Dean's wife] had asked his sister why Adlai had not used Dean as foreign relations advisor. He said he had not seen Dean for a good many years.

One of the most important points Adlai told me was that they never expected Khrushchev to fold so easily and pull his missiles out of Cuba. They expected him to crack down on Berlin with a quarantine, and this was one of the points raised regarding withdrawal of American missiles from Turkey and Italy. Adlai argued that when a showdown came over a blockade of Berlin, we could bargain with these missile bases. He said Tommy Thompson had actually drafted a letter to Khrushchev holding out the promise of negotiation regarding these bases if Khrushchev withdrew missiles from Cuba. The letter, however, was never sent. Kennedy felt we should keep the Turkish and Italian missiles in abeyance for future bargaining.

Adlai had three reasons for Khrushchev's prompt withdrawal of the missiles: (1) the fear we might go to war—atomic war; (2) the prompt and unanimous manner in which the OAS backed up the United States (at the Punta Del Este conference there had been five Latin American holdouts against us); and (3) the effectiveness of the UN debate.

He said the overwhelming reaction in the UN was not an accident. He had used his emissaries to drum up all the African, Asian, and uncommitted nations and made sure their delegates were present when he confronted Zorin with the evidence of the missiles. The reaction, he said, was overwhelmingly favorable to the United States.

**WEDNESDAY, DECEMBER 12** | Princess Hohenlohe came to lunch. She tells me that Capt. Fritz Wiedemann, Hitler's military aide, is living in Bavaria with about half his stomach removed from an ulcer operation and would like to publish his memoirs. He has written them, but they are humdrum. Actually, according to the princess, Wiedemann's life with Hitler was both exciting and amusing. He hated Hitler yet served under him for eight years. It all came about because Wiedemann, after World War I, went into dairying and lost his shirt. During his troubles a friend said, "Why don't you get some help from your old friend Hitler?"

Wiedemann at first didn't know who he meant. "You mean to say that little Austrian with the droopy mustache we had so much trouble with?" he asked. Hitler had been a corporal under Captain Wiedemann during the war but was a lousy soldier. Wiedemann's friend pointed out that Hitler had now become a big man in Bavaria, with his picture hanging everyplace.

He was about to speak in a nearby city, so they both went to see him. When Hitler saw Wiedemann, he clicked his heels, saluted, and said, "Hauptman" (Captain). Apparently, Hitler had forgotten or didn't know that Hauptman Wiedemann had once blocked his promotion. At any rate Hitler made Wiedemann his military aide.

She showed me a letter from Lady Lawford, mother of Peter Lawford, complaining that Peter gave her an allowance of only $150 a month, that she was never permitted to see her grandchildren, and that if she left the United States, the Kennedy family were ready to withdraw her reentry permit. They have never forgiven her for wearing a big campaign button during the 1960 election, "I like Nixon."

THURSDAY, DECEMBER 13 | I am sixty-five years old, and after losing a lot of sleep on the West Coast, I find I sometimes feel my age.

FRIDAY, DECEMBER 14 | Averell Harriman came to lunch. He is just back from India and Pakistan and says the Chinese advanced so fast that the Indian troops couldn't work the bolts on their rifles fast enough. His theory behind the Chinese advance in the Ladakh area is similar to that given to me by George Yeh, former Nationalist Chinese minister of foreign affairs; that this area is actually Chinese; and that it is a high plateau over which the Chinese have built a highway necessary to reach Tibet. The other advance into Assam was for psychological reasons in order to show that India is not the strong nation it has claimed to be. The effect on Southeast Asia of a setback by India has already been felt. The Chinese could go through Burma like a knife through butter, Averell says, and all the small neutrals in that area are beginning to hesitate about supporting India. Before the Chinese penetrate into Southeast Asia, they first have to show that India is a paper tiger.

During the Cuban crisis the Supreme Court was notified that a helicopter would stop and pick them up in case of war but could not take their wives. The chief justice and Arthur decided that in this case they would stay behind. This was how close the country was to war after Kennedy gave his ultimatum to Khrushchev.

I gather that Arthur is fed up with his job on the Court. He says Bill Douglas came in see him and said, "For the first two years I felt like resigning every other day." During the Cuban crisis Arthur particularly felt out of things. He would have given his eyeteeth to have been back in harness. He felt that the present secretary of labor, Wirtz, could easily have stepped into the New

York newspaper strike and prevented it. He could have rallied the president and public opinion behind the papers.

I learned today that probably the *New York Mirror*, which has been using my column for thirty years, will not reopen following the strike; also probably not the *New York Post*. The Christmas season is the only time when these newspapers can make real money. If they don't make it now, they run in the red heavily the rest of the year.

Arthur explained how Chief Justice Charles Evans Hughes had assigned opinions to associate justices on the basis of speed. If they hurried and finished a case, then they immediately got another opinion to write. Thus, at the end of the year Felix Frankfurter, by dillydallying, came out with only four opinions, as against twenty or twenty-five by Douglas and Black. Warren has changed this. Each justice gets so many opinions regardless of speed. If he finishes them quickly, he gets some time off. Apparently, what changed the procedure under Hughes and Stone was an article I wrote some years ago pointing out that Burton had written only two opinions during the year and Frankfurter only four.

Apparently, Hugo Black is getting crotchety, and this is one reason why he and Bill Douglas are not getting along. Hugo is a bit dictatorial about his views in his old age.

TUESDAY, DECEMBER 18 | Georgi Bolshakov, who is being recalled for his part in the Cuban deception, came to lunch. He is the editor of the Russian propaganda journal in the United States—the equivalent of *Amerika*—and became a friend of Bobby Kennedy. In fact, Bobby, after warming him up quite a bit over the period of weeks, told him to defect. I asked Bolshakov about this at lunch. He laughed, denying it rather unconvincingly. Prior to the Cuban showdown, Bolshakov had gone to Bobby supposedly with word from Khrushchev that there were no missiles on Cuba. This was one reason why President Kennedy was so sore.

I did not ask Bolshakov about this, but we talked frankly about the problem of getting the U.S.-USSR relations on a better track. He suggested that before there was another summit conference, Jack McCloy should sit down with the appropriate man in the Kremlin to iron out the problems. Then Kennedy and Khrushchev could put the stamp of approval on them. He remarked that Vienna was not a good time for Kennedy to have met with Khrushchev. It was too soon after the Bay of Pigs disaster.

**WEDNESDAY, DECEMBER 19** | Ken Galbraith, ambassador to India, came to dinner. He substantiated what George Yeh had told me, that the Chinese Nationalists supported the Chinese Communists regarding the squabble with India. Ken said he discovered that the United States had been very cautious about taking a position regarding the McMahon line, the boundary set by the Scotsman between India and China some years ago. The only statement the United States made was a cautious one by Secretary of State Chris Herter that we didn't recognize the line. Galbraith wanted to put the United States flatly on record behind the Indian position in the boundary dispute, but when he consulted the State Department, he got a cable in reply stating, "We are giving the matter further study."

Ken then wired Kennedy direct, asking his permission to make a statement. "Must I be pecked to death by ducks?" Ken asked Kennedy, referring to the State Department policy of ducking issues.

The president replied by return cable, okaying the statement, whereupon Galbraith wired the State Department that he was proceeding with a statement. They replied okay, but there was a notation at the bottom of the cable that a copy was being sent to Taipei. Galbraith's assistant caught this notation and warned him that the Nationalist Chinese government would be squawking to high heaven. So, within thirty minutes Galbraith summoned a press conference and gave a statement putting the United States squarely behind the Indian position.

It was none too soon. Shortly thereafter came a cable from the American embassy in Taipei asking him to hold up his statement until it could inform him of the Nationalist Chinese position. Later he learned the Taipei government was raising hell. The position of the Chinese Communists regarding Ladakh is understandable. They needed to reach the province of Sinkiang. In fact it's the only place where they can build a road. The other drive to the east into Assam Province, according to Ken, was to show that India was not a great nation. The Indians have been boasting that they dominate middle Asia and would drive the Chinese out. So, the Chinese decided to show them by invading these two provinces right down to the tea plantations of Assam. The Indians lost some twenty-five thousand men in the first part of the fighting—as many as the United States lost in the Normandy invasion.

At first no one in Washington was interested in the Indian war, only in Cuba, but when Cuba eased up, Galbraith got attention for his cables. When

Krishna Menon, then still India's secretary of defense, asked him for a list of weapons, Ken replied that he would get them faster if the request came from Nehru. Nehru made the request officially on a Monday. By Friday afternoon U.S. planes were landing at Calcutta every four hours delivering the requested supplies. The Indians were greatly impressed. This occurred at the height of the crisis, when the British were still selling Viscounts to Red China, the Canadians selling wheat, and the Australians selling cotton and wheat. It put the United States in the position of being India's sole friend.

At that time Galbraith was practically making military decisions for the war. At one time he was asked whether India should use its tactical weapons against China. He replied they should not. Reason was that if India lost its tactical weapons and the Chinese retaliated, the United States would then be expected to come to the rescue. Nehru he described as an intellectual snob who would like to have his daughter succeed him but is realistic enough to know that the leaders of India would not take her. Indira was once president of the Congress Party. At one time Khrushchev told Nehru: "Our short-term problems are with the United States. Our long-term problems, with China." "What do you mean by *short term*?" Nehru asked. "Ten years" was Khrushchev's reply.

**FRIDAY, DECEMBER 21** | Finished three columns in advance of Christmas and left for Portland, Oregon. After our Wednesday dinner Galbraith left the next day for Nassau, for conferences with Macmillan and Kennedy. Kennedy is firm that he will not develop the Skybolt missile. The British press is raising Cain. Kennedy hasn't said this, but the real reason he's dropping the Skybolt is economy and a tax cut. Apparently, he's serious about a tax cut and realizes the only place to cut the budget is the military. He could have used a good argument additionally in the record of Douglas Aircraft, which is one of the worst highbinders in the whole defense racket. I wrote a column today pointing to Douglas's record in selling the DC-4 blueprints to Japan before Pearl Harbor and lobbying to take over the missile industry and in charging through the nose for the Nike launcher loaders.

**TUESDAY, DECEMBER 25** | Christmas was pleasantly hectic. The Freedom Fighter prisoners have finally been released by Castro at a ransom of $53 million in drugs and food. This is the first time in modern history that the United States has paid to ransom prisoners. Although technically the money is being paid by private individuals, actually it's going to come out of Uncle

Sam's pocket in lessened taxes. I also understand that the White House emergency fund is picking up part of the tab.

**FRIDAY, DECEMBER 28** | Bobby and Teddy Kennedy have flown out to Aspen, Colorado, to ski. The rest of the Kennedys are in Florida. When you consider the amount of money used up to take staff members to Florida for conferences to see Kennedy, it leaves a bad taste in the public's mouth.

Kennedy has won some great victories in Cuba, and his popularity is high but can dissipate "quickly with a few stupid moves." One of them is the spending of a lot of money at Palm Beach and Aspen when about four million people are out of work. Another was the pardon given to Jake "The Barber" Factor after he had paid $22,000 to the Democratic Party. Another is the fact that the *Mona Lisa*, just arrived from France, is being kept in a crate in the basement of the National Art Gallery until Kennedy can come back from Palm Beach. Meanwhile, thousands of other people who have never seen the masterpiece are kept from seeing her.

**SATURDAY, DECEMBER 29** | Kennedy flew to Miami, where he talked to the Cuban Freedom Fighters at the Orange Bowl. Jackie also spoke to them in Spanish. She said: "I hope my son, John, will grow up to be as courageous as you have been. When he grows up, I shall tell him about your courage." Already Castro has frozen up on the release of any more relatives—for understandable reasons.

For one brief hour of publicity in front of the Freedom Fighters, Kennedy kissed away his immediate chance of bettering relations with Cuba.

**SUNDAY, DECEMBER 30** | Spent the weekend at the farm but came to town to have dinner with Averell Harriman. Both he and Clayton Fritchey, and even Bill Walton, who thinks the Kennedys can do no wrong, thought it was a great mistake for the president to address the Freedom Fighters. "Jackie only said what they'd told her to say," explained Bill.

Clayton called my attention to a *Miami Herald* story that the CIA paid $4 million to the families of Freedom Fighter prisoners. He had some figures showing that the drug companies which put up the money for the ransom would make money in the end by tax deductions.

Bill says that Kennedy has a guilt complex regarding the Cuban prisoners, that he is down on Smathers and rejoices in any criticism I write about Smathers. He also says that Kennedy knows Washington DC better than any other city, even Boston. He's spent fifteen years of his life here. He favors subways to freeways, and the only real force locally favoring subways apparently is Phil Graham of the *Washington Post*.

Had an interesting talk with Averell Harriman. I asked him about an incident that Ken Galbraith had reported in India when Duncan Sandys, former son-in-law of Churchill, had tried to persuade the Indians to desert their position as a nonaligned nation. Averell and Galbraith had talked the matter over and decided they should speak to Sandys about this. So, Ken approached the matter rather diplomatically, saying that it was rumored around the Indian foreign office that he (Sandys) had urged that India desert its neutrality and line up with the western NATO powers. At this point Averell interrupted. "What the ambassador means," he said, "is that you shouldn't have done it." When I asked Averell about it, he said: "It was much stronger than that. I told Sandys that as long as this is a joint mission, you're not going to speak for me without prior consultation.

"The greatest mistake we made was when John Foster Dulles formed the SEATO [Southeast Asia Treaty Organization] Alliance, and the smaller nations had to pick and choose as to whether they were going to be aligned with us or not. Prior to that, all the neutral votes lined up for us over Korea. After Dulles made them choose, we lost the neutral support. Since then Iraq, Pakistan, and Iran have figured they were doing us the greatest favor in the world by being for us. They never cease to remind us. The last thing we want is for India to make a public declaration that it was no longer a neutral nation."

**MONDAY, DECEMBER 31** | Chester [Chet] Bowles came to lunch. He has now been in semi-exile for a year and a half, having been eased out from undersecretary of state to ambassador at-large for Latin America, Africa, and Asia. He says the chief defect of the administration is that it doesn't do any long-range planning but makes decisions from day to day and week to week. The decision to push President Tshombe out of Katanga was made only two weeks ago at the urging of Bowles and Soapy Williams, with an assist from Adlai Stevenson. McGeorge Bundy was opposed. He doesn't care much about the UN. Actually, the anti-UN advisors to Kennedy almost pulled the United States out of the Congo, but the pro-UN group managed to win out and put across a go-for-broke policy. The British have been trying to undermine the United States in the Congo and even tried to persuade Nigeria to withdraw its two battalions from the UN forces.

One year ago, just before Christmas, Chet said the UN was about to win a complete victory over Tshombe and Katanga when it got cold feet and stopped. If its troops had pushed ahead, all the trouble would have been over. I showed Chet a press release just issued by Sen. Tom Dodd of Connecticut, whom I suspect is in the pay of the Katanga forces. Chet agreed. Dodd was the man whom Governor Ribicoff picked to run for the Senate in Connecticut instead of Bowles or Bill Benton because Dodd was a Catholic and Ribicoff was running on a Jewish-Catholic ticket. Sen. Styles Bridges, who was in a position to know, once remarked that Dodd was a crook. His operation for Katanga has all the earmarks of being a paid job. Chet agrees.

Dean Rusk is trying to get Walter Judd, the right-wing representative just defeated in Minnesota, appointed to the State Department. According to Chet, the administration is always looking for someone who has never been mixed up in liberal controversy or taken a vigorous stand to act as the figurehead for major moves. Kennedy doesn't want anyone who has been in battle stepping up to the plate to go to bat for him.

Chet feels that 1963 will be a critical year and if we're going to accomplish peace, we must do it then. In 1964 elections will obscure everything. This from a man who once was head of the Benton & Bowles advertising firm and has been elected governor, to Congress, and served as ambassador to India. I thought this was not only a wise observation but one grounded in experience.

We agreed that Kennedy had been carried away with the Cuban Freedom Fighter rally. Chet said that Muñoz Marín's young understudy, Arturo Morales Carríon, now in the State Department, had submitted to Kennedy the draft of a speech in which he pledged that Cuba would never return to the old Batista regime but that the United States was determined to bring social reforms and a new deal to all of Latin America. This would have electrified the rest of the continent and cut the ground out from under Castro. Kennedy spurned it, except for a small, indirect reference.

He gave a wonderful description of how the White House does business on Capitol Hill, with Ken O'Donnell going up to a member of Congress saying, "We just gave this job to your brother and just made your uncle a judge, what more do you want before you vote for this bill?" Eventually, you run out of jobs with which to reward blackmail.

# 1963

In January, Alabama governor George Wallace—standing where Jefferson Davis took his oath as president of the Confederacy—said in his inaugural address, "I say segregation now, segregation tomorrow, segregation forever."

By June, Wallace had become a national figure with his "Stand in the Schoolhouse Door" slogan. He attempted to stop the first African Americans from enrolling at the University of Alabama. President Kennedy nationalized the Alabama National Guard in order to get Wallace to back down.

In 1963 Martin Luther King Jr., along with other civil rights leaders and activists, effectively shut down the city of Birmingham through civil disobedience. This effort unleashed a reaction by Eugene "Bull" Connor, the city's commissioner of public safety, who ordered that firehoses and dogs be used against the protestors. There were also mass arrests, and the national news coverage forced Connor's resignation. King's reputation soared with his arrest. President Kennedy said: "The civil rights movement should thank God for Bull Connor. He's helped it as much as Abraham Lincoln."

In June, Kennedy gave a national speech on civil rights. While he did, civil rights leader Medgar Evers was killed by Byron De La Beckwith. An all-white jury reached no verdict and was dismissed. (The case was retried in 1994, and this time Beckwith was convicted. The former Klansman would spend the rest of his life in jail.)

Through 1963 King emerged as the most important leader in the civil rights movement. He became a legend with his "I Have a Dream" speech before more than two hundred thousand people at the Lincoln Memorial in late August. In it he said he dreamed that his children "will one day live in a nation where they will not be judged by the color of their skin but by the content of their character."

Sonny Liston, an African American, would be the first boxing champion to win $1 million for a fight. Elizabeth Taylor would be the first actress to be paid $1 million for a movie. The average American annual salary was $5,800.

Valentina Tereshkova became the first woman in space. Her flight, along with the publication of Betty Friedan's groundbreaking book *The Feminine Mystique*, reflected the changes in women's roles in society. Surgeon James Hardy performed the first lung transplant.

In Europe, France and West Germany would sign a treaty of friendship. While West Germany's "economic miracle" was discrediting the system of central planning in East Germany, President Kennedy gave a speech at the Berlin Wall in which he said, "Freedom has many difficulties and democracy is not perfect, but we have never had to put a wall up to keep our people in."

Along with West Gemany's Konrad Adenauer, many Western leaders were replaced in 1963, including Harold Macmillan (Britain), David Ben-Gurion (Israel), and John Diefenbaker (Canada). In Italy, the government fell twice, and Pope John XXIII died. He was replaced by Pope Paul VI. In South Vietnam, President Ngo Dinh Diem was assassinated in a coup supported by the CIA.

On November 23 President Kennedy was killed by Lee Harvey Oswald. Lyndon Johnson, his successor, formed the Warren Commission to investigate the assassination. Oswald himself was killed by Jack Ruby before we could learn more from him. While the Warren Commission concluded that JFK had been killed by a lone gunman, many were skeptical. Aldous Huxley, who died on the same day as Kennedy, took the title of his most famous book from a line in Shakespeare's play *The Tempest*, "How beauteous mankind is! O brave new world! / That has such people in't!"

Some basic facts in 1963:

World population: 3,209,535,906

U.S. population: 189,241,798

U.S. gross domestic product: $617.8 billion

Makeup of U.S. Congress (based on 1962 election):

Senate: Democrat 67, Republican 33

House of Representatives: Democrat 258, Republican 176

Number of women in the Senate 2 (2%), House 12 (2.8%)

—Ed.

# THE DIARY

**SUNDAY, JANUARY 6** | Agnes Meyer came to dinner, also George Baker. We discussed the influence of sex in the Kennedy administration. It's become contagious. When the president of the United States is laying every girl in sight, it sets a precedent for people around him. [Justice] Bill Douglas is now hell-bent for a divorce, Ted Sorensen hasn't seen his wife in two years, and now Pierre Salinger is making passes all over.

In New York, after the speech before the [National] Economists Club, Earl Smith, the former ambassador to Cuba, staged a late dinner for the president and the attorney general. There were so many beautiful girls there, apparently imported models, that it resembled a chorus line. At about 2:00 a.m. Bobby started dancing with one of the waitresses—also beautiful.

During the course of the evening we did not mention the effect sex has had on Agnes's son-in-law, Phil Graham. He has now sent for his girl from Paris and is flaunting a couple of other mistresses almost openly before his wife.

**TUESDAY, JANUARY 8** | Dined with Agnes Meyer and then drove to the National Art Gallery to participate in the unveiling of *Mona Lisa*. The place was packed. All Congress, the Supreme Court, and the diplomatic corps were present.

In the rotunda, somewhat removed from the ceremony, a group of Republican congressmen were milling around. Rep. Jerry Ford of Michigan had just won a victory over the old guard Republicans by being made chairman of the House Republican Conference. I talked to him and Rep. Bill Ayers. Bill confided that this was not a revolt based on policy but on youth. The Republicans were tired of having old men, namely Everett Dirksen and Charlie Halleck, appear on television as their spokesmen. They had to compete with the youthful image of the president. If the Republicans change their policies as well as their image, they might get somewhere.

**THURSDAY, JANUARY 10** | Marian Frelinghuysen came from New York, and we took her to the vice president's party for new members of Congress. Bess was officiating in the hall and gave us the privileged treatment when it came to hanging up our wraps downstairs instead of traipsing upstairs. I don't see how Bess handles two children and all the social activities of Lady Bird Johnson—but she does them well.

It looks like a pretty good new crop of congressmen. Claude Pepper is on top of the world, and Mildred, not looking as buxom as in the past, seems beamingly happy over returning to Washington. She was even polite to Luvie and me. It's been a long time since my story about the "beautiful, buxom Mildred," who usurped a seat on the dais of the Democratic dinner. She hounded Luvie for days afterward and once laid in wait for me when I went to see Claude on Capitol Hill.

After the cocktail party we dined at the Russian embassy. Deputy foreign minister Kuznetzov was the only other guest. Apparently, they wanted to talk confidentially. The dinner was uneventful though very friendly. Kuznetzov said that he'd had a fine talk with the president and was impressed by the president's desire for peace.

Kuznetzov studied at Carnegie Tech in Pittsburgh and knows the United States well. He has a considerable understanding of Kennedy's political problems—the ambassador likewise; however, the ambassador is inclined to let his sense of humor outrun his observational abilities. Not so Kuznetzov. I suggested to both of them a plan I have been toying with to take the Harlem Globetrotters from Alaska, where they would entertain American troops, over to Siberia to entertain Soviet troops. I got nowhere with the idea. They seemed to think it was amusing but made the point that the Harlem Globetrotters would be sure to defeat a Russian basketball team and that national prestige therefore would be involved. I tried to explain that the Globetrotters would play their own American team, but I don't believe I got this point across.

SUNDAY, JANUARY 13 | We gave a party for Sen. Tom McIntyre, new from New Hampshire. Lyndon and Lady Bird Johnson were the first to arrive. I didn't tell him I had a column coming out the next day pointing to him as responsible for the fighter plane contract going to General Dynamics instead of Boeing. He will be sore as the dickens.

We did, however, talk about Phil Graham. Phil had been to see the president two days before and told him he was going to be like a Buchanan and a Harding, that his tax program was lousy, and called him various names that you don't call a president of the United States. And on the night of Lyndon's party, Phil sat in Lyndon's limousine outside the house for about thirty minutes telling him he was not going to be president of the United States. The conversation, according to Lyndon, went something like this: "You're through. The Kennedys will tolerate you for 1964, but after that you're through, and you might as well make up your mind to it. You haven't got a chance. The Kennedys don't like you."

Lyndon said he had to get in to his own party, but Phil wouldn't let him go. Jerry Siegel, the *Post* attorney, was in the car. Phil railed on. Finally, Phil asked for Lyndon's limousine, even though his own with chauffeur was right behind. When Siegel pointed to that fact, Phil said, "I've got to have a car with a phone." So, he departed in Lyndon's limousine.

Lyndon thought Kay should have Phil committed. He said that Phil had a tumor which was pressing on his brain and that his brother had had the same problem. Phil is now demanding a divorce and has announced that he is going to get married on February 13.

The Kefauvers came to the party and recalled how Myrtle McIntyre had campaigned up and down New Hampshire in the ice and the snow for Kefauver in 1952, after which she became Democratic National Committeewoman. Tom McIntyre was a delegate to the convention in 1956 and was asked to switch to Kennedy. He was pledged to Kefauver and couldn't switch.

"I think I helped elect Kennedy in 1960," McIntyre said. If New Hampshire had switched in 1956 and made him vice presidential candidate, he would have been defeated and not in line to be nominated again in 1960.

Teddy Kennedy also came to the party. His wife told me they had taken a house two blocks up on Dumbarton Avenue. She is beautiful and will be a great asset to him. Teddy is going about his business in a quiet way. Other senators seem to like and trust him. He has a square jaw of determination and a great sense of humor. After all the guests had left, except for the McIntyres, Tyler, Bess, Florence Mahoney, and George Baker, we had a beef stew supper, during which the chief topic of conversation was Styles Bridges, whom McIntyre replaces. Bridges was senator for a quarter of a century and became about the most powerful member of the Senate, though also the most crooked. The fact that he took money was known by nearly all his Senate colleagues, and yet they did nothing about it.

McIntyre pointed out that Bridges came to the Senate penniless and died with an estate of half a million dollars. I recalled that on one occasion the Chinese Nationalists had sent half a million dollars in cash up to Bridges in Concord to be used for Republican candidates. This was one way the Chinese Nationalists were always able to get what they wanted in Formosa [Taiwan]. There was also the famous case which came to light of the manner in which a defense contractor had paid for much of the construction of

Bridges's house. When a weekly paper uncovered the facts and was about to publish them, they suddenly received a handsome offer to sell out. Dwight Perrin was the editor and told me about it. At one time he was with the *St. Louis Post-Dispatch*. I explored the story several years ago but couldn't pin it down in libel-proof form.

**THURSDAY, JANUARY 17** | Senator McGovern telephoned, obviously worried; said he hadn't known whether he should talk to me or not but that he had an unfortunate and disturbing trip to South Dakota with Phil Graham.

Luvie was scheduled to fly to South Dakota, together with Kay and Phil, where he was planning to buy the *Sioux Falls Argus Leader*. When Phil telephoned Kay that he was demanding a divorce and later telephoned Luvie calling the trip off—also announcing his divorce—naturally the two ladies did not go. McGovern, however, did go and said that the purchase of the paper fell through because of Phil's queer behavior. He had his *Newsweek* girl from Paris on the plane, an Australian. McGovern described her as a pathetic creature who was obviously in love and bowled over by Phil's personality.

In Sioux Falls, Phil addressed the chamber of commerce, but at dinner prior to the speech, he used the filthiest language imaginable in talking to them, calling them the same names he had called President Kennedy. His language was so obscene and his behavior so peculiar that one representative of Northwestern Bell Telephone remarked, "If that's the nut whom Kennedy has placed in charge of the communications satellite, I don't want to have anything to do with it."

Phil flew on to Phoenix with the girl to the Associated Press meeting, leaving McGovern to come back alone. George wanted my advice as to whether he should talk to the president. I told him he should—that Kennedy was going to get some very bad publicity out of the whole thing if he wasn't careful and that it would be a favor both to the president and to Phil. I felt that the only thing that might stop Phil was a strong reprimand from the president over a request for his resignation. I said I would check with Kay to make certain and call him back.

Meanwhile, Johnny Hayes, who was in Phoenix, said he and his wife had called on Phil and found his girl doing the Twist in a sheer nightgown in front of a strong light. Phil insisted that John and his wife sit down and enjoy the show. Phil has now announced to the AP that he will be married in Mexico, yet not a word has appeared in any newspaper. There is no union tighter than the publishers' union. Some years ago it was Phil who telephoned me and implored and finally persuaded me not to publish the story about Mike Cowles and the row inside the Cowles family over Mike's wife being appointed ambassador to the Court of St. James's for Queen Elizabeth's inauguration, in return for giving Nixon a front cover story in *Look* magazine. Mike had appealed to Phil. Phil, much against my better judgment, finally persuaded me to kill the story. I have always regretted it.

Kennedy sent his budget message to Congress today—$99 billion, the largest peacetime budget in history. Taken along with tax reduction, it's a daring move and has brought him a lot of criticism. The tragedy is that he is calling for a big military increase and almost nothing for education.

**SUNDAY, JANUARY 20** | Phil Graham arrived at Washington airport at about 7:00 a.m. in his private plane and promptly escaped. The doctors got into the ambulance and drove to Georgetown Hospital. Phil got into a limousine and drove to George Washington University Hospital, of which he is a director. The psychiatrist had flown all the way to Arizona to bring him back.

Later in the day, after a lot of certification and rigmarole, Phil was sent to Chestnut Lodge in Maryland under heavy confinement. It now develops that the U.S. Air Force had sent a plane to Arizona with the psychiatrist. McGeorge Bundy got into the act when his wife, who is a trustee of Radcliffe [College], arranged for Lally to skip her exams in order to go to Phoenix. Bundy then got the president to order out an air force plane. On one occasion Phil talked directly to the president and even insisted that the president talk to his girlfriend. He still remains chairman of the Communications Satellite Board of Directors.

**WEDNESDAY, JANUARY 23** | Sam Kauffmann, publisher of the *Washington Star*, called in his top brass the other day and told them that if anyone published anything about Phil Graham, they would be fired. Phil's girlfriend is now coming back to Washington, and no one knows quite what to do with her. She confided to John Hayes that she had been planning to walk into the editor of *Newsweek* after the marriage. "What will he say when he meets me as the wife of the publisher?" she said. Phil had ordered reservations at the King David Hotel in Jerusalem for the honeymoon.

One of his prize lines, when speaking before the chamber of commerce in Phoenix, was "I don't know what you bastards are going to do now, but I'm going home to sleep with my secretary." One of the worst things that happened was his sexual exhibitions in front of other people. Everyone was afraid he might stage one in front of his daughter, which was one reason they kept the girl off the plane on the return trip.

He also phoned for his other mistress to come to Phoenix. She turned out to be a former maid to Mrs. Cafritz and Mrs. Meyer, who claims she also slept with the president.

The president sent his tax program to Congress. It is detailed and voluminous and has so many concessions to so many people that it may well pass.

**SATURDAY, JANUARY 26** | Kennedy has suspended our underground nuclear tests in Nevada. It looks as if he was making an effort to meet the Russians halfway in the current talks on suspension of all nuclear testing.

I spent the day at the farm and was so tired that when we went to dinner with Senator Morse, I almost fell asleep. The Mennon Williamses were there. Nancy Williams says that the new governor, George Romney, immediately fired all his secretaries and found he had no one to handle the payroll. He then asked one to come back, but she had gone to another job and refused. He also made quite a splash about getting rid of his limousine and driving in a small car. In fact, he kept the limousine and merely added an extra car—the small one.

Wayne [Morse] was tight-lipped about Russian arms in Cuba. Both Rusk and McCone testified before the Senate Foreign Relations Committee yesterday. Wayne remarked that most senators had forgotten that Cuba has the right of self-defense. Senator Kuchel of California has been one of the Republicans yapping about the arms buildup of Cuba, despite the fact that only two weeks ago he was telling me the Republicans must take a moderate, bipartisan course.

**SUNDAY, JANUARY 27** | Met Stewart Udall at Representative Reuss's. He remarked that it looked as if Mr. K. was going to do what he and I wanted him to do—that is, stop nuclear testing

**MONDAY, JANUARY 28** | Went to see Udall, who told me about his talks with Khrushchev, and also his trip through Siberia. The Russians, he says, have been building the biggest power dams in the world and have developed some fine techniques and engineers. This is one reason they don't want a war. They don't want to blow up the things they've built.

The U.S. embassy in Moscow, Stewart said, is probably the worst place in the world to get a real picture of the Kremlin. Its members are virtual prisoners. They hate the country, and the reports they send back to Kennedy unfortunately are the ones on which he fixes his judgments. Shebab of the *New York Times*, who lives in the suburbs and sends his kids to Russian schools, sees the real change which has come about in the Kremlin. Shebab took the trip with Udall to Siberia.

Even such older revolutionaries as Khrushchev and Mikoyan are convinced that the world has changed and there can be no war.

I asked whether Khrushchev had given him any inkling of the missile buildup in Cuba. He had not, but Khrushchev did say coyly that he understood Kennedy's problem with the elections and therefore was not going to raise the issue of Berlin. Obviously, Khrushchev knew about the missile plans for Cuba then because they must have started in June or July; however, he played out his poker hand.

SUNDAY, FEBRUARY 10 | Agnes Meyer had a dinner last night for Secretary of Defense McNamara and Soviet ambassador Dobrynin. Only a few hours before, Dobrynin had been called to the State Department to be grilled on the removal of Soviet troops from Cuba. The two men, however, were cordial and animated dinner companions. After dinner Madame Dobrynin sang quite beautifully, not only some Russian songs but some of the latest from the American jukeboxes. The public, and particularly old John D. Rockefeller, would have been surprised to see that his grandson, John D. IV, now a member of the Peace Corps, enjoyed the dinner.

Adlai Stevenson, also present, confessed when I asked him if it was his old "friend," McGeorge Bundy, who had balled up the brusque statement to Canada which caused the current crisis.

I sat at dinner beside Mrs. Robert Oppenheimer, wife of the Princeton scientist, whom I had not seen since we lunched with Governor Meyner in Trenton with the duke and duchess of Windsor. Mrs. O. asked me to help get her husband reestablished with the Kennedy administration. Apparently, his security clearance is still at issue. I didn't remind her that after I had gone to bat day in and day out when Oppenheimer was on trial, he turned me down for a TV interview and went on Ed Murrow's program instead.

Dr. [Leo] Szilard, the man who carried to FDR the letter from the atomic scientist that it would be possible to make an A-bomb, was also present. He has just recovered from cancer and is now working on a plan to raise money to help worthwhile candidates for Congress. He raised about $100,000 in the last election.

Mrs. Oppenheimer remarked, when she heard Szilard was coming, "When you have a Hungarian for a friend, you have an enemy." These scientists certainly love one another. Also present were Jerome Wiesner, Kennedy's scientific advisor, and Harrison Brown of Caltech [California Technical Institute].

**WEDNESDAY, FEBRUARY 20** ∣ During the thirty-seven years I've been in Washington, I have not yet attended a White House dinner or social function—until last night. This was because of misplaced conceit on my part and partly because I was not asked. In the early days, particularly under Roosevelt, I was invited annually to one of the receptions but always declined.

I had the idea that when you went out to dinner with people, you became obligated to them and this influenced your news judgment. As I get older, I am convinced this idea is more correct than I did when I was young, but either I am willing to yield to pressures or at times consider myself strong enough to rise above them. Of course, in later years, especially under Truman and Eisenhower, I was not asked.

Nor had Luvie and I been asked to the White House under John F. Kennedy until President Betancourt of Venezuela came on a state visit this week. When the invitation arrived, I suspected he was responsible for nudging the White House. Now that the dinner is over, I'm not so sure.

I almost didn't make the dinner. I was talking before the Michigan Retail Hardware Association in Lansing at breakfast. And while the weather was excellent in Detroit, it was terrible in Washington, and when I arrived at the Detroit airport, Northwest Airlines told me there was only a 40 percent chance of landing. I made some exploratory soundings about hiring a private plane but found it would have even less chance of landing, so I got on Northwest, and after some skirmishing around in the fog over Virginia, we finally landed.

Luvie and I ordered a limousine, which actually we didn't have to do. Immediately, on the sidewalk I skidded and almost fell, taking Luvie with me. Fortunately, she propped me up. By this time we were in the limousine about ten minutes early; we had to drive around the corner in order not to arrive at the White House at four minutes of eight instead of two minutes after eight. En route I had a sickening feeling that maybe this was a white-tie affair. I had on a black tie. Luvie assured me that my memory of the invitation was correct.

We drove in the south entrance. A little scooter belonging, no doubt, to John F. Jr. stood by the door, reminding us that the White House is also a home. Upstairs we joined the guests in the Blue Room, which has been redecorated by Jackie.

Wayne Morse, Representative Pilcher of Georgia, and Representative Selden of Alabama were there ahead of us, together with the new Venezuelan ambassador and his beautiful wife, whom we had met in Caracas. At that time she was having a baby. Assistant Secretary of State Martin for Latin American Affairs was also present, and the American ambassador to Venezuela, Tom Stewart, with his wife. I was glad when I shook hands that I had not written a story about her getting drunk at state dinners in Caracas and falling asleep with her head in the plate.

Representative Pilcher immediately gave me a speech about his junkets abroad and how hard he was working on them. (This is true.) He remarked to his wife that "Drew was wrong about me only once," referring to the time when he almost got the American ambassador to Israel fired because the ambassador had not come out to the airport to meet him.

Luvie and I, and the other lesser guests, had a cocktail in the Blue Room, while the honored guests, the Betancourts, Vice President Johnson and Lady Bird, and Secretary of State Rusk and wife, foregathered upstairs with the Kennedys. There was a trooping of colors in the main hall as the presidential group came down, and then we were arranged to pass through the receiving line.

This was the only time in my life where I have preceded my beautiful wife. According to protocol, husbands precede their wives when passing through the White House line. Luvie and I were last in line, being the only newspaper people or, for that matter, the only nonofficial guests present. When I shook hands with Mrs. Kennedy, who was second in line, I said, "I am trying to look benign tonight."

This referred to her greeting when I met her in Caracas and she had remarked, "Oh, Mr. Pearson, you look so much more benign in Venezuela than you do in Washington." I had replied, "That's because you don't see me much in Washington."

Dinner was not in the State Dining Room but what is called the Family Dining Room. We were seated at little tables of eight. I had a choice seat, once removed from President Betancourt and twice removed from Jackie Kennedy. Someone had worked out the seating with considerable care because Mrs. Moscoso, a Puerto Rican who had been stationed in Caracas as wife of the American ambassador and who speaks Spanish (and whose husband is now head of AID [Agency for International Development] and the Alliance for Progress), sat between Betancourt and me. An interpreter sat in the background between Jackie and Betancourt, while another interpreter sat between Kennedy and Mrs. Betancourt. They were fast and efficient.

On my right was Mrs. Stewart and on her right Secretary of State Rusk. The foreign minister, Falcón Briceño, was on Mrs. Kennedy's left. Most of the dinner conversation was between Jackie and Betancourt, and once Betancourt lifted his glass and toasted, "To Drew." Jackie then explained to me that she had been telling the president of Venezuela what I had written about her Pakistan necklace. "I told your wife," she said, "I was going to give her that necklace. Now I have on my Venezuelan necklace." She pointed to a very attractive pearl necklace of about five strands. I made a remark about it being very beautiful and did not suggest that it be auctioned off for the benefit of Junior Village, as I once had suggested should be done with the Pakistani necklace.

I now understand why these official dinner parties are . . . frequently a bore. There was almost nothing constructive or important said at the table. Later President Kennedy proposed what I thought was an excellent toast. Betancourt replied, and that ended the first phase of the dinner.

The men adjourned to the Red Room, the ladies to the East Room. I talked to Lyndon, while Kennedy got Betancourt in a huddle with the senators and representatives. Lyndon told me that upstairs, before dinner, Kennedy had remarked to Betancourt, "We have a distinguished American as our guest tonight," referring to me, "[who] gives you better publicity than he does me."

I suspected that Lyndon dressed this up a bit, but Mrs. Angier Biddle Duke told Luvie after dinner that the chief subject of conversation upstairs before the dinner was about me.

Lyndon also said that Rockefeller was beginning a campaign against the administration both on Cuba and civil rights. He said that Javits had come to him and apologized for his speech denouncing Lyndon's ruling on the filibuster.

He and I pulled a chair over to the group. Albert Gore of Tennessee was asking Betancourt about the feasibility of a Latin American army, similar to the UN army in the Congo, which would help to police certain areas against communism. Betancourt replied that national individuality was so strong among countries such as Colombia, Ecuador, and Peru that this kind of army would be difficult to form.

President Kennedy listened carefully. When Betancourt stopped at one point, he said, "Tell some more about that." It was obvious that he was using the senators and representatives to bring out various points from Betancourt. Betancourt remarked at one point that he was a "lame-duck president" and was now merely trying to make sure that free elections were held and that a free democratic government was installed to replace him.

After we joined the ladies, I had a chance to congratulate Kennedy on his toast. He talked for a couple of minutes rather eloquently about the importance of Latin America. The gist of what he said was "Crosby Noyes in the *Star* this afternoon talked about de Gaulle going to Latin America as if it was a threat to us. I'd like nothing better than to have de Gaulle go. We've been trying to get the Europeans interested in Latin America. The tragedy is that we've put all our money into Europe—$12 billion in four years—and now we've about reached the end of our resources."

Kennedy kept punching with his arms while he talked in the same way he does when he's making a speech on the stump. He then made what was an amazing statement: "I don't think there's any danger of Russia marching into Europe. I am not worried about it. And I don't think the atom is important anymore. Everyone is going to get it. It's passé. We just don't need to worry about the Russian army in Western Europe, but we do need to worry about Latin America."

Jackie came up to me after that and asked whether my column was published in South America. She said she had read the column on Betancourt and hoped that it was read in South America. I assured her it was widely read in Venezuela. She said she had talked to de Gaulle, Adenauer, and others but that to her the greatest men of all were Betancourt and Lleras Camargo, the former president of Colombia. She had visited both in December 1961 (the trip I also took). I had the feeling she meant what she said.

Representative Selden asked Betancourt, during the male huddle, what the United States should do in case of a situation similar to that in Guatemala, when a pro-Communist or leftist president took over. Betancourt was forthright. He replied, "The American ambassador should not go out with a pistol on his hip alongside the revolutionary junta which is trying to throw the president out." He referred to "Pistol-Packing Peurifoy," an old friend of mine who was ambassador to Guatemala. He participated in the CIA revolt which threw President [Jacobo] Arbenz [Guzmán] out. Betancourt said the thing to do was let the Latin Americans work out their own problems.

The Betancourts departed at 10:00 p.m. When we got home, Luvie said she had never attended anything so disgraceful. Instead of having a white-tie state dinner in the State Dining Room, we had been crowded into the Family Dining Room at little tables with no entertainment after dinner. Latin Americans like a show, she pointed out, and this was by no means a show. The reason, she claimed, is that Jackie is just plain lazy. I argued to the contrary and pointed out that Betancourt had had an interesting talk with various senators. Luvie was not convinced. She said that the highest compliment to a president is to bring in top guests, and these were not top guests. Maybe she's right. Anyway, I had a good time.

**MONDAY, MARCH 11** | Dr. Szilard, one of the original developers of the A-bomb, came to tea. He has been wanting to get up a group of senators who will support Kennedy with regard to Cuba and nuclear testing and some of the other tough problems which have become bogged down in partisan politics. He said that Kennedy was the victim of his own politics. He had aroused the American public opinion against Russia at the time of the Cuban crisis by accusing Khrushchev of deception. Now Kennedy wants the American people to go along with him in trusting Khrushchev regarding nuclear testing. [Szilard said:] "The worst thing Khrushchev could do to Kennedy now would be to agree to Kennedy's terms for a nuclear test treaty. Kennedy then couldn't get the treaty confirmed. He has aroused too much suspicion. The United States wants the treaty much more than Russia. You are way ahead. If you stop testing now, you stay ahead. Khrushchev is under pressure from the Red Army not to stop testing. They want to catch up."

**WEDNESDAY, MARCH 13** | The newspapers are getting querulous about the speed with which Khrushchev is taking his troops out of Cuba. Kennedy left himself wide open on this at his press conference last week by stating that he was not satisfied with the rate of withdrawal. Actually, he has scored an amazing victory by even getting Khrushchev to withdraw any without simultaneously K. demanding that some American troops withdraw from Turkey, but Kennedy is always playing this from the easy way politically. He doesn't seem to have the courage to stand up and state the real facts.

**SATURDAY, MARCH 16** | Khrushchev is taking about two thousand Russian troops out of Havana today. The Scripps-Howard newspapers begrudgingly admit this but say that it's too slow. In this they are merely echoing Kennedy.

Two Russian planes flew over Alaska for about thirty minutes yesterday, and the State Department sent a formal protest. This was the first time any Soviet planes have flown over U.S. territory since the end of the war. When I was in Alaska some years ago, both sides were very careful to keep well away from the approximate middle of the Bering Sea. When American reconnaissance planes flew out in that general area, they could see Soviet planes taking off in Siberia and coming out in their general direction to meet them; however, there was never any crossing of each other's territory.

SUNDAY, MARCH 17 | Averell and Marie Harriman came to dinner, also Al Friendly. Averell said he was worried about his ability to fill his job because he had been given such a press buildup. He said everyone at the State Department was coming around wanting decisions made on this and that and presenting their problems. After dinner Averell took me aside to ask me what I thought of Khrushchev's present tactics. He seemed to think Khrushchev was somewhat off-balance, was making overtures to the Chinese one day and apparently rebuffing them the next. I told him if Khrushchev saw the United States following a stable policy in regard to some of our joint problems, he probably wouldn't be flirting with the Red Chinese.

Averell made a significant remark: "A diplomatic victory that you crow over is not a diplomatic victory." He was referring to our getting Khrushchev to withdraw missiles and now troops from Cuba.

Phil Graham is back in town after a vacation in San Juan with his girlfriend. He has written notes to some of the directors of the Satellite Corporation saying that his mental difficulties are due to the fact that his wife would not give him a divorce.

WEDNESDAY, APRIL 10 | Chet Bowles came to breakfast. He is feeling much better since he became ambassador to India, says that India is like the United States prior to 1914, when we relied on the British fleet for defense. Hitherto India has relied on us for the defense of Asia and has now discovered it has to stand on its own.

Chet thinks that now is the time to strike for a ban on nuclear testing. "It's not the Pentagon which is opposing this treaty but the State Department," he said. He went on to explain that Rusk seems to have a fear of sticking his neck out too far. "Every morning Rusk wakes up and pinches himself to see whether he's the little country boy from Georgia who has finally become secretary of state. He can't really believe he is secretary of state, and he doesn't want to destroy that illusion by doing anything too courageous."

**FRIDAY, APRIL 12** | It's finally come out that Mercedes Douglas is suing Bill for a divorce. They haven't been living together since last summer, and Mercedes finally decided to give in. As Luvie remarks, sex seems to be a mark of senility, a sort of disease with older men, and she should have ridden out the storm. This morning one of Bill's girlfriends, Doris Santora, a waitress in a cocktail lounge in Portland, was due to leave Portland to see him. The man who introduced them was Damon Trout, a Portland sportsman and well-known procurer. Luvie says she has been skeptical of Bill ever since our party in the country when Bess remarked, "Why is a Supreme Court justice messing with my legs?"

I received a photograph in the mail today of a young man who doesn't have the excuse of senility for sex: President Kennedy. Mrs. Florence Mary Kater, who lives down the street, used to be the landlady for Pamela Tenure and got an idea that she should protect the young lady from the advances of then–Massachusetts senator Kennedy, who was a frequent caller. Finally, she and her husband waylaid him outside with a flashbulb camera. The result, which she sent to me, is unquestionably Kennedy. She had the photograph enlarged and tried to picket the White House at one time. The *Washington Star* checked up on the story and found that Bobby Kennedy and the then-senator had threatened Mr. Kater with his job if he pursued the matter further. The *Star* was convinced the story was true. Mrs. Kater wrote to me in rather intemperate language, claiming I had chickened out in exposing Kennedy and enclosing a letter she had written to Bobby Kennedy regarding the fact that Pamela is now in the White House as secretary to Mrs. Kennedy. I don't know whether I shall ever write that book on "Love in the White House," but certainly I have enough material.

**MONDAY, APRIL 22** | Gave a dinner for Karl-Heinz Hagen, editor of *Quick*, the German weekly. Lyndon Johnson, Salinger, Secretary of Agriculture Freeman, and quite a few senators were there. Hagen held forth briefly, after some prodding about the situation in Germany. For the first time, he said, the United States has begun to lose its popularity. De Gaulle's visit contributed to this. De Gaulle didn't say much but is a superb actor and sentimentalist, and the Germans are sentimental people. They loved the idea of making friends with an old enemy.

**WEDNESDAY, APRIL 24** | Back to Washington by train from Boston. Up early to finish an article for *Quick* on Kennedy's trip to Germany. I delivered it to

Hagen at lunch. He seemed to like the original installment, which he had shown to Salinger the day before. Salinger had promptly taken it in to the president and had asked that one paragraph be censored, in which I referred to the fact that Secretary of Defense McNamara believed in reducing American troops in Germany and that Secretary of the Treasury Dillon was worried over the dollar balance and therefore wanted to reduce troops.

Hagen had a pleasant twenty-minute talk with Kennedy, who told him that this trip was not aimed at counteracting de Gaulle. Hagen, of course, saw through this.

FRIDAY, APRIL 26 | Yesterday Khrushchev made a speech in Moscow stating he was sixty-nine years old, could not last forever, and would resign from one or both of his jobs before too long. Ambassador Dobrynin came to lunch. I asked him about it. Dobrynin said that if he were in Moscow, he would have the scuttlebutt and would know the answer, but in Washington they don't send him cables on this type of subject.

He said Khrushchev was quite discouraged over the problem of working out relations with the United States and was now taking the hard line.

"When he decided to permit three inspections per year," Dobrynin said, "he had opposition. He argued that this would win some results in Washington. There was quite a debate over it. We debate these things today. Things are not the way they were in Stalin's time, when the word was passed down from above. Now there's very free debate. Khrushchev won the debate and made the proposal to the United States, thinking it would be accepted.

"Instead, Kennedy began to negotiate. He wanted ten inspections, then eight, and as a result, I don't think Kennedy could get a treaty ratified by the Senate. I think if he had accepted the three inspections proposal immediately, the Senate would have agreed. Today I don't think there's any use for us to propose five or six or some other figure."

I said I'd heard that Arthur Dean, Dulles's former law partner, had suggested to the Russians that if they agreed to two or three tests per year, this would be acceptable to the United States and that the Russians immediately bought the idea, thinking that Dean spoke with authority.

"This is correct," Dobrynin said. "We thought Dean spoke for the president. Khrushchev told his people this is the president's idea; let's accept it, and we will make some progress. Then we found he was not speaking for the president."

I said I thought Secretary of Defense McNamara was more in favor of a nuclear test ban than was Secretary of State Rusk. He said he had met McNamara only twice, but in the Soviet Union McNamara was pictured as a warmonger. He added that he supposed this was because McNamara had to go before Congress and justify his appropriations; TASS had carried these statements to the Russian press. When I noted that it was the job of a government news agency to carry complete reports, Dobrynin said: "TASS only has three correspondents here, in contrast to many more by the other agencies. They don't have time to edit. They just carry the statements as they come."

I told Dobrynin that the chief justice, Mrs. Meyer, and Luvie and I were planning a trip to the Black Sea, where we hoped to call on Khrushchev. He was interested in this and wanted to know whether Phil Graham, Mrs. Meyer's son-in-law, was coming along. I explained that there was a separation in the family and that sex had reared its ugly head. We got to talking about sex as a problem among public officials, and he emphatically denied that Madame Furtseva had been Khrushchev's mistress. He said she had been a secretary of the Central Committee in 1957, when Khrushchev had his showdown with Molotov, and had been very vigorous in rallying votes for K. in the Central Committee—but sex, he said, was not involved.

"There is so much sex around in this country that you have a different problem," he said. "You feature sex in your magazines, movies, newspapers, and advertising. Wherever I go, I see pictures of beautiful half-naked women. No wonder you go in for sex. We don't have this problem. We don't feature sex in our advertising, movies, and newspapers the way you do."

I inquired about our old friend Zhukov, who had accompanied Luvie and me to the Black Sea. Dobrynin said that he was very happy now with *Pravda*. "He was not a very good executive," Dobrynin commented. "He liked to do things himself too much. He is much better as a writer."

SATURDAY, APRIL 27 | Dinner last night at Mary Russell's, where I got into an argument with Ed Morgan and others over citizenship for Winston Churchill. I argued that Churchill deserved citizenship less than almost any other Briton and recalled how the war could have been won about four months earlier if he had not cut off the gasoline for Generals Bradley and Patton when they were racing toward the Rhine in October and November 1944. Had it not been for Churchill, there would have been no Battle of the Bulge.

Someday I am going to write a book on the way men with Madison Avenue techniques, such as Churchill and Eisenhower, have changed history.

Fidel Castro has arrived in Russia. Averell Harriman got there one day earlier and seems to have had some success with Khrushchev in getting Russian cooperation on Laos. At least Harriman got a communiqué out of Khrushchev pledging cooperation, though I doubt if Khrushchev or any other Russian can get the Chinese to do what they want in Southeast Asia.

**TUESDAY, APRIL 30** | NEW YORK—Luvie and I dropped in to see Adlai Stevenson at his apartment at the Waldorf. It is a beautiful place, and he took us on a tour.

I tried to sound out Adlai on the latest talks with the Russians, but he seemed uninformed and I gathered had lost interest in what the Kennedy administration was doing in foreign affairs. He said he had lost touch with the latest Kennedy attempts to get a nuclear test ban or any talks on Berlin. He seemed much more interested in the Graham divorce troubles. Phil has now gone abroad, and Kay, for the first time, has really made up her mind that she is not going to get him back. I believe she came to this conclusion after Lally had a long talk with her father and told her mother that she should give in to him regarding relinquishing the *Washington Post*.

Kay also was set back when Clayton Fritchey went to a party given by Phil. Yet Clayton was supposed to be the great friend of the Meyer family and has been on two trips with Agnes abroad. Luvie had been telling Kay for some time that people don't stick with their friends; they stick with power. And the *Washington Post* means power.

Adlai said that when he was in London, [Ambassador] Dave Bruce received a note from Phil wanting to come around to the embassy. Dave had ducked any invitation but offered to come to see Phil. Prime Minister Macmillan also received a note from Phil inviting him to lunch or dinner with his concubine. He replied that he was engaged but would be happy to see Phil at No. 10 Downing Street.

**FRIDAY, MAY 3** | Averell Harriman has flown back from Moscow. He has reported to Kennedy that Khrushchev will not be thrown out or resign.

The Dominican Republic has mobilized troops on the edge of Haiti and threatens to go in to throw out President Duvalier. This is one case where a Dominican move might be helpful. I suspect the State Department is not unhappy.

Bumped into Johnny Hayes at WTOP, where I was doing my new TV production recording. John has been holding Phil Graham's hand. Phil has just come back from Europe and is taking Daisy Harriman's old house on Foxhall Road. Agnes has sent word to the *Washington Post* that no *Post* money is to be spent for "a house of prostitution" (though I believe Agnes used less elegant language). The battle lines are now drawn. Agnes has made it clear that the . . . man who was made with Meyer money is not going to get away with the *Washington Post* and a divorce at the same time.

John Hayes recalled to Phil the other day the story that Phil has long told as his formula for success, namely, "Be smart, work hard and marry the boss's daughter." John reminded him, "The formula worked, but now you can't get rid of the boss's daughter and have people think you're a hero."

**SATURDAY, MAY 4** | We finally bagged some manure, "Drew Pearson's Best Manure, All Cow, No Bull." I don't know how it will work, but it looks like an attractive and certainly non-odorous product.

**TUESDAY, MAY 7** | Went to a big reception by Agnes Meyer. Dean Rusk was there and talked to me about his recent visit to Belgrade. He said he'd had lunch with Tito and a good visit with Popović, the foreign minister, who had entertained us last summer. Rusk described him as the ablest foreign minister in Europe. He also emphasized that Tito was building up a new young generation which wants to do business with the West and that under the new constitution the prime minister will succeed Tito.

I remarked that George Kennan had been rather clumsy in lobbying the Congress last summer regarding aid for Yugoslavia. Rusk says the most-favored-nation trade treaty is now before the House Foreign Affairs Committee and the Senate Foreign Relations Committee and that unfortunately the Yugoslavs in this country don't want relations with Tito, while the Poles in this country do want relations with Communist Poland.

**WEDNESDAY, MAY 8** | Talked to Ed Reid (who is in Montgomery) regarding the Birmingham riots. Ed, despite all his moderation, is inclined to blame the trouble on Dr. Martin Luther King. He told me in passing that he'd had a talk with Bobby Kennedy, who remarked that I was unfriendly to his father. "My father was of great help to Drew when he had trouble with his first wife," Bobby said, "but Drew has been very unfriendly to Father."

"He's a great friend of yours and a great friend of Jack's," Ed reminded him. "But he's not a friend of Father's," said the attorney general.

This illustrates the unity of the Kennedy clan. Bobby was probably referring to the fact that when Joe Kennedy was ambassador to England, he did offer to help me, not with my first wife but in the custody battle over Tyler. Actually, he was of no help whatsoever, though I am sure he still thinks he was.

THURSDAY, MAY 9 | The Alabama race riots are continuing. The president, at his press conference yesterday, was cautious; urged both sides to get together. Governor Wallace came out with a blazing statement resenting Kennedy's so-called interference. Wallace is following the pattern I predicted when he came to see me in February. The minute a head of a state tells the people of that state that he will stand up and encourage violence before he will submit to integration, the people below him take the cue.

FRIDAY, MAY 10 | Lunched with Averell Harriman at the State Department. He told me about his recent trip to Moscow. Khrushchev was very cordial. He spent about three and a half hours with him. Khrushchev had not known that Harriman was coming, largely because the trip was decided upon at the last minute. Khrushchev explained he was sorry he could not have more time with him, but he was very "engaged." Next day Averell found out why. Castro was arriving.

Averell thinks Khrushchev has had a lot of trouble with his right wing and the Red Chinese but is still very much on top. He doesn't think Khrushchev has any intention of resigning. His recent statement about getting old and appointing a successor was said in connection with his admonition to industrial leaders that they would have to step up production, and as sort of an afterthought, Khrushchev added that he wouldn't be around indefinitely.

Averell feels Khrushchev is in no mood to negotiate with the United States on anything constructive and there's no chance of getting a test ban agreement. He feels Khrushchev made quite a concession when he proposed three inspections and had reason to believe the United States would accept this. I expressed the opinion that Kennedy missed the boat on this and should have accepted it without haggling. Averell agreed. He added that none of the advisors around Kennedy had recommended acceptance. They had expected the Russians to negotiate. We were ready to come down to five inspections and figured they would come up to five. Instead, they stood pat, and as of today, it would be almost impossible to get a treaty through the Senate, even based on five inspections.

Khrushchev can't point to any accomplishments with his policy of moderation. They have lost Africa. Nasser has been flirting with the West. They have given the impression to many Communist leaders that they let Castro down. They have no new missiles or Sputniks to show in the May Day parade, and this was why they suddenly brought moth-eaten Castro to Moscow to parade him in front of the Communist world. Significantly, Castro, in his speech replying to the welcome, did not mention Khrushchev once.

As of today, Khrushchev doesn't have any expectation of a test ban pact and won't even discuss the matter.

Gromyko sat beside Khrushchev during the conversation with Averell and kept stopping him when he thought Khrushchev went too far. It was obvious that Gromyko was not enthusiastic about real negotiations with the United States.

**SUNDAY, MAY 12** | KALAMAZOO MI—Arrived yesterday for a bonds talk. Spent one hour searching for my broadcast script on Alabama, due to the fact that it looks as if there was peace in Birmingham and my prediction, due to run at 6:55 p.m., would be cockeyed. Couldn't find the script. Two hours later, unfortunately, it became unnecessary. I learned that all hell had broken out in Birmingham last night. The Ku Klux Klan had met just outside of Birmingham. The Negro motel, where Dr. Martin Luther King had his headquarters, was bombed, together with King's brother's home. My prediction that trouble will continue in Birmingham looks all too true.

**MONDAY, MAY 13** | WASHINGTON DC—Talked to Tommy Thompson at the State Department about his reported differences with Foy Kohler, the U.S. ambassador in Moscow, who is reported tougher than Tommy. Tommy, according to information Jack picked up, was advising Kennedy to write conciliatory letters to Khrushchev in order to give him something he could show around the Kremlin to indicate progress with the United States.

Tommy denied any differences with Kohler except possibly on two minor things. He said he had proposed having minor functionaries of the U.S. embassy at the May Day parade, where Fidel Castro was the honored guest, rather than boycotting it. Kohler boycotted it in toto.

I asked Tommy about the May 28 meeting of the Soviet Central Committee at which a harder line was in prospect. He said this meeting would probably be postponed because of the pending visit of the Red Chinese. He believes the Chinese will not get anywhere in patching up relations with Khrushchev and that it's probably a good thing to postpone the May 28 meeting. Khrushchev is scheduled to go to Yugoslavia in June, so the Central Committee will have to meet sometime in between or later.

Khrushchev is having a battle with the Red Army, somewhat similar to that which McNamara is having with the American military. In 1960 he proposed a cut of 1.5 million men, which would include 250,000 officers. He had to suspend this after the U-2 incident and after our tough Berlin policy. The Red Army was too powerful for him.

Khrushchev, on the other hand, argues that the day of the big mass army, big navy, and big bombers is gone in view of modern missiles. He wants to spend more money on agriculture, which is lagging.

The people of Russia, according to Tommy, now won't read the government's propaganda. In Stalin's day they read propaganda carefully in order to see which way to jump. Now they're not worried. They don't expect any purges or punishment. In government circles you now find statements that the propaganda is ineffective. It's just as effective as it used to be, but the people are tired of it. They still want a Socialist-Communist regime, but they don't want to be pressured and exhorted all the time. This is one of Khrushchev's problems.

Another problem, and one reason for his row with the writers, is that they were turning out more critical stuff. Khrushchev had okayed Solzhenitsyn's book on the prison camps, *One Day in the Life of Ivan Denisovich*; also, he okayed [Yevgeny] Yevtushenko's famous poem critical of Stalin.

Following publication of these, however, every other writer wanted to come out with criticism. Khrushchev is the No. 1 censor and personally okays publication. When he got this barrage of criticism, he figured that things were going too far; however, the writers circulated their material among themselves, even though not published, and this became quite a cult. It became so fashionable to be critical that Khrushchev is now on his hardcore line.

**TUESDAY, MAY 21** | I spent two hours talking with Dr. Robert Erdman, who was indicted during the investigation of Vincent Keogh, brother of the congressman, for taking a $30,000 bribe from "Ducks" Carollo. Erdman was the intermediary. He tells a disjointed, bitter story of corruption in which Representative Keogh was involved up to his eyebrows. If we can get him to put this on the record, it will not only blow Keogh but also Attorney General Kennedy out of the water. There is evidence that Kennedy was protecting Keogh. In case after case Erdman told the assistant U.S. attorney who was investigating the matter to talk to Gene Keogh, the congressman, but both Handler (the assistant attorney) and the FBI man laughed. "What do you want to do, get me fired?" remarked the FBI man.

This is going to be a hard nut to crack because Bobby Kennedy is ruthless and vindictive. The minute we start trying to take Dr. Erdman's deposition, they will go ahead with their indictment and haul him up for trial.

THURSDAY, MAY 23 | Eisenhower's judge in Atlanta, Elbert Tuttle, has overruled a Kennedy-appointed judge in Birmingham and ordered the public schools to readmit the schoolchildren fired for their sit-in.

The Republicans are missing a bet by not going all out on civil rights. Kennedy has played this so cautiously that the Negro vote is beginning to slip out of his fingers. A smart and courageous Republican could become a hero. Sen. Cliff Case's administrative assistant called me the other day suggesting Case for president. I am going to suggest that if Case wants to be president, he assume some leadership now.

FRIDAY, MAY 24 | In Moscow, Khrushchev said good-bye to Fidel Castro and criticized with vigor the Chinese concept of war. Significantly, Castro came out for Khrushchev's more moderate position. In the past he had been flirting with the Red Chinese and is reported to have threatened to bolt to the Chinese unless the Russians were more amenable, especially regarding the proposal of UN inspection of missile removal. Khrushchev also took a good crack at the United States in warning us against war in Cuba. Thus, Mr. K. has taken a shot at his Chinese critics, also shot at his critics in the United States, and bolstered his main satellite in the Western Hemisphere—all at one time. This is about as clever politics as John F. Kennedy would put across. Yet most Americans don't seem to realize that politics is important in the Kremlin too.

SUNDAY, MAY 26 | Averell Harriman came for dinner and bridge. He remarked that the Russians were now using Cuban sugar at such a profit that they are paying for all the aid they are sending to Fidel Castro. This is amazing but probably true.

FRIDAY, MAY 31 | The pope is sinking fast. Last rites were administered today. He is eighty-one, and of course, the end has to come, but I have the feeling that we have all lost a very great leader, and I personally have lost a friend. While I never knew the pope, it was a real satisfaction to have a leader in the Catholic Church whom one could applaud and sincerely admire. He was such a contrast to the late Pius XII, who played ball with the Nazis in Germany until Hitler began to turn against the Catholics. As long as Hitler was only anti-Jewish, it didn't make any different to Pius, who was then cardinal in Germany, but Pope John has jogged the Church out of its reactionism.

Had lunch with Paul Healy of the *New York Daily News*, who is writing a book on Cissy Patterson. The conversation brought back many memories. I confess I was always a little bit in love with my mother-in-law, and I think there were times when she had real affection for me. I remember that when Elmer Schlesinger died on the golf course at Aiken, she telephoned me to come to Aiken, and I was the only one with her in her car when we brought Elmer's body back.

She gave me a lot of leeway writing editorials, and I have always remembered the editorial when I defended Hugo Black even though he was a member of the Ku Klux Klan. Nearly every other newspaper in the country was jumping on him, but the *Times Herald*—thanks to my editorial leeway—came out emphatically for Hugo's right to take his Supreme Court seat.

Washington was a lot different in those days. There was a small circle of society leaders, and you were not kept busy by two-bit embassy parties every other night. Those who cracked the whip socially were only about four people—Cissy, Alice Longworth, Daisy Harriman, and Evelyn McLain. Cissy, of course, fought with all of them but made up with all of them.

**SATURDAY, JUNE 1** | Arthur and Dorothy Goldberg came to dinner. He wanted to talk to me about Bill Douglas, and I wanted to talk to him about the report that Senator Stennis of Mississippi is going to be appointed to the Court replacing Douglas. Arthur had heard the rumor but couldn't believe that Kennedy would do it, though Stennis and Bobby K. are close friends.

Douglas is not very communicative with other members of the Court. He is magnificent in expressing himself in opinions but not in conference. He writes lucidly but can't argue effectively for what he stands for. The Court has developed a certain amount of camaraderie. It must, according to Arthur. When only nine men are thrown together, they cannot afford to have personal antipathies (though this was not the case with Felix Frankfurter).

Therefore, even Justice Harlan, who differs with the majority most of the time, is considered a great guy.

Arthur considers Bill Douglas the soundest man on economic matters. The chief justice and Hugo sometimes get emotional. Arthur observed that "Kennedy has never studied the Court as you have. He doesn't realize its history; otherwise, he would never have appointed a Whizzer White and me at the same time." We got to talking about Lyndon Johnson and his great speech at Gettysburg and whether or not the Kennedys will dump him. If Kennedy decides to write off the South, then Lyndon will probably be sacrificed, according to Arthur.

Bobby has always disliked Lyndon. Jack was never enthusiastic. The wisdom of their picking Lyndon was borne out by the fact that he helped carry some of the southern states. Kennedy would not have been elected without him.

Lyndon may be in for some trouble on the TFX [Tactical Fighter Experimental] contract. We have information that he met at the Carroll Arms Hotel with the chief executive of Grumman Aircraft and "Matty" Mathews, who runs the Senate Campaign Committee. Ross Gilpatrick, the undersecretary of defense, was also present, and Arthur recalled that lawyer Tom Moore had been embroiled in the bribery of Judge Johnson of Pennsylvania in the Bethlehem Steel case. Lyndon practically runs the Defense Department, aside from McNamara. Korth, the secretary of the navy, is a Texan recommended by Lyndon. The secretary of the army, Vance, is Lyndon's man, and the secretary of the air force, Gene Zuckert, is also close to Lyndon.

MONDAY, JUNE 10 | Kennedy spoke at American University in a bid to Russia for a test ban agreement. He said the things I have been wanting him to say for a long time. He came out flatly for coexistence, pointed to the twenty million casualties lost by Russia in the last war, and said that countries could be friends even when their governments were based upon different principles. In this speech Kennedy was trying to undo some of the distrust he spread with his speeches during the Cuban crisis. At the time he built up—deliberately I'm sure—a distrust in the Kremlin. Possibly it was justified. There had never been any definite commitment that Russia would not put missiles in Cuba, and most people forgot that we had missiles in Turkey, Italy, and England. Kennedy, at that time, needed to build up the big, bad Russian bear in order to win the November election.

SATURDAY, JUNE 15 | Returned from Nebraska just in time to see George

Brown, deputy leader of the British Labour Party, who, with his wife, dropped in at the house on Dumbarton Street. I compared her with the Christine Keeler type, which has caused a political revolution in England and will be the main cause of dumping the Conservative Party. Mrs. Brown is plump, plain, quiet, modestly dressed, and lets her husband do the talking.

I had seen George just a year before at lunch with Arthur Goldberg at Camp David. He is now almost certain to be the next British minister of defense and has been talking to the top cabinet members here as well as the president. They went out of their way to woo him. He wanted to know about the political atmosphere in this country, and I reported that Kennedy was by no means a shoo-in and that if the Republicans had a strong candidate, said candidate could probably win. George said he had the same impression but could see no evidence of a strong Republican emerging.

His opinion of Kennedy was that of a man who had no great convictions or dedication but was interested in the techniques of politics rather than great social achievement.

Brown's most interesting contribution to the Conservative Party's sex scandal was the fact that Dr. Stephen Ward, the society osteopath, had given a letter to Harold Wilson, the British Labour leader, weeks ago telling about the Profumo scandal and the fact that the Russian naval attaché was mixed up with Christine Keeler (Profumo's inamorata), along with the minister of defense. Wilson asked Brown what he should do with the letter, and Brown's reply was, "Give it to the prime minister, of course." This was done weeks ago, yet Macmillan did not act.

Macmillan, according to Brown, is a man who never had very much on the ball, except for a certain amount of political shrewdness, but has now lost the political touch. He bumbles and procrastinates and will undoubtedly be out of office around August. George thinks the Conservative Party will stick together when the showdown comes on Monday but then will ease Macmillan out so they can have a clear deck for the election, which must come before 1965.

Most of Brown's talks in Washington have been devoted to opposing the surface nuclear fleet which the United States has proposed as the new arm of NATO. George said that in his opinion it had been brought forward in order to give Macmillan a substitute for the Skybolt missile, which the Kennedy administration had suddenly pulled away from the British. I told him that Gen. Lyman Lemnitzer, the new head of NATO, had just written a report to the Pentagon strongly critical of the surface nuclear fleet as impractical and vulnerable.

He has had several vigorous arguments with Walt Rostow. He also had some arguments with McGeorge Bundy and made the observation that when a young president is surrounded by older advisors or an old president is surrounded by young advisors, it's a good idea, but when a young president is surrounded by young advisors, it can be bad. I observed that this was what had led to impetuous moves such as the Bay of Pigs operation.

George said that when he met with Kennedy, he thought he had succeeded in killing the whole surface fleet idea—unless Macmillan, in his meeting with Kennedy on June 30, accepts it. Macmillan needs something to bolster his shaky political career.

The remark Kennedy made to me in February, that he thought there was no danger of a Russian attack on the Continent, apparently was disturbing. George thinks we should goad the British and the French into strengthening NATO.

[Handwritten note.] Brown said he advised Kennedy his trip to Europe was poorly timed. He got the impression that the president's heart is set on going to Ireland, so he is going ahead with the entire trip.

**TUESDAY, JUNE 18** | Lunched with the Soviet chargé d'affaires, Kornienko, in preparation for our trip to the Black Sea. The Soviet Union has not yet given permission for the *Lisboa* to touch at most of the Black Sea ports on the ground that these are inaccessible to foreign ships.

Kornienko wanted to know what I thought of Kennedy's speech at American University—whether it was tactical or strategic. He said he had picked up comment in the *New York Times* that it was made because there was bound to be failure in the nuclear test negotiations anyway and Kennedy wanted to put himself in front early and on the record for a friendly, favorable settlement.

I said this was wrong, that Kennedy was sincere, and reminded him of the internal politics Kennedy faced. I said I had just come back from Nebraska, where there is strong isolationism and suspicion of the Soviet Union. I told him of Ernest Cuneo's advice to me not to go to see Khrushchev again and his advice to the chief justice along similar lines. I am not sure that I made any impact, but I think I did.

Kornienko said my recent columns were wrong in reporting that the Red Army was influencing Khrushchev's policies. I asked why Khrushchev had become less cooperative and more difficult. Kornienko said it was because we had gone ahead with a tough policy and organized the multilateral nuclear force. I asked whether it would be of any help if the MLF [Multilateral Force] was dropped. He said it would. He also said he didn't believe it would be dropped. I did not tell him about my conversations with George Brown, but my opinion is that it will be dropped.

When I agreed with Kornienko that there would be no chance of settling Berlin, he said that last year the United States had started to make some proposals regarding Berlin, but they were leaked by the Germans to the press. "We never got the proposals," he said, "but we read them in the press, and they seemed to be very close to our position." He referred to the recognition of the Oder-Neisse line and apparently the establishment of a neutral commission to regulate traffic up and down the highway to Berlin.

[The following undated entry begins midsentence.]

... Harriman carried on that notorious affair that almost caused Marie to divorce him. Bernie Baruch advised her to sit tight, which she did, and Averell finally got over it, thanks in large part to the fact that Roosevelt transferred Averell from London to Russia as ambassador.

In fact, it was a transfer which influenced history. Largely because of the friendships he established in Russia at that time, Averell is going to Moscow next month as chief negotiator for a test ban agreement. What most people have forgotten is that immediately after the war it was Averell who sold Truman on a very tough anti-Russian policy, thereby knocking down Morgenthau's policy of friendship.

Mrs. [Leland] Hayward, who is still quite beautiful, was present at the White House ceremony awarding American citizenship to Churchill, a ceremony where almost everyone that attended had slept with everyone else. She had served under Randolph [Churchill] and Averell, both of them present, together with Jock Whitney, also present. Mrs. Jock Whitney had served under Jimmy Roosevelt, who was present. And apparently there was some kind of an affair between Bill Paley, head of CBS, and Mrs. Hayward, to say nothing of course of Kay Halle and her affairs with Averell and Randolph.

According to the Haywards, it's Douglas Fairbanks Jr. who served naked with a mask on at one of the Dr. Ward parties. Fairbanks also paid the duke of Argyll 20,000 pounds ($60,000) to keep him out of the divorce suit. The British newspapers carried columns and columns over the Argyll divorce with all the quotes from the judge's opinion, which are too frank to record here.

Profumo had quite an affair with the duchess of Kent long before he married Valerie Hobson, the actress. The irony is that Profumo is a dull and deliberate guy who took twenty-five years in the House of Commons to work up to become minister. Now he has threatened the entire Conservative government. Apparently, it was due for a defeat anyway, having been in office longer than any other government since 1810. The man who will succeed Macmillan for the Tories will be Iain McLeod, who is witty, liberal, and very much like the Labour leaders in political philosophy.

Some years ago, while flying to Albuquerque to see Luvie, I was on a TWA plane which was grounded in Kansas City because of weather. I had to take the rest of the trip on the Santa Fe. On the train was Douglas Fairbanks Jr. We got acquainted. He seemed like a nice guy. His father, who was married to Mary Pickford at that time, was having quite an affair with a British countess. Perhaps that's where Doug Jr. inherited his extra activities. Apparently, he has developed a knack of setting a camera and then getting back in bed with a dame to take a picture of himself. No wonder the British Empire is slipping. A lot of these pictures were placed in evidence at the Argyll divorce.

**WEDNESDAY, JUNE 26** | I have spent most of two days being cross-examined by Representative Keogh's attorney. I don't think he's discovered anything new. I suppose I could have saved myself this time and money with a face-saving apology, as suggested by Cuneo, but I am convinced that Keogh is one of the crookedest members of Congress. Last week I sent Jack to New York to confer with the Rockefeller forces to have an investigation made of the various tips we have received from the doctor regarding skullduggery between Keogh, Abe Multer, and the links with the Kennedy family. There is no question that Bobby Kennedy pulled the FBI off the congressman when it was investigating his brother, Judge Vincent Keogh, later convicted of accepting a $30,000 bribe.

**FRIDAY, JUNE 28** | President Kennedy was given a tumultuous reception in Ireland. I called the White House regarding a special jet sent to Ireland to carry the Irish members of its staff for the big jamboree but got the runaround. No one would admit the plane was sent or who was on it. Almost everyone has gone to Ireland, and I wasn't quite sure whether the runaround was deliberate or just plain inefficiency. After persisting, I got a call back which gave me the facts. The alibi was that they had to send papers to Kennedy to be signed by the end of the fiscal year—apparently not trusting the mails, which are very good to London and Ireland.

Larry O'Brien was one of the "Irish Mafia" who took the trip. In my being cross-examined by Representative Keogh's lawyer, it developed that O'Brien had run to Keogh immediately after my talk with him a month ago. I had gone to see Larry about a column Jack Anderson wrote on Keogh's lobbying. Obviously, O'Brian is much closer to Keogh than I had suspected.

At dinner the other night Liz Carpenter surprised me in her bitterness toward the White House. She described the Kennedys as the most ruthless, scheming family ever to occupy the White House; as watching every public relations trick; all out for themselves and nobody else. This has been my opinion for some time, but to have it come from Lyndon Johnson's right-hand assistant is significant.

MONDAY, JULY 1 | Kennedy is in Rome—with a lackluster reception. The Romans were bored. The big difference was that Khrushchev had not passed the word to the Communist Party as he did when Ike arrived in Rome in 1959, at which time all the Communist children were out en masse to greet him.

There are reports from the Vatican the pope wants to come to the United States. This would be a political catastrophe, as far as Kennedy is concerned, if it occurred before 1964. Kennedy did a good job during his first two years in shunning Catholic politicians, but the word I get from the Hill is that there is resentment against him for dealing only with the Catholics and the Irish. John McCormack is a large part of his trouble. Almost everyone you talk to in the White House who is close to Kennedy is Irish.

TUESDAY, JULY 2 | Kennedy is in Naples. He went there at the last minute to get an enthusiastic reception after the poor one he received in Rome. In Naples he made a speech which sounded like coexistence. In Berlin, at the City Hall, he stormed against the Communists and said nobody could trust them. Three hours later, at the Free University of Berlin, he talked once more about peace. Now, in Naples, he has gone back to more or less the American University theme, that we must get along with the Russians.

Kennedy is suffering from the same mistake he made after the Cuban crisis. When he broadcast to the nation, he went out of his way to tell how Gromyko had sat opposite him in the White House and not disclosed the presence of missiles in Cuba. The whole purpose of his speech was to plant distrust in any statement made by the Russians. Since January, however, Kennedy has been trying to reverse this distrust. He wants a test ban badly, and in order to get one, he has to preach the idea that you can trust the Russians. He did this in his American University speech, then cut the ground out from under his own thesis in Berlin. Now, in Naples, he's trying to create trust again.

At dinner the other night I talked briefly with the Dutch ambassador, who certainly is no lover of the Soviets. He remarked briefly on this phase of Kennedy's speeches and said that he knew of no case where the Russians had made an agreement and violated it. He felt they had always kept their word. American scientists in the space program also say they have never caught the Russians lying about a space achievement.

The Spanish ambassador lunched with me. I've had cool relations with the Spanish embassy ever since the Franco regime took over, but Antonio Garrigues is a new type—a straitlaced lawyer who seems to believe in religious freedom and does not go in for the brazen lobbying of the other ambassadors. He married a Des Moines girl, and his daughter is about to marry an American. He seems to be a genuine booster for the United States and recalled one of my columns regarding the Spanish-American War, in which I had noted that the United States did not have to go to war with Spain over Cuba.

He was in the Republican cabinet under Foreign Minister Rodriguez prior to the Spanish Civil War. He had an interesting alibi for the fact that Spain has been so long under a dictatorship—namely, that the Spaniards feel things so passionately that they cannot always operate a democracy.

**WEDNESDAY, JULY 3** | Khrushchev has announced in Berlin that he will accept a test ban in the air, under water, and in outer space—everything except underground. He linked his statement to a request for a nonaggression pact between NATO and East Germany, Czechoslovakia, and Poland. This is a reasonable request, but it gives indirect recognition to the Oder-Neisse line between Poland and East Germany. Kennedy told me in September 1961 that he favored the Oder-Neisse line, but the West Germans do not.

Several months ago the United States proposed almost the same test ban agreement, but it was turned down from the Russians.

**THURSDAY, JULY 4** | Kennedy worked at his desk most of the day considering Khrushchev's test ban proposal and indicated through Pierre Salinger that he was favorable. This is a big plus.

This morning Khrushchev delivered another diatribe against the Chinese, calling anyone who would try to make war against capitalism "a lunatic."

**FRIDAY, JULY 5** | There has been a rash of spy cases this week. A British newspaperman named Philby has gone behind the Iron Curtain. Almost simultaneously, the State Department has called for the deportation of a Soviet cultural attaché who approached a CIA employee. On top of this the FBI has arrested two Americans and two UN Russian employees for espionage. The interesting thing to me is that the FBI pounced on them at this particular time. In the old days I have known J. Edgar Hoover to keep a case of Nazi espionage on the griddle for a year or two to try to get more information. The fact that he cracked down on the Russians at this time would indicate he and some of the anti-Russian clique in the State Department were trying to poison public opinion just before Kennedy tries to get a test ban agreement.

**SATURDAY, JULY 6** | Kennedy has sent a very friendly message to Khrushchev, a reply to Khrushchev's congratulations on the Fourth of July. In the message Kennedy expresses his hopes for peace.

[From July 27 through September 5 the Pearsons were traveling, largely on a yacht chartered by Agnes Meyer, widow of Eugene Meyer, who had bought the *Washington Post* in the early 1930s. Their daughter Katherine "Kay" Graham was married to Philip Graham, who had become publisher of the *Post*. Among those in the party aboard the yacht were Chief Justice Earl Warren and his wife, Nina, as well as the Graham's daughter, Lally, who was a college student at the time, and her classmate.

The yacht departed Pireaus, the port of Athens, Greece, on the thirty-first. It headed through Greek Islands to the Dardanelles and Istanbul. There, on August 4, the American consul came aboard with a message for Mrs. Meyer: Phil Graham had committed suicide after a long period of bizarre behavior, apparently caused by a brain tumor. Also during the trip, on August 15, Pearson learned that his good friend Sen. Estes Kefauver had died.

After two days in Istanbul, the party proceeded to Bulgaria for a brief visit, then to Romania for a four-day visit, including a meeting with its president. There Pearson found out that his scheduled visit with Khrushchev near Sochi had been called off because of a scheduling overlap. Later he found it had been restored. What follows is the August 16 diary entry covering the Khrushchev meeting.]

We arrived in Sochi at 4:20 p.m. I was napping. Suddenly I noticed we were boarded in a hurry. None of the usual delays. I went up on deck, and Ruth came running up to me with a letter. It said that "Sirs Pirson and Warren with Miss Mejer" were invited to see Khrushchev at 1800 hour and a car would be ready to take us at 1600 hour. That meant we were to leave at 4:00 p.m., and it was already four thirty, for a long drive to get there by 6:00 p.m.

I tried to get Luvie to come, but she said no. The chief, for once, was late. He had been down in his room asleep, and we forgot to tell him.

We piled into the car at 5:00 p.m. for the breakneck ride over the winding road to Gagra. The tires squeaked, the rear end of the car swayed, as we went around hairpin curves. The countryside along the Black Sea is beautiful, but we had no time to enjoy it.

The Khrushchev place is located in the Soviet Republic of Georgia, at Cabe Petsunoe, a Greek word meaning "cape of the Pine Trees" (the Greeks colonized it in the fifth century). Old foundations of Christian churches have been found there.

The big iron gate around Mr. K.'s place was opened in a hurry when we arrived, and a servant inside motioned us over to the swimming pool. The pine trees were just as beautiful as before, but the grass was completely uncut.

We were twenty-five minutes late. Khrushchev and his son-in-law, Adzhubei, were standing in front of the playhouse at one end of the pool and immediately showed us the pool. Khrushchev pushed a button, and a great glass wall came out on a track to enclose the pool for cold weather. I had to help Agnes around with her broken foot, so I got no chance to take any pictures.

Finally, we went upstairs to a balcony looking out over the Black Sea, and the interview began. I was not required this time to submit my texts in advance of cabling. Apparently, they trusted me more than last time. The interpreter, whose name was Vasili, was slower than Victor. He wrote all that Khrushchev said on a pad before translating, and this gave me more time to take notes. It had been terribly hard to take accurate notes at the Shivkov and Gheorghiu-Dej interviews because they were so fast and informal.

Khrushchev seemed tired and not as jovial as before. Perhaps this was because we weren't with him so long as last time. You can get to know a man better in two days than in two hours. But he was frank and friendly, though careful not to say anything which might upset the new friendship with the United States.

Khrushchev asked about Luvie and expressed regret that she hadn't come. He said, "When I see her, I'm going to blame you for the fact that you didn't bring her." He obviously remembered her *Saturday Evening Post* article. He referred to our previous swim by saying: "There's where we swam out to Turkey. You swam like a seal. I wore an inner tube. I couldn't catch up with you."

We departed at eight fifteen. I had the feeling that Khrushchev is more tired than we realized and that he may not be too long for the leadership of the Soviet world.

We had tried to get the Sochi harbormaster to let us sail the ship to Gagra to save us the long drive back and so the rest of the party could perhaps sail past Khrushchev's palace. He had remarked that we could have dropped anchor off his beach and even asked the draft of the ship, but when we returned, we found the harbormaster imbued with red tape. The ship was not permitted to move.

[The voyage proceeded back to Turkey with visits to Troy and Pergamon and the Greek islands of Rhodes and Mykanos. The Pearsons then went on to Rome and Spain before returning to Washington.]

MONDAY, SEPTEMBER 9 | Talked with Senator Morse about Kefauver's death. Kefauver was on the Senate floor making a speech against the communications satellite. The satellite corporation proposes to get its experimentation done at government expense by NASA, and Kefauver was blocking it. Suddenly he asked for a quorum call and, while this was taking place, sat down.

It was obvious he was not well. He told other senators that he had had a severe stomachache. It was not until eleven that night that he went to the hospital. The doctors said there was only a one-in-a-hundred chance of saving Estes without an operation, though a fifty-fifty chance if he had a major operation. They were preparing an artificial heart, and the operation, when he died.

TUESDAY, SEPTEMBER 10 | Dined last night with Averell Harriman, who is worried over the test ban treaty confirmation battle. Senator Stennis of Mississippi yesterday leaked to the *Washington Post* a damning report by the Senate Preparedness Subcommittee blasting the treaty. Stennis did not make it clear that there was opposition to his committee report by Saltonstall and that Symington would vote for the treaty anyway.

Averell said he tried to get Secretary McNamara to go on *Meet the Press* on Sunday night to blanket at least part of the Stennis report on Monday morning. He could not get the White House to back him.

Kennedy takes time to call his pals on relatively minor things. Just before dinner he called Bill Walton, who was at dinner, to ask him if he had read the new Victor Lasky JFK book. It takes both Kennedy and Walton apart. The president was able to waste time over his public relations and his book, yet Averell didn't feel qualified to call him on the vital question of the test ban treaty.

Walton, who had read Jack Anderson's Sunday piece on the Irish Mafia, claimed there was only one real member of the Irish Mafia, namely Ken O'Donnell. Larry O'Brien, he felt, was a straight-shooter. But O'Donnell is the man who is the chief guardian of the White House gate and the toughest confidant, and the most unscrupulous one around the president.

I told Averell I had been up on the Hill checking with three senators and that in my opinion there would be thirteen to fifteen Democratic votes against the test ban treaty ratification, plus about ten Republican votes. It was the consensus that Kennedy was paying the price of southern opposition because of his firm stand on civil rights. Russell of Georgia, who is bitter over civil rights, is determined to block anything that comes along with Kennedy's name on it.

Averell said this is a battle for the survival of the big bomber. General LeMay is against the treaty because the only way to deliver the big bomb is by the bomber and the United States has no big bomb. With the test ban treaty in force, we could not experiment to build a big bomb. Dr. Teller has pooh-poohed the effectiveness of the big bomb; nevertheless, General LeMay is fighting for it. If there is no big bomb to carry, the air force is out-of-date and gives way to guided missiles.

Averell was still critical of Dean Rusk as secretary of state, says Rusk thinks . . . as if he is running a foundation. Most of those present, including Ken Galbraith, were thanking their lucky stars that Adlai had not been elected president. I disagreed and told Averell, "If he had been, you would be secretary of state." I also told Averell how I had called Adlai in the 1956 campaign and told him Kefauver was willing to come out for him if they could have a private conference. Adlai's reply: "That wouldn't be fair to Averell." Averell hadn't known about this and seemed touched.

I argued that sooner or later Kennedy had to do what Roosevelt, Truman, and other presidents had done: tangle with Congress head-on. To this Walton observed, "Let's face it, our president is not one to engage in battles he can avoid."

Galbraith told how he'd negotiated the Voice of America treaty with India which Nehru now wants to cancel. Galbraith had proposed a radio station to be operated jointly by the United States and India on the Andaman Islands south of Calcutta. "Won't this mean political problems for you?" asked

Galbraith. Nehru didn't think so, so the treaty was negotiated and probably will now have to be canceled. I asked Ken how Nehru liked Chester Bowles. He replied that the ambassador Nehru liked most was Sen. John Cooper because he was such a good politician. Nehru, himself, one of the best politicians in the world, has respect for a fellow member of the trade.

**MONDAY, SEPTEMBER 16** | Sen. Strom Thurmond of South Carolina delivered a speech on the Senate floor attacking me for following the pro-Khrushchev line. He meant it to be scathing, but his oratory did not come up to that of some of my other critics.

**THURSDAY, SEPTEMBER 19** | Foreign Minister Gromyko made his speech at the UN. It was mild and hopeful—in fact, amazingly so, considering that Gromyko has been a very tough customer in the past. Most people don't realize how much he's changed. I think I had better dig up all of the sour performances of the past.

Gromyko proposed an eighteen-nation disarmament meeting in Moscow—nothing new. I talked with Harry Truman on the telephone. He agreed to serve on our Birmingham church committee. He was rather negative, however, regarding that deposition I want him to give in the Alaska libel suit.

Mrs. Stennis, wife of the senator, telephoned to weep on the girls' shoulders in the office over my column this morning. I told about her husband's junket, which was worse than Adam Clayton Powell's. I've been writing a series of columns on the influence of the military on the Senate in the test ban treaty vote, especially those who are reserve officers. Margaret Chase Smith of Maine, who usually has excellent reactions, seems to be sour on the treaty. She is a reserve officer. More importantly, she has been flirting with Goldwater, I understand, to run for vice president on a Goldwater ticket.

**FRIDAY, SEPTEMBER 20** | Kennedy made a fine speech at the United Nations, proposing more cooperation with Russia in outer space, particularly in reaching the moon. This was significant because earlier in the week the NASA official in charge of the moon project dumped on the proposal of cooperation with the Soviet—at the National Press Club.

Kennedy also accepted Gromyko's proposal of yesterday that the two countries join in barring nuclear weapons from outer space. He is sloughing off some of his old timidity.

Last night, when Kennedy's car was parked in front of Earl Smith's hotel, somebody threw a paint bomb against it. I have detected some loss in Kennedy popularity around the country, and this may be one straw in the wind. Kennedy has certainly not lost his ingenuity in being able to dine with Ambassador Smith and at the same time make love to the ambassador's wife.

**FRIDAY, OCTOBER 18** | Back to Washington for breakfast. There were pickets in front of the White House yesterday during Tito's lunch. Today he is confined to bed with a touch of flu and a fever. They flew him back to Williamsburg immediately after the luncheon. Apparently, Kennedy wanted to get rid of him as soon as possible. The trip to California and the speech before the Commonwealth Club in San Francisco have been called off.

Foreign Minister Gromyko, en route back to Moscow, stopped at Prestwick, Scotland, and told newspeople that negotiations between the East and the West to ease the Cold War "couldn't be worse." I suspect that some of the sticklers around the State Department have been trying to negotiate their last pound of flesh. Certainly, when I saw Khrushchev on the Black Sea in August, he was anxious to ease tensions further. It is a fact, however, that Moscow has not yet replied to Kennedy's joint moon proposal. It's also a fact that Gromyko is a bit more recalcitrant than Khrushchev and sometimes inclined to pop off.

**SATURDAY, OCTOBER 19** | Returned to Washington, arriving just as Kay Graham came by the house for a visit. Kay went to the Tito luncheon, where Kennedy, in introducing her to Tito, said, "Mrs. Graham has visited your country many times." Obviously, he confused Yugoslavia with Romania.

Kay said that at the end of the dinner Kennedy mentioned to her privately my column that morning on Jackie Kennedy and Onassis. He was obviously displeased. Kay said she thought I had to write the column and went on to give her explanation of the trip to Greece: that Jackie is so fed up with the Kennedy family and so fond of her sister, Lee, that she had to go to see her. It was her only escape. The two sisters are very close, and as I am pointing out in a column on Tuesday, Lee has been living with Onassis all summer.

Kay told of the warm feeling she has for Jackie. You only have to talk to her for a couple of minutes to feel it.

Last fall, when Phil was on one of his tantrums, he would go see the Kennedys. This time he took Jackie a present of an original manuscript of [the poem] "Sheridan's Ride," which Eugene Meyer had given him. While Phil was talking to Jackie, Kennedy came in the room and expressed interest in the manuscript and quoted from some of the stanzas.

Later Kay got a six-page letter from Jackie telling how much she appreciated the manuscript and how she had copied it in order to recite to the children. She said she got tired of telling them stories so that this would be very apropos. She also wrote that inasmuch as the manuscript came originally from Kay's father, she knew she would like to have it back, and she returned it. Kay also mentioned the warm letter she received from Jackie after Phil died.

**WEDNESDAY, OCTOBER 23** | Saw Tommy Thompson, former ambassador to Moscow, to find out what had happened regarding Gromyko's statement that "negotiations couldn't be worse" and the holding up of American troops on the *autobahn*. Tommy is a man who knows his onions and tells the truth. He said Gromyko had been misquoted by the British newspaperman at Prestwick, who had omitted the word *disarmament*. These negotiations have been going badly—in fact not at all.

Yet in Gromyko's talks with Dean Rusk and Kennedy, he indicated complete satisfaction with the talks. Tommy said Khrushchev had to have something to show his colleagues in the Kremlin that it did pay to get along with the United States, as opposed to the belligerent policy of the Red Chinese. Khrushchev could now point to the test ban treaty and agreement to keep arms out of outer space and the purchase of American wheat. The next step, according to Tommy, will be the signing of a consular treaty between the two countries and a commercial air route between New York and Moscow. We may not establish consulates immediately in Russia, but we will sign a consular treaty. So far, the American embassy handles all consular work.

Tommy said Kennedy faced a tough decision in regard to wheat but would be in a very difficult position if he refused to sell wheat to the Russians when they needed it badly. This would have played into the Chinese hands and proved to them that we did not mean it when we talked about coexistence. I expressed the view that Kennedy had been timid by hesitating so long about wheat. Tommy did not agree.

I also said Khrushchev was in a position to "win" the next U.S. election, Kennedy having gone out on a limb for coexistence. This put Khrushchev in the position where, if he wanted to create a real disturbance or get tough over Berlin a few weeks before the election, the American public would react against Kennedy and Republicans could yell, "We told you so."

He gave me the lowdown on the *autobahn* incident as far as he knew it. He said Khrushchev was out of Moscow, probably on the Black Sea, when the event occurred. It looked as if it was an incident inspired by some junior officer. Tommy felt there was no connection between Gromyko's statement at Prestwick and the *autobahn* incident. "If Gromyko wanted to be tough and inspire an *autobahn* incident as a bargaining move, he would have done it earlier—just before he started talking to Dean Rusk," Tommy said.

I asked why Gromyko and Rusk hadn't gone ahead with Khrushchev's idea of putting observation teams inside both countries to guard against surprise attack. Khrushchev had outlined this to me at the Black Sea, and it seemed like a useful, easy step.

Tommy said Gromyko had attached conditions to the proposal which Khrushchev had not previously mentioned: that there be a simultaneous reduction of U.S. forces in West Germany. I asked if this would not be possible following "Big Lift," the operation now taking place of sending one armored division from Texas to West Germany to illustrate how easy it is to transfer troops in a short period of time. Tommy replied there was going to be no troop withdrawal as of this next year.

He said Khrushchev understood this, that he and Gromyko were realists. "With Kennedy facing an election, with a new prime minister coming into power in London, and a new chancellor in Germany, Khrushchev knows he can't expect any action in regard to Berlin or U.S. troops in Germany."

**MONDAY, OCTOBER 28** | LOS ANGELES—Had a brief visit with Pat Brown at his office, the first time I've seen him in his office. He asked how I thought Kennedy was doing. I said he wasn't showing enough courage. Pat agreed. "What's the matter with Kennedy?" he asked. "He doesn't seem to have the oomph. He doesn't drive."

I felt there was a new self-confidence in Pat. When I asked him about state assembly speaker Jesse Unruh and Jesse's representation of the harness racing interests, Pat told me how Unruh had proposed a bill for the harness tracks. "You can introduce it," Pat told him. "I can tell you right now it will never get my signature. I'll veto it. The bill will never get out of the legislature." It didn't.

We reminisced about Earl Warren. Pat described the chief as "the strongest man in the United States. He plays his cards close to his chest—like this," and Pat made a gesture. "He told me to do the same—never to let people know what I was doing in advance, but I can't do that. Perhaps I should, but I can't. Perhaps my way helps me at election time.

"When I was elected attorney general, I wanted to take over crime cleanup, but Warren had appointed the crime commission. He had campaigned for it. Just before he was about to announce its continuance, he and I had a showdown. I urged him not to appoint a commission. He said he was going to anyway. I said I'd oppose it.

"'Let me give you some advice,' he said. 'There are a dozen newspapermen outside the office waiting to make headlines: "Pat Brown Breaks with the Governor." This is my third term and probably my last. It isn't going to hurt me to break with you.'

"'Governor, you've got your crime commission,' I told him."

Pat invited me to speak briefly to his Governors' Council, which I did. On the front seat was Max Rafferty, the new director of education, whom I had chastised vigorously during last year's election. When Pat introduced us, Rafferty remarked that he had met me at Needles, California, two years before. I had forgotten that the Needles people invited me to speak, paid me a nice fee, and were extremely hospitable. Rafferty was the man who was my host in Needles.

In talking to the Governors' Council about the state of the world, I let drop the fact that Warren had been with us when we interviewed Khrushchev. When I learned that newspapermen were present, I asked them to keep it off the record. Later in the day, however, just before I spoke in Salinas, I heard that CBS had reported the story. This illustrates something that I hate to admit: you can never trust a confidence with a newspaperman.

SUNDAY, NOVEMBER 3 | We held a Republican luncheon in the country for Bazy Tankersley, who has disagreed with me on almost everything for years and who is now the chief shareholder of the *Chicago Tribune*; also Sen. Frank Carlson of Kansas, a very decent senator, and Sen. Ken Keating of New York, brilliant and witty, who can be very effective when it comes to needling Kennedy on Cuba. Representative Mac Mathias of Maryland, a Republican liberal, was also there. I'm afraid Baisy felt the Republican friends we had were almost Democrats.

Luvie played bridge with the Harrimans, and I went over for a brief supper. Averell said he dined with the Udalls last night. Dobrynin, the Russian violinist, and the Venezuelans, the Tejera Parises, were also there. Udall complained that if Kennedy would only spend a fraction of the money on making freshwater out of saltwater, instead of racing for the moon, the United States would score a tremendous victory. Harriman concurred. Averell seemed to be unenthusiastic over the moon project but said that since Kennedy had campaigned for it, he had to live up to his pledge.

State Department cables report that Gen. "Big" Minh, the top man in South Vietnam, had offered Diem and his brother asylum three times, and a convoy had come up to the palace to take both men to the airport. They had been promised safe conduct to any country they desired. En route to the airport, inside the car, the two were killed.

**WEDNESDAY, NOVEMBER 6** | DETROIT—The *Free Press* still has not published my letter taking issue with them over Governor Romney. Romney last night suffered a defeat at the hands of the Michigan Senate. It killed his income tax program. This is a pity because Michigan needs income taxes no matter whether a Democrat or a Republican passes them. They will never get them, however, as long as Michigan remains unreapportioned, with the legislative power in the hands of the rural areas.

Jack Shelley was elected mayor of San Francisco by a bigger margin than I expected, and Mayor Tate won in Philadelphia by about sixty-five thousand instead of thirty thousand votes. The slim leads for Kennedy don't look good for next year. The civil rights issue has hurt Kennedy with white suburbanites in the North. In Michigan a lot of autoworkers have migrated from Kentucky, Tennessee, and Arkansas and don't like the prospect of Negro encroachment on their suburban respectability.

**THURSDAY, NOVEMBER 7** | The American convoy on the *autobahn* was released yesterday. It is not clear who gave in. Khrushchev made a statement claiming that we did. The State Department says we didn't. Khrushchev gave a rambling interview to a group of businessmen. He warned that if the American convoy had proceeded up the *autobahn*, it would have touched off world war. This is probably true. He also gave his ideas for settling the German problem and again emphasized it should be done under socialism. None of these things will help Kennedy's coexistence policy. It will probably scare Kennedy, especially because Nelson Rockefeller announced his official candidacy for president today and, in doing so, blasted Kennedy's Russian policy.

Luvie and I went to the Russian embassy reception commemorating the forty-sixth anniversary of the 1917 revolution. Ambassador Dobrynin was all smiles. The Russian wheat delegation was there and not smiling. Khrushchev issued a pessimistic statement in Moscow regarding the wheat deal, and it may be off. Carrying wheat in American bottoms at twelve dollars a ton extra seems to be the stumbling block.

FRIDAY, NOVEMBER 8 | Yesterday the Senate slapped the State Department by refusing aid to Yugoslavia, Egypt, and Indonesia. The slap against Yugoslavia was engineered by Bill Proxmire of Wisconsin and took place two weeks after Tito was here. It was done by voice vote, which indicates the irresponsibility of the Senate these days. Dean Rusk held a press conference afterward (amazingly vigorous for him), in which he pointed out that Congress acted only once a year, while foreign policy had to be fluid to change with day-to-day events.

Lunched with Ed Morgan, who had previously received an amazing fill-in from Bobby Baker's attorney. Lawyers apparently talk to each other just as priests talk to each other. The lawyer to whom they talk is not bound by any confidence. At any rate Bobby was the pimp, apparently, for President Kennedy, Lyndon Johnson, George Smathers, and various others in procuring girls. A lot of this happened when Kennedy was in the Senate and may have eased up now that so many women are throwing themselves into bed with him.

Bobby Baker apparently realized that the way to get ahead in Washington was through sex and thereby gained a lot of influence. How much of this is going to come out at the Senate hearings remains to be seen. Certainly, Rockefeller knows about it and figures that he can counteract the sex in his life by focusing attention on the sex in Kennedy's life. Obviously, he won't do this himself.

Baker was in Las Vegas the other day where Dean Ellston, the FBI man, confided to him that his wires were being tapped twenty-four hours a day. The FBI, as usual, was playing politics. Bobby and Lyndon are on the telephone about thirty minutes a day, and Lyndon is worried over the developments. This, of course, could knock Lyndon off the ticket for 1964.

Representative Torby McDonald of Boston has his mistress on the payroll. She was with McDonald and Kennedy when Kennedy got into trouble with the landlady of Pamela Tenure. I have known about the McDonald matter for a long time but hesitate to bring it out. She got pregnant, and Bobby Kennedy and Jack Kennedy both helped to arrange the abortion, which would certainly damn them in the eyes of their church. McDonald's girlfriend has been two-timing him and made a complete confession to the other guy when some of her checks from McDonald's office failed to arrive.

After the Pamela Tenure incident, when the landlady was picketing the White House with a midnight photograph of the president leaving Pamela's apartment, Jim McInerney got into the act. He told Byron Cowans, the attorney for the landlady, that she could have a $25,000 portrait if she would call off the pickets, with more financial reward to come.

Jim confided to friends that he felt like a social fixer. For the past ten years his chief work has been handling the girlfriends who got Jack Kennedy into trouble. Jim had an annual retainer from old Joe Kennedy.

MONDAY, NOVEMBER 11 | This is what we used to call Armistice Day. It is now called Veterans' Day. It has been forty-five years today since I was doing Squads Right and Squads Left as part of the Students' Army Training Corps on the Swarthmore College athletic field, when suddenly the whistles started blowing and people came running up to tell us the war was over. We were disappointed.

I was then almost twenty-one. I am now almost sixty-six. I have learned a little about war, but I am not at all sure the American public has. The trouble with us is we have never fought a war on our home soil since the Civil War. That was the most gruesome war in history up until that day. It was so long ago, however, that people have no recollection of it. I used to hear my grandfather Pearson tell about it, but he never really got his feet wet. He enlisted as a drummer boy because he was young and they paid a big bonus. Oliver Wendell Holmes, later associate justice of the Supreme Court, was wounded three times, once in the Battle of Balls Bluff opposite our farm. He used to tell his young clerks—with tongue in cheek—that war was a lot of fun: "You had those big champagne cocktails every morning for breakfast."

Agnes Meyer is back from Mount Kisco and came to dinner. She wants us to go on a sailboat cruise in the Caribbean next February.

TUESDAY, NOVEMBER 12 | Today I had lunch with the new Hungarian minister. He was late. He had been summoned to the State Department to receive a note restricting his movements in the United States. Previously, Hungary had lifted all restrictions on American travel, but we are restricting their movements. We also restricted the movements of all other Communist bloc nations, even though there had been no bars by Bulgaria, Romania, Yugoslavia, and Poland against us. I ascertained later that this was the Pentagon's doing. The State Department had opposed it, but Kennedy hadn't been strong enough to buck the Pentagon.

The Hungarian minister suggested that the United States and the bloc countries might arrange a long-term wheat and grain deal. They need the extra food, he said, and we have the food for sale. He emphasized that West Germany was selling many products to Communist bloc countries at the same time they were complaining about our wheat deal.

He recalled that I first suggested last summer that one way to break down antipathy in the United States, especially in the Midwest, was the purchase of grain and that Hungary had been the first to act on this. He noted they were getting their money through the Chase National Bank and this had been deliberate in order to help Kennedy, in case Rockefeller criticized him for the wheat deal. The Chase Bank, of course, is owned by the Rockefeller family, and David is the president.

I had a surprise anniversary dinner for Luvie. She was completely fooled until I made the mistake of writing her a note of congratulations for putting up with me for twenty-seven years. Then she began to wonder whether the invitation Bess had given her to play bridge with Lady Bird Johnson was a phony. It was.

**WEDNESDAY, NOVEMBER 13** | Yesterday I did a television interview with Sen. George McGovern of South Dakota, who is the one senator with the courage to introduce a resolution for a long-range plan to get the country back on a peacetime basis. Other members of Congress run in the other direction when they see a resolution of this kind.

In view of the restrictions on socialists' diplomatic travel and the worsening atmosphere, our interview may not be very timely—especially when McGovern faces one of the most unmitigated rabble-rousers in the Senate, Karl Mundt.

**SATURDAY, NOVEMBER 16** | The Russians came promptly at 8:00 a.m. . . . Luvie had been busy the night before setting up a Russian-type breakfast with black bread, cottage cheese, yogurt, sliced cucumbers, and sliced tomatoes. She had tea and coffee, though I told her the Russians would prefer coffee. They did. We also had scrambled eggs and bacon, which I think they enjoyed most.

The two-hour discussion which followed was extremely friendly and, I think, stimulating.

The men who led the discussion were Boris Polevoi, an author of war novels; Nikolai Polyanov, deputy editor of *Izvestia*; and Nikolai Inozemtsev, deputy editor of *Pravda*.

Also present were Lev Bezymensky, editor of *New Times* . . . Professor Nikolai Mostovatz, the historian, and a man from the embassy named Morivov, who acted as interpreter. I told them that one of the reasons for Kennedy's concern over *autobahn* incidents and the arrest of Professor Frederick Barghoorn was Republican and right-wing criticism and told them about my conversation with Khrushchev when he said that "We figure we elected Kennedy because he had such a narrow margin."

I explained that Kennedy was in a position where in 1964 Khrushchev could defeat or elect him because the president had tried to follow a line of coexistence and peace, so that an incident on the Berlin *autobahn* in October 1964 might defeat him.

I said the American people were overwhelmingly for peace but there were enough people who were suspicious and very vocal who could switch a close election in case of last-minute trouble. I also mentioned my conversation with Gromyko at the UN in October 1960, when he asked me who was going to win and my reply was "Kennedy—if you don't praise him."

"Not a word," said Gromyko, putting his finger to his lips.

Most of the breakfast was centered around how we could improve American-Soviet relations. Inozemtsev said: "After the Moscow [test ban] treaty last July, the Russian people thought we had [launched] a very important era. They sincerely welcomed it. Now they are worried and wondering what has happened and what can be done to get back to permanent good understanding. What do you suggest?"

"Now you're asking me to be secretary of state," I said; however, I proposed three things: first, observers on foreign soil prevent surprise attack. "This was Mr. Khrushchev's proposal when I saw him last summer. I know the American government welcomed it, but when Gromyko began talking with Rusk in New York, he attached to it the proposal that American troops be simultaneously reduced in Germany. Actually, we would like to reduce these troops, and we're ready to do so, but [it] aroused resistance in Germany, and we decided not to do it just as Chancellor Erhard came into power.

"I still think Khrushchev's idea for these observers is a good one. Right now, if it were proposed, it would not be welcomed in this country, but in a few months it would be.

"Second, an understanding regarding Cuba—I don't know what to propose regarding Cuba, but I do know this hurts our relations. The American people are sensitive about Cuba. We once fought a war over Cuba, just as you fought a war over Finland in 1940, and they are as sensitive about it as you are about Finland.

"Today Cuba needs food, and we have food. Russia is hard up for wheat, and there is no reason why we cannot supply the food direct to Cuba. I think the United States and Russia could come to an agreement about this if it were not for Castro, who is a difficult man. When I talked to Khrushchev, I had the impression that he, too, felt Castro is difficult. He did not tell me this, but I got that impression."

This aroused a great deal of discussion. Author Polevoi said he had been to Cuba, and he wondered if the United States could not change two things—the raids on the Cuban coast and the boycott.

"These raids don't do any good," Polevoi said, "they just make the Cuban people nervous and bitter. They cause you antagonism with no results. If you could eliminate these raids and the boycott, I think it would be fairly easy to work things out regarding Cuba."

I said the raids should be eliminated but that a lot of them are made by independent Cuban refugees who were beyond our control. Regarding the boycott, I explained that this was something the American people felt strongly about and probably could not be changed without a major settlement of the entire Cuban situation.

The Russians were sympathetic with this point and did not regard Cuba as a great victory for them with which they could needle the United States.

The *Pravda* editor said he had talked with Castro in Moscow last May, and Castro made it clear he must cooperate with the United States. Inozemtsev added that he did not agree with me that Khrushchev disliked Castro.

Several Russians made the point that when we backed Erhard, we were backing the return of German borders to 1937. I had not known that Erhard made this statement, but apparently he did in his initial speech. This matter came up when we discussed the nonaggression pact between the Warsaw Pact nations and NATO. The Russians could not see why we could not accept this pact. I replied that I agreed but that such a pact would mean the automatic recognition of East Germany and for that reason West Germany was opposed. They said they thought some face-saving device could be worked out regarding this, but it was very important to get away from the threat of West Germany.

They asked me what I thought of a summit conference of the heads of the eighteen nations interested in disarmament. I said I was leery of big conferences but that I felt there should be two meetings a year between Khrushchev and Kennedy which should take place automatically, whether the two nations had problems or not. This appeared to create considerable interest and approval.

One of the most significant statements came from Inozemtsev when he said: "Let's be frank. You have your right wing. We have those who say that we can never get along with the imperialists, that it is foolish to talk to them. So, we have to show them some progress. We have to show them that we can."

At the end there was picture taking and invitations to come and stay in Moscow. Polevoi told us that he lived in the former stable of Count Rostov. "When you come down from the peak to the valleys, come and stay at the horse stable of Count Rostov," he said.

FRIDAY, NOVEMBER 22 | Having worked until about one, I set my alarm for five thirty, got up and wrote one column on the Bobby Baker oil scandal, said good-bye to [grandsons] Lyndon and Danny, and caught a 9:00 a.m. plane to Dallas. En route [to the airport] Tyler told me I should accept an invitation from the Lyndon Johnsons to stay all night tomorrow after the president and Jackie have left the [LBJ] ranch. I am scheduled to speak at Southwestern Teachers College at San Marcos, where Lyndon graduated, and the next day at Wichita Falls, so it would be very difficult for me to go to the ranch.

We arrived at Austin [from Dallas] at approximately one thirty, twenty minutes late. The Braniff [airline] manager met me at the steps of the plane to tell me that President Kennedy had been shot and killed in Dallas; that Governor Connally had been severely wounded . . . At first I thought he was joking. Only when he repeated the information did I realize that he was not.

Three students from San Marcos met me, together with the AFL-CIO representative, and they confirmed the news. We drove to the Hotel Driskill, where the lobby was full of Texans, also silent, also helpless. I went to my room and started dictating a column to Washington in tribute to John F. Kennedy. It was not easy to do. It was easy to pay tribute because I think he deserved great tribute. But to remember the high points in his life in fifteen minutes was difficult.

. . . San Marcos canceled my lecture, which was a relief, and the Wichita Falls people canceled too. The nation is stunned.

. . . The news came in that a man had been apprehended named Oswald, who had been a Castroite and had gone to Moscow to live for five years. He has a Russian wife. It looks to me a little bit too much as if the Dallas police, who are not known either for their efficiency or their lack of prejudice, are taking the easy way out.

**SATURDAY, NOVEMBER 23** | WASHINGTON DC—Bess and I arrived at Dulles Airport, having flown from Dallas, with a raft of luggage belonging to the new president and the new first lady. The White House car met us, and for the first time I realized that the new president of the United States was in office who had been an old and very dear friend of mine and that possibly I might now have some entrée at the White House. I have been thirty-seven years in Washington and still have never been really in the good graces of any president. Probably I won't be in Lyndon's graces very long.

We dined at the Averell Harriman's. George Baker, Averell's old manager, was there, together with Clayton Fritchey . . . when Ken Galbraith, former ambassador to India, came in after dinner, we talked in a most intimate manner about Johnson.

At his [Johnson's] first cabinet meeting, held today, Ken said that Johnson had made the point that he was for civil rights as a general principle of human achievement, not merely because it was part of the Kennedy program.

**SUNDAY, NOVEMBER 24** | Luvie and I were at the farm, where I was trying to write my TV show . . . when suddenly she called for me to come to the television. In Dallas the police were transferring Lee Oswald from the police station to the city jail when someone shot him . . . The killer turned out to be a Jack Ruby . . . operator of two striptease night clubs and a man with a police record for carrying concealed weapons and assault.

**AFTER FRIDAY, NOVEMBER 22** | [The following entry is undated, although from the content it clearly was written the week of November 25.]

The threats are coming in against anyone who testifies against Jack Ruby in Dallas. I'm afraid Tyler is right that he will get off by pleading temporary insanity. Earle [Clements] says that even if he gets the death sentence, John Connally will commute it. He isn't going to let the man who killed the man who wounded Connally burn.

Evidence has come in which apparently nails Oswald closer to the assassination, and yet there are some disturbing clues in the other direction. It develops that he did not get the job with the Dallas School Book company expressly to be on the line of Kennedy's [parade] route, first because a Mrs.

Paine, a Quaker, who was helping the family, got the job for him; secondly because the line of procession was not announced until the morning Kennedy was killed.

The librarian in New Orleans says Oswald took out some anti-Communist books last fall and also a book on Huey Long which told of his assassination and another book on the life of John F. Kennedy. He had a run-in with the anti-Castroites in New Orleans, was arrested and fined ten dollars, which should have been another reason why the FBI—or the Secret Service—should have been conversant with him and kept him under scrutiny.

I have written the story of the Secret Service and the FBI for release on Monday with instructions to the syndicate to keep the story off our wire so it wouldn't be stolen in advance.

FRIDAY, NOVEMBER 29 | There were 200,000 people at the Kennedy grave yesterday.

Last night Lyndon made a short Thanksgiving Day telecast in which he renamed Cape Canaveral "Cape Kennedy." I understand that Jackie asked him to do this.

A lot of people are discombobulated who live around Cape Canaveral, and the sentiment is beginning to swing just a little bit against Jackie. The *Washington News* published a front-page picture of her yesterday grinning like a Cheshire cat as she entered the cemetery. It was a picture which would not win her friends or sympathy. Alongside was a picture of the Averell Harriman house, where Jackie is now going to live.

Today the *News* published a front-page sequence of the assassination showing that after her husband was shot, Jackie scrambled out over the back of the car. The caption said she was running for help, but to the intelligent reader she was obviously running away. She wanted to get the hell out of that car before any more shots were fired. I wonder what the public reaction will be to this.

The pictures were taken by an amateur motion picture photographer, who sold them to *Life* magazine for $40,000. *Life* has now made them available to the press.

Joe Borkin came to lunch. He says the tide has begun to turn against Jackie on several points. One is that she demanded the heads of state march behind the body in the funeral, which could have meant a heart attack for Lyndon, pneumonia for de Gaulle, and risked the lives of the free world chiefs if an assassin had wanted to risk his own life.

There is also some opposition to the eternal flame, according to Joe. There's only one other eternal light burning in front of a grave, and that's at the Paris Tomb of the Unknown Soldier. Some people think that Kennedy doesn't rate this yet. Of course, Lincoln didn't get a memorial for about seventy-five years, and Teddy Roosevelt and FDR still don't have one, nor does Andrew Jackson nor most of the presidents outside of Jefferson, Washington, and Lincoln. Yet already they want to name the Cultural Center the "Kennedy Center."

I came out to the farm early to go over some planning with the New Holland Farm Machinery representative. In the middle of it I got a call from Al Friendly proposing to kill my story on the Secret Service drinking at Fort Worth. He said I should name names, that the story wasn't fair to the Secret Service. If it had been any other agency of the government, Al would not have squawked. Finally, Russ Wiggins came on the line, and I could see that it was really Russ more than Al who was concerned. I finally persuaded them to run the story with the addition of an extra line urging the Secret Service to make public the names.

Immediately thereafter, I got a call from Ed Ryan of WTOP, who wants to query the Secret Service and get their side of the story. I did not do this because I knew the Secret Service would come out with a protective denial; however, I finally agreed to pursue the matter myself in the morning with the Secret Service. I suppose the fat will be in the fire long before the story appears on Monday—if it appears at all.

The *New York Times* reports from Moscow that Mikoyan was pleased with his visit with Johnson and the Russians want a summit conference between Khrushchev and Johnson.

**SATURDAY NOVEMBER 30** | Pierre Salinger phoned protesting the column on the Secret Service. He claimed the Secret Service men at the Fort Worth Press Club were probably off duty and not in the shift which was to protect the president the next morning. I argued that no matter what shift they were on, they needed rest and to be on the alert. I asked for the names of the six men who were at the Press Club. He didn't know them and refused any comment. I offered to publish any comment. He said he was just calling as a friend. I pointed out that I had praised the Secret Service over the years but that conditions had become lax; that neither a locomotive engineer, a newspaperman, or a doctor could afford to drink before going on duty.

George and Helen Vournas came to dinner. Helen reported being at a ladies' luncheon, where the resentment against Jackie is mounting, especially the renaming of Cape Canaveral. I received a telegram today from Miami, signed by several people, proposing that the Bay of Pigs be renamed "Bahía de Kennedy." The telegram had been sent to President Johnson.

The ladies seem to think that Jackie's five visits to the grave were too much, and also there has been a lot of comment about the fact that Bobby Kennedy, her brother-in-law, accompanied her on some of these trips. She always hated Bobby. During the funeral procession Rose Kennedy, mother of the president, walked behind while her two remaining sons walked ahead of her with Jackie.

There has also been comment over the fact that immediately after the funeral, Jackie invited LBJ to hold the meeting of the Latin ambassadors in the East Room, where the Alliance for Progress was born, and she came down to greet them personally.

Marie Harriman is now regretting having given up her house to Jackie. She talked to Luvie today, complaining that she was now cleaning out her drawers, putting away her toilet articles, and preparing to move to the Georgetown Inn, where, she said, the food is terrible. Marie is wondering why Jackie couldn't have gone down to Virginia for one month of mourning and then come back and found a house for herself, but Jackie likes Georgetown and "has" to stay there. She declined Bill Walton's house because she doesn't like dogs and he had no polished servants—only Katie, who is lame.

The Soviet grain deal is snagged again. The shipping companies have refused to reduce their rates to the equal of foreign carriers, and the long-shoremen refuse to load grain if there is insufficient use of American carriers. The American farmer gets rooked by the unions, whether he's selling milk or shipping wheat. The Teamsters have increased the retail cost of milk while the wholesale price of milk to the farmers was going down.

Johnson has appointed a commission to investigate the Kennedy assassination. He picked the chief justice to head it. This means it will probably be an impartial investigation, despite the fact that Dick Russell of Georgia is on it.

A lot more is coming out about the strange, mixed-up character of Lee Oswald. He started writing a book on Russia which was very critical and gave an interview to a radio commentator in New Orleans in which he claimed the only real type of communism was that of Fidel Castro. George Vournas raised the question as to whether he wasn't a CIA agent when he went to Russia. Most Americans who spend two years there are. His purchase of the

Italian-made rifle, and his carrying of a long, wrapped-up package to work on the morning of the assassination, suggests he was an instrumental part of the plot. I continue to doubt whether he was alone. A French sailor claims that he took a photograph of two men in the window of the building from which the shot was fired. I have not seen the photograph, nor has it been published.

**MONDAY, DECEMBER 9** | CHICAGO—I slept briefly in the motel near the airport and caught an 8:30 a.m. flight headed for Marquette, Wisconsin, which is on the shore of Lake Superior, one of the northernmost cities in the United States. When we got over Marquette, however, there was a snowstorm, and we had to fly back to Escanaba, a little fishing town where I once spoke before the Michigan State Teachers Association and simultaneously sold the column.

We took a bus the rest of the way to Marquette, arriving four hours late. I spoke before a very large audience and afterward had a stimulating party at one of the faculty member's homes, where they asked me . . . intelligent questions considering the fact that they are isolated way up in the backwoods of the Northern Peninsula.

**TUESDAY, DECEMBER 10** | Yesterday the subway bill for the District of Columbia was defeated by an overwhelming vote, obviously the work of Roy Chalk, head of DC Transit. Roy was actually in the House Press Gallery lobbying to the last minute. His stooge, whom I'm sure he's paid off in the past, Abe Multer of Brooklyn, introduced a bill on the floor which would provide that if the subway was built, it could only be operated by a private enterprise, not by the government.

The Teamsters also had something to do with killing the bill. They want to continue buses and gasoline fumes. Incidentally, Jimmy Hoffa refuses to fly the flag at half-mast over the Teamsters building. His refusal to respect Kennedy's death has caused Harold Gibbons, No. 2 man in the Teamsters, to resign. There's been some speculation that Lyndon might pull his punches on the prosecution of Hoffa because of the fact that Hoffa supported Lyndon at the Democratic convention in Los Angeles. I was there and recall how hard Hoffa worked to swing the Pennsylvania delegation away from Bill Green [Jr.].

Up to the very end Hoffa thought he was going to switch the Pennsylvania delegates away from Kennedy, but Bill Green won out. Hoffa was working with John Connally, now governor of Texas and Lyndon's floor manager and [who] I suspect put up some of the money for the Johnson campaign.

Despite this, I am certain that Lyndon will go ahead with the Nashville trial in which Hoffa is indicted for jury tampering.

**WEDNESDAY, DECEMBER 11** | WASHINGTON DC—Saw Pierre Salinger at the White House about getting an interview with the president for Hagen, the editor of *Quick*. Salinger was much more cordial than in the past. I wondered how the Secret Service would feel when I came into the White House, but they were quite cordial. Salinger thought that it might be possible to arrange the interview. He told me he was staying on as press secretary, and I understand from other sources that Lyndon has found it difficult to put anyone else in the job.

Lyndon has been putting the bee on Congress and finally got the vocational training bill passed by persuading Rep. Adam Clayton Powell to break the deadlock. Adam was opposed to so much money being voted for Alabama and Mississippi, compared to that going to northern cities. Lyndon told him that thousands of Negro boys would lack training if the bill was still deadlocked.

Lyndon also put the bee on Senate leaders, and they passed the college construction bill today, without any safeguards regarding aid to Catholic colleges. Thus, Catholic schools will get considerably more under a Protestant president than under a Catholic president.

The Red Chinese have issued another blast against Khrushchev, accusing him of being a tool of U.S. imperialism and warning him that the United States would not cooperate. Simultaneously, the State Department seems to bear out the Chinese accusation by refusing to talk, at least constructively, regarding a nonaggression pact for NATO and the Warsaw Pact countries. This has now been hanging since last July, and the Russians recently brought it up again. The State Department has put out stories saying, "No talks."

It looks as if some of the ideas I've planted about the Russians getting together with Johnson on Cuba may be bearing fruit. Jack Anderson picked up scuttlebutt at the Pentagon that the Russians want to dump Castro. This goes further than my talk with Dobrynin. At the Pentagon they even think Khrushchev might start a revolution to get Castro out. Of course, Khrushchev could handle such a revolution, whereas we couldn't, but I doubt if he will go that far.

There's no question, however, that the Russians are tired of Cuba and its drain on them and would like to patch up the whole business if they could save face sufficiently. It would be a great thing for Johnson if he could go into the next election showing that Castro was out and that normal relations had been resumed with Cuba.

**THURSDAY, DECEMBER 12** | Florence Mahoney telephoned to say that Jackie Kennedy was upset over a couple of lines in the column, saying that the reason Bobby and Teddy Kennedy had walked beside her, rather than with their mother, during the funeral procession was because she had taken tranquilizers, and her doctor had given instructions to look after her. Florence says Jackie claims it isn't true and was quite emotional about it.

I called Jack Anderson, who had written the item and who swears it is true. I am not sure. I wish I had used better judgment editing it. Ed Guthman telephoned on behalf of Bobby to say that he was sore at the same item and would not see me.

Khrushchev has made a friendly statement about Lyndon Johnson. Simultaneously, the Chinese have made a vicious statement attacking Khrushchev. They say he can never make peace with the West, that the U.S. "imperialists" will always double-cross him. This is something Averell Harriman and Adlai Stevenson used to pound home to Kennedy—namely, that Khrushchev has his political worries. Sometimes I think his worries are greater than the domestic problems of the American president.

**SATURDAY, DECEMBER 14** | Pierre Salinger says, about an appointment for Hagen of *Quick*: "The president wants to make a trade. He'll see Hagen if you'll get him out of the December 22 speech. He's been working at a terrible pace and wants to go to Texas that Sunday. He would handle the Christmas tree celebration by remote control."

I was too flabbergasted to argue, but I told Pierre that this would really knock the bottom out of the ceremony and that the memorial services had been planned all over the country. I said I would consult the churchmen and advise him. I did consult Monsignor John Spence, who was heartbroken.

**SUNDAY, DECEMBER 15** | Earle Clements drove me to the airport. On the way I told him about Johnson's proposed trade regarding the German editor and the December 22 ceremony. "That's typical of Johnson," Earle remarked. "He always wants to trade."

Earle also bore out my information that Bobby Kennedy is bitter against Johnson. In fact, he thinks the whole Kennedy family is bitter. They had been in great power. They regarded Johnson as an upstart. Now they are on the sidelines, while Johnson is doing a good job of taking over. The smartest thing Johnson has done, Earle thinks, is to ask the entire cabinet and staff to remain. Earle agrees with me, however, that the Irish Mafia in the White

House is out to gut Johnson. Ralph Dungan was always anti-Johnson, Dick McGuire was against him, and the worst of all was Ken O'Donnell.

Luvie had dinner with Kay Graham. Abe Fortas had just been to see Kay to try to persuade her not to write anything further regarding the embarrassing fact that Bobby Baker secured a life insurance policy for Lyndon after his heart attack and that this was charged up to the LBJ radio and TV stations in Austin. The insurance company, which has headquarters in Silver Spring, Maryland, and no business in Austin, thereupon took some ads with the radio station.

**TUESDAY, DECEMBER 17** | The churchmen have been worried because there's been no official announcement from the White House about Lyndon's speaking at the Lincoln Memorial next Sunday. It's been difficult for them to organize in view of the lack of publicity. I called Pierre Salinger asking for an official announcement, and he said, "I'll tend to it right away."

An hour later I got a call from Liz Carpenter, who moaned over the fact that Lyndon would have to remain in Washington on Sunday when he wanted to get back to Texas. I was pretty tough about it, argued that this was something that was good for him and the nation and that the Negroes were very anxious to have the ceremony in order to promote civil rights. I finally said that if the president wanted to cancel, we would cancel the whole meeting and blame it on him. "You sure do trade rough" was Liz's comment.

**WEDNESDAY, DECEMBER 18** | Lyndon made an excellent speech at the United Nations—making a hit with the delegates. He is beginning to look more and more like a president. I felt remorseful during the night and called Liz Carpenter this morning to say I had been too tough on Lyndon and would let him off the hook discreetly and diplomatically regarding the Lincoln Memorial ceremony. She replied that she thought everything was all set but suggested that I talk to Jack Valenti. I did so and told him the same thing. He called back around noon that the president had just announced at his press conference that he was going to remain in Washington to light the candles and then fly back to Austin that night or the next morning.

We still don't have a member of the Kennedy family to join us, and Monsignor Spence thinks that it's a deliberate boycott. I talked to Sargent Shriver to invite his wife, but she is expecting a baby in February and is not anxious to participate in public appearances. Sargent suggested Ted Kennedy, whom I tried to get—without success.

Luvie and I had dinner with Bess and Tyler. Bess doesn't seem to be feeling the effects of her big new job [White House social secretary]. I asked her how she kept her thirty-five stenographers busy, but she said the mail was overwhelming—and most of it favorable.

[What follows is an entry with a duplicate date of Wednesday, December 18.]

Lunched with Averell Harriman at the State Department. He . . . said that the career boys had boxed him in on everything pertaining to Germany and Russia. "They are delighted to have me work on Africa, Latin America, Southeast Asia, or any other part of the world except Europe. They seem to be afraid I might prevail in working out a solution for Germany."

He said that in March 1961 Adenauer had been ready to accept an easing of tensions over Berlin. In the past Adenauer had followed a policy of keeping the Berlin situation hot as an excuse for keeping U.S. troops in Germany and a no-recognition policy of East Germany. Then suddenly Dean Acheson was appointed head of Kennedy's advisory board, and the Adenauer policy went back to that of Cold War tensions. Adenauer had found Dean to be just as tough as Foster Dulles.

Averell thinks Dean has a guilt complex. He was accused of being pro-Russian as secretary of state, and now he goes out of his way to be anti-Russian. He was accused of being pro-British as secretary, and now he's anti-British. He was accused of being too soft at the end of the Berlin blockade when he didn't get sufficient guarantees for commercial traffic to enter Berlin—only military. Now he's tough regarding Berlin.

The only solution for Berlin, Averell argued, is the easing of tensions. If Willy Brandt had not taken the initiative, there would have been no crossing of the Berlin Wall this Christmas. The Bonn government would never have worked out the agreement if left to them. Averell argues, as I have in the past, that the only solution is to let East and West Germany gradually grow together.

Averell [is] quite bitter about the Europe clique in the State Department. He described them as worshipping everything European. Chip Bohlen, now ambassador to Paris, seems to think that de Gaulle is God. Dean Acheson, Averell pointed out, hated everything Latin American, and now we are suffering from that neglect.

THURSDAY, DECEMBER 19 | Dined with the Orville Freemans. Eugenie Anderson was there, together with the Harrimans and the Walt Rostows. I had written a column after Lyndon entered the White House warning him not to rely on Walt's advice and indicating Walt was a warmonger. Mrs. Rostow, as a result, was quite cool. I sat beside her at dinner, and it took her some time to warm up. Walt, however, took the criticism in stride. It may even do him some good.

Orville, as an ex-marine, claimed it was easy to understand how Lee Oswald was able to shoot with accuracy in such rapid succession.

**FRIDAY, DECEMBER 20** | I was supposed to have gone to a meeting to wind up details for the Candlelight Services but got so bogged down I couldn't make it. I managed, however, to get Sargent Shriver to agree to be present to receive the flame from the president's candle. I had tried Teddy Kennedy and earlier Jackie. All had refused. Teddy claimed he had to go to New York, but I am beginning to think that Monsignor Spence is correct that the Kennedy family wants to boycott this service.

**MONDAY, DECEMBER 23** | Up early for breakfast with a South Vietnamese political leader named Van Tran who wants to go back and become prime minister and wanted me to help him. I don't think either I or the United States should be endeavoring at this distance to pick political [winners].

Liz Carpenter telephoned to say the president was delighted with the ceremony yesterday. He wants me to work on the peace portion of his State of the Union message.

Went to lunch at the Press Club in honor of David Lawrence, who is now seventy-five years old. It's been snowing heavily, and I was afraid that a crowd would not turn out; however, the place was full, and Dave made quite a speech—much more human than he appears to be from his column. Perhaps he is like me. Part of the speech was devoted to his efforts to keep the *United States Daily* alive. I had started out in Washington as foreign editor of the *Daily*, and I never really understood how hard Dave had worked to raise the money for its publication.

Last night, driving with the president from the Lincoln Memorial, he asked me: "Tell me about that son-in-law of yours (referring to Tyler); what kind of a fellow is he? I'm thinking of appointing him to a very important job. How old is he? Has he got judgment?" I said that Tyler was thirty-two, not thirty-five, as Lyndon had thought, and that he had excellent judgment. The best training, I said, was working for me.

Today Lyndon called Tyler to the White House and to bring a biographical sketch of himself. Tyler handed the sketch to his secretary, but she said the president wanted to see him. They talked for about five minutes, and during the course of the talk, Lyndon motioned in the other direction. Tyler turned and saw a photographer. It was the official White House photographer who took their picture. This apparently meant that the appointment was set for Tyler to be assistant postmaster general. The president said it would be announced from Texas.

**TUESDAY, DECEMBER 24** | Johnson won his battle with the House of Representatives at seven o'clock this morning. After frantic telephoning all over the United States, he got enough congressmen to come back yesterday to ensure a vote early today. The House met at seven for probably the first time in history in order to permit its members to go to the Bill Green funeral in Philadelphia. Johnson flew up to the funeral and then off to Texas. I don't know of any congressmen to whom he owed less—because it was Bill Green who tipped the scale in Los Angeles against Johnson's nomination. Bill delivered Pennsylvania to Kennedy, despite the fact that Jim Clark, Green's biggest backer, was pulling all sorts of wires at the behest of Jimmy Hoffa to switch the Pennsylvania delegation the other way.

I spent most of the day shopping and taking the children around town. I delivered them to the White House at about ten forty-five, where Bess took them on a tour, including the president's office. They were impressed with the bulletproof glass around the president's office and the pockmarks on the floor where Eisenhower used to go out with his golfing cleats.

We had dinner with Agnes Meyer. Scottie Reston of the *New York Times* was there as well as Kay Graham. Scottie proceeded to give his views rather vigorously that the *Post* and the *New York Times* had published the recent John Birch ad blaming the assassination of Kennedy on a Communist plot. Most of the ad was devoted to quotes from J. Edgar Hoover, and all of it was geared to make Kennedy's and Johnson's policy of coexistence more difficult. Kay had been undecided about the ad, though actually I think her business staff put it over on her.

One of the things Johnson emphasized to me on Sunday night was the fact that Halleck's attempt to beat him on the wheat deal was part of the old isolationist clique and its attempt to get back into power. Yesterday Liz Carpenter telephoned me. She emphasized the same point in detail. Obviously, Johnson is anxious to have it highlighted.

CHRISTMAS DAY, DECEMBER 25 | We were supposed to go to the Al Friend-lys' party last night, but around 10:00 p.m. I took a brief nap with my clothes on, and it turned out to be an all-night sleep. We never got to the Friendlys' party. At 8:00 a.m. the children opened their stockings, and I awoke. After that I finished wrapping some presents and shifted two merry-go-round horses I had purchased at the Thieves' Market in Alexandria into the living room in front of the fireplace. After breakfast we had a hectic but wonderful time opening presents. Luvie liked the horses, though we don't quite know where we will put them.

Bill Walton came in during the morning, having just returned from Russia. He had tea with Mrs. Khrushchev, who told him that her husband had received a personal handwritten note from Jackie, which touched him very much. All of the Russian people are grieved and upset over Kennedy's death. They felt that he sincerely wanted peace and are not quite sure how Johnson will be. They regard him somewhat suspiciously as a big businessman.

They want to see some evidence that there will be new moves to ease Cold War tensions under Johnson. The wheat deal is not quite enough. I told Bill that Johnson had felt strongly—and so told me—that if he had not won a victory with Congress over the wheat, it would have shown the Communist world that he was not sincere about his speeches.

He talked to both Adzhubei and Zhukov, to whom I had given him letters. Adzhubei was quite frank. Zhukov gave him a propaganda lecture. Adzhubei told about a Russian visitor going through the White House being conducted by Mrs. Kennedy and seeing on Caroline's bed a Russian doll alongside an American doll. Adzhubei remarked that this was proof to the Russians that there was no hate in the White House, that if children could learn to grow up together with Russian dolls playing with American dolls, there could be peace and coexistence.

Mrs. Khrushchev spent some time telling about her trip to the United States and laughing over the fact that she had been taken to see a dry cleaning plant in Bethesda. She laughed over this and said she couldn't understand why she had been taken through a dry cleaning plant. Later Bill said that on the plane going to Poland, he discovered the reason why. He met a dry cleaner from Los Angeles, Roman Fielding, who had made a deal with Mikoyan to set up eight dry cleaning plants in Russia. These are automatic, where the people can do their own dry cleaning.

Mrs. K. deprecated her role as a teacher. She said this was a figment of the imagination of the American press. "I only taught a little while and was a very poor teacher," she said.

I called Liz Carpenter, urging her to get Averell Harriman invited to the LBJ Ranch before Erhard arrives, in order to counteract the pro-German policies of McGeorge Bundy, who is flying to the ranch tomorrow. I don't know whether it will work, but it's worth trying.

The Clementses, together with Tyler and Bess and their children, came for a later Christmas Day dinner. It was very pleasant, and the children were reasonably well behaved. Tyler and Bess are flying to the ranch at ten o'clock tomorrow morning, and I presume Tyler will then be proclaimed assistant postmaster general.

# 1964

## ANNALS

As the year began, the nation was still getting over the shock of President Kennedy's death. Attention soon turned to the upcoming presidential election.

In November, Lyndon Johnson won in a landslide election over Sen. Barry Goldwater. No twentieth-century president matched Johnson's popular vote victory of 61.1 percent. (His vote total was 43,129,784; Goldwater's was 27,178,188.) With solid majorities in both houses of Congress, LBJ could push vigorous legislative program.

For the first time residents of the District of Columbia could vote for president. It was also easier for African Americans to vote, with ratification of the Twenty-Fourth Amendment, which banned poll taxes.

While the outcome of the general election was never seriously in doubt, there was a battle for the Republican nomination between conservative Barry Goldwater and moderate Nelson Rockefeller. Rockefeller's loss in the nomination contest was likely affected by his divorce from the mother of his four children and then quick marriage to a recent divorcée with children of her own.

The most-watched election in the U.S. Senate was that of Robert F. Kennedy in New York. His candidacy began just as he won a conviction and prison sentence for Teamster boss Jimmy Hoffa. Although it was a good year for Bobby, brother Teddy was nearly killed in a plane crash in June. Several major figures died in 1964, including Herbert Hoover, Douglas MacArthur, and Jawaharlal Nehru.

Nikita Khrushchev was ousted as general secretary of the USSR and replaced by Leonid Brezhnev. There were coups in Brazil and Saudi Arabia; in Saudi Arabia, King Saud abdicated in favor of his half-brother, Faisal.

At home the nation was captivated by the British music invasion, led by such bands as the Beatles and the Rolling Stones. The music signaled a rise in the 1960s counterculture. Almost one-third of U.S. households tuned in to *The Ed Sullivan Show* in February to see the Beatles perform.

While Johnson inherited from Kennedy sixteen thousand military advisors in Vietnam, the war intensified with the Gulf of Tonkin incident. On August 2 the destroyer USS *Maddox* exchanged fire with North Vietnamese torpedo boats. With the help of four navy F-8 Crusader jets launched from the USS *Ticonderoga*, the *Maddox* forced the North Vietnamese to retreat.

Two days later the *Maddox* and USS *Turner Joy* were sent to "show the flag" in response to the first incident. The commander of the *Maddox* was facing tough weather conditions, while his crew believed they detected radar, sonar, and radio signals that indicated an imminent attack from the North Vietnamese navy. Captain Herrick would later say that "freak weather effects" interfered with radar and that the second attack was questionable.

LBJ ordered a retaliatory response. Congress passed the Gulf of Tonkin Resolution, which authorized the president to take "all necessary measures to repel any armed attack against the forces of the United States and to prevent further aggression." From then on the war steadily escalated.

—Ed.

# THE DIARY

**FRIDAY, JANUARY 10** | This morning there were front-page headlines about rioting in Panama over the fact that American teenagers had flown the American flag in front of their school without the Panamanian flag alongside it. The situation has been brewing for a long time, and American bureaucrats in the Canal Zone, plus diehard employees of the canal, have resisted concessions to Panama.

Harry Truman was undoubtedly right when he proposed to Joe Stalin at the Potsdam Conference that all the great waterways be internationalized.

**SATURDAY, JANUARY 11** | Johnson has flown the secretary of the army and Ed Martin, the retiring assistant secretary of state, together with Tom Mann, the new assistant secretary of state, to Panama. This may be a tough break for Johnson because the diehards in Congress will demand tough action, and if he takes it, it will alienate all of Latin America.

**MONDAY, JANUARY 13** | Lunched at the Russian embassy. The ambassador and Mrs. Dobrynin, Luvie, and I were alone. The main thing he apparently wanted to talk about was who was likely to be the Republican nominee. I still think it will be Nixon.

I suggested the Soviets should do something in the way of better understanding of the United States in order to strengthen Johnson's hand. I made the suggestion after the ambassador said that he had a high opinion of Johnson and felt that Johnson was sincere in wanting peace. He also said that Mikoyan gained a high opinion of Johnson and had so reported back to the Kremlin. I didn't get any immediate response from Dobrynin regarding my suggestion. I pressed a little further, suggesting that a solution of the Cuban situation would be the biggest help to Johnson, but he passed this over.

Mme Dobrynin, however, did not pass it over and came back with a reminder to her husband that I had mentioned Cuba. At this the ambassador, in effect, threw up his hands, indicating that nothing could be done about Cuba. I did not know at the time that Castro was on his way to Moscow.

We talked about the possibility of Johnson's going ahead this spring with a meeting with various heads of state, including Khrushchev. I thought that it would take place; Dobrynin didn't. He mentioned that Johnson was bound to listen to his career advisors. I said he'd overruled Rusk and some of his advisors in writing a letter to Khrushchev thanking him for his cooperation regarding the Lee Oswald file. Dobrynin also mentioned that Johnson would have to call on de Gaulle or else purposely slight him if he went to Europe and that he wouldn't want to be in the position of doing either. Dobrynin has studied these things carefully.

I said that Khrushchev had made a fine proposal, both publicly and to me when I saw him last summer, regarding the placing of inspectors on the other country's soil to prevent a surprise attack, but that Foreign Minister Gromyko, in talking to Rusk, had attached this to a requirement that U.S. troops be reduced in Germany.

Dobrynin did not deny this, said there was no reason we shouldn't ease troops somewhat in Germany. He repeated the Russian fear of a new and powerful Germany and emphasized particularly the shortsightedness of the United States in placing the multilateral force [MLF] at the disposal of Germany. His argument was that we appeased Germany more and more, and before long we would have another powerful military nation on our hands which we could not control.

I argued that the alternative was a multilateral nuclear force in which Germany could participate with us or risk having Germany get the atomic bomb. I noted that German scientists were smart and they also might get help from de Gaulle and that if they got the atom bomb on their own, they would be a real threat. Dobrynin seemed to think they would be just as great a threat as participants in a multilateral force.

I had to confess to myself there was no reason why we couldn't reduce troops in Germany by at least a token amount.

Significantly, Dobrynin said that he had sat in various councils in Moscow at which they discussed moves that could be made to better relations with the United States, but they were always fearful that these moves would be rebuffed because of the political problems inside the United States.

**TUESDAY, JANUARY 14** | The Panamanian government is getting tough about not negotiating with the United States unless we agree to consider revisions of the Panama Canal Treaty. This Johnson has refused to do. The result is a stalemate. Johnson has his political problems with Congress, and President Chiari has his political problems back home. Panamanian public opinion is really aroused.

It now develops that the American teenagers had hoisted the American flag on Tuesday, January 7, and no one in authority in the Canal Zone had forced them to take it down until the Panamanians hauled it down on January 10, after a lot of taunts from the teenagers.

In other words, a bunch of high school kids have the United States in the most serious predicament in Latin America in perhaps sixty years.

**FRIDAY, JANUARY 17** | A break has come with Panama. President Chiari has ordered out all U.S. personnel in our embassy. This is a blow to American prestige in Latin American, even though the American public doesn't realize it. Panama is a country which we created, just as we created Cuba. Johnson could have avoided this if he had not been too quick on the trigger and had not listened too much to another Texan, Tom Mann.

I suppose that the Congress will be happy with the development. I suppose also that a few Republicans will have enough knowledge of it to make an issue of this.

The story, which Bundy gave me, of French recognition of Red China has already begun to leak. So also has the story that Johnson will send a message to Khrushchev in reply to his round-robin at Christmastime. I suspect that

Bundy leaks only stories to me which he knows are going to break soon, or else he goes out and breaks them just after he's given them to me.

SATURDAY, JANUARY 18 | Luvie and I went to Howard K. Smith's for lunch. I had not wanted to go, first because I don't like to interrupt my Saturdays; second because I suppose I am too sensitive about friends who forget. After years of going to bat for Smith when he needed help, he put Jack Anderson on the air some time ago to give him all the credit for focusing attention on congressmen who cheat. I suppose it has been about twenty years since I started this crusade.

I was glad, however, that we went. Sen. Paul Douglas, Secretary Wirtz, and Jimmy Roosevelt were there. Jimmy and Wirtz expressed some concern over the fact that Lyndon is working too hard, but Wirtz said you can't stop him—he has never been so happy. Jimmy felt Lyndon had made no mistakes. I said that Panama was his first mistake.

WEDNESDAY, JANUARY 22 | The *Washington News* carries a big feature story this afternoon that Johnson is going to give aid to parochial schools in poor areas. This is what frequently happens to a Protestant president: he knuckles under to Catholic leadership in order to get votes. Kennedy would never have dared to do this.

THURSDAY, JANUARY 23 | The president finally held a press conference to meet the Bobby Baker charges. I was not there, and I did not see it on television, but the reports are he did not do well.

The president first made an announcement about Panama, in which he reversed his previous position and did what I urged him to do one week ago. He said he was willing to discuss all questions with Panama after diplomatic relations were resumed. This was an ignoble retreat. Last week he could have said very easily that since the United States had to consider the problem of a new route or improving the canal, obviously we would discuss these matters, but today he put himself in the position of being blackmailed by the Panamanians.

FRIDAY, JANUARY 24 | Liz Carpenter finally called back to say that the president had not leaked the story on aid to Catholic schools, but she went on to quote him as saying that "Catholics get hungry too." Of course they do, but apparently the president doesn't understand that this can be relieved not through schools but by direct aid such as FDR administered.

I didn't argue this with Liz because I had another very important query to give her, which obviously she didn't like—namely, that Bobby Baker had arranged the mortgage on The Elms when the Johnsons purchased it from Perle Mesta and also had financed one of the Johnson swimming pools, probably the one at the ranch. Liz said at first that she couldn't take this up with the president. I noted that if this was going to come out, it was better to have it come out now rather than later. She argued that probably the Bobby Baker involved was Robert G. Baker, head of American Security & Trust, who had arranged the mortgage. Anyway, she finally promised that she would discuss the matter with the president.

Personally, I hope neither is true. The fact is that Lyndon has been something of a wheeler and dealer in the past but nowhere [as] bad as either Nixon or Eisenhower. I remember the sleight of hand he helped Brown & Root get away with on their income taxes, after the company had contributed $100,000 to his Senate campaign. This, of course, was part of the machinery of getting elected, which has come to be so undermining to honest candidates and which Lyndon himself would not remedy when Tom Hennings wanted to introduce and pass a new Corrupt Practices Act governing campaign contributions. Lyndon was probably the man who did most to block that bill because it would have prevented contributions from the big oil companies.

Just before Kennedy was assassinated, I wrote a story on oil contributions and how Lyndon adroitly blocked an investigation of the attempted bribery of Senator Case of South Dakota by Superior Oil. It was John Connally who would have been shown up by such an investigation, and it was John Connally who was almost killed one day after I wrote the story. I held the story.

Yesterday Walter Jenkins telephoned Bess that she was not to drive the children to school in the White House car. It was Walter Jenkins who arranged the insurance kickback whereby Don Reynolds, who took out the insurance on Lyndon, placed advertising on the LBJ TV station in Austin. Walter's call is certainly locking the stable door after the horse has been stolen.

Jackie Kennedy is back in town, still occupying the Harrimans' home. Luvie invited the Harrimans to dinner for next Tuesday and also next Friday. Marie warned that you couldn't depend upon Bill (Walton), for he would get a "command"—meaning an invitation—from Jackie. "I wonder," said Marie, "when he will wake up to the fact that when you're out of the White House, you can no longer command."

Sure enough, Bill called a day later to say that he had been commanded to go to Bobby Kennedy's welcome home party. Bobby's coming back from Indonesia not too much of a hero in British eyes because apparently he bowed to Sukarno in the completely untenable demand Sukarno is making on British Commonwealth member Malaysia.

MONDAY, JANUARY 27 | We lunched at the White House. This time we knew the ropes better than the first—the dinner given by Kennedy for President Betancourt of Venezuela. This time we did not hire a special limousine. We parked our old Chevy in one of the private lanes of the White House along with the other folks. [Sen.] Maurine Neuberger of Oregon was just ahead of us. I did not mention the cigarette report, which was quite a triumph for her, and she did not mention my little item, which was rather mean of me, that she occasionally smoked a cigarette in her kitchen.

We were ushered into the East Room to the tune of a loudspeaker. The Betancourt dinner was quite small. This time there were about one hundred guests for the queen of Greece, including most of the Greek Americans who run restaurants from Corpus Christi to Sacramento.

We were ushered into a long semicircular line alphabetically. Then, as the line increased, we moved up to the P section. Meanwhile, the president and the queen were upstairs. Cocktails were served while we stood in the line, and at about 1:20 p.m. the president and Lady Bird came down and stood at the head of the line, where we filed past. The queen was also in the line, together with Princess Irene.

While we were standing in the line, Lynda Bird Johnson, who has just returned from the University of Texas, sauntered along the line shaking hands with people she knew. She is quite a charmer. Someone asked her about her younger sister, Luci, who had gone out to Wisconsin to see a boyfriend, and a picture that was taken of Luci. "Oh, Luci's just a ham," said Lynda Bird. Then she added, "Of course, there's a little ham in each of us" (she did not mention her father).

The White House is a goldfish bowl in which to bring up children. She is coming through it apparently very well.

As we filed past the president, he said to me, "There's about as much truth in that story as some of those other Drew Pearson columns." I wasn't sure what he was talking about and didn't care because at this point the queen had recognized me and gave me a very cordial double-handshake. Johnson, seeing this, said, "A great friend of your country."

Lady Bird was much more cordial than the president. I had just written a piece on Saturday defending him regarding the stereo/hi-fi, but he obviously had forgotten this and apparently was thinking about a query I'd sent him at the end of the week asking about his plan to give federal money to parochial schools. I did not get a clear answer from him on this and so went ahead and wrote a story, which is scheduled for publication on Wednesday. He will not like it.

We filed into the main dining room. Luvie was at table 1 with Kay Graham, Elia Kazan, and others. I was at table 8, much nearer to the center table, and on my right was Lois Hunt, who had just flown up from Houston to sing. On my left was Mrs. John Pappas of Boston, whose husband owns the Meadowbrook Downs Race Track. Directly across was Princess Irene and beside her Lynda Bird. I last had seen Irene at the luncheon in Corfu at the summer palace, when there were about fourteen members of the royal family present.

The opera singer on my right had spent the night on the plane with her baritone partner, a man named Wrightsman. When they arrived about 6:00 a.m., they went to bed, and afterward Dr. Janet Travell gave them a shot of vitamins to pep them up. Miss Hunt seemed to have plenty of pep. As the luncheon ended, she took off her belt and left it on the chair. Fortunately, it was not serving a useful purpose, so it did not unhinge her wearing apparel. She has a beautiful voice, and I can understand why she didn't want a belt hindering her respiration. She and her partner walked through the tables singing. She told me she was flying back to Houston that afternoon to fill the balance of a nightclub engagement.

After the entertainment a microphone with a podium was moved in front of the president, and he gave a toast to the queen. He read the toast. It was well done, but I remember Kennedy's toast was pretty much impromptu when he honored Betancourt.

The queen responded, impromptu because she referred to "a former citizen of our country" who had told the president when he was a little boy that he would become president of the United States. "I did not know that we had lost the Oracle of the Delphi," the queen continued, "though I am glad this prediction came true."

She spoke well. She was referring to an elderly Greek restaurateur from Corpus Christi, who had been draping his arm around the president at the head table and started to drape his arm around the queen, when Johnson put his arm around her first. The gentleman, named Govatos, had come at the president's invitation.

Johnson has a way of remembering people who do things for him, and he had remembered—thanks in large part to Bess—most of the Greeks who had ever helped him.

The lunch broke up right after the toasts, the queen having toasted the president and the president having toasted the king. Lady Bird and the president mingled with guests afterward, and it was three twenty before we left the White House.

Went to Abe Fortas's for dinner. He was more than an hour late arriving. He'd been kept at the White House because of new developments in the Bobby Baker investigation, which may put Walter Jenkins in danger of perjury. Some letters have turned up regarding the advertising contract between Don Reynolds and the LBJ television station in Austin, showing that Jenkins was consulted. Previously, Jenkins said he knew nothing about the deal.

Abe asked me if I did not think Walter was a dedicated, honest idealist. My reply was no. I said he'd been mixed up in the TFX contract, though he had lied to Jack Anderson that he knew nothing about it. I hope I am wrong about this, but I just don't believe Walter is as innocent as he said he is. Abe pointed out that the affidavit which Walter signed was actually written by the Senate Rules Committee investigators and taken back to him for approval. He then signed it.

Stuart Symington was at the dinner with his wife, Eve, who is the granddaughter of John Hay, the secretary of state who negotiated the Panama Treaty in 1903. I asked her whether her grandfather's papers were available in the Library of Congress and whether it was true he had written a letter to his daughter criticizing the treaty. Eve said that the papers were open to public scrutiny and that the letter he had written said they had better hurry up and ratify the treaty or the Panamanians would get wise and refuse to do so—or words to that effect.

TUESDAY, JANUARY 28 | (Private lunch at the Greek embassy for the queen.)

The queen was animated and charming in her conversation. She said that the interview I'd sent back for approval for *Quick* magazine had been edited and reedited by all the bureaucrats. She thanked me for the piece I had written in the column which was published on the day of her arrival and said that the pickets had not really bothered her. My story was calculated to discourage the pickets.

I told her that Chief Justice Warren, who had lunched with her two years before at Corfu, had been picketed both in New York and San Francisco and that I was sometimes picketed when I lectured. She seemed surprised at this and asked who the pickets were. I told her, "From the extreme Right." Of course, she has been picketed by the extreme Left on the charge that she is a member of the Right.

The queen talked about ex-premier Karamanlis, whom she described as a fine man and foolish to have left for Paris when he was defeated. She said he was a little too impulsive and should not have taken the defeat so badly. We talked about the situation on Cyprus, where she said the Turks had refused to integrate with the Greeks. She described the situation as "explosive."

On the way to New York I wrote a new lead for the Wednesday column and phoned in a kill of the critical piece on Johnson and parochial schools. The new lead dealt with the danger of war over Cyprus. It was a good story and timely, even if I did chicken.

**THURSDAY, JANUARY 30** | Tyler was sworn in as assistant postmaster general. It seems a long time since I drove him and his mother back from the hospital in my old Lincoln convertible in 1932.

**SUNDAY, FEBRUARY 2** | The Averell Harrimans came to lunch at the farm. I had to leave early, first to handle a Big Brothers press conference on the Sonny Liston–Cassius Clay fight, second because Jack has just obtained the documents we've been trying to get for some time on Don Reynolds. Reynolds is the former McCarthy witness with a very unsavory background, who has been the key witness recently before the Senate Rules Committee against the president in the Bobby Baker case. Jack whipped up a quick column with some serious charges against Reynolds. It will be libelous if untrue or if we are called upon to produce the documents. Nevertheless, I let it go.

Luvie went to play bridge at the Harrimans, and I joined them later for dinner. We didn't sit down to the table until 9:00 p.m. due to the fact that two State Department men came in to get Averell's okay on some last-minute decisions regarding Zanzibar.

After dinner I read Averell a copy of part of an air force report on Reynolds's record when a major in the air force and suggested that the State Department had been sitting on its fanny when it could have helped the president regarding the chief witness against him. Averell said he would look into the matter at the State Department tomorrow.

Earlier in the evening I telephoned Bill Moyers and told him what I had in mind, and said I would like to see the president. He ducked this request.

The Harrimans have just moved back into their old home. Jackie Kennedy got out last night. They were irked at her for keeping them waiting about two months in a hotel, while she reclined at Palm Beach, spent weekends in Virginia and only about two-thirds of the time in the Georgetown house. Tonight Marie showed me a leather-bound copy of the test ban treaty, which Averell had negotiated in Moscow last July, together with a beautiful note from Jackie expressing her appreciation for the house. It more than made up for all of the past discomfort.

**THURSDAY, FEBRUARY 6** | Johnson and Adlai have been getting along like two long lost souls. When Secretary-General U Thant came to the Kennedy funeral, Johnson was introduced to him by Adlai, and Johnson remarked to U Thant, "This man is the man who should be in my shoes today."

Adlai has been singing Lyndon's praises ever since. Lyndon asked him to write a foreword to his book of speeches, and Adlai turned it over to Bill Attwood. Adlai, however, actually dictated part of it, and it's turned out to be a glowing description of Johnson.

This is an interesting contrast to the derogatory remarks Adlai made to me about Lyndon during the 1962 cruise. He said that when Lyndon came to Stockholm for the Hammarskjöld funeral, he sat around the luncheon table with other distinguished visitors telling Texas jokes. These did not go down well.

Castro late today cut off the water for our Guantánamo naval base. The action was in protest of the seizure of four Cuban fishing boats south of Key West. The boats were spying on the operation on the Dry Tortugas Islands, where the CIA has set up a base from which agents take off with fake passports for Cuba. Central Intelligence has got us into more trouble regarding Cuba than anybody wants to admit.

Bill Moyers telephoned me from the White House yesterday to say that the *New York Times* was trying to track down the source of my information on the Reynolds case and wanted to pin the blame on him. He was quite panicky. The president is in New York and panics over press relations more easily than most people in high places. Today the *Times* carried a story but did not mention any news leaks or try to pin the blame.

**FRIDAY, FEBRUARY 7** | The Bulgarian minister, a pleasant, roly-poly man named Popov, came to lunch. It's rather embarrassing that the Communist diplomats seek me. I suppose the reason is that they know I won't quote them, and they also are hard up to talk to Americans. I told Popov about the CIA situation inasmuch as I'm writing it for the column anyway. He in turn seemed to be frank about the Chinese-Russian debate. He said it had gone so far that they could not retreat. I asked if there would be a break in diplomatic relations. He said no, but he described it as a Trotsky-Lenin debate all over again.

Popov said Hungary has developed a very prosperous trade and that 600,000 Hungarians visit the West every year as tourists, out of a population of 8 million. They must have hard currency to do this.

I had to make a prediction today on Guantánamo for use Sunday night on TV. It was difficult. The Johnson cabinet met during the afternoon, and he later announced that the United States would supply its own water to Guantánamo indefinitely. He is also dropping a large number of Cuban personnel on the base. Obviously, Johnson is playing a cautious and wise game. He is not being stampeded by Barry Goldwater, who announced today that we should send in the marines.

**SATURDAY, FEBRUARY 8** | The *New York Times* today came out with a blast against the White House for leaking the Don Reynolds story. It was only a short time ago that the *Times* was editorializing against McCarthy's placing of irresponsible witnesses on the stand. Now they are chiefly worried that they've been scooped. Yesterday Arthur Krock published a long column denouncing me—without mentioning my name—claiming that the Reynolds columns were not the result of reportorial diligence but a gift from the White House.

I have written a letter to editors, reminding them that when the *Times* published the inside story of the Wake Island conversation between MacArthur and Truman four months after I published it in 1951, they got a Pulitzer Prize, but I did not go around complaining either about the prize or the fact that the *Times* got a White House handout.

Al Friendly of the *Post* made a serious error, in my opinion, by killing the Friday column, in which I told in some detail how the White House had been unable to defend itself regarding these documents and had not known about their existence. Such a column would have taken a lot of heat off the White House, but Al killed it.

**MONDAY, FEBRUARY 24** | SAN MARCOS TX—Filling the engagement that was canceled on November 22, when President Kennedy was assassinated.

I took the same plane and stopped in Dallas. Then I flew on to Austin to the same airport where I was met that fateful noonday by the Braniff manager to say that Kennedy had been killed. People had been wandering around the airport in a sort of a daze that day.

A lot has happened in those three months. Kennedy, who was extremely unpopular in some quarters, has now become something of a saint. I still think that his death saved him from serious scandals and perhaps ignominy.

The new president, naturally, is very popular in Texas and will carry the state in November. Otherwise, I am informed that Kennedy would have lost Texas. The Republicans are already leveling a steady drumbeat of criticism against Johnson on foreign policy, even though he inherited all the problems from Eisenhower. And some of the Kennedy people, who have left the White House, are beginning to make wisecracks about the Texas drawl and corny manners of the president. It looks as if Bobby Kennedy was out to become vice president on the Johnson ticket, whether Lyndon wants him or not.

**THURSDAY, FEBRUARY 27** | Bobby Baker this week took the Fifth Amendment. This has had terrific impact around the country. In Fresno people were saying that he must have taken the Fifth in order to protect Johnson or someone in high places. People don't seem to realize that Bobby Baker was protecting only himself. It looks as if the scandal will really hurt Johnson in the long run.

**FRIDAY, FEBRUARY 28** | Yesterday the Republicans let loose with a fusillade against Johnson's foreign policy. Senator Dirksen, Rep. Charlie Halleck, and Nixon issued blasts against Johnson for vacillating. Significantly, Nixon issued his blast from the offices of the Cargill Company in Minnesota, whom Nixon represents. Cargill is the biggest shipper of grain to the Soviet Union and other Communist countries. Of course, Nixon didn't mention this in his blast.

Lunched with Enrique Tejera París, the Venezuelan ambassador, who had just spent an hour with Ambassador Dobrynin. Enrique reported that Dobrynin seemed worried that Castro would get Russia into trouble in the Western Hemisphere. He didn't want anything to rock the boat between the United States and Moscow.

Enrique had called on Dobrynin on instructions from Betancourt to urge that there be a steadying hand on Castro. Dobrynin claimed that the cache of arms found in Venezuela from Cuba had been planted by the CIA, which, of course, is absurd. On the whole, however, he seemed cooperative and concerned.

This fits in with the conversations I have had both with Dobrynin and the Russian newspaper editors, that they would like to get off the hook with Cuba and would like to see the United States patch up its relations. They cannot, however, throw Castro overboard.

Enrique told me that the ambassadors of the United Kingdom, France, and Spain had all been called in by President Betancourt and told they would have to make up their minds between Castro and him. In other words, if they kept on trading with Castro, he would cut off imports from those countries—which are considerable.

**MONDAY, MARCH 2** | (Traveled to Virgin Islands and Barbados en route to Granada with Luvie, Agnes Meyer, and Dr. and Mrs. David Paton.)

**TUESDAY, MARCH 3** | [From March 3 through March 17 the Pearsons joined Agnes Meyer on the sailing yacht *Pandora*. Drew Pearson interrupted the cruise from March 10 to March 12 to attend, as a state guest, the inauguration of Venezuelan president Raúl Leoni in Caracas.]

[The *Pandora* is] a beautiful two-master, once owned by Emperor Bao Dai of Vietnam. The captain, Tim Hickman, described her as the best sailing ship in the world and told how he had sailed her from the Canary Islands to New York in a record ten days.

[On March 6 the ship's radio received a message from the White House inviting Agnes Meyer to be President Johnson's special ambassador to the inauguration, an appointment that Pearson had engineered. Mrs. Meyer firmly declined and pleaded illness in her radio reply. After the inauguration Pearson met the *Pandora* on Barbados on March 13, as did Adlai Stevenson.]

**THURSDAY, MARCH 19** | WASHINGTON DC—Luvie and I dined with the Franklin Roosevelts. Jimmy Roosevelt was there too, together with John Sherman Cooper and the French ambassador. I sat beside Nicole Alphand, who is a gorgeous creature. On the other side was another gorgeous blonde, Joan Gardner. The Roosevelt boys have always had an eye for beauty.

Earlier in the day Pierre Salinger suddenly resigned. Simultaneously, it was reported that Dean Rusk was going to bow out after November. All of this threw Washington in a tizzy.

Salinger had sounded out Jimmy a few days ago as to whether he should run for U.S. Senate in California. Jimmy tried to warn him of pitfalls. Pat Brown had just persuaded Stanley Mosk to get out of the race, largely because Stanley has had woman troubles and transported one to Tijuana, who has turned up with a criminal record as a prostitute. Jimmy warned Pierre that he personally was committed to Alan Cranston and that Pierre should take a good look at what he's up against. Pierre said he had Jesse Unruh, the big California political boss, behind him.

We all agreed that Salinger had been a good foil for Lyndon. Franklin and Jimmy argued that Lyndon has a soft spot regarding any man's problems and will do his best to help out even though it's against his own welfare. They thought Lyndon had jumped in to help Pierre hurriedly in this case. Franklin also felt that Lyndon was in a very bad spot strategically, with members of the White House staff, chiefly picked by Bobby Kennedy, in a position where they can resign at their pleasure, not the president's. While this is true, I don't see how Lyndon can avoid it. He has decided to try to keep the Kennedy team.

Franklin gave an interesting comparison between Lyndon and his late father. He said, "The old man understood political timing better than anyone else in American politics, and Lyndon does too." The comparison was interesting since Lyndon has frequently quoted FDR Sr. to me.

Most of the conversation regarded Johnson's goofs on foreign affairs, particularly Panama, where I said he was following the lead of Sen. Dick Russell. Jimmy told how in flying to Los Angeles with the president to meet [Mexico's President Adolfo] Lopez Mateos, Lyndon remarked, "I'll be goddamned if I'll agree to the State Department's formula on Panama." This was just after an official announcement that there had been no disagreement between the State Department and the White House on Panama.

Franklin suggested that Averell Harriman should take over the State Department, but Jimmy pointed out that he had been present at a meeting between Lyndon and Averell, when Averell lost his temper over some foreign situation. Apparently, it made a bad impression on the president.

After dinner, at about the time that the top-ranking guest should have broken up the dinner, Hervé Alphand got me aside and talked about de Gaulle. He made the point that the United States should not be miffed at de Gaulle, when de Gaulle was carrying out our own ideas on the unity of Europe, getting interested in Latin America, and building up a strong contingent.

Joan Gardner was indignant with the Kennedy tribe for sitting around poking fun at the Texas corniness of Lyndon. The Harvard professors who once worked for Kennedy had been having a field day imitating the Texas drawl of the new president.

**TUESDAY, MARCH 24** | Dave Karr came to dinner. He has spent about a week in Texas talking to people about Lyndon's past and came up with a bushel of data, some of it rather appalling as far as a favorable book is concerned. He spent several days with Harold Young, whose wife, Louise, used to work for Lyndon. Harold hates him, and Louise is the opposite. Her sister lived for five years with Lyndon and divorced her husband over Lyndon. I ask what Lady Bird had done all this time. There was no answer except that she is a saint.

Dave found evidence linking Lyndon closely to Brown & Root. Land around the LBJ Ranch was purchased by Brown & Root, then deeded over to Lyndon by various dummies.

We discussed when Lyndon began to go liberal, whether he really had gone liberal or not, and who was responsible. We came up with no concrete answers. Hubert Humphrey claims he helped to get Lyndon on a liberal path. I have claimed that I helped a bit—though I really doubt it. I suppose the real fact is that Lyndon is a complete opportunist with no firm convictions, except that now that he's in the White House, he has the convictions which I think every president has, namely to make history.

Dave is supposed to do a book on Lyndon but doubts whether he can turn anything out that will be halfway honest. I am also supposed to do a book. I don't see how I can get it done before the election.

Lyndon delivered a good speech before the UAW [United Auto Workers] convention in Atlantic City. He came out for holding the price-and-wage line. This is going to make George Meany and Walter Reuther very sore.

**THURSDAY, MARCH 26** | Fulbright delivered a great speech in the Senate yesterday. He criticized the Johnson policies on Cuba and Panama, in fact ridiculed them, and called for junking of the Cold War myths. He dissected the differences inside the Communist world and put his finger on the problem which has plagued the State Department. That is, the fact that Congress doesn't realize that the Communist world has changed and emerged from Stalinism and has just about as many differences as the free world.

Fulbright is a peculiar mixture. He votes wrong on civil rights, signed the Southern Manifesto, was in favor of Dixon-Yates, votes against the Walsh-Healy Act and all labor legislation. Yet he was the only man who stood up and opposed Joe McCarthy's appropriation, when even the late Senator Lehman voted for it. And consistently over the years he has shown real leadership on foreign affairs. He was the man who stood up to John Foster Dulles repeatedly when Dulles was lulling the American people to sleep with his platitudes on brinksmanship and massive retaliation.

FRIDAY, MARCH 27 | Attacks on Fulbright have started. They began with Bill Miller, the Republican National committeeman, who called him an appeaser. Today Dean Rusk got off a more dignified attack aimed particularly at Fulbright's statement that our boycott of Castro had failed and that we should recognize his existence. Johnson had gone to Texas for Easter so wisely said nothing but, in fact, probably was behind the Rusk statement. I am out on a limb with a prediction to be aired on my broadcast on Sunday that Johnson will support Fulbright's general ideas. I guess I have given Lyndon too much credit for courage.

SUNDAY, APRIL 5 | [Here Pearson notes news of the death of Gen. Douglas MacArthur.]

In the biographical highlights of MacArthur's life flashed on the screen today, there was nothing of the Bonus Army, which he shamefully kicked out of Washington; nothing of his mixing politics in his career in the Pacific; nothing of the way he took his Chinese nurse out of the Philippines when he could have taken an American officer instead; nothing of the way he rehearsed his landings for the photographers hours after his troops had gone ashore; and finally, nothing of the disastrous retreat from the Yalu River, when he claimed he faced a bottomless pit of Chinese but actually faced only about 150,000.

WEDNESDAY, APRIL 8 | All the papers last week featured a story about Lyndon's speeding in Texas with a can of beer at his side with Marianne Means and a couple of other newspaperwomen. A trip like this will lose Johnson more votes than any other thing he could do. Dave Karr thinks Lyndon is rapidly coasting downhill. I don't quite agree, but he could if he gets any more publicity like this. The last time I saw him I warned him not to give any favors to individual newspapermen (apparently I didn't stress newspaperwomen). Since then, he has been out on several parties with Marianne Means, Betty Beale, and now this one in Texas.

Bess was disturbed over the poor publicity and said that the president should not pal around with either of these gals or any other individual newspapermen except, she was polite enough to say, except such solons of the press as Walter Lippmann and me. I learned later that Lady Bird was quite distressed about the whole thing and doesn't want to go back to the ranch in Texas. There are too many newspapermen hanging around there. She also doesn't like Camp David—too isolated and confined. I can understand why. There's a golf course which Ike enjoyed. Although it's beautiful, it's also lonely.

**FRIDAY, APRIL 10** | The Soviet ambassador came to lunch. I told him that in view of Khrushchev's friendly speeches in Hungary and the Republican attacks on Johnson to the effect that he didn't know how to handle foreign affairs, the time was ripe for some Soviet-American understanding. I thought this would help Johnson prove to the Republicans that he was a statesman, and it might help Khrushchev with the Chinese to show that he could get along with the West.

We discussed several ideas. Dobrynin seemed to think that Khrushchev's proposal to me of last summer, of observers to prevent surprise attack, would be too difficult because it was linked with the reduction of troops in Germany and the scrapping of our multinuclear force for Germany. He suggested that the two countries were on the verge of signing a pact for direct flights between Moscow and New York, when suddenly they were called off by the United States. This could be revived, Dobrynin said.

He also suggested that the easiest form of quick understanding was to reduce American troops in West Germany and Russian troops in East Germany.

He said that his government had been under the impression that the United States didn't want to discuss anything during an election year, and this was the reason why they had sat on the sidelines in Geneva. He said that if I found the Johnson administration was ready to move ahead on some of these things, it could be accomplished immediately.

Shortly after lunch, I saw headlines that the Russians had tried to force confessions out of four American naval attachés and later confined them to Moscow. The immediate reaction was that the Russians were not trying very hard to get along with the United States. Later in the same day, also, the United States announced the withdrawal of seventy-five hundred troops from West Germany.

When you examine the reports out of Moscow—not the headlines—you discover that there were two incidents, one occurring February 14, the other March 17, not while Khrushchev was making his friendly speeches last week in Hungary. Why the American embassy chose to leak the information, in one case two months later, in the other case one month later, remains a mystery. Perhaps it was the usual technique of the career boys undercutting attempts at better understanding by the higher-ups.

The American troop reduction went off without a ripple of protest in either the United States or West Germany, except for a disgruntled statement from the ex-minister of defense, [Franz Josef] Strauss. The only trouble is that it should have been accompanied by some simultaneous moves by the Soviet. If they had reduced their troops simultaneously, it would have meant a big plus for Johnson. Apparently, no one in the White House or the State Department is thinking about these things.

Last December Khrushchev reduced his troops . . . by about 4.7 percent, and Johnson made a somewhat similar reduction, but neither one bothered to link these to get some mileage for better understanding.

**TUESDAY, APRIL 14** | PEORIA IL—Stayed in the famous Pere Marquette hotel, where Joe McCarthy was conducted up the back elevator to Eisenhower's suite and persuaded him to delete the favorable references to Gen. George Marshall from the speech which Eisenhower was about to deliver in Milwaukee. I remember getting this story. I had already come to the conclusion that Ike had no guts. This confirmed it.

**THURSDAY, APRIL 16** | WASHINGTON DC—I took Hagen to the White House for a private interview with Lyndon. First, however, we attended the White House press conference. It was the second conference Johnson has staged on television, and he did well. He is more at ease and less verbose. He still lacks Kennedy's succinctness. Hagen, who had listened to both presidents, remarked that Kennedy summarized a situation more brilliantly than any expert and packed more information into a few short sentences than anyone he had ever heard before. When you have finished listening to Johnson, you have to sort out the kernel from the chaff. And sometimes there isn't much kernel. Nevertheless, compared with the past, Lyndon did well.

When newswoman Sarah McClendon asked him about the classified documents being published regarding General MacArthur, Johnson replied that he had inquired about this from the military and they told him everything published so far had been from books. This was aimed at me. Afterward I chided the president about it. He replied that he only wanted to keep me out of jail. "You wouldn't want to go to jail for publishing classified documents, would you?" he said.

We met Johnson in the Cabinet Room, where he was talking to two Texas editors, Jackson of the *Corpus Christi Caller-Times* and the editor of the *Texarkana [Gazette]*. Johnson introduced me and Hagen to them, remarking: "You say I persuaded all your Texas papers to cancel the column. Here is one [in] Corpus Christi that has been publishing you for years." I had to admit this was correct. The *Caller-Times* never did cancel—but what a memory Lyndon has to recall this.

He repeated what he'd said in the press conference that the Pentagon told him the MacArthur documents had previously been published. "You were there, Walter," he said, turning to Walter Jenkins, "isn't that what they said?" Walter nodded in the affirmative. Later, however, Jack Anderson told me how he had laboriously copied these documents from the classified texts.

The president first took us out into the Rose Garden, remarking how Mrs. Paul Mellon had contributed the beautiful crabapple trees. We posed for some photos together, during which Lyndon pulled a letter out of his pocket from the Secret Service regarding Mrs. Johnson's alleged speeding. The Secret Service said she had not been speeding, and Lyndon added that sometimes when newspapermen were traveling in a caravan with the president or first lady, they had to speed up to pass a truck, and it gave them the impression that the whole caravan was speeding.

We went inside and settled down for the formal interview. Hagen, who speaks English pretty well, was nervous, but the president helped him out and was quite expansive. The highlight of the interview came after Secretary McNamara called the president to congratulate him on the press conference. The president had refuted Barry Goldwater's claim that we had insufficient bombers, and McNamara told Lyndon that he had handled the whole thing just right. After this Hagen asked the president about further troop withdrawals from Germany. He referred to the seventy-five hundred troops which the Defense Department had withdrawn last week.

"We take some troops in and take some out," the president explained. "This was the extra troops we had sent in during the Berlin crisis. I didn't actually know about the withdrawal until I read it in the papers." He then picked up the telephone and called Secretary McNamara. "Are we planning to withdraw any more troops from Germany?" he asked. "I have with me Mr.

Hagen, editor of an important German magazine, and I wish you would tell me what plans are for the future."

The president then held the telephone out away from his ear so that Hagen could hear McNamara's reply. McNamara stated that there were no troop withdrawals contemplated, except for approximately five hundred men who were on a special mission and would be taken out in September.

"You heard what he said," continued the president. "I can assure you that we are not going to reduce our military strength below our commitments. We have made a commitment to keep six divisions in Germany, and we will keep it.

"A lot of people over here don't understand why we should have so many troops in Germany," he continued. "They believe you breed enough young men yourself to handle your defenses, and they claim the United States should not spend so much money on the defense of Germany."

The president then explained he had just taken a thousand troops out of South Vietnam, but it didn't mean reducing our overall strength there. "They have been over there to train military police. Now that they have accomplished their mission, they are not needed anymore."

Hagen asked whether the United States was contemplating any more important trade moves with Soviet Russia. President Johnson said: "No, we have just concluded a wheat deal. We had some difficulty getting Congress to okay it. We thought it was important to show that we were willing to feed people who needed food. This had nothing to do with military power. We wouldn't like it if Germany sold military supplies to Cuba, but we are not going to object to her trading around the world.

"We built Germany up from a shattered nation after the war so that now she is competing with us all over the world. We don't object to that competition. We don't ask for any payment for our help. All we want is for Germany to do the same with her knowledge and her skills and her treasure for the underdeveloped countries.

"Today I sent Sargent Shriver to Germany to see about organizing the German Peace Corps. We want to get your ideas and give them any that may help."

On the subject of peace Lyndon spoke eloquently. "We want to examine every avenue for peace," he said. "I told the chancellor when he was here around Christmastime, 'Ask yourselves what you should do to improve relations with the Russians. I am not trying to advise you. I shouldn't be advising the German people, but remember that the Russians are nervous about you. They suffered heavy casualties during the war. You can understand why they are nervous. So, examine your relations to see how they can be improved.'"

The president asked whether Hagen had read his plan about freezing nuclear weapons. He said, "The Russians have reacted negatively as usual, but there are some features in this which they may not entirely appreciate and may come around in the end. Just imagine what it would mean if we could give up the production of atomic weapons entirely."

Hagen asked about the reunification of Germany. The president replied, "Naturally, I am for reunification but not for negotiations with East Germany. I don't want a Communist Germany. I favor negotiations between West Germany, the Soviet [Union], and the United States."

He reiterated his support for the multilateral nuclear force, which is, of course, what the Russians object to.

After about forty-five minutes I broke up the interview. The president had been generous with his time. I took him aside and told him, "As you know, I am always trying to tell you how to run the world. I see you're going to speak down at the memorial for General Marshall. I assume you're planning to take that opportunity to remind people about the wonderful job he did with the Marshall Plan and make up for some of these tributes to General MacArthur?" Lyndon indicated he would.

"Also, I was down in Staunton, Virginia, awhile back at Woodrow Wilson's birthplace," I told him, "and they have been anxious to get you down there for Wilson's birthday. It seemed to me that October, during the campaign, might be a wonderful opportunity for you to go down there and talk about the international ideals of Woodrow Wilson and the manner in which the isolationists gutted him. It will be a time when the Republicans will be taking out after your foreign policy."

Lyndon seemed to think it was a good idea and asked George Reedy to make a note of it. He took me over to his desk to show me the latest Gallup poll, which will be published Sunday. It showed him running about 73 percent even in the South and higher in the North. The president pointed out that even Eisenhower in his most popular day hadn't run that high.

MONDAY, APRIL 20 | Johnson delivered a speech at the Associated Press pretty much per schedule, announcing a dramatic cutback of nuclear raw materials. Simultaneously, Khrushchev announced another cutback of the same proportion.

Went to see McGeorge Bundy to try to get to the inside story of how Lyndon had put this across. He was not too helpful. I told him that the president would be far more helpful and give me all the details, and Bundy admitted this was correct, but he added, "I am not the president." He said, however, that Lyndon had begun working on this problem as early as last Christmas and kept probing Khrushchev and the Defense Department. He told Secretary of Defense McNamara that he wanted something concrete to offer the Russians, and McNamara had proposed this, together with a cutback on bombers.

I asked Bundy what other steps could be taken to create a more favorable atmosphere before the elections. I inquired about Khrushchev's plan for observers to guard against surprise attack. Bundy said that Johnson was very much in favor of this but that Khrushchev had attached some reservations to it, particularly the reduction of U.S. troops in Germany and the abandonment of the multi-nuclear force. He said the United States could do neither; we were obligated to Germany on both points, but the president was anxious to explore any other channels of agreement.

Later I had lunch with Dobrynin. He was friendly and open-minded regarding avenues of further discussion but emphasized that the United States seemed to be taking its policies from the West Germans. He pointed out that at first, during the test-ban talks, the United States had seemed favorable toward removing nuclear weapons from both the Warsaw Pact and NATO countries. Then, suddenly, we reversed ourselves, apparently after we had heard from Bonn.

THURSDAY, APRIL 30 | While in New York, I telephoned Adlai Stevenson to ask him whether he was interested in running for the Senate. He was frank. "I could have been vice president or secretary of state in 1960 if I had come out for Kennedy, but I didn't—out of loyalty to Johnson. I don't know whether he will remember this or not."

"I'll remind him," I interrupted.

"My field is foreign relations," continued Adlai. "I don't know whether I want to go back in on the combat line in a new state or leave this job— even though I shouldn't continue indefinitely. Whether I run for the Senate will be up to Johnson. It's a question of where I can serve him best. We have finally got around to scheduling a meeting in Washington on East-West trade.

"We have made some needless mistakes, Johnson never should have announced the nuclear cutback to the Associated Press luncheon without telling the Geneva arms negotiators about it in advance. Yet on the whole we are doing all right."

I gathered that he definitely did not want to run for the Senate and had his eyes on being either secretary of state next year or on the Johnson ticket as vice president.

**WEDNESDAY, MAY 13** | (Lunched with Czech ambassador, Dr. Karel Duda, along with two Russian newspapermen, Sergei Vichnevski of *Pravda* and Victor Krapovic, editor of USSR, a Russian propaganda magazine published in English; joined at lunch by Tyler Abell.)

I talked about Khrushchev's speeches in Cairo and that his politicking there in favor of the Arabs and against Israel made it more difficult for Johnson to follow coexistence and more difficult for me in writing favorably about coexistence. Vichnevski reminded me of the paragraph in Johnson's speech at the AP luncheon, which I had said the State Department had inserted. "*Pravda* did not carry that paragraph," he said.

He also brought out that *Pravda* had dealt with the Bobby Baker incident in a routine way. "We did not play it up as illustrating the decadence of the capitalist system," added Krapovic.

After Tyler and the Czech ambassador left, the two Russians asked to talk to me a bit further, and we went into the garden. They were curious about the *Quick* magazine interview and wanted to know whether I had inspired it. Particularly, they wanted to know whether I had inspired President Johnson to make the statement he had made to Hagen that Erhard should find ways of getting along with the Soviets. They said they had heard that Reedy did not want to go ahead with the interview but that Johnson had proceeded when I insisted on it. They also said they had heard that I had arranged for Johnson to talk about détente, the diplomatic phrase for easing East-West relations.

I told them I had not persuaded Johnson to talk on this subject, that this had come spontaneously from him without any prompting, and that I was convinced he meant it. I said I had helped arrange the interview and that its origin took place when *Quick*'s editor met Johnson at my house at dinner the year before.

[From approximately May 26 through June 25 the Pearsons traveled to Ethiopia, Kenya, and Israel.]

**[PAGE UNDATED—PROBABLY WEDNESDAY, MAY 27]** | ADDIS ABABA, ETHIOPIA—It was hot on the parade ground. Fortunately, we rated a large umbrella. His Imperial Majesty sat solemnly and very small on his throne, handing out medals as an officer read out the citations and as a court functionary handed HIM the medals.

After it was over, HIM spoke briefly from his throne, then we were led over to meet him. He said in English, "Does the hot weather bother you?" The ceremony had been pitched in such a low key, and I had been whispering to Luvie, that I found myself whispering to the emperor, "No, Your Imperial Majesty, the weather is fine."

They rolled up the red carpet, put a red velvet robe over the throne, and then began carrying away the trappings of royalty. We marked time for about an hour, then went to one of the summer palaces to attend a luncheon given by HIM for air force units, which were decorated.

**THURSDAY, MAY 28** | The emperor put a special plane at our disposal to fly to Bahr Dor, the headwaters of the Blue Nile. The governor met us and drove us to the Tesissat Falls, a beautiful waterfall where the Nile falls from the tableland around Lake Tana down to a deep gorge and then cascades down toward Egypt.

We drove through flat bush country, a lot of livestock, a few farms, not much land tilled. This area around Lake Tana is one of the most promising yet least developed. They have made a brave start, however, by building a textile mill, and the Russians have built a technical training school.

Imagine the frustration of the Russians, building a magnificent school of this kind, far better than I have seen built by the United States, then to have the teaching done by an Ethiopian trained at Menomonie, Wisconsin, and directed by a graduate of the University of Michigan. Even the signs on the toilets read "Ladies" and "Gents."

**DATE UNCERTAIN** | NAIROBI, KENYA—We are staying at the American embassy, whose front door is barred with a huge iron bar and whose windows have iron latticework, a remnant of Mau Mau days, when the natives murdered whites indiscriminately.

Today Jomo Kenyatta, leader of the Mau Mau, is prime minister, and the white plantation owners all swear by him.

WEDNESDAY, JUNE 3 | [Ambassador and Mrs.] Attwood had the Soviet ambassador, Lavrov, the Israeli ambassador, Eillen, and British governor-general, Malcolm MacDonald, to dinner.

Earlier that day the British announced a sixty-thousand-pound aid program for Kenya, which far surpassed the Russian aid proposal of a hospital, technical school, and fish cannery.

After dinner I told the Soviet ambassador that I'd had good talks with Khrushchev and with Johnson, and both had expressed the hope that the United States and USSR could work toward better understanding. I said, however, I was surprised to find a cutthroat rivalry between the United States, China, and Russia over Somalia which could start war. Lavrov squirmed a bit but replied that the British had just announced army and aid programs to Kenya today.

"That is exactly what Mr. Pearson is talking about," said the governor-general. "We are offering arms to Kenya in competition with you, when we should be working together with you so these little countries won't be building up armies which they can't afford."

We had a long argument with the Russian, with me doing most of the arguing. I recalled [Italian] President Gronchi's proposal to Khrushchev that Russia and the United States should cooperate in foreign aid, also LBJ's proposal that we scrap all bombers instead of selling them to the smaller nations with which to start wars. The ambassador parroted the usual Communist line of having total disarmament, not piecemeal disarmament. I argued that piecemeal disarmament was necessary in order to allay American public opinion, and I told of the criticism I got after my first Khrushchev interview. I doubt if it made an impression, but Bill said everything would be reported back to Moscow.

SUNDAY, JUNE 7 | ISRAEL—The Mediterranean Sea outside my hotel window is blue-green and pounded so rhythmically that I slept late; then up for a swim and a kosher breakfast. It is invigorating to be back in Israel. The last time was in 1957.

I drove at 10:00 a.m. with three Israeli engineers north to see the hook-up of the long pipeline from the Jordan River down to the Negev desert—a project to which the Arabs object vigorously and have threatened invasion.

I was surprised to learn that Israel has also drilled twenty-three hundred deep wells, about one thousand feet, at a cost of $100,000 each, to take subsurface water, and these will be hooked up with the Jordan pipeline. The Israelis are careful not to over-pump and bring in saline water from the sea.

As we flew over the country, I was amazed to see the amount of overhead irrigation. The contrast between green Israel on one side and barren Jordan on the other is striking.

We walked around the military fortifications at the point where the Jordan enters the Sea of Galilee and where Syria joins Israel. The hills above Israel are rocky and barren, but a group of Israeli army-agricultural troops are manning the defenses and at the same time doing some farming.

Below, in Syria, the delta of the Jordan is green and fertile. Israel owns a ten-meter strip completely around the lake and much wider strips in some places. Syrians are allowed to fish at the north end of the lake, which is about sixty-five square miles and twelve feet deep. It's a beautiful lake which looks placid and peaceful. A great deal of history has been spelled out here, from the time Christ walked on the water to the present.

MONDAY, JUNE 8 | Drove to Jerusalem with David Landauer, the Israeli PR man, to call on Abba Eban, who is now deputy prime minister. He is a South African, with a beautiful Oxford accent, who was brought back from Washington by Ben-Gurion in order to bring him up the political ladder. He is resented by some of the old-timers, who were here digging in the desert and fighting with the Arabs when Eban was in knee breeches. Despite this, he has come up to be No. 2 man in the government.

Though a Ben-Gurion man, he and the Eshkol government balk at the belligerency of Ben-Gurion and seem more anxious to get along with the Arabs. Eban wanted to know what I had found out in Cairo. I expressed the opinion that the Egyptian people had no real enmity for Israel and recognized it was here to stay.

Eban said he sat beside Nixon on the shuttle to New York a month or so ago and Nixon unburdened himself about the GOP nomination. He discussed various deadlocks—all of which pointed to Nixon as the logical candidate.

Mrs. Golda Meir, the foreign minister (from Milwaukee), had just come back from signing a Common Market agreement in Brussels. I had not talked with her since I interviewed her in Jerusalem in 1956. She has the same strong face and this time talked frankly—though off the record—about the Arabs. She seemed to think they were softening a bit toward Israel but that if Hussein said anything favorable about Israel, he would be shot immediately. She added, "His grandfather was."

His grandfather, King Abdullah, was shot after he had held two secret meetings with Mrs. Meir in Jerusalem. Hussein, then a small boy, was beside his grandfather in the great mosque of Jerusalem as the shot was fired.

The Israelis saved Hussein in 1958, when their intelligence got wind of a Nasser plot against him. They tipped off the British, who rushed troops into Jordan by U.S. transport planes.

"We know Hussein would like to get along," Mrs. Meir said. "We also suspect Bourguiba (of Tunisia) would like to get along. There have been Nasser attempts on his life too. And when he sits in an Arab summit meeting, he has to speak out against Israel or he would be suspect."

[HANDWRITTEN TEXT DATED "LATE JUNE '64"] | WASHINGTON DC—
Lunched with Arthur Goldberg. He is upset over Hugo Black's vote against Negro restaurant sit-ins. Hitherto Hugo has been the swing vote in favor of civil rights and the minorities, but this time he swung the other way.

Bill Douglas is disgusted. He told Arthur, "They've cut our nuts off, and I don't think I'll stick around for the interment."

"What do you mean by that?" Arthur replied. "The whole world is watching us. You can't get out in the middle of this fight." Arthur said that Bill is lonesome. Mercedes would leave her husband in a minute and come back to him.

Hugo is getting lots of conservative praise. Great as he is, his instincts as a southerner couldn't quite bring him to the point where he believed the Fourteenth Amendment called for public accommodations for Negroes.

TUESDAY, AUGUST 18 | Flew back from Fairbanks last night, a long, beautiful trip over the Alaskan mountains, which are still snow-topped, with glaciers running down between them into the sea.

Flying up to Alaska on Sunday, we kept pace with the sun. Most of the evening we flew about as fast as the earth turned on its axis, so that we could see the sun setting for almost two hours. It hung motionless just above the rim of the earth while the plane hurried to catch up with it. Finally, just before we arrived at Fairbanks, the sun dropped down behind the earth; however, it was light at Fairbanks most of the night.

I arrived in Baltimore at 9:40 a.m. On the plane was Bill Miller of the Democratic Senate campaign committee, who had been out working for the reelection of various senators.

Miller has long worked on Capitol Hill, and he believes LBJ has done an amazing job and wondered why because, as a senator, he [had] conducted a parochial operation and was unhappy unless his ego was being constantly massaged.

The three years he spent as vice president were probably the most unhappy of Lyndon's life, according to Bill. He had nothing to do. That unhappiness probably gave him more insight and more time for introspection. I remarked that it gave him some chance to become familiar with foreign affairs.

FRIDAY, AUGUST 21 | The Democrats have now nominated Lyndon Johnson for president. Hubert Humphrey finally got the vice presidency. The convention was held at Atlantic City and, perhaps because I am getting old and jaded, thought it was a humdrum affair. There were the parties, the fight over seating southern delegates, the suspense until Hubert was finally picked, and there was the tawdry boardwalk, which hasn't changed since the days when I came to Atlantic City as a boy.

Lyndon flew to Atlantic City on Wednesday to nominate Hubert Humphrey in person. Hubert had come to Atlantic City full of confidence, even had Humphrey-Johnson buttons prepared in advance, but he was kept waiting until the last moment. Even Wednesday afternoon, Sen. Tom Dodd of Connecticut was summoned to the White House, along with Hubert, and speculation arose that Dodd would be the man. If he had, I think I would have cut my relations with Lyndon; however, it was just a gesture to help Dodd in his race for reelection, and an hour or so later the president appeared in Atlantic City with Hubert on the same plane and announced that Hubert was his choice.

Southern delegates took it rather badly. My old friend Donald Russell, now governor of South Carolina, who used to represent me in libel suits, got off some sour remarks on the convention floor. The Mississippi Freedom Democratic delegates, who were bitterly disappointed over being excluded, blamed Humphrey for their political demise.

David Karr came down from New York, but the fiery days when he organized rallies for Henry Wallace in Chicago are gone. In the first place, there isn't much chance to fight here. Secondly, Dave has become sedate and affluent. Ernie Cuneo was more youthful and irrepressible. He had come to Atlantic City trying to promote Sen. Claiborne Pell of Rhode Island, who had about as much chance as I did. Ernie hung around the Mutual Broadcasting studio, where I was doing some work.

[Walter] Winchell was there too, manufacturing big items out of trivia. I felt rather like a has-been, nibbling around the edges of radio in comparison with the TV coverage I used to give ABC. The *Atlantic City Press* and the *Philadelphia Bulletin* play up the column big, and I had plenty of friends and boosters in Atlantic City. It makes all the difference in the world when your column is given full play or when it's cut to ribbons.

Bobby Kennedy got a tremendous ovation on the last day of the convention, and so did Jackie Kennedy when she attended a reception given by the Harrimans. I think Lyndon was probably right in putting Humphrey across the day before. Otherwise, the convention would have stampeded for Bobby.

**THURSDAY, SEPTEMBER 3** | The chief justice and Nina Warren came for dinner, together with the Tom Kuchels and the Paul Douglases. The chief does not look well—tired and old, and his color is not good. Nina says that he has been working all day, every day, on the Kennedy assassination report and doesn't get home until 7:00 p.m. He seemed rather subdued compared with his old self, whom we had known for the past three summers. I don't know what the Court and the country would do if anything happened to him.

**FRIDAY, SEPTEMBER 11** | Yesterday the Senate voted down Everett Dirksen's cloture petition, aimed against the Supreme Court's decision on legislative reapportionment. I telephoned various senators from Alaska, Edmondson of Oklahoma, Symington, Tom McIntyre of New Hampshire, to persuade them to vote against cloture.

I have written several columns on the subject; however, this is probably the most important battle of the entire session—more so than the civil rights bill because this gets to the question of power. And if you can change the economic power in the states, you can really change poverty. The power of Illinois Light & Power and Mississippi Light & Power and all the other utilities and gas and oil companies in the various states derives from their control of the legislatures. This is what few people understand about the Supreme Court's decision, including some of my Freedom Fighter friends. If the Supreme Court is going to be knocked on its can by Senator Dirksen, it will be in no position to strengthen the civil rights law and continue its valiant battle for human rights. There has never been a period in history when the Supreme Court has carved out such important legislation affecting the pocketbook, the welfare, the dignity, and the freedom of the average American. Without the Court there would be no wedge in the door of Mississippi to permit Freedom Fighters to go down and broaden the wedge.

FRIDAY, SEPTEMBER 25 | Late last night Mrs. Quinn, one of the Negro ladies from McComb, Mississippi, telephoned me, quite upset. She had talked to a friend in McComb, who had warned her not to return home. The tension was too high. The stories that the three ladies had given to members of Congress, and later to the president, had gone back to McComb, and there was a great deal of tension in the city. Mrs. Quinn wanted to know whether the president would really follow through in getting them protection. She said they had had a very sympathetic visit with him and he had promised to get some additional FBI men there.

I was unable to get Lee White at the White House, so I telephoned chief of police George Guy in McComb, and had a long talk with him. He said it was true that he could not guarantee the safety of the three women. He advised that they "ease into town without anyone knowing it and stay with friends." He said he was distressed over the violence and admitted there had been a great many bombings. His distress seemed to be not so much with human life as with the bad name it was giving to McComb. He repeated this several times. I asked him why he couldn't plant a man inside the Klan or the White Citizens' Council [aka Citizens' Councils of America], which should be fairly easy to do. He said he was working on that. I relayed the information back to Mrs. Quinn.

The Warren Report was published at 9:00 a.m. this morning and shows conclusively that I was right about the drinking of Secret Service men in Fort Worth early in the morning before the president's assassination and also regarding the FBI's failure to give the information on Lee Oswald to the Secret Service.

The report shows in great and conclusive detail that Lee Oswald alone was responsible. It will be interesting to see what the reaction is in Europe, especially from men such as Khrushchev, who, in Cairo, told me just the opposite.

Lunched with Leonard Marks. He told me he had never had such an intriguing time in his life and that "You're responsible." He referred to my selling the president on the idea of a small brain trust and suggesting that Leonard and Tyler be members of it. Leonard is devoting most of his working time to this enterprise.

When I went into the White House yesterday to see the president, I went a bit early in order to meet Tyler and was somewhat embarrassed when I walked upstairs, past an open door, where Tyler, Leonard Marks, Bob Martin, and other members of the brain trust were sitting. They are doing a good job. They devised the idea of passing out copies of Bill Scranton's devastating letter to Goldwater in every audience where Scranton introduces Goldwater. It sets Bill Scranton crazy.

They have also devised the idea of a cartoon book containing all the devastating cartoons against Goldwater, which is to be sold or passed out at supermarkets. They even got up in a hurry, a dummy company, "The Robert Luce Publishing Company."

They have also been working on various rebuttals to Bill Miller, part of it the manner in which he had a pocketbook interest regarding the Lockport Felt Company. I have been trying to stir up a debate on the floor of the House to put Miller on the spot regarding this conflict of interest, but so far no member besides Wayne Hays has had the guts to do anything.

Leonard wanted to know what I thought was the best way to combat the McClosky–Bobby Baker hearings, which apparently are going to start soon in the Senate Rules Committee. I suggested at first an investigation of the big contributions to the Gettysburg farm, but Leonard thought this pulled down the stature of the presidency too much and would give the impression that all big shot politicians, including presidents, were crooks.

Leonard asked what worried me most about the campaign, and I replied: first, the low level of Johnson's speeches; and second, the fact that while people don't love Lyndon, they fear Goldwater. Unlike the campaign of Franklin Roosevelt, whom people loved, or of Eisenhower, whom people liked, or of Truman, whose spunk people admired, the public really doesn't get enthusiastic over Lyndon. To them he's an able strategist and a political operator but not a great figure.

Bess picked me up at the house to drive out to the farm. We got to talking about the trip to Greece and my column on Lynda Bird and her press-shy activities there. Bess confirmed what the president had told me the day before, that Lynda was jealous of her younger sister, Luci. This apparently has increased ever since the *Life* cover story on Luci. This had been okayed by the president for both Lynda and Luci jointly, but at the last minute Lynda ducked out and refused to cooperate. So, the story was about Luci alone. Since then she has been more sensitive than ever.

She's going on the whistle-stop trip with her mother, and the hope is that she will get accustomed to the photographers. I suggested that her mother ought to take her in hand a bit, but Bess said Lady Bird is much too gentle. She would never be very firm; her father's the only one who can.

Bess described Lynda as bright, sweet, and a wonderful person when you get to know her but who has the habit of antagonizing people.

Representative Keogh of Brooklyn has sued me for another $2 million.

SUNDAY, SEPTEMBER 27 | The Warren Report was aired on TV, and I confess that when I saw it, it raised some of the doubts I once had as to whether there was not some kind of a conspiracy behind Oswald. He behaved too coolly, looked too innocent; however, the weight of the evidence is to the contrary, so I suppose I am wrong.

At dinner at the Johnny Walkers, Bill Walton and I discussed the fact that JFK, now a hero, was hated just before he died. He was approaching one of the most unpopular periods of his life. Bill, who knew him well, said that Kennedy was thoroughly familiar with this fact and also knew how hated he was by the average middle-class American.

Bill thought part of the enmity of 1963 resulted from the new civil rights bill. I argued that it was more from Kennedy's stand against the steel industry and the general feeling that he was the enemy of business. We both agreed that he was not, that he wanted to get along with business, and that he hated the word *liberal*. Yet in a showdown he always took the liberal course.

WEDNESDAY, SEPTEMBER 30 | Secretary Rusk announced yesterday the long-awaited and somewhat dread news that China now has the makings of a nuclear device, which she will set off shortly. The information came from photographs we have taken from satellites over China which show the Chinese building a detonation platform. Presumably, they want to touch off a bomb during their annual celebration of the Chinese revolution, October 10.

Dined with Averell Harriman. He is not worried about the Chinese A-bomb. He thinks it will be some time before an effective weapon is developed.

Bill Sullivan from Saigon was at dinner. He pointed out that the French had sent their missionaries into the area in advance of the troops. The troops followed when there were massacres of the missionaries. As a result of these tactics, North Vietnam is largely Catholic, and under the 1954 agreement, they have the right to migrate south. This is one reason Cardinal Spellman has always been so concerned about this part of the world and has discreetly, but successfully, urged American intervention. It's the clash of the Catholic refugees with the Buddhists which has caused the trouble. Sullivan said that in the latest street rioting teenage boys on one side were killing teenage boys on the other. Part of this, of course, is quietly encouraged by the Vietcong.

I asked why the Communists had such a hold in this part of the world. Sullivan replied that they had used clever tactics with youngsters in the rice fields. They will take a boy, who has a career of planting rice in the village, and give him a job as a Vietcong courier. After beginning at the bottom, he is gradually promoted until he becomes a dedicated Communist operator. On the other hand, the South Vietnamese don't bother to train or indoctrinate their people.

**SATURDAY, OCTOBER 3** | Fred Sontag came to supper. He has some amazing information regarding the attempts of the Goldwaterites to take over the Republican Party; says they are playing not for the 1964 election but for '68 and later.

During the civil rights battle, according to Fred, the Republicans spent so much time on getting this passed that they neglected the routine work of the party and let Miller and Goldwater take over the machinery. Miller, then national chairman, stole the papers, looked in the files, served as an inside spy for Goldwater when he should have been neutral.

Goldwater is now harping on the theme that "Johnson is soft on communism." Apparently, he is making some headway, or he wouldn't harp on it so much. His latest gimmick is to claim Johnson is soft on the Red Chinese because of a proposed test ban treaty, which has been under discussion in Geneva for some time and last week was made public by Sir Alec Douglas-Home with considerably more fanfare than at Geneva. The hope of the British and the United States is to get the Red Chinese to sign it—something that is sorely needed. Goldwater makes it out as an act of secret submission by the United States—especially the Johnson administration. So far Lyndon is sticking to his guns and has even advised our NATO allies to try to straighten out their relations with the Communist countries.

**WEDNESDAY, OCTOBER 14** | Luvie has been slightly under the weather, so I went with the Elliott Roosevelts to the Kuwait embassy for a foreign students' money-raising dinner. Afterward we were supposed to go to a big sports jamboree. I always feel guilty when I meet these very nice Arabs. I have pounded the hell out of Nasser, and I think he deserves pounding. I have not criticized the emir of Kuwait, who has done a wonderful job of governing his people. Nevertheless, the Arab world somehow gets all lumped together in this unfortunate battle between Israel and the Arab states. Actually, they're all Semitic, and they all should work together.

The Kuwait ambassador told me he had studied journalism at the American University of Cairo, where my name was something of a byword. Whenever a young journalism student got too ambitious, somebody else told him, "Who do you think you are, Drew Pearson?"

Elliott recalled that he was the man who first got a gangling, young Texan named Lyndon Johnson on his father's presidential train when FDR was fishing down on the Gulf of Mexico. Yet today Elliott can't get in to see the man who he helped to start up the political ladder and who is now president of the United States.

I talked to Tyler about the smears against Johnson and ways to counteract them. One would be to have Harry Truman give a televised broadcast counteracting these smears—as only he could do. Harry, however, fell in his bathtub last night and broke two ribs. He is in the hospital, apparently doing well. I also suggested Adlai Stevenson and Cabot Lodge. Cabot Lodge is sitting out the election. I think I can probably get him to do a first-rate exposé of Republican smears in regard to foreign policy, particularly the Goldwater charge that Johnson is "soft on communism."

Returning home after the Kuwait dinner, we got telephone calls that Walter Jenkins, the closest White House assistant to Lyndon, had been arrested on a morals charge at the YMCA. At first I couldn't believe it. Walter has six children, and he has always seemed to me a very quiet, dedicated, self-effacing man. Johnson once told me that Jenkins was the most faithful assistant he had and he could be trusted with anything.

Apparently, though, Jenkins has been nursing this personal problem for many years because he was picked up by the police also in the YMCA in 1959. Jenkins was caught with an old man from the Soldiers' Home. I wonder if this could have been a plant.

THURSDAY, OCTOBER 15 | Never has so much happened to turn the tide of history in a single day. On top of the Walter Jenkins scandal, which is really going to hurt Johnson, British Labour won the election, and Khrushchev was kicked out of the Kremlin.

Khrushchev's exit did not break until late in the afternoon, and I had to come back to cut a special edition of the radio tape. Meanwhile, I had to write a special immediate release column on Khrushchev. Despite it all,

Luvie and I went square dancing at Marjorie Post's. Marjorie indicated that her fifth husband, Herbert May, now relieved of duty, had the same trouble as Walter Jenkins. Marjorie is still a sexy old gal and likes her husbands to do valiant service. I think she is now about seventy-seven, but when I danced with her, she didn't act it.

The Jenkins incident is hanging like a pall over the Johnson administration. The president took the news badly in New York last night. He was fifty minutes late to make his speech at the Al Smith dinner at the Waldorf. The general public really doesn't realize how close Jenkins was to Lyndon. He handled the TFX contract deal, where I would suspect Lyndon did a little political maneuvering to get the contract awarded to Fort Worth, Texas. And Walter also got Lyndon life insurance after the heart attack, when no other company would award it.

Walter was also handling some of the investigation into Barry Goldwater, including the time a Houston girl blamed Barry for getting her pregnant and shook him down for $25,000. In the end she wasn't pregnant, but Barry paid up anyway.

Walter is a member of the Goldwater reserve air force unit, the 999th Squadron, and has taken many junkets with Goldwater. They like each other, but Walter confided that whenever Barry gets to town in the evening, he goes out on the town with the girls. Barry is making a great issue of morality, but there is no morality on either side in the Goldwater family.

Leonard Marks came to lunch. He was on his way to the hospital to talk to Jenkins. He recommended that Walter be put under psychiatric care but ran into a roadblock immediately with Mrs. Jenkins. Leonard says that one of her problems is drinking. Bess says that her husband is away every night working, which of course is true. Walter has really knocked himself out during this campaign. I am fairly sure that Lyndon had no idea of Walter's weakness. Lyndon is a guy who really loves the gals and wouldn't tolerate anyone around who had a weakness for men.

Khrushchev has been replaced by his understudy, Leonid Brezhnev, and Alexei Kosygin. The former is the man whom I have predicted would replace Khrushchev, though I had no idea it would come this soon. The State Department has put out unofficial backgrounders to newspapermen saying that the two new Kremlin leaders would follow Khrushchev's coexistence policy. I hope this is true; however, I hear rumblings in the background that [Mikhail] Suslov, who belongs to the old Stalinist clique, was behind this changeover.

Luvie and I never dreamt, when we saw Khrushchev in Cairo in May, that he would be out so soon. He looked the picture of health. He was talking about new plans for cooperation with the United States after the election. He was quite willing to wait. He talked about some of the "small things" he and Johnson had put across, rather minimizing them, but said that the big things would have to come after the election, such as Berlin.

I have always felt that the Kennedy administration made a serious error in not taking advantage of Khrushchev's overtures. Strangely enough, Eisenhower realized much more clearly the possibilities of peace with Khrushchev but had the ground cut from under him by the semicolon men in the State Department. They were also nitpicking around Kennedy, but Johnson got above them and really started to make some progress with Khrushchev.

Looking back on it, there was one suspicious conversation in Cairo which may have indicated the pressure by the Kremlin right wing on Mr. K. Adzhubei said he was coming to the United States, and I suggested an interview with Johnson. He shied away and explained, "You know, it's no secret that we are waiting to see how things go." Later Adzhubei did not come to the United States. In retrospect this may have been the first telltale sign that Adzhubei's father-in-law, Mr. K., was getting pressure from the anti-American forces inside the Kremlin.

FRIDAY, OCTOBER 16 | The full force of the Russian changeover is now being realized in Washington. It looks as if the new regime would be following a harder line. It now appears from our intelligence reports that the Red Army was partly behind Khrushchev's ouster. They objected to his cuts of conventional weapons. He told me about this in our Black Sea interview in 1963. Suslov was also against Khrushchev because of his more complacent [view] and his refusal to make peace with the Chinese.

Finally, our policy in wooing the satellites away from Moscow has just been too successful. Despite the fulminations of Barry Goldwater that we were soft on communism and the attempt of Representative Rodgers of Texas to cut off wheat sales to the satellites, the satellites have drifted more and more our way. The reports from Moscow are that there have been some tough table-pounding sessions between Khrushchev and the satellite leaders to try to get them back in the fold.

Even though Khrushchev trained the men who have now taken over, they are giving him the full force of the back of the hand. A statement was issued from the Kremlin that he had been guilty of bragging and temperament. He is to be retired on a pension of three hundred a month. A man of his activity, after eleven long years of running the second most powerful country in the world, can't retire easily. You can't talk to a man as we have on four different occasions, and on one occasion for two days straight, without getting to know him fairly well.

The men around Khrushchev, especially the pro-Americans, are also being fired. They include Adzhubei; Oleg Troyanovsky, who went to Swarthmore and is very pro-American; also P. Satukov, the editor of *Pravda*, with whom we had lunch in Moscow.

*Pravda* has been playing down American critical news of late. The riots at the University of Alabama, the Panamanian difficulties, the street riots in Harlem, were given inside play.

About noon today it was announced that China had finally detonated its first A-bomb. It was not unexpected, and it gave Lyndon something with which to take the play away from Walter Jenkins. He immediately went on television with a statement. He also received Ambassador Dobrynin, who assured Johnson of the continued policy of coexistence. This also helped to take the news away from Jenkins.

I was afraid that Lyndon would really have a new heart attack as a result of the Jenkins case. He has been working at a terrific pace, almost eighteen hours a day, and as long as things are going well, there is no danger to his heart, but when things don't go well, the doctors say it can be the opposite.

He is taking things in his stride, however, and a few phone calls I have made around the country indicate that the Jenkins case will not cut as deeply as I anticipated. Inadvertently, the Red Chinese and the Kremlin have really come to Lyndon's aid.

I talked to Pat Brown in California last night. He still thinks Lyndon will carry the state. Some of the New York politicos seemed worried, but Lyndon had tremendous crowds in New York yesterday and today.

It now appears that Walter was picked up several times, but not arrested, by the police. It also appears that the Secret Service knew about it but failed to pass the word on to Lyndon.

MONDAY, OCTOBER 19 | Khrushchev is still absent, and the United States is still stunned over the quick changeover in the Kremlin. There is much speculation as to what happened. I have written one column blaming a lot of it on the military, plus the farm program, plus the independence of the satellite countries, plus the impossibility of getting an agreement with Red China as long as Khrushchev remained in power. I fired an article to *Quick* magazine in Munich by telex.

No question but that Khrushchev and the Chinese A-bomb have saved Johnson embarrassment over the Jenkins case.

**TUESDAY, OCTOBER 20** | Saw McGeorge Bundy. He gave me a fill-in on Johnson's talk with Ambassador Dobrynin, also said that Johnson was in excellent form and really let his hair down talking to Dobrynin straight from the shoulder. Johnson talked for about forty-five minutes or an hour and took advantage of Dobrynin's call to give a message to the new leaders of the Kremlin, assuring them that the United States very much wanted peace but was not going to surrender.

Bundy read to me from the Mem-Con [memorandum of conversation] prepared by Tommy Thompson, who was present at the interview and obviously took copious notes.

Thompson came to lunch. He said he was still mystified as to the reasons for Khrushchev's exit, but he thought it might be in connection with the forthcoming Khrushchev trip to Germany. He said that Brezhnev had been in Germany just before the shakeup in the Kremlin and that Kremlin leaders were worried over K.'s trip. Sometimes Mr. K. went off half-cocked, and they might have been worried over his selling out East Germany during some ebullient session with the West Germans.

Obviously, the mustard gas used on the West German attaché in Moscow was deliberate and probably a put-up job by the right wing of the Kremlin, or the military, in order to kill Khrushchev's visit to West Germany. [The Associated Press reported that embassy aide Horst Schwirkmann, an electronic engineer, had been attacked with mustard gas while attending a September 6 church service. The USSR denied any involvement.]

Tommy told of his visits with Khrushchev, how he is gregarious and friendly and frequently lonesome. Once he called Tommy in the evening to go with him to the Ice Follies. Mrs. Thompson and Mrs. Khrushchev were along. They saw one act and then went out someplace for dinner. Khrushchev remarked: "I didn't invite you just to see the Ice Follies. Let's talk about Germany."

Sometimes Khrushchev would call up Mikoyan, the closest man to him in the Kremlin, just to have a chat.

We speculated as to what the Kremlin leaders would do with Khrushchev. If he strolls down the streets of Moscow, people will come up to talk with him, and there might be a chance of his staging a comeback.

Tommy told how he once attended a big rally where Khrushchev was speaking. He could see the high command of the Kremlin sitting behind Khrushchev, watching him intently. When he strayed from his text, they would start exchanging anxious glances at each other, wondering what he would say next. When he got back to his text, you could see from their faces that they felt better.

Tommy thinks the Kremlin means it when they say they will continue Khrushchev's policy of coexistence. Tommy has tried to bring Kosygin over here for some time without success.

Herbert Hoover died today. His passing brought back many memories—how I exposed his building of his cottage at the Rapidan River, how I razzed his foreign policy, how eventually I helped defeat him with the book *Washington Merry-Go-Round*. Looking back on it, I was unfair about [Camp] Rapidan. Hoover was extremely honest, kept receipts for everything, even the nails used at Rapidan. Yet he was so timid in the face of great challenge that the United States was set back for decades, and the world was set back by the inevitable drift toward World War II.

When a man dies, people write only the good about him, but history eventually shows him in retrospect. And I suppose that history in retrospect will show Hoover as a man with one great failing—namely, that he didn't understand the machinery of politics. He couldn't get men to work for him, couldn't get the Senate to move, couldn't get ambassadors to negotiate. It takes not a mechanical engineer but a social engineer to make our cumbersome democracy work. It takes a man who has been a senator or a governor and has the courage to crack the whip.

As a young newspaperman covering the State Department, I watched Hoover. I suppose I was one of Hoover's greatest critics at the time. Perhaps no one did more to undermine him politically than I did, with the exception of Franklin D. Roosevelt during the 1932 campaign. Yet I was sorry to see him go. He must have been a very lonesome old man sitting in solitary splendor in the Waldorf Towers looking back on history.

WEDNESDAY, OCTOBER 21 | The backlash has begun to set in against the new leaders of the Kremlin. Premier Kádár of Hungary and Premier Gomułka of Poland have both spoken in defense of Khrushchev and want to know why he was kicked out with such a diatribe. It was Khrushchev who first gave the satellites a lot of independence, and now it is Khrushchev, in his exit, who has given the satellites even more independence. Never before have they dared publicly question the Kremlin. Now not only the satellite countries but the French and the Italian Communists want to know why Khrushchev was kicked out.

FRIDAY, OCTOBER 23 | U Thant, secretary-general of the United Nations, has made quite a surprising statement—namely, that Khrushchev be invited to speak before the UN on his policies of peace. On top of this, the French Communist Party has raised Cain over Khrushchev's removal and is sending a delegation to Moscow.

The Republicans are astounded over J. Edgar Hoover's report on Jenkins, saying that he had violated no secrets. What the Republicans are really up in arms about is the fact that Hoover sent Jenkins a bouquet of flowers at the hospital with a card, which he said could be prominently displayed. The Republicans, of course, don't seem to realize that Hoover has been in the same category with Jenkins for some years, only has been careful not to use the YMCA.

Late in the evening I got a telephone call from McComb, Mississippi, that twelve freedom workers had been arrested on the charge of cooking. They wanted me to raise bail. I telephoned police chief George Guy, whom I have gotten to know through previous conversations, and asked him if he would release the prisoners on my word and that I would get him the money in the morning. This was about 11:00 p.m. He said he would.

SATURDAY, OCTOBER 24 | I got a call from McComb early this morning that police chief Guy had not released the prisoners as per his promise. When I called him back, he said that he wasn't able to find the judge. I reminded him that McComb was rather a small town and suggested that he look under the judge's bed. Chief Guy admitted that perhaps the judge just didn't want to be found. At any rate I sent the $1,200 down by Western Union, then caught a plane to Miami. I think I shall go to McComb tomorrow.

MIAMI—I spoke at a Bonds [for Israel] dinner which raised about $700,000. Claude Pepper was there and made a wonderful tribute to me. He recalled that some years ago he'd been invited to my home and that I had arrived very late and very agitated to report that Senator McCarthy had just delivered an hour's speech attacking me. I said that I was probably going to lose my radio sponsor. Claude said that he remarked to me, "Drew, you're going to be in business a long time after Senator McCarthy's gone." And Claude reminded the audience that this had come true.

SUNDAY, OCTOBER 25 | Flew into Orlando about 10:30 p.m. and drove to the Sherry Plaza Hotel. The lobby was packed, and it took me twenty minutes to get a room. Lyndon had arrived about thirty minutes before.

Jack Valenti took me upstairs to see Johnson at about eleven thirty. He was in the same large suite in which I rattled around two weeks before, and I was a little taken aback by the fact that George Smathers was sitting on the sofa alongside him, his long, spindly legs stretched out on the coffee table. With the president also were Martin Anderson, publisher of the *Orlando Sentinel*, and his cartoonist.

Lyndon was in a blue shirt, no necktie, and looking a little tired. He'd had a full day at Miami, which apparently went well. When I came in, he was talking about Charlie Marsh, who had given him his first boost up the political ladder and who had also helped to put Martin Anderson in the newspaper business. Charlie is a great liberal who has never changed his colors. Martin started as a liberal but became a vigorous reactionary, who now finds himself in the embarrassing position of trying to swing the city of Orlando back to a liberal policy behind LBJ.

Lyndon told the story of Lady Bird's TV wealth. He said that Lady Bird had studied journalism in college and wanted to acquire a newspaper. So, Charlie and the Fentress interest, with which he was then associated, had picked out a paper at Baytown, the *Sun*, which she could acquire. The cost, however, was too high, so she bought a one-third interest in an Austin radio station instead. The other partners were Sid Richardson, a close friend of Sam Rayburn's and the Fentresses.

In the end her two partners sold to her, and thanks to efficient management, according to her husband, she got the radio station up to a point where it was making about $4,000 a month. Around 1950 she decided to apply for a TV station. At that time, according to Lyndon, everyone was losing money on television. The *San Antonio Light* dropped its license because of losses. Oveta Culp Hobby of Houston was losing so much money she almost dropped her license, while Amon Carter in Fort Worth was also losing; however, Lady Bird hung on. She used her profits from radio to make up her losses on television.

"Bird had a smart lawyer, Leonard Marks," said the president, "and she was the only one who applied for that television license. If Drew Pearson or anyone else had applied, then the FCC would have had to hold hearings, but no one else applied. That's the big monopoly scandal they're accusing me of today."

Anderson recalled how he had written me after Lyndon assumed office to say that the first person Lyndon called upon after becoming president was Charlie Marsh. He also said that Charlie was keeping himself alive only to watch Lyndon get reelected.

I reminded Lyndon how, after I had written a story that Marsh had backed him for the Senate, Jesse Jones had "called" [for payment of] a $50,000 loan which Marsh had in a Dallas bank. Jesse had pressured the bank, and as head of the RFC, he was in a position to bring pressure.

After the others (except Smathers) left, I told the president about the evidence we had that Lou Guylay had come to Washington to set up the Jenkins case. He was very interested and told me to pursue it with Valenti in order to have a speedy FBI investigation.

He also told me something about Hoover's investigation of the Jenkins case. The 1959 file on Jenkins was marked: "arrest—suspicion." There was no other clue regarding the nature of the arrest at that time. Hundreds of cases have been booked that way, and there was nothing in the file to arouse suspicion.

He also pointed out that for many months Jenkins had sat under Sen. Barry Goldwater and received briefings from Goldwater as head of the air force reserve unit on Capitol Hill, which Goldwater commanded. During that time Goldwater found out nothing about Jenkins as a security risk any more than did President Johnson.

He expressed appreciation for the column I had written defending Jenkins, which, incidentally, the *Washington Post* failed to publish. I left after about thirty minutes with a guilty feeling that I had kept the president up.

I then called Lee White, the minorities' staff member of the White House, finally locating him at Clearwater, Florida. By this time it was 1:00 a.m., but he did not mind being wakened. I suggested that he ought to get somebody from the civil rights division down to McComb, Mississippi, on Tuesday when the COFO [Council of Federated Organizations] workers come up for trial on a charge of cooking. I confess that I went a little further than I had a right to do in calling Lee because I indicated that the president wanted something done. Actually, he was too tired and sleepy to register regarding this, but I figured it would be good from both the point of view of the Freedom Workers and his point of view to have at least one lawyer down there. Of course, if there is a big civil rights hullabaloo, it could react against him in the South just before election. Lee said he would get busy.

**MONDAY, OCTOBER 26** | Lyndon was down in the hotel lobby promptly at 9:00 a.m., shaking hands en route to the big supermarket where he is to speak. I parked my bags in the press bus and joined the parade. In these press buses it is almost impossible to find out what is going on. You are so far behind the president that all you can see are some of the squealing crowds when he gets out of his limousine to shake hands. They rushed down the street to see if they could get a glimpse of him. He stopped about four times en route to the supermarket.

It is also impossible to get very close to the speaker's stand. I hung around on the fringes of the crowd and bumped into three former students at Stetson University who had heard me speak there around 1945. One of them is now a local judge. They say the state was going for Goldwater and that the city of Orlando is still rather strong for Goldwater, but the tide is turning.

We hopped back in our press buses and scurried aboard the big Pan American jet, which was bogged down with motion picture and television equipment, again with more newspapermen than I have ever seen on a presidential plane before. Looking them over carefully, however, I noted that a good many were technicians and AT&T representatives. Also Western Union. The number of actual working reporters on the plane was small.

I hardly recognized anyone, which would seem to date me. Pete Lisagor of the *Chicago Daily News* was there, also Phil Potter of the *Baltimore Sun*, and one AP man I knew.

Unlike a commercial flight, the press jet starts rolling whether you're strapped in or not. In this case we started off while I was still trying to get my typewriter and briefcase bedded down someplace. People were still standing in the aisles as the jet got off the runway.

It was only a few minutes when we arrived in Jacksonville, piled out, jammed into three press buses, and followed the president downtown. This time I was a little more on my toes and got into a press section very close to the bandstand where he spoke. There was a tremendous crowd in the park, but I would say two-thirds of them were Negro children. This is no compliment to him, and later some of the Floridians remarked that it would lose him votes. They referred to it as "the dark cloud."

Also, right under his nose almost were some rather insulting signs brought in by the Goldwaterites. One of them read, "Loved by Jenkins."

The president ignored them, though during one part of his speech, he did stop and say, "To those of you of opposite philosophies, I would say . . . ," and then he gave a very brief plea for harmony after the election. His face is more deeply lined than I have ever seen it before, and obviously he is tired. At one point he waved to me from the bandstand, as did Haydon Burns, the mayor of Jacksonville, who will be the next governor.

On the whole I thought Lyndon handled himself well. The speech was good, and I was particularly interested in a statement he made regarding bipartisan foreign policy. He referred to the fact that he supported Dwight D. Eisenhower in the crisis in the Formosa [Taiwan] Strait. This was all too true and was one of the issues that I used to argue with him about when he was Senate majority leader.

I left the press plane, got settled in my hotel, had a press conference myself, and finished the column. I got some critical questions in the press conference, indicating the strength of the Goldwater sentiment in this state.

At night I spoke to about a thousand city officials from all over Florida at the Florida Municipalities Convention. Mayor Burns sat on my right. He says that his stand for Johnson will cost him about 200,000 votes. This seems a little high; however, he admits he'll win handily, though he isn't sure whether Johnson will carry the state. I did two TV shows after my talk and then caught a 1:48 a.m. plane for home.

**TUESDAY, OCTOBER 27** | WASHINGTON DC—We have finally nailed down an affidavit in the case of Lou Guylay setting up Walter Jenkins. The affidavit quotes Guylay's prospective son-in-law, John Witt, and when Jack Anderson got Witt on the telephone afterward, he claimed that he had been talking just as a joke; however, it was obvious that this was not the case. I am sure the affidavit is accurate, but I am also sure that we haven't got enough evidence to be conclusive. I spent the evening mulling the thing over and talking to Leonard Marks, who advises strongly against using the story.

Jack also nailed down Cassie O'Connor, Goldwater's mistress. He located her in a hotel in Scottsdale, Arizona. She admitted freely that there was a $25,000 shortage in the Senate campaign funds when she was in charge of the books. She was frank in saying that Barry was a guest at her home frequently, that she liked to cook for him, that he was the godfather of her son, and that Peggy was away so much she had to take care of Barry.

I suspect that we will not use this story either. I am still deciding. Certainly, I will not use the sex part of it. If we had developed it earlier in the campaign, I would certainly have used the fact that Barry made up the $25,000 deficit for Cassie out of his own pocket. Now it will look like a last-minute smear.

The president is off to Boston, Pittsburgh, and Albuquerque to speak. He needs votes in Boston and Pittsburgh as much as I need less sleep. He is ignoring Virginia entirely, despite about three times I have urged him to go down to Woodrow Wilson's birthplace. One trip down there, and he would carry the state. Otherwise, he will not. I have been wondering whether he is keeping out of Virginia in order not to disrupt the Byrd machine. There is no machine in the country which needs disrupting more, and it would mean votes in the Senate if Lyndon could put it in its place.

FRIDAY, OCTOBER 30 | Ambassador Dobrynin came to lunch. He usually accepts a lunch invitation with alacrity, but this time he was slow. The reason was obvious. The shakeup in the Kremlin is not easy to talk about.

At lunch we sparred to see who could get the most out of the other. He was interested in the American elections, I in the Kremlin shakeup. On the whole I think he did better than I, though actually there is no secret about the elections. He inquired about the Jenkins case and why it had attracted so much attention, also why there was so much homosexuality in the United States. I asked him about its extent in Russia. He said there was very little.

I predicted that Johnson would sweep most of the United States but perhaps lose three southern states. I told him a little about Mississippi and the extent of racism there; that the description of Mississippi as a police state was not exaggerated.

When we got down to the real nub of our talk, I said that some of our reports from Moscow had indicated that he, Dobrynin, was a member of the Central Committee and that Suslov had failed to notify him and other members of the Committee to come back because Suslov didn't want pro-Khrushchev men present. I also said that I understood the majority in the Central Committee was only one vote against Khrushchev.

Dobrynin denied he was a member of the Central Committee. He said he had been made ambassador after the Central Committee was appointed.

Ordinarily, the ambassadors to England, France, and the United States would be members, but he was not. Regarding attendance of the Central Committee, he said this was obligatory on the part of every member unless he was ill or there was serious sickness in the family. He did not answer the question as to whether Khrushchev lost by one vote, but he did point out that Khrushchev was presiding at both meetings, the Presidium and the Central Committee. He emphasized that Khrushchev's removal had been done in a legal manner. I said that while this may have been true, I thought it was too bad that they had to proceed with a campaign of degrading him. After all, he had done a pretty good job for the Soviet Union in the peace of the world. Dobrynin was noncommittal about this.

I asked if it was true that Khrushchev had ordered the Russian missiles into Cuba. Dobrynin said they could not have been put in there without his consent. He was evasive, however, as to whether Khrushchev was the main reason for their placement.

Regarding my request that I get an interview with Khrushchev and with the new leaders of the Kremlin, Dobrynin remarked on the first point that he would try, though he seemed skeptical. On the second, he said that five newspapermen were already ahead of me with requests to see Brezhnev and Kosygin. He indicated I would wait in line. "There is always an argument between the Foreign Office and the Press Office as to whom our leaders should see. The Press Office will argue that it's time for him to see an Indian newspaperman or an African newspaperman and that not too many interviews should go to Americans." Dobrynin recommended that my request for interviews be sent after November 7 since the Kremlin was so busy getting ready for the big holiday [USSR holiday celebrating the "Great October Revolution" of 1917] that any request would be lost in the shuffle.

It was reported by military intelligence that Dobrynin was going back to Moscow to help organize the Friends of Khrushchev, not to restore him but to make sure his policies were continued and perhaps get even with Suslov. I did not quite bring myself to ask this question, but I did ask whether he was going back to Moscow. He was doubtful. Madame Dobrynin is arriving here on Election Day.

The United Press printed the summary of a memo supposedly handed to Gomułka and other satellite leaders to explain the reasons for Khrushchev's ouster. One of the reasons was that Khrushchev had given the Medal of Lenin to Nasser plus a credit of $280 million without the okay of the presidium. I suspect this is true.

The *Washington Post* has refused to use my Sunday column on Bobby Kennedy and the manner in which he failed to act on two pro-Nazis in the United States—[Nicolae] Malaxa and [Andrija] Artukovic. Al Friendly put it on the high-level basis that it was an attack on somebody at the last part of the campaign. I argued with him but lost the argument. Later I discovered that the real reason was a call from the Justice Department. The Justice Department even had the temerity to call the assistant Sunday editor to ask whether I was going to kill the column in other papers beside the *Post*. These people at the Justice Department are naive. They seem to think that once they persuade one paper to kill the column that I am going to kill all the others.

I even got word that President Johnson was going to call me personally to ask me to kill the Bobby Kennedy column. He has not, and I am sure he won't. If he did, this would be one request I would agree with.

Jack Anderson suggested some time ago that Bill Huntley, in charge of the Criminal Division of the Justice Department, prepare a report on crime for Johnson's use. Huntley is a Republican hangover. The report is now in, and Johnson is tickled with it. I tried to pry the report out of the White House so we could use it also but failed.

Katzenbach, the acting attorney general, has been wiring newspapers denying my Bobby Kennedy story. He has dished up the same old camouflage that was used when Bobby first refused to take action on these war criminals.

**MONDAY, NOVEMBER 2** | The town is quiet. Campaign oratory is over, and the die is cast. The president has put on a prodigious show of campaigning during the final days—far beyond what was really demanded—but he doesn't want to do what John F. Kennedy did in 1960, coast during the final days. JFK almost coasted to defeat.

Bess is now in Texas with the Johnsons. Tyler's brain trust has stopped work. And I am writing Mississippi columns to be published right after the election. Suddenly I have become a great Mississippi specialist, when I used to steer as far as possible away from anything pertaining to Mississippi.

**TUESDAY, NOVEMBER 3** | Election Day: dull from the point of view of no news. I voted for the first time since 1928. That was the campaign between Al Smith and Herbert Hoover, when I was a very active Al Smith protagonist, and I remember going all the way to Swarthmore to vote. I kept my residence there for some time in order to vote, but I finally estimated that it cost me ninety dollars a year in taxes, and I, being an impecunious young bachelor, finally gave it up. I don't think I could have really kept it since, beginning with 1926, I was a bona fide resident of the District. This is the first year residents of the District have been allowed to vote.

We went to Agnes Meyer's for dinner and to listen to election returns. Tommy Thompson and Jane were there, also Herb Block. The returns were sufficient to know the outcome before we sat down to dinner.

In the last election that I covered for ABC in 1948, we did not know the final returns until well past midnight; however, I could see as I looked at the big board that a couple of key states were going heavily for Truman, and early in the evening, I think about eight thirty, I made a prediction that Truman would win.

Tonight the computers do this for ABC, NBC, and CBS. Even by eight they had pretty good predictions regarding the outcome, and as the evening wore on, they proved to be accurate. It's a landslide for Lyndon.

Lyndon did it practically by himself. He handled the strategy, the planning—everything except the speeches and the travel details—out of his own breast pocket.

**WEDNESDAY, NOVEMBER 4** | My predictions came out reasonably well: namely, that Vermont, Maine, Kansas, and all the Northeast, Middle West, and Rocky Mountain states, except Arizona, would go for Johnson. I was wrong, however, on the South, where I predicted three states would go for Goldwater. He carried five. Georgia deserted to the Republican column for the first time in history, and Alabama elected five Republican members of the House for the first time.

Actually, this is a good thing. It will mean the emancipation of Lyndon Johnson as a southern president. He will no longer be beholden to Dick Russell, the man who really made him Senate majority leader, and to the various other southern committee chairmen. It's also a healthy thing because it brings the two-party system at long last to the South.

His landslide has been much greater than anyone had ever predicted, even me. He has rolled up the biggest plurality in American history, about twenty million votes ahead of Goldwater. [Official tally: Johnson, 43,129,484; Goldwater, 27,178,188.]

The night before the election, Rep. John Pillion of Buffalo sued me for libel for $2 million. He has now been defeated. No wonder he was nervous.

Lyndon stayed up nearly all of election night. He was on television as late as 5:00 a.m., went to bed briefly, then was up again around eight. The astrologist who predicted he would have a stroke early in the morning of Monday, November 2, was wrong. I marvel how the president keeps it up.

**THURSDAY, NOVEMBER 5** | I went to see Secretary of Defense McNamara. He was working in his shirtsleeves at 5:30 p.m., when most people in the Pentagon had left for home. I said: "The president's been telling me what a great cabinet officer you are, and I have been telling him the opposite, but I haven't convinced him. He says I've gotta 'hep' you so I've come down to hep you, but before I hep you, I want you to hep me first."

I then explained the situation in Mississippi and the fact that the only force Mississippians would listen to was economic force. I gave McNamara a list of textile firms operating in Mississippi (though owned outside), together with a list of locally owned firms, and suggested that he do what he had done when Johnson was vice president and in charge of the Equal Opportunities Committee. At that time Lyndon told me how he had McNamara call in the one hundred top defense contractors for a lecture by the vice president on giving equal jobs to Negroes.

I suggested the same thing might be done with some of the textile firms in Mississippi that sell to the Defense Department. They could be given a friendly warning and then some firm follow-ups that they have to exert some economic pressure on the local community for better race relations.

McNamara didn't make much comment but seemed sympathetic. He looked over the list carefully, commented that he didn't see any big defense contractors on it but he would investigate. I then asked him about the economy program which the president had been bragging about and which was saving the government about $4 billion. McNamara explained it in some detail, also told how every shipyard and every air base was bringing pressure to prevent demobilization. Apparently, McNamara is standing up to the pressures. He said he hadn't changed his mind about one single surplus base.

"I hope you're going to remain on," I said just before leaving. "That's up to the president," he replied. "But the president tells me he is demanding that you stay." McNamara didn't reply. I had gathered he had agreed to stay on.

**TUESDAY, NOVEMBER 17** | Oliver Emmerich of the *McComb (MS) Enterprise Journal* phoned me to say 650 McComb citizens had signed a declaration of principle against violence and for equal treatment of Negroes. He said very few ministers had taken part in this, that the initiative came from businessmen.

This is a great victory for Emmerich, an editor with a lot of courage; however, though I didn't say so, and can't say so, it also is a certain victory for the column.

When I talked to Emmerich and told him of plans to check on Mississippi textiles with a view to an economic boycott, he immediately began taking notes. I cautioned him not to spill the beans on this as far as I was concerned, but I am quite sure he did so anyway. I am also quite sure that this is what counted with McComb businessmen more than anything else.

I am still getting hell from some editors, partly as a result of Mississippi, partly as a result of standing up for Lyndon. The *Meridian Star* has canceled. This is a paper which ordered the column back in 1933. The *Vicksburg Post* canceled some time ago. Nevertheless, I think the tide has begun to turn in Mississippi, and these 650 signatures are indeed a triumph.

Lyndon has flown back to Washington, and I asked Jack Valenti to get me an appointment.

**THURSDAY, NOVEMBER 19** | Yesterday McComb integrated without incident. A group of Negroes walked into various restaurants and were served. My friend police chief George Guy was on hand to preserve order, and there was no problem. The power structure had spoken.

J. Edgar Hoover had a press conference with some women reporters yesterday and really blew his top. He made an ass of himself by criticizing, first of all, the Warren Commission, secondly the Reverend Martin Luther King. Criticizing the Warren Commission won't really hurt him, but he called King "the most notorious liar" in the country. This will get every Negro leader in the United States down on Hoover and could finally prevent Lyndon from reappointing Hoover after January 1, when Hoover reaches the age of seventy.

Took early morning plane to Phoenix and read the papers. The most interesting item, aside from Hoover's press conference, was a report on captured Nazi war documents, finally made public by the British, showing that Pope Pius XII was pro-Nazi while he was archbishop in Germany shortly before the war started. I had always known this, but it was worth one's life to report it. The British report spells it out in rather conclusive detail.

**FRIDAY, NOVEMBER 27** | The Russians are getting tougher. They have blasted our aid to Vietnam and the Belgian paratroop invasion of the Congo, done with our blessing.

Bill Attwood, the ambassador in Kenya, had been negotiating with Kenyatta, president of Kenya, to try to rescue the American missionaries, but the talks broke down. Following this, Bill apparently gave word to Washington, and the paratroop invasion took place.

When Luvie and I were in Kenya last June, the main thing we noted was the rivalry between the Chinese and the Russians to give aid and win influence in East Africa. Since then I understand there has been even more Chinese concentration on the Congo. The recent statements from the Kremlin, critical of us, would indicate that the Chinese and the Russians were getting closer together.

Clayton Fritchey has been staying with us during the festivities for Lally Graham, who is getting married on Saturday. We had a "shower" for Lally Wednesday night. Clayton believes that any bombing by the United States of North Vietnam would be tragic. He fears the president is falling for the Joint Chiefs of Staff recommendation; points out that the French spent eight years fighting in Vietnam and the surrounding area; that we have spent ten years fighting there. Obviously, there is no military solution. The solution should be to put the whole matter before the United Nations.

Agnes had a big reception and dinner for Lally tonight. It was held in the old home at Crescent Place. I gave a toast, as did McGeorge Bundy, Adlai Stevenson, and others. The grandiose party, attended by the secretary of defense, Alice Roosevelt Longworth, Tommy Thompson, and Adlai, reminded me of the party I had attended at the same home in 1930, just thirty-four years ago. Tonight Alice, who for a long time didn't care much for me, was at the dinner, eighty-one years old and looking quite well.

SUNDAY, NOVEMBER 29 | Clayton is quite pessimistic about the deadlock in the UN on Tuesday when the General Assembly meets. The Russians have refused to pay $50 million in dues for police operations in the Congo and elsewhere. We have demanded that they be denied the right to vote unless they pay.

The deadlock originated when the Kennedy administration asked for a bond issue for the United Nations to pay for police-keeping operations. At that time congressmen asked why Russia wasn't doing its share, and Dean Rusk promised to get tough with the Russians. If the bond issue was okayed, he said, we would collect from the Russians.

Now we're stuck with this decision. We don't want the Russians to pull out of the UN. It would be catastrophic. We don't think the Russians want to pull out, but in turn they have their own political problems with the right wing in the Kremlin and with the Chinese. Furthermore, we are now backing Tshombe, the right-wing leader, who was anathema to us and the Communist world only a few months ago. So, the Russians are adamant against any money for Tshombe's support directly or indirectly.

Adlai flew back to New York this afternoon to try to iron things out. Rusk and Gromyko are having a lunch in New York to do likewise.

TUESDAY, DECEMBER 1 | The UN session opened thirty minutes late. Gromyko adopted the hard line and refused to compromise, though he finally went along with U Thant's plan to avoid any votes. Thus, the new president of the General Assembly, Alex Quaison-Sackey from Ghana, was elected by acclamation.

Tommy Thompson explained to me this morning that there seemed to be considerable dissension inside the Kremlin and a lot of influence by the hard-liners. Thus, Brezhnev and Kosygin are leaning toward Suslov, who represents the Stalinists. The split apparently is about fifty-fifty.

Tommy said that regardless of some of the tough speeches, the Kremlin definitely wants coexistence. He also said that Khrushchev was quite changeable and frequently popped off one way, then another. At least the present Kremlin leaders are being consistent. The Chinese, he says, are pushing them hard.

I tried to get Tommy to let me have the reports on the first Geneva Summit Conference in 1955 insomuch as they are now almost ten years old. He was reluctant.

TUESDAY, DECEMBER 8 | [At home Pearson was host over coffee for the women's editor of *Pravda* and others.] The Russians took notes as if I was giving a very important interview. The main point the Russians wanted was my opinion as to what President Johnson would do. I find myself embarrassingly in the position of being a spokesman for the president, though I have not actually seen him since Orlando, Florida, in late October, at which time he was busy reminiscing over a highball.

I think my diagnosis was correct that Johnson, having been elected by a tremendous majority, and despite the right wing, nevertheless was a cautious man and was feeling his way. He could not come out with cure-alls overnight, first because he didn't know what the Russian position was on many matters, second because he had to talk to his main allies, especially the British. I said that Johnson had issued a moderate statement regarding North Vietnam and was not going to be pushed into any extreme position there by his advisors. I reminded them that he had been much more conciliatory toward Khrushchev than the State Department last year and had tried to take various steps to build for peace all during the year. I said he would continue to do so if he got any sort of cooperation from Moscow.

**WEDNESDAY, DECEMBER 9** | Sandy Gottlieb of SANE [National Committee for a Sane Nuclear Policy] brought two young Fair Dealers to lunch, Marc Raskin, who once worked for McGeorge Bundy, and Richard Barnet, who worked on disarmament with Bill Foster.

They argued that MLF was now outdated, that Von Hassell, the German foreign minister, didn't want it in 1962, when he first came here, and that the whole problem of arms must be connected with a political settlement.

Secretary McNamara has a much more fluid mind when it comes to disarmament than Rusk, who is a bureaucrat. They reminded me of Johnson's statement of January 21, 1964, to the Geneva Disarmament Conference, offering to cut back missiles and bombers. Rusk's statements on disarmament were described by the British arms expert as "woof." The State Department is opposed to arms reduction because it hurts the Cold War, which is needed to keep our alliances together. Without it the alliances would fall apart.

Being the most powerful nation in the world makes us poor negotiators. We depend on brawn, not brains. Countries without power, like France, have been skillful and done well. It has become a major power today just by brains.

**SUNDAY, DECEMBER 20** | CHICAGO—Took Charles Evers, head of the NAACP [National Association for the Advancement of Colored People], to lunch in the Pump Room. Some years ago Charles was in charge of the men's washroom at the Ambassador East Hotel. His brother was killed in the cause of states' rights, and his father was beaten up so that he got a brain tumor and later died.

The Pump Room is the swankiest restaurant in Chicago, and it was interesting to take Evers to it for lunch. He remarked, rather pathetically, as we sat down and scanned the menu, "I tell my children one of the problems of integration is to get used to eating the white man's food."

He tells me that the NAACP cannot work with COFO and that COFO, the young students, are seriously spoiling the integration movement in the South. I think this is probably true. Certainly, in McComb the white leaders, liberal as they are, will not talk to COFO. They will talk to the NAACP.

Yet these young students who came down last summer have put Mississippi and civil rights on the map. They have advanced the cause of civil rights perhaps twenty-five to fifty years in Mississippi. Evers paid tribute to them by saying that he was very glad they were there, that when they were present it took the heat off him and he was in no great danger.

This was the night of our big entertainment. Sammy Davis Jr. flew all the way to be the star attraction. The other stars were Dick Gregory, Eartha Kitt, George Gibson. It was quite an evening; however, many people who ordinarily would have come were at a Bonds-for-Israel dinner in the same building—seven thousand of them—each having bought a $1,000 bond to get in. I went over to see Hubert Humphrey, who was the guest of honor, and asked him to come over and say a word or at least plug our show in his speech. He declined, said the Israeli hosts had told him not to.

It was an all-Negro cast in our show and virtually all Negro assistants behind the scenes. I was one of the few white men in evidence. It gave me a strange feeling. Yet the Negro performers were terrific, and the show was one of the best I have attended. This was really a case of Negroes helping other Negroes, which has not happened too much in the past and is what we need.

**MONDAY, DECEMBER 21** | LBJ is going to Texas. He sent us some honey and home-cooked bread. Since we had no servants this evening, Luvie cut some of the bread, and we enjoyed it.

Rusk is still trying to collect some dues from the Russians for the UN; the Vietnam situation is bogged down worse than ever; the Congo is revolting; and the Republicans are still churning, trying to decide whether to kick out Dean Burch as chairman. Barry Goldwater is back in town to help with the churn.

**WEDNESDAY, DECEMBER 23** | Harriman came in at seven thirty for a drink. Things have been going from bad to worse in the international field, and he gave me a little pep talk about it.

Today Nasser told the United States to jump in the lake because we disagreed with him about sending Egyptian arms to the Congo. Three days ago the military threw out the civilian government in South Vietnam, and today General Khanh blasted Ambassador Maxwell Taylor by name and also told the Vietnamese people that his country would rather remain poor than knuckle under to a powerful foreign nation, that is, the United States.

Averell argued that despite the kick from Nasser, we should not cut off aid. He pointed out that the Russians would give anything to have us break relations with Nasser and that during the period since the Suez crisis, the Russians had got very little for the money they had poured into Egypt. Averell said we had to turn the other cheek and remember that we were playing for the support of the Egyptian people, not the Egyptian dictator.

He talked about President Sukarno of Indonesia and said we had to wait until Sukarno goes, which should not be long. Then he corrected this and asked me not to use it. What he had in mind, of course, was the fact that Sukarno is terribly ill.

Averell said the oil properties we have in Indonesia are far more important than the food we send to the Indonesian people. If Indonesia goes Communist, he argued, all of Southeast Asia goes Communist.

"When I was in charge of the Marshall Plan in Paris," he said, "I used to tell the French, 'This is your project. We're putting in one-fifth. You're putting in four-fifths. We are only helping you.'

"I told Congress later that our plan was to get people to help themselves. Gratitude, I told them, is very fleeting. We don't expect people to be grateful. We want people to be on their own.

"The president is very understanding on these matters. He does not go off on tangents and crack down on countries because they burn a library or denounce us publicly."

As Averell was about to leave, he said that Dean Acheson was a bad influence and asked me to help counteract him. "Dean's great field was Europe," Averell said. "He turned up his mustaches at almost every part of the world except Europe. He has been telling the president we must follow a hard policy, and I am afraid he influences Johnson. I want you to help counteract him."

I told Averell of my recent talk with the president, at which he remarked that a very "wise man" had encouraged him by pointing out the difficulties of the Kremlin and saying that Johnson was lucky not to have the same difficulties. Just the same, I agree with Averell that Dean is a bad influence and should be counteracted.

FRIDAY, DECEMBER 25—CHRISTMAS DAY | Abe Fortas called while we were at breakfast to say he had been talking with the president in Texas and the president wanted him to tell me how much he appreciated my help. In the course of the conversation Abe remarked, "Poor guy, what troubles he has." I think I shall have to write a column about Johnson's troubles and the fact that the average American citizen not only doesn't realize his troubles but expects everything in the world from him, including the answers to his mail.

In addition to the Congo and Vietnam, Senator Fulbright of Arkansas kicked over the traces today by announcing that he would not handle the foreign aid bill under the administration's present plan. It is rather complicated, but this is a blow to the president.

**WEDNESDAY, DECEMBER 30** | LBJ has sent a greeting to the Kremlin for the New Year—rather a comprehensive and enlightened one. He proposes a complete ban on nuclear arms tests and goes about as far as he can in wooing the Kremlin. I must say that in his relations with Moscow, Lyndon has been surprisingly liberal.

# 1965

## ANNALS

President Lyndon Johnson used his mastery of the legislative process to steer the 1964 Civil Right Act. He opened this year with a series of measures dubbed the "Great Society," which were passed by large congressional majorities. This year would prove to be the zenith of Johnson's influence and power.

With college campus antiauthority demonstrations increasing, 1965 would also become a year in which "radicals" of the New Left would question the legitimacy of the nation's "social compact." The rise of the counterculture movement, along with the growing feminist movement, showed that America was at the cusp of changes in social norms that would strain the traditional framework on which Western culture had been based.

Daniel Patrick Moynihan, an assistant secretary in the Labor Department, issued a report about the collapse of family values. It showed that in 1965, 3.1 percent of whites and 24 percent of blacks were born to a single mother. (By 2009 over 29 percent of whites, 73 percent of blacks, and 53 percent of Hispanics were born to single mothers.)

Among Moynihan's staffers was Ralph Nader. In 1965 he gained notoriety as the author of *Unsafe at Any Speed*. The book was influential and led to mandatory seat belt laws.

At the University of California–Berkeley, the Free Speech movement began during the 1964–65 academic year, with demonstrations paralyzing the campus. Despite the dean's imposition of restrictions on political activity, by spring thousands of students were protesting the war.

By the end of the year the number of U.S. troops in Vietnam had increased to nearly two hundred thousand. Students on many campuses burned their draft cards and turned against Johnson, while he was scoring legislative victories.

In the first session of the Eighty-Ninth Congress, LBJ proposed eighty-seven bills, eighty-four of which eventually became law, including the creation of Medicare and Medicaid and the Voting Rights Act. Despite Johnson's legislative achievements, Vietnam overshadowed his domestic legacy.

Some basic facts in 1965:

World population: 3,350,250,014

U.S. population: 194,302,963

U.S. gross domestic product: $719.1 billion

Makeup of U.S. Congress (based on 1964 election):

Senate: Democrat 68, Republican 32

House of Representatives: Democrat 295, Republican 140

Number of women in the Senate 2 (2%), House 11 (2.5%)

—Ed.

# THE DIARY

**TUESDAY, JANUARY 5** | The Senate Democrats yesterday picked Russell Long as whip. They will live to regret this. Russell is an improvement over his father, but there is a streak of insanity in the Long family. It cropped up in Huey midway in his career and led to his assassination. It cropped up in Earl when he was governor, though he was for the most part an excellent governor; however, he drank himself to death. And it crops up occasionally in Russell. He seems to have licked his alcohol problem, and he's done a terrific job on some things.

Dick Gregory and Charles Evers of Mississippi came to dinner. Dick had been in town rallying the Mississippi Freedom Democratic Party, and Evers had been in New York attending the national meeting of the NAACP.

Evers has been under attack from leftist Negro groups, including SNCC [Student Nonviolent Coordinating Committee] and COFO. Charles maintains it isn't necessary to demonstrate and resist arrest in the South anymore to integrate restaurants. "The law is on our side," he says. "All I have to do is to go into a restaurant, and if they turn me away, I call my lawyer and tell him to get the facts."

Gregory told me how he'd gone to Patterson, New Jersey, during the Negro riots last summer, also to Philadelphia and Cambridge, Maryland, to quell riots. "For four hundred years the Negro has been nonviolent," he said. "When he was pushed around on the street by the white man, he didn't push back. His wife told him, 'Don't get into a fight. You just stay with me.'

"But when he saw television and those police dogs in Birmingham and the cops pushing the Negroes around, that's what changed him."

I hadn't realized before how much Gregory had done during the riots last summer to prevent bloodshed. He really deserves a medal for standing up before thousands of angry people and quieting them down.

**WEDNESDAY, JANUARY 6** | Lunched with the Czech minister, Duda. He wanted to quiz me about the president's State of the Union message and what the president had in mind regarding an exchange of visits with Moscow. I told him Johnson had always wanted to improve the peace. I said I understood there had been some diplomatic feelers regarding an exchange of visits which hadn't gone far. Therefore, Lyndon had taken the bull by the horns with his public invitation.

I told Duda I thought Johnson would try to go to Europe in late spring or early summer, then on to Moscow if the invitation was extended. He said the Kremlin leaders would be busy with their March 1 conference for the Communist world, then with their trip to England later in the spring. He also said there was some talk of a meeting at the UN next September, attended by all heads of state, in order to bolster the prestige of the UN. This was to take place on the twentieth anniversary of the UN, so we speculated that Brezhnev and Kosygin might want to come to Washington at that time to see Johnson.

So far the Kremlin has not published in the Moscow press any word of Johnson's invitation. Later in the day part of the State of the Union message was published. Meanwhile, *Pravda* came out with a blast against the main part of the message, calling it a hodgepodge. I supposed this was aimed at trying to appease the Red Chinese and also at reversing Khrushchev's more friendly policy; however, it isn't going to set well with Lyndon.

We discussed the subtle byplay between the White House and the Kremlin in reducing arms budgets. He said he had known all about the manner in which Dobrynin had gone to the White House to ask how much the American military budget was to be reduced, and following the reply, the Kremlin announced that it was going to cut and that the U.S. budget was going to be cut, likewise. We agreed this was constructive and skillful diplomacy.

**FRIDAY, JANUARY 8** | Sukarno has finally pulled Indonesia out of the UN. The State Department informs me he has cancer and that it's a matter of waiting until he finally bumps off.

**MONDAY, JANUARY 11** | CHICAGO—My niece and nephew, Julie Lang and her husband, didn't turn up [at the cocktail party to market "Pearson's Farm" products], and a lot of other guests were no-shows. Dick Gregory did come. He has a delightful sense of humor as well as a crusading fervor, and he can turn one or the other off at will.

After the cocktail party we went to the Ambassador East's Pump Room with Herb Cobey and bride and a couple of other people, plus Dick Gregory. The waiters fawned over Dick.

**WEDNESDAY, JANUARY 13** | WASHINGTON DC—Had my first real talk with Humphrey since the election. He has an office in the old State, War, and Navy Building just across West Executive Avenue from the White House. His desk was clean of papers. This is new for Hubert.

I reminded him he had promised me over the telephone to see a German editor, Hagen of *Quick* magazine. Hubert remembered immediately. "I'm not vice president yet. I'm not a senator, but after I'm vice president, then I'll be able to talk to your German editor.

"Lyndon is going to be a great president. He is working like hell. No one knows government better. He calls me several times a day. I go over to the White House every day, but I have to be careful. You've known him longer than I have. He watches every little thing. He's going to forgive me if I make some mistakes. He knows that's human nature, but he isn't going to forgive me if I nudge him or compete with him.

"I told Muriel the other day, 'I've got a one-man jury sitting on me. If I am nominated again in '68, it will be up to one man. After three months and we both make it together, I won't be worried, but for the first three months I'm going to be careful.'"

I told him that the president last spring told me he wanted a vice president who could take a lot of burdens off his shoulders. I also told Hubert, for the first time, how the president had asked me to make a survey around the country and come up with a recommendation for his running mate. I told him who I had recommended, but I also added that I was sure the president would have picked him anyway. I told him how the president has rehearsed all the potential candidates with me and weighed their virtues and liabilities.

Hubert remarked that he was sure that my recommendation had carried some weight because he recalled the president was on tenterhooks trying to make up his mind.

Hubert went on to tell me about his relations with the president. "You come into his office. He doesn't ask you how you are. He gets his nose right down close to your face and says, 'What have you done?'"

Hubert then pulled out a letter signed, I believe, by Kermit Gordon, director of the budget, which said the Agriculture Department would require a supplemental appropriation of $1,742,000,000 right away.

"The Agriculture Department already has a budget of $8 billion, and now they've got to have more," Hubert said. "The reason is that every farmer has taken a loan on his crop. The farm market is even more sensitive than Wall Street. The rumor is around that this administration is going to reduce farm price supports, so every farmer has decided to get rid of his crop at the highest price right now. He can't lose. If the price drops, the government is stuck with his price. If the price goes up, then he can pull his crop back and sell it at a higher price. So, all the corn, cotton, and rice is now dumped on the government, and the Agriculture Department has to have the money to pay for the loans."

Humphrey then outlined his proposal to curtail price supports on a graduated scale for the big farmers. Second, he planned to keep supports and relatively higher ones for the little farmer.

"Kermit Gordon was right when he said the other day that one million farmers could support all the people of the United States, but we can't do that; it would just swamp the cities. And we can't cut off subsidies from these big farmers too soon. Some of them now get a subsidy of $750,000. I plan to take a figure, say $20,000, for subsidy, and when they go beyond that, they can't get any. It will be like the graduated income tax, with more help for the little farmer just to keep him on the land.

"If we let him go off the land, our small towns will become skeletons. I'm not talking about towns of two or three hundred; I'm talking about towns of ten to fifteen thousand. They'll be ghost towns. So, it will pay us to keep the small farmer on the land rather than pay for retraining programs if he goes to the city.

"No one man can run the Agriculture Department. Commodities policy is fixed by committees. Out of twenty-five men on a committee, twenty-two are producers. They fix the policy. And once they decide what the price support should be, they plant their rows of corn a little closer together or apply more fertilizer, and they can swamp the government with extra crops.

I told Hubert that Martin Luther King had come to see me early in the week and had a plan for boycotting products manufactured in Mississippi. I didn't tell Hubert I had helped to inspire the plan. I said King would probably begin with Sears, Roebuck, which had five factories in Mississippi manufacturing women's underwear, and would start with a boycott of these products. I said King and other Negro leaders were tired of trying to persuade the Mississippians to permit Negroes to vote the long hard slow way, by registration drives, and wanted to go for the kill right at the top.

Hubert said that you had to hit the power structure and agreed this was the best way to do it.

I told him I'd seen Secretary McNamara about cutting off the purchase of textiles for Defense Department uniforms if manufactured in Mississippi and urged that the DOD follow the same tactics that Johnson had done as vice president in charge of the Equal Opportunity Commission. Hubert agreed. He said: "Write a one-page memo for the president and have Jack Valenti put it on his desk. He'd like to know about this, and he'd appreciate a memorandum from you. He respects you tremendously."

At one point Hubert said: "The president is a man who can bawl the hell out of you and then take you in his arms and love you. Perhaps it's because he feels sorry that he bawled you out." I thought this was an accurate description of Lyndon.

SATURDAY, JANUARY 16 | Today in Jackson, Mississippi, a federal grand jury has indicted sixteen white men in connection with the murder of the three civil rights workers in Philadelphia, Mississippi. They will probably be acquitted when they finally go to trial. At least the Justice Department is trying.

I sent a memo yesterday to the president, telling him about my conversation with Martin Luther King and plans for a boycott of Mississippi products. It was really a boycott of the South that won the Civil War. The South couldn't ship cotton, couldn't import manufactured goods, couldn't buy arms from the outside. Its troops were indomitable in battle, but its industrial system was nil. Today, if Martin Luther King succeeds in putting a boycott on Mississippi goods, Mississippi will have to surrender.

TUESDAY, JANUARY 19 | Luvie and I went to the inaugural concert with about eight guests. It began on the dot of eight thirty, with the president entering his box a little early. It was a good concert, and Lyndon seemed to enjoy it.

After the concert we went to a reception given by Abe Fortas and Mary Lasker at the State Department. The president and Lady Bird dropped by briefly, and he danced. Lady Bird came through to shake hands with people. She has an amazing memory. She called many people by their first names, including me.

**WEDNESDAY, JANUARY 20** | This is the big day. The sun came out and smiled on the inaugural. About fifteen minutes before noon, the ceremony started with the [U.S.] Marine Band, the Mormon Tabernacle Choir, and the swearing-in of Humphrey. At 12:00 noon the president's term expired. Four years before, Kennedy was so late taking the oath that for twenty-nine minutes the United States was without a chief executive. This time our country lacked a president for only three minutes.

It was a simple and beautiful ceremony. I felt personal pride in the fact that Lyndon was finally taking office completely on his own, for a four-year term, after one of the greatest victories in history. When you have been through all sorts of tribulations with a man, sometimes opposed him but always helped him at the crucial moment, you almost feel that you were part of his victory.

The first time I helped Lyndon was when he was running for the Senate against Coke Stevenson, then governor of Texas, and I sent David [Karr] out to the airport to interview Stevenson regarding the Taft-Hartley Act. Lyndon later claimed this interview tipped the scales in his favor and elected him to the Senate. Since he won by only eighty-seven votes, a lot of people could claim credit for his victory. In every election since then, I have gone all out for him, though there have been times in between when he wished he had never heard my name.

**FRIDAY, JANUARY 22** | I took Hagen to see Secretary Rusk for a background session. Rusk was eloquent.

Among other things he said he expected the NATO and Warsaw Pact nations to come through the next fifty years without war. The statement did not surprise me for its factual content, but it did surprise me that Rusk said it.

We later interviewed Hubert Humphrey. He showed us through his office, which was once occupied by Franklin D. Roosevelt when he was assistant secretary of the navy.

At the end of our talk, which chiefly dealt with American and German agriculture, I talked to Hubert about civil rights in Mississippi. I told him that Internal Revenue ought to crack down on the sheriffs who had been taking graft and that the Mississippians had found a loophole in the Civil Rights Act, whereby if they got into litigation with the government, they would not have to integrate their schools until the court order was finally issued.

Hubert asked if I had seen the president lately. I said I had not. "You ought to see him. These southerners are so charming and adroit that they get in the opposite point of view, and you need to get over there. He talked about you last night and said he hadn't seen you lately."

**SATURDAY, JANUARY 23** | At about 2:00 a.m. the president was taken to the Bethesda Naval Hospital. The bulletin said he was suffering from a bad cold with respiratory complications and a temperature of one hundred. Luvie and I can hardly believe this. When you are suffering from a cold or lung congestion, you don't go to the hospital at 2:00 a.m. We remembered the president's previous heart attack. It was a serious one, and only a long rest in the hospital brought him back.

Yesterday Hubert told me he and Johnson had signed a letter, on file at the Justice Department, that in case the president should become incapacitated, the vice president would take over. The Constitution is vague on this point.

**SUNDAY, JANUARY 24** | Tyler says the president is just suffering from a bad cold. Why, however, did he scare everyone by going to the hospital at 2:00 a.m.? The town is rife with rumor. The president is sensitive about his health and knows how much people worry about his former heart attack. Personally, I can't believe he was suffering from only a bad cold.

Winston Churchill died about 8:00 a.m. My column about his wartime mistakes will be published tomorrow morning.

**TUESDAY, JANUARY 26** | There has been more hoopla over Churchill's death than any other man in years, even more than Kennedy's. Churchill even wrote his own funeral directions and specified that his body was to be carried on a barge up the River Thames, the first Briton to be so honored since the days of Lord Nelson.

**SUNDAY, FEBRUARY 7** | Early this morning the United States sent a squadron of navy bombers from carriers in the Gulf of Tonkin over North Vietnam. The raid was in retaliation for a surprise attack on an American military compound at Pleiku in South Vietnam, about two hundred miles north of

Saigon. The Vietcong were able to sneak up to the wall of the compound and touch off bombs, which killed eight Americans and wounded a hundred. There was also some mortar shelling from a distance.

Washington is full of speculation as to what will happen next. The raid took place while Kosygin was in Hanoi, and the early reports are that American planes raided the outskirts of Hanoi.

The mystery is how the Vietcong were able to penetrate to the walls of the American barracks without being detected by the South Vietnamese guards. I suspect it was a matter of desertion and an inside job.

There is also some feeling that the American military were looking for a chance to crack down on North Vietnam. They have been itching to bomb for a long time, but Johnson wouldn't let them.

**MONDAY, FEBRUARY 8** | Saw the president at 8:00 p.m. The appointment was set for seven fifteen, but he had a long meeting, first with Acting Secretary of State George Ball and McGeorge Bundy and later with Secretary of the Treasury Dillon and William McChesney Martin. When I got in, he ordered two Sankas, seemed very relaxed, and said, "Let's talk." I apologized for taking up his time, but he said, "No, I just want to visit with you."

When I came in, he was on the telephone with Orville Freeman and remarked, "Your friend Drew Pearson's just come in, so you better not say too much. You probably were leaking to him anyway." Orville said something to him in reply, to which the president said: "He doesn't give away his sources. He told me that thirty-five years ago."

He began by talking about the balance of payments. "This is the toughest problem we face," he said. "We're losing $1.7 billion on tourists. We've got all these schoolteachers who've saved up their money . . . and want to go to Europe. They eat de Gaulle's French food and drink de Gaulle's wine and spend their money, and you can't blame them, but we have got to do something about it.

"But you have papers in all these states, and all these states have beautiful tourist attractions. Look at Wyoming. Lady Bird said she went out to Idaho and Wyoming and had never seen such beautiful places. Even Mississippi has wonderful old mansions. You can write about all of 'em, and your papers will be pleased, and you'll help to keep the dollar at home.

"Lady Bird's had a slew of mail ever since she started this beautification program. She's got Mary Lasker, who brought flowers and trees to New York, to come down here and do the same thing for us. Today I sent a message to Congress, one of the best I've ever sent, on improving the United States. We've got machines developed to take all these cars along the highway and crush them so they won't be an eyesore. We're going to take all this mud and filth that comes down the river and clean up our rivers. We've got to make the companies that are pouring their waste into these streams quit doing it. I've got some boats here. I haven't been down to the river much because it smells like a garbage can. We'll try to clean up the Potomac so we can enjoy it."

He picked up the telephone, got Marvin Watson, and asked him to bring in the message he'd just sent to Congress. Then he had me read the first paragraph, then turned through the message and showed me some of the old army bases and old parks that Udall was going to acquire.

The president leaned back and said: "You're smart, and you're public spirited. I want to get your advice. I've been looking for a Republican who can serve on the Federal Communications Commission. I want someone who'll buck the networks. I want someone who'll work with the Democratic commissioners, but he's got to be a Republican or an independent."

I told the president that there was considerable speculation as to whom he was going to appoint to the Federal Power Commission [FPC]. "A lot of people are watching you to see whether you appoint some oilman from Texas."

The president then discussed Charles Ross, the Republican holdover on the FPC, and said he had planned not to reappoint him. "However," he said, "George Aiken wants him, and George Aiken always votes for me. He's the salt of the earth. And the other day I was talking to Governor Hoff of Vermont. Hoff is my type of man. He's a white-haired Scandinavian, just the salt of the earth. He said he was for me because I helped him carry Vermont for the first time in a hundred years. I asked him to recommend a good public servant, and he recommended Ross. He said he had roomed with Ross at college and there was no man he would trust more. "Some of the critics say that Ross has been too prejudiced and that he goes out and lobbies for his own reappointment. I don't like to be pressured. When a man is lobbying for himself, I am not for him.

"But when a man like Governor Hoff tells me he's for a man, I have to go back and reexamine the books, and that's what I am doing now."

I said Ross had never pressured me and that I was strong for him.

He went on to indicate—I was reading between the lines—that he would probably appoint Dolph and reappoint Ross and that the two would counterbalance each other. He remarked that Woodward, whom Dolph would replace, was a utility man and that the balance on the commission would still be tipped in favor of the public.

It was getting late, but I asked him about Vietnam. "You've done such a good job on improving relations with Russia," I said, "that I've been worried that you were going to lose it all in this Vietnamese crisis. I know what you're up against, and I sympathize completely."

"Well, I'll tell you about this off the record," he said. "About two weeks ago we had our fleet in the Bay of Tonkin ready for operations. We were going to put some patrol boats out along the shore and make some raids on the shore. Then we heard that Kosygin was coming over, and I called everything off. I gave orders that there was to be nothing that could possibly upset Kosygin's visit. No pictures taken from the air, nothing.

"I also sent McGeorge Bundy over there to coincide with Kosygin's visit. When he got there, Kosygin made a speech in Hanoi which, according to our intelligence, didn't really satisfy the North Vietnamese.

"Our intelligence reported that the North Vietnamese deliberately staged that attack on American personnel in order to put Kosygin in a box. They wanted to make it so that he would have to go much farther by deliberately provoking us. So, they brought down their mortars, all of them made in China, and attacked our base from about two miles away.

"If I had let a hundred American boys be wounded and some of them killed and hadn't done anything about it, I would have been ridden out of here on a rail. I did let one attack down in the South go without doing anything about it. I figured that if we retaliated, too many women and children would have been killed. This time I couldn't stand by.

"So, I sent for Tommy Thompson and told him to get hold of Dobrynin and tell him exactly what we were going to do. I told him to assure the Russians that we were not going to go any farther, and this was retaliation for a deliberate attack upon us.

"Tommy had Dobrynin come over to his house and explained everything. He pointed out that we figured they had mousetrapped Kosygin and that this was a deliberate attempt to stir up trouble between us. Tommy reported that Dobrynin had taken it very well and seemed to be satisfied. I don't want you to write this now, but you can say that we did communicate with the Russians." He added that this afternoon Moscow put out a statement which was much milder than we had expected.

By this time it was almost nine o'clock. I asked him when he ever got a chance to eat and how he was feeling.

"I'm feeling all right. I'm working too hard, but there doesn't seem to be much I can do about it." We went over to his desk, where there was a pile of papers. "I've still got to get this out of the way tonight," he said.

I said I understood Orrick was leaving as head of the Antitrust Division, and this prompted the president to tell me about Katzenbach and how he appointed him attorney general. "Last September, Bobby asked me to keep Katzenbach on until after the election so that he could get a better job later, having served as acting attorney general. I thought this was only fair to honor the request of a retiring cabinet member, so I told him I would keep him until the inauguration.

"On January 20 I talked to Katzenbach and asked him what he wanted to do. I told him I could find a judgeship for him, though nothing was open on the Supreme Court. He said he would like to stay in government service. He said he would be glad to do anything. I told him that Central Intelligence was open, that John McCone was leaving, and how would he like that? He replied, 'If my president asks me to serve, I'll be glad to serve.' So, I told him I'd think it over and be in touch with him. He came to dinner at about that time, a farewell dinner for Luther Hodges. I told Bird to keep an eye on his wife and see how she got along. Bird said she was considerate and the height of courtesy.

"So, one night I invited the Katzenbachs to come over and have supper with us. We didn't go into dinner until 10:00 p.m. I finally asked him, 'How would you like to stay on and be my lawyer?' He said he'd like to do anything I wanted him to. I told him, 'If it's all right with you, I'd like to have a young fellow named Ramsey Clark be your deputy.' He had already told me that he thought well of Ramsey.

"So, that's how I happened to appoint Katzenbach. It was because he didn't pressure me and was so willing to take any job at all."

On the way out, Marvin Watson, the new assistant to the president, was there, and the president said to him: "Any time Drew wants to come in to see me, you arrange it—but don't fix a specific time. Tell him 'about' seven o'clock or something like that because I'm always a little late, and he gets impatient."

I arrived late to Abe Fortas's dinner for the governor of Puerto Rico. Ben Stepansky, former U.S. ambassador to Bolivia, was present and said that

Enrique de la Lozada was hard up and looking for a job. Enrique used to be one of the wealthier members of the Bolivian aristocracy but gave all his property to the Bolivian government in the spirit of agrarian reform.

TUESDAY, FEBRUARY 16 | We are in Barbados, British West Indies, and I have succumbed to inertia. We flew down on Sunday after I spent most of Saturday night writing two columns. It was at the height of the Vietnamese crisis, and I wasn't sure I should come; however, I took some material along and in a spurt of energy wrote three columns yesterday, which I cabled to Washington. Now, suddenly, I have given in to the tropics. I do nothing but sleep. We are staying with Agnes Meyer in a place she has rented from Jack Heinz of 57 Varieties fame.

[This trip concluded with the Pearsons' return to Washington on February 28.]

MONDAY, MARCH 1 | Arrived home last night from the West Indies.

I found upon arrival that Lyndon had been putting the heat on me and various senators regarding Vietnam. There was a barrage of letters here for me, all obviously inspired by the president: one from George Ball, another from Art Sylvester, neither of whom ever write letters unless under instructions; and another to Luvie from Assistant Secretary of State Bill Bundy accusing her in effect of leaking information to me regarding Vietnam, dating back to a Potomac Marching Society Dance which I didn't attend.

Meanwhile, the president has been calling Dirksen to thank him for his support and sic him on George McGovern and Frank Church.

The *Post* this morning also published a little encounter which happened between Lyndon and Sen. Frank Church of Idaho in which the president asked Frank where he got his information on Vietnam. The reply was "Walter Lippmann."

"Then the next time you want a dam, talk to Walter Lippmann." In other words, the president is using all the techniques on Vietnam that he learned as Senate majority leader.

Meanwhile, in East Germany, Kosygin sounded off against the white paper the State Department issued over Sunday to show that the Vietcong guerrilla warfare was directly connected with Hanoi. I had written a column on Friday claiming just the opposite. I suspect my column had something to do with rushing out the white paper. At any rate Kosygin called it a "black paper."

In Moscow the Communist countries are meeting to try to get a solid front against China. None of the Asian countries sent representatives, nor did Romania. I suspect that the only country which can draw them together is the United States. Certainly, the Kremlin can't.

**TUESDAY, MARCH 2** | We sent 160 planes on a bombing raid over South Vietnamese targets last night. The *New York Times* has a story from Saigon, with all the earmarks of authenticity, that the Defense Department had planned a series of unannounced raids some time ago which were to continue until the guerrilla warfare stopped. They were not to be publicized.

**WEDNESDAY, MARCH 3** | Dick Gregory came to lunch. I wanted to talk to Dick about raising the money which he owes me so I can repay the $21,000 I owe to Jim Carey and Dave Dubinsky for the Mississippi turkey pilgrimage. Dick was much more interested in talking about the assassination of President Kennedy. He claims the Warren Commission is a fraud, that Warren wrote it in order to calm American suspicions and keep the country from being pulled apart.

The real culprits in the assassination, Dick claims, are Texas oilmen and J. Edgar Hoover. I wouldn't put it past the first; however, I can't believe that Hoover had anything to do with it, evil though he frequently is.

Luvie was so flabbergasted over the Gregory luncheon that she repeated the points at Bill Walton's dinner. Bill pointed out that Bobby Kennedy had read over the Warren Report in great detail and was convinced it was accurate.

**THURSDAY, MARCH 4** | [Meeting with Ambassador Tommy Thompson.] We discussed the Vietnamese crisis. Tommy said, "It will leave a lot of scars." While he didn't say so, I got the impression he was not in favor of these raids. I gather Tommy had made a report that the chances of Chinese intervention were slim. His reasoning went like this: Ho Chi Minh will not call upon the Chinese for help because if he did, they would occupy his country afterward, and he doesn't want to be occupied. He will use supplies from China and conceivably call upon the Chinese for some "volunteers" but doesn't want outright Chinese intervention.

Tommy believes the Russians would support the Chinese in case of war, though they have not said so and the Chinese don't know it yet.

Tommy doubts that Vietnam will come up at the Communist meeting in Moscow this week. The satellites are irked about foreign aid and don't want to supply any more to Vietnam or anyplace else. The Czechs are in bad shape economically and don't want any further drain on their resources.

Kosygin went to East Germany, Tommy believes, in order to downgrade the Communist meeting. They know it won't succeed so they don't want it to attract too many headlines. Not even Brezhnev attended, according to reports.

Kosygin apparently did not get along well with the Chinese during his recent trip to Asia. Tommy said that whereas he went back to Peking after being in Hanoi, Kosygin did not return to Peking after his trip to North Korea. He flew directly home. What has really irked the Russians about the Chinese was their attack on new Russian postwar boundaries and their suggestion that Bessarabia be given back to Romania. The Bessarabian border is extremely sensitive. I suspect that this is one reason why the Romanians have been cozying up to China and did not send an emissary to the Moscow meeting this week.

**FRIDAY, MARCH 5** | Bobby Baker came to see me late this afternoon. He reports that the Justice Department has put three hotshot lawyers on the Baker grand jury with a view to impeaching—or at least to smearing—LBJ. For the first time Bobby really let his hair down, and this is what he reported:

At the start of the investigation Bobby wanted it to go to Sen. John McClellan of Arkansas. He said McClellan could wind it up in a few days, but McClellan and Lyndon are not friendly. And Lyndon, looking over the makeup of the committees, pointed out that there were more Democratic friends on the Rules Committee than any place else. So, Lyndon had switched the probe to the Senate Rules Committee.

Bobby told me some revealing things about the past. He said the TFX contract was actually put across by Kennedy. Johnson, as vice president, had nothing to do with it. Jack Kennedy wanted to swing some contracts to Massachusetts to help his brother Teddy, and the Grumman people had promised a lot of TFX contracts would go there.

Bobby also said Kennedy had been behind the General Motors–DuPont tax deal which was worked out with Sen. Bob Kerr of Oklahoma. Unquestionably, this must be true. There was too much support for that tax giveaway at the time it came up, and Kerr, Bobby's close friend, was on the inside of these things.

The most amazing story of all, however, was one involving Sen. Styles Bridges.

Bobby says that Bridges had received approximately $1 million in contributions from various people and passed part of the money out to other senators, keeping part for himself. When Bobby Kennedy started to investigate, a very high Republican called Jack Kennedy and told him that if the investigation proceeded, the Republicans would declare all-out war on the Kennedy administration. "We will go into your sex life and a lot of other things that won't bear investigation. On the other hand, if you want some cash in the bank with me, you can have it. We can support you on most things. You're doing all right so far, and we'll go along."

Jack Kennedy bought the deal. Bridges was never investigated. Bobby did not reveal who the high-up Republican was, and I didn't press him—but I shall later.

At first the Baker grand jury investigation was handled by a Justice Department attorney named Taylor, who was fair, methodical, and not a witch-hunter. Before Bobby Kennedy left as attorney general, however, he apparently wasn't satisfied with the investigation and appointed three of his crack witch-hunters who had been working on the Hoffa case. They have been calling in key witnesses and interviewing them in a rather alarming manner.

One they interviewed was Jose Benitez, a Puerto Rican who was working out a deal with the Murchisons for the sale of meat from the West Indies. The three attorneys talking to Benitez said something like this: "What can you tell us about Bobby Baker's dealings with the president? Will the president try to impede the grand jury if we go all out? We're the ones who got Hoffa, so you know we can get anyone in the United States, even if it's the president. If Baker is indicted and convicted, what would he do? Would he squeal on the president?" Baker suggests that I talk to the president and warn him.

**WEDNESDAY, MARCH 10** | Dr. King marched across the bridge in Selma, then stopped and turned his followers back. There was no showdown with Alabama state troopers. Jane Ickes, Emily Douglas of Illinois, and Mrs. Tobey, widow of the New Hampshire [senator], went along. The president worked frantically behind the scenes to avoid a riot, which would force him to call out the troops. He succeeded.

**FRIDAY, MARCH 12** | I find myself in the difficult position of having been in the vanguard on civil rights but now being considered somewhat conservative. It's hard to explain to people that you can't send federal troops all over the nation to keep law and order when no federal law or federal court decree has been violated.

The tragedy is that northern business has been sending more and more investment money into Alabama because of the hard-boiled tactics . . . of Governor George Wallace.

Wallace wired Johnson today asking for an appointment. Lyndon wired back telling him, "Anytime." He would have been much smarter to have named a definite time and couched the telegram in rather tough, cold language.

SATURDAY, MARCH 13 | Talked to Ed Reid in Montgomery last night, who told me that Wallace was scared over recent developments. He was afraid that his image was being spoiled in the South and that the Selma situation was getting out of hand. Lyndon will also bail him out on this.

Ed says Martin Luther King wasn't able to get anyone to follow him in the parade in Montgomery, so he had to move it to Selma. The mayor of Selma, according to Ed, is a New Dealer and was trying to work out better race relations before King barged in.

I don't know how true this is, but I do know that prior to Selma, the civil rights organizations were flat broke. The NAACP was about $250,000 in the hole and had cut off all funds for SNCC. It wasn't even planning to spend legal money to defend the young COFO workers in Mississippi, as previously. The SNCC people were giving up their central headquarters and curtailing staff. Now the Selma incident has bailed everyone out. The money is pouring in.

SUNDAY, MARCH 14 | I suspect that as a result of Vietnam and the Alabama riots, Johnson has lost about 30 percent of his popular following. Seldom has the rating of a president dropped so rapidly as his in February and early March.

MONDAY, MARCH 15 | I stopped by . . . the Czech embassy for a reception in honor of a trade delegation. They are trying to improve relations with the United States economically and change the most-favored-nation trade agreement, which only Yugoslavia and Poland of the Communist nations now enjoy. At the embassy I was quickly surrounded by the Polish and Romanian ambassadors, plus the Yugoslav minister. They tried to pump me regarding Vietnam. Later I talked to the Bulgarian and Yugoslav envoys. They also were deeply concerned over Vietnam. All made the point that it was very difficult, if not foolish, to try to bomb another country into a negotiable frame of mind. I pointed out that Hanoi had not been willing to negotiate and therefore Johnson was giving them an alternative of either aerial punishment or the conference table.

The Yugoslav mentioned that Tito had sent an appeal to President Johnson and Johnson had replied with a long letter, reasonable in tone. The Yugoslav said the uncommitted nations were now meeting in Belgrade, ranging from India to Cuba, to decide what steps they could take to end the war.

Driving to the farm, I got to thinking that this might be the excuse that Johnson needed for negotiations. So, I telephoned the Yugoslav ambassador and suggested that I might send a cable to Tito myself urging a dual appeal to Johnson: first, a cessation of the bombing until a conference could be arranged; and overtures to Hanoi to come to the peace table.

The ambassador seemed to think the idea was a good one so, around eleven thirty, when his guests had thinned out, I read him a cable, which I then cabled to Belgrade. I thought I might get hooked on the old act which forbids American citizens from interfering in the foreign affairs of the United States.

WEDNESDAY, MARCH 17 | Lunched with Soviet ambassador Dobrynin. There were four policemen outside the Soviet embassy, as contrasted to the usual one. I told the ambassador Luvie and I were leaving for Moscow next week. He tried to discourage the trip, pleasantly but definitely. He remarked that when Scotty Reston went to Russia last December, he came back disappointed and bitter because he had not seen either Kosygin or Brezhnev. He said that he didn't want me to come back from Moscow bitter. I assured him I had spent some time in Slavic countries and I was accustomed to delay.

As usual, the ambassador pumped me for the position of the president regarding Vietnam. I traced the history of the president's patience in the whole matter.

I said the president had asked the Canadians to sound out Hanoi on the question of negotiations in January, at a time when both U Thant and de Gaulle thought the North Vietnamese were ready to talk. The Canadians came back with a negative report. This, I said, was why the president had finally engaged in his present bombing operation.

Dobrynin then gave me a pleasant but firm dissertation on the futility of bombing. In brief he said: "We cannot come forward to mediate as long as you are bombing. We are not going to be a party to these kind of tactics. This is not the way to bring someone to the conference table."

"I thought we were making real progress with the United States toward better understanding and friendship," the ambassador said. "I felt that President Johnson sincerely wanted this. We seemed to be making more progress than ever before, considerably more than Kennedy.

"In Russia, Johnson was hailed as another Roosevelt. The newspapers pointed out that he had studied and worked under Roosevelt. We felt that he would usher in a new era of understanding."

"Perhaps we built him up too much," he said. "Now people are saying: 'What's happened to Johnson? Why has he changed?' The Soviet press has not been critical of him. We have been very careful not to criticize, but we have raised questions."

The most important statement the ambassador made was "You must decide whether Vietnam is worth more than better relations with the Soviet."

THURSDAY, MARCH 18 | Jack Anderson was at the White House yesterday and bumped into the president in the corridor. The president complained good-naturedly: "Why does Drew keep writing these columns about Vietnam? Doesn't he understand that we have to draw a line someplace? If we don't draw the line at South Vietnam, we will have to draw it at Thailand. If we retreat from Thailand, we'll have to draw a line at Burma. If we retreat again, we'll have to draw one at Indonesia."

I had not written anything about Vietnam for some time, except rather favorable articles. In fact, the vice president had complimented me on the articles and said I was the only newspaperman who was correctly interpreting the situation and it was good for the president to have this interpretation given to the public.

FRIDAY, MARCH 19 | The president is jockeying with Governor Wallace about who will protect the freedom marchers as they trek from Selma to Montgomery. Wallace says he hasn't got the troops to protect them. Johnson replied that he had the power to use the Alabama National Guard. Wallace now wants Lyndon to pay for the National Guard. He says Alabama doesn't have the money.

If I were writing an immediate column release, I would point out that Alabama pays $1 billion in taxes and the United States sends back $3 million in federal aid.

TUESDAY, MARCH 23 | Called the White House to say I was leaving for Moscow. The president came on the line to tell me his views on Vietnam.

He talked so fast I could hardly take notes. He seemed harassed and worried but very determined.

He said he had kept the British foreign minister waiting twenty minutes already and had to go into a luncheon shortly with McNamara and Rusk. At the very end he asked me how I liked his message to Congress. I had not written him about it. I figured he gets too much mail, but I did say in the column that it ranked with the Emancipation Proclamation.

I feel awfully sorry for Lyndon. He has done such a terrific job on the domestic front. He was on the way to becoming one of the greatest presidents. And then he gets bogged down in Vietnam—a morass in which no president can win. He inherited it. He could have pulled out immediately after the election, but now he's listened to the Pentagon and the Bundys, and he's in deeper than ever. There is only one group that can get him out—the Communists and neutrals.

We went to the airport to catch a 5:40 p.m. plane. (It didn't leave until seven thirty.) Our Air India plane was supposed to leave at eight thirty from Kennedy. Fortunately, the Indian ambassador, B. K. Nehru, was with us. The plane waited.

I recalled proposing to [Prime Minister] Nehru . . . in 1962 that we promote a "Peace Year" on the pattern of the "Geophysical Year." Nehru made a speech in the United Nations that week, and this year the UN followed his idea by proclaiming 1965 as "International Cooperation Year." It has been anything but.

WEDNESDAY, MARCH 24 | We are in Moscow again, this time at the Hotel Metropole, and I am writing from a big mahogany desk, just as big and cumbersome as Lenin's desk, which I used at the Hotel National four years ago.

We have three rooms, two of them furnished with a grandfather's clock, massive Teutonic furniture, and a piano. The third, our bedroom, is warm, and we are glad to be here.

Outside, across Red Square, is the Kremlin. Immediately below our window, on both sides of our corner room, is construction. Moscow is building—everywhere. The road into town from the airport is lined with new apartment houses. Our guide said that 314 families move into new apartments every day—including Sunday.

This is one reason the Russian people don't want war. Their standard of living is higher than ever before. People on the streets look far better dressed than when we were here in 1961. There are more automobiles, and the stores feature canned foods in their windows. There are more restaurants, more hotels, and a really startling innovation, billboards and electric signs. Madison Avenue has come to Moscow—a sure sign of competition and capitalism.

There is a new airport, where we were received courteously and efficiently. Intourist even had a complete itinerary mapped out for our party of Americans under the auspices of Air India. What immediately strikes you about the airport is that it isn't busy. Ours was the only plane arriving, unlike Kennedy Airport, where planes line up to land.

**THURSDAY, MARCH 25** | I awoke at 1:00 a.m. The big window had swung shut, and it was hot under the one big blanket. I got up to read and take a closer look at our parlor. The desk is eight feet by four, with carvings of helmeted knights and ancient goddesses on the front. It is so big that it is difficult to pull the huge armchair up to it.

We had lunch with Mrs. Tamara Mammedova, long in the Soviet embassy in Washington, now head of the Soviet Friendship Committee. She reported that Khrushchev was terribly upset by his demotion. Once, when he presided over a meeting, Kosygin told him he'd made a mistake. "Then I'd better resign." "Yes, you had."

This was the first time they'd all told him together of his mistakes. They never had the courage before. The greatest blow to Khrushchev was drought and the wheat failure. He'd been telling people to expect great things, and instead they had to buy wheat.

Accustomed to making decisions himself, he's now spending all his time at a dacha near Usova. He has an apartment in Moscow but has only been there once or twice. His wife is there much of the time.

Hitherto, when a man was kicked out, he was jailed, but he [Khrushchev] has a good pension, servants, and cars.

Watch for a younger set of pro-Americans which may come into power. Shelepin is one of them. Suslov is still powerful and still anti-American. Kosygin is a detail man, colorless, sharp, disagreeable, efficient. Brezhnev is charming, broad-gauged, easier to get along with. Kuznetzov is labeled as pro-American. Because he was educated at Carnegie Tech, he is under constant suspicion. Mrs. M. advised us strongly not to embarrass him by trying to see him. Some of the pro-American Russians can lose their jobs if we talk to them. Mrs. M. said that her husband, who is No. 2 in the radio-television setup for the Soviet Union, was being very aloof and not getting mixed up in pro- or anti-American policies. She said that she could easily lose her job but she wasn't worried about it because the principle of Soviet-American friendship was too important.

President Mikoyan received the cable from Cyrus Eaton that I had asked him to send. Eaton went very far, described me as "a friend of the Soviet Union." Mrs. M. laughed at this and said she hoped it would not be published in the United States; however, because of Eaton's cable, she said she was fairly confident Mikoyan would see me. He was now in Romania at the funeral of [Romanian Workers' Party leader Gheorghe] Gheorghiu-Dej. Mikoyan, she said, is old enough to be above the others and not worry about criticism for being pro-American.

The Vietnam crisis couldn't have come at a worse time. The new Soviet leaders are just finding themselves. Bombing while Kosygin was in Hanoi isn't understood, except as a slap at the Soviets. People don't read the fine print or the diplomatic explanations.

People who see you can lose their jobs. Ambassador Dobrynin is the son of a peasant and therefore has protection. He was slated to be foreign minister under Khrushchev, but now his career has leveled off.

Menshikov, the former ambassador, was not pro-American and was antagonistic to his staff who were. He even sent a critical report to Moscow on Mrs. Mammedova, who was the No. 1 American booster in the embassy.

We went to a Verdi opera in the famous Bolshoi Theater. The curtain went up promptly at 7:00 p.m. People checked their coats and were in their seats in ample time. There are plenty of cloakrooms, and there is no tipping. The performance was a bit dull, but the opera house was beautiful. Afterward we had dinner at the Metropole, which featured a very loud jazz band which played the "Twist." A lot of people danced the "Twist" or tried to.

FRIDAY, MARCH 26 | During the arrest of Professor Borghorn, the Yale professor who was nabbed in Moscow as an intelligence agent, I entertained [in Washington] a group of editors at breakfast. This was on November 16, 1963, just before Kennedy was assassinated. Immediately after Borghorn's arrest (incidentally, I think he was acting as an intelligence agent), the State Department froze relations with the Soviet. They canceled all engagements between U.S. officials and the delegation of visiting editors, authors, and scientists. Madame Mammedova was in charge of this delegation. She called me at that time in desperation to ask me to entertain the editors, which I was glad to do, even though it went in the face of State Department policy.

At the breakfast in November 1963 was the deputy editor of *Pravda*, Inozemcev. I recall that he asked me many questions and seemed to be most intelligent. Madame Mammedova in Moscow arranged to have him come to lunch. She described him as a very influential man in the new administration who had the courage of his convictions and believed that there should be Soviet-American friendship and understanding.

The luncheon was held in a room of the Soviet Friendship House, where we were reasonably certain there were no wiretaps. Before the luncheon we had a briefing session in the middle of another room, an art gallery, with an occasional tourist coming in to look at the pictures. We stood in the middle of the room, and Mrs. M. explained that we could be safe there as far as Dictaphones were concerned.

There is a completely new atmosphere in Moscow. When we were here before, we didn't worry about Dictaphones or wiretaps or espionage. Now it's the Russians who are afraid—that is, Russians who are pro-American.

I read to Inozemcev the notes I had taken over the telephone when Lyndon called me on Tuesday to explain his Vietnamese position. Since I am putting this in a column for Friday, I saw no reason why I shouldn't give the same information to Inozemcev. The Russians are so down on Johnson that I wanted them to understand the president's point of view.

"I don't see very much to be encouraged about from that statement," Inozemcev said after I finished. On rereading it, I didn't either. It chiefly showed how Lyndon was following a mandate from Congress.

Inozemcev, who was in the United States for Fred Warner Neal's "Peace on Earth" Conference, said he'd talked to newsmen who said Kennedy was cooler, conferred with many people, and took their advice and that Johnson made his own snap decisions.

"You've been talking to Kennedy's friends," I said. I also pointed to the fact that Kennedy and Johnson had the same advisors, McGeorge Bundy, for example, and that in regard to most things, such as the MLF, he had been cautious and strong for peace.

I told how Johnson had sounded out North Vietnam through the Canadians last August about negotiations and got a favorable response. At that time, however, Goldwater was heckling him for not bombing North Vietnam, so Johnson was hesitant to stick his neck out in the heat of the election by urging a trade. This wait was probably Lyndon's greatest mistake, and I suppose he has regretted it.

Madame Mammedova reemphasized to us privately that everyone was afraid of Americans. "I don't care if I lose my job," she said, "but I don't want my husband to lose his. He laughs at me and says, 'Why do you care so much about the Americans?'"

She went on to tell us about her fear that all the goodwill built up in the past was rapidly going down the drain. "There are weak men at the top," she said. "And they are afraid. They are suspicious and worried, and your policy in Vietnam has embarrassed them. Your only hope of seeing anyone at the top is through Inozemcev. He is a good man, and he has influence with the new crowd."

**MONDAY, MARCH 29** | A day of waiting. This was the day when the Central Committee was no longer meeting and when . . . Madame Mammedova was sure the meeting with Mikoyan, possibly with Kosygin and Brezhnev, would come through. It didn't. We were told to wait all morning in our hotel room for a phone call. We did.

Actually, I didn't mind much when the interviews failed to come through. I figured they wouldn't. The lid is on in Moscow. The climate has changed. It's risky to be seen with Americans. The people at the top are giving the cue by seeing no Americans, not even for unofficial talks.

I did a broadcast on tape to be taken home; got word that the Polish embassy would require a couple of days for a visa and decided to come home. The Poles and Hungarians had been urging us to go there, but when you walk up and knock on the door in Moscow to get visas, it's a different story.

Dined at the American embassy. The Belgian ambassador, a mincing career diplomat, more interested in two weeks' extra leave than improving Soviet relations, was there. He kept interrupting when Ambassador Kohler tried to say something juicy. Also present were Mr. and Mrs. Walter Stoessel. He is minister of the embassy and seemed intelligent. She had read a recent column of mine on Vietnam. It was an old column taking strong exception to U.S. policy in Vietnam, so I suspect her husband had suggested she read it before sitting by me at dinner. I suspect also that the State Department had sent it over to warn the ambassador of my views. Mrs. Kohler is one of these North Carolina ex-beauties who insists on transplanting Americanism to the foreign country to which she is attached. She has revamped the upstairs of the czarist castle . . . so it now resembles the Hilton Hotel. Downstairs, however, it keeps its original flavor—magnificent marble pillars, a reception saloon now used as a motion picture theater, and a beautiful collection of portraits made possible by the Stanley Woodward Foundation.

Kohler used to be head of the Voice of America, at which time I defended him from Joe McCarthy. He is a wispy little man, and I am not sure how good an ambassador he is. Certainly, he is not a Tommy Thompson. He speaks Russian well and generally does not seem worried about the Russian freeze.

"I have people traveling all over the Soviet [Union]," he said, "and they report that the Russian people are very friendly toward the United States and do not want war."

Kohler insists that even high Soviet officials of cabinet rank in the technical services had expressed concern over their own government's anti-American policy. On March 4, Kohler said, Gromyko had handed him a very tough note, insulting in tone, one of the toughest in Soviet-American relations.

At about that time Soviet policy hardened. The ambassador thought it was word from Hanoi that there would be no yielding and no negotiations. Hanoi was confident of winning. The Moscow press ever since has been beating the tom-tom against the United States with scathing editorials in *Pravda*.

The Brezhnev-Kosygin administration made a serious mistake in calling the all-Communist conference on China. It was a flop, and the Chinese have been rubbing it in ever since.

TUESDAY, MARCH 30 | Mme Furtseva, minister of culture, was supposed to see us but was "in a meeting" in the same way others have been.

Went to say good-bye to the Henry Shapiros, where we got the news that the American embassy was bombed this morning in Saigon, with eight people killed.

Henry confirms Kohler's statement that Americans are generally popular with the Russian people still, though the government has stiffened considerably in the last two weeks. The Rusk statement, justifying the use of gas,* was just as stupid as Ike's statement taking responsibility for the U-2 incident. [*On March 22 the State Department confirmed that the United States had supplied "South Vietnam armed forces with non-lethal gas which temporarily disables, for use in tactical situations."] On top of this, the White House, or someone, announced that gas would be used again.

Madame Mammedova drove us from the hotel to the airport so she could talk to us where there would be no microphones. She was very frank. Madame Popova had been on the phone all day Monday, she said, hammering at Kosygin, Brezhnev, and Mikoyan, trying to get them to see me.

She failed. She, as a member of the Central Committee, could raise hell with them, and she did.

Meanwhile, Madame Mammedova was phoning their assistants, among them Troyanovsky, assistant to Kosygin and a former Swarthmore student. He was all for the interview but was powerless. Mikoyan said he wouldn't see us unless Brezhnev and Kosygin did.

The reasons for all this, Madame Mammedova explained, was they had kicked Khrushchev out for seeing American newsmen, and they didn't want to be criticized for doing the same thing. They want to keep a stiff front against all Americans at this time. To see us would indicate approval of our North Vietnam bombing—and "How do we know," asked Kosygin, "that he has any standing with President Johnson? He has no credentials from the American ambassador."

The man with real influence in the Kremlin now is Suslov. Madame Mammedova took out her purse and wrote the word "Suslov" on a piece of paper. She did not dare mention his name for fear the chauffeur in front would understand what she was talking about. Suslov is the Stalinist who led the purge of Khrushchev. He has TB [tuberculosis] but is still powerful.

If you don't show your opposition to Americans, you are likely to lose your job, she said. Dobrynin, for instance. Here Madame Mammedova used his first name, Anatoly, and cautioned me not to use his last name. She said he had called on Rusk to talk over American policy in Vietnam. The *New York Times* and *Washington Post* reported that he had not been tough and had not mentioned the use of gas. The reaction was so sour in Moscow that Dobrynin had to cable an explanation that he had talked tough. He is anxious to keep his job.

The men at the top in the Kremlin are divided: some for the United States, some not, but the Vietnam bombing has united them on an anti-American course. Kohler has no real idea what's going on. The chief Russians he sees are the wives of American newspapermen. Only unimportant Russians go to the U.S. embassy dinners.

Some Russians are saying that all cultural exchange should be stopped with the United States. Madame Mammedova is arguing that this is the time to do just the opposite. She added that it's conceivable the United States might stop the visa of Mme Nina Popova, which would be a catastrophe, as she is one of our best boosters and is fearless.

The second secretary of the Polish Embassy phoned to say they would give us a visa tomorrow. I couldn't resist being rude to him in telling him we were leaving today. We departed from the Moscow airport at 3:15 p.m. for London.

Got to London in time for dinner with Albert Carthy. He's the secretary of the Socialist International, which is the link between the Labour Party of England, the Loyal Democrats of Italy, Germany, and Scandinavian countries.

We talked about Willy Brandt, the mayor of Berlin, who is leader of the party in Germany and is pushing for power. I was surprised to hear Carthy say he believed in modifying the Oder-Neisse line in favor of the Germans, at least in one or two places. After this was done, the Russians would not have such bargaining power over the Poles. Carthey also favored modifying the Sudetenland border in favor of the Germans. These are fighting words with the Czechs.

Carthy was with Prime Minister Harold Wilson when he phoned Foreign Minister Stewart in Washington to tell him to make strong representations to President Johnson against the use of gas in Vietnam.

Carthy thinks the Labour Party will continue in office until May 1966, partly because the Conservatives don't want elections before that time. (They aren't ready.)

**WEDNESDAY, MARCH 31** | WASHINGTON DC—(Arrived in time for dinner at the White House in honor of Douglas Dillon, retiring as secretary of the treasury.)

I told both Lady Bird and Bill Fulbright about the anti-American atmosphere in Moscow. They seemed surprised. The reason, I said, was the bombing of North Vietnam. Lady Bird made no comment. Bill suggested I talk to Secretary McNamara, rather than the president, because McNamara has influence with the president.

Fulbright, of course, has opposed the president's policy of bombing North Vietnam and thinks we ought to get out. He said he'd kept quiet but was trying to influence policy from the inside.

I got Hubert Humphrey off by himself and gave him the brief story on Moscow. He listened carefully and seemed surprised that the Russians were so sour. Obviously, our ambassador has not been sending back very objective reports. Unlike Hubert's earlier concern about the situation before I left

Washington, this time he seemed more complacent. Later I learned from Fulbright that Hubert had been sat on by LBJ regarding Vietnam. When Hubert and Fulbright were together with the president, Lyndon turned to Fulbright and rasped, "Are you going to be on our side or Hubert's side?"

Hubert asked me, "Are you going to talk to The Man?" I said I was. Hubert added that Lyndon was not going to go off half-cocked regarding the bombing of the American embassy in Saigon, that he was taking things very coolly and would act deliberately.

I only had a chance to exchange a few words with the president. He looked tired and puffy in the face. When I asked him how he felt, he said he was tired—quite an admission for him. He said he hadn't slept much lately.

He gave an excellent toast to Doug Dillon. I have never seen him in better form in after-dinner speaking. Dillon replied in a rather stuffy manner.

I was afraid there would be entertainment after the dinner and I would fall asleep. Fortunately, we danced instead. Although it was 8:00 a.m. Moscow time at 12:00 midnight in Washington and I had been up all night, I felt amazingly well. I also discovered that there were some remarkably good dancers present, including my wife.

FRIDAY, APRIL 2 | Long talk with Senator Fulbright. He spent the morning listening to General Taylor's report from Saigon. He and other senators tried to pin down Taylor regarding the additional troops being sent to South Vietnam. All he would say was "some." He denied the dispatch of 350,000, as reported.

Fulbright said he had written a ten-page memo for the president on a plan for getting out of Vietnam altogether. He argues we have to help restore Russian prestige in that part of the world. We have given them a slap with our bombing of North Vietnam and knocked the props out of their coexistence argument with the Chinese. Therefore, he proposes we entrust the Russians with supervising an election in Vietnam, previously called for by the 1954 Geneva treaty. "The elections were to be held in 1956," he said, "but John Foster Dulles sidetracked them, and we have been in violation ever since."

Bill argued that if we could reinforce Ho Chi Minh and make him another Tito, we'd be much better off. He pointed to the healthy position which Yugoslavia occupies in southern Europe even though it's a Communist country. "I would rather have a Communist country friendly to the United States—and independent of Russia—in southern Europe than the moth-eaten dictatorship of the former king," Bill said.

Fulbright has sent his memo to Secretary McNamara and is to see him on Sunday. He is doing this because he figures that the president will not listen to him but will listen to McNamara.

Fulbright said he had no luck talking to Rusk, who gave him the usual line about protecting a small freedom-loving country. This was the experience I had with Rusk at the White House dinner. When he asked me about Moscow, I told him bluntly that we had played into the hands of the Chinese by bombing North Vietnam and knocking the Russians' coexistence argument into a cocked hat. "But," said Rusk blandly, as if he was rattling off a rehearsed speech, "we cannot sit by while another country is violating the territory of the freedom-loving South Vietnamese."

Something peculiar has happened regarding Ambassador Taylor. When he first arrived in Washington, Lyndon did not see him, kept him waiting a couple of days. Meanwhile, the president has not retaliated for the bombing of the American embassy. He has waited. Intelligence reports show that there is considerable uncertainty as to whether the bombing was done with the knowledge of North Vietnam or whether it was done by South Vietnamese Communists in order to stir up our retaliation and therefore solidify and strengthen the North's support for the South.

Jack Valenti called to say I had an appointment with the president at twelve thirty Thursday. He wants me to brief McGeorge Bundy first on Moscow and be briefed by McGeorge in turn. This will be a doubtful pleasure but I think an important one.

THURSDAY, APRIL 8 | Met with the president, supposedly to report on Moscow, but he did most of the reporting. When I arrived at the White House, he was out on the lawn taking a hike with newsmen. It was a wonderful April day. I sat in the Fish Room for about twenty minutes and noted for the first time that the Fish Room now had two copies of the *Washington Post* and one copy of the *Congressional Record* on the reading table, both stamped with the words *Fish Room*. There are some new decorations in the room, with the picture of President John Tyler having been removed to a reclining position on the floor, replaced by a modern portrait of a missile or satellite in flight. There were some other modern gadgets on a table. I spent my time rehearsing the things I was going to tell the president.

When I got in to see the president, he was seated at his desk reading a memo. We went over to sit in his big rocking chair, and he brought the memo along. I could see that it was captioned "Memorandum for your talk with Drew Pearson" and signed "McB" (McGeorge Bundy). Lyndon ordered a root beer for both of us, and I opened up by telling him he looked better than when I had seen him the other night. He replied that he felt all right and then told me about his schedule.

"I work from six to four," he said, "then take a good nap, then get up and have a shower and go to work again about six or seven. It's a good idea to break up the day. The doctors like it, and I like it. McNamara gets to his desk about seven. I start reading the papers at six. I finish up at my desk about ten [at night], have something to eat, look at the eleven o'clock news, and then go to bed and read the reports and the papers."

"When do you swim?" I asked.

"I haven't lately. Now that it's warm, I'll start again. Usually around noon."

I gave him a report on Russia, emphasizing that the new leaders were green and nervous and we had put them in a bad spot by our bombing of North Vietnam. "They've got problems with the Chinese," I explained, "and we have put them in a very tough position."

When I came in, I had congratulated Lyndon on his speech, and later I went back to it, telling him that it was a great thing to have opened the door to mutual Soviet-American foreign aid.

During the first part of our talk a photographer was busy snapping pictures of us. While I was flattered to be shot with the president, it was a bit disconcerting because I labored under the impression that what I was reporting was confidential. I'm not sure I gave him a very penetrating or worthwhile report. At any rate he launched into a vigorous discussion of why he had to continue bombing North Vietnam. Some of it was repetitious. He had told it to me before, except this time his language was stronger and he put in some unrepeatable cuss words, plus Texas colloquialisms.

One remark was "I'm not going to be a donkey out in a hailstorm." Another was "I'm not going to scratch my ass while they kill American stenographers. Walter Lippmann and Wayne Morse and John Ochs and Drew Pearson want me to sit there scratching it.

"I haven't killed anybody. I have bombed concrete bridges, which can't bleed. I have bombed radar installations and munitions dumps, but that isn't killing people.

"Walter Lippmann, John Ochs, Frank Church, and George McGovern don't say anything about the women and children killed by the Vietcong. I haven't seen you write anything about that, but you don't want me to bomb bridges. It may not stop them from coming south, but it does make them get off and unload and cross the river on foot and then load up again.

"We haven't committed any atrocities, but they have been slitting women's throats and cutting off men's peckers and throwing kids in irrigation ditches. They have killed I don't know how many mayors of villages.

"We've lost only 400 Americans in four years. Only 100 since I took over. Truman lost over 160,000 in Korea. And in Texas, during one Fourth of July, we'll kill about 400 people during a weekend.

"I had Walter Lippmann in here confidentially and talked to him for an hour and a half. I had John Ochs of the *New York Times* in here. Yesterday I had Frank Church, George McGovern, and Magee in here. I asked them what policy they wanted me to follow.

"Last week I had a group in here and read my speech to them. They got up and applauded when I finished." I asked the president who they were. He replied, "I won't tell you, or you'd publish it." Then he went on to tell me that it was the ADA (Americans for Democratic Action).

I congratulated him on his new position of being willing to hold "unconditional" negotiations. He said this was not really new. "I have been willing to go anywhere at any time to see anyone," he said, "but I changed the wording. Where can I go? If I offer to negotiate with Russia, they say, 'Go —— yourself.' If I offer to negotiate with China, they say, 'Go —— yourself.' If I offer to negotiate with North Vietnam"—here, the president ran out of diversified profanity and lapsed back to the conventional—"they say they're not interested."

The president was talking so vehemently, and his profanity was so strong, that I couldn't help smiling. Obviously, he was trying to convert me and had not liked a lot of the things I'd written, even though he really aimed his fire at Walter Lippmann and John Ochs of the *New York Times*.

"We have to take our Tyler Abells and our other pink-cheeked boys and send them out there," he said. "And then one night, at Pleiku, the Communists come in and kill them while they're sleeping in their barracks. And has Walter Lippmann written anything critical of that? Has Drew Pearson?"

I kept telling him that it was a great speech. He said that he had received a telephone call from Bob Kintner this morning, reporting that the speech had a 96.4 percent listening audience, which is the greatest listening audience in television history. Lyndon said he had begun to report to the nation at 9:00 p.m. in the State of the Union message, another on the voting rights message, and the one of last night. "No president in history has given that many messages to the American people in prime time at 9:00 p.m.," he said.

Lyndon talked about his domestic program. He said this week he would pass an aid-to-education bill and a Medicare bill—"if your friend Joe Clark doesn't make a speech on Vietnam to hold up the whole thing. You . . . tell him to shut up until after we pass these bills, and then he can talk all he wants." I said that I would call Joe. I started to tell him that I had saved some other senators from making speeches on Vietnam until after he spoke, but the president interrupted.

"I think you're a hell of a president," I finally told him. "In fact, one of the greatest presidents of history, but I think once you get this Vietnamese problem settled, you can go on to much more important things and really win the peace. What I want you to do is to be one of the greatest peacetime presidents in history. You've got the vision and the ingenuity to do it. There's no other president, not even Kennedy, who had."

I thought afterward I had made a mistake in throwing in Kennedy because, actually, Kennedy didn't do anywhere near as much as he was cracked up to have accomplished.

Toward the end of the talk Lyndon picked up the memo with my name on it. Clipped to it were some other reports on conditions in Russia, which he read to me. I asked if they were from Ambassador Kohler. He replied they were not but declined to tell me the source. The content of the memo was rather similar to what Kohler told me—namely, that American observers traveling around the Soviet had found people friendly and had held meetings with intellectuals who were quite favorably inclined toward the United States. They avoided discussing Vietnam, however.

"You've got to think about riding Russia," he said. At the very end his secretary brought him a sheaf of reaction to his speech, including a cable from Chester Bowles in India, which he read with considerable satisfaction. We then went over to his desk, where he showed me a pile of telegrams which were favorable and another pile which were not. The favorable telegram pile was not much larger than the unfavorable one.

As I left, the president growled, "Well, you made me miss my lunch." He ducked out of the room into the cabinet meeting ten minutes late. As he left, however, he said, "Thank you for coming in."

**TUESDAY, APRIL 20** | Bobby Baker came by. His tail is not dragging. He explained that ever since I talked to Katzenbach, things were picking up. Abe Fortas was answering his calls, and he wasn't so worried about the grand jury anymore. I am not sure he is right. At any rate, if he does not go to trial, he confided that he would probably run for the Senate from South Carolina in 1967. "Nobody has the guts to take on Strom Thurmond," Bobby said. "I was down in my hometown not long ago, where I got a wonderful reception. There will be two openings for the Senate in South Carolina. Donald Russell won't have the courage to take on Strom, but I will."

Bobby made a good point: the power structure in the South was being shaken as never before, partly by the death of Sen. Olin Johnston and by the illness of Sen. Dick Russell, who has emphysema.

Bobby should write his memoirs. He knows where more bodies are buried on Capitol Hill than anyone outside of Lyndon Johnson.

The most interesting thing he told me was the inside of the big DuPont–General Motors tax deal. The DuPonts had hired Clark Clifford and probably paid him a million dollars over a period of ten to twenty years. Clark, in turn, sold Sen. Bob Kerr of Oklahoma on carrying the ball for the tax giveaway. Clifford had been on Kerr's strategy board in promoting him for president. Kerr, in turn, worked with Allen Frear when the Democratic senator from Delaware put across the tax concession. Kerr siphoned $27,000 through Bobby Baker's bank account into Frear's political campaign. This was only part of the money put up for Frear. "If I go to trial," Bobby said, "I will show how this money went through my bank account."

Kerr also would develop oil wells, sell them to Frear for ten cents on the dollar. They turned out to be very profitable wells. Because Frear was carrying the ball, the Republican senator from Delaware, John Williams, balked at the DuPont–General Motors tax bill and helped to kill it. He hadn't been consulted. Later he was brought in on the act and helped to carry the ball.

Obviously, Bobby has been preparing for his trial if it takes place.

**FRIDAY, APRIL 23** | Dan and I went to dinner at Rep. Hale Boggs's. We were only supposed to go for drinks, I having declined on the excuse that we had another appointment. Actually, I wanted to get home to the farm; however, the company was so engaging that we stayed for dinner anyway. Present were Secretary McNamara, Joe Fowler of the Treasury, Attorney General Katzenbach, and Undersecretary of State George Ball.

Hale said he had been interested in my columns from Moscow and that, after publication of one of them, had been at the White House for breakfast and asked the president, "Did you read Drew's column this morning about your prestige dropping in Russia?" The president said he had.

"What did you think of it?"

"I think Drew was right," replied Lyndon.

Hale said that the president had a deep affection for me. I admitted that I had one for him. We agreed that he is in a hell of a spot on Vietnam and we hated to criticize him regarding it. There was some good-natured jousting between Gene McCarthy of Minnesota and George Ball and me about George being the only dove left at the State Department.

TUESDAY, APRIL 27 | The vice president said he'd been down in the dumps over Vietnam, especially when he talked to me at the White House some three weeks ago, but he felt better now. He said there had been no real peace feelers from Hanoi. Jack seemed to think there were. He said Lyndon's policy of standing firm would, he thought, pay off in the end. The president had gone through turmoil and taken a lot of criticism, but if the policy won out in the end, he would come out on top around the world.

I raised the question of the criticism the United States was taking from our friends and allies, but Hubert said that after the Baltimore speech, the reaction had been much better.

Hubert said that the president fretted over Vietnam as no other problem. He raised hell with the military over accurate bombing and insisted they confine their bombing to strict military targets. Hubert said the new South Vietnamese leader, Premier Quang, had been getting around the country and winning some support.

Jack told Hubert that one of the president's handicaps was that he had the image around the country of being cold, whereas Kennedy had the image of being warm and responsive. Jack asked Hubert to give us some human interest about Lyndon.

"The best stories about him are these sessions he has at the White House for members of Congress. He's had ten groups of them down for dinner with their wives, and they get a terrific thrill out of it. When these wives go down to the White House, it really sends 'em. After dinner Lyndon grabs 'em and swings 'em around the floor, and they can go home and say they danced with the president.

"In the old days they walked through the White House perhaps once a year and stayed there a few minutes. Now he takes them around, and even some of the old-timers tell what a thrill it is to go upstairs and see the residential part of the White House.

"And he puts on a great show in talking to these congressmen—many homely stories. For instance, he introduces Dean Rusk and says, 'I don't know why we have him around here. He can't even carry Georgia.'

"Right in the middle of a briefing by Rusk or McNamara, Lyndon will get up and say, 'I want to answer that one,' and he'll come in and argue with the congressmen. So, the member of Congress can go back and tell how he argued with the president, and the congressman's wife can . . . tell how she danced with the president.

"You might say that's high-pressure lobbying and public relations, but there has to be some cooperation between the White House and Congress.

"Once he said to me, 'I'm tired. Hubert, you take over.' I talked for fifteen minutes, and then suddenly the president comes in and talks for thirty minutes."

**SATURDAY, MAY 1** I LOUISVILLE KY—[Derby Day.] Up later than usual. Was reading reports when Mary Bingham knocked on the door to say I had a phone call and she thought it was the president. It was. He said he thought I was in my office or he wouldn't have bothered me. He said he wanted me to do something for him. "Wayne Morse has just made a fine speech on the landing of marines in the Dominican Republic. He didn't ask me about it. He just went ahead. I wish, when you talk to him, you'd tell him you had been conferring with me on another matter, and I mentioned the speech to you and said it was a great speech. I don't want to do it myself, but you can do it for me. There is no great hurry about it, but when you get back, I'd appreciate it if you would mention it to him."

The president added that it was a Communist outfit that had stirred up the revolution in Santo Domingo but that it wouldn't do any good for him to start name-calling and say so. "We've got to get the bloodshed stopped," he said.

I was in the dark as to what Wayne Morse had said, so I asked the president. He explained that Wayne had described the president's motives in landing marines as only for the purpose of getting Americans out. "His speech was very helpful. It was somewhat contrary to his position on Vietnam."

"Wayne is like you," said Lyndon. "He's mean as hell, but when the chips are down, he's always there."

The Binghams entertained at lunch—a mixed crowd, much more interesting than the Kentucky cave dwellers we met last night. Ed Pritchard was there, just as roly-poly and optimistic as ever, though he has really taken a shellacking as a result of that ballot box stuffing case and his conviction for it. A good many people in Kentucky still won't have anything to do with him.

SUNDAY, MAY 2 | WASHINGTON DC—Enrique Tejera París came by the house. He had been conferring with other OAS ambassadors on "how to bail the United States out," as he put it, in the Dominican Republic. The reaction of Latin American ambassadors was as I expected. They felt that Johnson had turned back the progress of Latin American friendship by three decades.

"Johnson could have waited two hours and saved himself a lot of ill will in all the hemisphere," Enrique said. "Now you're being called an imperialist power."

Enrique said that in September 1963, when Bosch was kicked out by the military, he'd gone to see President Kennedy and Assistant Secretary of State Martin. He said their diaries will show that he warned them that if the army took over, there would be another revolt and that the Castroites would take over the Bosch regime in part. This is what has happened.

"Now there are two factions among the rebels, the Castroites and the non-Castroites. The speaker of the House leads the latter. He could call on the OAS to send in an international police force. Venezuela would be delighted to send in such a police force to help out the United States. Chile and Mexico have said emphatically, 'No—not until the United States gets its troops out,' which, of course, is impossible. The Venezuelan army and navy have already been alerted."

MONDAY, MAY 3 | I telephoned Wayne Morse and asked him about his speech. He said he'd pounded the hell out of the president, though he'd said that the president was on safe ground if he merely protected American marines. Wayne went on to tell me about a session he'd had with Johnson, when other senators had been called down to confer over the State Department's recommendation that the military junta, which threw out Bosch in September 1963, would itself in turn be overthrown unless the United States recognized it. The meeting at the White House was in December 1963. Wayne said he registered his protest vigorously, but the president went ahead shortly thereafter and recognized the junta.

I had to leave that evening for Manhattan, Kansas. Things are breaking so fast that I hated to go.

**THURSDAY, MAY 6** | Arrived home. As I walked into the house at 7:30 a.m., I found a huge photo of Lyndon Johnson and me with a very nice inscription below it. I know he will be irked, even hurt, at some of the columns I have been writing on both Vietnam and the Dominican Republic. He is such a wonderful guy and trying to do such a good job that I hate to be critical, but the fact is that he has kissed off one of the most important policies we have built up in Latin America and done it within a few hours. He has also jeopardized the friendship we have developed with the Soviet Union to which he himself contributed much. I simply must be critical. His portrait, however, made me feel rather mean.

I'm not sure whether I can continue indefinitely to travel all night and work all day. This time I was bushed; however, I had a column and a broadcast to finish. I wrote a column about Lyndon's sincerity in offering the Mekong River dams to the Vietnamese. This column at least was more friendly.

During the morning Bill Moyers telephoned from the White House with a poll taken by Oliver Quayle showing that about 69 percent of the American people supported Johnson in landing troops in the Dominican Republic. I did not tell Bill, but this is the real trouble with Lyndon's foreign policy. He plays it according to what he thinks the American people will like, not according to what is good for the country. And he called in the Senate leaders to tell them about landing the marines instead of calling in the OAS ambassadors. It would have made all the difference in the world if he'd done the latter.

During the late afternoon I saw ex-president Figueres of Costa Rica and Luis Muñoz Marín, ex-governor of Puerto Rico. Both have been hastily summoned here to help rescue the Dominican fiasco. I suspect Hubert Humphrey had a lot to do with it, together with Abe Fortas.

"In 1958," Figueres said, "I wrote a report on a UN trusteeship for the Dominican Republic. Trujillo was alive then, and I thought the only way to get him out and restore order in Santo Domingo was a UN trusteeship. When I showed it to Juan Bosch, he said it will come in twenty-five years perhaps.

Now, only seven years later, the OAS has voted for a police force. I never thought it would happen. The UN perhaps but never the OAS.

"This will be an important organization all over the Caribbean. The day will come when Castro will be ousted and there will be chaos in Cuba. We've got to have some way to hold elections in the Dominican Republic. This is a country which doesn't even have registration for voting. Anyone can start a party. All you have to do is to get a card and have it printed, such as 'Drew Pearson, president of the Christian Dominican Democrats.'

"There is bound to be trouble in Haiti, also in Honduras and Colombia. So, this OAS commission can serve as a means of stabilizing the Caribbean."

We discussed communism in the Dominican Republic. "There was some," Pepi said, "but nowhere near as much as Johnson indicated nor as influential. After all, what is communism? If it wasn't for the fact that two big military powers, Russia and China, were promoting communism, it would be a doctrine and a theory but not too dangerous."

Muñoz was less communicative. He said he had urged the president to let a Latin American general command the OAS military force in Santo Domingo. Johnson had argued mildly against this, saying there was too much jealousy among the Latins. I suggested that Briceño Linares of Venezuela be the commander. "That was what I suggested to the president," said Muñoz.

**TUESDAY, MAY 11** | NEW YORK—Had a brief talk with Adlai Stevenson at his apartment in the Waldorf, chiefly about the Dominican crisis. He has been battling in the Security Council to protect the American position on the Dominican Republic against a Russian resolution, severely critical, which is supported by the French and Uruguay. Adlai is trying to prevent a vote on the ground that the matter is now before the OAS. So far he has been successful, but the whole thing has been embarrassing.

He said he was at the White House the evening that the decision was made. "They had received some alarmist cables from our ambassador, who said the Communists were going to take over. The president said: 'We've got to send troops into the Dominican Republic. It's very bloody. We've got to get the Americans out.'

"Rusk was there, also George Ball and Hubert Humphrey. No one spoke up to oppose this decision."

"Lyndon stuck a sheaf of cables in my hand," Adlai said. "It would have taken me half an hour to read them. Tapley Bennett, the ambassador, has been a good man in the past, but he was certainly on the alarmist side. He sent some very strong cables. In addition, the Dominican government had cabled that it could not guarantee law and order or protect American lives or those of other embassies.

"Lyndon called in the senators and representatives of both parties. Something was said about a meeting of the OAS at ten o'clock the next morning because they weren't available that night. When the leaders arrived, the first to speak was Russell Long of Louisiana. He said, 'Mr. President, if you let Castro take over one other Latin American country, the American people will never forgive you.' Dirksen then spoke up (Adlai imitated his deep voice): 'Mr. President, I am in favor of getting at the source.' He didn't say what the source was," Adlai added, "but I suppose he meant Cuba."

"Nobody was against the intervention; everybody was for it."

I asked if Ellsworth Bunker was there since I'd heard he was not enthusiastic over the landing of troops. Adlai said that Bunker was off preparing a statement to give to the OAS the next day. I asked Adlai if he or Hubert had objected. It was obvious from his explanation that he felt he could not object. Also, he was sensitive over the criticism of him in the *Saturday Evening Post* for allegedly being an appeaser during the Cuban missile crisis.

"I've got to handle this bloody mess now after the White House gums it up and without ever being consulted. It's the toughest job I've ever had. I think Lyndon owes me some consideration on this as one of the Democratic elders."

WEDNESDAY, MAY 12 | Things look worse in the Dominican Republic. They can't get [Gen.] Wessin y Wessin to resign. He's the big reactionary on the military government's side. The Mexican foreign affairs ministry has come out with scathing criticism, comparing American intervention with the Russian occupation of Hungary in 1956.

I was about to go to bed at midnight, when I noticed one light on the telephone blinking. I answered it. It was somebody in Juan Bosch's office in Puerto Rico. He told me that Bosch was directing the troop movement and was always in control, also that the influence of the rebels was increasing. Then Bosch himself got on the line. He thanked me profusely for my articles.

"I am trying to save democracy in the Dominican Republic and also American democracy," he said. "I have been careful not to destroy the image of President Johnson. He is the leader of democracy all over the world. President

Johnson is misinformed, but I have confidence in him, and I always have confidence in the honor and honesty of the people of the United States."

"This is not an isolated democratic revolution," he said, "but part of the revolutionary plan in Latin America."

It was a touching conversation. Bosch is, as so many people describe him, an idealist, a poet, and completely unpractical.

FRIDAY, MAY 14 | On Wednesday I asked to see the president "within the next couple of days" and yesterday got a call from Marvin Watson that he would see me today. Watson is trying to cut out the long delays and therefore this morning telephoned to say that my appointment would be changed from eleven thirty to twelve "if I had no objection," as if I was doing the president a favor by coming to see him. This is pretty much the Texas attitude which is used around the White House these days—rather unlike the curt one of Ken O'Donnell in Kennedy's day.

The president, as usual, was standing at his desk when I walked in, and as usual, he said, "Hello, Drew," just as cordially as if I had not been panning him on the Dominican crisis.

He looked much better than when I had seen him in early April. Lyndon then replied by telling me once again about his sleeping routine, only this time he added the fact that as a truck driver in his youth, he had learned to get up early and go to sleep in a hurry.

"I wake up almost every morning at six. It doesn't make any difference how late I go to bed. I suppose it's habit. Then, in the afternoon, I knock off for a good long nap. I suppose it's the siesta habit I got from the Mexicans. Anyway, when I wake up, I feel like a new man. I watch the eleven o'clock news, and then a man comes in and gives me a rubdown. He works on me for about an hour, and for about forty minutes of that time I sleep. It's only when he twists my legs . . . that I wake up.

"Then I get up and go to work reading reports. It all depends on how many Central Intelligence reports I have to read as to when I get to bed. Sometimes it's one, sometimes two. I almost always wake up at three and call the Pentagon to see how my bombers are getting along. They don't call me. I call them."

He was referring to the bombing raids over North Vietnam, and I asked him about the difference in time. He said that 3:00 a.m. was about the time the bombers were getting back to their bases.

"Then I go to sleep. I can get to sleep in about ten minutes. I suppose people would say that I just wasn't worried about the war, but I've got to relax when I can. Last night I worked until after three, and this morning I just slept until 10:00 a.m. Don't tell anybody that. I don't often do it, but I just kept on sleeping."

I told him that perhaps it sounded sentimental but I wanted to see him become a great president and that I hated to criticize him. He immediately picked up on this.

"You didn't have to be critical of me on that oil shale situation," he said. "You know that the Texas oil companies always oppose me in every election. Yet you had to bring me in as having all those Texas oil friends."

The president went on to say he'd referred all oil matters to Stewart Udall. "Ickes once told me that when he became secretary of the interior, he didn't know anything about oil, so he got Major Partin to come from Texas and Ralph Davies to come from California and let them run oil. I turned all oil matters over to Udall, a real liberal and a Kennedy appointee. I announced I wasn't going to have anything to do with it. I never heard of oil shale—didn't know anything about it until I read it in your column. You just didn't have to bring me in with my Texas oil friends."

I protested that I had not brought him into the oil shale story, except to say what the oil people were saying about him. My chief difference with him was over the Dominican Republic, where I thought he had made a mistake of not properly consulting with the OAS. He then went over to his desk, saying he would give me a play-by-play account as to what happened in the Dominican situation and how carefully he had consulted with the OAS, but he couldn't find the paper he was looking for and telephoned Marvin Watson. "Where's that paper I had on the Dominican Republic?" he said. "You tell Jack Valenti to quit taking it off my desk. If he wants it, tell him to make a copy. Tell him to get it in here in a hurry, or I'll have his ass." Marvin came back a minute or two later, a carbon copy of several telegrams, but the president said: "No, that isn't it. I want the mimeographed sheet with all the notes in the margin. You tell Jack Valenti to get that paper back here in a hurry."

By this time his secretary came in with a paper, and Watson came back with another, neither of which satisfied the president; however, he made do with the first rather poorly typed sheets of thin paper, on which were a series of summarized telegrams from the Dominican Republic. "Our ambassador there called us some time ago to say that things didn't look good and to suggest that he come up and tell us about it. He did. On the way he stopped to see his family, and the crowd down there, knowing he was gone, began to get out of hand. Almost by the time he got back, trouble began.

"On Sunday, April 25, I was at Camp David and ordered American ships to lay offshore, not to do anything but just to be there in case things got bad.

"On Monday the fighting started. We notified the OAS ambassadors what might be coming, but the OAS, I can tell you, isn't worth a (expletive)." They just frittered around, talked, and consulted with their governments. They had a formal meeting on Tuesday, by which time things were getting hot, and they didn't do a damn thing.

"By this time we had reports that the Communists and the rebel crowd were getting the upper hand. There was a Castro member who defected and gave us the plans of exactly what they were trying to do in the Caribbean. We had their names, numbers, photographs. Bosch was the leader behind the scenes, but these fellows were the ones who were really taking over.

"You liberals have got your Tad Schultz [Sculz], your *Christian Science Monitor*, your Drew Pearsons, who are cutting my throat. You all say Lyndon Johnson doesn't understand Latin American problems. I was debating the marine occupation of Nicaragua in 1928 in high school, and I always won when I took the side against intervention. You people talk about Kennedy understanding Latin American affairs and Tom Mann being the hard-nosed militarist. Kennedy had six revolutions when he was in office and the Bay of Pigs. Up until now we haven't had any.

"Tom Mann wanted to quit. You fellows said I mishandled the Panama situation. Tom Mann said let's hold everything, let's not promise them the moon, let's not kowtow to 'em. You fellows were scolding him, but I followed his advice, and now things are fine with Panama. We couldn't be better friends."

I did not interrupt to point out that the president's Panamanian policy had now come around to exactly what I had urged him to do back last January 1964, when I suggested that he tell the Panamanians he would negotiate not merely a new treaty for the old canal but negotiate for a new canal as well, possibly in another country. This is exactly what he's now doing. When Lyndon starts talking, however, it's very difficult to interrupt him.

"You said I was listening to Tom Mann, a hard nose, and you praised Bunker and Jack Vaughn. They were all in on this," the president said. "We've got the best Latin American staff the State Department has ever had."

The highlight of the crisis in the Dominican Republic came apparently when the rebels, whom Lyndon described as Communists, distributed ten thousand rifles indiscriminately to anyone who wanted a rifle in downtown Santo Domingo. The president said this created chaos, with indiscriminate firing back and forth, and no protection of American lives.

"What would you have done if Tyler and Bess and your wife and your grandchildren had been down in that hotel? You would have been cussing me out if I hadn't acted. Meanwhile, the OAS had been meeting and getting nowhere. Finally, on Wednesday, April 28, I got this telegram from Bennett."

He pulled Ambassador Bennett's last telegram from his pocket. This one was neatly typed, and apparently he had kept it in his pocket to pull out and show to people in explanation of the Dominican crisis. He showed me where he had marked, in his own handwriting, the hour, "5:15," when it was received. It had left Santo Domingo at four thirty. The last sentence in the telegram was "I recommend that we intervene."

"I was sitting in that little room over there with my staff discussing Vietnam when this message came in. I told them to notify all OAS ambassadors immediately and to bring the leaders down from the Hill. I then gave the order to land four hundred troops."

A couple of times I said I had written that the OAS was weak, and I suggested that it ought to be bolstered with top men including ex-presidents. Lyndon, however, didn't really listen. He said the OAS members down in the Dominican Republic right now wanted to come home for the weekend.

"They haven't got a staff," he said. "They are completely unorganized. They won't even give an answer to Honduras, which has had two hundred men ready to come and be part of the OAS army."

I asked about Betancourt, Figueres, and Muñoz Marín going down to help establish order. "The OAS won't let 'em come. They're too jealous of them. I have had them in here—the three wise men, they call them—I have expressed my complete cooperation, but they can't get the OAS to cooperate.

"We've got two hundred soldiers from Nicaragua and twenty policemen from Costa Rica. That's all there is in the OAS army. I'll take a Latin American commander; I'll take anything, but we can't get 'em to move."

"I've got troops down there," he said. "We've had eighteen men killed. These Communists get up in the buildings and snipe all day. They're ruthless. If an American patrol goes out and asks whether they should turn right or left, they don't understand Spanish too well, and they turn the wrong way; they get killed."

He said that the day after he had landed troops, on April 29, the OAS Council met in Washington and then adjourned. "We had to call 'em back and make 'em meet again. They weren't going to meet again until Friday. Finally, they voted for an OAS army to go there."

At one point I told him that his exposition of the Dominican crisis had made me feel mean for criticizing him. "You're not mean," he said. "You just don't know all that's happened."

I said good-bye, much to the relief of Marvin Watson, who, however, smiled good-naturedly as I walked through his office.

**WEDNESDAY, MAY 19** | The Dominican problem has seesawed. The OAS mission has become huffy and returned to Washington, partly because the United States sent Tom Mann and Jack Vaughn down to look over their shoulders, partly because the UN sent ex-ambassador Mayobre down to do the same. I knew Mayobre well when he was ambassador here. He is a good man and once considered a Communist, just as Betancourt was.

I am sure Lyndon was responsible for sending the American truce team there because he was impatient and irritated with the nonperformance of the OAS. He wanted results in a hurry. The American team has changed the signals in a very interesting fashion. They are now willing to deal with the rebels. The United States now proposes a coalition cabinet headed by ex-agriculture minister Guzman, formerly in the Bosch cabinet. General Imbert has suddenly become very high and mighty and has said, "No dice." He even issued an indignant statement claiming the United States was intervening in the sovereignty of the Dominican Republic, when it was only a few days ago that we were protecting him with U.S. Marines and keeping him in power.

**MONDAY, MAY 24** | The president telephoned to deny rumors of irritation with Senate [Majority] Leader Mike Mansfield.

**WEDNESDAY, JUNE 2** | Secretary McNamara, in Paris for a NATO meeting, has told our NATO allies that the United States is doubling its nuclear stockpile in Europe because of a Russian nuclear buildup there. This may be psychological warfare; however, intelligence reports received at the Pentagon show a steady drift inside the Kremlin against the United States. The military are also leaking information to the press about Russian SAM [surface-to-air] missile sites and Russian Ilyushin bombers, now in North Vietnam. Our military want Lyndon to bomb both immediately. It's more or less what the military did during the Cuban missile crisis. At that time Kennedy had the Republicans on his neck. This time the Republicans are with Johnson, but the military are on his neck, and since Lyndon is inclined to be pro-military, it really doesn't mean much of a clash. I suspect, however, that he is getting worried. He doesn't want to be known as a war president. I can tell from the way he acts each time I talk to him that he is becoming increasingly worried about the impasse in North Vietnam.

**THURSDAY, JUNE 3** | Bill Moyers telephoned this morning, asking me to see the president at twelve thirty. I learned from sad experience before that this does not mean lunch, so I took the precaution of some sandwiches and a glass of milk at twelve. The president was giving some citations to corporation executives who had hired teenagers during the summer and was only about thirty minutes late. Marvin Watson suggested that if we strolled in slowly, the president, who was on the telephone, would see us and hang up. We did so.

He was in the little green room, just off his main office, telephoning Luci. After he hung up, he said that Luci was concerned as to whether she should go with her father this afternoon to Chicago or go with a boyfriend on a date. She had asked her father whether she should stand up the boy since she could not get hold of him in time to tell him about the trip to Chicago. Her father advised that she not stand up the boy but, if she could get hold of him, to bring him along on the plane.

I began by saying: "I wrote you a letter after I was here last time about oil and gas, which I gave to Bill Moyers. He said I should talk to you direct instead of sending you a letter, and here I am.

"The chief point I wanted to make was that you are vulnerable on oil. People are suspicious of the stand you are going to take. This is unfair to you. Nevertheless, it's a fact, and I want to see you avoid these pitfalls. As a newspaperman, I get around and hear the criticism, and I can report to you that you are being watched very carefully in regard to oil."

I then mentioned Chairman Swidler of the FPC and the fact that he was being dangled in midair over his reappointment. I had planned to say a lot of other things, but the phone rang. The president answered it, after which he took over the conversation.

He said: "I never knew Drew Pearson being tongue-tied. It looks to me as if you're pretty good at expressing yourself. I am aware of what you say. I know that I am on the spot regarding oil. And that's why, when I became president, I asked Stewart Udall to take over all oil problems. I think Udall's a pretty good man, and he's not going to sell me down the river. He was not originally my friend. He stole the entire Arizona delegation away from me.

"I have been appointing Kennedy men and reappointing them," Lyndon continued. "Sometimes I think I've got too many of them. There are too many leaks. There was a leak over at the State Department the other day to the *New York Times*. Max Frankel carried a story on my foreign policy. Sometimes I think there ought to be more Johnson appointees instead of so many Kennedy men."

"You've got to realize that people aren't always fair," I said, "and it doesn't make any difference that you're divorcing yourself from oil problems. They're going to pin oil on you."

"The liberals can get away with anything when it comes to oil," Lyndon said. "But you can bet I'm not going to do anything wrong about oil, or you can kiss my rear end. Take the Kennedys. I was in a meeting with Bobby and Jack Kennedy and the old man when he told them that if they sold their oil properties at that time, they would lose $10 million apiece. He told them to keep their oil. They've got a field extending all the way from Corpus Christi to El Paso that's worth millions. Bobby Kennedy himself is probably worth $10 or $15 million. All I've got is about $200,000 in bonds, and my wife's got a radio/TV station.

"But did you ever hear of anyone criticizing the Kennedys about oil? When Kennedy took office, he announced he was putting his properties in a trust. But when I assumed office, I asked them in the White House to find a trust so I could make out one for myself. We then talked with Clark Clifford, who said there hadn't been any [Kennedy] trust. Old Joe Kennedy wouldn't let Jack Kennedy's oil property be put in trust."

Lyndon was irritated over the newspapers trying to tell him how to run foreign policy and went into some detail on the Dominican crisis. "The *New York Times* tried to tell me how to run Panama last year, and after they got finished, we got the Panama business all straightened out. We're going to get the Dominican Republic straightened out. There were about five thousand Castro Communists in the ranks of the rebels on Sunday, plus seven thousand men who had been trained in the Spanish Civil War or in Cuba. They were beginning to take over. Now that we have intervened, they have gone underground again. Casmano is not a Communist, and neither is Bosch, but there were plenty of others, and we could have had a Communist government on our hands. Then the fellows who were criticizing me now would be talking out of the other side of their mouths."

He said the leaders of Latin America were with him and told how. Just yesterday the foreign ministers of Brazil and Paraguay sat where I was sitting, expressing their approval of what he'd done. I was tempted to tell him what the Latin American ambassadors had told me at the Venezuelan embassy the night before: that only the dictator governments were supplying troops to the OAS, among them Paraguay and Brazil, and that all the democracies were voting against the United States.

Lyndon recalled that yesterday there was a two-to-fifteen vote in the OAS, with only Uruguay and Mexico opposing the United States on the question of okaying the three-man team which will negotiate a peace. "After the Mexicans voted, we got a note from them giving us their private blessing," he said.

"I need the support of fellows like you," Lyndon said. "So, the next time you write about Lyndon Johnson and oil shale, just remember you can pick up the telephone and talk to me. And if I ever am tempted to denounce you, I'll pick up the telephone and call you. Just remember, your poor old president is working for all the country, and he's got to have your help.

"I have put across an aid-to-education bill; we're going to have a Medicare bill; we've got an antipoverty bill; we've put across appropriations for the colleges and universities; we're going to make this country over. They told me the Catholics would never stand still for that aid-to-education bill, but they did. Then I got a protest from the Jews and then from the Baptists. You try getting the Jews and the Catholics and the Baptists all to stay still in one room. Bill Moyers is flying down to Baylor University this afternoon in order to talk to the Baptists.

"I put across my first foreign aid for Vietnam yesterday with only a couple of votes against it. I have already increased the number of schoolchildren in South Vietnam from 500,000 to 1.5 million; I've doubled their rice production."

"How did you do that?" I asked.

"Just by opening the schools," Lyndon replied, "and I'd do the same for North Vietnam if they'd let me."

This was the only reference, during our long talk, to North Vietnam. I'd written a column, published yesterday, regarding the futility of the Vietnamese war and the fact that McGeorge Bundy and General Taylor had euchred Lyndon into the decision to bomb the North. A letter from Secretary McNamara appeared in the *Washington Post* this morning claiming that I was unfair to these two gentlemen since he and others had participated in the decision. Obviously, the letter was inspired by the president. McNamara does not go out and write these letters on his own.

Lyndon has a habit of keeping on talking even when you get up to relieve him of your presence. As we were on our feet, he told me about his continuing problems to keep the economy stable. He referred to the aluminum strike which had been prevented two days ago by a wage hike and a price increase. He said he wasn't satisfied with it but wasn't quite sure what could be done about it.

"The dockworkers now want to strike," he said. "We've persuaded them to call it off for two months. We can't afford to have the ships tied up. We've got the balance of payments coming our way.

"Still, the dockworkers want theirs, and the aluminum workers want more money. You want more newspapers. You're not satisfied with four hundred; you want six hundred."

The president referred to the fact that he'd cut unemployment down from 4.5 million to 4.2 million last month. "But," he said, "I've got a terrible problem with getting teenagers jobs. Just a few minutes ago I had ten executives in here to give them citations and show my appreciation for what they had done in hiring youngsters during the summer. I departed from my text and told the AT&T executive: 'When you go up to Saint Peter to get into Heaven, he isn't going to ask you how many times you went to church or what church you belong to or what tithing you paid. He's going to ask you what you did to put boys to work. He's going to ask you what you did to help your fellow men when kids needed help and employment. That's what Saint Peter's going to ask you.'"

This ended the session, except that on the way out, he looked behind the door, where several framed citations were and picked one up. It was a citation from A. Lincoln, which he handed me with this advice, "When you think about criticizing your poor old president, read this first." The framed citation read: "If I were to try to read, much less answer, all the attacks made on me, this shop might as well be closed for any other business. I do the very best I know how—the very best I can, and I mean to keep doing so until the end. If the end brings me out all right, what is said against me won't amount to anything. If the end brings me out wrong, ten angels swearing I was right would make no difference." Signed A. Lincoln.

**THURSDAY, JUNE 10** | Walter Lippmann has just come back from Europe and written a story of the dismay and distrust of Lyndon Johnson. We saw Walter in his home. He told me he had stopped going to see the president. He found the president demanded complete support and that the conversations were too one-sided. So, Walter only goes to the White House when the president takes the initiative.

Bob Wagner has announced his decision not to run for mayor of New York again. This means Bobby Kennedy will take over the New York Democratic machine and have a big leg up to put his brother or himself in the White House after 1968. It's also a blow for Hubert. Hubert went to New York last night and tried to persuade Wagner to run again but failed. Bobby will probably pick Franklin Roosevelt Jr. for mayor—the man who castigated Hubert's war record during the West Virginia primary in 1960.

**FRIDAY, JUNE 11** | Went to see McGeorge Bundy to invite him to participate in the IPA [International Platform Association] debate on foreign affairs. He was cordial but said he was sure Lyndon would say no on the grounds that he did not permit his assistants to testify before a Senate committee and therefore would not permit his assistants to participate in a debate with senators before the IPA. I can see the justification for this but suggested that Bundy persuade LBJ to act as a substitute for him. "That," said Bundy, "would be like substituting an elephant for a rabbit."

I had not seen Bundy since some potshots I took at him in the column, especially on sucking the president into the Vietnamese impasse. He did not refer to this until toward the end of our talk, when I rose to go, apologizing that I had kept him too long. He said: "Don't be in a hurry. You're so much pleasanter in person than in print." I mumbled something about getting up too early in the morning when I wrote those disagreeable columns.

The most important question I asked him was how we are going to get out of the Vietnamese impasse.

"What would you do?" Bundy returned the question.

"I don't know. I didn't get the president into this," I was unkind enough to say. I suggested, however, possibly turning the matter over to the UN or getting the three-power commission—Poland, India, and Canada—back into authority.

Bundy replied that the UN didn't want it and that North Vietnam and China both had emphasized they would not cooperate with the UN if it were brought into the picture. He said that the tripartite commission had been restricted in its movements in North Vietnam and that the Canadian members had not been paid due to a holdup of money by China. He didn't think they would have any power to conduct an election.

I asked if he'd studied the Fulbright proposal. He hadn't. I said that its thrust was to let the Russians supervise elections and let the country go Communist under a sort of Tito independence. "Who's going to be elected in 1969 in that case?" asked Bundy.

I told him that some ambassadors were irked at the fact newspapermen were having long sessions with the president, whereas they could not get in to see him. I mentioned in particular Alistair Cooke of the *Manchester Guardian*, who had three hours with the president this morning. Previously, the British ambassador was required to see Johnson in company with the Chilean and Danish ambassadors.

Bundy asked if he could relay this suggestion to the president. He agreed it was bad policy for Lyndon to waste so much time with newspapermen. He explained that Scotty Reston had asked for an appointment and the president said for him to come on over to the White House last night. Scotty said he couldn't because he was having dinner with Alistair Cooke, whereupon Lyndon told him to bring Cooke along. This resulted in the meeting this morning, which extended from nine twenty until after twelve noon. Cooke came away glowing with praise for the president.

FRIDAY, JUNE 18 | Early today the air force sent twenty-seven B-52s on a bombing mission from Guam, about twenty-five hundred miles, to blast South Vietnam. They flew back without landing, a total of five thousand miles. This was the first time the B-52, the prized new plane of the air force, has ever been used. It was built in the 1950s and has been considered outmoded by the missile. The mission was a failure. Two planes collided over the Pacific and were lost, and one B-52 wasn't able to get the bomb bay unfastened to drop its bombs.

An area north of Saigon was bombed, but the Pentagon admitted it accomplished almost nothing. One Communist soldier was found dead. Later—and I strongly suspect as a cover-up afterthought—the State Department announced that the bombing mission had broken up a concentration of troops . . . about to raid Saigon.

[Meeting with Russian ambassador Dobrynin and Sen. Wayne Morse.] I reminded the ambassador there had been a lot of progress under Johnson during 1964 toward a better understanding, but he deprecated this. I pointed out the cutback in plutonium stockpiles, but Dobrynin said that we would probably have done this anyway. We had too much. I pointed to the military budget cuts, but he remarked, "Who initiated that? And look what's happened to your budget cuts now. You have just appropriated an extra $700 million for Vietnam."

He went on to say the Russian people were still friendly toward the American people. He pointed to the reception given to the Cleveland Orchestra right now.

"The Russian people are friendly and want to be friendly . . . Nevertheless," he said, "we have taken a firm commitment to defend the Socialist nations. It is similar to your commitment to defend your friends and allies. And if the war goes too far, we will have to fight the United States. We are regretfully ready to do this, and the Chinese know it."

I pointed out that the president had got himself in a box and the problem was how to get out. I got no suggestions from the ambassador. Wayne Morse, however, had made this proposal: the United States cut out bombing North Vietnam, not withdraw but wait for peacekeeping machinery to take over South Vietnam.

Dobrynin listened carefully but didn't seem enthusiastic. When I pressed him on this, he said: "Do you realize what impression this constant bombing makes—your mission of B-52 bombers today? How do you expect the Russian people to turn around and help you out of this predicament in view of the impression you have created?"

TUESDAY, JUNE 22 | I asked Hubert [Humphrey] about how we were going to get out of the Vietnam impasse. His reply was that after the monsoon rains he thought both sides would be willing to negotiate.

"The president is changing his mind a lot about this thing," he said. "He's changed quite a bit just in the two weeks since you last saw him. So has McNamara. You talked to him after you came back from Russia. Others have talked to him. All these talks are like drops of water on a stone. They don't make any impression at first, but in the end they do."

I told Hubert about the conversation with Dobrynin and his blunt warning that Russia would go to war with the United States if pushed too far in Asia. He said he did not think the Russians were bluffing. "There is a certain amount of bluffing on both sides," he said, "but I think they mean it."

**THURSDAY, JUNE 24** | Some of Dobrynin's warning seems to be borne out. Moscow has refused the British peace overture. Prime Minister Wilson has been hatching a plan with Nigeria, Ghana, and some of the British Commonwealth countries to visit Moscow, Peking, Washington, and Hanoi to discuss the Vietnamese war. The Russians today refused to see them.

Simultaneously, there is trouble over Berlin. Whenever the Russians want to get tough, they turn the screws in Berlin, while the Chinese turn the screws in Asia.

Bobby Kennedy has proposed a nuclear treaty to stop the spread of nuclear weapons that would include even China. It was his maiden speech on the Senate floor and an excellent one. The White House, however, was chilly. Bobby Kennedy has always been fairly enlightened on Soviet relations, but unfortunately, the more he proposes, the more Lyndon backs away.

Dean Rusk has made a speech urging North Vietnam to divorce itself from Peking when it comes to peace negotiations. I am sure the suggestion will get nowhere.

**SATURDAY, JUNE 26** | Agnes [Meyer] is looking much better after a sojourn at Saratoga Springs, where she got partially on the wagon. She is now able to walk reasonably well with only her stick. Spending the weekend with her were Marietta Tree, ambassador to the UN; the Harold Taylors, who took the first trip with us to Norway; and Donny Graham, Kay's eldest son, who is spending the summer at Cambridge buying presses for the *Crimson*.

Harold Taylor was chairman of the big SANE rally at Madison Square Garden, where Wayne Morse spoke earlier this month, and naturally we got into an immediate argument over Vietnam. Kay was about the only defender the president had. She came back from Saigon more convinced than ever that his policy was right. She reported that the Vietcong blew up a fashionable French restaurant on the waterfront yesterday and would do more of this kind of thing. They systematically figure out the key spots, such as the American embassy, an air force compound at Pleiku, or a choice restaurant—just enough to keep us in constant fear.

Last night the Vietcong radio declared they would kill Ambassador Maxwell Taylor, General Westmoreland, Assistant Ambassador Alexis Johnson, and one other top American.

The most interesting thing Kay reported was that the young stenographers at the American embassy water-ski every afternoon on the Mekong River, and a few months ago the Vietcong took some potshots at them. Since that time you see beautiful young Americans, around twenty-two years old, going to ski with machine guns over their arms.

FRIDAY, JULY 2 | Lunched with Constantine Brown, who used to be full of information, most of it coming from his friends in the navy. They tell him troop morale in Vietnam is bad, that officers have no arguments to give their troops as to why they're fighting, that the Vietnamese people, originally under President Diem, have had so many changes of government that they don't know who their government is or what it stands for.

Most interesting information from Brown was about a session with LBJ last spring. The president told him he had seen de Gaulle during Kennedy's funeral, had two sessions with him, and [that] "we hit it off very well, but now he gives me the needle every chance he gets. What's wrong with him?"

Connie told the president that de Gaulle had been much impressed. Then, when he was about to go to Mexico, he figured he would not stand on protocol but would fly from Mexico to Texas to spend a day or two at the LBJ Ranch.

"Then he read a speech by Senator Fulbright excoriating France and de Gaulle, which was broadcast over the Voice of America. If Fulbright had spoken in the Senate, de Gaulle understands American politics, and it would not have meant anything, but coming over the Voice of America, which had to have the blessing of the U.S. government, de Gaulle was angry. He called off his plan to visit the ranch and has been sore ever since."

Connie picked up from French sources this account of Hubert Humphrey's talk with de Gaulle: when de Gaulle told Humphrey that the United States should get out of Vietnam, Humphrey replied with the usual two reasons— prestige and the domino theory—as to why we couldn't.

Regarding prestige, de Gaulle allegedly answered: "I faced that problem in Algeria. I have been elected on a pledge to stay in Algeria, but when I studied the situation carefully, I decided to get out. My prestige was on the line. I was nearly murdered. I experienced an army revolt. I was in danger for my life. Yet we went ahead. Look at my prestige today. Has it been hurt? Also, look at the prestige of France. It is higher than ever."

As to the domino theory that other Asian countries would go Communist if Vietnam falls, de Gaulle argued that you can't win wars against national liberation today any more than the British were able to win the American war of liberation in 1776. History adjusts to communism, just as history adjusted to republicanism, considered dangerous by the crowned heads of Europe in 1776.

**MONDAY, JULY 5** | To dinner at Gwen Cafritz's. Sat near Bill Rogers, and we discussed his first big libel case, which he handled for me against Frederick N. Howser, the attorney general of California. We discussed Nixon and Eisenhower.

Bill admitted there was no love lost between Nixon and Eisenhower during the 1952 campaign after the revelation of Nixon's $18,000 personal expense fund. Bill denied my belief that the friction continued. I maintain that if Eisenhower had delivered some speeches for Nixon in 1960, Nixon would have won.

Bill contended Nixon never called on Ike to speak because he wanted to win the race on his own. He said one factor which had killed Nixon in the election was Ike's inability to remember anything important which Nixon had done as vice president. This, Bill said, was an accident.

"I talked to Eisenhower about that afterward. He said: 'You know, Bill, ever since I was sick, I have had trouble speaking. I am rather slow. I was about to tell of Nixon's accomplishments when somebody in the press conference said, "Thank you, Mr. President," ending the conference, and all the newspapermen rushed out.'" I can understand how this might have happened, though I am skeptical.

**WEDNESDAY, JULY 7** | Lunch with Leonard Marks and Jackson Leighter. Got a call from Jack Valenti that the president was trying to get me in this week and wanted to know whether I had finished my lunch yet. I told him I had finished and would be available in five minutes. Valenti called back about five minutes later and asked me to come right away. I did.

There was almost no wait. The president looked well, although I was rather startled by the grayness of his hair. His face is a little fuller, but he has gained no weight. If anything, he's lost some. On the whole he looked rested.

I said I was going to tell him some things he might not like—for example, that he was worrying too much about the press and seeing too many newspapermen. They were bragging how they had seen him and how they didn't really appreciate seeing him.

"This sounds as if I thought I was the only newspaperman you should see," I said, "but I think you know I don't mean it that way. Some of the

*Newsweek* people were in here during the Dominican crisis and bragged they had lunched with you and remained until 6:00 p.m."

The president denied that had happened. "They came in here about two o'clock. I couldn't refuse a man like Buck Rodgers of *Newsweek*, who has been a good friend of mine, and we felt we also had to include some of the others, including the *Time* correspondent. He's a Kennedy worshipper and will never write anything good about me, but we felt we had to have him. We had a late lunch, and I was interrupted part of the time, and they actually left here a little after five. I heard that they were bragging about the amount of time they had spent, so I looked up the log."

From here on the president grabbed the conversation, and I was unable to say much.

"I've got a letter on my desk raising hell because I'm seeing you," he said. "They want to know why I am seeing that fellow Drew Pearson, who isn't friendly to me." I interrupted to say I would forgo the visits if they caused him any embarrassment. He ignored this.

"You fellows are a bunch of prima donnas," he said. "You're all jealous of each other. You all go around bragging that you've been in here to see the president. I have made it a policy that what goes on in government, unless some danger to the United States is involved, should be open to the press, and I have made it a practice to see most any newspaperman who wants to see me. I've had luncheons for *Time* and *Newsweek*, luncheons for Cowles Publications. I have even seen the *Dallas News*, which is against me, and the Copley Press, which pans me all the time. Scotty Reston called the other day and said he hadn't been able to see me for a long time, so when I got through my work at 6:00 p.m., I called him and said to come on over. He said he was giving a dinner for Alistair Cooke and would love to bring him along. The next morning I was going to Houston to welcome the astronauts, and I told them to come on before I left. They told me in Houston not to go down there until after the astronauts had held their press conference, which meant that I didn't have to leave until around noon. So, I spent two hours with Reston and Cooke, not three hours.

"Cooke sat there telling me how to run the world, and I listened to him. Bill White won't come in to see me unless I ask him. He's sensitive about imposing on our friendship. Walter Lippmann has come in from time to time when I invite him. He gives me the benefit of his advice.

"Merriman Smith came in the other day to ask about an announcement that I was going to attend the governors' meeting. I told him I wasn't. I met with them twice, and that's enough. They wrote me several months ago, inviting me to attend, and I told them I couldn't. Despite that, they put out an announcement. What they were trying to do, of course, was build up interest in their conference.

"When I told Smith this, he growled something about having to go back and check with the governors. I then picked up a letter on my desk, dated last spring, in which Jack Valenti had told them I couldn't come. Merriman still said he'd have to go back and check with the governors."

I said the president's time was too important to be spending on these things. I didn't tell him, though I should have, that George Reedy was the man to handle this type of query.

Lyndon ticked off a group of newspapermen who were always in Bobby Kennedy's corner. He included Ben Bradlee of *Newsweek*; Ted White, the White House correspondent for *Time*; and the *New York Times* people.

"Teddy White accused me of lying to Bobby Kennedy about the vice presidential race. I had Bobby in here and told him, 'Bobby, you're not going to be on the ticket,' just as frank as that. Within a few hours afterward, before he got to New York, he had leaked the story to his friends."

"Is it true that you had a tape recorder in here?" I asked.

"No," replied the president. "Of course not."

I asked about Joe Alsop's story on Monday that the president had spent six hours indignant over Scotty Reston's scoop on Johnson's UN speech and the report that Johnson changed it at the last minute.

Lyndon replied: "It just didn't happen. He spent the last few days complaining because the secretary of state wouldn't see him and that he couldn't get information out of Central Intelligence. I'll tell you exactly what happened.

"A good many months ago, when they asked me to speak at the UN in San Francisco, they explained it was a very important birthday. I am for the UN, though I think when we need it most, it isn't around, but I didn't make a promise to speak. I said I would try; however, they assumed I was going to speak and put out a press statement along that line, just as the governors' conference did—but I never made a commitment.

"Later someone suggested I talk about Article 19 and the Russian-French debt. I told them that this involved Congress, and also our allies, and I couldn't do it. I never had any idea of making a speech on this at San Francisco. Reston sent his man in here, John Pomfret, and we told him it wasn't true, but the next day Reston wrote the story anyway."

I said I'd almost written this story myself, that the UN speech was to be a ceremonial occasion and that he, Johnson, had no intention of talking about Article 19 or making an American contribution to the UN.

"The trouble is you only read stories that needle you, and you don't read my stories that praise you."

"I don't read any of these stories," the president said, obviously fibbing. "I get the *Washington Post* Bulldog edition when I'm having a rubdown at night, and I am too sleepy to read much. The next day I read the *Baltimore Sun*, the *Philadelphia Inquirer*. They have less propaganda in their columns."

"Don't you read the *New York Times*?" I asked. He said he did not. "They pan me all the time," he added.

"We are having trouble in Vietnam. The Republicans now want me to bomb Hanoi. We're going to have to send more ground troops in, and things are going to be pretty bad. Your friend Dobrynin has been talking to you and Wayne Morse and other people about what the Russians may do. He's been talking all over town, but he hasn't talked to me.

"The Russians are calling me a thief, a bully, and a warmonger. I am keeping a list of their names. Someday I'm going to tell the American people what they're calling me. I'm not calling them names, and I don't think the American people are going to like it when they see what the Russians call the president."

I argued that it was foolish for him to reply. "You have done an excellent job in keeping calm," I said. "And after this is all over in Vietnam, you're going to need to sit down with the Russians and work things out. The peace of the world depends on it." The president did not listen.

"I slept with an eighteen-year-old girl last night," the president continued. I didn't quite know what he was leading up to. I didn't think he went around bragging about sleeping with young girls.

"Luci was up to one o'clock in the morning with her fan mail. She had about five hundred letters," explained the president, "about forty of them against her for being converted to Catholic. 'This is a personal matter,' she said. 'I don't see why people have to be concerned with my religion.'

"I told her to come on to bed with me, and she said she had to go to Mass at seven. So, I woke her up. And when I got up in the morning, here was all this stuff on the newsreel about the fact that she shouldn't have been baptized. This fellow Bishop Pike just wanted to get his name in the papers, I guess. The Episcopalians lost Luci when Dean Sayre came out with that statement last October. That was when Luci made certain she was going to become a Catholic."

At one point, when we were alone, the president looked at the news ticker to note that Jerry Ford of Michigan was demanding that he bomb Hanoi and that Rep. Paul Findley of Illinois had come back from a trip to Europe to give advice on our NATO policy.

"This is the damnedest piece of politics I've seen," he remarked. "These Republicans aren't even members of the Foreign Affairs Committee, yet they go to Europe to try to give advice. If they had some advice, why don't they come down and tell me about it?"

"If we bomb Hanoi, they'll bomb Saigon. Then American public opinion will demand that we bomb Peking. Then the Chinese will retaliate by sending a land army into North Vietnam. Then we will have escalated into world war. That's what I've been trying to avoid. Why don't you write a story about the foolishness of that idea?"

The president then told me about a stag dinner he'd held, regarding which Bess previously had been very secretive. It was attended by some industrial and labor leaders, including George Meany.

"We passed the cigars," explained the president, "and inside each cigar wrapper was the word *talk* or *write*. Those who received the instruction to write have been writing me letters. I received a fine letter from Henry Ford. The others got up and made brief speeches about the state of the world. George Meany made quite a speech. He usually isn't very grammatical. He mixes up the *dems* and *dose*, but this time he didn't. 'I like this system,' he said. 'You might describe it as a piece of pie. This pie is worth $660 billion of the gross national product. And we all carve it up. We in labor want to see you in industry get your share. We want you to get enough to take care of dividends, take care of depreciation, take care of a reasonable profit. We also want you to take care of us. I, for one, expect to be around to make sure that labor gets its share of the pie. It's a good system, and it works. I am for it.'"

"A lot of big executives were there," continued the president, "but when Meany sat down, they gave him a tremendous ovation."

I asked him whether he was going to go see de Gaulle in the fall. He replied in the negative. "Hubert's got that all fixed up," he said with a grin.

He went on to talk about the South. "The South deserves a pat on the back for the way it's accepted the civil rights law," he said. "Everyone predicted there would be rioting and bloodshed, but they've taken things in stride. On the whole the schools have been integrated. Most of the officials are enforcing the law."

I had been sitting with the president, watching the clock tick away well beyond my three o'clock deadline, when the wire opens to send my column. He seemed in no hurry, however, and as long as he was dropping nuggets of information, I didn't feel like running away from them.

The president showed me a letter he had just received from David Dubinsky—thanking him for the get-well message that Lady Bird and he had sent Dave. "The reason Dubinsky was for me at Los Angeles was because Maury Maverick and I were the only Texas congressmen who voted for the minimum wage bill.

"Dubinsky sent $2,500 down to Maury, and he got indicted and almost convicted. The only thing that saved him was when I got Alvin Wirtz to defend him. Maury had taken that $2,500 to a poor section of San Antonio and poured it out on the table and told all the Mexican women to come up and get 50 cents apiece, but he didn't report the contribution, and what he did was completely against the law.

"When the case went to trial, Wirtz didn't deny anything. They had witnesses to show where Maury cashed the check and witnesses to show how he dumped the money on the table. Wirtz got up and asked the jury, 'Tell me when any Texan has been able to go up to New York and get some money from those northerners and bring it down here and give it to Texans. Tell me any other Texan who has been able to get this much money out of anyone in the North. This man should get a badge of honor, not criticism.'

"The jury was out twenty minutes before acquitting Maury."

By this time I was on my feet and walking to the door. We had left the little green room and gone back into the Oval Office, where the president looked over the papers on his desk. It was three thirty. Usually, he takes a nap at this time. Earlier he'd told me that when the *Newsweek* people wanted to talk to him about the Dominican Republic, he told them, "I'll give you my nap."

**TUESDAY, JULY 13** | Lunched with Hal Raskin, former assistant to McGeorge Bundy, and Richard Barnet, formerly with the State Department and the Disarmament Commission.

The most alarming report they gave me was that the Joint Chiefs of Staff had unanimously recommended using germ warfare in South Vietnam. They learned this from a State Department official, who reported that the papers had come from the Pentagon to the White House with the unanimous approval of the JCS.

The recommendation went to the Science and Technical Section of the White House and to the Bureau of Intelligence and Research and the Policy Planning Council of the State Department, where the ideas are being discussed.

Specifically, the recommendation is to use tularemic fever, a disease contracted from rabbits which spreads quickly and is not fatal, except occasionally to very young children or old people. It has the same effect as undulant fever, giving you a low fever, sapping your energy, and making it very difficult for you to do anything energetic.

The State Department and the White House have not approved the Pentagon recommendation. They feel that tularemia, if spread through North Vietnam, would hurt our friends in the South, that it could be somewhat isolated but not entirely.

Raskin and Barnet were very depressed. They said things were going to pot all over the world. The Communists were taking control of the Tokyo area, due in part to resentment against the American policy of bombing North Vietnam. They predicted that the Berlin crisis will get worse. The Russians will heat it up just as much as we heat up North Vietnam. It's been a long time since Khrushchev said: "Berlin is a bone in my throat. It will continue to be a bone in the throat of peace."

There is increasing sentiment for unification of East and West Germany in Bonn. And the revanchists are stronger than ever and demanding the return of the Sudetenland and parts of Poland. Even Willy Brandt, head of the Social Democrats and a moderate, is now for the return of the Sudetenland. At one time the United States could impose its will on Germany to accept the Oder-Neisse line between Poland and Germany but not today. The Germans now see that the United States needs them. They also see that the détente between the United States and Russia is over, and as a result, the Germans are asking higher terms. Foreign Minister Schröder, last Sunday, made a speech saying Germany must now get nuclear weapons if there was to be no multilateral force.

WEDNESDAY, JULY 14 | During luncheon Marian called from the office to say that Adlai Stevenson fell dead on the streets of London this morning while walking with Marietta Tree. All over the room, from the telephone operator at the Cosmos Club to the waiters to the people at lunch, the news spread. I had not realized before how much Adlai meant to so many people.

This evening I talked to Clayton Fritchey in New York. He denied that Adlai had been thinking of leaving the UN, as reported from London by Eric Sevareid. Clayton said Adlai was determined to build up the UN and get it back on the track when the General Assembly meets in September. I went back to the office after lunch and tried to write a column about Adlai. It was hard to write in a hurry. I had known him in the latter years so well, though I opposed him vigorously when he and Kefauver were battling it out for the nomination in 1952. I wrote a long column, then drove out to the farm and sat on the terrace in the sunset, to realize that I hadn't really written very much and couldn't write very much that was adequate about a great man who had been a dear friend.

In a few days, I suppose, the newspapers will have forgotten about him. He'll be just another marker on a grave. So, you have to write a story in a hurry, but this doesn't prevent your thinking and wondering what would have happened had Adlai been elected or had he been appointed secretary of state.

The first time I really met Adlai was when he appeared as a witness against me at the libel suit trial in the case of Monroe Kaplan. Adlai appeared on behalf of Secretary of the Navy Frank Knox, and while he didn't particularly want to be against me, he was defending Knox, and his testimony was somewhat damaging.

As Adlai came down from the witness stand, I adopted an old technique. I reached out and shook hands with him very cordially, as if to thank him for his testimony. He couldn't do anything but smile and shake hands back. The effect on the jury was very good from my point of view.

That summer, during the war, Adlai occupied the Hagner log cabin next to our farm with some other bachelors. I think Adlai, though married, was not getting along with his wife. I never saw anything of them and never got to know Adlai at all well until our trips together on Agnes's yacht.

After Adlai lost, I also lost my sponsor, both on radio and television, and tried to make a go of a new syndicated TV program. Adlai was good enough to be one of my guests at a time when I needed a distinguished guest or two. After that we saw more of each other and became friends.

THURSDAY, JULY 15 | When Adlai was alive, I suppose that more newspapers kicked him around than they did any other presidential candidate since the days of William Jennings Bryan. Now, in death, newspapers are singing his praises.

He was right when he advised Kennedy to run with the Berlin ball immediately after his inauguration. Kennedy ignored the advice and suffered some humiliating defeats, such as the pullout from Laos and his showdown in Vienna with Khrushchev. These were all avoidable. Kennedy didn't get American foreign relations back on the track for two years. If he had followed Adlai's advice in the winter of 1960–61, the world would have been a better place.

Adlai was an interesting mixture. He loved young people, and the women all loved him. Yet he was never happily married and probably never would have been. Marietta Tree, who tried to resuscitate him when he fell dead in London, was madly in love with him, and so was Alicia Patterson, who traveled with him all over Europe.

The last trip with Adlai was in the West Indies on our sailing schooner in the winter of 1964. Adlai came on for just a couple of days with his son Borden, who is his youngest boy and something of a problem child. Borden wanted to start a hotel and go in for tourism in one of the British islands, I think Antigua. At the end of the trip Adlai flew there with Borden to check into it. Adlai seemed a little restless and not as happy on that trip as on the others.

Adlai used to complain to me about the State Department and the fact that they never let him in on policy decisions, that he only knew about them after he was given a speech to deliver in the UN, defending some mistake in Washington. The last time I really had a talk with him was in May this year. About the Dominican crisis he said he was in on the decision at the White House when the president rushed in with a sheaf of telegrams saying, "We've got to land troops in the Dominican Republic."

Adlai said that of course he could have objected, but it was difficult to argue when apparently the president had already made up his mind and when he, Adlai, didn't know all the facts. Well, Adlai is gone now. I shall miss him, and the world will miss him.

FRIDAY, JULY 16 | After dinner Luvie and I went to the Cathedral, where Adlai's body lay. There was a long line of people coming in from the hot summer night passing the bier. It was draped with an American flag, without flowers, but with an honor guard standing at attention. The crowd was silent.

SUNDAY, JULY 18 | Lunched with Howard Morgan, former Federal Power commissioner. He has an idea for trying to settle the Vietnamese crisis—namely, a proposal by Johnson, in tribute to Adlai Stevenson, that the problem be referred to the organization which Stevenson battled for during the year, the UN. Johnson would propose a cease-fire and the end of bombing until the UN could tackle the situation.

I said that the UN in the past had not wanted to take over the Vietnam dispute, also that China was not a member. I suggested that Johnson might say that the United States would be willing to have China participate for the purposes of this discussion as a UN member. I realize this might be hard for Lyndon to take, but nevertheless war would be even harder.

Morgan argued that Lyndon was on the hot seat, that he was getting nowhere, and that a sentimental appeal in the memory of Adlai Stevenson, if made within the next forty-eight hours, would carry great weight and also be publicly smart. We went to see Wayne Morse to sell him the idea. We found him putting red Devon cows through his cattle chute to check on their pregnancy and ear tags.

He bought the idea, and we agreed to discuss it at lunch tomorrow on Capitol Hill. Wayne is convinced Johnson wants a war, that the military have sold him on the idea that now's the time to knock out China. Wayne doesn't think Johnson will buy our idea, but nevertheless it's worth trying.

**WEDNESDAY, JULY 21** | Last night, at the Humphrey dinner, George Ball made a tough statement about the future sacrifices the nation will have to make in Vietnam. He said we were going to experience a period of austerity but that we would be equal to it. He spoke in such somber tones that some people were shocked.

Hale Boggs disagreed with him; however, it now becomes evident that George's somber note comes from a White House meeting between Democratic leaders and the president yesterday morning. Bob McNamara did not get back to Washington from Vietnam until this morning, yet twenty-four hours in advance it was decided to start warning the nation. This became evident today when Mike Mansfield echoed the same tough line given by George Ball and calling for unity. Mansfield, however, also gave a hint of his long-standing concerns about the war by calling upon the Geneva nations, especially Britain and Russia, to open peace talks.

**THURSDAY, JULY 22** | Joe Borkin came to lunch. He bemoans the fact that he's lost his walking partner. He and Arthur Goldberg used to walk down Connecticut Avenue every morning. Arthur was frank during these talks and made it clear—as he has with me—that he doesn't agree with Lyndon on Vietnam.

Later in the day Arthur called me, I suspect because he was afraid I might reveal the fact that he didn't agree with Lyndon on Vietnam. He said he needed my help. When I told him I knew how he felt, he said, "Yes, but for God sake don't publish that."

I outlined Howard Morgan's idea of a presidential appeal in memory of Adlai Stevenson, that the whole matter go before the United Nations. "Go ahead with it," Arthur advised. "Even if it doesn't succeed, it will show that the United States is not the big nation bullying the little nation. "You're the president's friend," Arthur said, "and he knows it. You've got to keep on influencing him. The worst thing is to let him get isolated."

The White House talks on Vietnam are continuing.

**SUNDAY, JULY 25** | Arthur Schlesinger has made the revelation that in 1962 Kennedy had decided to dump Dean Rusk as secretary of state after the 1964 elections. I am not surprised.

Adlai used to describe Rusk as a Buddha who sat and listened and said nothing. Kennedy wanted someone who could help him make up his mind. I recall, however, that John Foster Dulles made up his mind too frequently and too vigorously, and he was frequently wrong. In a way Rusk is the ideal secretary of state for Johnson, who is certain to make his own decisions. At any rate Lyndon, having endorsed Rusk only quite recently, is now stuck with him.

Averell Harriman has left Moscow for Bonn, where he is conferring with Erhard. Reports are published today that Kosygin expressed a desire for cautious cooperation with the United States despite Vietnam.

**THURSDAY, JULY 27** | Before I left Washington and just as I was writing a column on whether Johnson would okay a military paper on the bombing of SAM missile sites, the ticker carried the news that forty-six American bombers had flown over Hanoi and bombed these SAM sites. This is almost certain to mean a showdown with the Soviet Union. I suspect, however, that the Russians will not retaliate. Their bid for unity with the Chinese was definitely rebuffed. It's this split that we are counting on most.

**WEDNESDAY, JULY 28** | The president held his long-anticipated press conference to announce the result of his deliberations on the Vietnam buildup. He had a big audience and handled himself well. He's going to double the draft, increase troops in Vietnam by about fifty thousand, but not call up reserves.

**FRIDAY, JULY 30** | I tried to call Arthur Goldberg at the State Department [he had replaced the late Adlai Stevenson as ambassador to the UN], but he was tied up in conferences. Later I learned he had persuaded the State Department to broaden the appeal to the UN. As a result, he sent a second letter to U Thant offering American collaboration "unconditionally" with the Security Council for settlement of Vietnam.

The amazing thing is that Arthur has succeeded in going much further than Adlai Stevenson ever thought of being able to go, which sort of bears out the idea that Adlai, though eloquent publicly, was a timid negotiator privately. This is not really fair to him, but he wasn't anywhere near the salesman Arthur is. Of course, Arthur has an advantage in that he gave up a very important job at Lyndon's request, and he can now call the shots to a considerable extent.

Jack Anderson turned up a significant story at the Pentagon which we haven't been able to break. On Sunday or Monday we sent twenty-six bombers over a SAM missile site over Hanoi, losing six planes. At first the Pentagon tried to cover this up and announced only three planes but finally admitted the six. What has not been admitted is that it was a dummy SAM site. The Russians or the North Vietnamese, or both, had constructed a site which looked like a SAM missile launching base but actually wasn't. Then they surrounded it with ack-ack guns and lay in wait for American bombers. We came in at a low level to avoid missile fire, and six planes were hit by antiaircraft batteries.

**MONDAY, AUGUST 2** | Jack got a good inside story of the White House session with the leaders. Only Democrats were present. The president admonished the conferees that this was a strictly secret session which would discuss classified material. He said he was not calling out the reserves because it would incite the Russians, and apparently he felt he had some understanding with the Russians that if we didn't make any abrupt mobilization moves, they would not intervene further in North Vietnam.

I'm not sure this was the real reason for the president's decision not to call out the reserves. I rewrote the column in a hurry.

**TUESDAY, AUGUST 3** | Jack came in with a confirmation of the report that our raid on the SAM missile sites, forty miles west of Hanoi, were actually dummies and that we had been trapped into the raid, thereby losing six fighter bombers. He contacted Bill Moyers, who reluctantly confirmed the story after calling Secretary McNamara. McNamara was irate. He said, "There has been a leak, and we'll investigate who it was."

I was planning to hold the column for Monday release, but Jack was afraid it might not hold, so we rushed it out this afternoon.

THURSDAY, AUGUST 5 | (Hosted evening IPA debate over Vietnam policy with Senators Ernest Gruening of Alaska, Tom Dodd of Connecticut, and Frank Church of Idaho.)

An interesting dinner. I escorted the senators to the ballroom for the debate and then ducked out to have dinner with Averell Harriman. He'd just come back from Russia and Europe, and I was anxious to learn what he'd discovered.

He said he'd had some talks with Kosygin and Mikoyan together. He found Kosygin easy to talk with on this trip; however, he found them adamant against any role of peacemaker regarding Vietnam. Averell talked to Kosygin about LBJ wanting peace and emphasized it strongly; however, Kosygin would not buy it.

Our real problem with North Vietnam, Averell told me, is that they think they can take South Vietnam with no trouble; therefore, they don't want to negotiate.

He found China and Russia just as far apart as ever. "China is a 'have-not' nation; Russia is a 'have' nation. This is the basic difference." At the moment China is sitting pretty regarding North Vietnam. The more we fight there, the better she likes it.

Averell found that the Russians had kept track of Johnson's name-calling of them. Averell talked to them about calling a halt to the name-calling, explained that the president was quite sensitive. Averell feels he made some headway on this point.

I got the impression that he did not make much headway on any major problems and found the Russian leaders pretty much as I found them in March.

MONDAY, AUGUST 9 | Arthur and Dorothy Goldberg came to dinner. Arthur offered me a job as his deputy at the UN. Luvie immediately protested that I couldn't afford it, which was true. She also protested that I didn't agree with his policy in Vietnam, which was true, but Arthur replied, "He's a Johnson man."

I certainly agreed with this. I was half-scared that he would press the idea and I would have to accept—and half-hoped he would. After fifty years I would get back to what I once dreamed of doing when I got out of college— being a diplomat. I didn't go through with it at the time because I hadn't any money, and being an ambassador in those days required a lot of money. It still does. I am still too broke to become a diplomat. Luvie pointed out that we would have to sell the farm.

The conversation simmered along. Inasmuch as Arthur had left the Supreme Court for the UN and Leonard Marks had left his $200,000 law practice for the USIA [United States Information Agency], I confess that it made me look like a heel not to jump at Arthur's bait.

I made a weak suggestion that I couldn't be confirmed by the Senate, and Arthur said that he hadn't thought of that. Actually, of course, I would be confirmed overwhelmingly, but we let it drop, and Arthur never brought up the subject again.

Arthur told me how he had managed to get the UN in on the Vietnam crisis. He said he'd talked to the president on Friday to tell him he wanted to discuss the Vietnam buildup. This was well before the Wednesday press conference announcing the fifty thousand men to be drafted for Vietnam. Lyndon replied that he was going to Camp David. "You know you don't sit up there and rest," replied Arthur. "You go up there to talk to McNamara and telephone and discuss what you're going to do next week."

Lyndon was still reluctant to talk, so Arthur concluded, "I want you to know I am damned unhappy about it." Eight minutes later Dorothy got a call from Lady Bird inviting them both up to Camp David for the weekend. When they got there, Arthur didn't intrude himself, in fact rested and made himself generally scarce.

McNamara was also invited, arriving Sunday. Finally, about 4:00 p.m. Lyndon suggested that they take a walk. "I want to talk about this before McNamara," Arthur said. So they did. Arthur argued that Vietnam had to be placed before the UN, that it would give us a better image before the world, that we had neglected the UN too much, that the world feels we're the big power source pounding a little power and refusing to negotiate.

Finally, Arthur said: "I've got a way out for you in this. You can send a letter by me to U Thant." The president bought this immediately.

When Arthur took the appointment, he told Johnson that his position was the same as Sen. Dick Russell's. Dick had argued that we shouldn't be in Vietnam at all, that it didn't have a viable government, that we had no business being in the country unless we had a government which was able to support us. Arthur compared the situation to Malaysia, where, he said, the British had just as much guerrilla warfare but where the population was strongly for the British. In South Vietnam the population isn't with us.

I said the crucial mistake Johnson made was last November, immediately after the elections, when he did not announce that he had a mandate from the people and that we were getting out of Vietnam. Dick Russell was down at the LBJ Ranch at that time and should have so advised him. Arthur said the reason he didn't act was because nobody told him what he faced. Rusk didn't. McGeorge Bundy didn't, and he didn't have enough understanding of foreign affairs to act then.

I pointed out that Johnson had an unerring instinct and capability when it came to domestic affairs. He could plot a course years in advance. When it came to foreign affairs, however, he just didn't have the instinct or the know-how.

Arthur said the Republicans are playing it two ways: the Dirksen way, giving all the support possible to the president; and also playing it the Romney–Mark Hatfield way, by pointing out that we are bogged down in a disastrous war on the Asia mainland. Then, when election time rolls around, they can point out that they gave the president all the support he needed and that he has now got the country into a disastrous war with more and more men committed needlessly.

"Eisenhower will never stand with him in the last analysis," Arthur said. "Ike always puts a string to his statements of support. He puts in a reservation against a land war in Asia. He can always say that he recommended we send only a few advisors and that Johnson has now got land troops committed wholesale."

The president was pleased at the reaction to Arthur's letter to U Thant, offering American cooperation with the UN and asking for U Thant's cooperation. Letters had come pouring in, favoring the president. Arthur said, incidentally, that he'd received fourteen thousand letters himself following his appointment to the UN. We all remarked that this indicated how much people were interested in peace and how important the UN was.

Arthur presides over the Security Council September 1, at which time he expects a fusillade from the Russians, partly because Harriman talked too much upon his return to Washington and has put the Russians on the spot. Harriman went too far, in Arthur's opinion, in saying that the Russians couldn't make any moves toward peace negotiations because of their political problems with the Chinese. This is true and is what the Russians told me, but Harriman made a mistake by saying so publicly, and Ambassador Federenko is preparing, Arthur hears, to blast the United States at the next Security Council meeting.

Arthur asked my opinion of Jimmy Roosevelt as an ambassador to the UN as part of his staff. I told him I thought Jimmy would be good and that the Roosevelt name carried a lot of prestige. Jimmy apparently wants to leave Congress. Arthur has offered John Stevenson, Adlai's second son, a job as his executive assistant and has asked George Lodge to become an ambassador—also Eugenie Anderson of Minnesota, replacing Marietta Tree. I put in a mild demur against this, pointing out that Eugenie's husband was a pain in the neck and that he always insisted on hanging around. I didn't think her performance in Bulgaria was any too hot. I gather, though, that Arthur has already made his decision.

THURSDAY, AUGUST 12 | Earlier this week the *New York Times* reported that Henry Cabot Lodge, testifying before the Senate Foreign Relations Committee, said that even if the South Vietnamese government asked us to leave, we would not. The State Department has been busy denying this ever since, and Johnson put in his two cents' worth today, emphasizing that we were in Vietnam only at the invitation of the South Vietnamese government. I suspect that the vigor of the denial is motivated in part by a plan to leave ourselves an escape in case things are too hot and we want to be invited to leave.

SATURDAY, AUGUST 14 | Kay Graham, with Averell and Marie Harriman, came to dinner at the farm. After dinner, while the others were playing bridge, I had a long talk with Kay. The best visit we have had since we spent a day traveling through Romania together.

When I complimented her on the *Post*, she said she was shaking things up, putting Ben Bradlee of *Newsweek* in as editor and planning to develop some young men. Almost everyone in there, she said, was approaching sixty. It made me feel ancient.

Kay has become a lot better since Phil died. When he was alive, she used to radiate his philosophy—and sometimes his philosophy was cockeyed. I was surprised to hear her refer to George Humphrey, the ex-secretary of the treasury, as a "crook," and refer to his stockpiling of nickel, as brought out in the Symington report.

We discussed the Schlesinger-Sorensen books on Kennedy and the current feud between them. Sorensen has said that Schlesinger should not have told all—especially Kennedy's plan to fire Rusk. Schlesinger shot back by publishing a letter that Sorensen had written him, praising his book and saying he wouldn't change a word.

Averell said that he wouldn't dream of reporting some of the things that Franklin Roosevelt had told him because it would make Franklin look mean and petty. Of course, at times, FDR was that way. We kidded Averell about writing his memoirs, told him he ought to get busy, but he didn't seem in any hurry. Averell is seventy-four but doesn't look it.

Averell argued at the dinner table about Russia. He said Russia was out to communize the world, and until it had given up this goal, we must remain rivals, even enemies.

This is quite a different song from that which Averell was singing just after I saw Khrushchev and when he wanted to be ambassador to Moscow to try to negotiate a solution for the Berlin Wall. Averell said that Foy Kohler didn't know what it was all about and was treated by the Russians as a small boy.

The riots in Los Angeles are becoming bitter, vehement, and have burned millions of dollars' worth of property. Art Steuer, Dick Gregory's man in New York, telephoned me stating that the best solution would be to fire chief of police William Parker. Parker had said the Negroes were behaving like monkeys in a zoo and that he was determined to "turn the blotter black—arrest, arrest, arrest."

Yesterday Dick Gregory was shot in the leg. Fortunately, the assailant was not a cop but Negroes barricaded in an empty building. Dick wanted me to contact Governor Brown, who arrived in New York City this afternoon, to ask him to fire Chief Parker immediately. If done, this would leave a very sour reaction among the public generally, which doesn't know what Chief Parker has been doing. Like J. Edgar Hoover, he has a file on almost every important public servant, and in his opinion they can do no wrong. Parker is not going to be fired easily.

SUNDAY, AUGUST 15 | Dick Gregory called me about four o'clock this morning, asking me to arrange a secret meeting between him, Governor Brown, Lieutenant Governor Anderson, and me. He has been out on the street most of the night trying to calm Negroes and trying to get their guns away from them. His conversation ran something like this:

"I said before it happened, 'This is going to be the biggest riot in the history of America.' A Negro broke another Negro's store window. When I see that, I knew what was going to happen. The National Guard came in too late. They cleaned people off the street, and now the snipers are going to start. They are going to take potshots at the cops from the rooftops, and if ten cops are killed, they'll fire back into the crowds, and there'll be white bitterness. Every city is going to blow up. At present only Negroes have been killed, but when the white people start getting killed, then there will be white revenge, and the civil war starts.

"White America will get together to retaliate against the Negro, and then the Negro will retaliate against the whites. There's no guarantee that sticks of dynamite won't be thrown all over the place. If the Negro starts turning on water in New York with its water shortage and the white people start turning on the water to fill up their basins to protect their kids and then a fire starts—well, the biggest city goes up in smoke.

"What you've got to do is to win over the Negro—get some goodwill started. Bring out some soup kitchens and feed people the way you did in the Dominican Republic after you landed troops.

"If a Negro sticks up a bank and gets away with a million dollars, the Negro people grin. They're not going to help the white people. They've got nothing to lose through violence.

"And if one soldier gets scared and shoots into the crowd, the word goes all over to get the white man. You know what one Negro in Vietnam can do if he gets word that his mammy's killed. He doesn't know that she was killed while looting. You know what he'll do to one whole company."

I asked Dick about his leg wound. He said it had made him a hero, but it didn't happen exactly the way the newspapers reported it. "A cop knocked me down," he said, "and the Negroes started firing at him but hit me.

"There were some Negroes in a house, firing. I knew if I didn't go over there, the cops would start firing back. So, I stepped out in front. A hundred cops screamed, 'Come back, come back.' And a cop knocked me down. That's when the Negroes started firing at him and hit me. "I put the blame on the Negro. If I put it on the cops, fires would have broken out earlier in this town."

Later in the day I tried to reach Pat Brown but failed; however, things began to quiet down in Los Angeles. I talked to George Arnold. He said they'd experienced four days of hell. The rioting and the burning had come right up to La Cienega Boulevard, which is not very far from the district where he lives. He blamed part of the trouble on Police Chief Parker, whom he said had the same grip on Los Angeles businessmen that Hoover has on high officials in Washington. Parker has been making incendiary statements, calling the Negroes "hoodlums."

**MONDAY, AUGUST 16** | Pat Brown called back. He said that Chief Parker was a good, honest cop but had infuriated the Negroes by calling them "monkeys." The police were tired and shorthanded.

The trouble was poverty, Pat said, not civil rights. There had been a big migration from Louisiana, Mississippi, and Alabama to Los Angeles. "We have no restrictions here," Pat said, "but a lot were not able to adjust."

He asked me what I thought of John McCone to head up a blue-ribbon commission to investigate the whole Negro racial problem in Los Angeles. I said I had once been very critical of McCone but had come around to believe that he had done a good job at the CIA.

I suggested Dick Gregory's idea of having food distributed by the police in order to win back favor in the eyes of the Negroes. Pat said this wasn't practical because the police were worn-out. He is having the food distributed by the Salvation Army, with fifty markets open for them to buy food.

I suggested he talk to Dick Gregory regarding ideas on healing the wounds. One of them is to get the highest-priced defense attorneys possible for the Negroes arrested.

Dick Gregory called later in the day. "A new society has developed among the Negroes," Dick said. "It's the society of those who have been prosecuted and sent to jail. It's a badge of honor to have been sent to jail during these times. You ought to handle these prisoners as you handle prisoners of war," he suggested. "Cross-examine them, have sympathetic people do the cross-examining so you can get all the information you can from them. This way you can cure the problem and prevent another outbreak."

Dick said that 60 percent of the people in Watts were on relief.

**WEDNESDAY, AUGUST 18** | Dean Rusk gave a briefing on the Vietnam War and defined American honor as when the United States told the Russians, at the time of the Berlin airlift, that they were not going to get out of Berlin and mobilized an armada of planes to prove it. Again, American honor was illustrated when Khrushchev told Kennedy to get out of Berlin in six months or there would be war. "All right," said Kennedy. "If that's the way you want it, Mr. Chairman, that's the way it will be."

Or again, said Rusk, American honor was illustrated when the United States told Russia to get its missiles out of Cuba or there would be war. And today, said Rusk, we are illustrating American honor by defending a small country in Southeast Asia.

Rusk's eloquence was so contagious that one businessman came up to him afterward and said, "Mr. Secretary, you were magnificent."

"But," replied Rusk, "I am supposed to be dull."

**FRIDAY, AUGUST 27** | The Gemini astronauts are still in orbit, despite some difficulties. Today was Lyndon's birthday. He is fifty-seven. It has been exactly one year since the Atlantic City convention which nominated him.

Dean Acheson has just written his memoirs. He tells how in 1919 he became a liberal as a result of the mistreatment of coal miners in the 1919 strike. This brought back a flood of memories. It was 1919 that I, then a college senior, went to West Virginia to make a report on that same strike for the American Friends Service Committee. The Friends invested quite a bit of money in trying to help the semi-starving miners.

Later, when I came to Washington, it was Dean Acheson who befriended me perhaps more than any other person except Sumner Welles. Dean invited me to the Sunday night dinners held by Justice Brandeis. Dean was a young, energetic liberal in those days, and I was a young divorcé with not much to do. Sumner Welles, who never acted like a liberal but was underneath, also invited me to his place from time to time. In the long run I think that Sumner proved more of a liberal than Dean, though both in their way carved some important milestones for the United States—Sumner in foreign policy, in trying to head off the Japanese conquest of China and the march of the Hitler-Mussolini dictatorships, and later in laying the foundation for the United Nations.

Dean came along later and carved milestones in his firm stand against Joe McCarthy and in conceiving the Marshall Plan and NATO.

Significantly, I think Dean succeeded because he had as president Harry Truman, a man with great courage who was willing to follow Dean's advice. Sumner failed because he had as president Franklin Roosevelt, a man who thought he knew more about foreign affairs than Sumner.

**THURSDAY, SEPTEMBER 2** | Mike Mansfield spoke on the Senate floor, outlining the willingness of the Johnson administration to proceed with direct talks with the Vietcong. He could not have made the speech without either an okay from the White House or breaking with the White House. The fact that the administration has now shown itself willing to go very far in peace talks and the fact North Vietnam is not willing to talk has stilled much of the criticism of LBJ's Vietnam policy.

**WEDNESDAY, SEPTEMBER 8** | (Met with LBJ.) I asked whether he thought China would intervene in Pakistan. "We don't think they will, but we can't be sure," he said. "I cut off aid to both countries [Pakistan and India] some time ago, and they have been howling about it and calling me names, but I told them I wasn't going to give them any more aid until they send someone over and justify it.

"They say I am inexperienced in foreign affairs, but I am experienced enough to know that you don't give a lot of foreign aid to countries who may be at each other's throats, especially when you haven't got the foreign aid voted yet by Congress."

Lyndon said the Pakistanis were sore over the fact that he wouldn't go along with the consortium proposal last summer. "The State Department has been after me to aid India, and so has Chester Bowles, but I'm not going to move until this thing is straightened out."

I told him about the refusal of the Defense Department to make public the figures on aid to India and Pakistan. "We have never done that," he said. "We don't want one country to know what the other country is getting . . . If we told one what the other one was getting, they'd come in and demand more."

Marvin Watson came in as a signal that somebody else was waiting; the president, however, merely ordered some grape drink for himself and for me. I got up a few minutes later to leave, put the empty glass down on the little table in front of the couch where I was sitting. The president said, "Bring that glass along."

I handed the glass to the Filipino butler who lurks in a little closet just off the president's private passageway. As we were walking out, the president sighed as if he was tired. "I've had a hell of a week," he said. "First it was the maritime strike and then the steel strike. I'll be glad when this session of Congress is over. We've passed sixty-eight laws at this session," he said, "and Roosevelt passed only five laws up to 1935."

**SUNDAY, SEPTEMBER 12** | ABIDJAN, IVORY COAST—Slept late, 9:00 a.m. (a record for me). I have a room overlooking the lagoon. The view would be beautiful if Africans did not insist on closing the curtains and turning on air conditioning.

At ten we took a trip by helicopter over the city and surrounding country. We skimmed low over fishing villages built on stilts on the water's edge; people waving to us; over the jungle treetops—thick, dense growth which mankind has not yet penetrated; jungle clearings of villages with thatched roofs and pottery drying on roofs; clearings of trees with ashes showing where the trees had been burned down to make way for man's agricultural march; rows and rows of healthy rubber trees; palm trees for the production of coconut oil; banana trees planted in square plots about a half-acre in size with deep drainage ditches around each plot—because there is a six-inch rainfall on the coast.

Flying back to Abidjan, the city stood in contrast. It is as white as the ivory for which it is named—white skyscrapers with blue or red windows jutting up from a city which has sprung up from the jungle in a few brief years. Magnificent hotels on the banks of the lagoon; a new, modern market with varicolored earthen jars and bowls spread out in rows; and an older market with people thronging around the stalls.

Lunched with my chief host, who has been detailed by the president to accompany me. He says what the country needs is teachers. The Peace Corps, with only fifty people here, could do a terrific job if it could send in an army of teachers, but they must speak French.

Ghana next door is socialistic and has incurred the wrath of the British and most of its neighbors because of [Kwame] Nkrumah, who is a megalomaniac. He even calls himself "The Redeemer."

SATURDAY, SEPTEMBER 18 | Did a telecast by the marketplace. Also did a radio taping; called on the American ambassador.

We were supposed to leave on Nigerian Airways at four forty, but the plane was an hour late. When we got aboard, the passenger agent announced he was two passengers over. Ellen and I were asked to get off. At this point the captain took pity on us and invited me to sit in the cockpit, Ellen on the stewardess's jump seat in the rear.

WEDNESDAY, SEPTEMBER 22 | PARIS—What is troubling France today is memory—either too much or not enough.

Jean Beliard, who traveled with us across the United States with the Friendship Train, came to supper, and we discussed the past and future.

De Gaulle told Beliard—with great vigor—how, "If there is another war, French troops would be commanded by a Frenchman."

He [de Gaulle] doesn't remember that when a Frenchman did command those troops, France was pushed to the sea. He doesn't remember how Winston Churchill picked him from a crowded hotel lobby in Bordeaux to bring him back and groom him as the savior of France. He doesn't remember how Ike delayed the American entry of Paris one day so de Gaulle could march at the head of the troops. And he doesn't remember how Truman deliberately made a place at the Potsdam Conference for France and gave France a zone of occupation in Germany, though France had done no fighting for three years.

De Gaulle now wants to junk the carefully built NATO machinery of cooperation for the defense of Europe. He doesn't remember how the Allies pulled at cross-purposes before Hitler struck and how, if they had cooperated, he would not have struck. He doesn't remember how, in March 1936, the British cabinet debated all day as Hitler marched into the Rhine, trying to decide whether they would support the French. At the end of that day it was too late. Hitler had the Rhine, and a big start toward World War II had been taken. De Gaulle doesn't remember how cooperation at that time might have prevented war.

De Gaulle does remember how Chip Bohlen, our ambassador, was a pal of Ben Reber and the State Department group that coined the phrase "the so-called Free French" during the war. That's one reason he never sees Bohlen today.

And he remembers how FDR almost reinstated Laval, the traitor, as prime minister of France after V-E Day and how Anthony Eden had to persuade him not to.

I am writing to LBJ tonight suggesting he appoint Gen. Omar Bradley as U.S. ambassador to France—the man who retook Paris—in order to remind the French people of the bigger things and in order to talk back to de Gaulle.

FRIDAY, OCTOBER 1 | WASHINGTON DC—I've told my doctors that I probably have malaria. Having an aversion to air cooling, I opened my windows in Nigeria and found some mosquitoes inside the next morning.

SATURDAY, OCTOBER 2 | They finally took me to the hospital with a fever of 104.

SUNDAY, OCTOBER 3 | The doctors have diagnosed it as malaria.

FRIDAY, OCTOBER 8 | The president went to the hospital late last night and was operated on this morning. It was successful. It seemed to me, however, that he made too much of a show of the whole thing and that the doctors and the press secretary, Bill Moyers, went into too much detail. I am not interested in people's insides, even those of the president.

Before he went into the hospital, he had a reception at the White House and the State Department for Congress which proved a fiasco. Bess had gone to see him early in the evening to say that if he would get Congress adjourned and get the House members to the reception, "I'll pass your beautification bill for you."

Lyndon called John McCormack, but John was his usual grouchy self. He refused. Meanwhile, while the Republicans cussed, Lady Bird, senators, cabinet, and guests from New York waited at the White House and listened to the Ned Odum boys, who wouldn't stop singing, and finally the president said, "Let's go over to the State Department and have the show." Leaving Dirksen and Mansfield, who were supposed to ride with him in his lead car, behind, he swept Sheila MacRae and Fredric March into the limousine, and off they went. Bess had worked hard on the show, and Ernest Cuneo had written the lyrics. It was a great success.

Afterward they went back to the White House, where Lyndon was having such a good time he didn't want to go to the hospital. As Bill Moyers said, "The president's enjoying himself so much he wants Hubert Humphrey to have the operation."

My nights are long and lonely in the hospital.

WEDNESDAY, OCTOBER 20 | I have been having a wonderful time relaxing at the farm. The weather has been warm; the trees gold, green, and scarlet; the cows giving a fair amount of milk; and I haven't worried about the state of the world. Johnson is in the hospital, I am on the sick list, and General de Gaulle hasn't made up his mind to run for reelection. Therefore, aside from Vietnam and the problems of Sukarno, the world is at peace.

SUNDAY, OCTOBER 31 | Arthur [Goldberg] confessed he could understand how the UN job killed Adlai. He explained that there are 116 ambassadors, all of whom can see our UN ambassador at any time. It's their privilege, and they must be seen. On the other hand, the secretary of state in Washington only sees an occasional ambassador on very important occasions. Rusk also has a battery of . . . experts to help him with his homework, whereas Arthur has a very limited staff.

Arthur, however, is going about the job in a systematic way. He called on the Polish foreign minister on his own initiative to see whether the Poles had any word that the North Vietnamese were willing to negotiate.

Arthur's big problem is to try to keep the channels of communications open for the time when the North Vietnamese want to negotiate. That was why he was anxious to talk to the Poles—because they have direct communications with the Chinese. He could find no sign of willingness to conciliate, though the Poles were anxious to cooperate.

Henry Cabot Lodge and some of the embassy staff in Saigon apparently are opposed to Lyndon's policy of negotiation. They want to take the hard line and occupy South Vietnam for a long time.

I remarked it was significant that Russia had agreed to join in the World Bank talks regarding foreign aid for Indochina. Arthur said when the Russians joined the talks, they remarked to the Americans at Singapore in effect, "Don't make too much of this, and don't make too little of it either."

Arthur telephoned the president when students were tearing up their draft cards and gave him a little unsolicited advice on giving these youngsters the chance to be heard. He reminded the president that he, Arthur, had been called in to give advice when it was sometimes embarrassing, such as the strike negotiations, and therefore he felt he had the right to volunteer some advice. He told Lyndon that this country was founded on the right of free expression and that these kids had the right to express themselves.

"I don't agree with these kids, but they have a right to say what they think," Arthur advised. He told me that Johnson didn't like it much but followed his advice and kept hands off.

Arthur was optimistic about American-Soviet relations. In private conversations they are courteous and cooperative, though tough in public. They've become sophisticated and aren't going to make the mistake that Khrushchev did when he took off his shoe and pounded the table.

Foreign Minister Gromyko was fairly mild in his criticism of the United States over Vietnam, Arthur thought. They don't want the Chinese in there. Arthur suggested I check with Dobrynin regarding an incident he'd heard about where Dobrynin was asked by a small American group whether Russia wanted U.S. troops to pull out of South Vietnam. The answer, after some hesitancy, was reported to be no.

Tommy Thompson, Foy Kohler, and Averell Harriman maintain the whole trouble between the two countries is our policy in Vietnam. Arthur doesn't think so, believes it's the divided leadership in the Kremlin. Actually, the

Russians don't know exactly what policy to follow because they don't have one man guiding the country as they did with Khrushchev.

Lyndon is irritable these days. Talking to Arthur on the telephone, he complained that his back hurt and he couldn't sleep well. Apparently, he has had to have a catheter to urinate, which is extremely painful.

On one occasion Arthur was talking to the Poles when the president called. He refused to take the call. You don't do this with the president of the United States, but later Arthur explained that if he had taken the call at the Polish mission, the entire conversation would have been recorded.

The right wing is now in a position where they can play it either way and come out all right. They can quote their great hero, General MacArthur, that the United States should never get bogged down on the Asia mainland. Or they can claim that the Johnson administration wasn't tough enough in South Vietnam, was too ready to negotiate.

I got the impression that Arthur regrets leaving the Supreme Court. He said: "What I regretted most was leaving the chief justice. When I left, I got letters from every member of the Court but not from him. About six weeks passed, and I began to get concerned that I hadn't heard from the chief. Finally, he wrote me a long letter in his own hand telling me how much he would miss me." I gathered that the chief had leaned heavily on Arthur for support in some of the tough Court arguments.

I asked how Arthur thought his successor, Abe Fortas, would be. The reply was: "It will depend on whether he listens to the plaudits of the newspapers or to his own conscience. He can have all the plaudits of the newspapers and the bar associations. The latter will give you gold medals, but you will not be true to yourself."

THURSDAY, NOVEMBER 4 | Czech radio carried a Vietcong peace feeler earlier this week which has been taken seriously by LBJ and the Pentagon. It's started a hassle as to whether the president should entertain peace talks. The Pentagon has said flatly no; it would be a sign of weakness. Cabot Lodge in Saigon has backed them up.

Now I understand what Arthur Goldberg was saying when he warned that Lodge was very hard-core and wanted to make no concessions. Lyndon is going to stand by Lodge.

Meanwhile, we have almost as many troops in Vietnam as we had in Korea. The American people are not going to be happy when they find this out.

Lyndon issued a flat denial today that Clark Clifford and Henry Kissinger had been sent to Saigon on an official mission by him. He was irked because of news stories that they had found graft, dictatorship, and lack of real war effort at the top.

**FRIDAY, NOVEMBER 5** | Called on Tommy Thompson. I asked him about the articles running in the *Washington Post* by the Russian spy Col. Oleg Penkovsky, especially regarding his claim that Khrushchev was on a war policy. Tommy didn't agree.

Khrushchev, he said, was hipped on two subjects, the settlement of Berlin and trade with the United States. During Tommy's five years in Moscow, Khrushchev talked chiefly about these two subjects.

I recall that President Kennedy once told me, immediately after his Vienna showdown with Khrushchev, that he thought the East Germans were pushing Khrushchev and that this was why he pushed us so hard on Berlin.

Tommy didn't agree that the East Germans weren't pushing and even if they were, they had no hold over the Russians. They were supplying some specialized machinery, but this was not important enough to mold a policy over Berlin. Tommy felt that Khrushchev had gotten started on Berlin and let it become a fixation. Finally, he realized that we meant business and backed away. This occurred after Kennedy told him at Vienna, "It will be a long, cold winter," and then sent additional troops to West Germany. Tommy said that Berlin really hasn't been much of an issue since.

Tommy told me some fascinating history about what happened in Moscow on May 1, 1960, at the time of the U-2 crisis. He said that a member of the American embassy staff had seen a Red Army officer take a note up to Khrushchev on the Lenin tomb, which they later deduced was word of the U-2 flight. Khrushchev had told me at the Black Sea how he received this message while he was reviewing the May 1 parade and how he had given orders to shoot the plane down. He also said he'd given orders not to let anyone know that it had been shot down in order to entrap the United States.

Tommy said Khrushchev gave a report to the Supreme Soviet regarding the incident and that when he, Tommy, was ushered into the Supreme Soviet meeting, he was invited to sit in the No. 1 box. According to protocol, he should have sat in his own box, which was No. 2. He thought it was rather suspicious that he was urged by one of the Soviet foreign office to sit in the front row. He declined and sat in a rear row, partly because he was suspicious, partly because the Chinese ambassador was sitting in the front row. Later, when Khrushchev made his revelation regarding the U-2 and castigated the United States, everyone in the hall looked at the American ambassador. Tommy was glad he was not sitting in the front row.

That day or the next the Czechs gave a reception, which Khrushchev attended. When Tommy entered, Khrushchev was surrounded by a group of people but detached himself, took Tommy by the arm, and led him to one side, where they had a private conversation.

"We have invited Eisenhower to visit us," Khrushchev said. "We like to do these things in a big way, and we face a problem. In view of this incident I don't see how we can invite him." Tommy said, "I understand your problem."

I asked Tommy about the Czechoslovak peace feeler. He didn't attach much importance to it. I also asked him about the incident in which Arthur Goldberg had heard that Dobrynin, at one meeting, told Americans that Russia did not want U.S. forces out of South Vietnam. Tommy had not heard of it, but he did say he was quite sure the Russians did not want the Chinese in South Vietnam.

I mentioned the wholesome fact that the Russians were participating in the World Bank Development Plan for Southeast Asia, but Tommy said that although they sat in on the talks, they finally decided not to participate actively. They are keeping in touch but not putting up any money. Tommy thought it was because they couldn't spare the foreign exchange.

**TUESDAY, NOVEMBER 9** | (Beginning of New York City blackout.)

**WEDNESDAY, NOVEMBER 10** | A call from the newspaper syndicate that the post office had not been able to operate, the column had not moved, mail was piled high in the New York Post Office. In the syndicate they had operated the mimeograph machines by hand. Water pressure was low, toilets wouldn't flush, and even at noon, a day after the blackout, New York was partially paralyzed.

David Karr phoned to say that the scene last night was almost unbelievable. He sat in his office on Park Avenue and watched the lights go out. First they flickered in his office, then went out across the street, and one by one they went out in all the buildings around him. The people were very quiet, well behaved. There was little crime.

Some eight hundred people were stalled on the Queensboro Bridge in a subway train and had to be brought down by firemen with long ladders.

Ambulances ran out of gasoline because there was no electricity to operate the gas pumps. If there had been a fire, there was no water pressure for the hoses.

They still haven't been able to find out what caused the power failure. Nothing happened to the lights in New Jersey just across the way. It was only the New York power hookup, extending from Niagara Falls to Boston to Manhattan.

SATURDAY, NOVEMBER 20 | Last night Truman Capote, who has just written a book on a flagrant Kansas murder, came for tea along with Kay Graham, the detective in the case, and the widow of the judge who sentenced the murderers.

SUNDAY, NOVEMBER 21 | Agnes had a family luncheon. I sat beside Kay, and we diagnosed the distressing condition which is developing once again between the press and Lyndon. Walter Lippmann, according to Kay, thinks Lyndon is nuts. McGeorge Bundy definitely wants to leave. Kay noted that Bill White was the only newspaperman invited to the Princess Margaret dinner, as against all three of the TV network executives.

MONDAY, NOVEMBER 22 | It's reported that the Romanian foreign minister, when in New York, sounded out the United States on peace in Vietnam. Last week Eric Sevareid published in *Look* magazine a report on his last words with Adlai Stevenson. Adlai told Eric how Johnson had turned down some peace feelers put forward in fall 1964 by U Thant.

There were a lot of peace feelers at that time, and I reported some of them. It is hard to diagnose exactly what happened, and the only thing I am certain of is that Lyndon postponed the peace talks because he was then running for election and Goldwater was banging hell out of him as an appeaser.

WEDNESDAY, NOVEMBER 24 | There were 240 American casualties in Vietnam last week—a record. People are grumbling about Lyndon being in Texas. It's been six weeks since his operation, and some cabinet members are rebelling mildly and privately against the three-hour trip to Dallas, plus twenty minutes by helicopter, then the long flight back again. Chancellor Erhard has said he doesn't want to see Lyndon in Texas, only in Washington.

MONDAY, NOVEMBER 29 | Rumors have been increasing about Lyndon's health. McGeorge Bundy is leaving the White House, and rumors have started that Secretary McNamara may replace him as a sort of glorified assistant president. Bobby Kennedy is touring Latin America and obviously is already starting running for president.

**TUESDAY, NOVEMBER 30** | Had an appointment with Hubert Humphrey for 3:00 p.m. but as usual, he was late—by forty-five minutes. I was about to walk out when he finally arrived.

I started off by chiding Hubert about Bobby Kennedy getting all the headlines and nobody knew he, Hubert, was around. I told him I understood what he was up against, but still he ought to keep his name in the news. He got out a sheaf of clippings. "These papers in Washington won't print a thing. That's why I have to go out of town. They give me reams of space out of town."

"I went to New York and spoke for [New York mayor Abe] Beame, and the *New York Times* is so much for Lindsay, they printed hardly a word. They're so sore at the president's policy on Vietnam that they won't report what we're doing. I can't say that of course. It doesn't pay to tangle with the press."

I said Bobby was still stealing the headlines. Meanwhile, people were saying that Hubert had deserted his old liberal philosophy. I cited his speech saying that Communists were behind the student demonstrations against Vietnam.

At this Hubert almost jumped down my throat. He claimed he hadn't said that at all—rather, that a few Communists always attached themselves to any liberal demonstration and that it was too bad that the American demonstrations had to coincide to the very date with the Communist demonstrations in Moscow and other parts of Europe.

Then he went on to cite the different statements he'd made on the same subjects as Bobby Kennedy and had made them years in advance. "Nine years ago I was on the floor of the Senate as chairman of the subcommittee on disarmament and reminded people that disarmament must apply to all nations, including China. Stuart Symington stood and said, 'Do you mean to say that you would have us sit down with Red China?'

"'Of course,' I said, 'I wouldn't have my nation disarm and not have it apply also to China.'" Hubert was referring to the fact Bobby Kennedy had said that China must participate in any program to stop the proliferation of nuclear weapons.

"Bobby came out for a nuclear-free zone in Latin America," Hubert continued, "but I did that two years ago. I came out for the Alliance for Progress and urged that it be continued, linking it with political liberty. Bobby came out for this quite recently in Latin America. He also talked about rural development. It was in 1961 that I emphasized that the real problem was rural Latin America, not the big cities. Bobby is just catching up."

I asked when the president was going to deliver his message about a massive food program, and Hubert said it would probably be after Congress convened. "But I can't go around telling people that Hubert Humphrey said this and said that long before Bobby Kennedy."

"But you can tell your friends," I said, "and let us tell the world." Hubert agreed this should be done.

"You know how the president is," he said. "You keep trying to get in to see him. You keep sending him memoranda, and he doesn't pay any attention. Finally, he gets you on the telephone and asks you why you haven't done something about something, and you tell him to read the memorandum that you sent him several weeks ago. Then he wants . . . to know why you've been so lazy.

"I was supposed to take some trips abroad last fall. When the president got sick, that was wiped out. I had to cancel some speaking engagements in order to remain in town, and when I canceled them in advance, the president wanted to know why the hell I had done it. Nobody knew at that time that he was going into the hospital.

"I said, if I had done it after he went into the hospital, everybody would have been alarmed. 'They would have thought you were really sick. So, I figured that it was better for me to cancel the dates before you went to the hospital,'" Hubert added.

I asked about Lyndon's health and said there were rumors on Wall Street that he was not feeling well and that Bobby Kennedy had started to organize in all fifty states, figuring that he would be the nominee in 1968.

Hubert said the president seemed to be in excellent health. He talked to the president's doctor, who comes from Rochester, Minnesota. Dr. Cain told him that Lyndon should reduce but hadn't been worried about his health either then or now.

Hubert said he'd heard rumors that Bobby didn't expect Lyndon to live out his term. "I tell my friends that the president's going to run again in 1968 and if I am a reasonably good vice president and don't try to hog the limelight, I'll be renominated on the ticket. If not, I won't be renominated, and that's that."

I asked about the report that McGeorge Bundy was going to step down. Hubert said it was true. "I had misgivings about Bundy at first but not anymore. He is a good influence around the White House. He helped to sell the president on his April speech at Johns Hopkins, putting himself on record in favor of negotiation."

I asked who would replace Bundy, whether McNamara might do so and become sort of assistant president. "I think that's about right," Hubert said. "McNamara is a great secretary of defense, but with the Pentagon spending billions of dollars, anyone could be a good economizer."

He said McNamara was probably the closest man to Lyndon in the cabinet and that the president consulted him on everything. Hubert was disparaging that McNamara had spent one day crossing the Pacific, one and a half days in Vietnam, and one day flying back yet acts as if he knows exactly what's going on in that period of time and makes recommendations to the president.

I told Hubert I had noted his speech of a week or so ago regarding the civil rights program and that I was distressed at his statement there was not a thing the federal government could do further about civil rights. He denied he had said this. He said, "We have passed some great laws, and we now have to enforce them."

I argued that school funds were not being withheld as required by law in southern states where there was no integration. Hubert denied this. He pointed out that school funds had been withheld from Boston, Chicago, and much of Alabama. He also argued that under the law there had to be congressional hearings before the federal government could cut off funds to the southern states.

As I was about to leave, Hubert gave me an eloquent description of the president. "You know how he is," he said. "First he loves you, then he rides your tail off. My job is to work for the president—and he is a good president. He put across a terrific program in the Eighty-Ninth Congress. I helped, but I can't brag about it. I introduced the Wilderness Bill back around 1958 and got all the lumbermen in Minnesota so mad they called me a Communist. This year, though, by a little adroit maneuvering, we got it passed.

"I don't think they would have gotten foreign aid passed if it hadn't been for my work. I went to see some of our southern Democratic friends and told them, 'You may not like foreign aid, but we're the party in power, and we've got to be responsible. The people want foreign aid, and we've got to pass it.' So they voted for foreign aid.

"I'm no longer the Hubert Humphrey of the old Senate days. I can't speak out the way I used to. I can't claim credit for the achievements of the

Eighty-Ninth Congress. We got 'em passed, and I am glad the president is getting the credit."

**THURSDAY, DECEMBER 2** | Arthur Goldberg sold Lyndon on the idea of including China in the disarmament talks proposed by the UN, but today the Chinese refused unless they were members of the United Nations.

Patrick Stewart is in Moscow talking to Foreign Minister Gromyko about peace. He's gotten nowhere. Meanwhile, the CIA reports that the premier of North Vietnam went to Moscow and Peking to ask for aid. The Chinese promised no aid but urged that North Vietnam keep fighting. The Russians told him to take his country out of the war.

The pressure on Johnson to bomb Hanoi is increasing, both from the military and Republican leaders, especially Nixon.

**SUNDAY, DECEMBER 12** | This was made my birthday as far as the family was concerned.

**MONDAY, DECEMBER 13** | Lyndon flew in from Texas at 2:00 a.m. and is going to stay through the visits of Ayub Khan of Pakistan, UK prime minister Wilson, and Chancellor Erhard. He has already started chopping the Great Society portions of his budget to get money for Vietnam. Instead of talking about a further tax cut, the Treasury is eyeing ways and means of raising more money. The deficit is going to be terrific.

Many newspapers are speculating as to how Lyndon can ever get himself out of the Vietnamese war and what it will do to his political chances. It's true that the public is still behind him, according to the polls, but my political sense tells me they're getting very tired of this war.

Jack Anderson informs me that the Pentagon is familiar with Arthur Goldberg's proposal of a moratorium on bombing, but they believe he only has in mind the effect on public opinion and that he's not sincerely of the opinion that this might lead to peace. Jack also reports that Lyndon knew last July, when he started the American troop buildup, that he would need a total of 400,000 men this fall.

**THURSDAY, DECEMBER 16** | (Departed for Tel Aviv.)

**SATURDAY, DECEMBER 18** | (Toured Bethlehem.)

**SUNDAY, DECEMBER 19** | (First day of shooting on film—interiors of nuclear reactors. Discussed atomic issues with Dr. Ernst David Bergman, chairman of the Israel Atomic Energy Commission; interviewed [Israeli] chief of staff Maj. Gen. Yitzhak Rabin.)

MONDAY, DECEMBER 20 | (Toured seaport south of Tel Aviv; dined at the American embassy with visiting senators.)

TUESDAY, DECEMBER 28 | (Filmed Jewish immigrants for documentary; lunched in Haifa with Leo Herman; discussion of intensive Soviet spying operations in Israel due to strength of Israeli scientific community; discussion of possibilities of Israel's acquisition of atomic bomb.)

THURSDAY, DECEMBER 30 | (Drove to Dead Sea area to interview soldier-farmers.)

FRIDAY, DECEMBER 31 | (Reinterviewed Ben-Gurion.)

# 1966

## ANNALS

It was a year for the advancement of women and minorities and decline in public support for the war in Vietnam. In India the daughter of Jawaharlal Nehru, Indira Gandhi, became prime minister. Mrs. Gandhi was only the second woman to be an elected head of government. (The first was Sri Lanka's Sirimavo Bandaranaike.)

Indira Gandhi came to power at a tense time. India had just negotiated a peace agreement with Pakistan after another war over Kashmir.

Tensions in the Dominican Republic were solved by an election. Fearing another Cuba, the United States had sent forces in to end a civil war there. Along with forty-two thousand U.S. troops, the Organization of American States achieved peace. An election brought Joaquín Balaguer to power.

Lyndon Johnson's approval rating fell below 50 percent for the first time. (It had reached almost 80 percent in his first months in office.)

In France, when President Charles de Gaulle withdrew his country from NATO's military command, the French also demanded that all American military personnel leave. Johnson had Secretary of State Dean Rusk ask de Gaulle if the bodies of buried American soldiers must also leave France. That settled the argument.

In Oakland, Huey Newton and Bobby Seale founded the Black Panthers. Betty Friedan helped found the National Organization of Women (NOW). Labor unions in the private sector were declining. This was the last year in which union members made up at least one-third of the workforce. The Supreme Court continued to expand civil liberties with the *Miranda v. Arizona* decision. Mao Tse-tung launched the Cultural Revolution. Millions of Chinese were to perish.

The debut of *Star Trek* was an event. As astronomer Carl Sagan said,

"The visions we offer our children shape the future." The vision of *Star Trek* was that there would be a day when an interracial crew would be able to work together and explore the universe. In the midst of the Cold War and racial violence at home, *Star Trek*'s starship *Enterprise* included a Russian navigator, an Asian helmsman, and an African American communications officer.

—Ed.

## THE DIARY

JERUSALEM—(Shot footage for documentary; interviewed [Israeli] minister of finance Pinhas Sapir; met with Jerusalem mayor Teddy Kollek.)

**TUESDAY, JANUARY 4** | Drove to Ashdod, the new port just south of Tel Aviv, where I had previously interviewed stevedores. This time I visited the residential part of the town. A whole colony of apartment houses for new refugees has sprung up.

I interviewed a Polish woman, Regina Gwozdiewicz, who had been here only two months and spoke neither English nor Hebrew; however, she understood my Serbian—somewhat. She told a tragic story. We shot the conclusion of the film on a sand dune outside Regina's apartment house. This was my last day of work—a strenuous one.

**SATURDAY, JANUARY 8** | WASHINGTON DC—Talked to Arthur Goldberg in New York. He asked me to call LBJ and congratulate him on his peace moves. I could not press Arthur over the telephone for the part he had played, but I gather it was considerable. He said the president finally called him and said, "Let's get going."

He told me in early December that he had urged the president to come to the UN before Christmas, declare a truce on bombing North Vietnam, and announce that he would continue it while, and as long as, peace talks continued. The president obviously did not do the first part of it, so I assume Arthur came forward with the second installment—namely, an intensive public drive for peace.

Lyndon has transferred his future son-in-law, Pat Nugent, from Texas to Fort Andrews, Maryland, just outside of Washington, the same mistake that Sen. Pappy O'Daniel made with his two boys during World War II. Pappy screamed to high heaven when I exposed this, and I suppose Lyndon will do the same when I say something about Pat Nugent.

**MONDAY, JANUARY 10** | Earle Clements came to lunch. We talked about Bobby Baker and the fact Earle had used Bobby to make substantial campaign contributions around the country. Sometimes cash contributions didn't always turn up intact, but they always did with Bobby. He was one of the most trusted envoys of the Senate.

Earle made a pathetic remark about his own lobbying activities. He said he was now out of things, didn't see the president, and that he had to because he represented certain clients "that you write about from time to time." He referred to Superior Oil, which tried to bribe the late senator Francis Case of South Dakota. I was active in exposing this.

Here was Earle, once the majority leader of the Senate, once governor of Kentucky, now reduced to lobbying. I am sure Lyndon would have given him a good job. The only trouble was that Earle started lobbying during the Kennedy administration.

I talked to the president on the telephone, congratulated him on his peace offensive. He was rather noncommittal, remarked that he'd held 226 peace talks in all but it was necessary to dramatize them in the open.

He talked in a very low voice, without his usual exuberance. Arthur had warned me that he seemed to have changed since his illness. Today was the first time I have talked to him since the operation.

**THURSDAY, JANUARY 13** | Jack Gordon and Arthur Courshon, who have been sponsoring my program in Miami for about ten years, came to lunch, along with Joe Borkin; Henry Schultz, former counsel for the Anti-Defamation League; and Matty Rosenhaus, my old sponsor (Serutan). Jack and Arthur talked about some of the problems of liberalism in Florida. Jack has been on the school board for some time in Dade County. It's an uphill battle, but he has managed to keep the local witch-hunters from purging the textbooks, has completed integration, and says that things are going liberal now. Jack was Hubert Humphrey's campaign manager, and Art was Johnson's chief money raiser, also Kennedy's, in Florida.

George Smathers has announced he'll not run for reelection to the Senate. Significantly, he made the announcement not one day after Bobby Baker was indicted. George, of course, was one of those involved with the call girls. He claims to be ill and apparently is.

**THURSDAY, JANUARY 20** | Had an interesting talk with Bobby Baker about his defense and his book. He plans to get his book published about October this year. The first chapter will deal with the selection of LBJ as vice presidential candidate in Los Angeles in 1960.

I asked Bobby about certain things that came up in his indictment, particularly the $100,000 paid by my friend Mark Taper of Los Angeles, a savings and loan executive, which the Justice Department claimed Bobby stole.

Bobby said that during the 1962 session of Congress some savings and loan executives had come to Washington, that the Kennedy tax program meant a $32 million increase in their taxes, which they could not absorb at one time. They proposed a more graduated tax so that the increase would not hit them all in one year. Bobby took their idea to Sen. Bob Kerr, then a power on the Senate Finance Committee, who immediately said no.

Bobby pressed the point. Later Kerr said that if the savings and loan people would bring $200,000 in cash as a campaign contribution, he would introduce their tax amendment. Bobby said they delivered $100,000 and he sat in Kerr's office while counting the money. About $50,000 of it went to finance Mike Monroney's campaign for reelection. Bobby said this would hurt Mike when the whole thing comes out at Bobby's trial.

It occurred to me that the $40,000, which Bobby says came to him as a gift from Senator Kerr, came out of this $100,000 in cash, and I asked Bobby if he had any witnesses to show that this money to him was a gift from Kerr. He said that Kerr's partner, McGee, was ready to testify that it was a gift and that McGee would be Bobby's best witness. He added that he had paid income taxes on all of the funds received. Of course, a gift is not taxable by the recipient, only by the donor, and I suspect that Bobby is on thin ground here.

I told Bobby I thought we may have made a mistake in the column when we reported, just about the time Kennedy was killed, that Lyndon Johnson had been mixed up in the TFX contract and that he had made some calls to Gene Zuckert, the secretary of the air force. The column was due for publication about the day after Kennedy was killed, and because of the assassination, we killed it in most papers in order to carry the story of Kennedy's death.

Bobby said word had come from the White House to swing the TFX contract to General Dynamics and that Lyndon had nothing to do with it. He said there were two factors behind the White House decision. First was the fact that Boeing had been grabbing all the contracts and that General Dynamics faced a grave financial crisis and growing unemployment. He said Boeing had the benefit of the K-17, the air force tanker which became the B-707 but on which the U.S. government had done all the preliminary work. After that Boeing got all the big contracts. Bobby said that at one time Donald Douglas complained to him that Douglas would be in serious straits if Boeing kept on getting the big contracts. General Dynamics was in the same boat. So, the contracts had to be passed around.

In addition, Grumman, one of the prime contractors along with General Dynamics, was going to do a lot of work in Massachusetts, where Teddy Kennedy was running for election.

Lyndon had nothing to do with the whole matter, though of course he was interested in having work done in Fort Worth. When the word went to McNamara from Kennedy to switch the TFX contract to General Dynamics, McNamara simply found reasons for overruling the recommendation of the navy that the contract go to Boeing.

Martin Marietta was at the top of the list to get the contract with the best bid, and North American was about fourth; however, Jimmy Webb, head of the space agency, had once worked for Bob Kerr and, when he got the word from Bob, simply switched the contract to North American. It was as simple as that.

MONDAY, JANUARY 24 | After Jack Anderson had put in a week to work up the series on Sen. Thomas Dodd's finagling with Gen. Julius Klein, the *Post* did not use his column this morning. Later in the day, and after several phone calls by me, which were ignored, Russ Wiggins called back to complain not about the first column, which was omitted, but the second column, which has yet to be published. He complained that the series might look like malice because of repeated criticism of one man, also claimed that Jack was unfair in comparing Dodd with the late Senator Lundeen of Minnesota, who was a spokesman for Germany in 1940, when the United States was on the verge of war, and thus Lundeen had committed close to treason. Russ argued that our relations with Germany are far different today. I agreed with him on this point and also told him that I had inserted the stuff on Lundeen into Jack's column. We finally compromised on leaving out the references to Lundeen, and he agreed to use the column.

Later it occurred to me that the *Washington Post*, time after time, has belabored one person in various articles—for instance, Representative McMillan of South Carolina and Bobby Baker. I did tell Russ that we had documentation on Dodd and the fact that he was being used by a German agent and apparently was being paid.

Kay Graham, who has never hitherto telephoned me about anything in the column, called this morning about my story on Luci Johnson. She said that Jack Valenti had been tearing himself into ribbons to her last night, claiming that the army had transferred Pat Nugent, Luci's fiancé, without any prompting either from the White House or Luci and that any man had a right to secure such a transfer. Kay said that the *Post*'s Ben Bradlee had checked into the White House denial of my statement that Luci was failing in two subjects and found she was getting one F and two Ds. Liz Carpenter, in calling the *Post*, said, "Luci has the right to fail." Liz always did have a sense of humor.

Dick Goodwin, former White House advisor on Latin America for both Kennedy and Johnson, was at Kay's, helping her with a speech. He is now at Connecticut Wesleyan with a fellowship which requires him to do almost nothing. He says he doesn't even have to talk to the students. He made it clear that he got out of the White House because he couldn't stand Johnson's policies on Latin America, especially in the Dominican Republic. "You and I are about the only two people left in Washington who are interested in Latin America," he said.

**TUESDAY, JANUARY 25** | Had a date with Hubert Humphrey at 3:00 p.m., but he was busy being photographed with the National Dairy Council—drinking milk—and also by *Newsweek* for a "Day with Hubert Humphrey." Finally got in to see him at three thirty. I told him that while in the Near East, I had read about his troubles with his press relations man, whom he had fired, and the Evans-Novak pieces about his image.

"Yes," said Hubert. "It didn't help me a bit. Bob Jensen is still out trying to knife me. I had to call him in the other day. The fact was that Bob just wasn't doing any work. He had some personal problems, and he just wasn't around when I needed him.

"This business about polls and my popularity came from a man named John Carroll, who is my CIA liaison. He doesn't know anything more about public relations than a rock.

"Last fall he began telling me that I should spend more time hunting and fishing and not so much on politics. He said my image was bad, that a lot of people liked to think of me as a fisherman or a hunter, not as a politician. He wrote me a memo along this line and made carbon copies for different members of my office, one of them going to Bob Jensen. That's how it happened to appear in full in *Newsweek*. And that's how the idea got around that my image wasn't good. To hell with my image. I'm not going to go out and hunt and fish just because I'm vice president, when I've never done it before. I have a good time playing with my grandchildren. I have a good time with my wife. And I'm not going to change my way of life just for my image.

"I am jacking up my office. It hasn't been too efficient. This morning I had a meeting at 8:30 a.m. with some civil rights leaders. I had a memo giving me the background of the different leaders and what we were to talk about, and when I arrived at the meeting, the memo wasn't there. Someone goofed.

"I was in New York late last night with the American-Jewish Council and got home at 2:00 a.m. I had another meeting at 10:00 a.m. with congressional leaders. I opened the Senate at twelve. I had to rule on parliamentary matters."

"To hell with my image," he concluded. "After all, I'm working. I'm getting things done. And I am the vice president of the United States, which is a hell of a lot more than I ever thought I'd be twenty years ago."

We discussed the pressure on the president to resume bombing North Vietnam, and Hubert said it was terrific. "It comes chiefly from the military," he said. I told him that it also came from Henry Cabot Lodge, to which Hubert replied, "Yes, but Cabot is a good professional, and he'll go along. The military aren't so easy to handle.

"McNamara has used a restraining hand on the generals. He's realized his mistakes of the past. Somebody told me the other day that McNamara was all out for resuming bombing again. 'Look here,' I said, 'I was there. I have just come from a White House meeting where McNamara was present, and I know that he isn't for the resumption of bombing.'"

When I got back to the office, I called Wayne Morse to get the lowdown on the Senate Foreign Relations Committee meeting of yesterday where, Hubert had said, "they gave Rusk a very bad time." Wayne said he hadn't been at the meeting . . . He said that a meeting of congressional leaders had been called at the White House and right now they were probably en route to get the news from the president that bombing would be resumed.

Wayne said, "This is the beginning of the greatest mistake the president has ever made. You remember what the Russian ambassador told us at your house—that if we bomb Hanoi, Russians are going to be hit, and it would be very difficult for Russia to stay out."

Luvie and I were due at seven thirty at the Averell Harrimans' for dinner.

We arrived on time, but Averell did not arrive until about eight fifteen. He had been detained in part by the White House meeting with congressional leaders.

I asked him when we were going to resume bombing North Vietnam, and he said he had no idea. He argued, however, that we were losing too much military advantage by delaying the resumption of bombing. I argued to the contrary.

"You know well from having been ambassador in London during the war that bombing doesn't pay," I said. "It merely stiffens the determination of the nation that's bombed."

Averell argued that the United States could resume bombing and then break it off later, after it had destroyed some military targets. I said that to resume bombing and then break it off made us appear to be vacillating, that we would lose face and peace negotiations would be much more difficult. He disagreed.

He told us about his talks on the recent trip. He found Gomułka of Poland an old-fashioned Communist out of tune with the times. The Polish government, he thought, was far more out of step with its people than other Communist governments. The theater, music, the universities, had made tremendous progress in Poland, but the government has not. On the other hand, the Yugoslav government and the Yugoslav people are very much together.

He described Tito as a tough old warrior who had impressed upon him the importance of getting Russian cooperation for peace pressures on North Vietnam. Tito had his differences with Russia and perhaps for that reason was anxious for further cooperation

WEDNESDAY, JANUARY 26 | NEW YORK—I dropped in to see Arthur Goldberg. He occupies the old office of Adlai Stevenson but has turned his desk around so he looks out on the UN building and the East River. Adlai sat with his back to the river.

We talked about Humphrey. Arthur said that Hubert must never lose his strength with the liberals. This was his great anchor to windward—the Jews, the Negroes, and labor. I observed that Hubert felt he had only one constituent—LBJ. Arthur agreed but also pointed out that LBJ respected power and that if Hubert lost his political power, Lyndon would be the first to dump him.

There was no doubt in Arthur's mind that the president would resume bombing. "It's a decision he hates to make," he said. The question was the timing. Arthur remarked that the minute bombing was resumed, he and Dorothy would take a trip to the Virgin Islands, partly for a vacation, partly because he wanted to get away when the policy of bombing was resumed.

"The military want us to go in with 600,000 to 700,000 men," Arthur said. "When they get a certain number of troops in, they immediately ask for more." Arthur said that McNamara had become somewhat disillusioned with the military, though he has not yet really argued against bombing. If he had, Lyndon would go his way.

Mike Mansfield argues for small enclaves along the coast, similar to the proposal of General Gavin. We now occupy a few cities along the coast, and all Johnson would have to do to adopt the Gavin policy is to stop big offensives in the jungle and sit tight where we are. Arthur seemed to think this was what we would do.

Arthur felt Mansfield had a lot of influence with Lyndon, while Fulbright didn't. "He's too lazy," said Arthur. "He doesn't work at the job of opposing Lyndon from the inside. It's much easier for him to come out with a public statement opposing Lyndon instead of arguing at the conference table.

"The Foreign Relations Committee is split—one side wanting war, the other peace. There is no cohesion. Lyndon respects Fulbright's brains, but Fulbright just doesn't know how to handle Lyndon."

I showed Arthur a copy of Andrew Tully's confidential note to editors stating that Goldberg had no confidence in U Thant. "Absolutely untrue," commented Arthur. "We enjoy a complete trust and cooperation. U Thant told me the other day, 'You get me a yes or no answer in one day. Adlai didn't get me an answer for six months.'"

FRIDAY, JANUARY 28 | Luci Johnson called to thank me for the column this morning, written about Pat Nugent and how he arranged for his transfer to Washington on his own.

There is still no decision regarding the bombing. Lyndon was curt in replying to fifteen senators who asked him to continue the moratorium.

The Senate Foreign Relations Committee held a public meeting, with TV cameras present, to grill Rusk on Vietnam. They gave him a very bad time.

MONDAY, MARCH 7 | Talked with Senators Hartke, Young, and Morse about the session of "dove" senators, in which Gene McCarthy went almost berserk against Lyndon. In the end, however, they all backed down except Fulbright, Morse, McCarthy, and Young, who voted to rescind the Bay of

Tonkin Resolution. I was surprised that Wayne Morse, who is usually critical, this time is laudatory of Fulbright. Most of the time he's rather lazy and complacent, but when the big crises come along, he stands and fights.

Wayne gave me a full account of what happened in the Foreign Relations Committee when Fulbright tried to move toward the ousting of Tom Dodd from the committee. Claiborne Pell turned out to be Dodd's chief supporter—also, of course, Russell Long, which I expected, and Stuart Symington, which I didn't.

Talked with FDR Jr. about running for governor of New York. He confirms he will run but doesn't want any public announcement. He was interested in the reaction of the Buffalo Jewish community when I told him that on the whole they would be for Rockefeller. I told him that Frank Sedita, the mayor of Buffalo, was strong for him.

FRIDAY, MARCH 11 | Sukarno appears to have been kicked out of Indonesia—at long last. He had been president since Indonesia became an independent state in 1946 or '47. I remember the first time he came to Washington. Joe Borkin, who was then plugging for him as a public relations man for Indonesia, held an early morning session for him at the Indonesian embassy. Present were Justices Felix Frankfurter, Hugo Black, and Bill Douglas, one or two friendly senators, and two or three newspapermen. Sukarno came in, very jaunty, wearing his black Muslim fez at an angle, and proceeded to speak in excellent English about all sorts of things but chiefly about Borneo. Indonesia wasn't satisfied with getting independence for its vast island empire; it also wanted Borneo and wanted it immediately and wanted it badly. Sukarno made an ineffectual argument about needing Borneo, which was then under the Dutch and obviously unable to govern itself. It had a population not at all similar to the Indonesians; however, he indicated he was willing and able to fight for Borneo if necessary.

Sukarno made several other trips to the United States . . . His other trips were partly to the UN and partly on junkets over the United States when he flew to Mexico or on to the Pacific. On one occasion he collected several American women and proceeded to enjoy them on the route west. His plane was known at the time as "the high-flying whorehouse." In Russia the Soviet government planted a brunette on him, whom he took back to Indonesia and kept her as a sort of third or fourth wife, until the army objected and made her go home.

I saw Yolanda Fox at the big Democratic jamboree, which Luvie helped to stage at the Shoreham to raise money for the Democratic Women's Club. She and Luvie were selling all sorts of things. I bought a pair of African sandals, which I claimed were formerly used by ex-president Nkrumah. I hope I shall not follow in his footsteps.

I also bumped into Gene McCarthy of Minnesota and Hubert Humphrey's sister. I expected fireworks from both. The sister was most pleasant, despite the mean column I had written about her attempt to get out the police patrol to take her from Columbus to Dayton during the big blizzard.

Gene did not deny the story I wrote about him that morning on the meeting of doves and the very critical statements they'd made about the president. I had quoted him as saying, "We have a wild animal in the White House, and we have to treat him as such." He went on to discuss the tactics to be used against the president in Vietnam and said: "At least we have made him pause a little bit and think twice before he goes any further. He's going to have to nod to us in passing."

I hope he's right. I think Lyndon is really trying hard to confine the war. I learned yesterday he had sent messages to the Chinese indirectly through the French and, I think, the Poles, saying that he had no intention of attacking the China mainland.

TUESDAY, MARCH 15 | The Senate Ethics Committee has finally decided to investigate the Dodd case and is sending its counsel around to see Jack's files this morning. They have decided not to go into Dodd's campaign contributions. As I have been telling Jack, this is a sensitive point with every senator. They have interviewed Dodd, whose chief defense is that he did not do the things that Julius Klein asked him to and, second, that Klein imposed on other senators as well.

Had a visit with Pat Brown, who says, "I'm having a great time being governor of California, but I sure have a tough time getting my contract renewed." He had just finished a session with Sargent Shriver, from whom he was trying to get $250 million to help place unemployed Negroes to work. There are about fifty thousand unemployed in Watts and other areas. Their wives can get jobs, but the men can't because they migrated from Alabama and Mississippi and have no skills. Brown said he had the jobs ready for them as janitors, doorkeepers, etc., and in various government offices, but needed federal funds. Shriver turned him down; said that if he did it for California, he'd have to do it for other states, and with the war in Vietnam, they didn't have the dough.

Pat is worried about the amount of money he'll have to raise and spend first to defeat Sam Yorty in the Democratic primary and later to defeat either Ron Reagan or George Christopher. He thinks Reagan is the better TV personality but that Christopher is the better politician.

Talked to Orville Freeman at the Agriculture Department. He said he was feeding more people in Mississippi than in any other state. He had as his chief opponents the Delta Ministry, a part of the National Council of Churches, which did not want too many people fed there because, they said, they would lose the issue. The issue, of course, is unemployment due to the firing of the Negro sharecroppers by the big plantation owners.

THURSDAY, MARCH 17 | I called on Bill Moyers. Hadn't seen him since I went to West Africa last September. He said the president had telephoned him a week or so ago about the memo I'd sent on the chief justice. He said the president had a deep affection for the chief. I said it was reciprocated.

Bill said the president was not responsible for chopping the salary increases for the Supreme Court, which, of course, I knew.

I took up with him the idea of a visit by Hagen, editor of *Quick*, to the Texas ranch, which Bill said he thought was a good idea.

He mentioned the columns on Dodd, and I said we had left out some things pertaining to Jake Jacobson, whom, I said, attended one meeting with Dodd but that we had called him up, and in view of his denial, we had omitted his name; however, I said that Jake had lied about this.

During the course of our talk the telephone buzzed, and Bill got on with the president for a long conversation. I suppose I should have ducked out, but I didn't think it was going to be that long. During the course of the conversation Bill told him, "Drew Pearson is here and says the chief justice worships you."

Obviously, Bill and LBJ were talking about press reaction to something or other—I think one of Walter Lippmann's pieces, because Bill remarked that Kay Graham said she thought the president's statement was the best rebuttal he had [ever] given to Walter.

Later in the evening I ran into Kay, who said she had Bill Moyers to lunch that day. She added: "I'm back in. I've been invited to the White House for the dinner with Mrs. Gandhi."

Jake Jacobson called me at home after I'd returned from the White

House to say the president had just read him a memorandum stating that he [Jacobson] had lied regarding the meeting with Tom Dodd. He claimed that he had not been there, though he had talked with Joe Resnick at a White House reception about the Dodd affair, which he said was a mistake; he shouldn't have done it.

Incidentally, Moyers made an interesting remark that Jacobson and Marvin Watson haven't been around Washington and don't understand some of the things here. Marvin and Bill have been reported at odds over various things, ranging from monitoring White House phone calls to ousting Abba Schwartz from the State Department.

FRIDAY, MARCH 18 | The Indian ambassador, B. K. Nehru, came to lunch.

I said Orville Freeman had told me he was sending eight million tons of wheat to India. B. K. expressed surprise at this since so far the deal was only for two million tons of wheat, with one million tons of milo. Milo, he said, was a surplus crop which was raised in Texas, and the United States wanted to get rid of it. The people of India had never eaten it, didn't know how to use it, and if forced to eat it, they would riot; however, the gentleman in the White House had said in effect if they are starving, they can eat anything.

The ambassador was a little sour on the whole question of American aid and the American tendency to ignore India in the past.

"What you do in South Vietnam," he said, "we'll ignore because you have helped us in regard to China. We are your friends. The Indian people are so worried about China that we are 100 percent with you, but underneath, when you talk to people individually, you can find no one who is really for your position in South Vietnam. They don't like the idea of a big country picking on a tiny country.

"Personally, what I am worried about is that you will concentrate on one small part of Asia and forget the main part. India has five hundred million people. Laos has seven to eight million, Cambodia five million, and South Vietnam fourteen million."

The ambassador said there were only four countries in Asia which really amounted to anything: China, India, Japan, and Indonesia. The rest could slide into the Pacific, and no one would really miss them. The United States was in danger of alienating all four of the big powers.

He pointed out that we had given foreign aid to Formosa [Taiwan] at the rate of $7.68 per head and to India at the rate of $.65 per head; we had sent aid to Libya at the rate of $20.69 per head and Korea at the rate of $8.71.

We discussed the prospects of peace in Vietnam and the fact that an Indian envoy had just come back from North Vietnam after getting nowhere. "The trouble is they regard us as stooges of the United States," said the ambassador.

"We have fairly good intelligence there, however, and during the Christmas holiday on bombing North Vietnam, our people reported that the doves in North Vietnam were beginning to gain strength. In North Vietnam they have their doves as well as their hawks, just as you do. During the moratorium in the bombing the doves were able to tell the hawks that they were wrong in their all-out policy against the United States. Then suddenly you resumed the bombing."

He said the president had asked to confer with Prime Minister Indira Gandhi, alone, when she arrives at the end of March. He said he didn't want any advisors around "telling us what to do." I speculated as to who would win that argument, Lyndon, who can be a passionate wooer, or Mrs. Gandhi, who is quite stubborn.

We agreed that Lyndon didn't know much about India, except that he had delivered a Texas yell on the steps of the Taj Mahal when he visited there as vice president, but we agreed that he was learning.

The ambassador described Lyndon as a man with a heart of gold, great passion, and compassion. He told how he had bumped into two Americans in India who were selling pumps. They said the president had called up the head of their firm and told him to get down to India and peddle some of the old-fashioned pumps which could pump water out of shallow rivers for irrigation.

The ambassador remarked that one of the problems was finding someone in the State Department who would stand up to Lyndon and disagree with him. Rusk, we both felt, does not do so; George Ball did to some extent. B. K. said that when he talked to the president, he got an average of about five minutes in for thirty minutes of conversation. I had to agree that my ratio was about the same.

The ambassador described Mrs. Gandhi as not particularly well qualified to be prime minister but that she had several important things going for her: first, her tremendous popularity; and second, her strength. When the Calcutta riots broke out recently, she refused to bow to disorder, sent word that she would listen to any grievance, provided the rioters observed the law. If they did not, she said, they would be met by force and would be shot. This enhanced her popularity.

**MONDAY, MARCH 21** I Early in the day Jack told me the FBI had called him this morning to say the attorney general had ordered an investigation of us for the alleged theft of Dodd's files. Deke DeLoach, the caller, said the investigation had been ordered indirectly by Bobby Kennedy because of his hatred of me. I can't really figure out how Bobby would have that much influence over Katzenbach, and I suspect the FBI was just trying to cross a few wires; however, I told Jack to call Rosenthal, the press relations officer at the Justice Department, and ask him whether the Justice Department had investigated Sen. John Williams of Delaware for his possession of unauthorized documents; whether it had investigated Senator Dodd for his possession of the Otepka papers, etc. Jack said he had quite a conversation with Rosenthal today.

**WEDNESDAY, MARCH 23** I At 5:00 p.m. Jack Anderson and I had a session with Attorney General Katzenbach and Jack Rosenthal regarding the Justice Department's investigation of us regarding theft of the Dodd papers. I was surprised to see Fred Vinson Jr., chief of the criminal division, there. I had not seen him since he pitched baseball on the St. Albans team when Tyler was in school there. His father was one of my best friends when he was chief justice of the United States, and he played bridge with Luvie on the average of once every two weeks.

Fred's presence lent some credence to the report which Morris Bealle gave my two Reidsville friends that a grand jury was being called to indict us for the theft of the Dodd documents.

I was inclined to laugh it off in talking to Katzenbach and told him how I had been investigated by the Justice Department under Eisenhower when Roy Cohn had tried to get me indicted for possession of the secret intelligence reports on the strength of the Chinese army during MacArthur's disastrous retreat from the Yalu River.

Jack was somewhat bellicose—too much so in my opinion. He talked vigorously and indiscreetly about the manner in which Dodd's employees had come to him with these documents.

Luvie and I made a quick call on Soapy Williams, who was holding a farewell reception at the State Department and is going back to run for the

Senate from Michigan. Mayor Cavanagh of Detroit is running against him in the Democratic primary, which may well mean a Republican victory in the fall. The *Detroit Free Press* has yet to publish my story on Cavanagh's police record.

From the State Department we went to the White House for the chief justice's birthday party. I think my memo to the president may have had something to do with his scheduling of this reception. In addition to friends of the Warren family, a lot of judges from both the District of Columbia and New York were there, together with members of the House and Senate Judiciary Committees.

There was some comment regarding the Dodd columns. We bumped into Mrs. Katzenbach, who, remembering our last dance at the White House, said something about "May I have the next dance?" to which her husband said, a little ominously I thought, "Mr. Pearson has already danced."

The president seemed in a good mood and looked well. When I complimented him on how well he looked, he said something about having a pretty hard day, beginning with "de Gaulle in the morning, the Celler funeral during the day, and this tonight." [He had flown to New York for the funeral of Rep. Emmanuel Celler's wife.]

There were howls from some of the newspapermen that Lyndon hadn't given them advance notice regarding the trip and didn't even tell them where he was landing; however, he didn't know that Mrs. Celler was going to die and certainly has the right to make up his mind at the last minute, also to keep his destination secret when police problems are so difficult in New York.

THURSDAY, MARCH 24 | The Yugoslav ambassador came to lunch. He'd arrived back from Belgrade two days before, after a month at home. He said he'd had a long talk with Tito, who is very understanding about American affairs and well pleased with them. He said I would be welcome back in Yugoslavia and hoped that I could come soon. He said Tito would be pleased to see me. He also mentioned that they were planning to invite the chief justice to visit with the chief justice of Yugoslavia. I told him the chief was going to Israel in July and possibly could stop off en route.

The Russians and the Chinese have finally reached an open break regarding the Twenty-Third Party Congress in Moscow next week, with the Chinese refusing to attend. On Tuesday the bitter letter addressed to the Chinese by the Russians was published by a Hamburg paper and picked up by the

*Washington Post*. Today the equally bitter Chinese reply was published, accusing the Russians of collaborating with the United States in deserting the principles of communism. The ambassador felt that the Twenty-Third Congress would be better off without the Chinese present.

When I mentioned that fifty thousand Chinese troops had gone to the Sinkiang border opposite Kazakhstan, he pointed out that what the Russians really feared was a trek of a million and a half people across the border, Chinese civilians, whom the Russians couldn't fire on. They would swamp the economy of Kazakhstan.

Secretary of State Rusk was at the Russian embassy, the ambassador said, when he received a telephone call which canceled the signing of the cultural agreement between Russia and the United States. The luncheon was held for the purpose of toasting the signing of the pact, but Rusk suddenly called it off. The president, according to my information, was irked because the trip of *Hello, Dolly!* to Russia had been suddenly canceled, and he wanted assurances from the Soviets that there would be no more sudden cancellations of this kind.

The Yugoslav ambassador remarked that to him the significant fact was that Russia had gone ahead and signed the agreement despite this sudden disruption at luncheon. They might well have waited until after the Twenty-Third Party Congress but didn't. They signed two days later. I gathered he felt this was an indication of how much the Russians wanted American friendship.

FRIDAY, MARCH 25 | I saw Tommy Thompson regarding the Russian-Chinese split and specifically the question of whether this did not give Johnson a very important opening to cement better relations with Russia. I said Lyndon had done a terrific job of improving relations during his first year in office but lately had been crotchety regarding the Russians. I suggested that the present impasse and the public refusal of the Chinese to attend the Moscow conference might be a way to get the North Vietnamese to the conference table.

I pointed out that the problem of Germany was now pretty well taking care of itself and that disarmament was pretty well disrupted by our war in Vietnam. Tommy agreed. He also agreed that Johnson had been able, by mutual consultation, to cut back on arms with the Soviet but that this was now out the window as a result of Vietnam.

He said the Chinese-Russian showdown was an old row which possibly began in 1956, when Khrushchev began downgrading Stalin and talking about coexistence. It really got bad, Tommy said, however, after the Camp David talks in 1959.

"When Khrushchev went to Peking," Tommy said, "they were really rude to him. They didn't meet him at the airport, and they treated him badly. I think the row between China and Russia all began then."

Tommy confirmed that Rusk had been called away from the luncheon table at the Soviet embassy, though it was not, he said, to break up the treaty. He said he'd phoned Dobrynin at nine thirty the morning before the lunch to tell him that the treaty would have to be held up. He said that it was difficult to get papers of this kind on the president's desk in time for action.

SUNDAY, MARCH 27 | In the evening Clayton Fritchey and the Chester Bowleses came to supper. Chet is back in New Delhi for his second tour as ambassador and says he doesn't have time to travel around the country as much as formerly. There are two thousand people in the American embassy, or attached to it, and much of his time is taken up with routine administrative problems.

He has been around among Indian farmers. At first they were against fertilizer; now they're crazy for it. They remarked to Chet: "You're from America. When are we going to get this fertilizer you've been talking about?" Chet thinks that with fertilizer and more agricultural know-how, India can be self-supporting for food in three to four years.

The Russians have been making a tremendous play for India and, in fact, for the rest of Asia. They have been wooing Japan also, but their biggest bid is India. Thanks to some important weapons at a time when India was threatened by Red China, Russia has made an impact.

Hank Byroade is now ambassador to Burma, a rather dull assignment. Chet described Burma as one country where China might conceivably move in, in order to flank India on one side and Vietnam on the other. Aside from this Chet doesn't think that China has any aggressive intentions.

He reminded us that the Nehru family has a soft spot for Chiang Kai-shek since he was the first to advance and champion Indian independence. We speculated that probably Madame Chiang has had more influence on modern history than any other woman of this generation. It was she who repeatedly came to the United States to preach the doctrine of "hate Red China" and the idea that an independent Formosa [Taiwan] might eventually retake the mainland.

Chet recounted some of his troubles with Representative Rooney of Brooklyn, whom he considers the worst influence on State Department policy. Everyone is scared of him. Rooney will not permit blocked currency in Poland, Yugoslavia, or India to be spent for education or for the travel of the American staffs to see the country. In India it's important to have the staff of the U.S. embassy get around and understand Indian problems, but this is expensive. Meanwhile, Indian rupees, accumulated from the sale of American wheat to India, lie idle.

This week Rusk stated that the United States was contemplating the recognition of Mongolia. Clayton predicted this would bring such opposition from Chiang Kai-shek that Rusk might retreat again. He recounted Rusk's cowardice, during the Kennedy administration, when Kennedy planned to recognize Mongolia in order to strengthen American influence in Asia; however, he got an ultimatum from Senators Mundt and Hickenlooper, both members of the Republican minority on the Senate Foreign Relations Committee—hereupon Rusk backed down.

**TUESDAY, MARCH 29** | Flew to Rochester and found myself sitting in the plane just in front of Jim Farley and beside Bob Hill, former ambassador to Mexico during the Eisenhower administration. Bob was the protégé of the late senator Styles Bridges of New Hampshire and, after he got out of the diplomatic service, went to New Hampshire to serve in the legislature. He told me he was disillusioned and got out. The reason was the heavy use of campaign funds in influencing the legislature.

Bob said that Sherman Adams was opening a ski jump behind his home and had collected money from Sinclair Weeks, former secretary of commerce, from him, Bob, and other members of the Eisenhower administration. Adams had been a recluse ever since the vicuña coat incident but now was coming out of his shell.

I thought that compared with Tom Dodd, Adams had been a relative saint. Hill said that the columns on Dodd had caused concern in the business community among those who had previously relied on Dodd to handle problems for them.

**WEDNESDAY, MARCH 30** | Spent the day in New York and had an interesting talk with Arthur Goldberg. He told me about his trip to the University of California, where he was greeted unfavorably by demonstrators against the Vietnam War. In his speech he justified the American position in Vietnam on the grounds that the UN was not yet ready to police all the areas of the world, especially this one, and therefore the United States had to protect a small country from aggression.

I thought Arthur's reasoning was a bit labored but did not say so. Obviously, he is having a hard time reconciling his personal conscience with the official position of the Johnson administration.

Arthur told me about a visit he'd had with the president the same day he had to cancel an appointment with me in New York in order to testify before the Rooney Appropriations Committee. I believe it was on the day I came to speak before the Intercollegiate Editors at Columbia, March 11. Arthur said that instead of attending the Rooney hearings, he spent four hours with the president. Lyndon just wouldn't let him get away. It was in the little room just off the president's office where I have sometimes talked to him—or rather he to me.

Arthur said he told the president: "You ought not to be rowing with Fulbright. His hearings were part of his job, and he conducted them in a very dignified way, a way which will help you by giving you some alternatives regarding China.

"And you never should have let Gene McCarthy, Hartke, and the Senate liberals stray away from you. They are your friends. You should have talked with them instead.

"Don't just take the advice of [Gen.] Bus Wheeler regarding Vietnam. You've got to see other people aside from the military men. The circle of men around you in the White House who will really tell you the truth is becoming smaller and smaller. You've got to see more of your old friends and not just have around you people who agree with you."

"Who do you suggest?" asked LBJ.

"You ought to see more of Drew," replied Arthur. "He's your friend."

"Drew's not my friend," replied the president. "He hangs around with the Russian ambassador until two or three in the morning. He does anything the Russian ambassador wants him to. He's a peacenik. He's always criticizing my policy in Vietnam."

Arthur said he disagreed. "I have read his column," Arthur told Lyndon. "He hasn't been critical of you. He's been quite objective. He's a newspaperman. He's criticized me when I did something wrong, and he has the right to criticize you. He's not a press agent. I hire a press agent, and you have Bill Moyers as your press agent. We wouldn't respect Drew if he always agreed with us. He's got to be independent."

"He writes about Luci," the president expostulated. "Why did you keep your son's marriage so secret? Drew hasn't written about that. Did your son marry a Jew?"

Arthur explained that his son had married a Christian, but she had been married by a rabbi and was taking studies in the Jewish faith, with a view to becoming a Jew. "When I am asked whether she is Jewish, I say I don't know." He said that obviously the president was sensitive about Luci becoming a Catholic.

I racked my memory as to whether I had ever seen the Russian ambassador late at night. Arthur asked me whether I had ever seen him at two or three in the morning, and I was able to say that I hadn't. The last time I saw him was at luncheon on Dumbarton Avenue shortly after I came back from the Near East. The only other time I have been to the Russian embassy in the evening was last November 7, at the big reception, when Luvie and I left around 8:00 p.m. About two or three years ago, I believe during the Kennedy administration, Luvie and I had dinner at the embassy and later stayed to see a movie filmed by Mrs. Dobrynin, but I think we left at about ten.

I suspect that the FBI, which has a camera across the street from the Russian embassy on Sixteenth Street, made a hazy shot of someone coming out of the embassy at two or three, probably someone with a mustache, and thought it was me.

Luvie suggests, however, that the president may have read an FBI report on a luncheon which broke up between 2:00 or 3:00 p.m. instead of 2:00 or 3:00 a.m. Lyndon can jump to conclusions.

Arthur said Bob McNamara was getting fed up with the warped advice his military men had given him on the war and was becoming a dove instead of a hawk.

Arthur thought I should see the president more often. This is a little difficult because I don't like to barge in with my hat in my hand. Furthermore, Lyndon will never be satisfied if you don't give him about 99 percent support. Bill White has been writing columns supporting him on everything. It makes Bill look like a White House public relations agent. I'm afraid Lyndon, when beset with difficulties, is going to get more touchy about criticism. The war has been going reasonably well in recent weeks, but . . . agitators have been demonstrating from Boston to Washington.

**THURSDAY, MARCH 31** | (South Vietnam's) Premier Ky appears to be in more and more trouble. Ambassador Lodge has cautioned Washington not to praise him publicly because it increases the public impression in Vietnam that he's the stooge of the United States.

All of this indicates that Lyndon's trip to Hawaii to meet Ky was a blunder. It was motivated, undoubtedly, by a desire to take the headlines away from Fulbright, and while it may have helped Lyndon politically here at home, it didn't help in Vietnam. The trouble with Lyndon's policy in Vietnam is that it's almost entirely geared for domestic consumption and based on American political reaction.

(Attended USO [United Service Organizations] dinner in honor of comedian Bob Hope.) I sat beside a navy corpsman who had been slightly wounded in Vietnam. He was attached to the marines and said he liked Vietnam and would be glad to go back.

Another veteran, an air force master sergeant, had been badly wounded in both legs. One of his legs was cut away almost to the bone, and he rather enjoyed pulling up his pants leg to show it frequently during the dinner. He also enjoyed Vietnam and said he would like to go back. The women, he said, were beautiful, partly French, partly native, and he had lived with one for about a year, in fact had a son by her. I asked him how she was getting along, and he replied that an army captain was taking care of her and that he was sending the boy some money.

The sergeant described the Vietnamese army as completely undependable. "They run over to the other side and fight against you if things get rough. I would rather have one Vietcong fighting on my side than five of the Vietnamese army.

"On the other hand, the Rangers, especially trained by the United States, are excellent fighters and the equal of the Vietcong."

The sergeant said the trouble with fighting the Vietcong was that you couldn't see them. They were hidden in the jungle so they could see you but you couldn't fire back effectively. He was rescued by helicopter at night after he and about fifty men had fought off the Vietcong in a small area almost completely surrounded by the enemy.

The president came in toward the tail end of the dinner and paid a tribute to Hope.

**FRIDAY, APRIL 1** | Pat Brown telephoned from Sacramento to praise my column on preserving the redwoods. He said Doris Duke telephoned him from Honolulu to say she'd read my column and wanted to contribute to the purchase of some of the redwood land before the trees could be cut down. While she couldn't go for the $45 million necessary to establish the Redwood National Park, she said she was willing to buy up some of the land.

"You don't realize how much power you have and how much good you do," he said. "When you get behind a thing, it really moves."

We agreed that next week I should call Doris Duke and see if she would consent to have a story written.

WEDNESDAY, APRIL 6 | Had a cocktail party for Milton Shapp, who is running for governor of Pennsylvania and will probably get the nomination, though I suspect will be defeated by the Republican lieutenant governor in the general election.

Orville Freeman dropped in. He said Lyndon was sore over my reference (in a recent column on Madame Gandhi) that he had required the Indians to take Texas sorghum (milo). Lyndon apparently blamed Orville for what I wrote, though it came from the Indian ambassador. What I said was that the Indians suspected Lyndon has required them to buy milo because it came from Texas. This was a fact. They did. It's funny how the president will take time to explode over a two-line item of this kind.

THURSDAY, APRIL 7 | The anti-Ky, anti-American riots in South Vietnam are getting worse. The city of Da Nang in the North is now out of control. Ambassador Lodge has urged Premier Ky to send troops up there to control it; Ky is opposed. He fears it would result in a lot of bloodshed, with the United States and his own administration being the goats. The Joint Chiefs of Staff are again pressuring LBJ to bomb Hanoi and Haiphong.

FRIDAY, APRIL 8 | The Ky government looks extremely shaky. Lyndon staked all or nothing on him at the Honolulu conference.

SATURDAY, APRIL 9 | The riots in South Vietnam seem to be getting worse. Earlier in the week all American troops were ordered off the streets, but over the weekend one American civilian was stoned, two American cars burned, and it looks as if the Buddhists were out to end the regime of Premier Ky. One of the things held against him is that Johnson built him up and embraced him at the Honolulu conference. Of course, this conference was held in haste, with no thought behind it. I'm convinced it was called in order to offset Bill Fulbright's Senate Foreign Relations Committee hearings.

Late in the evening four members of Senator Dodd's staff came to see me. Jack brought them because they were terribly discouraged over recent events. They had been willing to stick out their necks, and two of them have lost their jobs. It seems to them the administration has ganged up against them and to some extent that we have let them down. It's obvious that the FBI is conducting a whitewash of Dodd. It's also reported that the Senate Ethics Committee will do the same, though with more deliberate speed. I have purposely held up a couple of the Dodd columns, partly because I thought they could be better written, partly because some editors felt we were overdoing it.

Dodd's former staff members say they can see he is more confident now, getting back on his feet, and feels he is no longer on the defensive. General Klein sent a two-thousand-word letter to all editors blasting me. It is full of misstatements and relies largely on the fact he is Jewish.

I assured the former staff members that we were not running out on them and we would renew the battle next week. Meanwhile, James Boyd, former assistant to Dodd, has been fired from the House Public Works Committee, thanks to Speaker John McCormack's intervention with Representative Fallon of Baltimore, who is chairman of that committee.

SUNDAY, APRIL 10 | Easter Sunday. In the late afternoon we stopped at Kay Graham's to meet Winston Churchill's offspring, who are here for the dedication of their father's statue yesterday. Randolph Churchill and I don't get along, but I had a nice talk with Christopher Soames, who married Mary Churchill and who Winston used to call "the brewer."

MONDAY, APRIL 11 | The riots in Vietnam have calmed down. Yesterday George Ball said on TV that the riots had not affected the war. Today Art Sylvester of the Defense Department says the war has been slowed down, partly because ships have not been unloaded, partly because South Vietnamese troops have been awaiting the decision of the riots.

Jack and I went to see several members of Congress to get action on Dodd. First, we called on John Moss of California to suggest that he, as chairman of the Government Operations on Suppression of the News, hold a hearing regarding the fact that the FBI had tried to intimidate us, investigate our news sources, and intimidate witnesses. This was a strategy which we had worked out Saturday night with the former Dodd staff members. Moss listened carefully and at first seemed favorable, but the more Jack talked, the more he shied away from the idea. I think we drew a blank.

We went to see Sen. Wayne Morse, who listened for five minutes and gave us an immediate affirmative answer. We asked him to make a speech on the Senate floor expressing concern over reports that the Ethics Committee was going to whitewash the matter. This is difficult and delicate because the Senate rules do not permit the criticism of another senator; however, I suggested that he do it without mentioning Dodd's name, merely saying that the reputation of the entire Senate was at stake.

Later I called Sen. Steve Young of Ohio, who also agreed immediately to support Wayne. I tried to contact Fulbright, George McGovern of South Dakota, and Senator Smith of Maine—all out of town.

**TUESDAY, APRIL 12** I I sent a long letter to Kay Graham taking issue with the recent *Newsweek* story very critical of me. I am sure she had nothing to do with it.

It seems to me that if the Dodd case fails of action, it will be impossible ever to improve the ethics of the Senate—and cynicism about Washington throughout the nation will spread. There will be a green light to cheat. If they can cheat in high places, we can cheat down below. There will be a feeling of one standard for Senate employees, as in Bobby Baker's case, and another standard for senators.

Some of the facts given us by Boyd's staff are shocking. Jim Boyd worked for Dodd for twelve years. It was not until latter years that he became convinced that Dodd was dishonest. When they broke, Dodd told him, "I'll drive you out of Washington."

I think the greatest scandal regarding Dodd is one we really haven't scratched: his contributions from insurance executives. These were carefully recorded on his statement, either because they came by check or because they came from Republican insurance executives. Significantly, this was the only occasion on which they ever contributed to a Democrat. Dodd has delayed investigation of the insurance companies for five years.

**WEDNESDAY, APRIL 13** I Telephone call with Pat Brown. He was cheerful despite all the brickbats thrown at him. He said there might be some chance to persuade Doris Duke to spend $2 million on a small plot of redwood trees to save them as a national park. He suggested I call her. I'm afraid I wasn't too kind to Doris when she and Jimmy Cromwell got their divorce, but I'll try.

**FRIDAY, APRIL 15** | Wayne Morse followed through on his promise to speak on the Senate ethics. So did Steve Young. They delivered statements that made headlines the next day, and strangely, Senator Fannin of Arizona, a Goldwater man and the only Republican present, got up to join them in the debate.

These speeches, plus the column published yesterday, have bolstered our witnesses and given us the initiative again in the Dodd case. The FBI, however, is still determined to whitewash the matter.

When I was in Beverly Hills, David Karr recalled how closely the FBI works with ex-FBI men and how close it is to Schenley's and Judge Irving Kaufman. [Schenley Industries Liquor Company, based in New York City, with a distillery in Indiana, owned several brands of whiskey and other beverages.] It was easy to understand, he said, why Dodd should hire Schenley's private eye to come to Washington to shadow us. Lou Rosensteel hired Lou Nichols, former No. 2 man in the FBI, as vice president of Schenley's.

Dave reminded me that Walter Winchell and I had built up J. Edgar Hoover in the old days, and now we had a Frankenstein monster with whom we had to live.

The Iranian ambassador came for lunch. I extended an invitation to the Shah to come to our IPA convention. The ambassador was realistic. He said the Shah would probably not come unless there was an invitation from President Johnson.

**SATURDAY, APRIL 16** | Johnson has been getting a tumultuous reception in Mexico City, and I am predicting he will take more trips like this through Latin America. I have written a column saying he should fire Tom Mann. I am sure the effect will be to solidify Mann in his job. Lyndon doesn't like to get ideas from anyone else, especially when it pertains to an old friend from Texas.

**MONDAY, APRIL 25** | Louis Johnson died yesterday. He was seventy-five years old. I had known him intimately when he was assistant secretary of war. When he was so eager to become secretary of war, it was pathetic. I remember at the Chicago Democratic convention in 1940, when Roosevelt was renominated for a third term, Louie came there full of expectancy that he would become secretary of war. Harry Woodring was on his way out. It was my sad job to tell Louie that the president had made up his mind to appoint a Republican to fill Woodring's place in order to give his administration some bipartisan flavor. Henry L. Stimson got the job. Louie was crestfallen.

Later, after Truman took office, Louie achieved his great ambition. He was made secretary of defense. This was in spring 1950, as Jim Forrestal became non compos mentis. Truman was criticized for firing Forrestal and appointing Louie, who had been his campaign manager; however, the fact was that Forrestal was out of his mind and unable to make sense at cabinet meetings. He called Tom Clark on one occasion to tell him that little men were shadowing him and for Tom to get the men off his trail.

Louie dutifully cut the budget as the Republicans and the defense experts recommended and then was caught short for the Korean War in June 1950. He never recovered from the criticism. Truman fired him in September that year, and Louie told me that after he had been fired, he walked out of the White House, up Sixteenth Street, just walking and trying to figure out what had hit him and what he would do next. It was a tough blow for a man who was so ambitious.

I was always grateful to Louie for allocating one of his best lawyers to defend the Sweeney suit in Clarksburg, West Virginia. It was the first case (we won) and a real setback to Sweeney.

Tyler and Bess had a housewarming for their new home on Twenty-Fourth Street last Friday, and Luvie reported that it was a huge success. The president came early. Tyler was dressed in red pants and a suede coat with an ascot tied around his neck. The president looked at him and remarked, "Now I see why the mails are late."

I asked Luvie if she had told the president her views on Vietnam, but she said, "No, he stopped me with a big kiss."

Mary Rockefeller and Bill Walton came to dinner. Bill said that Ken Galbraith, who testified today before the Senate Foreign Relations Committee generally supporting the administration's position on foreign aid, was invited by the president to fly back to Washington on the presidential plane from the Celler funeral in New York. The president wanted to talk to him about India before the arrival of Madame Gandhi. Ken found himself in the private compartment of the plane, at dinner with the president, Lady Bird, and J. Edgar Hoover. Hoover didn't open his mouth during the trip.

Galbraith has kept up his contacts with Johnson and gave a glowing speech in his defense before the ADA [Americans for Democratic Action]. Ken seems to be the only important member of the Kennedy crowd close to Lyndon. I wonder if he might later become secretary of state. If so, he would be an improvement over Rusk.

Jack Valenti is leaving the White House to become head of the Motion Picture Producers Association. About two weeks ago Jack Anderson gave me a story that the two men were feuding and that Valenti had been placed over Moyers. We held the story because it looked as if Moyers would win out in the end. Apparently, he has.

**WEDNESDAY, APRIL 27** | Called on George Ball, undersecretary of state. I had told him I hoped he wouldn't resign. His reply was that he had been in office longer than any other undersecretary of state in history, except Sumner Welles, and that eventually he would have to get out to make, as he called it, a "dishonest living."

He said there was no secret that he had been "fighting a lone battle for almost six years against involvement in the Vietnam War. The president listens; he reads what I say. He is careful to ask my judgment. The press has respected my position and not played it up, which is one reason I have been able to stay on.

"The amazing thing is that for almost six years Rusk and I have disagreed, and yet it hasn't hurt our personal relations. Nor has it hurt my relations with Bob McNamara or McGeorge Bundy." I asked if it was true that McNamara had become quite a dove recently. George confirmed this.

He went on to say that he thought the Bay of Pigs was responsible for the whole mess. "After the Bay of Pigs, Kennedy felt he had to show strength. Before that he had only six hundred military advisors in South Vietnam, which was under the figure permitted by the Geneva treaty. After September 1961, however, we began pouring in troops. And we've continued to pour them in ever since. I was alone in opposing this, and I'm still alone."

"We're in a desperate situation," George said. "I don't see a light at the end of the tunnel. There is real danger of escalation. I think the MIGs, which have been fighting over North Vietnam, are Chinese, or they could have been North Vietnamese trained by the Russians. At any rate they're not Russian. People don't realize that these things can creep up and up until very soon you are in a war.

"The North Vietnamese are adamant in refusing to talk. They think they're winning. And when they see what's happening in Hue and Da Nang, they may be right. I can't tell you how many approaches we have made to them, but they won't budge."

He was referring to the recent dogfights taking place between American bomber fighters and MIG-21s—the first time MIGs have appeared defensively over North Vietnam. Meanwhile, the Seventh Fleet has been alerted for possible submarine attack by Chinese or Russian subs in the Gulf of Tonkin in retaliation for our intensification of the war.

The newspapers have been playing up Dodd's testimonial dinners and the fact that Dodd didn't pay taxes on approximately $200,000 received from dinners which everyone else thought were campaign dinners.

Jack called today to report that the FBI yesterday suddenly began reversing itself and was examining the witnesses whose names we had given it a month ago. On Monday my column, telling how the FBI had used police state methods in investigating Dodd and how the FBI was close to the president, had quite an impact. We heard from many people.

THURSDAY, APRIL 28 | Jack had a talk with the vice president yesterday and was informed that Lyndon had completely reversed himself on Dodd. He now feels that Dodd let him down. He had tried to save Dodd and was undoubtedly behind the prejudiced manner in which the FBI was investigating. He now feels Dodd took advantage of his friendship by having him come to those two fund-raising dinners when Johnson was vice president.

The president is making Katzenbach the goat. The word is he will fire him, replacing him with Ramsey Clark, who is a good man and also is a close friend [of the president]. He comes from Texas.

FRIDAY, APRIL 29 | The dogfights continue over North Vietnam. The president, however, has held back against bombing the North Vietnamese MIG bases, despite urging from the air force. Joe Alsop has a column this morning which could push the president into action.

The Senate Ethics Committee announced today it would hold public hearings on the Dodd case, though confining it only to his relations with Gen. Julius Klein. This should be the easiest to prove. Naturally, the senators don't like to get mixed up with the matter of campaign contributions. Apparently, they are leaving this to the IRS [Internal Revenue Service]. I am beginning to understand why Sheldon Cohen called me. Undoubtedly, it was at the suggestion of the White House. At that time last week the White House was still in Dodd's corner and undoubtedly wanted us to know that the IRS could be too.

THURSDAY, MAY 5 | The White House staged its annual diplomatic reception and buffet dinner last night, inviting the ambassadors only after a lot had booked other engagements. The Mexican ambassador, for instance, had already invited most of the Senate to the ceremony for Mike Mansfield. As a result, the ambassadors were late getting to the White House. The Hungarian and Romanian ambassador each had his picture taken . . . with Johnson. It's not often that a Communist ambassador can get this kind of a trophy.

Mrs. George Wallace has won an overwhelming victory in Alabama in the Democratic primary for governor, which means her husband will be in power for another four years. There is a close election in Selma, Alabama, between Sheriff Clark and Safety Director Baker, a moderate. The Justice Department has intervened to seize some of the ballot boxes. It looks as if Baker has won, thanks to Negro votes.

SATURDAY, MAY 7 | Senator Dodd has hired attorney John Sonnett, formerly assistant attorney general in the Truman administration, now with one of the biggest Wall Street law firms. Sonnett apparently knows his way around Washington, especially with Judge Holtzoff, who was in the Justice Department at the same time. He appeared before Holtzoff and secured an order (without our knowing it) to attach our records and produce them in court [in Dodd's libel suit against Pearson and Anderson], including not only documents but copies of documents. Holtzoff issued the order, and Dodd's attorneys promptly issued mimeographed press releases in the Senate press gallery. It's obvious that Dodd, who had his tail between his legs, has been bolstered by outside support—or else by desperation. What he's doing now is attempting to take the play away from the Senate Ethics Committee.

MONDAY, MAY 9 | Premier Ky upset the carefully negotiated plans to hold national elections in South Vietnam in August by stating, in a press conference, that he expected to hold office for another year regardless of the elections.

TUESDAY, MAY 10 | Ernest Cuneo, who says he has been in touch with the White House, reports that the president is sore at Dodd for bringing suit. Senator Stennis of Mississippi, chairman of the Ethics Committee, is reported also to be sore at Dodd. Hitherto he has called Dodd regarding every move the committee has made. Now he says Dodd can paddle his own canoe.

Franklin of the *New York Times* called to discuss the case. He says Dodd is going to make a motion on Thursday to set aside his own deposition, which we had noticed for Monday the sixteenth, and also to close the depositions from press attendance.

Clayton Fritchey came to dinner last night. He has just returned from the Kentucky Derby, where he saw Sen. John Sherman Cooper of Kentucky, a member of the Ethics Committee. He emphasized to John that the Senate's name would be mud if the Ethics Committee did not crack down on Dodd. John agreed.

THURSDAY, MAY 12 | This morning I gave instructions to the girls in the outer office not to interrupt me even if President Johnson called. They did interrupt me. Lady Bird called.

Lady Bird said she had read the letter I had written to her husband about his going to the national parks with foreign ambassadors. I thought it was interesting that she referred to LBJ not as "the president" but as "my husband," which to me is a much better way of talking about him than the way the Kennedy family referred to Jack as "the president."

Lady Bird continued that she wanted to talk to me about Lynda. Lynda Bird, she said, "has never been abroad. In 1964 there was the campaign, and in 1965 she took that trip through the Far West, where she shot the rapids and climbed mountains and visited all the national parks to try to emphasize the importance of seeing America first."

"So, I am not one to tell her that she can't go abroad now," she said. "She's twenty-two and has almost a straight A average at the University of Texas. She won't get a Phi Beta Kappa because we had her come up here for one year, and that's our fault.

"She's going to stay with some of our old friends like Carol Duke in Spain so she won't really be draining many dollars out of the United States.

She concluded by saying that she wanted Luvie and me to know, once again, how much they appreciated the "imperturbable efficiency of Bess. I don't know what we could do without her."

I told her that we had nothing to do with it, that Bess was a great gal on her own with no help from us. "Yes, I know, but you take the children over the weekends so she can help us," said Lady Bird. I didn't tell her that as far as I am concerned, this is a real treat, though Luvie does get tired sometimes.

We went to dinner in honor of the chief justice and Arthur Goldberg—the big annual dinner of the American Jewish Committee. I sat on the second dais, just below Nina Warren, who looked very sweet and lovely. Much to everyone's surprise, the president arrived at about 9:00 p.m. I didn't know he was coming. He was given an award and made an eloquent reply about freedom. He kept looking at me about half the time while he was delivering it, as if the speech were meant chiefly for me.

He and Lady Bird left immediately afterward to go to the big Democratic meeting at the Armory, where he delivered a rousing defense of the war in Vietnam.

At our dinner Judge Proskauer, now eighty-eight years old and the former brain trust for Al Smith, delivered a stirring introduction of the chief justice. He didn't have a note. Probably it was the best speech of the evening. The chief, in turn, introduced Arthur, who had some important things to say but did not say them very well. His main point was that the United States was now pushing for the ratification of the genocide convention, making it a crime to conspire for the mass murder of any group [of] people. This was initiated in the Truman administration long ago but has been gathering dust in the State Department.

**FRIDAY, MAY 13** | Spent most of the morning in court listening to arguments before Judge Holtzoff regarding the Dodd depositions.

Yesterday we served notice on Dodd to produce about forty documents from his files when he appears for deposition on Monday. We retained Duffy, the famed process server, who nailed Pegler and others when I badly needed to get them. Duffy handed Dodd the subpoena just as he was entering the Senate Judiciary Committee hearing. Duffy, who is not adverse to some good publicity, tipped off the TV camera people and the photographers so that a striking photo was in the papers this morning. This made his counsel, John Sonnett, see red.

Sonnett blasted me for conducting this trial in the press. He read my letter to Holtzoff. It was a reasonably good letter, but letters like this are always dangerous and could be improved. I was against sending it in the first place but deferred to Jack.

The judge, however, sounded bored and told Sonnett to go ahead with the argument. In the end Holtzoff ruled against us on two important points— namely, that Dodd's deposition should be taken first and that the deposition should be open to the press. I did not care about the latter, but I did about the former. Holtzoff ruled against Dodd that all of his depositions should be completed. He said that the sides should alternate.

Arthur Goldberg came to lunch. He said that after our dinner he heard indirectly that at least five senators had stated he would probably resign soon. Arthur's point was that you can't trust senators. They always talk. I'm afraid he's right. He had said at the dinner that every president should have an ambassador at the UN who was part of the career team (not a political figure) and thus inclined to be independent of the State Department. Obviously, this was interpreted as meaning he would get out.

He told me he missed the Court, especially the chief justice. I told him that Abe Fortas had not been taking his place and that I had noted this in the column; and that Thurman Arnold had become sore as hell over it.

Talking frankly, he said he thought his leaving the Court for the UN had been justified by several developments he had achieved; that they weren't entirely accomplished but were "on the train."

He said he'd persuaded the president to accept the theory of two Chinas. Johnson always said, "Get Rusk aboard." He had not had too much trouble with Rusk, himself, though there was opposition by some of the China experts in the State Department. We discussed whether the Chinese would be mollified by the adoption of this new policy. They had been insistent that Taiwan be included in China and have made it clear that they didn't really care much whether the United States now recognized them or not.

Arthur argued that the old order must change in China, that Mao Tse-tung could not be propped up forever, and that we needed to meet China halfway.

Arthur said the second thing he had put on "the train" was a proposal for a joint meeting between the Chinese and the United States at the foreign minister level. Again, he had no trouble getting the president to approve. I gathered that he had been busy this morning getting Rusk to give his okay and had succeeded.

Arthur also said he got the genocide convention off the shelf and put it back in for ratification. "In this case I called Bill Moyers and said I assumed that the president would not be opposed to a policy which had been endorsed by two previous presidents, Truman and Kennedy."

Moyers agreed. The State Department didn't protest because it figured that Arthur had cleared it with the president. In the past the State Department has opposed the genocide convention, Arthur said, because of probable objections from Russia.

Next, he'd been able to get an agreement on Ribicoff's proposal to send UN advisors to Vietnam. "I discussed this with Rusk today. Probably the UN will turn the idea down. The Russians will be opposed, but we will press it."

The next accomplishment at the UN that Arthur listed was the American position on Rhodesia. "We wouldn't have done anything if I hadn't taken a firm stand on this," he said. I am sure he is right. In the past we have run in the other direction when the question of South Africa and Rhodesia have come up, and I recall vividly how hard Wayne Morse had to press on this when he was a special ambassador to the UN during the Eisenhower administration.

Arthur is concerned that Clark Clifford is going to replace George Ball as undersecretary of state. Clark is a hawk and an effective one. Arthur says he sits in on National Security Council meetings as the chairman of the Intelligence Committee, that he is succinct, effective, and forceful. He will have an influence on the president.

Arthur sends his letters direct to Lyndon, with a carbon copy to the secretary of state. Rusk never opposes him. They get along fine, but this is probably due to the fact Arthur can talk to the president direct.

Arthur noted that Clark Clifford was close to the president, and it was Clark and he, Arthur, who settled the last steel dispute. They brought it in to the Labor Department, Arthur representing labor and Clark representing industry.

Arthur says Bill [Douglas] called him up the other day and wanted him to help get a visa to visit China. "Talk to the president yourself," Arthur replied. "He's your friend. You were for him in 1960, and he has a good memory."

Arthur said he knew Bill had seen the president because late one evening he got a call from Lyndon, who said: "Bill Douglas is here, and we've been braggin' on you. Bill wants to go to China. Is there anything wrong with it?"

Arthur replied there was nothing wrong, but he didn't think the Chinese would let him in (so far they haven't). They take the position that since we don't recognize them, they're not going to recognize any of our people as visitors. He does think, however, that the present situation in China is the equivalent to the era in Russia just before Stalin died and that big things are stirring.

The most hawkish one around the president, according to Arthur, is Henry Cabot Lodge, who has just come back from Saigon to confer at the White House this week. Cabot actually telegraphed Washington urging that we bomb Cambodia. The president decided against him, as he usually does in risky cases of this kind.

When I mentioned Premier Ky's statements that he was going to remain in office another year, this did not disturb Arthur. He indicated that at the right time the United States would kick him out or help the Buddhists take over.

The worst influence of all is Dean Acheson. He is always hovering around the president and doesn't think it's possible to have peace with the Communist world.

Arthur wanted to know whether Chief Justice Warren was involved in the Dodd matter. I told him I thought not, except through friendship. Arthur thought that Katzenbach had handled the matter poorly.

"Crime," Arthur said, "does not decline because of police efficiency. It declines because there are more jobs. The reason crime has been reduced 12 percent in Washington is because we have full employment."

SATURDAY, MAY 14 | Brezhnev has returned to Moscow from Romania after what appears to be a difficult session. There are reports that Romania may bolt Moscow. Kosygin is still in Cairo. He was invited there apparently because Nasser has to dicker with the United States for a new food agreement, which comes up June 30.

Bess has flown to Texas on a mysterious mission. Both Lady Bird and Lyndon are in Washington, and Luvie suspects that she has gone down to persuade Lynda Bird either not to get married or else to remain in the United States this summer. We are taking care of the boys.

Late yesterday Sonnett filed a new motion with the court, completely disregarding some of the rulings the judge had made.

MONDAY, MAY 16 | (Held press conference regarding libel suit against former San Francisco mayor George Christopher.)

FRIDAY, MAY 20 | We dined at the Greek embassy, where I met Tom Sullivan, a Dumbarton Avenue neighbor, who is in the Treasury and told me that only on Monday the sixteenth had Rheinmetal paid restitution to the Jews for using slave labor during the war. I think he said Rheinmetal had paid $600,000. Obviously, the payment at this late date resulted from the publicity over Julius Klein.

Sullivan said that Klein had been a pain in the neck with the Treasury on various matters, particularly the Rheinmetal contract to manufacture the German gun which the Defense Department wanted. I think it's called the M-20. This is the reason the Springfield, Massachusetts, arsenal was closed down.

TUESDAY, MAY 24 | The situation in Vietnam has become chaotic, with the Buddhists bucking Ky in every major city. Lyndon roped in Speaker McCormack, whom he doesn't particularly like, to speak before the International

Labor Press Association. McCormack, who left the White House for a legislative strategy meeting, and the president stepped into the East Room to talk to the delegates. McCormack told them, "This country has never left the field of battle in abject surrender."

I received an invitation to a White House civil rights conference next week. SNCC has turned down the conference invitation. It has also kicked out its former leaders, John Lewis and James Forman. Over a year ago, when I was in Atlanta, I had a session with the SNCC people, and it seemed to me that Lewis and Forman were way over on the left side. They had been invited to go to Guinea by President Sekou Touré to study the question of black Africa and had come back with ideas about a segment of the South which was to be run entirely by Negroes. I remember Dick Gregory warning me of the militancy of the Negro movement and how the old line and the moderate conservatives could not keep them in check.

Apparently not even Forman and John Lewis have been able to keep SNCC in check because both have been chucked out and replaced by a new radical West Indian, Stokely Carmichael, twenty-four years old.

**FRIDAY, MAY 27** | The Dodd deposition has unearthed some evidence that Dodd had backing for stirring up trouble in the Congo. Secretary Rusk has written a letter, dated only a few weeks ago, supporting his position. This is contrary to what Pierre Salinger had told me, and Salinger, as the right-hand man to JFK, was in a position to know. Also Dean, then with the UN, had told me the contrary. Obviously, Rusk is either an inept dumbbell or was acting on the president's orders when he wrote the letter to Dodd; however, it's going to cause us some trouble.

**SATURDAY, MAY 28** | Allan Witwer came to lunch at the farm. He is a former employee of Clint Murchison Sr., who operated the motel near the Del Mar race [track] at La Jolla, California, where J. Edgar Hoover used to spend his vacations on the cuff. At one time Witwer was going to give me the bills and receipts showing that Hoover was the long-standing guest of the Murchisons and affidavits that Hoover placed bets at the hundred-dollar window through Murchison, not the two-dollar window, as he claims. After spending a lot of time with Witwer, he backed out, and today I learned why. The Murchisons had paid him off.

He told me that he had more recently worked for Hill & Knowlton and that he had prepared a book on the bribes, secret bank accounts, and underworld activities in the Bahamas. Hill & Knowlton gave him $55,000 not to publish it. He seemed to think that Jack Anderson or I might be interested in using some of his documentation. I looked over his outline.

I would be much more interested in his files on Hoover. He recalled one of the prize remarks made by the late Sid Richardson, the big Texas oilman, who was a close friend of Lyndon Johnson and Sam Rayburn. As Sid and the Murchisons were sitting around the swimming pool patio with J. Edgar Hoover, Sid said to the latter, "Edgar, get your ass over there to the bar and mix me a bourbon." A remark like this, in view of the rarified atmosphere in which Hoover lives today, would be considered sacrilegious.

Allan wanted to know why Hoover enjoyed the confidence of Lyndon Johnson and John F. Kennedy. He had been reappointed by Kennedy one day after Kennedy was elected, and Johnson has kept him on two years beyond the statutory requirement age of seventy. I replied, "Blackmail."

Hoover has more on Johnson and had more on Kennedy than he had on any other president. He knew every girl Kennedy had laid and every oil lobbyist Lyndon cavorted with.

**SUNDAY, JUNE 5** | Held a legal conference at the farm, attended also by Jim Boyd and Marjorie Carpenter, who was Dodd's private secretary. She told some shocking stories about how Dodd would get tight in his office—so drunk that they would have to cancel appointments. At one time, a real estate man was coming in from Maryland to give him a large wad of dough, but Dodd was so drunk he had to be laid on the couch for the better part of twelve hours.

I was impressed with both Boyd and Marjorie. She said the atmosphere in the Senate was like the atmosphere of the underworld: suspicion, intrigue, under-the-table operations. She amended this to say this applied only to Dodd and those he palled around with, such as Hruska of Nebraska and Eastland of Mississippi.

Boyd said Dodd was always talking about loyalty and that he, Boyd, didn't understand what he meant at first. Later he realized Dodd was saying that his staff should not squeal on him. He was getting away with murder. Finally, most of the staff did rebel.

**THURSDAY, JUNE 9** | Luvie and I skipped the British garden party for Queen Elizabeth's birthday—the first time we have done so. We came out to the farm instead. The children are having a wonderful time here. It's good for them and for us.

I talked to Arthur Sylvester at the Pentagon about [Rep. Mendel] Rivers's confinement in the Bethesda Naval Hospital. He confirmed that Rivers was drunk. He expressed some concern that defense salaries were tied up in the bill which was hung up as a result of Rivers's inebriation.

FRIDAY, JUNE 10 | Spent the morning working up a column on Representative Rivers and his binge. Talked to Representatives Jed Johnson of Oklahoma, Nedzi of Detroit, and John Blandford, clerk of the Armed Services Committee, to button down the details, libel proof. I also talked to Jerry Siegel, attorney for the *Washington Post*, to warn him the column was coming. Called Ed Ryan, news editor of WTOP, to warn him.

Later in the afternoon, when I went to WTOP to transcribe for television, I got an abrupt notice that the Rivers item had been killed. I haven't walked out of a radio or a TV show ever in my life, but I almost felt like it then. The excuse was "Rivers has given us trouble before."

Here is a congressman who places himself above the secretary of defense and proposes the appropriation of $930 million of the taxpayers' money, which the secretary of defense doesn't want, and yet is so inebriated he cannot show up on the House floor to pilot his bill through the House. Yet an important TV station ducks out on its responsibility to report this to the public.

I had a session with Secretary of Defense McNamara at five forty-five. I stuck a copy of the column I'd written on Rivers in my pocket to show to Art Sylvester, his assistant, but Art was tied up. I never planned to show it to McNamara and did not.

I congratulated him on his speech in Montreal, at which he advocated two years' service by every young American—if not in the armed services, then in some peacetime project. I said I had spent two years, after serving briefly in the first war, in doing something like this with the American Friends Service Committee.

McNamara seemed pleased and said he had received a fine reaction to his speech. The letters were about 100 percent favorable, and he had received many from colleges and universities. He seemed especially pleased at a speech delivered in San Francisco by Tom Gates, former secretary of defense. McNamara said Gates telephoned him to ask if he could adopt his idea in a speech, and McNamara naturally gave his permission. He said he thought it was a fine thing that a man now a representative of big business should propose this. I wondered what McNamara thought he was, as he was former president of the Ford Motor Company. Still, McNamara is still more of a teacher than a big businessman, and I think he would like to go back to teaching.

I asked him whether he had any plans for revising the draft. He said the Draft Act didn't expire until next year and it was too early to begin working on it.

We talked about NATO and the switch from France. He remarked that the president had been astute in not wanting to push our NATO allies on taking any fixed position in a hurry. They didn't want to remove the political organization of NATO out of France, so we didn't remonstrate. We also left a place for the French to come back should they change their minds, McNamara pointed out. After all, de Gaulle will not live forever.

I asked what we were going to do about the pipeline which crosses France to supply NATO, and he said there had been no decision. "I suppose you will not dig it up the way the French yanked all the telephone lines out of Guinea when they departed," I said.

As I was about to leave and headed toward the door, the secretary rather hesitantly said: "I'd like to ask you to do something for me. I understand you're writing a story about Rivers. If you do, it will murder me."

"I've already written it," I said.

McNamara didn't ask me to kill it, as some cabinet members would have done. I assured him I thought it would not hurt but would help. I said I had merely quoted some of Rivers's vituperative statements against him, together with describing his behavior.

SUNDAY, JUNE 12 | Came into town early to meet with thirty Russian students visiting the United States who had asked to see me. I expected some hot questions on the Vietnam War, but everyone was quite friendly. They had heard I was a friend of Johnson's and asked me about him and whether or not I was influenced by the president's views. I replied that I couldn't help being influenced on some matters and cited Mrs. Johnson's telephone call to me about Lynda Bird's trip to Europe. On the other hand, I said I have not been influenced regarding Vietnam, where I had differed vigorously with the president.

Toward the end of the session, which lasted almost two hours, one young man asked me whether I thought Russia would gradually veer over toward the political position of the United States and the United States would gradually veer over toward the political position of Russia, until they both went along the same line. I replied that I felt this was true, as did many other Americans.

After it was over, they were quite charming in the way they showered me with small tokens of appreciation: postcards of their hometowns, pins purchased in Moscow, etc. We posed for photographs out in the garden. I did not tell them that the garden had been designed by Alice Acheson, wife of the secretary of state, who had been among the most vigorous critics of Soviet Russia.

MONDAY, JUNE 13 | I had an interesting interview with U Thant (the first time I had met him). He told me he considered me one of the two or three most courageous newspapermen in the world. He turned down my invitation to speak at the IPA convention, but we had a very interesting conversation about Vietnam. He said he had been living in Hanoi in 1955 at the time of Dien Bien Phu, that he knew Ho Chi Minh and considered him a real independent as far as China was concerned.

He said that in August 1964 he received the green light from Ho Chi Minh for peace discussions with President Johnson; however, Johnson waited five months and in January 1965 had turned Ho down. His excuse was that any peace talks the United States had with North Vietnam would immediately leak out and cause trouble for the Quang government in South Vietnam, which had recently come into power and was shaky.

I asked about Canadian prime minister Lester Pearson's visit to the LBJ Ranch, where I reported Johnson had asked Pearson to sound out the North Vietnamese (the Canadians have a man on the International Control Commission in Hanoi). U Thant said there was nothing to this, that he, not the Canadians, had been the chief negotiator.

This was contrary to my previous information, and later I asked Jack Anderson about it. His explanation was that U Thant probably did not know that Johnson had brought in some other emissaries to double-check on U Thant's information. If U Thant is correct, and I am sure he must be, the United States started bombing North Vietnam shortly after we turned down the offer of peace talks in January 1965.

U Thant gave one basic reason for Hanoi's unwillingness to talk peace now: they are convinced the United States is going to stay in Vietnam for twenty to fifty years.

He recommended the following steps as an effort to bring about peace: (1)

stop bombing the North; (2) de-escalate the war. He said he was encouraged that his latest proposal brought no response from Hanoi or Peking. There have been no editorial criticisms, in fact no reaction, pro or con. He talked at length regarding the untenable position of the United States in bombing North Vietnam. He said there would be no peace as long as we continued bombing—"and I don't mean a let-up of thirty-seven days."

He indicated, without saying so, that he would probably retire as secretary-general of the UN. "I have to make up my mind this month," he said. "I doubt whether any man should hold this position for more than five years. Back in my country, civil servants retire at the age of fifty-five. This was something the British put into effect in order to make room for younger men. I am now fifty-eight."

I pointed out that Arthur Goldberg's proposal made before Catholic University was now close to the terms of Hanoi, but U Thant said, in turn, Hanoi would not trust us sufficiently to talk peace as long as we were bombing the North and as long as Ho Chi Minh was convinced we were in the country for up to fifty years.

TUESDAY, JUNE 14 | Talked with Pat Brown by telephone. He was worried, as I am, that Sam Yorty will come out for Reagan in return for a deal whereby Reagan knocks out Sen. Tom Kuchel with Yorty later. "I have been spending about three days reading Reagan's speeches," said Pat, "everything I can find about him. He shouldn't be underestimated. He takes direction well. He listens to his handlers. People don't remember that he came out against public schools, against the Tennessee Valley Authority, against almost everything we stand for in California."

MONDAY, JUNE 20 | Dodd hearings opened before the Senate Ethics Committee, in executive session. Jim Boyd was the chief witness. According to the news coverage we got, the committee was extremely friendly. Jack had advised him not to ask for a lawyer, that the senators would become his lawyer and defend him in view of the battery of lawyers Dodd had defending him, which was what happened.

Cooper of Kentucky, Bennett of Utah, and Stennis of Mississippi were especially vigorous in defending Boyd. Mike Monroney looked unhappy during the hearing, also Gene McCarthy. Mike is one of my oldest Senate friends. I helped elect him to the Senate when we exposed the conflicts of interest of Sen. Elmer Thomas. Mike, however, has been getting old, tired, and less courageous—and his state, Oklahoma, has been turning conservative.

TUESDAY, JUNE 21 | Had a talk with Dean Rusk. I asked him whether it was true, as rumored, that there had been feelers from Hanoi for peace. His reply was emphatically negative.

"There have never been any overtures from Hanoi at any time," he said. I asked him about U Thant's widely quoted statement that there had been feelers during the late summer and fall of 1964. Rusk said that U Thant's sources were questionable and that he had not been in direct contact with Hanoi. "During that time we also had some contacts which did not bear out his reports."

I asked whether these were through the Canadians and whether they had not been affirmative and that Hanoi was ready to talk. Rusk said the Canadians were among those who had taken some soundings for us but never got back an affirmative answer.

We discussed the general Indochinese situation, dating back to 1961-62, when Laos was under discussion. Rusk said the United States had accepted Khrushchev's candidate to become prime minister of Laos, namely Prince Souvanna Phouma, and that Khrushchev had generally been cooperative, but the Vietcong never did carry out their pledge to remove troops.

When I said I understood the situation in Laos was good, Rusk replied, "Hanoi is just busier now with South Vietnam, so they don't have the time or energy to worry about Laos; however, the International Control Commission has never been able to police certain parts of Laos. They just won't let the ICC in."

"Prince Sihanouk in Cambodia," Rusk said, "had decided about two years ago that the wave of the future was with China. The United States has no relations with him whatsoever."

We discussed Egypt and food to Nasser. I said that when I was in Israel, I found that Mrs. Golda Meir was reconciled to food to Egypt. "The Israelis know we have no alternative to keeping some contacts with Nasser or letting him go all the way to the East. The Israelis don't want the latter. The only trouble is that Nasser keeps on making speeches. If you keep on kicking the old cow in the flank often enough, she'll just quit giving milk."

When I asked whether Moscow had given us any help toward peace in Vietnam, Rusk replied that Russia couldn't do very much without being castigated by China. "When Hubert Humphrey went to New Delhi for Shastri's funeral, Kosygin was there too. And the Red Chinese saw this as a plot.

"Again, when Russia accepted our proposal for a moratorium on weapons in outer space, the Chinese sounded off against the so-called Russian-American conspiracy."

Rusk did not know what to make of the situation in China but thought the advent of the military into power might be healthy. They had common sense and realized the futility of getting into a war with the United States.

Jack and I went to see Senator Javits, who was irked over two recent columns linking him with Gen. Julius Klein. I have never seen a newspaperman give a senator such a skillful cross-examination as Jack gave Javits.

The senator started out by telling us of his letter to Klein, which he said was written because he really believed Klein had done something for German reparations to Israel. He kept protesting that he didn't really care about Klein and had just done this to get Klein out of his hair. He denied he had any other important relations with Klein. Whereupon Jack asked him if he had not written a letter endorsing Klein for appointment to the War Battlements Commission and whether he had not given joint luncheons with Klein on Capitol Hill for German foreign minister Brentano. Javits admitted this was true. Jack wanted to know whether Javits—or Klein—had paid for the luncheon. Javits didn't remember but said he was reasonably certain he had paid for it.

Jack then accused Javits of receiving thick sealed envelopes from Klein, which assistants said had contained cash. Javits denied this emphatically but promised to make a search of his office.

Jack did not tell Javits that Klein's former secretary, Ellen Batheson, is going to testify before the Senate Ethics Committee that she sent large sealed envelopes to Dodd and Javits from Klein. I was on the whole convinced that Javits was not telling the truth.

**THURSDAY, JUNE 23** | Flew back from Los Angeles last night. I attended the first public hearings of the Ethics Committee, where Boyd was a witness. He did very well. He made a good statement as to why he hadn't given the documents to the Senate but to Jack Anderson instead. He pointed out the respect which senators have for each other and referred discreetly to the so-called Senate club. He said he was familiar with the fact that the Senate rules barred senators from criticizing one other. Marjorie Carpenter, who followed Boyd, was nervous but effective. She testified that when Dodd returned from his trip to West Germany, David Martin, who accompanied him, remarked to another aide, Zeiller, that "Klein must have paid Dodd a lot of money for that trip—at least $10,000."

Dodd made a fool of himself by demanding that Marjorie be prosecuted for perjury and was promptly rebuffed by Chairman Stennis.

FRIDAY, JUNE 24 | I called Hubert Humphrey. The following dialogue took place.

DP: Which side are you on, Hubert, in the Dodd case?

HHH: Why?

DP: You wrote a letter to Dodd just two days ago giving him an out for going to West Germany.

HHH: Well, I had to tell the truth. I did give him permission to go during the civil rights debate. He called me, reminded me of it, so I wrote him a letter. Of course, I didn't know he was going to spend so long or why he was going. He told me he would only be away one weekend plus one day.

DP: Why didn't you put that in the letter?

HHH: I didn't write the letter. My assistant wrote it; I signed it.

Averell Harriman came to the farm for dinner and reminisced about General de Gaulle. Rusk, he said, is a pain in the neck. He is still living in the past, when he was an expert on the Far East. George Ball, he said, was pretty good but not the man to send to see de Gaulle since he had been Monet's lawyer.

De Gaulle, Averell thinks, has been a tragedy for Europe. He recalled how de Gaulle was really the product of General Speers of the British Broadcasting Company (BBC). General Speers was the British military attaché in Paris during the early war years, before the United States entered the conflict. After de Gaulle came to live in England as a refugee, it was the BBC which built him up with frequent statements. Roosevelt almost fired de Gaulle at Casablanca, but Anthony Eden saved him. Anthony was his chief champion, not Churchill. Anthony flew down from London to Casablanca to urge that de Gaulle be given another chance.

Later Roosevelt and Churchill both wanted to fire him when de Gaulle told the French general in Syria not to obey the orders of the British general there. Despite all this, Roosevelt arranged to let de Gaulle march into Paris ahead of Eisenhower. And later, at the Yalta Conference, Roosevelt definitely did not want de Gaulle present and barred him. He wanted to iron out the intricate problems of Europe direct with Stalin, without being handicapped by a stuffed shirt—de Gaulle.

**SATURDAY, JUNE 25** | Bob Kintner telephoned, saying I should tell Pat Brown, if he had any requests to make of the federal government that were not too "outrageous," to send them along and they would be honored immediately.

**SUNDAY, JUNE 26** | Michael O'Hare, former accountant for Senator Dodd, and Glenn Cooper, who worked for him briefly, came to the farm to see me. Cooper said he'd received a call from Dodd's attorneys, John Kenney and Nate Bickford, asking if he would see them in the Sheraton-Carlton Hotel. He obliged. They sat around, ordering champagne, giving one-dollar tips to the bellboys. Cooper said he remarked, "I suppose Senator Dodd is paying for all this." Bickford replied, "Oh yeah."

Cooper said he had been badgered by [the] two young attorneys asking him to testify for Dodd in the libel suit before the Senate committee. Dodd's lawyers seem desperate for witnesses, but Glenn was not obliging. They asked him if he had talked to Michael O'Hare about Mike's May 23 conversation with Kenney, in which Kenney had threatened him unless he testified. They wanted to know what Michael O'Hare had told him.

"What I read in the paper today was very much like what he told me." At one point Kenney wondered aloud whether O'Hare had taped the conversation Kenney had with Michael.

O'Hare told about Judith Berling, who had been his secretary. During the controversy she resigned, though she had not been implicated. She also refused to take two weeks' notice.

O'Hare told me a lot of things about Dodd that I didn't know before, particularly how he had padded the juvenile delinquency payroll. Out of eighteen members on the juvenile delinquency staff, ten worked for Dodd in his office as of January 1965. There is a turnover of ten to twelve people each month. One of the staff members is Elizabeth Knipe, a graduate of Trinity College DC, with Dodd's daughter Martha. Elizabeth's mother graduated with Mrs. Dodd from Trinity College and was at first turned down as a secretary because she failed in the civil service examinations; however, she was given a job on the Juvenile Delinquency Committee.

Also on the Juvenile Delinquency Committee is Roger Lowe (son of Florence Lowe of Metromedia), a consultant at about $5,200 a year. Anne Ketcham, a friend of Dodd's from Connecticut, who worked with him in the

National Youth Administration in Connecticut, was given a job for ninety days on the Juvenile Delinquency Committee. She's still there—approximately two and a half years later.

**MONDAY, JUNE 27** | It was Dodd's big day in court with the public attending. He made a poor move at the start by attempting to disqualify Senator Bennett of Utah. Chairman Stennis, a Democrat, promptly overruled him.

Before we went into the hearing room, I dropped in to see Senator Pearson of Kansas.

Ernest Cuneo had written a resounding statement about the attempts of Dodd and his attorneys to intimidate witnesses, which Ernest thought a Republican senator should deliver before the hearings opened this morning. It was a good statement, but I had misgivings whether I could get any senator, Republican or Democrat, to deliver it; however, I made a stab at Pearson. He was cordial but didn't think a freshman senator should stick his neck out so far. He did deliver a rather modified statement about intimidating witnesses, though in the afternoon, not the morning.

Later in the day I suggested to Steve Young and Wayne Morse that they deliver speeches on the floor. They took the matter under consideration.

Mrs. Dodd testified first regarding one of the much publicized errors we had made in an early column, namely that Klein had given them an expensive Persian rug. She testified that she had bought all the Persian rugs in their home; none came from Klein. She mentioned the famous Christmas postcard "Persian rug," which made us look like fools.

Dodd himself was a reasonably good witness. He didn't lose his temper. He talked rather convincingly about the staff he had helped to develop and hire just after they were out of college and trained them and depended upon them and placed his confidence in them—and how they went back on him. He implied without exactly saying so that it was because he had fired Jim Boyd and Marjorie Carpenter that they turned against him

**THURSDAY, JUNE 30** | There was another raid on the oil depots around Hanoi and Haiphong. I told Jack we had been deficient in covering this important event and that we could not devote the column entirely to Tom Dodd. He finally came up with a fairly good story of the background reasons for the raids, the chief one being that the Joint Chiefs of Staff were terribly depressed and that their morale had to be bolstered because we had been losing.

**MONDAY, JULY 4** | Lyndon is in Texas with most of his family. Lynda Bird is in Spain, where she ought not to be.

**FRIDAY, JULY 8** | Lunched with Leonard Marks and Jack Valenti at the Motion Picture Producers Association, the offices so long occupied by Eric Johnston. Valenti thinks the best undeveloped market for American pictures is among the Iron Curtain countries and is planning a trip to Moscow, Prague, and others.

We talked a lot about Johnson. I told them there were some things Johnson could do to improve his popularity. These pertained to relations with his family, namely Lynda Bird's trip abroad and the big wedding for Luci at a time when other American boys, unlike Pat Nugent, who has a cushy job with the National Guard, are going to Vietnam. I agreed there wasn't much Lyndon could do about the draft status of George Hamilton [the actor whom Lynda Bird was dating], but there were things he could do about the other matters.

"He knows this better than anyone else," said Valenti. "He knows how the public reacts. He writhes over this publicity. He talked to Lynda about the trip abroad, while she was still in Texas, and pointed out that he was trying to persuade other Americans not to go. She said: 'Why should I be punished? I am no different from anyone else.'

"'But you are different,' her father told her. 'We're all different. When you're in the White House, you have to serve as an example to everyone else.'"

"Lynda is a strong-willed girl," said Jack. "She's like her father. Luci's approach is different. She gets up in her father's lap and strokes him and cuddles him and gets what she wants out of him.

"As far as he's concerned, he'd rather have Luci go off and get married in a chapel or before a justice of the peace. He wishes she would elope. He finally persuaded her not to have the wedding in a big church. But he can't help the publicity. He's given orders to Liz Carpenter to cut out the publicity. He bawls Liz out every time he reads the paper, but Liz is surrounded by all these women who want the news. Every time the boss sees it in the paper, he hits the ceiling. The leaks probably come from Luci."

Valenti talked vividly about his relations with Johnson. "I'd go in to see the president about seven thirty in the morning. First I'd call up the communications center and ask, 'Did the president call you this morning?' 'Yes,' they'd say, 'at three and three thirty, four, and five thirty.'

"I'd say, 'How did you sleep, Mr. President?' He'd say, 'All right,' in a sort of noncommittal way, but he looked tired. Then the phone would begin to ring. First it was Rusk with a problem on Indonesia. Then Udall would call up with a water problem. Larry O'Brien had a problem regarding a bill on Capitol Hill that had to pass. HEW had a problem over hospitals and integration. They all called him. He was the one man who had to decide things.

"Then I'd read the newspapers. Alsop was panning him because he didn't go far enough in Vietnam. Lippmann was panning him because he went too far. Joe Kraft was panning him for something else. Doris Fleeson thought he'd made political blunders. There was just no way of pleasing them."

**WEDNESDAY, JULY 13** | Had a session with the president this morning at his suggestion. I'd written to him about the importance of the right kind of ambassador for Bolivia.

He talked instead about Vietnam. "Jack Burns (governor of Hawaii) was in this morning and told me that reaction was good in Hawaii. They are losing more men there just as they did in Korea. The closer they are to the seat of conflict, the more important it is to them." . . . He talked at length about the war and said Arthur Goldberg had just explained to the pope that we were not bombing civilians, only enemy targets. The pope has now written the president a nice letter, which was received yesterday.

"You quoted the generals about Vietnam as being against me," the president said. He went to the telephone and called General Goodpaster at the Joint Chiefs of Staff. He did not answer. "I asked Goodpaster to find out whether you were right or not. You're probably right about General Ridgeway because he's a good friend of General Gavin's. Gavin came out with that statement about holding the enclaves along the coast in South Vietnam. All during 1964 that was the policy I followed. All we did was to hold enclaves. We didn't increase the war. We didn't do anything except defend ourselves. And at the end of that time we figured we were not serious, and I finally decided we either had to pull out or fight. Since then we have been showing that we meant business.

"We're not hitting civilians. Roosevelt killed civilians right and left in Germany, but we haven't killed twenty civilians; we haven't killed a dozen.

"Fourteen Communist nations criticized us for hitting oil tanks. Suddenly the Communist world has become vitally concerned about oil, but from now on we're not going to have these big trucks taking oil south. I saw 'em the other night, truck after truck, barging down the highway carrying oil. From now on they'll have to carry oil on their backs. They may be able to do it, but it will be a lot slower.

"McNamara came in to see me the other day with a map. It had a circle around Hanoi and Haiphong and another line at the Chinese border. We're not bombing China. We're not bombing these cities. McNamara said we had to bomb with a pinpoint to get in between these circles and the line, but that's what we're doing. It takes a mosquito to get in there. This is the most amazing pinpoint bombing that's ever happened. Out of twenty planes we've only lost one. We've sent our best pilots and our best planes, and we are careful not to hit civilian targets."

He talked at some length also about his main objectives in Asia, namely the development of civilian resources. He pointed out that the Asian Development Bank was now a fact and functioning efficiently. He referred briefly to a report on the thousands of children who have been inoculated. "This is the kind of thing the public doesn't know about. This is the kind of thing you fellows ought to write about."

He gave me a couple of reports to read, one of which was marked CONFIDENTIAL, and asked me to copy parts of it in the next room and then give it back, which I did. Two other reports he let me keep.

He referred rather vigorously to Bill Fulbright. "He says we ought not to be in Vietnam because the people over there are different from us. They may be of a different color, but they're human beings just the same. He says we've got to be careful about the Chinese because they're different. They're human beings too, and we don't want to go to war with them. I'm being very careful about that. And I have gone further than any other person in this office to show that we want to be friends with them."

I told Lyndon that I thought he had a great opportunity in the Western Hemisphere to do some constructive things to iron out the troubles between Bolivia and Chile, Chile and Argentina, Venezuela and Guyana. I told him that Assistant Secretary Gordon could give him the details.

"I think Gordon's doing a good job," he said, "and we're going to try to get some good ambassadors, as you suggest. One fellow who is doing a very good job is your friend Leonard Marks.

"When I took over here, Edward R. Murrow was supposed to be the great executive, but he made a mess at the U.S. Information Agency. He is a great television star but no executive. Representative Rooney went around the world visiting U.S. Information offices and came back to cut hell out of the budget. Leonard has now come in and very quietly made it one of the greatest organizations in government. He's cut expenses, cut out the dead wood, proved his effectiveness 100 percent. You ought to write something about it. He can't do it himself. You have to do it for him. Tell him to get the facts and give them to you."

The president mentioned a letter which John Steinbeck had written to the *New York Times*. "It's a great document," he said. "Steinbeck has a boy over in Vietnam. He answered one of his Russian friends, who wanted to know why we bombed Hanoi and Haiphong. He told his friend, 'You only get part of the story.' You get that letter and read it and write something about it. Not many people have seen that letter. You and Steinbeck have got something in common. You're both crusaders.

"We hear from our negotiators that these speeches by Fulbright and the other people are definitely delaying peace. They think we're going to give in. They tell us they're waiting for the opposition to force us to stop. Well, we are not going to stop. We are in this thing to stay. I am not going to pull out, and the quicker the other side knows this the better. You ought to write that. Also that we want to help build a better place for people to live, and that's exactly what I intend to do as soon as we can get this thing over. You write that, and it will help. Write something like John Steinbeck did. It's the best thing that's been written about this war so far."

I asked whether there was any chance of Harold Wilson getting the Russians to move for peace. The president shook his head. "No, but we think they've tried; however, they have about as much influence with the Chinese as you have with Senator Dodd."

I asked how we were getting along with the Russians now. "They're not calling me names anymore. They're not being personal. Ever since you were in Moscow and told them not to, they've been much better; however, they're very difficult. They've been spying. They've been buying secrets right inside of our Joint Chiefs of Staff. They pulled out of a track meet in Los Angeles. That was uncalled for. That's something we would never do. We would never try to buy secrets inside their Joint Chiefs of Staff. How do they think we feel about this?"

I asked whether this was recent or dated back some time. The president said it was still going on. I asked whether Dobrynin knew about it. "He's pretty high up," the president said, "and we think he's friendly. We don't know whether he knows about it or not, but we know it's going on."

Twice during the conversation the president said, "How can I defend Israel with one and a half million people if I don't defend a nation of fourteen million?

This is a test of our commitment, of our word. What will my word be good for if I don't make good here? I made Israel put it in writing that we should sell tanks to Jordan in order to keep Russian tanks out of Jordan," he said.

Obviously, someone had been telling him about my network troubles and my inability to get the Israeli picture on a network, which was why he mentioned Israel. He went on to say: "You've got a lot of friends among the generals. There is General Klein and General Sarnoff. You tell the networks to get off their asses and get busy. We gave 'em six hours' notice for McNamara's press conference, and they got their wires crossed. We gave 'em three hours' notice for my press conference, and they missed out on the first couple of minutes. Last night they said they weren't going to televise my speech, which I made by telephone to White Sulphur Springs, but when they read the speech and saw what was in it, they decided to carry it live. Why don't you write something about these networks and how high-handed they are?"

Several times Marvin Watson came in to hold a card in front of LBJ reminding him that his next caller was outside. I could read from a distance that the caller was Sen. John McClellan of Arkansas, who certainly does not like me, and he would blow his top if he knew he had to wait because of me. I made a couple of motions to go, but the president said, "Tell him we're running behind today."

Then the president gave me a couple of memos and told me to telephone him after I'd read them.

Outside his door in the hall I waited to see which room I should go into to take notes on the confidential memo, when Senator McClellan went by. I am sure he saw me. I hope he doesn't vote against the president on the next round because he was kept waiting.

THURSDAY, JULY 14 | I telephoned Senator Fulbright about when he would speak at the IPA convention. He had a sour reaction to the president's speech in West Virginia, said that Walt Rostow had probably written it and that Rostow was a bad influence on the president.

"The public has no idea," said Bill, "that in that speech the United States replaces Britain in assuming the white man's burden. Do you think the American people want to do that? This is not a matter of stopping communism. It's a matter of colonialism. This is the reason North Vietnam will not talk peace. They see us heading for colonialism, exactly what they fought the French to abolish.

"The last line of the speech is the most significant, where he quotes Teddy Roosevelt. Does the president realize that Teddy Roosevelt was the most jingoistic president we ever had? He started the Spanish-American War. He seized the Panama Canal. He waved the big stick all over the world."

"The trouble with a declaration like this," continued Fulbright, "is that a year or so from now it takes on the quality of unchangeable gospel. It becomes the policy of the United States. It's like the Bay of Tonkin Resolution, which is now quoted as the reason for our being in the war."

I cited the *New York Times* story from Moscow that Kosygin had made a bitter commentary against the United States in front of Prime Minister Indira Gandhi, saying that Russia was ready to offer volunteers to North Vietnam.

"We don't seem to realize that they mean what they say," commented Fulbright. "And the president doesn't seem to realize that he's getting in deeper and deeper so that the next step may be catastrophic. If the North Vietnamese execute the American flyers, public reaction will be to bomb China. It will be difficult for the president to resist this."

Fulbright said he was terribly discouraged. I tried to cheer him up by pointing out the investigation he undertook in 1963 regarding Gen. Julius Klein was now being confirmed. "Yes," he said, "but it takes weeks of testimony to bring out the facts."

WEDNESDAY, JULY 20 | We drove to the Bolivian embassy and from there direct to the White House for lunch, which put me in the position, for the first time, of entering the White House through the front door. It has not been since I was a young reporter that I have stood on the White House portico in the front to welcome distinguished visitors—but only as a reporter. As a guest, I have come in the South entrance, or back door. This time we drove up in the front entrance, waited a few minutes in the cars until President Johnson had come down to the front entrance, and then got out of the cars to be greeted by him. I tagged along with the president of Bolivia, as if I was part of his party.

During the toasts that followed the luncheon, Barrientos, who spoke in English and, though halting, obviously spoke from the heart, led off by saying, "I have come here on the invitation of Drew Pearson and the International Platform Association to participate in its discussions." This must have been a surprise to about one hundred of the guests present—in other words 90 percent of them—and on the way out, President Johnson, who had his arm linked with President Barrientos, said to me, "What's the plug worth to you, Drew?"

New York mayor Lindsay and I sat at the same table, though Bess, either in deference to me or as a slight to Lindsay, placed me on the left of the table's host, the secretary of the treasury, Joe Fowler. Lindsay sat across the table.

It occurred to me during the day's proceedings that Lindsay would make a far better Republican candidate for either president or vice president than Romney or Javits, who basically are phonies. I think that Javits is already washed up as a result of the Julius Klein hearings, which began yesterday and ended today. Klein hemmed, hawed, and lied. The committee had great difficulty pinning him down and more or less gave up in disgust. Jack had given the committee counsel, Ben Fern, a lot of quotes in which Klein had obviously lied, but Fern did not use them.

The senators also avoided the embarrassing question of asking him which senators he had contributed to in the past, and when he referred to his close relations with Jack Javits, the Republicans on the committee came to Javits's defense.

Some of the Jews who know Javits well have said happily that the Klein testimony has washed up Javits as a vice presidential candidate. I also got a call from Cy King, editor of the *Buffalo Courier Express*, suggesting that I go into the Javits-Klein relationship further. He said Javits had gotten away with murder and should be exposed for what he really is.

At the IPA conference we debated the war in Vietnam, with Fulbright and I sitting in on the panel to cross-examine Wayne Morse and Gale McGee; the latter two did an excellent job of presenting opposite points of view. Morse was shaking his finger in Gale's face when the chairman, Sen. Clarence Dill of Washington, adjourned the meeting, much to the disappointment of the crowd.

FRIDAY, JULY 22 | Dean Rusk spoke at the IPA in the morning. When I told him we had the alternative of written or oral questions, he said we could use either one, but he wanted the questions screened, if written, by someone not connected with the government. Since Dr. Glenn Seaborg, chairman of the Atomic Energy Commission, was introducing him, I was given the job of screening the questions. Most of them pertained to Vietnam, and Rusk did well. Before he arrived that morning, his press officer, Bob McCloskey, called to discuss whether Rusk would be on or off the record. He was rightly concerned as to whether what he said would leak to the press even if the statements were for background, so Rusk finally decided to go on the record completely.

One question was whether China would be admitted to the UN. I was surprised when his answer was a firm no. He based this in part on the fact that China demanded that it be the sole representative in the UN and that we could not abandon Formosa [Taiwan]. This, of course, is true, but the vigor of Rusk's reply made it clear that Arthur Goldberg had not yet converted Rusk to his point of view.

The situation regarding captured American prisoners in North Vietnam continues [to be] tense. The Indian chargé d'affaires confided at the Bolivian cocktail party the other day that he had urged Premier Gandhi, when in Moscow this week, to make a plea with Kosygin to use his influence with Hanoi against the prisoners' execution. She had done so and apparently received a sympathetic response from Kosygin. Wayne Morse, in arguing before [the] IPA, pointed out that North Vietnamese prisoners have been turned over to the South Vietnamese by us and have been tortured and murdered. Therefore, we were in no position to appeal for humane treatment for our prisoners. I made a recorded prediction for WTOP that the American prisoners would not be executed.

Just before dinner Bob Kintner telephoned from the White House to say that the president wanted to inform me regarding the latest Gallup poll showing that his rating had gone up to 56 percent from 50 percent since his bombing around Hanoi and Haiphong. The president was pleased, but he is relying too much on these polls. He should be picking policies which are right rather than those which are popular.

SATURDAY, JULY 23 | The story on Dodd's trip to the West Coast, in which he charged the Junior Chamber of Commerce, the Senate Juvenile Delinquency Committee, and his own campaign for the trip, is beginning to break ahead of our column, but it's not a bad idea to have some other newspapers in on the story. Public reaction to his refusal to have his campaign funds and testimonial dinners investigated has been very sour. The Senate Ethics Committee is also down on him and is going ahead with the financial investigation despite Dodd's objections.

WEDNESDAY, AUGUST 10 | Jimmy Hoffa called with his formula for settling the airline strike. He says [International Association of Machinists and

Aerospace Workers president] Siemiller has lost control of his men because they have other jobs and don't care whether the strike continues or not. Hoffa estimates that only one-third of the Machinists will go back to work when so ordered by Congress.

**THURSDAY, AUGUST 11** I The column on LBJ as a weak father was published today and got some sour reaction. Significantly, the White House called Jack and told him that the president would agree to an interview for *Parade* or else do a signed article. Jack interpreted this as punishing me by favoring him, which is more or less standard procedure around the White House.

Earlier this week U.S. planes bombed a Cambodian village by mistake, killing 150 people. Today U.S. planes bombed a U.S. cutter off the coast of Vietnam by mistake, killing two Americans. This pretty well knocks down Lyndon's claim of pinpoint bombing to avoid civilian casualties.

Averell Harriman is due to leave for Cambodia and other Southeast Asia areas to explore prospects for peace.

The Joint Chiefs of Staff have recommended to Lyndon that he close off the demilitarized zone (DMZ) between North and South Vietnam; otherwise, northern troops will keep infiltrating south. It was on February 7, 1965, that the Joint Chiefs recommended bombing North Vietnam in order to prevent infiltration, but now the infiltration has doubled. It's estimated that the enemy has 282,000 men in the South, some of them native South Vietnamese Vietcong. We have 286,000 men, and the Joint Chiefs want an additional buildup of 250,000—at least. I suspect Lyndon will take their advice.

**WEDNESDAY, AUGUST 17** I The House Un-American Activities Committee is still stewing over the witnesses called to testify regarding their opposition to the war in Vietnam and their aid to the Vietcong. Today the committee threw the attorney for the witnesses, a Professor Kinoy of Rutgers (a member of the Civil Liberties Committee), out of the room and had him arrested for disorderly conduct. He had been shouting at chairman Joel Pool of Texas, a rotund, unsavory-looking character, whose picture, if it is shown anywhere in England and France, will convince the average person that we are a bunch of Fascists.

**MONDAY, AUGUST 22** I Canceled lunch with Jimmy Hoffa in order to see Pierre Salinger. Then Salinger canceled lunch to go to the White House. He dropped around later to say he had seen Lyndon Abell lunching at the

White House with Bess and Liz Carpenter and that Liz was sore at me over the column I had written on the president being a weak father.

Salinger was loath to help me out of the Dodd suit regarding the intercepted cable which Dodd sent to the Katanga government. Salinger explained that his boss, Bob Six of Continental Airlines, is a great friend and admirer of Dodd.

I was surprised to hear Pierre Salinger defend Johnson. He pointed out that there was every reason why LBJ should have an obsession about Bobby Kennedy when Bobby rates ahead of him in the Gallup poll. He also noted that there was no Kennedy man who had a kind word to say about Johnson except him, Pierre. I pointed out that Arthur Schlesinger, Ken Galbraith, and Dick Goodwin were all brain trusting for Bobby now. Pierre remarked that he never did think much of Schlesinger, but he had a high opinion of Galbraith, whom he had asked to read over his new book on Kennedy. Ken did and made only one suggestion—namely, that Salinger omit a crude remark made by Kennedy just before the Cuban missile crisis.

We talked about managed news. Pierre remarked that the best press secretary in history was Jim Hagerty, who had a tough time with Eisenhower but nevertheless did a superb job. I remarked that he was aided by the fact that 80 percent of the newspapers were Republican.

FRIDAY, AUGUST 26 | We had been lunching once or twice a week at the Cosmos Club to organize the Washington Community Service Broadcasting Company to compete for the license of a Negro station, WOOK. Today was our last luncheon. I was encouraged. We managed to get together some Negro leaders of the community. They will take 60 percent of the stock; the white group will take 40 percent. We even had a Negro station owner from Detroit, Dr. Wendell Cox, who once dropped me from the air on his WCHD because I couldn't get a sponsor; however, he was anxious to participate in this venture, and we let him come in for 5 percent.

Lyndon left for Idaho this morning and made an excellent speech this afternoon, proposing that the United States and Russia call off the Cold War and get together on a new atomic treaty. It would have been a great speech were it not for the fact we are pounding the hell out of the Communists in North Vietnam, and it's difficult for the Russians to cozy up to a country which does this.

Martin Luther King has won a great victory in Chicago. The real estate boards have opened up the suburbs to Negro housing. Mayor Daley put it across—a tribute to him and to King's persistence.

**THURSDAY, SEPTEMBER 8** | DETROIT—Jimmy Hoffa, with whom I was supposed to have lunch, came in at five instead. He said I should use a private plane instead of the regular jets and offered to loan me his. I can see myself getting more involved with Jimmy Hoffa. Besides, he finally admitted it cost $500 an hour to operate a private plane as against $47 commercial to Detroit.

I asked Jimmy why it was that Johnson didn't have a bigger crowd in Detroit. He said that twelve thousand was a pretty good crowd to get out for Cobo Hall, and he had predicted there would be only three thousand. The trouble was that Cobo Hall had parking space for only five thousand cars, and labor today was not going to go out to a meeting unless it could park. (What a change from the 1930s, when labor in Detroit was on its uppers.) I reminded Hoffa that Roosevelt and Truman used to pull crowds of a hundred thousand in Detroit. "Yes," he said, "but they were hungry then. Today they're not hungry. Today my men won't work on holidays, even though they get ninety-six dollars a day. They've got a house, a cottage at the lake, a boat, and that's all they want. You go down the list of men with seniority and give them a chance to work on a holiday at triple time, and they'll pass it up.

"My Teamsters are guaranteed $168 a week for five days when they start on Monday. They get time and a half for overtime and triple time if they work holidays."

He remarked that Walter Reuther was having trouble inside his own union and explained that he hadn't got enough for his men. "A rigger for the Teamsters gets $5.10 an hour plus some fringe benefits. One of Reuther's riggers gets $3.84. So, naturally, he's dissatisfied. Naturally, he wants to leave Reuther."

One trouble with Johnson's reception in Detroit was that one of Reuther's men, head of his political action committee, was in charge of mobilizing the crowd and had failed to invite the Teamsters or the trade unions. Thus they boycotted the reception. "We stayed home and saw it on television," said Hoffa. "Why should we get out and wrestle for a parking space when we're not wanted?" said Hoffa.

He said he had been invited by the Russians to go to Moscow to confer on union problems. A secretary of the Soviet embassy had invited him, and recently one of the lawyers from the Teamsters had returned from Russia with a renewed invitation. He wanted my advice as to whether he should go. I told him to try to get the State Department to invite him, then he would get some public relations value in this country. He had argued that it would be unwise to go when the Supreme Court was going to argue his decision on October 12 and when a decision was expected momentarily in the Chicago federal court on another phase of his case.

During the conversation Hoffa said that if he were the president, he would put Bobby Kennedy in his place and take him out of the running. He said there was a fairly simple way to do this—namely, to have the FBI get the dope on Bobby's girlfriends. He said that the Teamsters made it a point to check on Bobby's activities and had found that whenever he went to Los Angeles, one of his girlfriends registered at the hotel one day in advance. When he went to Chicago, another girlfriend joined him, and altogether he had four girls scattered around the country.

"I would have the FBI bring in the facts on these women," said Hoffa. "They're crossing state boundaries, which is against the law, and it's about time Bobby was put in his place."

Hoffa looks at you with those baby blue eyes as if he had never driven a tough bargain with an employer and never turned over a truck. And almost in the same breath, he'll tell you how he deals with employers when they get too rough. He said that the Mennen Company of New Jersey had had three strikes, and he was inclined to blame Soapy Williams. I told him that Soapy owned only a minority interest in the company and that his cousin, Bill Mennen, whom I knew, would never permit any interference from an outsider, even his cousin.

Hoffa went on to tell how Mennen had used helicopters to try to break the strike, but it was too expensive, and he caved in. "One time we made him come around by mixing up his bills of lading. Shipments to Houston were sent to New Orleans, and shipments for New Orleans were sent to Houston. It took them weeks to unscramble these orders. When you have forty thousand pounds of orders going to the wrong city, and this takes place with several cities, it can put you out of business. All we had to do was to change the zone from zone 1 to zone 2.

"Another thing we've done is to pull out the computer operator on a Thursday. We've studied the operations of different companies, and if you pull the computer operator out on a certain day, it can knock a company out on its accounts receivable for twenty days.

"All you have to do is have the computer operator get sick and not show up for one night. Then the shipments go to the wrong place, the bills aren't paid, and a company can be thrown into bankruptcy. This was how the Yale

Company, a $75 million corporation, went bust. It expected its bills to be paid at a certain time; it had so many goods out, and it had to go to the bank to borrow money.

"We have studied the computer systems and the accounting methods of various companies to know when we should pull the computer operator. We don't resort to violence anymore. It doesn't pay. We just gum up the computer."

Jimmy said his wife couldn't take the long wait to see what the Supreme Court and the court of appeals in Chicago would rule in his criminal cases. "It's all right for a man but not for a woman. She has to sit there all by herself with nothing much to do. It's hard on my daughter too. My son has just finished his law degree and is starting to work in the Michigan State Senate as a legal clerk. He can take it better than his mother and sister."

Jimmy was full of praise for Governor George Romney, who had put sixteen bills through the legislature, all favoring labor, and once marched in the picket line on a fish cannery strike.

FRIDAY, SEPTEMBER 9 | Had a talk with George Ball, who is getting out shortly. He was frank about Vietnam and repeated with even more emphasis what he'd told me before, that we got into Vietnam in the fall of 1961 chiefly because Kennedy was looking for some way of impressing the public and the world with his strength after his Bay of Pigs fiasco. George generally agreed with me that Kennedy's foreign policies had been poor and that Johnson's foreign policies had been better up until the time he started to escalate the Vietnam War after 1964.

Ball said in 1962 he'd predicted to Kennedy that if we went into Vietnam, as he was then doing, we would need three hundred thousand troops within five years.

He said until General Westmoreland took over, Washington had no real information as to what was going on there. The reports were fragmentary and didn't give any real idea of the picture. At that time we were being consistently defeated, but the public thought the opposite; so did Washington.

All during 1964 we were losing, George said. Early in 1965 we were on the ragged edge and very close to losing. He did not say so, but this fact was the real reason why Johnson bombed North Vietnam after the Pleiku surprise attack in February 1965. It was not really to stop the infiltration of Communist forces south but to bolster the South Vietnamese government and South Vietnam morale.

**SUNDAY, SEPTEMBER 11** | My nephew Drew is back from Saigon, where he had been for two and a half years, first with NBC, now with ABC.

When I asked him what was the chief danger to a television man in Vietnam, he replied that it was going along the highway and that the greatest danger came from your own troops.

"When you're in action and you hear the artillery commander say that artillery support is coming your way, you know that in about five to ten seconds an artillery shell will burst right in front of you, and you wonder whether it's going to fall too short." Drew said, however, that our aim is accurate and the calculation of the artillery commanders is amazingly good.

He reported that American troops left a good impression in the villages they occupied, especially as compared to local Vietnamese troops, who requisition chickens and pigs and never pay for them, and the Vietcong immediately use this as propaganda with the villagers. In contrast, the American army comes along with extra supplies, which it hands out. It pays for what it takes, and its field hospitals are always willing to take in some of the local sick or wounded. This is in contrast to the generally sour note which the American army leaves in the big cities. There, away from the battlefront, the American troops are not popular.

Drew estimates that the United States will be fighting in Vietnam for at least another eight years, maybe ten.

He pointed out that Premier Ky is from North Vietnam so naturally wants to go back and retake that country. Most of the members of the Vietnamese embassy in Washington have been from North Vietnam, so we have North Vietnamese fighting against each other.

**MONDAY, SEPTEMBER 19** | BOSTON—Spoke at the United Givers luncheon at Swampscott. Afterward I went back to Boston and had tea in Cambridge with Ken Galbraith, who immediately wanted to know what I was doing about writing my memoirs. He emphasized that probably no one else had been around the Washington scene as long as I had and that I shouldn't delay. He made a rather uncomplimentary reference to Schlesinger's book on Kennedy and said that if I took some time, I could turn out a masterpiece by comparison.

About the Vietnam War and China, Ken feels Johnson is the prisoner of the State Department. He says Johnson went out on a limb with his speech on better relations with China, following which the State Department cut off the limb. There was now to be no admission of China into the UN. This could have been left open so China could have turned it down over Taiwan.

Dean Rusk is still living back in the days of the Korean War and is still trying to save his old friend McConnaughey, now U.S. ambassador on Taiwan. They worked together in the Korean War.

Ken thought the president should play down the news of the Vietnam War for several months so that the public would lose interest. Then we should slide out. Galbraith has written a letter to the president along this line.

We discussed the manner in which both Kennedy and Johnson became embroiled in the Vietnam War. Ken disagreed with the version, given to me by George Ball, that Kennedy sent some thirty thousand troops into Vietnam in the summer of 1961 following the prestige blow he took at the Bay of Pigs. Ken placed the date of escalating the war by Kennedy a year or so later.

He said, however, that Walt Rostow and Gen. Maxwell Taylor had been sent to Saigon by Kennedy in September 1961 to make a report on what the United States should do. Rostow then went on to Baguio, the Philippine summer resort, and wrote a report recommending that we send one full army division into South Vietnam. In order to get around the Geneva treaty, limiting troops to one thousand, Rostow recommended that the division be camouflaged as engineers to control the Mekong River floods. General Taylor signed the report, and this may have been the beginning of his career as a hawk.

Galbraith said after receiving the report, Kennedy sent him to Saigon to double-check Rostow's recommendations. He, Galbraith, recommended against it.

We agreed that Rostow was a bad influence on Johnson, and Ken recalled how JFK had arrived at the same opinion and had demoted Rostow, relegating him from the White House to the State Department. I told Galbraith of Rostow's remark to me after the Vienna conference, in which he praised Kennedy for being ready to look down the barrel of a gun vis-à-vis Khrushchev. Galbraith didn't believe it. He recalled that Kennedy had told him, "Khrushchev was the most difficult bastard I ever dealt with." Nevertheless, said Ken, we did get something at the Vienna conference, namely agreement on Laos.

FRIDAY, SEPTEMBER 23 | Gromyko blasted Goldberg's speech at the UN this morning, despite the fact Rusk had invited him to dinner and tried to get some cooperation.

What made headlines was his criticism of Goldberg's speech, though actually this was relatively minor compared with Gromyko's main thesis, namely that there is increasing danger of trouble in Europe. His whole emphasis was on Europe. This is something which the average American forgets—namely, that our involvement in Vietnam makes us vulnerable in Germany. If the Russians wanted to raise Cain around Berlin today, we would be widely divided between Asia and West Germany and completely unprepared for any showdown.

SUNDAY, SEPTEMBER 25 | We came in from the farm early to go to a reception given by Kay Graham for Pamela and Michael Berry. She is the daughter of Lord Birkenhead, and he is the owner of the *London Daily Telegraph*. He recalled that the last time we had met was a few days before the 1960 election, when I had told him in advance that I was going to break the story of Don Nixon's $205,000 loan from Howard Hughes.

We took Agnes Meyer to the party, but I had to take her home about thirty minutes after we arrived and never had so much difficulty loading her in her car. She weighs about two hundred pounds and was pure dead weight. I have never seen her quite so drunk.

TUESDAY, SEPTEMBER 27 | Breakfast with Adam Malik, foreign minister of Indonesia, who is here to bring Indonesia back into the UN. We discussed Johnson's forthcoming trip to the Philippines to meet with other Southeast Asia nations. Bill Fulbright had some caustic remarks to make about the trip, saying that Lyndon would only confer with "our boys" so wouldn't really get down to the heart of Asian problems.

Malik said he didn't think it would be wise for Lyndon to go to Indonesia because he would have to be received by President Sukarno, who was in an ambiguous position. "Sukarno hasn't been able to adjust himself," said Malik. "Before, he had too much power. Now he has hardly any power."

Malik is getting a certain amount of foreign aid, chiefly in the form of rice and spare parts. He isn't asking for too much, and the State Department is being coy about offering anything at this time.

I didn't ask Malik about the three hundred thousand Communists who were massacred, but I did ask him about the Chinese still remaining in Indonesia. He said about half a million of them were Red Chinese and they had been given permission to go back but were still there. Another half million or more are Nationalist Chinese. There's another million who have become Indonesian citizens. They all still remain a problem.

Clayton Fritchey, together with two men from *Pravda*, came to lunch. One was Sergei Vishnevski, their correspondent in Washington, and [the other was] the head of the American section of *Pravda*, whose name is Ratiani. Ratiani had been to the farm to look at Khrushchev's peas a couple of years ago.

Vishnevski expressed hurt that I had written about Russians who might defect. He referred to the two columns on the FBI and how J. Edgar Hoover had broken three spy stories. Vishnevski said he himself had an offer to defect, which included a large amount of money, but that Russians were not defecting. This, he said, was one of the problems when Stalin created the Iron Curtain. He was afraid of defections. Vishnevski said it's not happening anymore.

He said the young secretaries of the Soviet embassy had been flabbergasted over my columns and asked him what kind of a guy is this man—how does he dare write these things about Hoover? How can he stay in business? Vishnevski replied that he's a very fierce man with a very big mustache. I suppose that to buck the secret police in Moscow in print, if you are a Russian, is quite something. And I must say that Luvie has been a little nervous since I took on J. Edgar Hoover. He has the habit of spreading stories that you're a homo or stole from your grandmother or have Communist connections if you tangle with him.

The Russians asked me whether I had a bodyguard and had ever had threats on my life. I've had a few, but the only time I bothered much about it was some years ago when I was worried about the Mafia and had the police check on my car from time to time. It's when you start your car in the morning that the biggest risk is involved. I'm not worried about the FBI planning to bomb my car, but somebody else might figure that this would be a good time to do something along this line because it would certainly be blamed on J. Edgar Hoover.

We talked about Vietnam and the effect it had on American-Russian relations. Clayton pointed out that there was every reason why the Chinese should want this war to continue. The United States is spending $25 million a year on it. We are losing our allies. We're losing goodwill among all the African-Asian countries. It's costing us lives. It's spoiling the détente with Russia. It's costing political ill will for Johnson and costing inflation for the American public.

I recalled to Ratiani the irritation of the Russians toward us when we were in Moscow in March 1965, and I agreed the United States had made some mistakes, including the bombing of North Vietnam. I suggested, however, that in view of the overall Russian desire for world peace, which I was sure was genuine, they ought to step in vigorously with North Vietnam to try to end the war. The Russians listened but made no comment.

**WEDNESDAY, SEPTEMBER 28** | Riots broke out in San Francisco last night. Pat Brown called out the National Guard. A white cop shot and killed a fleeing Negro youth, who had stolen an automobile. The shouts of "black power" rang out all night. I wonder what this will do to Pat's reelection.

Luvie and I went to Howard University to attend a ceremony in which President Senghor of Senegal was awarded an honorary degree. It was an impressive ceremony. The hall was half-filled with university faculty, most of them Negro, a few white, one or two Pakistani Muslims, an Indian or two—all in caps and gowns. My old friend Dr. Mercer Cook, former U.S. ambassador to Senegal, was on the platform and translated Senghor's speech—a very good speech, incidentally. Senghor is a meek African who became quite a famous poet in France before he got into politics. It's too bad he is coming to Washington at such a crowded time, when dozens of foreign ministers are here from the UN General Assembly session.

I recalled what Dick Gregory told me on the telephone the other day, that the southerner understands Negroes because he has been raised with them. He is not afraid of a Negro doctor or a Negro preacher or a Negro in any walk of life. It's the second-generation whites in big cities, such as Chicago and Cleveland—sons of Polish and Italian immigrants—who have never seen Negroes before and who resent and fear them.

We were late getting to dinner with Agnes Meyer. By then she was stiff. We took her upstairs to bed, and I went—instead of Agnes—to the theater with Luvie. It's too bad that a woman of once remarkable talents and so much money with which she could do good should waste her life in these declining years. I suppose it's chiefly loneliness.

**FRIDAY, SEPTEMBER 30** | Dave [Karr] came for breakfast. He's going to continue with MGM, most of the time in Hollywood. He has a picture to be shot in Scotland next spring. He says that working in Hollywood is easy work, fairly good money, and fun.

Edgar Hoover apparently has thrown in the sponge. Deke DeLoach, his

No. 2 man, met Jack for lunch yesterday and reminded him that Hoover was an old man and that the doors of the FBI would always be open. DeLoach confided that Hoover was staying up late at night stewing over the columns, was scrutinizing Western papers to see whether there was any editorial reaction, and was more upset than he had been in years. My letter to him nearly blew the roof off the FBI.

DeLoach said that in investigating the Dodd matter, they were under instructions from the Justice Department not to go too far on certain aspects of the case and that privately the FBI was in our corner.

Cuneo came from New York for lunch. We discussed LBJ and the fact he has antagonized the press by almost announcing that if he got a scoop, he would undermine it. In contrast, the working press loved FDR. They did battle for him constantly against the wishes of their publishers. Now the publishers are more inclined to lean toward Johnson, while the working press more and more dislike him.

Eisenhower has made a statement which has more potential danger in it than anything in the Vietnam War so far. He said that once we resorted to force, we had to win and that we must take any action in order to win. We reported in a column two years ago that the Republicans had decided they would support Johnson in the war and then attack him just before election for not going through with the war fully despite their loyal support.

THURSDAY, OCTOBER 6 | Leonard Marks came by the house to tell me that Tommy Thompson was to be the new ambassador to Moscow. Tommy's appointment, he said, would keep for two, three, or four days. I wrote a special story and got it on the wire. Then the president announced it at three thirty. I also put it on the radio program in the form of an exclusive item, which will make me look rather sick on Sunday night, three days after Thompson's appointment was announced.

Leonard said that Tyler was going to Manila, ahead of the president, to help prepare the groundwork for him. He, Leonard, is leaving today to visit various capitals in advance and make sure the public reaction is favorable.

This afternoon the president announced an expansion of his trip, including stops in New Zealand, Australia, Thailand, and South Korea. He will not go to Japan, where Eisenhower was rebuffed after the U-2 summit conference failure of 1960 and where there is much opposition to the Vietnamese war today.

The trip is chiefly a public relations gimmick to help the congressional elections. Johnson was planning to spend most of October campaigning around the country but now finds that his name is mud in so many districts that the local Democrats don't want him there. This is really a crushing blow. He has to find some reason for not going to any districts other than the real reason, so the trip to Manila was invented.

It may also have some important results. I'm convinced that Gromyko, despite some sour notes struck in the Moscow press, will be conciliatory when he talks to Johnson at dinner next Monday night. I am also convinced that Johnson is desperately anxious for a way out of the war. If he doesn't find a way out, the Joint Chiefs are demanding that he escalate, and any real escalation will lead to serious complications, if not the involvement of the Chinese, which in turn could lead to World War III.

**SATURDAY, OCTOBER 8** | Johnson spoke in New York yesterday before the Editorial Writers Association. It was a surprise speech, and he actually asked to address this group. It set forth a new policy of cooperation with the Eastern Communist countries: more trade, most-favored-nation treatment, even American Export-Import Bank credits for some of them, and a proposed $30 million to help Fiat build an automobile factory in Russia.

This was going further than President Kennedy or Johnson, himself, had gone at any other time. The speech to some extent resembled Kennedy's American University speech on June 10, 1963, which set the stage for the nuclear test ban treaty and the improvement of American-Soviet relations.

The speech was a switch from Johnson's frequently bellicose private views on Russia, which he's expressed to me. And it got back to his earlier friendly views of his first year in office. Obviously, the speech was trumped up in a hurry in order to pave the way for the Gromyko dinner Monday night.

**THURSDAY, OCTOBER 13** | Johnson had a press conference today and announced that he would not go for a unilateral stop bombing. He said he was not going to have our men keep their hands in their pockets while the enemy continued bombing. Of course, it's a distorted picture. We continue fighting in the South and continue bombing in the South. The only thing we do is to stop bombing in the North, where we have not been very effective.

Lyndon did fairly well at his press conference, though I can see why the country is turning against him. He drawls along in a ponderous manner like a hick farmer standing in a pulpit pretending to be God. Most of what he said made sense. Most of what he said was good, but he just didn't say it the right way, and he seemed so sure of himself and so condescending.

**FRIDAY, OCTOBER 14** | Talked with Representatives Brooks of Texas, Mac-Donald of Massachusetts, Dante Fascell of Florida, and David King of Utah about subpoenaing the Ronald Reagan TV texts from General Electric to see whether GE had deducted this propaganda as a tax-exempt business expense and to find out what was in his various broadcasts. They are going to try.

**SATURDAY, OCTOBER 15** | A funny thing happened to me on the way to Kansas City. Shortly before I took off, I got a call from the TASS correspondent Petronssenko, wanting to see me on an emergency matter. I was intrigued, thought he must have something hot about the president's trip abroad or the Gromyko session.

What he wanted was to discuss this morning's column (which Jack wrote) about what LBJ told Gromyko on Monday. The column said that when the session was over, the president had put his arm around Gromyko and told Gromyko that during the last bombing pause over North Vietnam, "You kicked me in the groin," and that the president had referred to the bombing moratorium as a "Dobrynin pause," indicating that it was inspired by Dobrynin.

Petronssenko said the column had caused a great deal of comment in diplomatic circles and, further, that he had discussed it at the Russian embassy and Dobrynin said that the above points were not true.

I told Petronssenko frankly that I had not written the column and had been in Utah that day and that Jack Anderson had secured the information from reliable sources. I called Jack to get more details, and he told me that at the tail end of the Gromyko session, a group of senators had been brought into the room by LBJ, including Smathers, and that after Gromyko left, the president had briefed them on the session. I did not tell all this to Petronssenko, but I did tell him that either his embassy had given him the wrong information or that the president had been a little too exuberant in describing the session later.

What became apparent during my talk was that the Russians were worried over Chinese reaction to the column. Petronssenko made this clear when he mentioned the "Dobrynin pause" and kept coming back to it. The Chinese have been accusing the Russians of being the stooges for the American imperialist military, and this column, of course, would appear to substantiate their accusation. Petronssenko more or less admitted that the column would cause them trouble with the Chinese.

Petronssenko impressed me with his honest desire to improve American-Soviet relations. He is a sincere young man and was touched by the fact that Luvie gave him a beautiful child's book for his six-year-old son, which both Luvie and I autographed. I am also convinced that the story was about 90 percent accurate and that the Soviet embassy has been giving its TASS correspondent the slight runaround for political reasons.

WEDNESDAY, OCTOBER 26 | For the first time I was glad Hubert Humphrey kept me waiting. I was five minutes late arriving in his office from the chief justice's and, on top of this, had to wait twenty-five minutes, but it gave me a chance to write my notes from lunch.

Hubert said he had been talking to a group of civil rights leaders. Busing, they said, was not a good idea. When children were bused from one decrepit school to a modern school, it meant that the old school was not improved but went further and further downhill. The remedy was to improve the older schools in the old decrepit sections of cities rather than have the population expand into the suburbs.

I told him I'd just come from Minnesota, that I was concerned about the unfavorable comment I heard about him there and was also about the general reaction to him of late. I said I realized how difficult it was to be vice president, especially to play second fiddle to a man like Lyndon Johnson, who is an exacting taskmaster. Nevertheless, I didn't think he had played his cards to best advantage. Among other things it was not wise to put yourself in the position of running for president. People got awfully tired of hearing of a man being constantly talked about as a presidential candidate. I suggested that Bobby Kennedy would suffer from this. Hubert looked a little tired. For the first time I noticed lines in his face. Maybe this was because he dropped his usual mask of joviality.

He thanked me and went on to say he fully agreed it was a mistake to have your name put forward all the time as a candidate for president and that he had tried to discourage this. "I have avoided all these questions and comments except when I was too tired, and then once or twice I have slipped. I want you to know that I would be delighted if everybody forgot about me and the future.

"I am trying to do a good job as vice president, and that's all. Why do you think I spent an hour and a half today with this civil rights group, and why do you think I spend so much time with these other groups? It's to take the load off the president's shoulders. I have been making speeches around the country. I would much rather stay here, but I am under orders. I do what the president wants me to do. I think I have been helpful on some of the legislation up on the Hill." Hubert said the column account of the meeting between Johnson and Gromyko was the most accurate he'd seen. I told him how the TASS man had come to see me in some agitation, claiming that Dobrynin had denied the story, including the words "kick me in the groin," and that Johnson had patted Gromyko on the shoulder at the end. Hubert said this was absolutely true and that he had seen Johnson get up and pat Gromyko on the back as they walked out.

"When they blast us a little bit, it is pure politics, and you should discount it," Hubert said. "They have to do this to keep their position pure with the Chinese. Meanwhile, Arthur Goldberg is doing a wonderful job in New York, talking to the Romanians, the Hungarians, and the Poles. Arthur is a great negotiator, and he is making progress.

"I'm fairly optimistic," said Hubert. "After all, here are the Russians working for the same goal as we are, namely to stop Chinese militarism. Two years ago look what happened in India. We both came in without saying anything to each other and supported India against Chinese communism. We were silent partners."

Hubert told me how he'd met Kosygin in India when he went over for the funeral of Premier Shashtri and how he had given Kosygin a pair of his cuff links. He brought this up apropos the fact that Kosygin was not as outgoing as Khrushchev, not as pro-American, and played his cards closer to his vest.

"I met him in the garden of the presidential palace," said Hubert. "His daughter was with him. She spoke English and translated for us. I gave her a bracelet and gave him a pair of my cufflinks. Kosygin protested that he didn't think he could wear them because of the war in Vietnam.

"Later we met Dean Rusk, and I told Dean, in front of Kosygin, 'I have given him a pair of my cufflinks, and he said he didn't think he could wear them because of Vietnam, but I'm going to be watching him. And when he makes a speech and he lifts up his arms and I see that he's got those cufflinks on, then I'll know that we're getting along all right.'" Hubert talked about the importance of having the president specialize on foreign affairs. "I wish he'd leave these domestic problems to me. He needs to travel abroad and have more summit conferences."

"He ought to travel all through Latin America and visit every country there. He ought to go to Europe and talk to President de Gaulle. He and de Gaulle would make a great team. De Gaulle couldn't outmaneuver him.

"The trouble with the president is he takes the advice of these lace pants diplomats. Chip Bohlen is persona non grata with de Gaulle. He should have come home long ago. What we need over there is an ambassador who will cut some ice."

Hubert and I agreed that if Reagan won in California, Johnson's plan of cooperation with the Russians would be out the window. The right wing would be triumphant and would cramp the president's hand.

At the end of the day a Russian newspaperman, Victor E. Louis, who works for the *Evening News* of London, dropped in. I suggested that now is the time for the Russians to give Johnson a little help regarding peace, or otherwise right-wingers like Reagan would win. Louis's reply was surprising. In brief he said:

"If we had peace in Vietnam, then North Vietnam would become a Chinese satellite, and that's what we don't want. We would much rather have you continue in South Vietnam. It's a war that isn't going to expand. You are careful about it. We are careful not to send too many supplies, but if we cut off those supplies, China will send them instead.

"If the war continues, it keeps you busy in a part of the world where you can't bother anyone. We don't have to worry about Berlin, and we don't have to worry about Cuba. You're too busy in Vietnam. We understand your problem."

THURSDAY, OCTOBER 27 | Went to see Ambassador Dobrynin. He pointed to something I had not realized before—namely, that North Vietnam was the only socialist country with which Russia did not have a mutual security pact. "If we had signed such a pact with North Vietnam, then our missiles and rockets would be at her disposal immediately without any argument or discussion," Dobrynin said. He also pointed out that it was almost impossible for Russia to pressure North Vietnam as long as the United States was bombing it. This put us in the position of being the aggressor, and under such circumstances Russia could not very well pressure Hanoi to come to the peace table. This was why Foreign Minister Gromyko had proposed to President Johnson that we end the bombing of the North.

I replied that personally I was against the bombing and that some in the Johnson administration were also, but I said I thought Johnson was influenced only by the Joint Chiefs of Staff, who previously had advised that the moratorium on bombing in December of 1964–January 1965 had given the Communists a chance to mobilize their men and supplies for new attacks. The president didn't want to be under criticism from the Joint Chiefs of Staff for repeating this now.

We briefly discussed China. Dobrynin asked why we hadn't been able to improve our relations with China. I reminded him that Dean Rusk, Arthur Goldberg, and the president had all announced conciliatory moves toward China this past summer but had been rebuffed. They had proposed an exchange of professors and learned men and lowering the bars to Chinese visitors in this country. We got not a ripple of reaction.

Dobrynin remarked wryly that his country knew something about the difficulties of getting along with China. He added that the chief trouble at present was Taiwan. If we stopped doing business with Taiwan, he indicated without exactly saying so, Red China would melt its thaw and improve relations with the United States.

MONDAY, OCTOBER 31 | Had a good talk with Arthur Goldberg. I had not seen him for any length of time since last summer. He said that after his speech to the General Assembly, in which he expressed American willingness to withdraw and to include the Vietcong in the future government of South Vietnam, the president had chided him. "God damn you," said the president. "You gave a speech at the UN, and you don't say anything I haven't said before, but you get all kinds of favorable reaction. I say the same things, and there is no reaction."

"You wouldn't have made the same speech, Mr. President," Arthur replied. "By the time your people got through tearing it up, it would be in pieces." I asked Arthur whom he was referring to, and he replied, "Rostow." "When I prepared that speech, I started way off in left field," Arthur explained, "and gave 'em plenty to take out. By the time they finished, I had pretty much what I wanted in the speech."

Arthur referred, of course, to his old labor union technique of asking for a lot and then retreating to a point where you get about what you really wanted.

The most important thing Arthur told me was that he'd urged President Johnson to make a speech at the opening session of the UN General Assembly, in which he would pledge an end of bombing North Vietnam in the cause of peace. Lyndon refused to do this. He was willing to make the speech but not pledge a bombing moratorium. Arthur told him not to go to New York to make the speech unless he was willing to pledge an end to the bombing.

"If he had made this speech," Arthur said, "ninety-five nations would have supported him. Even the Communist nations would have had to go along. He could have said, 'I'm stopping the bombing. I turn this whole problem over to the assembly.'"

I told Arthur about my conversation with Dobrynin and his emphasis on an end to the bombing. I also told him of my suggestion that the United States get an advance commitment of peace talks, then stop bombing three or four days before any public announcement of peace conversations.

"We've talked about cutting out bombing if they gave us assurances," Arthur said. "But they won't give the assurances. We can't be sure whether the Russians won't or can't pressure Ho Chi Minh."

Arthur said that Federenko, the Russian UN ambassador, had been quite friendly in recent weeks. He thought it was not so much Johnson's proposals for relaxed trade but rather that he, Goldberg, had found housing for the Russians at Glencoe, Long Island. "Adlai did nothing about this," Arthur said, "but I put it across and they understand such things; however, they're not cooperating regarding Syria. We tried to get them to cut off arms shipments, but they refused. The situation is serious, and there may be war. The Israelis won't take many more incidents. The Arabs won't cooperate at all."

I asked him about Red China's admission to the UN. "I tried to get the State Department to agree to China's admission," Arthur said, "but they wouldn't go along with me. We'd be much better off if we took that position. China probably wouldn't come in anyway.

"The Russians are going through the motions of proposing Red China's admission, but they don't really care about it. I personally think we can't desert Taiwan but that we should propose Red China as a member."

SUNDAY, NOVEMBER 6 | Talked to Harry Lerner in Los Angeles about the Brown race and suggested that California labor leaders appeal to their membership. Harry seems rooted in the spirit of defeat.

At his press conference last week Lyndon went to town on Dick Nixon, calling him a chronic campaigner and slapping him down for his criticism of U.S. willingness to withdraw troops from Vietnam after six months of peace. Nixon had argued that the Chinese could put troops back in a few hours and we would have to go halfway around the world to return them. This is the old argument we used with the Russians over Berlin. Lyndon really did himself proud in slapping Nixon, but Nixon has thrived on it. Before, he was unnoticed. Now he feels important.

**WEDNESDAY, NOVEMBER 9** | Watched election returns last night on television until about 2:00 a.m. There were some serious and sad upsets for the old Democratic battlers for liberal government: Soapy Williams in Michigan, Paul Douglas in Illinois, and Pat Brown in California. I had predicted all of these. I was wrong regarding New York, where Rockefeller beat a last-minute trend by O'Connor and won by a substantial margin. This was a plus for good government. Nelson has been a good governor, despite his die-hard Republican opposition. O'Connor, the Democrat, was a booster of federal aid for parochial schools and in general a hack politician. In Maryland, Agnew, the Republican, beat George Mahoney, Democrat, for governor, as I predicted—again, a plus for better government. In Florida they elected a Republican governor for the first time in history, which I did not predict.

Talked to Jack on the telephone, who thinks George Romney came out of the election the big winner and is on the way to becoming the Republican nominee for president. (Jack, himself, is a staunch Mormon.) If the American public is going to go by brand names, then Romney is on the way up. If it's going to go for performance and track records, then it should take a man like Case of New Jersey, who, once again, was overwhelmingly reelected.

**FRIDAY, NOVEMBER 11** | Flew back from Los Angeles last night, arriving at Dulles at 6:00 a.m. It's a holiday, but I had to get out three columns and do a telecast. Lyndon had a press conference yesterday in which he admitted Republican victories in the House would make his program more difficult. His operation, scheduled provisionally for today, has been postponed until next week.

Had lunch with Joe Borkin and Alex Levin. Joe was worried about the prospect that Kurt Georg Kiesinger, a member of the Nazi Party in the early days of Hitler, may become the new chancellor of West Germany. Kiesinger was pretty young then. Much more significant, in my opinion, is the fact that most of the new candidates for chancellor are anti-American—at least favoring less cooperation with the United States—and lean toward de Gaulle.

It's significant that Johnson, when he received Chancellor Erhard here in late September and October, refused to make any concessions. He later emphasized to Foreign Minister Gromyko that the United States had not given West Germany any nuclear weapons and used this in order to try to get Soviet help for peace in Vietnam. I wonder how much Johnson's pro-Soviet policy, and his partial rebuff of Erhard, had to do with Erhard's resignation. I made a prediction that he would resign even before he arrived.

**MONDAY, NOVEMBER 14** | Took the Czech ambassador to lunch at the Cosmos Club. He wanted to be "educated," he said, regarding the next Republican presidential candidate and whether Johnson would run again. I do think that the Republicans are not going to pick Nixon again. He has too much scar tissue.

This morning the Bulgarian government issued a call for all Communist nations to meet, which was interpreted as another move by the Communist world to isolate China and perhaps break off diplomatic relations.

I told him now was the time for the Communist world to help Johnson regarding peace in Vietnam. I told him Johnson sincerely wanted peace, to which, for the first time, he heartily concurred. I also told him that Johnson's efforts to relax trade and secure most-favored-nation treatment with the Communist nations would depend on peace; that it would be very difficult for the president to get new trade relaxations through Congress, especially the new Congress, with the war still going on. The ambassador seemed to understand this fully.

The White House announced today that Johnson will be operated on in Bethesda on Wednesday.

News from Israel is alarming. Yesterday a small group of Israeli soldiers crossed the border in tanks, and with artillery, to a small Jordanian village, supposed to be the school for training saboteurs. An air battle developed, and finally, the UN truce team managed to invoke a cease-fire. Tension is high on both sides, especially in the Arab world. There is no telling what the Syrians will do next. The Jordanians are under better control.

**TUESDAY, NOVEMBER 15** | Last night we went to a party at the home of Bobby Kennedy in honor of Averell Harriman on his seventy-fifth birthday. We didn't want to go and almost backed out at the last minute, especially because we had to dress in costumes. I rigged up a semi-polo costume at the last minute, chiefly by wearing a polo hat and carrying a polo stick. Luvie resurrected an old dress with playing cards all over it.

When we got there, however, we found that it was the party to end all parties, chiefly because some of Lyndon's most intimate official family were present: Jack Valenti, Bill Moyers, Secretary of the Treasury Joe Fowler, and of all people, Hubert Humphrey.

Ethel was cordial, and so was Bobby. Ethel had apparently been doing some research on Averell Harriman's life because she recalled a column I had written about him when he was Marshall Plan administrator in Paris and adroitly euchred the French government into keeping a house the United States wanted. It was such an old column I'd forgotten it. Bobby was dressed in a coat, which he had borrowed from Marie Harriman, together with one of Averell's hats. He looked almost exactly like Averell. We were all supposed to come dressed in some stage of Averell's life.

Bobby made some magnificent toasts. He has his brother's charm and wit, and he lays it on with a deft hand. He introduced, among others, three guests, whom he said couldn't quite fit into the dining room, and the curtain was drawn on Joe Stalin, FDR, and Winston Churchill, all in wax, sitting outside the bay window in the garden. It was reminiscent of Averell's days at Yalta and Teheran, when he was ambassador to Russia.

Averell was taken by surprise and had no idea that a party was being given in his honor.

While we were talking with Averell after dinner, Dick Goodwin, formerly on Kennedy's and Johnson's staff, came up, and Averell gave him the worst bawling out I have heard in some time for criticizing Johnson's position on Vietnam. "You are killing American lives," he said. "The longer you talk, the longer this war is going to continue. Don't make any mistake that the other side isn't watching everything you say. You ate his bread, and now you are biting the hand that fed you." Dick looked unhappy but said nothing.

Bob Kintner said he had taken my column press release down to the president, who was quite pleased. I had not suspected that this much attention was going to be placed upon one story. It indicates how the White House watches its press relations. Bob says that the president was hopping around like a small boy and outdistancing all of them in walking around the LBJ Ranch. He took them in his car, which turns into a boat when driven in the water, and drove them around to see his deer. He also inspected his herd of three buffalo. Joe Fowler, who was also at the ranch, confirmed the fact that the president had kept him busy inspecting the place while talking budget figures.

**WEDNESDAY, NOVEMBER 16** | The president was operated on at 6:30 a.m., then, a couple of hours later, it was announced that the polyp on his throat was benign. A few hours after that, pictures were taken of him propped up in bed, looking a bit bedraggled but with Luci and Lady Bird looking on.

Last night I spoke in Philadelphia and drove back to Washington with Carl Levin, formerly of the *New York Herald Tribune*, now in public relations. We discussed the president's poor public relations and the fact he was slipping so badly. We agreed that what he needed to do was to have less exposure to the press, that the public had more respect for a president when they saw less of his intimate goings and comings. Roosevelt, for instance, was never photographed while being carried by the Secret Service up to the rostrum to make a speech. Very seldom was he ever photographed in his wheelchair. The public saw him only as a staunch figure with powerful shoulders standing behind the podium. The president, no matter who he is, should be a little bit aloof from the public. He should stand head and shoulders above. Furthermore, I think the public likes to feel some sympathy for a man who has an operation and not feel that he bounces back so quickly that he doesn't need sympathy. This president has done just the opposite.

**THURSDAY, NOVEMBER 17** | Yesterday Arthur Goldberg cracked down hard in the UN on the Israeli invasion of Jordan. The Israelis had it coming. They deliberately crossed the border and shot up a Jordanian town.

Bobby Baker has been contesting the right of the Justice Department to try him. Edward Bennett Williams is his lawyer, and he's contending that the case against Bobby has been nullified by the tapping of Baker's wires. Actually, Bobby's wires are not tapped, but a bug was placed in the Sheraton-Carlton suite of Fred Black, Bobby's friend and business associate, and the FBI listened in on their conversations.

Talked with Ed Williams on the telephone, who said the FBI was clearly in violation of Bobby's constitutional rights. He said the Justice Department had stipulated that Baker's constitutional rights were violated in order to avoid the revelation that the FBI had been guilty of housebreaking. He also said that the suite next door was the VIP suite, occupied by distinguished visitors, and that the FBI had listened in on it also, due to the power of the electric bug.

All this has come out in court, but there has been very little in the newspapers about it—indicating the fear of J. Edgar Hoover. Jack has been trying to tell me I shouldn't go after Hoover, that he's an old man about to retire; however, he is a symbol of the police state and in my opinion an ominous one.

Maybe it's what happens when you get to be too old and power goes to your head. Maybe it's one reason why I should retire pretty soon, though I don't think I have any power to worry about.

MONDAY, NOVEMBER 21 | Talked with Tommy Thompson, who is due to go to Moscow for his new post the first week in January. He did not go for McNamara's theory that the best way to have a thaw in American-USSR relations is to let the Russians build up to us in missile strength. McNamara argues that parity between the two powers would make for less nervousness on the part of the Russians and more willingness to cooperate. Tommy says we should continue to have superiority in missiles. This is Rusk's idea also.

We have been allies of the Russians in two world wars. We are now competitors of theirs around the world, but we do not want a war with them, and perhaps McNamara is right that parity would do some good.

TUESDAY, NOVEMBER 22 | This is the anniversary of Kennedy's assassination. Gov. John Connally of Texas stated he was not convinced that the same bullet which wounded him passed through Kennedy. He felt it was a separate bullet; however, he agreed with the main findings and saw no reason for another investigation.

The FBI has told Jack they can support me in my statements about Mark Lane. He has written a letter to the *Post*, attacking my recent column upholding the Warren Commission. I suspect the FBI wants to do a little trading. They undoubtedly suspect that I am going to sound off about their tapping of the Sheraton-Carlton Hotel suite.

TUESDAY, NOVEMBER 29 | NEW YORK—Dinner at the Jack Heinzes' and then to the Truman Capote ball at the Plaza. It was billed as the big event of the New York season. It became that way chiefly because Truman limited his guests to 540. Hundreds of others were clamoring to get in, and you had to go through a security check at the entrance. I think most of this was a good publicity stunt on Truman's part.

I seldom go out to dinner in New York, so the dinner at the Heinzes' was really more of an experience. They have a beautiful apartment overlooking the

East River: high ceilings, walls covered with Picassos, and every other form of modern art. The Edward Bennett Williamses had come up from Washington. John Gunther was there, looking quite old and thin. His books haven't been selling well of late. Herb Caen of the *San Francisco Chronicle* had flown in, together with a young and attractive wife, who is Spanish and beside whom I sat at dinner. The ball was supposed to begin at ten, but we arrived at eleven. I junked my mask shortly after arriving. I couldn't see—the eye slits were too small; however, the other masks, especially those worn by the women, were really something.

I got stuck with Lilly Guest, my fellow dairy farmer from Virginia, who is a good dancer, but even we got tired of discussing cows. The best dance I had was with Herb Caen's wife, who is terrific.

Actually, I spent most of the evening talking to the Kansas contingent. They were not having a good time. One of them was sour over the fact that New Yorkers had treated them as if they had arrived in a wagon train.

Alice Longworth, aged eighty-three, stayed until 2:00 a.m. Luvie and I [went] to bed about three. It was one of these parties that you don't want to miss.

Went to see Arthur Goldberg, who has been going from one crisis to another: last week the Israeli-Jordanian crisis; today it's the vote on admitting Red China.

Arthur said he'd gone to Texas and told LBJ, in front of Rusk, that the United States could not afford to get the reputation of opposing everything. We must be fluid, he said. We must agree to the Italian proposal to study Chinese admittance. Rusk agreed. The president okayed the U.S. backing of a study. Later, however, Rusk called Arthur and argued against it. He was quite nervous over the position of our allies—the Philippines, Thailand, and Korea—and tried to dissuade Arthur from going ahead.

Rusk's persuasion, however, was not very pointed; however, just as Arthur was about to go across the street to speak before the UN, he got another call from Rusk, who turned on the heat and asked Arthur not to go with the Italian resolution.

Arthur replied: "We can't go back to the president with this thing. It was all decided with him. I'll trim my speech, but it's time for me to go over and deliver it. I've got to go now."

With this he cut the conversation short. He had written a long, philosophical speech explaining the American position, most of which he junked in deference to Rusk. "If we had waited, Rusk would have gotten back to the president and the whole move to relax our position would have been killed," Arthur told me.

**WEDNESDAY, DECEMBER 7** | While in Chicago recently, I had a talk with Sidney Lovett, who did public relations work for Julius Klein in the Middle West in the 1950s and 1960s. He says we have only scratched the surface regarding Klein.

In 1961 Klein and his wife were talking in front of Lovett. Klein said, "We've got to get $10,000 quick for Tom Dodd." He was speaking in English. Then, realizing that Lovett was present, he switched to German, not realizing that Lovett understands German.

In 1964 Klein was telephoning Hubert Humphrey, with Lovett nearby. The conversation went like this. "Is it all right for me to talk over the phone?" The answer from Humphrey apparently said it was. "I put $500 on your campaign," said Julius. "You can have more whenever you need it."

**WEDNESDAY, DECEMBER 14** | Saw the president at about 6:45 p.m. Marvin Watson led me to the residential part of the White House after a short wait in the Fish Room, which has been cleaned up, with some of the old books left over from the Kennedy administration gone. In fact, there wasn't a book left, except the life of David Thoreau [*The Life of Henry David Thoreau*] and a big scrapbook given to Sen. Lyndon Johnson by his Senate staff at Christmas 1958. It is full of Texas cartoons.

The White House was dark and quiet. Marvin took me in the elevator to the third floor. There was a Secret Service man sitting at a table outside the Lincoln bedroom. I could hear some noises inside, which I thought was a motion picture being shown to the president. It wasn't. It was three sets of television in color. He was lying in the Lincoln bed in a set of freshly laundered gray silk pajamas, watching the news with a remote control in his hand. The announcement of Bill Moyers's resignation was being made, and Lyndon was obviously more interested in his TV sets than in talking to me—at first.

Jack Anderson had coached me on some of the things I should say to the president. I was prepared to let off a dismal report on the state of his political prestige, and although I started out, I got nowhere.

The president interrupted me by watching Bill Moyers and also telling about him. "Bill has a great opportunity," the president said. "He would probably never get one just like it. His brother died a short time ago of cancer. Bill has health problems too. He has two little boys his brother left him and his brother's wife that he has to take care of. And the *Newsday* people offered him all kinds of money—so much that I told him to get a lawyer and make sure that everything was tied down right. I couldn't believe they were offering that much. Mr. Guggenheim is in his late seventies and can't last forever. He's a man with $500 million, and Bill has a chance to really go places.

"Bill had two things he wanted to do, either run for office or do this kind of work. If he ran for office, he would have to run against Wright Patman. They come from the same district. When I came to Washington, my daddy told me, 'You watch what Wright Patman does and vote with him.' Wright, Mike Monroney, and I were the only congressmen from the Southwest to vote against an increase in the price of oil during the war. Everybody in Texas voted for it. I took a look at it. There weren't any oil wells in my district, but there were a lot of cattlemen and sheep men. I decided that if the price of oil went up, the cattlemen would come in wanting the same thing and everybody else would follow suit."

Jack discovered that the president had telephoned Wright Patman, asking him to investigate the Ford Foundation; however, one of our news sources was involved, and we couldn't investigate head-on without endangering him. So, I asked Lyndon why it was that Patman was investigating the Ford Foundation. "I don't know," said Lyndon. "Wright's up to all sorts of things, but you can bet he's always working on the side of the public."

By this time Dan Rather of CBS had come on the air with an interview with Moyers, which the president watched. Rather asked Moyers whether it was true that he was getting out because he was at odds with Walt Rostow on foreign policy. Bill denied this and said he was getting out for only personal reasons. He was also asked whether he had resigned because he had not been appointed ambassador to Saigon. I had never heard the latter, though I had heard the former. In fact, I'm sure that Bill wanted to take a stand in foreign affairs and was quite disappointed when he was not appointed undersecretary of state. His denial sounded a little rehearsed, though on the whole convincing. Then Eric Sevareid came on with a little spiel about Moyers, concluding with the line, "And thus retires the only man who has ever said no to Lyndon Johnson."

"That's a lie," said Lyndon, pointing from his bed.

Marvin Watson came in with the usual cue that it was time for me to go. And even though he stood at the foot of the bed for some minutes, I ignored him. "There are some things I want to talk to you about," I told the president. Marvin then left, and I made some points about shifting the interest of the nation away from the Vietnam War, if possible, to other things. I suggested that in the forthcoming Latin American summit conference, the president could do a lot of constructive fence-mending for long-range peace, such as getting a seaport for Bolivia, as originally proposed by Harry Truman. This struck no sparks whatsoever. I also talked about a visit to Paris with de Gaulle. "He's a difficult guy," I said, "but you're a very persuasive person, and you might bring him around to some of the old cooperation that our countries used to enjoy." No enthusiasm whatsoever. I had some other ideas, but I dropped them.

"What do you see for the chances of peace in Vietnam?" I asked.

Lyndon then launched into a rather careful diagnosis of some of the things he was doing. He referred to Harriman's trips and said, "Katzenbach, who is doing a fine job of administering the State Department, has reignited Averell. Arthur Goldberg is going over to Saigon just as soon as he can get away from the UN. Arthur has more imagination and more ideas and is more dedicated than almost anyone else I've got."

I asked whether he could get the Russians to give him some help. He said he wasn't sure, that Gromyko had been fairly cooperative. "Gromyko raised the question of all our bases over there. He said that nobody could believe that we were going to get out when we were building bases to last for fifty years. He was careful not to say that he didn't believe it but that others couldn't. This was why I made the statement in Manila that we would get out in six months. The Russians are having their problems with the Chinese, but we think they are winning out."

He then picked up some reports from his bed on the latest bombing raids and read them to me. He said they came from a nonaligned country, which he did not name. They pertained to the raids of last night, which the North Vietnamese claimed had killed women and children in the suburbs of Hanoi. The reports told of bombing a machine repair factory and a railroad. They did not mention civilian casualties. The most interesting thing to me was the report that within an hour a thousand workers were busy repairing the rail line and the prediction that it would be rebuilt within twenty-four hours. The report also referred to another explosion of a shell of foreign make. The president went on to say that some of the antiaircraft shells fired at our planes came back and exploded later and that we couldn't be blamed for all the casualties.

"Our pilots are very efficient," he said. "They can drop a bomb right into this cup." He motioned to a glass of water on his bedside.

"I don't know when we're going to get peace," he continued. "During the monsoon they think things are their way. Every so often there's a break in the clouds, and we stage a raid. Other days we can't do anything. When the monsoon season is over, perhaps they'll be more willing to talk. They thought they were going to be in a position after the elections where we would toss in the sponge, but they were disappointed. The next Congress is going to have more members against them than before. I think they got over the idea that I took a beating at the election as far as the war is concerned."

I suggested he go to the UN with a Christmas appeal for peace and offer to extend the truce indefinitely. I knew that Arthur Goldberg had suggested something like this earlier and that Senator Mansfield was proposing a longer truce now.

"A truce in bombing has to have two sides," he replied. "It can't be one-sided." I asked him if there weren't some reports on peace feelers from Algiers or Moscow that could be published to show what the status was. He said to wait until Averell Harriman got back and he might have some.

He told me how he persuaded Tommy Thompson to go back to Moscow as ambassador. "I got a lot of suggestions of good men, including yours," he said. (I had suggested the president of the Pennsylvania Railroad, Mr. Saunders, but I didn't think the president would remember it.) "I talked to some of the experts, who said that it was better to have an old hand go to Moscow than a fresh face. It's like having you rather than Jack Anderson. You've got the polish and the old know-how. Then I talked to Rusk, and he said the most experienced man on Russia was Tommy Thompson—but he said it would be difficult to get him to go back.

"McNamara was at dinner in Georgetown with some of you socialites, and he sat beside Mrs. Thompson. He asked her if her husband would go back to Russia. She said that her husband was a patriotic man and that if he didn't go back if the president asked him, she wouldn't live with him. McNamara telephoned me that night, and I had Thompson over the next day. He didn't want to go back. He wanted to hook up with an educational institution—but he agreed.

"It will be a great thing to have a man who knows the language so that when the chairman says come down and spend the weekend with me at the Black Sea, he doesn't have to take his interpreter along. The Russians don't like to have you ask to bring your own interpreter."

By this time Marvin Watson had come in several times, but each time the president said, "Give me five more minutes," and waved Watson out.

Earlier in the conversation Lyndon referred to the letter I wrote him about improving his press relations. He came back to it. "There isn't much I can do about the press," he said. "They are going to go after me no matter what I do. I've got to do the best I can without worrying about 'em too much. I'm going to try to be like Lincoln, who had everybody against him. I've got the Republicans knifing me and also Bobby Kennedy. Yesterday I had three columnists going after me. (All on the president's supposed deception regarding the cost of the Vietnam War.)

"I think part of the trouble is Rusk and the *New York Times*. The *Times* wanted me to fire Rusk, but I wouldn't. The *Times* keeps jumping on me. I can't fight back. If I did, they'd come at me all the harder. Suppose I called you in and said, 'Drew, I'm going to do this and this to you if you don't write some favorable stuff about me.' You'd go back and write the meanest stuff you could. I've just got to do the best I can and take it.

"You said in your letter that I shouldn't worry about the publishers. Well, I haven't been doing anything with the newspaper publishers for a long time. It is true that I had Mr. and Mrs. Norman Chandler in here during the summer of 1964 after their son, Otis, said that he was hoping the paper would not come out for Goldwater. I had them in for dinner but only because Otis thought there was a chance.

I asked if he'd seen Roberts's piece in *Newsweek*. The president had. "The credulity gap he's talking about is only in his own mind," he said.

I suggested one way he could counter the present unfavorable reaction was to let some of his cabinet take the gaff, just as Harold Ickes did for Roosevelt. Lyndon interrupted me.

"I wish I had an Ickes," he said. "I wish I had someone who could coin phrases like 'the barefoot boy of Wall Street,' but I haven't. I haven't got anyone in the cabinet who can raise hell like he can. I've got Joe Fowler, who's no politician, Gardner, Rusk. McNamara is the only one who can do it."

I pointed to Udall, and the president agreed. "Yes, Udall could do it if he wanted to stick his neck out, but he doesn't."

I suggested that Bob Weaver should take some of the gaff for the big city criticism.

"He went up to testify before Ribicoff's and Kennedy's committee the other day, and they wouldn't even let him finish reading his statement," said the president. "Imagine a cabinet member not being permitted to read his statement. He should have walked out of there and slammed the thing in their face, but he won't take on a fight."

I admitted that Weaver was something of a bureaucrat, but I thought he would take on a fight and said I would talk to him. "You talk to him and talk to these other fellows," said Lyndon. "Tell them this is not a one-man battle. We're all in it together.

"During the campaign I wanted to get someone to go after the Republicans on their heavy spending. Mansfield's a great guy, but he won't get out and fight. There isn't anyone in the Senate who can get out in the political arena and do battle. Jerry Ford was going after me on the President's Club. It was formed by Kennedy, not by me, to raise money. He even had them into the White House and passed the hat. I have never done that, but I have gone around to speak at dinners to raise money. And when Bobby was running for the Senate in New York, he wanted to tap the President's Club funds. He said that's what it was for. I said no. Whereupon he leaked to Evans and Novak some of the stories on the President's Club. That's the best way to discourage contributions.

"Meanwhile, we couldn't get anyone to show what the Republicans had contributed. They were far ahead of us. Finally, Representative Resnick put it in the *Congressional Record*. He made a speech on the floor. He showed that Rockefeller had contributed x thousand, the Mellons x thousand, Joe Pew x thousand" (the president named the exact figures, which I can't remember, but his memory seemed amazingly accurate).

"But even when we put it in the *Congressional Record*, do you suppose anyone would publish it? Not one newspaper picked it up."

At one point he remarked that Bobby is pissing in the wind. He also said that Bobby had come down to see him to oppose Weaver's appointment as secretary of HUD, saying there was no commitment to have him appointed. "I looked up the record, and there was a commitment by Jack Kennedy, and I appointed him."

He also mentioned that "if this economy keeps going down, we'll need to spend more money on steel and cement and public works." He pointed with some pride to the fact that there were only 1.7 million unemployed with the last Labor Department announcement, and he said: "When you figure people who are sick or being transferred from one job to another, that means practically no unemployment. Never in history has there been that little unemployment, and yet what do the newspapers say about it? Nothing."

Marvin Watson came into the room once again, about the fifth time. A Secret Service man came in with a message to call Katzenbach. I couldn't hear what the conversation was about, but apparently it pertained to Ambassador Gronowski in Warsaw. Lyndon told Katzenbach: "When you send him a message, tell him that you talked to me and I told you what a fine job he was doing. He left the cabinet to take this job, and he deserves some credit. Give him a little Christmas message." Earlier Lyndon had told me how well Gronowski was doing, that he was cheered in the streets when he walked through Warsaw.

Earlier, also, Lyndon referred to the fact that Tyler was resigning. "Tyler wrote me a letter saying that he was getting out. And I think it's a good thing. He's been in government long enough, and he ought to practice law for a while, then he could come back. He's one of the most efficient men I know—better than you are. Only his wife is better than he is. Last night she had a mess here. Planes were stacked up, guests were not arriving, Duke Ellington was supposed to be down here. She had tables where no one was sitting beside the women, and when she'd move men in to sit beside them, then suddenly the guests who were supposed to sit there arrived. Bess handled it all without getting disturbed or excited."

I mentioned that it was not easy to write for anti-administration newspapers, but before I could get the words out of my mouth, he interrupted. "Yes, I feel sorry for you with all your newspapers—you and Rockefeller. I weep for you."

As I got up to leave, Lyndon got up to go to the bathroom. He padded in with his bare feet and on the way thanked me again for my letter. "What you said was completely true," he said, "and we are going to follow your advice. We're going to keep out of the limelight. I showed your letter to George Christian, and we are going to hold one press conference a month.

"A lot of people don't tell you the truth, and I appreciate what you said. I remember Sam Rayburn telling Harry Truman, when he was about to come to the White House to be president: 'You'll have a lot of folks down there bowin' and scrapin' and tellin' you what a great man you are. Just remember, you ain't that good.'"

I had a hard time finding my way out of the White House and left to my own devices. The Secret Service guard was busy and told me to go down in the elevator, but I didn't know which button to push. Finally, I got to the ground floor and made my way back through the colonnade. It was dark and cold, but I finally got back to the Executive Offices, where my hat and coat were left. It was eight twenty when I finally got out.

P.S. At one point Lyndon emphasized what he had done to better relations with Russia. "In the past year," he said, "I have signed a consular treaty, a cultural exchange agreement, a space treaty, and we're on the verge of signing an anti-proliferation treaty. Yet they say I haven't done enough to improve relations with Russia."

**SUNDAY, DECEMBER 18** | (Drove to the airport with Jimmy Hoffa to discuss Hoffa's upcoming prison sentence.)

**THURSDAY, DECEMBER 22** | Kay Graham came to dinner with Clayton Fritchey. She razzed me a bit about my story on the Truman Capote party. Clayton, who has just come back from Saigon, said he had arrived at one of two opinions about the war: either that it was a major calamity or a complete catastrophe, and he wasn't quite sure which.

We speculated whether the amours of John F. Kennedy would now become public and, if so, whether they would hurt him. It was generally agreed that the one romance of FDR did not hurt but that the succession of dames who streamed in and out of the White House under Kennedy would.

Late this evening I telephoned New Hampshire to find that the jury had come in with a verdict of $10,000 against the *Concord Monitor* and $10,000 against NANA [North American Newspaper Alliance]. I would have to pay both. Millimet didn't want to appeal, but I told him that under no circumstances would we let the verdict stand without an appeal.

The judge permitted an instruction to go to the jury that even if Roy had been a bootlegger in his early life, they had to decide whether this was a fair comment. If you cannot dig into the record of a man who is running for U.S. Senate, it will be a sorry day for clean politics.

**SATURDAY, DECEMBER 24** | It snowed all day. I helped Ellen and the children trim their beautiful tree, and the kids got a great kick out of it.

Earlier Luvie had a luncheon for Lally Graham Weymouth and her husband, Yann. She is becoming the most spoiled brat between New York and Washington. When Adlai Stevenson was alive, he used to keep her somewhat in place, but now no one can. Joe Alsop, Clayton Fritchey, and several others came to lunch.

Dined at Agnes Meyer's, a family party with Kay Graham and her grand-children. Kay told me a little more about the tough time she had with Phil before he committed suicide. Apparently, he had started going off his rocker six years ago, and even the fact that she had tuberculosis didn't faze him.

**THURSDAY, DECEMBER 27** | Harrison Salisbury, who wrote an excellent series on the Khrushchev era in Russia, was able to obtain a visa for Hanoi and has been writing some dispatches on U.S. bombing. They show concrete evidence of churning up civilian sections of the city and [of] civilian casual-ties. His dispatches have been causing quite a furor and have been widely published all over the world. The Defense Department is trying to counteract them with a denial that we are bombing anything but military targets, but the denials don't seem to stand up. Certainly, they are not believed and have widened the so-called credibility gap.

As I look back on the denials of past administrations, I can't really see that Johnson's denials are worse than any others. If anything, the news is coming out a little straighter. Roosevelt put out some terrible canards and, immediately after Pearl Harbor, issued . . . lies regarding the damage, when every military attaché in Washington had cabled the real facts to his gov-ernment and the Japanese knew exactly what had happened. At that time, however, J. Edgar Hoover telephoned me with an implied threat that I would be jailed if I wrote the story. We had the facts ready to go out as a letter to editors when we called it back.

**WEDNESDAY, DECEMBER 28** | Ed Kenworthy of the *New York Times* tele-phoned to ask the status of our Dodd libel suit. It was supposed to come before Judge Holtzoff about November 22, to require Dodd to answer questions on his financial affairs, but we agreed to a postponement after John Cahill, the senior member of the Sonnett firm, died.

Kenworthy said that Edward Bennett Williams had been approached by the White House at one time to handle the Dodd case against us but refused. Kenworthy's brother-in-law is a member of the Cahill-Sonnett firm and says they have rolled up between $70,000 to $90,000 worth of law fees and expenses, which are being paid. It's not a free job, as publicized. The interesting question is who is paying the bill. Kenworthy thinks that Tommy Corcoran has been passing the hat. Of course, Tommy is not beyond tell-ing people that Lyndon wants him to do this. I suspect that at first Lyndon probably did.

We dined with Averell Harriman, and Luvie stayed to play bridge. The chief topic of conversation was the Manchester book. Naturally, the Harrimans are all for Jackie, though it seemed to both Luvie and me that Averell has regained some of his old detachment and was considerably franker about the state of the world.

We talked about Joe Kennedy, and Averell quoted FDR as telling him, when Joe was appointed head of the FCC, "You use a thief to catch a thief." Averell, who was then active in his family investment firm—Brown Brothers, Harriman and Company—said that the elder Kennedy had been flagrant in his shyster tactics of bidding up stocks so that a lot of widows and unsuspecting public investors came in, then quietly dumping the stocks, leaving the unsuspecting public to hold the bag. At that time, Averell said, it was legal. The SEC cured all this, and Kennedy was in charge of the SEC.

All of the Kennedy children, Luvie noted, adored their father, and Teddy was the only one who went to see Mrs. Kennedy when she was in the Lahey clinic in Boston. The old man treated Mrs. Kennedy shabbily, and of course, the boys got their lesson in philandering from him. The old man had more women than anyone else in public life during the New Deal days. He even made passes at Roosevelt's daughter, Anna. And it's reported that John Boettiger once caught him coming out of his and Anna's apartment in the Wardman Park Hotel. I still have in my files Gloria Swanson's statement on the manner in which Joe Kennedy looked after her career, she having been his No. 1 mistress.

Yet there was something in the Kennedy family which made for great ambition and public service. I think it was probably a drive by the old man to overcome the immigrant surroundings in which he grew up in Boston. There has also been a note of tragedy running through the family. Joe Kennedy Jr. was killed when the Nazis shot his plane down off the Portuguese coast. He was traveling with his girlfriend, a British noblewoman. One daughter is in a mental institution. John F. Kennedy was assassinated, and the Peter Lawford-Patricia Kennedy marriage is on the rocks.

Averell recalled that FDR had told him with some glee that he was appointing an Irishman to the Court of St. James. Joe, of course, was a terrible flop.

**FRIDAY, DECEMBER 30** | George Frasier of *Esquire* came to dinner. He's writing a piece about me. He brought his "researcher" along, a rather attractive Chinese American girl from Honolulu. George was so partial toward me, and so anxious that I win a Pulitzer Prize, that I suspect the story he writes will never see the light of day.

Frasier used to work in Boston, where he says the *Boston Herald* and *Traveler*, staunch Republican papers, are intensely pro–Teddy Kennedy. I noticed this myself. There is an iron curtain in Boston regarding any criticism of the Kennedys generally.

In the garden of Nikita Khrushchev's country retreat on the Black Sea, August 1961. (*Left to right*) Luvie Pearson, Drew Pearson, interpreter Victor Sukhodrev, Nikita Khrushchev, and stenographer. Photo by a Soviet photographer.

Pearson and Khrushchev pose for a photo by Luvie Pearson using her Kodak "Brownie," August 1961.

Yugoslavia, August 7, 1962. (*Left to right*) interpreter, Drew Pearson, and Marshal Tito. Pearson worked in Serbia in 1919, after graduating from Swarthmore College, and followed up with many visits to several Balkan countries. Photo by a Yugoslav government photographer.

Dizzie Gillespie was a special guest at Pearson's Maryland farm, one of several annual barbecues Pearson staged to raise funds for Big Brothers of Washington DC. Pearson was president of the organization from 1956 to 1968. In the summer of 1966 Bess Abell arranged for famed barbecue chef Walter Jetton of Fort Worth, Texas, to make the meal for three hundred people. City News Bureau.

Pearson with President Johnson, 1967. Pearson frequently visited with LBJ at the White House, sometimes in the Oval Office, also upstairs, even in the president's bedroom, and at the LBJ Ranch. Most photos of Pearson and LBJ were taken by White House photographer Yoichi Okamoto.

On many Christmases Pearson visited U.S. servicemen overseas, acting as master of ceremonies and organizer of entertainment (comedy, music, and dancing). Here he is dressed for the weather at Thule, Greenland, located seven hundred miles north of the Arctic Circle, ca. 1966. Photo by Wm. Berkeley Payne.

Pearson dictated his diary using a tape recorder, although columns and broadcast scripts were written on Smith-Corona portable typewriters, several of which he collected over the years, ca. 1962. Courtesy of the estate of Drew Pearson.

On a December 1956 trip to make a TV film about Israel and the Middle East, Pearson staged a publicity photo in the Dead Sea, which is so salty that people stay afloat much more easily than in freshwater or even the ocean. Courtesy of the estate of Drew Pearson.

Luvie and Drew Pearson with Emperor Haile Selassie in Ethiopia, 1964. Pearson recounted an amusing story about one of the lions guarding Selassie's throne who emphasized his duty by urinating on the visiting newspaperman. Courtesy of the estate of Drew Pearson.

Tyler and Bess Abell greet Luvie and Drew Pearson (Tyler's mother and stepfather) in Boston on the Pearsons' return from Israel in 1956. Courtesy of the estate of Drew Pearson.

Robert F. Kennedy and Drew Pearson (in costume) for a surprise birthday party for former New York governor and diplomat Averell Harriman held at the Kennedy home, November 14, 1966. Courtesy of the estate of Drew Pearson.

Supreme Court chief justice Earl Warren and President Johnson with Drew Pearson in the small "hideaway office" adjoining the White House Oval Office, March 1967. Several photos were taken of this meeting, but no one kept a record of what the three friends were discussing. LBJ Presidential Library. Photo by Yoichi Okamoto.

Pearson in Serbia, ca. 1920. From 1919 to 1921 he served as a volunteer with the American Friends Service Committee, helping rebuild war-torn villages. Courtesy of the estate of Drew Pearson.

Drew Pearson with his daughter, Ellen Pearson Arnold, and her sons (*clockwise from top left:* Joseph Patterson Arnold, eight; Drew Pearson Arnold, fourteen, and George Longan Arnold, eleven), Los Angeles, ca. 1962. LBJ Presidential Library photo.

# 1967

## ANNALS

Summer 1967 was the "Summer of Love." More than one hundred thousand hippies descended on San Francisco. It was also a summer of 159 race riots. For the hippies the focus was on drugs and free love; from Buffalo to Tampa it was on death and destruction from race riots. Newark and Detroit suffered the worst of them. In Detroit forty-three people were killed, hundreds injured, and more than two thousand buildings burned.

The Supreme Court, in *Loving v. Virginia*, struck down all race-based restrictions on marriage. President Johnson appointed Thurgood Marshall, the first African American justice, to the Supreme Court. As chief counsel for the NAACP, Marshall had won twenty-nine of thirty-two Supreme Court cases, including *Brown v. Board of Education*.

Only two decades after the Holocaust, the Jewish people once again had to fight to exist. Egypt's president Gamal Abdel Nasser declared, "Our basic objective will be the destruction of Israel." As troops amassed on the border, Israel engaged in a preemptive strike to cripple the Egyptian air force. With total air superiority the Israelis were able to capture the Gaza Strip and the Sinai within days. They also captured the Golan Heights from Syria and the West Bank from Jordan.

Meanwhile, the war in Vietnam was bogged down. In 1967, 11,153 Americans were killed. With almost a half million troops in the combat zone, the American people were having serious doubts about the war. By October a Gallup poll showed that a plurality for the first time believed the war was a mistake (47% to 44%).

Stalin's daughter Svetlana Alliluyeva defected to the West. She denounced the Soviet regime—a great embarrassment for the Kremlin.

Marxist leader Che Guevara was killed by the Bolivian army. In the earliest days of the Cuban Revolution he served as head of tribunals at La

Cabaña fortress. It was there that he ordered the executions of Cubans who disagreed with the revolutionaries' "ideals."

Ronald Reagan began his first year as governor of California.

The Twenty-Fifth Amendment to the U.S. Constitution was ratified. It established presidential succession. Under the amendment the president would appoint a vice president. It requires a majority of both houses of Congress to confirm a new vice president.

Some basic facts in 1967:

World population: 3,490,293,234

U.S. population: 198,712,056

U.S. gross domestic product: $832.4 billion

Makeup of U.S. Congress (based on 1966 election):

Senate: Democrat 64, Republican 36

House of Representatives: Democrat 248, Republican 187

Number of women in the Senate 1 (1%), House 11 (2.5%)

—Ed.

# THE DIARY

THURSDAY, JANUARY 10 | MOBILE AL—Last night I went on the Larry King radio show. It lasted until 1:00 a.m. King said he interviewed Nixon about a month ago. Nixon said at present no candidate could defeat Bobby Kennedy; that if the Democratic convention was left to itself with no pressures, it would nominate Bobby rather than Johnson.

Nixon also told a story of what happened to him on the day of the JFK assassination. He had been in Dallas that day but left about 11:30 a.m., not knowing the assassination had taken place. In the air he got no news and didn't know it when he landed at Kennedy Airport (then named Idlewild). In the taxi to New York City, the driver told him of the assassination.

When I got off the plane in Mobile, it was cold. All day I'd fought off catching cold. This is the first time I've ever really visited Mobile.

For about twenty years I've been critical of Frank Boykin, the representative from Mobile. He deserved criticism. He was in all sorts of real estate deals and was supported by the Ku Klux Klan and the White Citizens' Council, though he once conspired with Rep. Bill Dawson, the Negro from Chicago, to squelch an investigation of a Mobile road scandal. He was a likable but thoroughly no-good congressman.

Finally, Senator Tydings, then U.S. attorney in Maryland, and Bobby Kennedy sent him to jail on a nebulous (and probably unconstitutional) charge of making a speech on the floor on behalf of a real estate deal. The Supreme Court later held that no one can question the motive of a representative in making speeches.

Lyndon pardoned Boykin (after the judge had given him a suspended sentence) and once remarked to me that Bobby Kennedy never should have convicted Boykin. I was surprised to note in the paper the other day that Bobby had told William Manchester, apropos the book *Death of a President*, that there were three things he asked from Johnson when he retired, one of them being to pardon Frank Boykin.

Boykin is irrepressible in carrying out his own motto, "All is made for love," and to my surprise, he wired me a welcome message before my arrival. I called him, and we had lunch. He showed me around Mobile effusively, particularly Brookley Air Force Base, which he wants kept open but which Lyndon is going to close. He said Lyndon was going to close it because Alabama had voted for Goldwater. I doubt it.

I spoke at night before a lively young Jewish temple audience, which included a few Birchites who had come to heckle me. It was a good audience, and later I spent an hour at the home of my host, where we had a stimulating, enjoyable discussion. The Jews in the South are under some pressure because of their liberal stand on integration. Nevertheless, they remain on the whole liberal.

FRIDAY, JANUARY 13 | WASHINGTON DC—Ed Morgan came to lunch. He told how a man had come to him for legal representation when he was in danger of being called before a congressional committee regarding Cuba. The man was reluctant to say why he feared being called but finally said that around 1961, apparently after the Bay of Pigs fiasco, Bobby Kennedy had concocted the idea of assassinating Fidel Castro. Bobby had approached Central Intelligence, which in turn had approached this man. He in turn hired two underworld gunmen. They spent six months preparing to bump off Castro. They made a survey of the situation in Havana, working through members of the underworld who had run the gambling joints there in the past.

Castro's intelligence operation, however, was smarter than theirs, and the two men were apprehended, tortured, and killed. Before they died, they confessed that they were put up to the job by Kennedy. At this point Castro decided that two could play this game and . . . proceeded to hire Lee Oswald to kill Kennedy.

I am not sure whether there is a clear-cut connection between Castro and Oswald. It is true, of course, that Oswald was a Castroite and had been in Mexico with a view to going to Cuba. Certainly, he had contacts with the Cuban embassy in Mexico.

According to Morgan, one hood is apparently still alive and has promised that when the statute of limitations runs out, the first week of December, he will let me have the full story.

WEDNESDAY, JANUARY 18 | Ambassador Dobrynin came to lunch. I had not seen him alone for a time. He has just been given the Medal of Lenin, the highest award of his government. He didn't want it publicized and said that only he and his wife had celebrated with a bottle of champagne on New Year's Day.

He told me this apropos our conversation regarding the fact he had always served in the United States. First he was a secretary with his embassy in Washington, then went to the UN, where he was one of the delegates, then came to Washington as ambassador.

"Except for attending some conferences, such as the Geneva summit, it happens that I have always served in the United States," he said. I asked him if this didn't tend to destroy his government's confidence in him as being biased. I had in mind the fact that McGeorge Bundy had once told me that they couldn't request that Dobrynin stay on because it would hurt him at home.

Apropos the Geneva Summit Conference, I told him I was still struggling with my book on Khrushchev and Soviet-American relations. He said Khrushchev was now living in Moscow, where he had an apartment, and was frequently seen on the street.

When we talked about Vietnam and the possibility that the Soviet government might give Johnson a little help toward peace, the ambassador said his government had been trying. Then he revealed that on December 13 the United States had staged a raid over North Vietnam which knocked some negotiations into a cocked hat.

"We were all talking, and we seemed to be getting somewhere when the air force staged that raid." The excuse was that the raid was scheduled several weeks earlier, but the weather had intervened. So, the air force went ahead without knowing that the talks were in progress.

"The Red Army never would have done that. They would have rechecked with the civilian branch of government to make sure that nothing had changed the original order."

I recalled how Khrushchev had said the Red Army was pressuring him. The ambassador replied that the Red Army might argue with Khrushchev but they would always bow to his final decision.

We discussed . . . whether Kennedy or Lyndon Johnson had learned faster regarding the importance of East-West relations. I thought Johnson, despite his previous lack of experience in foreign affairs, had learned very rapidly and told the ambassador how I had dined with Lyndon one week after he became president and he was planning [then] to send a letter to Khrushchev thanking him for the Lee Oswald file, even though the State Department was opposed.

Last night at the White House dinner for the chief justice, the vice president, and Speaker McCormack, Lyndon let loose vigorously against the critics of these men.

Johnson probably won't like Jack's column this morning castigating John McCormack. I talked to John at Tyler and Bess's cocktail party. He was his usual pleasant self. I didn't tell him we had a column coming out ripping him. Jack is right; McCormack ought to retire, but human nature is what it is, and when I talked to him, I confess that I feel I could understand the president's defense.

THURSDAY, JANUARY 19 | Went to see the chief justice and reported on what Ed Morgan had told me, Ed having given his consent. There is one weak point in the connection between the attempted assassination of Castro and the assassination of Kennedy—namely, any definite link between Castro and Oswald. Morgan says that the secret agents set up around Castro were able to trace this contact.

Chief Justice Warren was skeptical. He pointed out that when Oswald started his propaganda mill for Castro in New Orleans, he was alone. They traced propaganda leaflets, which he had printed, and they were done by him, no one else. When he went to Mexico, he was frustrated because he couldn't go on to Cuba. He was in touch with the Cuban embassy in Mexico, but they rebuffed him. The chief also argued that if Castro had been operating through Oswald, he would have had more people involved; it would not have been a one-man job.

The chief said that inasmuch as he had been under considerable criticism for allegedly hushing up the facts in the assassination case, he would like to refer this information to the FBI or the Secret Service for them to investigate. Then, if it came out later, he could not be accused of withholding information. I said I would take this up with Ed.

FRIDAY, JANUARY 20 | Bobby Baker has taken the stand at his trial and testified yesterday that when he was hard up he went to Lyndon Johnson, then vice president, for financial advice. He was having trouble meeting the payments on his Carousel [Motel] at Ocean City, Maryland. Lyndon referred him to Sen. Bob Kerr, who immediately got him a $180,000 loan from an Oklahoma City Bank.

The testimony will be damaging to the president. To me, however, it was highly significant regarding the very close liaison between Lyndon and Kerr in the old days. I can see now . . . more vividly why Lyndon always sided with the oil companies on the depletion allowance and why he helped crucify Leland Olds as head of the Federal Power Commission when Olds cracked down on the oil and gas companies. Kerr carried the ball, but Lyndon backed him 100 percent. It's ironic that Lyndon now claims he had no ax to grind regarding the FPC.

Secretary Rusk has written a letter to J. Edgar Hoover, which was published today, asking him to make his position clear regarding the Russian consular treaty. Hoover replied briefly and cryptically that his previous position had been misunderstood. I am afraid the letter is so curt that it will not do much good. All the president would have to do is telephone Hoover and tell him to write a decent letter, and he would have to do it.

SUNDAY, JANUARY 22 | I flew back from Atlanta at 4:30 a.m., arriving home about six thirty. We had lunch with Agnes Meyer and took her to see *Dr. Zhivago*. It brought back memories of those crowded railroad platforms in Serbia, so packed with humanity that you could hardly step over the bodies; and those railroad wagons, bleak and cold, again stuffed with humanity; and the soldiers who would urinate in the ditch alongside the track when the train stopped and come running with their pants half up when the engineer whistled; and the terrible state of our prisoners' uniforms, their feet wrapped in burlap.

**SATURDAY, JANUARY 28** | During lunch Jack Anderson called to say he had the story of Bobby Kennedy's peace feeler attempts in Paris. Jack had seen a Pentagon cable telling in detail how Bobby had been told by the French to pay more attention to the statement by the North Vietnamese foreign minister to Australian newsman [Wilfred] Burchett that if there were a bombing moratorium, North Vietnam would be willing to talk peace.

The Johnson administration had explored this through the Poles, the Indians, and the Canadians; also through the Vatican and U Thant. They got nowhere. The feeling at the White House was that Bobby was cashing in on the present state of the war to act as the big peacemaker.

**THURSDAY, FEBRUARY 2** | The president held a press conference before TV cameras and the first since before Christmas. He still pauses and breathes audibly between sentences, but at least he's learned humility, which for him is an achievement. One reply in regard to a question from Ed Morgan as to his successes as president was particularly good. He said that sometimes when he went to bed at night, he felt he had been a failure because he couldn't end the conflict in Vietnam. "I do have disappointments and moments of distress, as I think every president has had. I am not complaining."

I saw Rostow shortly afterward to ask him about the various peace feelers. He claimed a lot had been received, many of them nebulous, but they had all been followed up carefully and diligently in the hope that one would turn out. I have usually distrusted Rostow, but I had the feeling he was telling the truth on this.

I asked him about the December 13 bombing on the suburbs of Hanoi, which had disrupted what Dobrynin told me had been definite steps toward peace talks. Rostow pooh-poohed this and said the other side was exaggerating.

**THURSDAY, FEBRUARY 9** | Kosygin has given an interview in London which was very effective. It was carried live via Telstar. He said that if the United States would stop bombing, there could be peace in Vietnam.

Leonard Marks and I went to the *Washington Star* to talk over the future of its syndicate. He was indignant at Bobby's attempt to be a peacemaker in Europe. Bobby had his press relations men out peddling the story that Bobby had turned up real peace feelers. Actually, Bobby, according to Leonard, wanted to be in on the peace if there was going to be one, or to make Johnson appear responsible for any failure.

Arriving back at the airport at the same time Bobby announced over television that Kasan, the Czech American travel agent, was released and returned home and brother Teddy Kennedy had been responsible for the release. Actually, Teddy had no more to do with it than I did.

**FRIDAY, FEBRUARY 10** | Secretary Rusk held a press conference yesterday which was about as hard-nosed as anything he has dished out to the American public. He made it clear there was going to be no halt in the bombing unless there was some move militarily to match it by North Vietnam.

Simultaneously, Kosygin in London emphasized the recent statement to the Australian newspaperman by the North Vietnamese foreign minister as opening the way for peace talks—"if the United States unconditionally halted bombing raids."

**WEDNESDAY, FEBRUARY 15** | The vice president's office called up earlier in the week and said he wanted to see me. The appointment was set for 11:00 a.m., and he was only fifteen minutes late. He has kept his weight down and is looking dapper. Probably he can never get over the fact that his face makes him look boyish and immature, and in these days, when the public is voting for TV stars, this is a handicap.

I tried to get some additional information from him regarding the Kosygin-Wilson truce talks in London. Jack had turned up a fairly good story of how Kosygin had sent a personal telegram to Hanoi, urging Ho Chi Minh to make some concession to the United States in return for our stopping bombing. Prime Minister Wilson and Kosygin had waited for the reply, and when it came, Wilson had gone to the Savoy Hotel late at night to confer over it. Unfortunately, the reply was negative.

Hubert either didn't have any additional information or else was being coy with me because he said that Wilson had given out more information in London than he had expected and that it was all true. Wilson merely gave out a statement that the United States had wanted North Vietnam to pledge their curtailment of supplies and men south in return for a bombing moratorium.

We discussed the *Newsweek* story reporting that the president had called Bobby in and lectured him on his peace pilgrimage to Paris. Hubert said that Bobby had first gone to see Undersecretary Nick Katzenbach, then had asked to see the president. Hubert said he didn't think the president would lecture Bobby because he knew that Bobby nursed grudges.

"Lyndon may scold me," said Hubert, "because he knows he can get away with it. Or he may scold you because you will take it, but he's too smart to bawl out Bobby. He knows Bobby would leak."

"The president wants the war over," Hubert said. "It's like a cancer. It's the worst political handicap he's got, but it has achieved some things. It's weakened the Japanese and got them out of their cocoon. It's given Burma a new sense of security, and it's changed things in Indonesia. Adam Malik, the new foreign minister, came here and told me that if we hadn't stood pat in South Vietnam, they would never have thrown the Communists out of Indonesia. And Prince Souvanna Phouma came here in 1965 and said that if we hadn't been in South Vietnam, there wouldn't be any Laos today."

Hubert is optimistic about developments in South Vietnam. He said the elections in the spring were going to be important and they would be even more important in the fall. For the first time a complete new government will be elected, and Premier Ky will either be in or out. Hubert said that Ky had learned a lot. He pooh-poohed Ky's earlier statement of admiration regarding Hitler and emphasized that Ky had not gone in for corruption but wanted to clean it up; however, Hubert thought the new premier should be a South Vietnamese, and Ky was from the North. "When the new government is set up," Hubert said, "a lot of the Vietcong or non-Communists should come over and join the government. This may cut the ground out from under the Vietcong resistance."

This was an interesting admission because we always claimed that we were fighting against the Communists, not intervening in a local civil war.

Hubert went into detail regarding the fact that he is keeping out of the war. He is making no more speeches on the subject. "I am going to concentrate on domestic problems," he said, "housing, civil rights, antipoverty, legislation. I am going to be Mr. Domestic. I am a New Dealer, and this war is not for me."

He thought the president was playing Russian policy very well. I asked who had sold him on this. He said he didn't know: "Maybe you did."

"I have talked to him," I said, "but I doubt if he remembers it."

"He's got a memory like a computer," Hubert said. "You tell him something, and six months later he remembers and quotes back to you as if it were yesterday.

"He's become less sensitive now. He used to carry polls in his pocket and peek at them all the time. Now he doesn't worry about the polls so much. I think at the time of his second operation he decided not to worry about criticism but do the best he can. He's become more philosophical and at ease—but he's all politician—and what a politician!"

**THURSDAY, FEBRUARY 16** | Arthur Goldberg came to lunch unexpectedly. Arthur told an interesting story about the differences between Bobby Kennedy and his late brother. Jack Kennedy, he said, didn't go in for some of Bobby's tough tactics.

"During the talks with the steel executives on rolling back prices," Arthur said, "they asked me whether, if they complied with our request, there would not be any retaliatory action. They referred to the grand jury, which the Justice Department had called to look into their price structure, and Kefauver's proposal to investigate them for antitrust. I had known these men for a long time and had sat opposite the bargaining table with them. I promised there would be no retaliation.

"Sometime later I got a call from Tom Patton, head of Republic Steel, who wanted to see me urgently. He came in to say that the Internal Revenue agents had been checking his income tax and going around to interview all of his golfing partners to see whether it was true that he had lost certain amounts of money to them. He said it was highly embarrassing, and he attributed this to Bobby Kennedy.

"I called the president and asked if I could come over and see him right away. I took Tom Patton with me. When we got there, I told Patton, 'Now, most people clam up when they're in front of the president. You tell this president what you told me.' Patton did, and after he had finished, the president went over to the telephone and said, 'Get me the attorney general.' When the attorney general came on the line, the president said, 'Bobby, cut it out.'"

**FRIDAY, FEBRUARY 17** | (Comments on Radio Moscow report of Soviet leaders rejecting LBJ's overtures on cooperation in missile defense; discussion of Sen. Karl Mundt's denunciation of Johnson policies; lunched with Sen. Claude Pepper and Hispanic activist Galal Kernahan; discussed with Pepper the Adam Clayton Powell case; conversation with U.S. ambassador to South Vietnam Ellsworth Bunker regarding Latin American summit; discussion with White House staffer Doug Cater regarding $3 million CIA payments to students and maintenance of Bay of Pigs exiles on CIA payroll, linked to Bobby Kennedy.)

**FRIDAY, FEBRUARY 24** | Up at 3:00 a.m. in order to write three columns before getting off. Worried about taking a government plane after I have been so critical of junketing but finally wrote a check for a little over $1,000 for two round-trip fares to Bolivia and will give it to the State Department escort officer.

Very cold. Got to Andrews Air Force Base at 11:40 p.m. The plane departed at eleven fifty-five. Air Force One is huge. It has three clocks, one giving Texas time, one Washington time, and one Greenwich time. There are a dozen upper berths and two lower couch berths. I thought the chief justice and Mrs. Warren would use these, but he gallantly climbed up into an upper berth, which he just about filled up, allowing Mme Sanjines, the ambassador's wife, to use the lower berth.

On the trip also are the Earl Warren Juniors; the State Department officer Mike Yohn; a White House doctor, Captain Voss; a White House aide, Maj. Haywood Smith. He had asked Bess how to handle me. She said, "Give him a martini and no onions." There are also several air force personnel and a Peace Corps member on board.

The State Department is quite efficient. They had a written briefing book prepared for both me and the chief, containing the background of every country, the American personnel, and the nation's leaders. The book even contained the speeches the chief justice was to make at the airport and his speech to be made at departure.

**SATURDAY, FEBRUARY 25** | Arrived at La Paz at 8:45 a.m. It was the first nonstop flight ever taken between Washington to La Paz.

The mountains below were beautiful, but the altitude was cruel when we got off the plane. I felt it much more than when I was here in 1954.

Herman Siles, the Bolivian vice president, was there to meet us. His father, who was president, is in exile. Victor Andrade, former ambassador in Washington, was there to meet us. He had run for president against Barrientos but only got a small percentage of the vote. The fact that he is still living in La Paz and gets along with this administration is significant. A few years ago it wouldn't have happened.

Lechin, former head of the miners' union and former vice president, is in hiding. Paz Estensorro, the former president, is teaching in Peru, but most of the political opponents are living in Bolivia, unmolested.

[The Pearsons and the Warrens took a three-day side trip to visit Gulf Oil Company facilities in Santa Cruz, in the east of Bolivia.]

We spent only an hour in La Paz. I felt a little woozy all the time and was glad to get aboard the DC-6 air force plane, which flew us four hundred miles down to Santa Cruz.

**TUESDAY, FEBRUARY 28** | They called us at 6:00 a.m. for an 8:30 flight. Luvie is still under the weather, and I am getting that way. We flew in a private plane with Ambassador and Mrs. Sanjines to La Paz, via Cochabamba, an Indian city halfway up the Andes—a quaint city which Tyler and I visited in 1954. It was the end of the new highway between the lowlands and the Andes Plateau.

We flew on to La Paz. Lunched with the ambassador, who put us up at the embassy.

I had to speak for an hour and a half before a journalists' seminar, then called on the vice president, then attended a cocktail party in my honor, standing for two hours, then to a dinner given by John Fisher, the counselor of the embassy, for Assistant Secretary Lincoln Gordon, who has just flown back from the Buenos Aires foreign ministers' conference. By this time I was bushed.

Jimmy Hoffa called during the cocktail party. The Supreme Court has ruled that he has to go to jail, and he wanted me intervene with the chief justice. I told him I couldn't.

**WEDNESDAY, MARCH 1** | (Breakfasted with President Barrientos and urged him to reconsider his refusal to attend the summit conference; discussion of Bolivian grievances against her neighbors; flew to Arica, Chile, then on to Santiago.)

**THURSDAY, MARCH 2** | (Interview with Chilean president Eduardo Frei; discussed Bolivian access to the sea; upcoming Latin American Summit Conference; lunch with Foreign Minister Gabriel Valdez; radio and newspaper interviews regarding Kennedy assassination. Dined with editors and television commentators.)

**SATURDAY, MARCH 4** | LIMA, PERU—(Arrived at 2:00 a.m.; flew at ten to Quito, Ecuador; remarks on death of Henry Luce and removal of Adam Clayton Powell from Congress; discussion with Chief Justice Warren regarding his battle against offshore gambling while governor of California; luncheon hosted by President Aresmeno; called in the afternoon on ex-president Galo Plaza to discuss politics.)

SUNDAY, MARCH 5 | (Rose early to drive to the equator with rest of party; discussed Peruvian and Ecuadorian politics with Galo Plaza; flew back to Bogotá; delivered report to Ambassador Sanjines on discussions with President Frei; met with U.S. ambassador Reynold Carlson.)

MONDAY, MARCH 13 | (Flew to New York; conversation with Mrs. Elliott Roosevelt en route; lunched with Bill Attwood; comments on de Gaulle's narrow victory in French election.)

TUESDAY, MARCH 14 | WASHINGTON DC—The Dodd hearings began yesterday. The Ethics Committee issued a detailed stipulation in which Dodd admitted spending approximately $175,000 of money raised from testimonial dinners but claimed that they were dinners for his personal benefit, not for his campaign.

Ben Fern, committee counsel, is putting on an orderly array of witnesses, showing impartiality. The committee itself is not really going into some of the fundamental questions, such as Dodd's law practice and conflicts of interest.

A Washington nightclub operator named Sanford Bomstein was on the witness stand, telling how he raised $13,000 for Dodd, which he turned over to Dodd's personal bank account. He had fixed up his alibis very neatly so that he said he had raised the money for Dodd to use in any way he wished. Obviously, he had been carefully coached.

Lady Bird has gone to Appalachia. It reminded me of the time when I once tried to persuade Lyndon, then a senator, to put some missiles and military bases out in Appalachia, instead of hogging them all for Texas and the South, but he declined. Now that he's president of all the United States, not just a senator from Texas, he's doing better.

Lyndon got his Soviet-American consular pact ratified today. It was a great victory. He probably had to give away a few judgeships in order to pay for it. Everett Dirksen got out of his hospital bed at Walter Reed and hobbled in to make a speech—a very effective speech.

WEDNESDAY MARCH 15 | Attended the Dodd hearings again. Michael O'Hare, Dodd's bookkeeper, testified and told a frank story about arranging to have money orders and cashier's checks used to pay bills so that people would not know that personal bills were being paid from Dodd's testimonial dinner fund.

Dodd's lawyer had been laying in wait for O'Hare, figuring he was the weakest witness and they could break him. O'Hare had been very loyal to Dodd up until just a few months before the big break started. He was the last to leave Dodd and had a hard time making up his mind to do so.

He did nobly on the witness stand this morning. Anyone who heard him could see that he was telling the truth. He even acquiesced in the statement that he had probably violated the law in taking money on behalf of Dodd out of the testimonial dinner account. Stennis told him he didn't have to answer this, but O'Hare said he wanted to answer it anyway.

**THURSDAY, MARCH 16** | Jack and Mary Margaret Valenti gave a dinner for us and Tyler. We dined at the Motion Picture Association headquarters, which Eric Johnston made famous in the old John Hay House.

We talked about Ev Dirksen and how such a strong friendship had grown up between him and the president. I remember when I used to be in Lyndon's office on occasion and Dirksen called at the front, Lyndon would let me out the rear door so that Ev wouldn't see me. I never told him that Ev and I had been friends longer than he and Ev.

**FRIDAY, MARCH 17** | Dodd testified this morning and did a pretty good job for himself. He admitted all the spending—he had to since he already stipulated [to it]. His excuse was, "I needed the money."

After he testified the committee suspended the hearings. All they have to do now is write a report. Three of the ex-staff came for lunch, together with Jack, and we held a strategy conference. Obviously, they were greatly disappointed. They felt the committee had done a poor job and leaned over backward to help Dodd. I recommended: (1) that they talk to newspapermen immediately to tell the story of all the facts which he committee suppressed; and (2) write a joint statement, signed by all of the ex–Dodd employees, to be sent to the committee, then publicized. The statement was to point out certain omissions and ask that the hearings be continued.

Lady Bird and Bess are going to the Virgin Islands for Easter, while LBJ flies to Guam. Tyler is going to Nassau with the children.

**SUNDAY, MARCH 19** | Ambassador Arthur Goldberg came for an early lunch. We hadn't seen him since he and Dorothy got back from their

Asian trip, which he said he didn't want to take but the president insisted. He was obviously unhappy about the war and said he felt strongly that we should not have bombed the steel mill in North Vietnam. It was not a military target.

He felt the president was too optimistic about the outcome of the war—but of course, he had been fed optimistic reports. Lodge he described as an optimist, Westmoreland not so optimistic. He thought the president had made a wise choice in Ellsworth Bunker to succeed Lodge, whom he described as a Brahmin and not too energetic as ambassador.

"The president telephoned me Saturday night to ask what I thought of Bunker. I told him I thought very highly of him. The president remarked that he was seventy-two. 'Yes,' I said, 'but he just got married, so apparently he's got plenty of sex appeal left.'

"Personally, I think the Vietcong can never win, but they can last a long time," Arthur said.

We discussed the trip to Guam on which the president embarked at midnight last night and agreed that he should not be taking these long trips. The others should come to him, either in Honolulu or Washington. We concluded that perhaps he didn't want the American public to see Premier Ky.

Arthur was worried about the Philippines, where corruption is everywhere and it appears to be creeping in at the top. When the Filipinos become disillusioned regarding their president—Marcos—anything can happen.

Arthur reported that Taiwan was thriving. He had a good talk with Generalissimo Chiang Kai-shek, who was watching very closely what we were doing but had no real plans for intervening on the Chinese mainland.

We discussed the chief justice. "The chief criticism of the Warren report is that it's been done by part-time commissioners," Arthur said. "This plays into the chief's hands up at Harvard. Harvard Law School is snobbish. They claim the chief is sloppy. They haven't given him a degree." Arthur compared the chief justice to John Marshall, who was given a lot of criticism when he was on the bench and was always called a politician. Now he's hailed as the greatest chief justice.

We discussed Adam Clayton Powell. Arthur thought Congress was making a fool of itself over Powell and that there should be a general understanding that once a constituency understood the transgressions of a congressman and elected him despite that knowledge, he should be seated.

**MONDAY, MARCH 20** | Talked to Ed Morgan regarding the underworld leaders he represents and whom the CIA got to hatch the conspiracy to assassinate Castro. While I was away, Jack wrote part of the story. It was a poor story and violated a confidence. Finally, it reflected on Bobby Kennedy without actually pinning the goods on him. The *Washington Post* and the *New York Post* did not run it. I think they were right.

Ed said when he was in Las Vegas about ten days ago the two gamblers involved had approached him with a clipping of Jack's column and were indignant. They indicated there would be no cooperation in the future. Ed and I had talked over a plan whereby they would get immunity from prosecution in return for full disclosure.

**THURSDAY, MARCH 23** | A three-judge federal court panel in Alabama has ruled that the state must integrate its schools by fall. Alabama has been taking federal money but not integrating.

In contrast to the backwardness of Alabama, Sen. Ed Brooke of Massachusetts made his maiden speech today, and it was a good one. He had just returned from South Vietnam and reluctantly changed his position on the war and went along with Lyndon. He also had some constructive proposals to make regarding the draft. It looks as if Brooke is going to be a force for good.

**FRIDAY, MARCH 24** | Jack came back from New Orleans much impressed with Jim Garrison. He spent six hours with him. Garrison pledged him to secrecy—we can't write anything—but unfolded his case as follows:

The CIA definitely had a plot to assassinate Castro and had approached Clay Shaw, a reputable, wealthy homosexual businessman, as a man who could execute the plot. Shaw was part of a homosexual ring, including Ferrie and Ruby in Dallas. Ferrie was an odd-looking character who wore a homemade wig and pasted eyebrows, usually at a cockeyed angle, so that he was easily recognizable. In Ferrie's papers after his death, Garrison's agents found that everything pertaining to the year 1963 had been removed, though papers were there for every other year.

Lee Harvey Oswald was picked as the man to execute Castro because he had come back from Russia very anti-Communist yet was considered to be pro-Russian and pro-Communist. As a blind, the Committee for Fair Play to Cuba was organized, and Oswald passed out leaflets on the streets of New Orleans.

The FBI, though checking on Oswald's activities at the time, didn't pay much attention to him. From other FBI interviews with Oswald, it was obvious they knew he was anti-Russia.

Oswald went to Mexico to get a visa from the Cuban embassy there—a transit visa to Russia. This was to be his excuse to get back to Cuba; however, the Russians are wary about admitting people in a hurry, and Oswald had to wait. After the assassination in Dallas, the Warren Commission, according to Garrison, asked Central Intelligence for a photograph of Oswald as he went up the steps of the Cuban embassy in Mexico City. (The CIA takes photos of everyone entering the embassy.)

CIA sent the Warren Commission a photo which obviously was not that of Oswald, and the commission made a second request for the proper photo. Garrison understands this was never received. The reason, he says, is that a thickset Cuban accompanied Oswald to the Cuban embassy. This Cuban was part of the CIA plot to assassinate Castro, and the CIA doesn't want him revealed in any picture.

When Oswald was refused his visa to Cuba, the conspirators then turned around and decided to assassinate Kennedy. They used Oswald as the patsy. He was the only non-homo member of their ring. They figured he was so mentally disturbed, and so at odds with the world, that he could be used for the fall guy.

On the day of the assassination (or perhaps it was the day afterward) Ferrie drove in a blinding rainstorm to Houston to go to an ice-skating rink. His alibi, when interviewed by the FBI, was that he enjoyed ice-skating. On that particular night, though, witnesses said that he didn't skate but stood for two hours against the wall. Garrison has investigated this spot and finds that the wall was adjacent to a telephone. Garrison figures that Ferrie made the trip so he could get a telephone call from Ruby without the call being traced long-distance. Ferrie, because of his eyebrows and weight, was easily identifiable.

On the day of the assassination Garrison points out that Ruby was everywhere. He went to the hospital. He went to the prison—and during a subsequent conference in which the background of Lee Oswald was discussed, including the pro-Castro activities in New Orleans.

Garrison points out that after Oswald took a shot at General Walker and missed, he came back to his wife, white and shaking. This proved that he was easily upset, also that he was a poor shot.

Garrison's theory is that two men on a hill over the Kennedy line of march fired two of the fatal shots at Kennedy. One witness saw two men on top of the hill hastily leave in a Nash Rambler. No cartridge was found on the hill.

In Ferrie's apartment was found an estimate on how far a cartridge would eject when a gun was held at a fifty-degree angle. Firing from the hilltop, the rifle would have been held at fifty degrees, and Garrison's theory is that the second man with the assassin on the hilltop was posted to pick up the cartridge after it was ejected.

Garrison points out that the police saw Oswald in the Dallas Book Depository Building on the second floor, standing beside a Coke machine. This was when they rushed into the building to investigate. He was calm. Garrison contrasts this with his emotional reaction after he tried to shoot General Walker.

It is Garrison's theory that Ruby killed Oswald for fear he would break. He [Oswald] was likely to squeal on the others. (According to Dr. Erdman, Dr. Alton Oxner had examined Ruby and had told him that he had cancer. Therefore, he was considered expendable.) [Garrison opened an investigation in 1966 claiming that the assassination was a conspiracy by the federal government. He arrested and tried businessman Clay Shaw as a conspiricist, but Shaw was acquitted.]

WEDNESDAY, APRIL 5 | Early morning appointment with Sen. George Aiken of Vermont, who told me how much Mike Mansfield was respected around the world. Even de Gaulle came to see Mike in Paris on Monday, though de Gaulle doesn't usually work on Mondays. The other senators accompanying Mike were not invited. In Japan the Socialists stopped rioting in honor of Mike, and in Cambodia, Prince Sihanouk was determined that the party stay all night. In Burma and Cambodia it was impossible for the Senate group to pay any of their own expenses.

Aiken said Johnson has become so unpopular that many senators up for reelection next year don't want to be identified with him. He cited as evidence Church of Idaho, Fulbright of Arkansas, Monroney of Oklahoma, McGovern of South Dakota, and Nelson of Wisconsin . . . are scared to death of their reelection chances and want to stay partly away from the Johnson administration.

Later, when I talked to the president about this, he said it was apparently true that there was a strong peace bloc in North and South Dakota, Idaho, and Montana.

Aiken said there had been a terrific hassle inside the Senate Foreign Relations Committee yesterday over the president's resolution to endorse foreign aid in advance of the summit conference for Latin America. Lyndon lost the battle.

"I am a Republican, but he's my president, and I don't like to see him lose prestige just before this conference," said Aiken. He said Stuart Symington was grousing against the president because he was worried over the balance of payments. "All we need to do is to tax Americans abroad, and we'll remedy the balance of payments," Aiken said, "but we don't want to do that. There are more companies doing business around the world than ever before. Some of the American farm companies now have to compete with their own imports coming back from their own plants abroad."

**MONDAY, APRIL 10** | CHARLESTON SC—After my lecture I had a question-and-answer period in the student center, where I got some live-wire questions from a couple of young students and some questions from the faculty as to whether the faculty should permit students to help direct the college. I also got acquainted with a young white professor at the Negro state college alongside, who had been dropped by the Negro president, together with two other white professors, because they had been too sympathetic to the Negroes. The Negro student body had then staged a two-week boycott in protest against their dismissal and threatened to march to Columbia to protest to the governor. It was the first real upsurge in any of the Negro colleges of South Carolina.

From this conversation, and from a subsequent talk I had at the airport with Bill Haddad, formerly of the *New York Tribune*, I gathered that there was real ferment in the Negro colleges of the South because progress was so slow. A young Negro with Haddad was vigorous on the subject. Bill himself praised Governor Robert McNair of South Carolina for promoting Negro job training. He said that McNair's program had been inspired by the desire to get northern industry to move south. They in turn had to have skilled workers. As a result, the economic status of the Negro was suddenly rising as never before.

**THURSDAY, APRIL 13** | The summit conference opened in Punta del Este yesterday. Lyndon made his opening statement today. As far as I can see, he used none of my ideas. The statement carried some meat, but he delivered it in his usual boring, uninspired manner.

Hubert Humphrey telephoned to talk about his European trip. Apparently, he did well with the Italians by taking a side run around Moro and Fanfani to the Socialist leader Nenni, whom he had known a long time ago.

Enrique Tejera París came to lunch. He thought my articles on Latin America were constructive, said that President Leoni had liked my general ideas on the summit conference, even though they are not being followed. The main point, however, is that Johnson has become interested in Latin America, and this is an important plus. If he can switch from Vietnam to Latin America as his major field of endeavor, the United States and the world will be much better off.

FRIDAY, APRIL 14 | Yuri Zhukov, who was instrumental in arranging my first interview with Khrushchev, came to lunch. At that time Zhukov was chairman of the Committee on Cultural Exchange and engrossed in the problems of a new cultural exchange agreement with the United States. He then had more or less cabinet status. Now he is the top columnist for *Pravda*. Khrushchev told me on one of our last visits that Zhukov loved newspaper work the most.

I got to know Zhukov during those two days at the Black Sea and during the trips back and forth. The last time I saw him was in a downpour at the Moscow Airport. Since then our paths have not crossed, though I have talked to him on the telephone.

I had offered to get some people together to see Zhukov, but he said he chiefly wanted to talk to me. Vishnevsky, a correspondent for *Pravda*, came along, and Luvie joined us.

Zhukov is a little stouter, and his English is just as ragged, though he understands most of what you say. It was interesting to note that he had been talking to various Republican senators, among them Percy of Illinois, an indication that they think Republicans may be coming in at the next election.

The conversation got around to the war in Vietnam. Zhukov remarked that relations were excellent between the United States and Russia and that the only thing hampering them was the war. He wanted to know about the prospects of the United States getting out of Vietnam after a peace, apparently not believing that it would.

I told him that the president had told me of his talk with Gromyko last fall, during which Gromyko had advised that the world did not believe the United States would get out in view of the tremendous warehouse and port facilities it was building. The president said he had taken this to heart and as a result had made his statement that the United States would leave six months after a peace. I said I was convinced he was sincere about this and, furthermore, that he wanted to end this war more than almost anyone else. I said he had made some mistakes but was not making any now and was determined to end the war. I also said the president had come around to the conviction that the peace of the world depended upon cooperation between the two great powers with nuclear stockpiles. It had taken him a time to make this decision, but he was now firm about it, and he had discussed it with me in detail.

Vishnevsky remarked that he was glad to see that I was on friendly terms with the No. 1 power, and Zhukov asked who had brought Johnson around to this point of view. I explained that I might have had something to do with it and that Tommy Thompson probably had the most to do with it but that it was the natural result of logic.

Zhukov reviewed briefly the latest efforts toward peace, when Kosygin was trying to persuade Ho Chi Minh to accept a truce. Zhukov said that Johnson had resumed the bombing before he received the final reply from Ho and that this had made matters difficult.

I related the conversation I had with the president about a week ago in which he reviewed these peace talks point by point, saying he had waited approximately eight days during the truce for a reply from Hanoi and had then noted that Ho had turned down the peace proposal of the pope. In view of this negative reply, the president resumed bombing one day later. I added that he had pictures of cars bumper to bumper, carrying supplies south, and that he had offered to show me these photos in the White House projection room.

This seemed to make an impression on Zhukov. He seemed to think Ho's reply to Johnson might have been couched in different language if we had not resumed the bombing. I don't know.

I pointed out during lunch that Johnson had really gone to bat to get the ratification of the consular treaty, that the vote was about two-to-one against him when he started, and that he had turned on the heat to get the Senate to go along. Zhukov acknowledged that this was quite an achievement.

THURSDAY, APRIL 20 | (In the hospital after a minor stroke.) I can now feel how Eisenhower felt when he suffered his first small stroke but kept it pretty well concealed from the public. Roosevelt also suffered several small strokes leading up to his massive one in April 1945. They were kept from the public.

I have fallen into the same pattern. We have released to the press that my illness is a return of malaria. Tyler guessed that it wasn't. He's had malaria. At any rate Dr. Lawn Thompson diagnosed this as a "strokelet," the bursting of a vein in my neck which affected my arm and speech. I am already beginning to recover. He has put me on an anticoagulant, originally designed to rid the waterfront of rats. It's so strong that when rats eat it, they die. With human beings the blood is thinned.

WEDNESDAY, APRIL 26 | Lyndon returned in time to attend the diplomatic reception at the White House late this evening. He had his photograph taken with de Gaulle in Germany. President Lübke of West Germany stood between them and held their hands in a three-way handshake.

I suspect de Gaulle must have been reluctant. I remember the time in Casablanca, in 1943, when Roosevelt could not get him to shake hands with General [Henri] Giraud, head of the Vichy French, until Roosevelt told Churchill: "You pay him. No photograph, no money." [Giraud had remained loyal to Marshal Pétain and the Vichy government but secretly communicated with the Allies to become head of the Free French Forces in North Africa. He feuded with de Gaulle over the issue of co-leadership.]

A junta of Greek colonels took over the Greek government a few days ago, arresting all its political opponents, especially Andreas Papandreou and his father, the ex–prime minister. Tonight I got a telephone call from a man named Schwartz in Los Angeles who has given me information on Papandreou before, saying that he was scheduled to be tried on Saturday for treason and might be executed.

I telephoned Walt Rostow, who had just returned from Bonn with the president. He hadn't slept for about twenty-four hours and under the circumstances was reasonably cooperative. He complained that somebody had unloosed a barrage of protests to save Andreas. At any rate he said he would get the U.S. ambassador busy in Athens. I sent a cable to the king. The king is probably sore at me for publishing pro-Papandreou stuff last year, but I sent it anyway.

THURSDAY, APRIL 27 | Talked with Rostow again. He has received urgent pleas from Dr. Walter Heller, former head of the White House Economic Council, and from Willy Brandt, vice chancellor of Germany. Rostow said that Phil Talbot was a strong and liberal ambassador who had made strong representations on behalf of An⸢

**FRIDAY, APRIL 28** | General Westmoreland addressed a joint session of Congress and did an excellent job. Unquestionably, he swung some wavering senators behind the president.

We've had a fairly good reaction to the Senate Ethics Committee's recommendation that Dodd be censured. The report came out Wednesday, for release Thursday. The committee pulled its punches on a lot of things; however, the fact that the report was unanimous and that Dodd admitted to so much diversion of funds has made a considerable impact.

**SATURDAY, MAY 6** | To the Bolivian embassy for lunch. Ambassador Linowitz asked me how serious Galo Plaza was when he said he would not become secretary-general of the OAS and suggested I sound him out definitely for the job. I suggested I would write to Nelson Rockefeller and get him to put the heat on Galo.

(Visited with Chief Justice Earl Warren to discuss case of Jim Garrison in New Orleans.)

I asked him whether he considered the role of the Supreme Court today to be chiefly that of protecting the Bill of Rights. He gave an interesting explanation dating back to John Marshall's day, when most of the decisions during the first thirty years of the Court pertained to "supremacy." The problem then was the supremacy of the Court to rule on decisions by the states and the federal government. "If it hadn't been for John Marshall's strong hand," the chief said, "we would have been a weak federation of rival states instead of a strong republic.

"During the next period, up through the Civil War, the Court was chiefly involved in states' rights. Then, after the Civil War, came the great industrial revolution, when the Court was busy protecting corporate rights. It twisted the Twelfth, Thirteenth, and Fourteenth Amendments, passed to prevent slavery, into a protective device for corporations. Then came the war and the Depression and the New Deal. The Court has been busy with all these things up until about the time when I took over, and now we have been busy in trying to protect some of the human rights of the country."

I asked the chief whether he considered the *Brown v. Board of Education* decision the most important or *Baker v. Carr*. He said that he thought *Baker v. Carr* would go down in history as the most important as far as the history of the United States was concerned. Had the Court not reapportioned state legislatures, the country would have limped along indefinitely with a lopsided government and no representation on the part of big city populations.

When the matter had first come before the Court, Justice Felix Frankfurter argued that reapportionment of state legislatures was a political matter, not a judicial matter, and that the Court had no right to take jurisdiction. The chief had argued to the contrary.

He said he had once talked to a state legislature lobbyist who confided that because of the domination of rural areas, he only had to worry about nine legislators when it came to a vote. If he could handle those nine, then he could swing the legislature.

The chief asked me if I had any news about who would fill the Supreme Court vacancy left by Tom Clark. He said he had no inkling any further as to Thurgood Marshall. He particularly wanted to know whether I knew anything about Arthur Goldberg and expressed the hope that he could be reappointed.

I told him about my talk with the president on behalf of Goldberg and the statement that Arthur could have the second vacancy but not the first. The chief said that when he had talked with the president on the same night that we both saw him, the president said he had given no commitments. The chief asked that I not mention to the president, if I saw him, the fact that he, the chief, was so much interested, but he hoped I might be able to do something.

WEDNESDAY, MAY 10 | The Bolivian ambassador is upset that a small guerrilla band has been loose in southern Bolivia. The Bolivian army has been unable to cope with it. It's unofficially listed at two hundred men, though the State Department tells me the size is nearer sixty. It is well equipped, apparently with Communist arms smuggled in through Argentina.

He remembers that it was a small band of Castroites, loose in eastern Cuba, which finally upset President Batista, took over the army, and put Castro into power. I told him I didn't think it was worth writing about; that these guerrilla bands also existed in Venezuela and Colombia. Incidentally, a Castro cadre of about a dozen men was recently landed on the Venezuelan seacoast.

SUNDAY, MAY 21 | Nasser has the bit in his teeth. He has stationed troops overlooking the Gulf of Aqaba and appears determined that this is I-Day, the time for Israel's demise. U Thant is flying to Cairo to see him.

**MONDAY, MAY 22** | Hume Horan came by the hospital to give me a briefing on the Middle East. He feels that Nasser is on a do-or-die course. His position at home has been eroding so rapidly that he had little to lose by a showdown with Israel. In case of war he can emerge as the No. 1 Arab—the only man in a thousand years to unite the Arab world.

Hume is pessimistic regarding the American position and said our only hope was to head off a conflict. He was stationed for a couple of years in Libya, for about a year in Beirut, and his father is the former foreign minister of Iran. So, he knows this part of the world.

Johnson has made a statement reaffirming the Straits of Tiran as an international waterway. It was a good statement, but simultaneously the U.S. ambassador in Cairo delivered a much vaguer statement to the Egyptian government.

Leonard Marks has been upset over the piece Jack wrote on Bob Kintner. I talked this over with Jack a good many weeks ago and thought I made it clear that we could criticize NBC without dragging in Bob, who has long left NBC. The president remarked to Leonard, "Have you seen Drew's column on Bob?" After all, Bob Kintner was the only man in radio who would put me on the air after Joe McCarthy lost his campaign to destroy me.

**TUESDAY, MAY 23** | I have been reading Anthony Nutting's book on the Suez crisis. He puts Sir Anthony Eden in a very sour light, as a conspirator with the French to return Britain's colonial empire. I am sure this was the case, but when you look back to the fact that Nasser had seized the Suez Canal in 1956 without even a "by-your-leave," you can understand somewhat the British position.

**WEDNESDAY, MAY 24** | They let me come home. I watched the UN debate from my bed all afternoon. Denmark and Canada called a meeting of the Security Council, but Russia has mobilized enough votes to make the margin close as to whether the Near East crisis should be put on the agenda. All afternoon was spent arguing merely over the question of whether the crisis should be discussed.

Arthur Goldberg put up a very uninspiring case for the United States. The British Lord Cartigan was brilliant in contrast, and so was the Russian, Federenko, even though he suffered from translation. The Russians are doing their best to stall and succeeded in postponing any vote.

**THURSDAY, MAY 25** | LBJ has flown to Canada to inspect the Montreal Exposition and also to see Prime Minister Lester Pearson. Abba Eban, the Israeli foreign minister, arrived here to point out that the Gulf of Aqaba was as essential to Israel as the Atlantic or Pacific Ocean is to the United States. Obviously, Israel is in a terrible predicament. The longer they wait, the less chance they'll have to win the war because they lose the element of surprise. This time the entire Egyptian army is already mobilized and active in Yemen and being withdrawn up to Sinai.

The Russians have now issued an emphatic statement supporting Nasser. Obviously, Nasser knew this in advance. The Russians have also made it clear that the United States is going to have to choose between the Far East and Vietnam or the Near East and Israel. They have Johnson in a serious bind. The American people aren't going to stand for American involvement in two distant parts of the world.

**FRIDAY, MAY 26** | Johnson is playing the Near East crisis very close to his chest. Obviously, he isn't going to be committed any more than he has to. Of course, when he was a senator, he was hell-bent for supporting Israel.

**MONDAY, MAY 29** | The Arabs are whipping themselves into a state of frenzy against Israel. It looks as if the entire Arab world has united behind Nasser and against Tel Aviv. King Hussein, who hates Nasser, flew to Cairo today and signed a pact with him. Their picture was taken in a fond embrace. Libya, Morocco, and Algeria, all skeptical of Nasser, today came up in full support.

**WEDNESDAY, MAY 31** | Security Council meetings are continuing. Arthur looks tired. He is no match for Federenko, who does a brilliant job of obstructing the Danes and the Canadians, who introduced a resolution for immediate Security Council consideration of the Near East crisis. Obviously, the Arabs and the Russians don't want any debate at this time. They are stalling on the plea that U Thant has gone to see Nasser and they should wait until he reports.

**FRIDAY, JUNE 2** | The president threw a big party for Prime Minister Holt of Australia. It lasted all night. Bess got home at 4:00 a.m. Australia is our one faithful ally in the Far East, and nothing is too good for Holt.

Another White House dinner is taking place tonight for Harold Wilson, who is supporting us in the Near East.

Chalmers Roberts has a front-page story today in the *Washington Post* to the effect that Rusk told senators that the United States would agree to a maritime police force to pilot ships through the Straits of Tiran, except for Israeli ships. No Israeli ships have been through the straits for two years, and Rusk apparently wants to appease Nasser with this formula.

Dodd's campaign is getting more intense. He's using every possible device to stir up public opinion in his favor and thereby pressure senators. He even asked to go on *The Joe Pyne Show*, with a trip to California for the taping. Jack and I taped a program in Washington to be aired Sunday night in Hartford as a rebuttal to Dodd.

**MONDAY, JUNE 5** | About 2:00 a.m. our time war broke out between Israel and its Arab neighbors. It was difficult at first to know who started the war, but I strongly suspected that Israel decided to get the first licks in, and as the day's developments unfolded, this appeared to be the case. Moshe Dayan sent the Israeli air force against all Egyptian air bases and not only knocked out planes on the ground but destroyed the runways so that those that got into the air couldn't land.

One Israeli force cut straight through the Gaza Strip, thereby pocketing a large part of the Egyptian army. For a time the Jordanians occupied the UN headquarters in Jerusalem but were pushed out. There was heavy fighting over Jerusalem, but toward the end of the day the Israelis seemed to be winning.

The State Department issued an immediate declaration of neutrality, but later in the day the White House hedged on this, obviously with heavy Jewish contributors in mind.

David Karr telephoned from Paris wanting me to wire him immediate credentials to the French Foreign Office. He said there were tremendous demonstrations for Israel, that the Rothschild family had sold their horse stable for $10 million to give to Israel, and that he wanted to fly to Israel.

**TUESDAY, JUNE 6** | The Jordanian army has collapsed. It had been trained by the British and was supposed to be the best army in the Middle East. The Israelis have now overrun the Old City of Jerusalem and much of Jordan, right up to the west bank of the [Jordan] river.

The Israeli army is also pushing across the Sinai desert to Suez and has taken the Gaza Strip.

Nasser has put out a statement claiming that Israeli victories were scored with the help of American and British planes from nearby aircraft carriers. As a result of this, the Algerian, Syrian, and Egyptian governments have broken relations with the United States, while crowds burned American libraries and attacked U.S. embassies and consulates. Actually, Johnson has been strictly neutral, and not one plane left any of our carriers of the Sixth Fleet.

The Security Council met this afternoon, and the Russians have suddenly reversed themselves in favor of an immediate cease-fire without a stipulation that Israel pull its troops out of the territory already occupied. This has the Arab countries raving mad. They called it a Russian double cross.

I talked with Senator Magnuson about the upcoming Dodd debate. He promised to check to see how many votes Dodd was likely to get. He is confident that most of the Senate will vote against Dodd, and Dick Russell of Georgia has already told him so.

WEDNESDAY, JUNE 7 | Jordan accepted the UN cease-fire proposal yesterday, and today Egypt threw in the sponge. This leaves only Syria, where there hasn't been much fighting. The Israelis apparently concentrated on Jordan and Egypt first.

I watched Arthur Goldberg on television. He did much better and seems to have his old oomph back. There is no question that Israel has won an outstanding victory. Israeli troops have retaken the mouth of the Gulf of Aqaba, have penetrated almost to the Suez Canal, and have one-third or one-quarter of Jordan under control. There is no question also that this was done by getting the jump on Egypt, a lesson which neither Russia nor the United States can overlook. If Israeli planes hadn't knocked out all Egyptian planes at the very start of the war, the results might have been different.

THURSDAY, JUNE 8 | It was broadcast from Tel Aviv today that the Israelis had intercepted a telephone conversation between Nasser and King Hussein in which they agreed that they would announce that ships from the Sixth Fleet had aided Israel and this was the reason for Israel's victory.

Talked with Tommy Thompson, who is back from Moscow supposedly for consultations, though he said the trip had been planned sometime before in order to take his thirteen- and seventeen-year-old daughters back from Holton Arms School. They are going to study at the University of Moscow and Russian schools this coming winter. Tommy says that Dobrynin, who is still in Moscow, is now called "The American" because he has championed and interpreted the American position so faithfully.

Tommy agrees there's not much chance of his doing anything constructive as long as the war is on; however, he said that people were coming to the American embassy as never before and from all walks of life. On the other hand, the political leaders of Russia are not going out much socially and are seldom seen. Tommy has talked to Kosygin, and he had some important talks with Gromyko. The Near East crisis started about May 22, and Tommy did not arrive here until June 1, so he was able to handle some of the preliminary note exchanges between LBJ and Kosygin. He shied away from telling me any details.

Tommy is not discouraged about Russia's failure to ratify the consular treaty. After all, the United States delayed over a year, and now the Russians don't want to appear to be hasty. Also, he feels that he may be able to do something regarding the ABM (antiballistic missile) Treaty. The Red Army is just as much opposed to this, as is Mendel Rivers and some of the right-wing leaders on the Hill. Since the Russian political leadership is weak, it's not going to be easy to put this across.

He [Thompson] is convinced the Russians didn't know Nasser was going to seize the Straits of Tiran, and they were embarrassed about it. Nasser got out of hand. They changed their ambassador in Cairo immediately after Nasser seized the straits, apparently because he'd failed to know what was developing.

The Russians also miscalculated the Arab strength. The Pentagon was right, predicting in detail how the Israelis would win. The Russians had trained the Arabs, given them tanks and jets, yet they didn't realize their weakness. As a result of this error, the Russians appear to want to quiet down the whole business—quickly.

FRIDAY, JUNE 9 | Nasser has resigned. He made his announcement to the Egyptian people in a broadcast—a shrewd move in which he took sole responsibility for the defeat. The reaction of the crowds was in his favor, and the National Assembly later rejected his resignation.

I made a prediction on tape yesterday that Nasser would either be kicked out or assassinated. The prediction will look phony by Sunday, but nevertheless I think in the long run it will be true. Israel has now ignored the cease-fire as far as Syria is concerned, has started bombing the outskirts of Damascus, and has sent three armored units deep into Syrian territory. Obviously, the Israeli military want to capture the Golan Heights, a large area overlooking the Sea of Galilee, before there is permanent peace.

Yesterday Israeli airplanes and torpedo boats killed about thirty American sailors and knocked a big hole in the communications ship,

*Liberty*, fifteen miles off the Egyptian coast. The *Liberty* was clearly marked with the American flag. I am convinced that the attack was deliberate. Obviously, the Israelis knew that the *Liberty* was intercepting their messages because Israel in turn was intercepting all messages itself between Nasser and the Arab leaders, so it must have picked up American messages.

The Israeli military are just cocky enough to take on the U.S. Navy. The Egyptians have no ships of this type, and obviously the ship would have had to be either American, British, Russian, Greek, Italian, or Scandinavian. None of these were belligerents.

SATURDAY, JUNE 10 | The Security Council met at 7:00 a.m. to deal with the continued fighting in Syria. Federenko blasted the Israeli ambassador, who was vulnerable. His government kept sending him assurances that the fighting had stopped, while U Thant kept getting messages from General Bull, the Norwegian in command of the UN police force, that the fighting was continuing. Obviously, the Israeli government either was lying or couldn't control the military. It was not until about 9:00 p.m. that the fighting in Syria appeared to have stopped.

SUNDAY, JUNE 11 | Stopped at Jack's on the way into town. Marjorie Carpenter and Jim Boyd were there, Jim having prepared a series of questions for senators to be asked of the Senate Ethics Committee. They are probably too detailed, but Jack and I will endeavor to get them asked.

Went to the Israel ambassador's ball. It was packed with jubilant people. Ambassador Harman was a little late arriving due to the fact that Russia has called another meeting of the UN Security Council, this time for the purpose of pinning the attack on Israel.

Bumped into Jim Scheuer, who said that Assistant Secretary of State [William] Macomber told him how, after the *Liberty* was fired upon by Israeli planes, the Israelis had immediately notified the Sixth Fleet of their mistake, planes from the Sixth Fleet had taken off to come to the *Liberty*'s rescue, and since the Russians were watching these planes, obviously they could not tell whether they were going to get into the war or perhaps attack Russian ships. When the Israeli flash came to the Sixth Fleet, it in turn immediately notified Washington, and the president got on the hot line to Premier Kosygin to tell him what was happening.

I also talked to Milt Friedman of the Jewish Telegraphic Agency, who says the ship was in CIA hands and failed to do what the Sixth Fleet usually does, namely notify local military commanders that the ship is in their waters.

I think the explanation sounds a little fishy and that probably the Israeli military got out of hand. The ship had been there since early dawn, and they didn't attack until 2:30 p.m.

MONDAY, JUNE 12 | Jack and I have been worried about the publicity barrage that Dodd and his "Justice for Tom Dodd Committee" have been waging. They have had some effect on Andy Glass of the *Washington Post*, who has had a series of pro-Dodd stories. I went to the Senate to see Sen. Steve Young of Ohio, who agreed to ask some questions during the Dodd debate.

TUESDAY, JUNE 13 | Senator Smathers has told Jack that Russell Long has an affidavit from a prostitute, swearing that Michael O'Hare tried to get her to frame Dodd. Russell plans to spring this on the Senate. Apparently, it's the big secret piece of dynamite he has been bragging about.

Knowing Michael, I am sure it's not true. I talked to him about it and warned him to brace for the attack. I was surprised to find he was not concerned. He's usually very nervous. He was more concerned over the attacks on him as a faulty bookkeeper who got Dodd into trouble and showed me a compilation of the air travel expenses for 1963. It was quite clear he had been very careful in pointing out to Dodd the legitimate airplane travel and the personal travel for the Dodd family and that for which Dodd was reimbursed. Michael even had some of Dodd's handwriting on the back of one list of expenses, which showed that Dodd had looked at the paper. Nevertheless, Dodd ordered Michael to have Ed Sullivan in Hartford (in charge of the campaign funds) pay the personal bills.

Various senators have received letters from Catholic priests urging humane treatment for Dodd. Sen. Eugene McCarthy, possibly influenced by this, has put a statement out tonight that perhaps the double billing case against Dodd should be dropped. Of course, it was the Senate Ethics Committee which bore down on the double billing in the first place. Jack and I never made too much of it, and certainly it was not as important as some of Dodd's gifts, which he took from those for whom he did government favors, which is clearly against the law. Nor was it as bad as the junket he took to Germany for Gen. Julius Klein, which the committee has chosen to overlook.

The Security Council in New York has voted down the Russian rebuff to Israel as the aggressor.

**FRIDAY, JUNE 16** | I went to Capitol Hill early this morning to try to persuade Sen. Steve Young to ask some questions showing that O'Hare was an honest bookkeeper. Steve was reluctant. He's not a very good cross-examiner.

I went across the hall to see Sen. Clifford Case of New Jersey, a Republican. I told him O'Hare was a resident of Jersey City and needed someone to defend him. I mentioned O'Hare's very careful bookkeeping. Case seemed impressed and indicated he would go to bat for O'Hare.

George Christian called from the White House to say he'd just announced to the press that the president was anxious to drop water to Egyptian soldiers and prisoners and had been in touch with the International Red Cross. This is Friday, and I made the suggestion on Tuesday. A lot of soldiers have died in that intervening time.

Senator Stennis got sore at Dodd yesterday and really pulled the facts on him. There seems to be no doubt that Dodd will be censured on his testimonial dinners, though they may drop the charges on double billing. Today Dodd was defended by Russell Long, who drooled on and on, while Dodd looked pained and unhappy.

Yesterday Russell accosted Jack Anderson outside the Senate and, in front of the photographers, put his arm around him to tell him that he didn't mean anything when he called me a crocodile. "After all, Walt Disney's crocodiles are good crocodiles," said Russell. Today on the floor, however, he repeated the charge that I was a crocodile and went further to say that Jack was a snake.

The Dodd debate has gone over until Monday.

Kosygin is coming to New York for the General Assembly meeting, and Johnson has indicated he would confer with him. The Russians are planning a showdown to save face for having not intervened to help the Arabs.

Dave Karr telephoned from London. He had just returned from Israel. He said the Israelis had decided on a Saturday to attack on Monday, but in order to throw the Egyptians off-balance on the timing, they had released one hundred thousand reservists over the weekend who had flooded the streets of Beersheba and Tel Aviv.

The Algerian ambassador telephoned yesterday wanting to talk to me, and I stopped by his embassy this afternoon. He was packing up. He lives in the old house that Lyndon Johnson occupied when vice president, and it looked empty.

On the hall table was an autographed photo of Johnson and the ambassador, halfway out of its frame. It looked as if the ambassador was debating whether he should take it home or leave it behind. Algeria has severed diplomatic relations.

The ambassador is quite young, quite intelligent, quite handsome, and quite wealthy.

He is friendly toward the United States and discussed Near East problems intelligently. "You never should have pulled the Americans out of the Arab countries," he said. "The State Department told them it could not guarantee their safety, but not one life was endangered and would not have been. Some of these Americans had been there for generations. They were an important factor in the country. Now the Arabs are saying you can't depend on the Americans; they leave in time of emergency.

"The exit of both the United States and Britain has left a void in the Arab world. The French will try to fill it but can't. The Russians probably can't either. This means a left trend in all the Arab states and possible communism."

The ambassador said the Russians had a black eye because they didn't come to the defense of the Arabs and would stage a show at the UN to make up for this.

We discussed solutions for the Near East crisis. "The Arabs must not get in the position of being anti-Jewish," the ambassador said. "The Arabs are not anti-Jewish. You must not drive them into this position."

He said the Israelis have not done a very good job with the Arabs inside Israel. They are second-class citizens. I agreed with him that the Israelis would have to treat the Arabs better inside Israel in order to show Arabs outside Israel that it was worth cooperating.

SATURDAY, JUNE 17 | Kosygin arrived in New York about five this morning. Arab leaders are arriving today and tomorrow. I suspect the United States is going into the General Assembly meeting with no comprehensive plan for a solution for the Near East. For twelve or fifteen years we have had fire brigade diplomacy, patchwork solutions for immediate problems with no overall plan. If there's going to be peace now, we must have an overall plan, but I doubt whether Rusk will come up with one.

THURSDAY, JUNE 22 | At 7:30 a.m. Bess called to invite me to a luncheon that day in honor of the Italian prime minister, Aldo Moro; Foreign Minister Fanfani; the Danish premier; and George Brown, the British foreign secretary. I learned afterward that she had been up part of the night inviting people. The president had decided to hold the luncheon only at four o'clock on Wednesday, and the principal guests had not accepted until about six thirty. As it turned out, the luncheon was a great success. I had a good time seated at the same table with Hubert Humphrey and George Brown, along with Kay Graham, and Representatives Selden of Alabama and Bates of Massachusetts.

When I went through the receiving line, I congratulated the president on being a grandfather. He replied, "Now I'm going to write letters to my grandson and print them in the paper the way you do."

Standing around in the East Room before the president and official guests arrived, I had a chance to talk to several guests. The room was stuffed with Italian American congressmen. Both George Meany and Walter Reuther were there, though they carefully avoided each other. Bill White—regarding whom we had taken a crack in the column for putting his daughter on the Dodd payroll—carefully avoided me.

The president rose right after the soup to give his toast. He was witty in talking about his grandson.

[Previously,] the president [had] sent word to me by Joe Califano that now that we had finished with Dodd, why not do the same to Representative McMillan. He referred to the South Carolina congressman who is chairman of the [House] District of Columbia Committee and whom I have suspected for a long time was in cahoots with the parking lot people and various filling station operators.

(Notes on the Johnson-Kosygin meeting in Glassboro, New Jersey.) Glassboro got its name from the fact that in the early days of the republic, it was the chief glassblowing center of the United States. Practically all the glass supplied to the thirteen colonies came from South Jersey. The sand there has an extra fine quality. Most of the glassblowers have long since died because glassblowing is now done by machinery. The industry has now moved to Trenton and Steubenville, Ohio. When I spoke at Glassboro State College two years ago, I found it a rather down-at-the-heel institution, barely struggling along. Glassboro pride, however, rallied to the occasion and made a great event of the Kosygin visit, and Kosygin appreciated this.

One hour after the meeting closed, Kosygin gave a press conference in New York at which he made it clear that he and Lyndon had accomplished almost nothing. He talked about the aggression of the imperialistic United States in Vietnam and the aggression of Israel in the Near East and repeated his demand that Israel withdraw its forces from occupied territory and pay reparations for damage.

He even balked at inviting Johnson to come to the Soviet Union, taking the same stand the Russians took when I was in Moscow in 1965—namely, that he could not come until after the war in Vietnam was ended.

To the American public, of course, this is going to mean a terrible letdown and a black eye for Johnson. On the presidential yacht yesterday his staff members were gloating over his success in getting Kosygin to talk and be friendly.

The interesting fact to me was that Lyndon took it in stride and continued to be hospitable and affable with Kosygin. Harry Truman would have blown his top, and the advisors around Eisenhower would have been sullen. Lyndon, however, has grown as a diplomat. He made a hell of a try, failed, but didn't react either publicly or privately as a result of that failure.

**MONDAY, JUNE 26** | The political reaction to the Glassboro conference is fairly even. A few years ago, had a Soviet premier blasted the United States after holding a friendly conference with the president, the reaction would have been very sour, but public opinion has changed a lot, and I think Johnson deserves credit for much of it. In all modesty I think that some of the articles I wrote, beginning with the Khrushchev interview, have changed public opinion too.

I have never seen Arthur quite so upset. Of course, the fact is that he has not been a particularly good debater, but I couldn't tell him this. He said: "I'll stick it out. There would be no compromise or retreat by me. I'm in this thing to win."

Premier Ky has been getting more high-handed. He has thrown a novelist in jail who criticized him. There is complete censorship of the press, and Ky is now campaigning around the country, though he is supposed, as head of the government, to refrain from doing so. I taped a blast at him in my radio program today.

**FRIDAY, JUNE 30** | Premier Ky has stepped down as a candidate for president in the September elections. He agreed to run for vice president, with the top military man running for president. This means a certain continuation of the military regime, duly elected however.

Obviously, the American embassy must have had much to do with Ky's step-down. Enrique told me at lunch this week that he met a man from the White House staff in the Kennedy administration who had sent the cable to President Diem which probably resulted in his assassination.

The White House had received a cable from the American ambassador saying there was no hope for stability in Vietnam unless Diem got out of the picture and that it was very difficult to make him disappear. The White House cabled back, "Don't abort." This is a term used among fliers which means, "Don't turn back." Two days later Diem was killed.

The Russians are complaining that American bombs hit another Russian ship, this one in Haiphong Harbor. The Pentagon has admitted it could have happened. After the last Russian complaint, the Pentagon denied the Russian charge immediately, but Johnson, a few days later, forced the Pentagon to admit it was true.

This last incident is certain to spoil most of the constructive effects of the Glassboro conference—at least as far as Moscow is concerned. When you let a war get into the hands of the military, you're in for trouble. Roosevelt and Churchill found this out, which was one reason World War II was won as quickly as it was.

Editorials have been coming in on the Dodd decision. Most of them have been constructive, urging a code of ethics for the Senate. Everett Dirksen, however, has stated publicly that no code could be adopted this year. This is a mistake. It would only take a few hours to draft a fairly forthright code.

**SUNDAY, JULY 2** | I stayed up late to listen to *The Joe Pyne Show*, who interviewed Jack Anderson. Pyne asked him why since he wanted congressmen to retire at the age of sixty-five, Pearson didn't retire at the age of sixty-nine. Jack replied, "That's up to him." Later he said that I was "moving over" to make room for him. I thought Jack handled the whole thing with inexcusable bad taste.

He also gave some lame answers regarding the usual right-wing questions as to whether he and I were pro-Communist and regarding the administration's policy of trading with Tito and other Communist satellites.

**SATURDAY, JULY 8** | LBJ RANCH, TX—We took a look at Johnson's buffalo and his longhorn cattle. The latter were brought over by the Spaniards in the early days and only remain now as relics of the past.

Finally, we pulled up at the ranch and waited inside for the president. The living room in the ranch house features a large stone fireplace with a leather rail around it upon which you can sit. It has wall-to-wall carpeting and on the whole is a modest room, furnished in good taste. Two portraits by Mexican painters were given the president by President Lopez Mateos and another similar to it by President Díaz Ordaz.

Immediately off the living room is a dining room, again modest, but looking out a beautiful picture window to the pastures beyond. The dining room is papered with a New England pastoral farm setting which could be Texas. Adjacent to the living room is a library, again rather modest, from which a pair of stairs go to the bedrooms.

The president has built an office adjoining the ranch house. It consists of one big room in which he occupies the main desk, and three secretaries have smaller desks. A huge silver saddle, given him by the president of Mexico, is mounted near the door, and his desk is littered with papers, though by no means as unkempt as my desk. There's a certain amount of orderliness about his desk and the office. He told us that when he came to the ranch, he got caught up with his reports.

Outside the office, on the veranda, are some comfortable cane rocking chairs. He had me sit in one of these, put my head back, and rock. I confess I would have gone to sleep in a hurry had I been alone.

As the president drew up, I introduced him to the three German guests and told him they had made the quickest trip between Hamburg, Germany, and San Antonio in history, having left Hamburg only yesterday noon. He went to the side porch to get some chairs and finally suggested that each one carry his own chair, which we did, over to the shade of a huge oak tree. It was pleasant and relatively cool in front of the ranch house.

He ordered soft drinks for us and ordered for himself a drink which I had not heard of before called Fresca. I tried some and found it delicious.

The first few minutes were taken up with ranch talk. LBJ told us how he had a chance to buy some property across the road for a small amount of money but passed it up. Soon he found that some enterprising businessmen planned to erect hot dog stands and souvenir shops and sell postcards to tourists. He and his friends bought up the land at a cost of $400 an acre, compared to about $10 an acre before.

Nannen asked the first real question. He said that Chancellor Kiesinger was grateful to the president for sending him a letter reporting on the Glassboro conference. He asked whether Glassboro was likely to launch a "Spirit of Glassboro," similar to the Eisenhower "Spirit of Camp David."

The president hedged on the launching of a new spirit of understanding between the United States and Russia; however, he did discuss the Glassboro conference. Parts of it came out in bits and pieces strung over the drive around the ranch. Later, at the lunch table, here is a fairly chronological account of what he said:

While Kosygin was in New York, Johnson asked his chief foreign affairs advisors whether he should see him or not. "You can submit memos, and later we'll put them in the Lyndon Johnson Library," he told his advisors.

He sent upstairs to get copies of three memos, and it was interesting that he instructed his secretary that they were in the bedroom, along with a telegram he'd sent to Patrick Lyndon Nugent. They were brought down, and the memos from Rostow, Rusk, and McNamara were read to us by the president. Rostow's memo was two and a quarter pages and talked about the importance of the two most powerful nations setting an example to the family of nations.

McNamara's was briefer, taking up one page only, and I thought more persuasive. I can't remember what Rusk said, but it was not as good as McNamara's. "Every one of my advisors recommended I go," the president said.

Meanwhile, he had Tommy Thompson, the U.S. ambassador to Moscow, up in New York talking to the Russians, and he also had Rusk there. Rusk called back to tell him he'd talked to Gromyko and that Gromyko was in favor of a conference.

"Did you talk to Kosygin?" the president asked. Rusk replied that he had not.

"Well, you go and talk to Kosygin and see what he thinks. He may have different ideas from Gromyko." Rusk did so and reported back in the affirmative.

Then, since the Russians didn't want to come to Washington, "my staff asked [New Jersey] Governor Hughes to find a good place. Actually, Hughes volunteered before we had a chance to ask him," the president said.

"He wanted us first to meet at the executive mansion in Princeton, but we had to consider security and the crowds. We couldn't afford to take any chances. Then Governor Hughes came up with the idea of Glassboro College. He said that the president of Glassboro was a Republican.

"Hughes wanted to announce Glassboro right away, but I said no; if the president is a Republican, we certainly have to consult him first.

"Finally, we got word from New York that Kosygin would come to Glassboro, and I tried to get Governor Hughes on the telephone. His office said he was en route home and couldn't be reached. Then I got a call from George Christian saying he has over a hundred newspapermen climbing up the wall, wanting to know if the meeting is going to be held and where it's going to be held and he has to have an announcement.

"Finally, I told the telephone operator, 'Look, honey, the governor must have a phone in his car. Get him on the phone and have him call me back.'

"So, Hughes stopped, went to a drugstore, and called me back. I told him we were going to announce Glassboro as the site of the Summit conference.

"'All right, I'll take care of the Republican president,' said Hughes.

"Then I called George Christian to tell the newspapermen the facts."

Johnson said he had seldom prepared so intensively for any meeting. "I got up at four thirty in the morning to read the position papers. Then, at seven thirty, I had breakfast with the men who had urged me to meet with Kosygin. On my right was Dean Rusk, then Nick Katzenbach, Tommy Thompson, Bundy, and on the side, Secretary of Defense McNamara, Walt Rostow—a total of six. They briefed me until ten thirty. And I was supposed to meet with Kosygin at eleven."

The president said much time was spent at Glassboro the first day just getting acquainted. Kosygin wanted to know whether Johnson was a real farmer, whether he irrigated, whether he supervised the work himself. The president told him how he had worked as a young man on a road construction gang for a dollar a day, and Kosygin told how he had worked in a textile mill as a young man.

"One of the most important things we got out of the meeting was to get to know each other better.

"Kosygin kept demanding that Israel withdraw its troops. I said we wanted her to withdraw her troops but not until after the conditions were remedied which led to the war. 'If a patient has a high fever,' I told him, 'you don't withdraw the medicine that has kept the fever down and then have the fever shoot up again to 105.'

"I told Kosygin that the United States and Russia could be compared to the heads of a family that must set an example to the world. I told him about my family. I belong to a family of seven. My mother was a cultured lady. My father was a hillbilly, something of a river rat. He only made $150 a month, and he had five children to support.

"When I was working at San Marcos College, I had one hour off between classes and rushed down to the college office to address envelopes for twenty-five cents an hour. This I gave to my sister to buy feminine things. I had a shirt and a pair of pants, but she needed feminine things which I didn't need.

"In our family, I told Kosygin, we children used to argue, but our father and mother never quarreled. They set an example to the rest of us. They held the family together. Russia and the United States must set the same kind of an example to the world."

One of the German editors asked whether the other nations should be disciplined. "No, we should just set an example," the president replied.

One guest asked whether it was Kosygin who suggested they meet the second time at Glassboro. "It was mutual," the president replied. "It was like a kiss. The girl always likes to claim that she was forced into a kiss, but she isn't going to be kissed unless she likes.

"Kosygin told me he knew I had an engagement in Los Angeles and he understood. He kept telling me that I should keep the appointment. I didn't tell him that some of the members of the President's Club in Los Angeles had complained that they hadn't seen the president in return for contributing a $1,000 each year to the President's Club, and they weren't going to contribute any more unless they saw the president. Instead, I told him that I was willing to cancel the Los Angeles dinner.

"He insisted I keep the engagement. I asked him when he had to leave the United States, and he said Monday or Tuesday. By this I knew that he would be available on Sunday, so I suggested that we come back on Sunday. He agreed."

The president said that three times during the talks Kosygin said that Russia wants peace, the United States wants war.

"I had my blood pressure examined that morning," the president told us. "It was 120 over 78. I knew I was in good shape. So, I waited ten seconds. Then I said: 'I don't know your country very well. I've never been there. I'd like to know it better. But I'm sure your people don't want another war. And I'm sure they don't want to go through another siege of Leningrad.'"

"I do know my people," the president told Kosygin, "and I can tell you that the American people don't want a war."

He noted that Kosygin at one point said: "China is accusing me of selling out. North Vietnam is accusing me of selling out. Some of my comrades in the Kremlin are accusing me of selling out. I am not selling out."

"Yes, you are," Johnson told him.

"To whom?" Kosygin asked.

"To me," the president replied. "I want peace."

Earlier, when the president and Kosygin first sat down at Glassboro, Johnson asked whether he would object if a movie cameraman came in and took some shots of them. Kosygin did not object. He held up his finger and said, "That's our first agreement."

Very early in the luncheon conversation, when Nennen first asked about a new "Spirit of Glassboro," the president quoted [the British writer] Charles Lamb, who was reading a book and suddenly threw it on the floor. His sister asked why he did that, and he replied, "I don't like that man."

"Have you ever met him?" his sister asked.

"No, if I did, I'd like him," Lamb replied.

The president was illustrating the fact that people had to know each other better if there was to be peace in the world. Time after time he came back to this point.

The president said he and Kosygin had some differences regarding the draft of a communiqué at the end of their Glassboro second talk. Kosygin didn't want to use the word "constructive" or the word "cordial" in describing their talks. He wanted to use the word "useful."

"It seemed to me that we ran that word into the ground. In the end we tore up the communiqué. Later he went to New York and used the same critical words at a press conference. In fact, he went much further than he had at Glassboro in talking to me."

"Were you upset by this?" a German editor asked.

"No, I knew that Kosygin wasn't a free agent," the president replied. "He had to think about China. He had to worry about North Vietnam. And he had his Arab clients to think about as well as his comrades in the Kremlin. In between the two Glassboro talks we learned that he communicated with Moscow and got instructions.

"On the other hand, I was in a position where the Fulbrights and the Mendel Riverses and the Drew Pearsons couldn't go after me. In this case Fulbright and Mansfield seemed to want me to meet with Kosygin."

Johnson indicated that in arranging the Glassboro talks, he had played hard to get and therefore considered himself in a better bargaining position than Kosygin, since he had 100 percent support from his people.

"Despite the war in Vietnam, I have negotiated, or almost negotiated, six important agreements with Russia, [for example] the space treaty, the consular agreement, the civil air agreement, and the cultural exchange agreement.

"A year or so ago Mary Martin was stopped from going to Russia with *Hello, Dolly!* There was a big stew about it. Everybody was upset. Nevertheless, we finally negotiated a new cultural exchange agreement."

He also mentioned that agreement was near on the nonproliferation treaty. When he was asked about the antiballistic missile agreement, he said he was hopeful there would be one.

Dr. Sommers asked, "Do you think that you can find a formula for nonproliferation that would be agreeable to both Germany and Russia?"

The president replied he was confident that this was possible.

"Mansfield and Fulbright have been demanding we reduce our troops in Germany. They said Germany could defend itself. So, I picked Jack McCloy, who knows Germany well, and asked him to study whether we can reduce our forces without hurting our NATO commitments. He went to Bonn, and he came back to recommend that we rotate two brigades of one division and parts of three air wings—a total of thirty-five thousand men and ninety-six aircraft. Redeployment would begin in 1968."

Johnson's secretary came out with a slip of paper, wanting to interrupt him. She was rather timid about it. He was talking enthusiastically and paid no attention to her. Finally, she gave the paper to George Christian, who poked it toward the president. He still didn't pay any attention. Finally, George said, "Secretary Rusk is calling you."

"I know what that's about," the president said. "Africa." He got up and took the call. When he returned, we got into the station wagon, and he drove us around the ranch. While driving, we continued part of the conversation on foreign problems.

At one point, while driving around, the German editors asked Johnson about Vietnam. He stopped the car and gave them a very pointed and vigorous lecture on the problem of bombing the North. Dr. Sommers had said, "Your critics have frequently criticized your failure to stop bombing North Vietnam."

The president replied, "Yes, I know, but put yourself in my place. I have boys up in the front line. Their safety is dependent upon airplanes coming over to support them. There are now five North Vietnamese divisions that have come through the DMZ. If I withdraw that air support, we don't have enough troops to withstand their greater numbers. We must have bombing. I am willing to end it the minute I get a promise of something in return.

"No one can say I haven't tried. I have had six bombing pauses—one for thirty-six days, one for six. And that's time enough for anyone to turn a thought in his mind."

While cruising around the ranch, Lyndon explained he had about 200 head of whiteface cattle but was going to cut his herd down to about 175, which was about what one man could handle. "I sell 50 to 75 calves a year," he said.

Part of the pastures were irrigated by wells, which the president said were buried from one hundred to one thousand feet in depth. "It cost $25 a month to pump water in here for these deer," he said. We saw a good many deer. "They're in a preserve with high fences, some divided off from other deer. There's the native Texas deer, which is small; the European deer from the Hart Mountains, which is bigger," and the president has also been sent Japanese deer (which are beautiful but small) and Cambodian deer.

The deer are fed from huge cylinders suspended from trees with a clock mechanism which goes off every twelve hours to drop corn below. Most of the deer are fairly tame.

Earlier the president was illustrating the problem of international relations.

"It's like my deer," he said. "If you don't come up on them suddenly and honk your horn at them, they're friendly, but if you scare them, they'll run. You can't be abrupt and sudden in international relations. You have to explain things and take things easy."

The most interesting house on the ranch was the home where Lyndon was born. He has preserved it beautifully. In his mother's bedroom is the old bedspread which his mother used and the quilt made by his great grand-mother. It looks like some of the quilts my grandmother Pearson quilted for me, though I'm afraid that long since they have been mislaid or worn out.

Lyndon's mother must have been a talented woman. On the wall is a framed account which she wrote of the day in which he was born. It's quite a beautiful tribute.

In the kitchen is the wood-burning stove. Outside, on the porch, is the old pump. Lyndon insisted on pumping some water from it, which he put in an old broken gourd.

We also paid a visit to Luci in a little ranch house which she and the new grandson and Pat occupy. The president explained that Pat got up at 6:30 a.m. to drive up to Austin every morning to work. He and Luci stay here only on such weekends as the President and Mrs. Johnson are here, which has been twice in the last month. The rest of the time they're in Austin.

Lyndon insisted on going in and interrupting his grandson's meal. Luci came out bearing Patrick Lyndon, who is quite a large baby, considering that he's only ten days old. He took this interruption without a squawk.

I have never seen the president so enthusiastic. He has a beautiful new grandson. He has done well with Kosygin. His political polls are up, and he's had a good rest.

[From Tuesday, August 1, through Wednesday, August 30, the Pearsons, along with Chief Justice Earl Warren and his wife, Nina, joined Agnes Meyer for a vacation at a house she had rented on Maui, Hawaii.]

MONDAY, AUGUST 21 | At eight o'clock this morning the chief got a call. It was conveyed by the maid since there are no telephones in our rooms. Nina said that the chief would call back in an hour. The maid returned to say, "It's the president calling you."

The chief dressed and hurried down to take the call. LBJ wanted him to go to Vietnam with a delegation of observers to make sure the election was conducted fairly and honestly. Senator Dirksen had approved of the idea and was appointing some Republicans. The delegation would also include representatives of the AFL-CIO [American Federation of Labor and Congress of Industrial Organizations], the League of Women Voters, members of the clergy, the press, etc., and the president wanted the chief justice to head it.

The chief told the president he thought the Judiciary should not get involved. "'This election is a political matter, not a judicial one. All my brethren on the Court would feel it was a great mistake for me, or any other judge, to get involved.'

'Your word is good enough for me,' the president replied."

Luvie and I afterward remarked to ourselves how quickly and firmly the chief had handled this. The average man, getting a request like this from the president, would either have accepted or hesitated and postponed a decision, but the chief was right to the point in a firm but kindly way.

Later he explained that he felt this was different from his acceptance of the Warren Commission. Both houses of Congress would have appointed investigating committees to probe the assassination. Therefore, Johnson had to move.

THURSDAY, AUGUST 31 | We arrived in New York on time and made the transfer to Washington. The capital seems a bit dull and complacent. Congress is out of town. The Labor Day weekend is approaching.

FRIDAY, SEPTEMBER 8 | Lunched with Charles Sullivan, who spent fifteen years with the Treasury and as political officer for the Defense Department. He recalled vividly briefing Jim Forrestal in early 1949 regarding the State

Department proposal that we recognize Red China. Forrestal walked up and down the floor, storming against the idea, but when he attended a meeting on the subject later, he didn't raise his voice.

Charlie Wilson was the first secretary of defense who had real power to crack down on the services, but he didn't know how to use it. Wilson did have some political sense. He wanted to keep out of Asia. He was always arguing against the offshore islands of Quemoy and Matsu.

Sullivan reviewed the history that led up to the war in Vietnam. He feels we are right in taking a stand in Vietnam and recalled that the discussion of taking a stand began during or immediately after the Korean War crisis. The Eisenhower administration felt that China was moving and the question was how to contain her.

I recalled that during the American Society of Newspaper Editors dinner at the Statler Hotel, Nixon revealed off the record that the United States was going into Indochina with land forces and that Clayton Fritchey, then editor of the *New Orleans Item*, went out and called the *London Telegraph*, which spilled the story. It then ricocheted back and forth across the Atlantic with ever-widening repercussions. This, I thought, probably helped Eisenhower change his mind.

Nevertheless, Sullivan said the decision had definitely been made, and it was hoped there would be a confrontation with China, during which we would drop the A-bomb. The strategy was to meet the crisis with China and get it over.

After Eisenhower ducked this showdown, Dulles proceeded to set up the SEATO pact, with the purpose of protecting Indochina, or rather, the new countries carved up out of it. Significantly, Charlie said, the French and British refused to permit the new countries, North and South Vietnam, Cambodia, and Laos, to become signatories of SEATO. The French and British knew there would be trouble and didn't want to get involved in the war.

He still thought that if we had not taken a stand in Indochina, the Chinese would have moved south and west. If they ever got into Burma, then Ceylon, India, Pakistan, and the Arab states would fall. He emphasized that the Chinese merchants, now Nationalists, in the Philippines to the tune of about three million, six million in Thailand, and several million in Indonesia, plus a couple of million in Malaysia, would turn Communist if they saw Red China coming out supreme in a struggle with the United States.

**THURSDAY, SEPTEMBER 14** | Yesterday the Pentagon released the fact that early this week there had been a raid on the port of Haiphong, the first. American bombers were careful not to bomb the docks where Soviet shipping would be endangered but did bomb railroads, warehouses, etc., in an effort to disrupt the flow of supplies. (A few days ago we also bombed the smaller port of Campha.)

**SUNDAY, SEPTEMBER 17** | Harry Ashmore, formerly of the *Arkansas Gazette*, and Bill Baggs, now managing editor of the *Miami News*, released a story late this afternoon on how they had gone to Hanoi to see Ho Chi Minh and thought they were doing a good job toward peace negotiations, when suddenly Johnson wrote Ho a letter cutting the ground out from under them. Johnson had given them a letter which was more conciliatory. Then he wrote a stiffer letter throwing up the obstacle of cessation of all North Vietnamese military activities if we stopped bombing.

**MONDAY, SEPTEMBER 18** | Had a talk with Hubert Humphrey in his office just off the Senate floor. He was rushing to New York to attend a dinner. He said he'd had a sad summer. His brother died; his mother, eighty-six, had almost died. His best friend died, and Muriel had become sick from drinking some kind of a parasite in the water, apparently from their lake in Minnesota. She had been in the hospital three times.

Hubert, however, went into enthusiastic detail about what he'd done during the summer to head off race riots. He named mayors who had done the best job, such as Daley of Chicago and Tate of Philadelphia, who he thought had probably done a better job than John Lindsay in New York. Hubert was enthusiastic about the contribution made by business in giving jobs and heading off riots.

We got around to Vietnam too late. By then he'd spent thirty minutes talking about riots, and his aides yanked him away; however, he said that the Joint Chiefs of Staff had eliminated thirty of their targets from the list and that McNamara had then accepted it.

"The strategy is to go through this list till all the targets are demolished and then open a terrific peace offensive," said Hubert. "You ought to see the boss. He's terribly upset over the Harry Ashmore story. He just hates to have anyone think that he would sabotage the peace. I was with him last night, and he was very blue about it. You ought to see him and get him to tell you all the things he's done to work for peace."

TUESDAY, SEPTEMBER 26 | Dinner for the new Yugoslav ambassador, Bogdan Crnobrnja. Among the diners were Sen. Joe Clark of Pennsylvania, with his new bride, and Rep. Ross Adair, Republican of Fort Wayne, Indiana, with his wife. Adair said he thought Johnson lacked warmth in his phone calls and personal conversation. I disagreed. The new ambassador told how Johnson had seen him only eleven days after he arrived in the United States and had been warm and understanding. Later in the same day Johnson had received Foreign Minister Nikezič on his mission to try to bring peace to the Middle East.

We talked after dinner regarding the war and Johnson's political future. Joe felt that if the president ran now without peace in Vietnam, he would be overwhelmingly defeated in Pennsylvania. When we began to talk about Republican candidates, Joe hedged and felt the Democrats could defeat Nixon or any other Republican candidate except Rockefeller, and it was generally agreed, not only by us but by Representative Adair, that Rockefeller could not be nominated by the Republican Party.

We tried to figure out why George Romney was such a dud. He has been a good governor of Michigan, we agreed, and a sincere fellow but is generally considered too gauche to be president.

I asked the ambassador what he thought of the State Department view that in the Kremlin there was a school of thought, now in control, that was delighted to have the United States bogged down in Vietnam. As a result, we couldn't move regarding Berlin, we couldn't move in the Near East, and we were losing friends in Asia.

The Yugoslavs understand the Russians probably better than any other Communist country. It was interesting to me that the ambassador made quite a defense of Khrushchev. He said Khrushchev had recognized the new spirit in the Communist world, the desire to have contacts with the outside world, and had given the greatest advance to the Communist world of any one man. Without Khrushchev there might have been very serious problems. The ambassador didn't say so, but he implied there would have been internal revolt. The old Stalin era could not continue.

He said that Khrushchev had been willing to admit his mistakes. He made a serious mistake in antagonizing President Tito and came to Belgrade to apologize for it. Afterward he was considered a bigger man than before. He also admitted his mistake in putting missiles into Cuba and withdrew the missiles. The ambassador said it didn't hurt him but, rather, increased his stature. I had given him the opening by making a comparison between Johnson and Khrushchev and suggesting that Johnson could increase his stature by saying he had made a mistake in South Vietnam.

**MONDAY, OCTOBER 2** | In the Senate, John Sherman Cooper of Kentucky launched another debate on bombing. He is a moderate Republican who has usually supported the administration, and this adds up to a series of moderate Republicans, including Case of New Jersey and Morton of Kentucky, who have all broken with the administration.

**WEDNESDAY, OCTOBER 4** | Kay Graham came to dinner, looking quite thin and quite well. Her dieting has done her good. We exchanged notes on who was or was not back in Lyndon's good graces. She was laboring under the impression that I had been out for a long time. It's funny how newspaper people love to criticize Lyndon but nevertheless do like to be in his good graces.

**FRIDAY, OCTOBER 6** | Sen. Vance Hartke of Indiana in a speech warns that the administration is considering an invasion of North Vietnam—the Inchon-type landing. The indication is that some of the Senate speeches, such as that of Thruston Morton, were made in order to head off such a landing. They may be right, though I doubt it.

The Bolivian ambassador wanted me to come over and see Foreign Minister Guevara D'Arze, who was so hurt by my story on the guerrillas and Che Guevara. I had known D'Arze before. He had been out at the farm with the previous ambassador, Victor Andrade. He had cooled down considerably.

D'Arze is here to get a credit from the International Monetary Fund, which he says Bolivia badly needs. He was irked over the fact that the CIA would not cooperate with him regarding intelligence on the Cuban guerrillas in Bolivia. The Argentine government, however, did cooperate and confirmed the fingerprints of Che Guevara, made when he was young, before he went to Cuba.

Wilbur Mills, chairman of the House Ways and Means Committee, has issued a statement that there will be no tax increase unless and until Johnson curtails spending. The interesting thing to me was that Johnson, at lunch with newspaper publishers about a month ago, had answered a provocative question from Jack Knight, wanting to know why the president had asked for a tax increase now when he had passed one up a year ago. Johnson's answer was that it would have been impossible to put it through the Ways and Means Committee. He was right.

David Karr came from New York for lunch. He had flown over from Paris for about a week and tells me he really enjoys living there and has found his marriage to his French wife very happy. They are going to have a baby in December.

Today Dave was pessimistic about the United States and the Johnson administration. He says that it's a shock to come back here and find you can't walk on the streets at night, that people are thinking chiefly of themselves, and that despite our terrific gross national product, we can no longer afford to be generous to smaller, underdeveloped nations.

He thinks the sentiment toward us in Europe has changed drastically. They used to admire Americans for their idealism and generosity. Now they don't. They see us as picking on little nations far away from our shores. We no longer stand for big things. The Johnson Great Society, which started out with a flourish of idealism, has now slowed down to a retreat and will not get going again as long as the war continues.

SUNDAY, OCTOBER 8 | The Soviet ambassador [Dobrynin], just returned from Moscow, came to lunch and engaged in quite a conversation with Senators Church and Magnuson. Wayne Morse was there, but silent. Magnuson told him that if his constituents knew he was having lunch with the ambassador, he would probably be defeated. Yet in the same breath Maggie told him that the Russians had been better at keeping their word on the preservation of faith than any other nation.

Privately, Maggie told me the ambassador had given him a tip for future fish conservation, namely that the United States call a conference in Geneva at which we would propose a twelve-mile limit for fishing. The Russians would back us, and with the support of the British, we could bring the other nations round, such as Peru, which claims a three-hundred-mile limit. Considering that Russian trawlers have been fishing within about four miles of the Pacific Coast, this is an amazing proposal. Maggie seemed quite pleased about it.

Frank Church told the ambassador that what was used against him in his reelection campaign was that he had voted for the ratification of the Soviet Consular Treaty with the United States. He asked the ambassador when Russia was going to ratify it.

Dobrynin gave an interesting dissertation on the fact that Russia hadn't wanted the treaty in the first place, that it had been proposed by the United States, and that the USSR had no reason to open another consulate in

Chicago or New York because there were very few Russians in those cities and almost no trade. He expressed surprise that the United States, during the Soviet treaty debate in the Senate, had not stated publicly that we were the initiators of the treaty, not Russia.

He felt that if Russia rushed in with ratification, it would play into J. Edgar's hands and seem to validate his contention that they wanted to open a consulate for espionage purposes. Someone asked him whether, if the United States opened a consulate in Leningrad, Russia would open one in the United States. The ambassador said that probably they would have to do so, though they were not much interested.

Magnuson asked him about the Aeroflot Aviation Agreement with the United States. The ambassador explained why it was not being put across. He said every foreign airline entering the United States had to agree in advance that if there was a crash, each family of a passenger killed would automatically receive $75,000.

The Soviet Union objected to this, claiming they should pay only if they were responsible for the deaths. Secondly, he said, Russia had just built some new, fast jets which were flying to Vladivostok and Montreal. The distance from Moscow to Vladivostok was just about the same as from Moscow to New York, and since these planes were quite busy and since they were short on producing new ones, they didn't want to open a New York route until they were better equipped. Finally, Dobrynin said that Pan American Airways had proposed opening the route to New York in the spring, when there was more traffic. Right now there wouldn't be enough to make the route pay.

After lunch the ambassador stayed to talk to me briefly. He wanted to know what the climate was regarding American-Soviet relations. I assume he wanted to know how I thought the president was feeling on this. I said that the president was still anxious to improve Russian-American relations and had spoken privately, with some degree of pride, regarding the fact that he'd kept them friendly.

The ambassador said he felt that, considering everything, the president had done pretty well. I told him I was convinced Johnson would like to get out of the war on the terms of an election in both the North and the South to see whether they would unite but that he had to have peace negotiations first; however, the report from the Canadian observer in North Vietnam was negative regarding such negotiations.

**MONDAY, OCTOBER 9** | [Pearson noted in the diary that British Labour leader Clement Attlee had died.]

**THURSDAY, OCTOBER 12** | Up early; to California, arriving in time for lunch with Pat Brown. With him was the new Democratic State chairman, Charles Warren, a nice guy but who struck me as being a flat tire politically. The state of California is in disarray as far as the Democratic Party is concerned. Pat is primarily worried about the peace movement, which threatens to cut the ground out from under Lyndon Johnson. His own son, "Jerry," a former priest, is active in the peace movement, and Warren's son was a delegate to the recent Democratic Peace Convention. If a good peace candidate starts campaigning on the Democratic ticket for delegates to the 1968 convention, it looks as if he might roll up considerable opposition to the president.

Pat told me that two of Governor Reagan's staff members, who were mysteriously fired last August, were homosexuals. When we were in Hawaii last August, we noted a mysterious item in the paper that two members of Reagan's senior staff had been dropped. No reason was given.

Pat also said that the *Los Angeles Times* was going to break the story shortly on a big harbor scandal involving appointees of my friend Mayor Sam Yorty. I got busy to see if I could break the harbor scandal myself but found it was moving too quickly and the *Times* apparently had it under wraps.

Pat thinks that Reagan is in some trouble because of curtailing money for mental health and increasing taxes. He thinks that Reagan's battle for tuition at California universities will not seriously hurt him; however, the people whose relatives have been making some progress in recovering from mental illness, and who were treated in clinics rather than going to hospitals, have now found the clinics cut off. As a result, they're going back to hospitals as regular patients, which will add to the taxpayers' burden.

**SATURDAY, OCTOBER 21** | I spent the morning at the farm and drove into town around noon because of a peace march. Luvie didn't participate this time. She decided that things were going a bit too all-out, but Drew did, and David Karr came down Thursday for the march. It all started peacefully and happily on the George Washington Monument grounds, then trekked past the Lincoln Memorial and across Memorial Bridge toward the Pentagon. I went down to the Watergate apartment owned by Herbert Sammons, who is a State Department legal counselor. We could see the long line of marchers as it slowly crossed the bridge.

After they reached the Pentagon, order and discipline apparently vanished. A minority of hippie demonstrators surged up against the troops around the Pentagon and for a time almost got in. Some of them had their skulls cracked with rifle butts. About 700 were carted away and arrested. Drew said that the MPs stood there very glum under their helmets as the hippies threw thousands of yellow flowers over them. It was a taunting, unruly crowd, which I think will alienate public opinion by their demonstration.

**WEDNESDAY, OCTOBER 25** | Up early to fly [from Minot, North Dakota] to Las Vegas. Temperature went from about thirty degrees in North Dakota to eighty degrees on the Nevada desert.

The Israelis have now blown up the oil refineries at Suez, the southernmost city on the Suez Canal. It was an act of retaliation against the sinking of their destroyer, but there's a lot of war fever on both sides, and the situation is becoming dangerous. The Russians have rushed some warships into Egyptian ports as protection for their allies.

**FRIDAY, OCTOBER 27** | Spent a good part of the morning on the telephone regarding the homosexual scandal in the Reagan cabinet. Apparently, he has been pretty ruthless in leaking the story in order to make himself appear as a forthright executive who cleaned house immediately. The story was leaked on the SS *Independence* by Lyn Nofziger, Reagan's press secretary [when the National Governors' Conference was being held aboard the ship]. It was given to various newspapermen and radio commentators. Actually, Reagan did not act in February (when he first learned of a homosexual orgy at Lake Tahoe); [it was not] until August when the two men were fired.

**SUNDAY, OCTOBER 29** | Telephone conversation with Leonard Marks. He says every member of the president's staff, contrary to *Newsweek*, has taken a private pledge to stay with him until after the '68 election. He says he was talking to the president, who was quite unhappy about some of the columns, including one by Marquis Childs which quoted him incorrectly. Finally, he said, "There's only one man who has been fair and friendly to me through the years."

Leonard said: "I hope you remember that next time you say Drew has been unfair. He has to needle you occasionally to keep his impartiality." Leonard said the president agreed.

**TUESDAY, OCTOBER 31** | My plane landed in the new, half-built Midcontinent Airport in Kansas City due to bad weather. A phone call was awaiting me from a TV station in Los Angeles, saying that Ronald Reagan had held a press conference that morning and blasted me as a liar in regard to the special release we sent out Sunday referring to the two homosexuals on Reagan's staff. I dictated a statement over the telephone to give out to the papers. Naturally, I stood pat on the Reagan story.

I drove to St. Joseph [Missouri], where the publisher of the *News-Press* was awaiting me. He and his father have used my column for about twenty-five years. It was Luvie's grandmother who introduced me to Dean Palmer, the broker who handled the sale of the paper and who got the column first introduced in St. Joe.

All afternoon I was busy answering phone calls from the West Coast regarding the Reagan story. I talked to Charles Roudebaugh of the *San Francisco Chronicle*, who had been investigating. He noted that none of the men on the ship who had heard Nofziger talk were now willing to talk. I talked to Bill Ames, CBS's man on the ship who had talked to Nofziger, but while he confirmed what Nofziger said, he took an aloof attitude. When I asked him why he didn't speak out [he said]: "I have to examine this one carefully to see what's to be gained."

I called Kay Graham to try to get her to run a piece in *Newsweek* wrapping up the whole thing about the California credibility gap. She was quite frank and was conversant with the story. She said she had talked to Evans and Novak, one of whom was on the ship and who said they would break the story if someone else wrote it first. She indicated that *Newsweek* would pass on the story. I may be sitting with another "lie" on my hands.

I called David Noyes in Los Angeles to suggest that now would be a good time for Harry Truman to come out with what he currently thought of me. I told Dave that Reagan had stated that none of the three presidents of both parties who had called me a liar had changed their position. Of course, it was only two presidents, both Democrats, and one is now dead. The other one had changed his position. Dave said he would try to get back to Truman, who was feeble and spending all his time in his home.

**WEDNESDAY, NOVEMBER 1** | Jack reports that the *Washington Post* story this morning carries a statement that Reagan's press conference denial came as a surprise to newspapermen on the SS *Independence*, who had heard Nofziger confirm the situation regarding the two homosexuals.

**FRIDAY, NOVEMBER 3** | Stopped in to see George Christian regarding the Reagan matter. He says the president is going to keep a thousand miles away from it. George did show me, however, a report written by the chief radio operator on the SS *Independence*, Charles Berger, who had signed and dictated a sort of confession as to how the message from Marvin Watson got into Reagan's hands.

George said it was a phony confession in the first place because Berger is an old Goldwaterite. In the second place he admitted he had gone six decks below to have the message Xeroxed. His only explanation was that he had two messages, one for Reagan and one to Price Daniel, and that he had put them in the wrong envelopes.

While I was with him, Christian called Price Daniel to get more details. Price said he had received a Xerox of the carbon copy, not of the original. He could tell this because there had been corrections on the original but no corrections on the carbon copy.

George showed me a copy of the Communications Act, states that it's a criminal offense to intercept a telegram or radiogram or to distribute one which was not intended for you. It's obvious, however, the White House isn't going to prosecute anyone or even conduct an investigation.

I talked to Ramsey Clark and to Fred Vinson, in charge of the criminal division of the Justice Department, about transporting boys across state lines for immoral purposes. They say that when the Mann Act was written, no one worried about this and the law applies only to females. Ramsey says it's difficult to enforce the Mann Act because so many men transport their secretaries across state lines, and if they really tried to enforce it, they would be arresting everyone.

Aside from politics this is getting to be a serious matter. Reagan's staff took two eighteen-year-old boys across the Nevada line to Lake Tahoe.

**SATURDAY, NOVEMBER 4** | Jim Corman was on the plane to Los Angeles, also Charlton Heston. A lot of people wanted Heston's autograph. Jim and I talked about the Reagan case and the do-nothing Congress. He says the trouble with the House of Representatives is that the Democrats don't have a majority. The Dixiecrats have gone over to the Republicans, and the leadership just doesn't have the votes. In addition, the leadership is clumsy and not really dedicated to the Great Society program.

Somewhat against my better judgment, I'd told American Airlines to set up a press conference in the International Inn near the airport in Los Angeles. It was [to be] Saturday [at] noon, and I doubted whether anyone would be there. The press room, however, was packed. I made three points: (1) I challenged Reagan to place the question of the homosexuals dropped from his staff before the California attorney general, Tom Lynch; (2) or, if he didn't want to do this, I urged that the Committee on Morals and Ethics of the California legislature investigate; (3) I challenged Reagan to take a lie detector test.

There were many questions, some of them unfriendly, some friendly. They bore down on whether I would name names and what additional information I had. The fact is that I can't name names without getting into a libel suit and also being unfair. Furthermore, there's no use hurting people who are already suffering.

**SUNDAY, NOVEMBER 5** | The *New York Times* has a front-page story today by Tom Wicker which calls Governor Reagan a liar. It calls the roll of newspapermen aboard the SS *Independence* who were told by Nofziger that two of the governor's staff were dropped because they were homosexuals.

**TUESDAY, NOVEMBER 7** | This is Election Day in several key cities where the race issue is uppermost, particularly Boston, Cleveland, and Gary, Indiana.

Ernest Cuneo came for lunch. The Reagan controversy is still ricocheting, and the *Washington Star* has an excellent editorial supporting me. The *Washington Post*, in contrast, has been silent. Kay Graham, on Sunday, said that *Newsweek* was going to pass up the story, but *Newsweek* came out with a piece today. *Time* had a reasonably good piece.

Reagan, last Saturday when challenged by newspapermen to comment on my press conference, remarked, "If Pearson's going to hang around California anymore, he better not spit in the street."

KGO, the ABC outlet in San Francisco, has been wanting me to come west this coming Saturday for their late interview program. I finally told them I would come a week from Saturday in answer to Reagan's challenge.

This is the fiftieth anniversary of the Bolshevik Revolution, and Luvie and I went to the Soviet embassy for their annual jamboree. There was a time when very few people went to the Soviet embassy, but today it was packed. Secretary Rusk even came . . . the first time that a secretary of state had set foot in the Soviet embassy in many years.

**THURSDAY, NOVEMBER 9** | Marvin Watson telephoned from the White House. I asked him if the president could come to the Big Brothers' dinner tonight in view of Hubert's being likely to be late. I thought for a time the president would come, but late in the evening, about 7:00 p.m., I called the White House only to find that he had flown to New York to attend the Jewish committee's dinner in honor of George Meany. This is a good indication that he is going to run again. There weren't many votes to be gained by appearing at our dinner.

King Hussein has been in Washington and New York talking a moderate line. He has made the amazing statement (for an Arab) that Israel must be recognized as a country which exists. The Algerians have sent word that they will not oppose Nasser if he takes a moderate line, and the reports from Cairo are that Nasser is definitely ready to go along with Hussein in admitting the existence of Israel; however, he's not willing to permit Israeli ships to pass through the canal.

The Senate yesterday slapped down the House on its redistricting bill, which postponed the one-man, one-vote formula until 1972. It was a heartwarming victory, led by Teddy Kennedy and Howard Baker of Tennessee (son-in-law of Ev Dirksen, who is the enemy of the one-man, one-vote Supreme Court decision).

**FRIDAY, NOVEMBER 10** | The Russians unveiled a huge new missile at their November 7 parade and have also launched a satellite which can fire missiles at the United States. McNamara has minimized the danger of the latter, but the drive has already started in Congress to combat Russia's new armament. It's going to be tough for Johnson to hold the line against an all-out anti-Russian drive in the United States, especially because Central Intelligence has just caught a Russian agent—or rather he's defected—which shows they have operated a very active espionage ring.

**SUNDAY, NOVEMBER 12** | We dined at the Harrimans'. Averell was franker than ever regarding the war and Lyndon's reluctance to explore peace. He said the president was leaning chiefly on Clark Clifford, Abe Fortas, and Walt Rostow, who are constantly telling him that hawks are in the majority in the United States and that he cannot retreat.

Averell went so far as to ask me to caution the president regarding advice from the above. I tried out on Averell the idea of sending Sen. Gene McCarthy, together with Fulbright and Bobby Kennedy, on a mission to Hanoi to negotiate peace. Averell seemed to think it was a good idea. He suggested, however, that McCarthy not be included. His taking the trip would look purely political. On the other hand, Fulbright, as chairman of the Senate Foreign Relations Committee, should go. He suggested also Sen. Bourke Hickenlooper of Iowa, the leading Republican on the committee.

We had a discussion about Bobby Kennedy, who is a great friend of Averell. Bobby's trouble, according to Averell, is that he has not been willing to treat Johnson as president. Averell said: "I've told him so. Ethel, of course, is worse than Bobby." Averell said he didn't consider Bobby the statesman that JFK was. "He's timid, shy, though he has the reputation of being brash."

The Reagan matter came up. Averell said that I had done a great service to the country in exposing Reagan. George Baker wondered why homosexuals in the California government were security risks. I told him that San Francisco Bay was one of the most strategic parts of the nation and that the governor of California handled all sorts of security information in cooperation with the army and navy.

Today was our thirty-first wedding anniversary. Despite Luvie's protests, Averell trotted out a bottle of vintage champagne.

Before dinner Tyler and Bess dropped around with the children. They had been out sailing all afternoon, and Bess came in barefoot. It's been a beautiful day. It doesn't seem like thirty-one years since we were married. I remember Tyler, age four, sitting on the floor of the big Santa Fe hotel lobby in Albuquerque, playing with a toy. His great-grandmother Butler had taken charge of him while Luvie and I were married in Bernalillo [New Mexico].

MONDAY, NOVEMBER 13 | Jim Jones telephoned from Air Force One on Saturday setting up an appointment at one thirty today with the president. At about one o'clock Marvin Watson called to say the president was running late.

The president explained that Ellsworth Bunker had so much information from Saigon that he was running an hour and a half late. "Some people say I talk, but I'm out to get the facts, and Bunker had so many facts that he was here much longer than I expected."

The president began by telling me about his trip to the various bases on Friday and Saturday. "First we went to Benning," he said, "where the general in charge said he had been through the Korean War and [the Battle of] Corregidor and that things were never as good as they are now. 'I'd like to think that I was responsible,' he told me, 'but I don't think that's the case. Our men are better. They receive better training, and they're doing a better job.'"

Lyndon then went on to describe his trip to the USS *Enterprise*, which had just returned from the Gulf of Tonkin. "They gave me a room as big as the room I have in the White House," he said. "I had about twenty people for dinner and got some enlisted men in.

"In the morning and at night I watched those planes fly in on the deck. They're just like clockwork. These fellows come in without ever making a mistake. There's a trigger mechanism that catches them and pulls them back when they land, and about one out of ten is supposed to miss the trigger. That's about par for the course; however, when I watched them, only one missed the trigger and had to fly around and come back again.

"I persuaded Dick Russell some time ago to let us take 12,000 draft rejects and train them. Now we've done 49,000, and the next batch will be 100,000. The results have been terrific. When a boy gets the right kind of food and fills out physically, it does something to his character. One officer told me that he had just come up with twelve officer candidates, all picked from the draft rejects.

"You ought to help Hubert," said the president. "Everybody wanted me to put him in, and now they're all picking on him. The ADA is picking on him. The liberals are all picking on him. Bobby picks on him most. Hubert hasn't changed his views. He's just as liberal as he always was."

Several times I tried to interrupt to ask questions, thinking that the president didn't have time enough to waste on me, but he was intent on talking to me, especially about Vietnam. He showed me some graphs given him by Ambassador Bunker, showing the progress in troop strength by the South Vietnamese army and the casualty rate of the North Vietnamese. One showed that the number of cadres placed in the villages by Bob Komer to carry on the work of rehabilitation had increased from 119 to 505 in one year by the third quarter of 1967.

I then suggested he appoint Fulbright and Bobby Kennedy, with possibly McCarthy, as envoys to North Vietnam to see if they could bring about peace. I said that while they probably couldn't succeed, this would at least bring unity in the United States and show Hanoi that we could be unified if and when such peace efforts failed.

The president said it wouldn't work, that he had asked Fulbright once to go to Saigon and he'd refused. He said he talked to Bobby about going to Saigon as ambassador, that Bobby toyed with the idea but finally backed out. I came back to the subject a second time, pointing out that a growing number of people were anxious for peace and that the president would be in a much better position if he explored the peace with some dove senators.

He replied that he'd had conversations with North Vietnam for two months. Beginning around August 25, a North Vietnamese person outside their government had been talking to American representatives, and during this time Johnson had not bombed Hanoi.

"The public hasn't noticed it, but I have been very careful not to bomb Hanoi. I have bombed around Haiphong but not Hanoi. I wanted to give a chance for these peace talks to succeed; however, they have now been broken off."

"There are nine thousand targets in North Vietnam," he said. "You can write that down. Of these five thousand are military targets. The military can bomb forty-five hundred targets without notifying anyone.

"There are five hundred strategic targets, and Washington wants to look at them carefully. Of these twenty-five have not yet been cleared. Of these twenty-five, one-half are in the Haiphong area, where Russian ships are tied up at the docks. This leaves about fifteen targets which are banned. These are around Ho Chi Minh's house in Hanoi. We are not going to bomb the ships as long as they are tied up at the docks. On one occasion the ships left the port, and we did bomb.

"Sixty-seven percent of the people, according to the polls, want the president to clean out Haiphong Harbor. I have asked the military, 'If you were president, would you bomb these docks?' They have said no."

"A lot of people think I listen just to Rusk and McNamara," continued the president. "Actually, I am seeing more people outside the government: Dean Acheson, Omar Bradley, Eisenhower, Arthur Dean, McGeorge Bundy, Bob Murphy (FDR's old ambassador), Averell Harriman, Clark Clifford, Abe Fortas, Douglas Dillon, Cabot Lodge, Maxwell Taylor, and George Ball."

This coincided with what Harriman told me last night—namely, that Clifford and Fortas were constantly advising the president and they had hawkish views. I told Lyndon that Clifford and Fortas were hawks, but he argued to the contrary.

"They are the finest advisors in Washington," he said. "Clark is sort of in the government because he reads all the intelligence reports. If you ever get in jail or have trouble with a woman, you call on Clark. He's got the keenest mind I know."

The president read me excerpts from Ellsworth Bunker's press conference that morning, and when Bunker was asked whether Westmoreland was going to be replaced, he denied it. As the president read this, he gave me a long look. Bunker was also asked about friction between Westmoreland and the Pentagon. There was another denial.

Then he picked up a memo from Secretary McNamara, which read on top, "Please get this to the president before he sees Drew Pearson." There was a point-by-point refutation of my column this morning. I had told Jack the president wouldn't like the column. He didn't and had taken some pains to have a refutation ready for me, though he took it good-naturedly.

Actually, McNamara's refutation admitted some of the points in the column. The chief denials referred to the reported crack of McNamara's regarding Westmoreland's tennis playing and the differences between the two.

"I think if Bus Wheeler were to drop dead tomorrow," said the president, "McNamara would recommend Westmoreland to become chairman of the Joint Chiefs of Staff. There are four men on whom we rely more than any others: McNamara; Creighton Abrams; Gen. Bruce Palmer, who took over in the Dominican Republic; and General Johnson. They are quiet-spoken. They don't throw their weight around. They stay out of politics."

I reminded the president that he had told me months ago that Westmoreland had to be relieved, that he had been there a long time and was getting tired. The president denied this emphatically.

The journalists' fraternity, Sigma Delta Chi, issued a report this morning panning Johnson's press relations. This was on LBJ's mind. He said it really boiled down to the fact that he hadn't always given sufficient notice to the press for his conferences. He noted, however, that he'd held an average of two news conferences a month, sometimes more. He read me a briefing which George Christian had given the press this morning regarding the general question of press conferences. The issue really turned on whether or not they had been given sufficient notice to attend.

"Just the day before yesterday, we had Ambassador Bunker and Westmoreland come here, and we offered them to the networks. They turned them down. The networks can supply time all morning for a hearing before Fulbright's Senate Committee, yet they didn't want to supply time to Bunker and Westmoreland. We had to arrange with *Meet the Press* to put Bunker on there. They talk a lot about television and how I have been reluctant on television, but when we ask them to cooperate, they run away."

Marvin Watson came in with a note that said the secretary of the treasury was waiting. I told the president I had two matters I wanted to talk to him about, one being a scandal in the Immigration Service, where I understood Ray Farrell was resigning, and the *Chicago Tribune* was revealing Thursday or Friday that several congressmen had been paid from $2,000 to $5,000 to pass private immigration bills. The president picked up the telephone and called Ramsey Clark, who was out. Then he got Ray Farrell and put the question to him. He leaned over so I could listen in and hear what Farrell said.

Farrell said that Jack Anderson had called him about this but he knew nothing about it. He knew of no congressman who had been paid and had nothing to do with private bills himself.

Lyndon recalled that when he was in Congress, it became a practice to introduce private bills to prevent deportations and that normally the Immigration Bureau would hold up a deportation until Congress had either acted or the session had adjourned.

Ramsey Clark telephoned and the president let me listen in. Ramsey said that Farrell had been in the Immigration Service for twenty years, had previously been associate director, and was regarded as an honest, though not very vigorous, executive.

I suspect that I'd acted on a bum steer. I also asked the president about the scandal involving the ex-governor of West Virginia, Barron, and his bagman, Don Brown. Jack thought LBJ knew all about this, but he didn't.

As I was about to leave, the president said to keep an eye on the British pound, that it was about to go off the gold standard. In that case, he said, prices would drop, and every other currency in Europe would also go off the gold standard. This would mean that the United States would be flooded with cheap goods, and we would have serious troubles with our monetary balance.

"You might write a paragraph," he said, "showing what Wilbur Mills and Jerry Ford are doing to the country. They entered a conspiracy to prevent new taxes until there was a cut in spending. I only asked for $4 billion in new taxes this year to help pay for the war and head off inflation, but they are adamant."

Toward the end of the talk Watson brought in the president's schedule for the next day. It called for a meeting with the premier of Japan between eleven thirty and twelve thirty. "We can't possibly finish that up in an hour," the president remarked. "And I don't see how we can get Linowitz in. Tell Rusk and McNamara that I want their staffs to stand by every Tuesday during the luncheon."

The president was highly critical of R. W. "Johnny" Apple, the *New York Times* correspondent. "He's a young fellow," he said. "He just dreams up these stories." I had always thought that Apple's reports were more penetrating than most from Saigon.

On the whole the president was in a more optimistic mood than on previous occasions. He had been through what I suspect was a very hectic morning, and I did not leave until 4:15 p.m. I think his trip to the military bases had buoyed him up. Also, Bunker's report was optimistic.

**TUESDAY, NOVEMBER 14** | I talked yesterday to Melvin Belli in San Francisco, who is still anxious to have me sue Reagan. I am skeptical. Harry Lerner thinks it would be a good service politically to keep Reagan on the ropes and under the constant fear of answering questions in deposition. Probably it would, but I've got a lot to do besides handle lawsuits.

Reagan held a press conference today in which he admitted the credibility gap and took back his threat to me not to hang around California or, if I did, to spit in the street. He called this an "injudicious remark, and I shouldn't have made it." This took some of the wind out of my sails, and I killed a column, written for Friday, in which it was announced I was coming to California Saturday to test out Reagan's warning.

Reagan tried his best to shut off questions about the homosexual matter and issued a blanket denial of the statement in my column that he had delayed for six months in firing two men involved. Apparently, he stood on the six months' delay portion of the column, but newspapermen quickly asked him whether the column was true except for the six months' delay. He stalled on this, and it was at this point that he said, "If there's a credibility gap, so be it."

Secretary McNamara has written me a letter, denying Monday's column that he has any differences with General Westmoreland. Jack insists that his facts are correct and that McNamara is covering up at the request of LBJ. I suspect Jack is correct. I have written a column regarding the tennis playing of General Westmoreland, which McNamara makes quite a bit about in his letter, emphasizing the importance of exercise. The basic differences between the two men that we reported earlier—over the number of combat troops needed and the building of the "McNamara Line"—we have not taken back.

SUNDAY, NOVEMBER 19 | Rep. Joe Resnick telephoned from New York. He got a pretty good reaction on his speech accusing Reagan of violating the Communications Act by filching the White House radiogram aboard the ss *Independence*.

Yesterday Liz Carpenter telephoned regarding the Lady Bird interview, a transcript of which I sent her on Friday. She made some rather inconsequential corrections and wanted to see the full text after it was written. I thought this was rather cheeky but didn't say so. Liz was in to see Luvie early in the week, wanting Luvie to use her influence to get Maxine Cheshire of the *Washington Post* fired. Maxine writes a society column every day and had said that young Robb, Lynda Bird's fiancé, would not be sent to Vietnam. I had always given credit to the Johnson administration for not using economic retaliation against newspapermen, as Herbert Hoover used to do. Apparently, I was wrong.

MONDAY, NOVEMBER 20 | I hope that the White House staff doesn't figure they can win the election with the new LBJ technique. He's got to do a lot more than look convincing at press conferences. One thing he must do is to organize the Democratic Party. [Bob] Kintner pointed out that it's in total disarray. There is no organization in New York, very little in Philadelphia, none in Ohio, none in California, and the Middle West will have to be kissed off politically. They need an organization similar to Mayor Daley's in Chicago.

Kintner and I reminisced briefly about the days when he was president (or executive vice president) of the ABC network. He said he had been with Ed Noble, chairman, and Bob Hinckley, his chief advisor, when I broadcast the news that Forrestal had gone off his rocker and rushed out of the house in Florida to report that the Russians were chasing him. Nobel, who didn't like my broadcast in the first place, was nonplussed. Bob Hinckley, who for years had pretended to be my friend and I think basically was, was critical. He was playing up to Nobel, to whom he owed a meal ticket.

TUESDAY, NOVEMBER 21 | General Westmoreland has been appearing before various congressional committees and spoke today before the National Press Club. Privately, he has urged Johnson to give him more men. He's not satisfied with a ceiling of 525,000. Publicly, he has played ball and not mentioned his differences with the president over this figure. LBJ has told him that an increase over 525,000 would mean calling out the reserves or increasing the draft.

**WEDNESDAY, NOVEMBER 22** | This is the fourth anniversary of Kennedy's assassination. The *Saturday Evening Post* has a new exposé by a young lawyer from Haverford who claims there were four bullets fired at Kennedy from three different directions in Dallas. I read the article rather hurriedly. It sounded convincing. Nevertheless, I continue to feel that the Warren Report is correct and that one man, Lee Oswald, killed John F. Kennedy.

Walter Lippmann had a piece in the *Washington Post* this morning regarding Kennedy, pointing out that his mistakes have now been forgotten and the memory is of his personality and his death. Walter touched on his mistakes, which were many. He dealt rather lightly, however, with the mistake of getting bogged down in Vietnam and his lack of courage regarding civil rights and aid to public schools. And of course, everyone has given a wide berth to the manner in which Kennedy made the White House a virtual house of prostitution.

**MONDAY, NOVEMBER 27** | Had an interesting talk with the editor at Simon & Schuster, Richard Kluger, who is handling our book, and Dan Green, the public relations man. They are both enthusiastic about the book. I hope their optimism is not misplaced. I always have my fingers crossed about books. I have helped to write four since *The Washington Merry-Go-Round*, which was the best seller of its time. None of them came up to it, primarily I suspect because *The Washington Merry-Go-Round* was new and the timing was right. Simon & Schuster says that it will take six months to publish this book. We got *The Washington Merry-Go-Round* out in two months, and Bobby Kennedy is having his new book put out by Doubleday-Doran in ninety days. It's a collection of speeches, for which he's getting $100,000.

I had a fairly long talk with Arthur Goldberg, who wants to resign. He told the president this last May, saying in effect: "I want to get out. I've had it." Arthur said the president replied with some flattering language, saying, "You're qualified to hold any position in government."

Arthur said there had been some cabinet sessions where he has found himself in vigorous disagreement. When they were discussing the bombing of oil depots, Arthur just got up and walked out. Later the president asked him why. "You know I don't go for this kind of stuff" was his reply.

Arthur asked me whether he should get out, and I told him I thought it would be a mistake to leave at this time. It would be a serious blow to LBJ politically. He told me he had gone to the court of appeals and been admitted to practice in New York. "They didn't make me write an essay on the Constitution and what it means, as they did Nixon," he said. "They were very nice and admitted me right away.

"Last weekend, with the General Assembly over and a resolution finally adopted for the Near East, Dorothy and I went to Virginia to visit our farm. We hadn't been there for a long time. I had barely got the windows open to air the place out when, thirty minutes after we arrived, I got a phone call that a Security Council meeting had been called on Cyprus. Ordinarily, I use the shuttle between New York and Washington, but I got Bob McNamara on the phone, and he got me a special plane. When war is threatening, I rate a private plane.

"I got to the Security Council one minute before eight—the first one there. The others straggled in. We debated all through the night. Finally, I got hold of Federenko and said: 'You don't want to be here all night, do you? Let's get together and work out a resolution.' We went into the UN restaurant and drafted a resolution which the council accepted.

"I got home a little after 3:30 a.m. About eight the phone rang. Dorothy answered it. It was the White House. She told the operator: 'My husband just got to bed at three thirty this morning. If it's the president calling, I'll wake him. If not, I want him to sleep.'

"It was Tom Johnson, assistant to George Christian, and later I called back to find that he wanted to ask me about the report that I was about to resign. The papers had picked up my being admitted to the New York Bar.'

"When I resign, I'll tell the president first, not the press," Arthur said.

About the Near East I expressed concern regarding the fact that the Russians were moving in so heavily, not only with arms experts to show the Egyptians how to use their weapons but also arming Somalia and obtaining port facilities at Aden in Yemen as the British move out.

Arthur expressed no great concern over this. "The more the Russians spread out, the more they have problems," he said. "When you get friends, you get problems. They can't control the Arabs. When Gromyko was here, he told me that the Syrians were impossible.

"The Russians have internal problems, just as we do. They have a lot of people against foreign aid and have to consider the home front first. There is nothing on our home front that can't be cured by the end of the Vietnam War."

Arthur was reasonably optimistic about the future of peace between Israel and the Arab states, though he said it would take a long time. The recent British resolution, he said, was actually drafted by the United States but given to the British to introduce because, first, they needed a buildup and, second, they were more neutral than we. The Arabs liked it, and so did the Israelis. It provided that the Israelis would withdraw to "secure and recognized borders." This gave them wide powers for negotiation. Arthur called attention to the fact that the Swedish diplomat was now arriving in the Near East to represent the UN to negotiate, that it would take some time but there would eventually be peace.

Personally, Arthur said he got along with the Arab leaders at the UN except for extremists such as the Syrians. The Egyptian ambassador always danced with Dorothy at UN receptions.

Arthur recalled that the Israeli crisis had come to a head last May, just at the time he had talked to Johnson about leaving. He said he had never worked so hard in his life, even when he was negotiating wage agreements for the steelworkers, but last May he couldn't leave because of the crisis. "How can you get me out of this?" Arthur asked.

He said, incidentally, that Rusk never disagreed with the president. He presented problems to him, which could be decided pro or con. He carefully outlined both sides so that the president could make the decision. On only one occasion did Rusk confide to Arthur that "confidentially, I think the president was wrong."

TUESDAY, NOVEMBER 28 | An editor of the *Jersey Journal* telephoned before breakfast to ask my reaction regarding the resignation of McNamara from the Defense Department. The *New York Times* and the *New York Daily News*, he said, were headlining the story. It began a hectic day.

The story made a fool out of me because only a short time ago Lyndon had told me how great he and McNamara were getting along, and McNamara had written me a letter expressing his confidence in Westmoreland and saying there were no real differences between them.

Jack came up with some good background. He is convinced that the president took the initiative in this and in effect fired McNamara or at least eased him out. I couldn't conceive that this was true in view of what the president has told me from time to time about McNamara.

I telephoned both Arthur Goldberg and Hubert Humphrey to get their reaction. Arthur had heard nothing about it and was as much in the dark as I. He said, "Would your advice still be the same to me in view of McNamara's departure?"

"No, I don't think it would," I said.

I asked Hubert point blank whether the initiative in McNamara's exit was taken by McNamara or by the president. Hubert caught his breath, then replied that McNamara had been thinking about leaving for some time. He had felt he was no longer an asset to the president. "He couldn't retire after the first part of the year. It would hurt the president," Hubert said. "So, he figured the best thing he could do was to retire now."

Hubert expressed some optimism about the chances of peace. He said the South Vietnamese were beginning to take the initiative in that direction. "The South Vietnamese," Hubert said, "have been working with the NLF [National Liberation Front] and with Hanoi. Remember that the Vietnamese are very closely related. Most of those in the South have families in the North."

"All this is our one ray of hope," Hubert continued. "Bunker feels it's desirable for these talks to proceed. Bunker is the most resourceful, reliable diplomat we've had out there. He engenders confidence. I thought his visit here was very helpful. He doesn't have to be on a short leash from the State Department. Johnson has confidence in him."

"Johnson is the one man who wants peace more than any other," Hubert continued. "Though most people don't realize it. He knows the war is a political liability. It's become an emotional problem with him. He worries about it all the time. It's bogged him down. He puts the great reliance on this ambassador. He found in Bunker a man of complete integrity, no bombast. Johnson is willing to put his trust in him.

"When I left Saigon, I told Ky, 'If your government fails, it will have an impact on the American people far more than you realize. There are forces at work in our country that could create great damage. It will so discourage people that they will withdraw into isolation.'"

"How did Ky take this advice?" I asked. "In good grace," Hubert replied.

We talked further, briefly, about the danger of isolation. Hubert had read some of my columns on this. "We can't retire into fortress America," he said.

**WEDNESDAY, NOVEMBER 29** | The town is still churning over McNamara. Tyler called and asked whether I had read Bobby Kennedy's two columns. He referred to columns by Joe Kraft and [by] Evans and Novak, both panning the president for firing McNamara. "I have known people to leak columns," Tyler said, "but never columns to two people on the same day."

Reston also had a column quite critical of Lyndon and ascribing the retirement to fear that some members of the Joint Chiefs of Staff might resign in protest against McNamara. Jack doesn't consider this conceivable. He does believe that the chief motive was LBJ's fear of attacks against McNamara from Capitol Hill. I recalled how Rep. Eddie Hebert had called me in just after Carl Vinson of Georgia resigned or retired from the chairmanship of the House Armed Services Committee, and when Mendel Rivers was about to take over, to urge me not to write about Mendel Rivers's alcoholism. Eddie said he thought he had Rivers under control, and if they could keep him under control, they could do a great job on trying to "get McNamara."

He went into some detail in describing McNamara as a no-good so-and-so who was ruining the defense of the United States. Actually, I think all that bothered Eddie was that McNamara wouldn't kowtow to Congress, wanted to abolish the reserves, and particularly wanted to curtail junketing by reservist congressmen.

I'm afraid McNamara's exit will start a train of other departures from the Johnson administration. More important, I'm afraid it will start an escalation of the war. Lyndon always did side with the top brass at the Pentagon, dating back to the days when he was a member of the House.

THURSDAY, NOVEMBER 30 | Lyndon held an off-the-record conference yesterday afternoon for Scotty Reston, Ben Bradlee of the *Post*, and other journalistic brass. The results were evident on the front pages this morning in a carefully documented series of stories telling how George Woods of the World Bank had approached McNamara last April, proposing that he take over the presidency of the bank, that Woods wanted to get out by January 1, and that McNamara was interested in the challenge the bank job afforded. I am sure the story was correct in part, though I still think that Lyndon could have easily argued McNamara into staying and that he put across the appointment in a rather sneaky manner. Jack and I did a radio broadcast in which I reported in effect that LBJ had surrendered to an alcoholic chairman of the House Armed Services Committee. This is probably too strong.

At Wednesday's National Security Council, just before adjournment, the president said: "In regard to those stories about Bob, those who have worked with him should know the facts. Last April 18 he was offered the presidency of the World Bank."

Johnson went on to explain how McNamara wanted to take the job but was willing to stay on. Then, referring to the animosity between McNamara and the Joint Chiefs of Staff, the president remarked, "Bus, I seem to remember that you have been at nearly all the meetings of the Security Council, but to make sure, I checked. It showed that out of fifty meetings, you were here forty-three times. Has anyone ever barred you from coming to see me?"

"No," replied General Wheeler. "You have all been here," continued the president. "You have all seen how the decisions were made. Has there been any animosity?" The answer was no.

In a conversation with Leonard Marks today, I pointed out that with McNamara's exit there would be other cabinet members leaving too and this would give the impression of men deserting a sinking ship.

"The president is about the best politician in Washington," I said. "He knows that McNamara's leaving will open a hole in the cabinet. He's a persuasive talker. He could have persuaded McNamara to stay on, but he didn't try.

"Maybe he isn't going to run again," said Leonard. This may be true. He has acted and talked like a candidate, but he could do what Harry Truman did in spring 1952, after Kefauver beat him in the New Hampshire primary and was about to beat him in the Wisconsin primary. Harry just bowed out.

FRIDAY, DECEMBER 1 | Long talk with Jack Valenti about McNamara's exit. The subject is still churning in Washington. Valenti said he called McNamara the morning he heard the news and that McNamara was all choked up. He described Johnson as a man who was always thinking about the other fellow and was trying to do things for McNamara, even at his own expense. Valenti said McNamara was almost emotional in his praise of the president.

This coincides with something Tyler told me when he went in to see Johnson to resign. He expected a hard time, especially inasmuch as Bill Moyers had been in just ahead of him to resign, but he said that Johnson was very considerate, talked over Tyler's plans, and said he thought he ought to get out of government.

I asked Jack why, in view of the idea that the president was trying to help McNamara, they didn't announce it right away and make such a mystery of it. We agreed that probably it was because of the president's passionate desire not to publish anything prematurely. Actually, the London *Financial Times* broke the story. Enrique [ambassador of Venezuela] told me that he had known the story forty-eight hours in advance. "What a pal," I said. "You hold out a scoop like that on me after all the piddling stuff you want me to write about Venezuela."

Valenti was concerned about the McCarthy race and observed that Eliot Janeway, whom I had seen working hard for Johnson at the Los Angeles convention, had now turned against him and was working for both McCarthy and Sen. Vance Hartke. There is a terrific battle going on between Hartke and Birch Bayh in Indiana, Valenti said. [He also said] that he had received my memorandum on Reagan's homosexuals but hadn't had time to read it. I told him the time for action had just about passed.

Valenti told me an interesting story about Bobby Kennedy, who has been preaching morality around the White House but is not exactly a paragon of virtue himself. When Bobby went to France for the visit with de Gaulle, Valenti happened to be there, and one of the motion picture companies, which was shooting in Paris, complained that their star, Candice Bergen, had disappeared from the set for four days. They finally traced her to a hotel on the East Bank where Bobby was staying. They tried to get her to come back to work, but she refused. In fact, she did not go back to work until after Bobby had left Paris. The hotel's majordomo said they were shacking up. Jack said that at the birthday dinner Bobby gave for Averell Harriman, Candice Bergen sat on Bobby's left, Marie Harriman on his right. Candice is the daughter of Edgar Bergen and beautiful.

**SATURDAY, DECEMBER 2** | Leonard Marks came to supper. We speculated as to who might become secretary of defense. We agreed that it might be Clark Clifford. He says that he sits in on sessions with Clifford and the president and that Clifford's approach is, after everyone else has discussed something, to say, "Now, Mr. President, if you're really serious about this, I'd like to be heard." Leonard thinks it's likely that Clifford was put in charge of reviewing Central Intelligence so that he would be steeped in foreign affairs and later could become secretary of state.

**WEDNESDAY, DECEMBER 6** | Flew back from North Carolina this morning. My column about Goldberg wanting to resign was published yesterday, and this morning the *New York Times* featured a story about his desire to resign and go with the law firm of Garrison, Rifkin, Wise et al. (Adlai Stevenson was associated with it before he was appointed to the UN.) The combination of my column and the *New York Times* story caused various speculative stories to appear on the news tickers. I tried to telephone Goldberg and finally got him about 5:00 p.m., hoping to tell him he should delay any resignation. I found he was in Washington, having come for a noon cabinet meeting and spending two hours with the president afterward. Apparently, he and the president had rubbed each other the wrong way. At one point the president told him that if he felt like resigning, he could resign today. Arthur said he thought this would be too precipitous following the McNamara resignation, so the date of December 20 was set for an official announcement, with the resignation to be effective February 1.

Leonard Marks telephoned earlier in the day to say that if Arthur would wait until spring, two openings on the Supreme Court would occur in April. When I told Arthur this, he said that he had heard the same thing, and I gathered that this had come from either the president or someone else in the White House.

Arthur also said he doubted there would be any openings in April since Supreme Court resignations usually occur at the end of the term, in June. At any rate the decision seems to be final. Arthur has been restless for a long time, and he's finally decided on a definite exit.

I called Leonard Marks back to report on this. I suspect that Leonard had called me at the instigation of the president. When I gave Leonard the report, he remarked that Johnson was becoming somewhat like Harry Truman when people talked about resigning. Truman had such great respect for the presidency that he resented it when anybody implied they were unwilling to serve under him, and he let them go immediately. I remember how abruptly he fired Henry Morganthau because I talked to Henry an hour or so after Truman had dropped him, when Henry had really not meant to resign but, rather, do a little dickering to strengthen his position. He had expressed some resentment at not being invited to go to the Potsdam Conference, and Truman accepted his resignation hardly before he got his squawk out of his mouth.

Leonard said that in a recent meeting of the National Security Council, Johnson had made a brief speech saying he had read that some members of the Joint Chiefs of Staff were thinking about resigning and that if they had this in mind, now was the time for them to do so. No one spoke up.

I called the chief justice to tell him about the conversation with Arthur Goldberg, inasmuch as the chief had asked me a year ago to use what influence I had to get him [Goldberg] back on the Court. The chief was puzzled regarding the statement that there would be two openings on the Court in April. He said he didn't know of any in the offing then or at any other time.

**SATURDAY, DECEMBER 9** | The most significant development of the week, I think, was Nixon's speech yesterday, in which he said that the race problem in the United States was more serious than the war in Vietnam. He implied that we should forget about the war and concentrate on the problems of race in the big cities. This is significant because in the past it was Nixon who was the No. 1 hawk of the Republican Party. If he's going to run as a dove and for the improvement of race relations, he'll get a lot of liberal support.

**MONDAY, DECEMBER 11** | Pat Brown is in Washington today for luncheon with Bobby Kennedy. He telephoned me afterward. I told him to be careful about cozying up to Bobby, that there was tremendous bitterness in the White House toward Bobby and he might get caught in the middle. I didn't tell Pat, but I remember vividly in 1960 at the Los Angeles convention when he was accused of being in the middle between Adlai Stevenson and Kennedy. He lost friends in both camps.

Pat said the political climate in California is not good so far as Johnson is concerned; however, Pat said that tomorrow he was going to announce behind Tom Lynch as the favorite son from California and a stand-in for Johnson.

Pat said George Wallace was having a hard time collecting enough signatures to get himself on a third-party ballot for the California primary. He was hesitant about advising me as to whether I should file a suit against Reagan. I also talked to Harry Lerner on the telephone, who had changed his mind and thought I should file against Reagan. He said that Reagan had rebuilt some of his fences and had done extremely well at Yale, even though the Yale boys were laying for him. He came out smelling like a rose.

**SUNDAY, DECEMBER 17** | Leonard told me yesterday the State Department had been in touch with the Vietcong but the latter were unwilling to talk peace. There was a meeting of the president, the secretary of state, George Christian, the Pentagon, and Leonard, at which it was decided to issue a story regarding the talks. The job was turned over to Rusk, who leaked it to Chalmers Roberts. He wrote a story in the *Washington Post* which had the effect of burying the whole business.

**MONDAY, DECEMBER 18** | Prime Minister Henry Holt of Australia has drowned, lost while skindiving off the Tasmanian Channel. The amazing thing is that they would allow him to go skindiving with only one companion. The Tasmanian Channel is one of the roughest waters around Australia, and skindiving is a sport which can very easily lead to trouble if there is not someone else along. Your gear can get tangled, or you can get in trouble with a shark or get hallucinations under water. I have never done any skindiving, but I did cross the Tasmanian Sea back in the days of the Australian Chautauquas. I got on the boat in Melbourne and confidently reserved a table. The steward accepted the reservation good-naturedly and with a look on his face which later I readily understood. He knew that very few people would be down to dinner. I spent most of the night flat on my back in my bunk, sick as a dog. We got to Tasmania the next morning, and only then did I crawl.

**THURSDAY, DECEMBER 19** | LBJ is flying to Australia for the Holt funeral.

We dined with Agnes. Dobrynin was to have been there but was called to New York for a Security Council debate to replace the Soviet ambassador to the UN. At the dinner were the Joe Krafts and the Ben Bradlees. Kraft said he had talked to Henry Slote, Rockefeller's press relations man, about the inquiry by newsmen as to whether Mrs. Slote was bedding down with the governor. Slote had replied, "No comment." He told Joe, however, that he figured that it was the only comment he could make and that it was absolutely untrue.

Ben Bradlee suggests that maybe Nixon is spreading the story to keep Nelson from running. Nelson has had a couple of other flings, and this fits into the pattern of the past.

**WEDNESDAY, DECEMBER 20** | Marcus Cohn came to lunch. Marcus confided that his firm did some finagling with the FCC to get LBJ's exclusive television license in Austin. I recall that I wrote something about it at the time only to have Marcus and Leonard vigorously deny that what I wrote was true.

**THURSDAY, DECEMBER 21** | The highlight of Johnson's TV interview, aired just before he left for Australia, was that it would be profitable for South Vietnam to sit down and talk with the National Liberation Front. Today, as he left for Australia, President Thieu issued a blunt statement that he was against talking to the National Liberation Front. Later, when he got to Australia, Thieu and Johnson had a two-hour session, after which they issued a joint communiqué, glossing over their differences; however, reading between the lines, it was easy to see that the differences had not been settled.

Leonard Marks tells me that the United States has already talked to the NLF. This no doubt was why Johnson was trying to put Thieu on the spot by publicly urging him to talk. It all adds up to the fact that we are more anxious for peace than are the South Vietnamese leaders. They know that once there is peace they are out of power.

FRIDAY, DECEMBER 22 | Spent part of yesterday on the telephone to Jackson, Mississippi, where the twenty-two Negroes elected to county jobs are having trouble getting bonded. If they don't get bonded by December 31, they lose their jobs. It looks as if there was a conspiracy by local insurance companies, with a certain amount of connivance by their northern offices, to prevent the Negroes from taking office. I called two of the executives in Philadelphia and Baltimore and found them more cooperative than I had thought; however, there is no question that tremendous obstacles have been put in the path of these Negro officeholders, in contrast to routine bonds given white officeholders in the past.

SATURDAY, DECEMBER 23 | Robert Mayhieu, PR man for Howard Hughes, called me back today, in reply to a query, to confirm that Don Nixon had defaulted on the $205,000 loan from Howard Hughes and had given the Hughes Tool Company the lot in Whittier which was put up for collateral. It's interesting that the newspapers never did follow up [on] what became of the Nixon lot or what was to happen to the $65,000 in cash that W. Alton Jones had in his briefcase when his plane crashed en route to see Ike in Palm Springs.

TUESDAY, DECEMBER 26 | The president flew back to Texas around noon today after celebrating the first Christmas he has ever spent in the White House. Just before he left, I told George Christian I wanted to get some of the human interest details of the trip around the world, plus the inside on the reported peace talks. He suggested Walt Rostow or Bill Bundy. I chose the latter, and he called me back in minutes. I went to see him. He talked openly about the trip, though he didn't give much regarding the peace talks.

Unquestionably, it was a tour de force and certainly proved that the president was not suffering from his old heart attack. Bill said that the most inspiring part of the visit was in Canberra, where LBJ sat opposite the Australian cabinet and told them in very friendly, frank, and rather appealing terms how much he thought of Henry Holt and how much the ties between the United States and Australia meant to him and to the American people. The Australian cabinet was deeply impressed.

LBJ then had a series of conferences which ran all day, beginning with the New Zealand prime minister at 9:30 a.m. and including C. K. Yen [Yen

Chia-kan] and the vice president of Nationalist China; the finance minister of Cambodia; the prime minister of Thailand; Thanom Kittikachorn, the finance minister of Laos; and E. G. Whitlan, the leader of the Australian Labor Party, the opposition, who has not been too keen about the war. He also called on Lord Casey, who used to be ambassador in Washington.

Lyndon also had a session with President Park of South Korea and had dinner with President Thieu of South Vietnam and other members of Thieu's staff and cabinet. At 10:00 p.m. he saw President Marcos of the Philippines, and at 11:15 he went to bed, at which time he had been up for about twenty-four hours. He also saw Foreign Minister Malik of Indonesia and Prime Minister Lee of Singapore, with whom he has developed friendly relations, and Prime Minister Razak of Malaysia. He was up at 6:15 a.m. to catch his plane, which left at seven forty-five to Melbourne, where he called upon Mrs. Holt at Government House, also on the new prime minister and Sir Henry Bolte at Victoria House (he represents the Crown) and on Sir Robert Menzies, the former prime minister. Then he added the memorial service for Holt and afterward spent three-quarters of an hour with UK prime minister Harold Wilson while the others were at lunch.

Bill said that the lineup in the front pews at the memorial services was most interesting. In the first pew were Australian officials; in the second pew, the president on the right and Harold Wilson on the left. In between them were the president of the Philippines, the president of Korea, and the president of South Vietnam.

Behind them, in the third pew, were the prime ministers of various other Asian countries. It was significant of how our ties had changed from West to East in recent years.

The president flew to Korat, Thailand, from Australia, arriving at about 10:00 p.m., where he had an hour and a half at the officers' club with U.S. officers. He talked to them until after midnight, which was 3:00 a.m. Melbourne time, and he had been up since six fifteen Melbourne time. When he went to bed, he remarked to Bundy, "I've never been so tired in my life."

Nevertheless, he was up at five thirty to speak before the enlisted men at the base, took off at six thirty for Cam Ranh Bay in South Vietnam, where he spoke again, conferring with the commanders for twenty minutes, then reviewing troops, going through the hospital with the senior commanders, and leaving at 10:20 a.m. Among other things he gave the Medal of Freedom to Ellsworth Bunker. I gathered it was the first time it had been given to a civilian.

Bundy said they had some trouble working out their appointment with the pope due to a couple of factors. One was that the presidential plane was equipped to put the entire Strategic Air Command into battle within eighteen seconds but was not equipped to communicate with any U.S. embassies. This had to be done through the State Department in Washington, and at times this was difficult; also, the State Department high-up officials were asleep. As a result, for four hours while flying over India, they were not able to communicate with the U.S. embassy in Karachi or New Delhi or Rome. They also had to work out a schedule with the pope which would not conflict with his Christmas Eve message. Bill was sensitive about this because there has been a lot of criticism that the president kept the press waiting—and the public in suspense—as to whether he was or was not going to Rome.

In Karachi he had a good talk with Ayub Khan, who insisted on coming to the airport to see him; and in Rome, a good talk with President Saragat and Prime Minister Moro before he saw the pope. Bill would not tell me anything about the session between the president and the pope, which led to my feeling that subsequent stories were correct that they had not got on very well and that there had been something of a brush between them regarding a bombing pause which the pope very much wants.

Bill was also sketchy about the various peace rumors, though he did confirm that there had been what was called "Operation Marigold"—talks between us and Hanoi. They had taken place via the Poles in Warsaw. The Russians were also in on it. They were broken off abruptly by North Vietnam despite the fact that the Poles and the Russians tried to keep them going.

Bill said the president got less rest than usual because he was not flying on the regular Air Force One but on a backup plane which did not have the special presidential cabin. This cabin was probably like the one on which we traveled to Bolivia, which had a presidential cabin astride the aisle so that when the crew wanted to pass back and forth, they had to walk through the president's bedroom. Bill said that at one point the president stuck his head out from between the curtains to give some additional instructions on the trip.

I contrasted in my mind the difference between George Washington's Farewell Address September 19, 1796, urging the United States to stay out of entangling alliances, with this round-the-world trip by the president of the United States—the first ever taken by a president—in which during four and a half days he cemented new alliances with Asia. Times have certainly changed in 171 years.

**WEDNESDAY, DECEMBER 27** | They took me to the hospital with a bleeding ulcer at noon today. I managed to transcribe the radio broadcast first, inasmuch as Jack is in Florida. This makes the fourth trip to the hospital for me in approximately three years.

The court of appeals handed down a Christmas present to us just before I left for the hospital—namely, a unanimous decision in the Liberty Lobby case deciding that we had not violated any constitutional safeguards for privacy when we published the Liberty Lobby papers.

**THURSDAY, DECEMBER 28** | It is snowing and raining. With LBJ at the ranch, Washington is relatively quiet. Senator Bartlett of Alaska is in the room next to me with a heart condition. He dropped in to see me. I did not remind him that he had testified against me in a Fairbanks, Alaska, libel suit, substantiating the defendant's claim that I was the "garbage man of the fourth estate." I had always written favorably about him.

We talked briefly about the state of the world, including the candidacy of Ernest Gruening, whom we both thought at the age of eighty should not run again. "However," said Bartlett, "nobody can tell him so."

Perhaps I, at the age of seventy, should be bowing out and nobody is willing to tell me so.

**SATURDAY, DECEMBER 30** | I finally persuaded Dr. Lawn Thompson to let me go out to the farm on the condition that I take life easy out there and really rest. The farm is snowbound, and the weather is bleak; however, it's beautiful.

# 1968

## ANNALS

On January 30 the North Vietnamese/Vietcong Tet Offensive began. By the time it was over, they had been defeated militarily but had won politically. Only a few months earlier Gen. William Westmoreland, the U.S. commander in Vietnam, told the National Press Club that the enemy could not mount another offensive.

By the end of the year the majority of Americans viewed the war as a mistake. CBS News anchor Walter Cronkite pessimistically concluded that the war was a stalemate. Following Cronkite's broadcast, President Johnson reportedly said, "If I've lost Cronkite, I've lost Middle America."

The president's approval ratings dropped, along with support for the war. In the New Hampshire Democratic primary, he defeated "peace" candidate Sen. Eugene McCarthy by 49 to 42 percent, but the media treated it as a defeat for Johnson. With the entry of Sen. Robert F. Kennedy into the race, Johnson announced on March 31 that he would not run for reelection. Vice President Hubert Humphrey entered the race with the support of most of the Democratic establishment.

On April 4 Dr. Martin Luther King Jr. was assassinated in Memphis. This precipitated race riots in 110 U.S. cities. This was in addition to the antiwar protests in the United States. Similar protests spread to Spain. In France protesters effectively shut down the country for the month of May.

In Czechoslovakia, twenty years after the Communists took control, First Secretary Alexander Dubček pursued liberal reforms, ushering in the "Prague Spring." The Soviet Union, with other members of the Warsaw Pact, invaded Czechoslovakia to make it clear that military force would be used to prevent the end of communism in any Soviet bloc country. This became known as the "Brezhnev Doctrine."

In June, Robert Kennedy was shot and killed by Sirhan Sirhan the night of Kennedy's victorious California Democratic primary election.

At the Democratic National Convention that summer Humphrey received the presidential nomination, with huge protest demonstrations going on outside.

In November, Richard Nixon narrowly won the presidency, climaxing one of the greatest political comebacks in U.S. history. (Nixon's vote total, 31,770,237; Humphrey's, 31,270,533.)

—Ed.

# THE DIARY

SUNDAY, JANUARY 7 | Today nephew Drew, who is just back from Vietnam, came for a visit. He's now working for ABC and has been in Vietnam three years.

He is discouraged. South Vietnamese top officials don't want the war to end. They know they would be kicked out of office after American troops withdraw. Meanwhile, they refuse to put across the reforms essential to combat communism. For instance, they have a land reform bill which has passed but is not being implemented. It permits each person to retain 250 acres of land, which would mean a family of four could keep about a thousand acres. There are vast areas owned by the Catholic and Buddhist churches, also by top officials, which have not been broken up under the Land Reform Act. When peasants don't own their own land, they're not willing to fight for it.

The pacification program is not progressing. Supplies aren't being used. There are some good leaders in the villages, but they are not being used. Army commanders sidetrack the supplies, sometimes selling them. They also block cooperation. In general the Vietnamese believe in taking men from traditional schools, the *lycées* established by the French, to handle pacification. The Vietcong, on the other hand, take qualified, though unschooled, men who know their business.

Anti-Americanism is increasing. Any plebiscite of the people would go strongly against us.

Drew thinks North Vietnam was smart not to put out genuine peace feelers. The minister of foreign affairs, in a reception, made a promising statement indicating there could be peace talks if bombing were stopped. He thinks the North Vietnamese have realized they can put us on the spot by genuinely talking peace for the reason that neither South Vietnam nor the Johnson administration really want it.

I asked about Westmoreland and the report to Johnson that things were better. "What he means," Drew explained, "was that U.S. supplies are moving more orderly, and troops are in a better position to fight. He's not talking about the minds of the Vietnamese people, which haven't changed. There are just about as many Vietcong as before, and they occupy just about as much of the country."

Drew made the point that the problem in Thailand is just the same as the problem in South Vietnam, one of land reform; just the same as in South America, Africa, Detroit, and Alabama—lifting up the poor. Taiwan and South Korea have done amazing jobs in this direction. The British in Malaysia have also done a good job, but the difference between Malaysia and South Vietnam is that the British were running the country when they made the reforms and they could give orders.

**WEDNESDAY, JANUARY 10** | Spent the morning at the hospital getting X-rays, which turned out to be quite satisfactory. Apparently, the ulcer has healed.

Chester Bowles has arrived in Cambodia and apparently is having productive talks with Prince Sihanouk to head off hot pursuit across the Cambodian border. There was some indication that this might have brought the Chinese into the war. Chet was certainly the right man to pick for this job. He was a dedicated and self-effacing ambassador to India, where he's taken a lot of punishment.

It's interesting that the *St. Louis Post-Dispatch*, though canceling my column, ran the column on Bowles yesterday. It was the only one they've run in months.

Ralph Nader came by with some interesting data regarding a row inside the new Department of Transportation and some documentation that the automobile companies, particularly General Motors, have the inside track at the White House and the Justice Department.

**THURSDAY, JANUARY 11** | Spent a good part of the evening talking to Averell [Harriman] privately. He thinks Lyndon is doing a better job on the domestic front than FDR. "He speaks about education as one of his greatest achievements," Averell said, "but I think his biggest job is antipoverty. Here he has really pioneered. We started it in New York when I was governor. We took the figure of $2,000 as the point where the poverty mark began. Today it's

$3,000. We started a study of how many there were, what they needed, and how they got that way. The study had been in progress for two years when Rockefeller came in and lopped it off. We found that in some slum areas, kids were being promoted in school automatically, never making any real progress but promoted by their teachers just to get them out of the way. And we found that through the system of welfare checks, men were drifting away from their families."

Averell described the seniority system as one of the worst evils of Congress. I said that Lyndon had a chance, when Congress convened in January 1965, to get rid of the seniority system by taking a stand against the Mississippi congressmen when they were challenged by the Mississippi Freedom Democrats. The latter had every constitutional right to be seated, and Lyndon had a chance to side with them and knock out seniority. At that time he had the votes. Now he doesn't.

Averell agreed but said that Lyndon had accomplished so much in that one year that it was worth it. "But," I said, "he should have set a precedent, not merely for himself but for his successors, by breaking up the rotten boroughs of the solid South."

He said Walter Heller, former chairman of the Board of Economic Advisors, had just come back from Greece, where he had secured the release of Andreas Papandreou to teach at the University of Minnesota. Walter told Averell, "They had a little trouble with him at the University of California, but sentiment was so overwhelming with the University of Minnesota faculty that we had to take him back."

THURSDAY, JANUARY 18 | NEW ORLEANS—I lunched with Bill Helis, Dr. Alton Oxner, the first man who really called attention to the link between lung cancer and cigarettes, and old friend Jimmy Noe. Noe was a candidate for governor when he helped me expose the Huey Long gang. It put him in the governor's chair and Governor Leche behind bars. Jimmy reminded me that he still owes me $5,000 on that oil investment of some years ago. I'll be glad to get it—if and when it comes.

I spoke in Baton Rouge and afterward had a brief but interesting session with Governor McKeithen at the Governor's Palace. It's quite a nice new job, quite different from the old mansion, where I spent a weekend with Earl Long when we dedicated the Merci Train boxcar. [In 1949 a train of forty-nine boxcars filled with gifts for the American people arrived in New York.

The cars were distributed to all (then) forty-eight states and the District of Columbia. Six million French citizens had donated the gifts in gratitude for the 1948 Friendship Train, which delivered over 250 railroad cars of food and relief supplies from American citizens. Drew Pearson first proposed the idea, then led the citizen campaign to create the Friendship Train.]

FRIDAY, JANUARY 19 | WASHINGTON DC—We went to dinner at Franklin Roosevelt Jr.'s. The chief subject of conversation was Clark Clifford. I had first known him as a naval aide to Stuart Symington when Stuart was assistant secretary of defense for air. Ben Bradlee of the *Post* said he got out various pictures of Clifford for use in the paper tomorrow morning, and they were so handsome that it looked as if Clark had a marcel wave. He decided it wasn't fair to use them.

According to Eunice Shriver: "Joan [Gardner] said that the president had been rather petty with FDR Jr. when he retired as undersecretary of commerce. He received Franklin in his bathroom while brushing his teeth and talked to him out of the corner of his mouth without taking the toothbrush out.

"'What's the matter with you fellows?' Johnson said. 'I fix you up with good jobs—you and John Connally—and then you get a hard-on to be governor.'"

FDR Jr. hates cuss words, and he had reported that almost every other word the president spoke was profanity. He never got a note of thanks.

The son of Rose Merriam was at the dinner. He brought back a lot of memories, though I didn't tell him so. His mother was the aunt of Wallis Simpson, now the duchess of Windsor. I used to go around to Rose's house to pick up Wally to take her out to dinner occasionally. I could easily understand why the king of England fell in love with her.

WEDNESDAY, JANUARY 24 | The seizure of the American ship USS *Pueblo* is a lot more important . . . than I had realized. It was an electronics ship, about sixty miles off the Korean coast, listening in on Communist messages and spotting Russian submarines. Its seizure puts the United States in a tough position because a vigorous retaliatory action by us might bring the Chinese into the war in Vietnam and into North Korea, where we are still enjoying only a precarious truce fifteen years after Ike brought "peace" to Korea.

Apparently, the ship's commander thought the North Koreans were just spoofing him when they brought some patrol boats around him. He did not call for help, and later he did not scuttle his ship. The electronic gear aboard was among the most secret.

Some of the junior officers in the Pentagon want us to go out and seize Russian trawlers, also equipped with electronic gear, off the American coast. Johnson has been meeting all day to decide what to do.

I have the feeling that the war has reached a crucial point and we may be in for serious escalation. Premier Kim Il Sung of North Korea has been advocating retaliation against the United States all over the world and has instigated six hundred incidents in the past year. The seizure of the *Pueblo* was a climax. Yet American naval officers were so complacent that they didn't send for help and didn't have an escort vessel along to guard this spy ship.

This afternoon the North Koreans refused to give up the ship, and the Russians have refused to lend their good offices to this end.

THURSDAY, JANUARY 25 | A tense day. Arthur Goldberg had breakfast with the president and then went to New York to call for a special session of the Security Council. This shows that the president is not reacting to the hawks on the Hill. I was afraid he might pop off in a hurry.

The North Koreans apparently have some kind of confession out of Commander [Lloyd M.] Bucher. It was read over the air, and although his wife denied it was his voice, obviously it was the voice of an American who was half-ashamed of himself reading a statement in very low key. He had probably been tortured or doped.

Luvie and I went to the White House for dinner in honor of the vice president, Speaker McCormack, and the chief justice. It used to be that the White House held three dinners, one each for the vice president of the Senate, the speaker of the House of Representatives, and for the Supreme Court with the judiciary. They were small dinners, with people invited to come to a reception later. Both Kennedy and Johnson, however, have rolled the three into one, and it makes for a crush. There were 190 people present, with little tables even in the Blue Room. The day of the state dinner around a horseshoe table in the White House apparently is gone forever.

We arrived only five minutes late. True, we did have to stand in line in the East Room for about twenty minutes, during which Rep. Mendel Rivers walked past me a couple of times and stood beside me for about thirty seconds, trying to stare me down. I refused to look at him, in fact pretended I didn't know who he was. At first I didn't. Then it dawned on me that the white-maned solon who was trying to pick a fight with me must be Rivers. My other old friend and critic Speaker McCormack was very gracious, and we exchanged pleasantries as I went through the line. His wife, who was seated in the receiving line—she's a semi-invalid—remarked something about "I'm not sure I like that name" when John introduced me.

Nina Warren looked very attractive in a white gown with pearls sewed around the [collar]. The chief, Luvie thought, looked tired. He said he had to go back and work for an hour after the party was over and would have to work two hours in the morning before the Court convened.

I sat at dinner once removed from George Meany on the left and Clark Clifford on the right. My first column on Clark had come out that morning and was rather critical. For a long time George Meany has been calling me a liar, and I have reciprocated; however, we got on pretty well.

Clark lived up to my column regarding his frugal diet by ordering milk. He eschewed all wine. I omitted the cocktail but didn't ignore the wine. George Meany gave a little sermon on wine. He noted with glee that no French wine was being served and went on to expound on the value of American wine, which apparently he knows something about.

Meany became eloquent over the problem of training unskilled youth. "Training is more important than unions, Drew," he said. "You may be surprised to hear me say that, but man has to have some training in life. We have been doing our best to help the training of unskilled labor in Africa. We sent a few dozen secondhand sewing machines to Kenya, together with a couple of representatives from the International Ladies' Garment Workers' [Union], and they have taught people to sew. If you can get the Africans able to work at a skill, you can revitalize the entire continent."

I was a little surprised at Meany's cordiality. In Florida about a year ago he excoriated me for saying that the AFL had received money from Central Intelligence for some of its operations overseas. Later the CIA admitted this.

I had a brief talk with Hubert [Humphrey] about the Korean crisis. He described it as very dangerous and [that it] could explode into war. The president, he said, spent the whole day "meditating." I asked Hubert whether this meant meditation by himself. Hubert explained it was a process of conferring and considering. "They'll strip the ship [the *Pueblo*]," Hubert said, "and after that they'll probably release it." He confirmed that a lot of secret electronic equipment undoubtedly had been captured.

"The president spent all day yesterday getting advice from the National Security Council," Hubert said, "asking each man for his advice. He has been very restrained. You've got to show some humility in this, the same humility that Khrushchev showed in the Cuban missile crisis. A big power can afford to be patient. We can't go off half-cocked."

There was a certain tenseness about the dinner, an uneasy feeling on the part of the guests. This was not true, however, of the president. He seemed relaxed and made a brilliant toast in tribute to the three branches of government and the importance of unity. When I went through the receiving line, he was his usual cordial self and said he'd been trying to get hold of me for a visit. He did call but obviously doesn't have time for a visit now. As he entered the East Room, there was applause from the assembled guests, which I have never heard before. And there was a lot after the toast.

Hubert gave a brilliant reply to the president's toast, one of the best speeches I've heard him give. He referred to the lonely man in the White House and to the stress and strain that he knew the president was under at this time. The chief also replied to the president's toast, straight from the heart.

Clark Clifford was cordial but restrained in his conversation. He expressed relief at getting two and a half hours of Senate [confirmation] hearings behind him. Incidentally, he was unanimously approved.

Bob McNamara was at the dinner, looking fit, though Arthur had said he looked tired and harassed the week before. Dean Rusk was the only top cabinet member absent. Leonard says he has been talking about getting out, and Leonard asked me whom his successor should be. I am sure he won't leave now.

After dinner Gordon McRae put on a skit. It was a bedroom scene, and for the first time in history a four-poster bed was in the East Room. Bess explained it was not the Lincoln bed. The acting, though good, fell like a wet rag on the group, which didn't know exactly what the next day would bring in the North Pacific.

FRIDAY, JANUARY 26 | Talked with the vice president on the phone about the Korean crisis. He emphasized that the Russians couldn't afford to have their communications ships picked up by small powers and that they had as much to lose as we in this argument. He said Kuznetsov had given a cold shoulder to Tommy Thompson's call, probably because the Russians hadn't made up their minds yet what to do. They always reacted negatively when taken by surprise. Premier Kosygin was en route to India, Hubert said, and he was the chief moderating force inside the Kremlin.

One of the advantages of these eavesdropping ships, Hubert pointed out, was that the two superpowers could know what each other was doing. This was important. If they didn't know, then the element of surprise and suspicion crept in. This was one reason for the hotline between Moscow and Washington.

He thinks the tough policy of the North Koreans in the last few days has been caused by the South Koreans getting ready to send more troops to South Vietnam. Premier Kim of North Korea is practicing what he preaches regarding the idea of diversionary trouble for the United States.

I talked with George Christian, who said Johnson had two objectives: (1) the return of the men and the ship; (2) discussion at the UN. At breakfast yesterday Arthur Goldberg had pointed out that the UN had long had a major interest in Korea and it was only natural for it to discuss the matter.

The UN Security Council opened late this afternoon, with Arthur making a comprehensive presentation. He showed conclusively that the *Pueblo* was located outside the twelve-mile zone. He did this with charts and minute citations of North Korea's own messages, which we had monitored.

The Russian, a new man named Morozov, answered with statements which will only rile the American public and I am sure are not true. He cited something like fifty-two thousand incidents inspired by the United States and South Korea across the 38th parallel. It's obvious that the Kremlin is following a super-hard line.

SATURDAY, JANUARY 27 | Senator Percy of Illinois was at the dinner [on January 25, hosted by the Goussans]. We had an interesting conversation. Kay Raley has been telling me that he is a great guy, and I'm beginning to think that he's not as bad as I thought he was.

He talked about Big Brothers in an obvious attempt to soften me up. He also talked rather intelligently about Henry Ford II being drafted to take over adult training to put unskilled Negroes and others to work. Percy thinks young Ford has a lot on the ball and can do a great job. I have long thought Ford was a step above some of the rest of the family.

TUESDAY, JANUARY 30 | Walt Rostow called from the White House to say the president had never received from the Joint Chiefs of Staff any proposal to bomb the USS *Pueblo* as it lay in Wonsan Harbor. Otherwise, Walt referred to my column of yesterday as accurate and helpful.

He is right. I didn't say the proposal came from the Joint Chiefs of Staff, however. It was proposed by some of their subordinates. I presume that it never got beyond the Joint Chiefs.

Had an interesting talk with Sargent Shriver. After he had put up a battle in Congress to keep his antipoverty money and won the battle, the president is whittling it down and transferring $135 million over to a new project, the "Urban Coalition" under Henry Ford, to train adult males. Ford is a close friend of the president. Shriver talked philosophically about it, though you could tell he was hurt.

The idea of having business train the unemployed is not new, he said. "I suggested two years ago that we have a $3 billion program with business doing the training. The only question in this case is whether business can get started fast enough to produce between now and July. It's a short time. Will business be able to get the paperwork done that the government requires, or will the government suspend it? The president is taking a risk. He can't afford failure this summer.

"We thought we had scored a victory with Congress. We were the only agency which persuaded Congress to vote more money than last year, but we got no response from the White House. It was as if we'd done something against the rules."

I told him I had called a friend at the White House—not the president—and urged that they have a ceremony at the time the bill was signed, but I got a blank reaction.

"The bill was signed," Sarge said, "when the Mental Retardation Bill was signed. They had quite a ceremony. It was not nearly as important, though it was a good bill. But they invited me down and had quite a show."

"What did the president think of your victory?" I asked.

"I don't know. I was going to ask you," he replied. "I have known Henry Ford for twenty-eight years or so," said Shriver. "He's a good man, but I don't know whether he is going to be able to get this done on time or not."

I asked if he had seen Bobby's statement today in which he said that "there were no foreseeable conditions" under which he would run for president against Johnson. He had not. "There is no question that Bobby was considering it," Shriver added. "He had people calling up around the country taking soundings. Frank Mankiewicz, Bobby's press secretary, used to work for me. When someone calls me from Denver saying that Bobby's people have called him to sound him out, you can't get away from the facts."

I asked whether he thought the feud between Bobby and the president could ever be resolved. "I don't know," he said. "I got into that buzz saw just a week or so after President Kennedy was assassinated. I decided I couldn't do anything about it. I have stayed out ever since. President Johnson's always been cordial and friendly to me."

The president yesterday submitted a budget to Congress of $186 billion, the highest in history. He toned down the Great Society program drastically, in fact had not mentioned it. He also said that war costs might go even higher.

**WEDNESDAY, JANUARY 31** | One day after the start of the Chinese New Year, the Vietcong started a concerted attack on provincial capitals all through South Vietnam and Saigon. They penetrated to the American embassy, blasted a hole in the wall, and apparently took over the ground floor and held it for about six hours. The attacks were at 3:00 a.m., when there were only three marines on guard. They have also taken over parts of Saigon and the old capital of Hue in the North. Apparently, American forces were caught by surprise.

The raids could not have been staged without inside help and if it had not been for the fact that Americans are unpopular throughout most of the country. This is going to be a setback for American prestige, especially in Asia, where they already deride the white man's alleged prowess; and also for Johnson's political prestige at home.

**THURSDAY, FEBRUARY 1** | Steve Young called to say he'd been at the White House the night before at a briefing in which the president had asked that there be no questions during the statements made by McNamara, Rusk, Gen. Maxwell Taylor, and General Wheeler, chairman of the Joint Chiefs of Staff. Senator Dodd, however, insisted on quizzing General Wheeler in such an antagonistic manner that the president interrupted him and told him that was enough. Dodd was obviously drunk.

General Westmoreland put out an optimistic statement that Saigon was now secure. Despite this, there are pockets of resistance holding out, and the old capital of Hue is still in Vietcong hands.

Tonight on television we saw my nephew Drew in Saigon in front of the American embassy, reporting on the attempt to retake the building. Suddenly, his soundman was shot, and we saw Drew pick him up and put him in a nearby truck. It all happened suddenly. Drew proved himself to be quite a hero. I wrote a column and did a broadcast, urging the president to fire General Westmoreland. I'm sure he will not do it; however, if he were to follow the precedent of Abe Lincoln, whom he's followed on other things, he will.

Jack sent his first column (mailed from Tokyo) regarding our thinly spread armaments in the North Pacific.

**SUNDAY, FEBRUARY 4** | Rusk and McNamara, appearing on *Meet the Press*, admitted the possibility that the *Pueblo* might have been in North Korean territorial waters. They noted that the *Pueblo* was out of communication with its headquarters in Japan for about fifteen days and might have strayed into North Korean waters during that time.

The immediate reaction to the Rusk-McNamara admission was that the United States was caught lying again. Some, however, interpreted it as preparing the groundwork for a face-saving statement which would win the release of the *Pueblo*. Negotiations have been taking place at Panmunjon between the United States and the North Koreans, but they have not been getting anywhere.

**MONDAY, FEBRUARY 5** | Boris Sedov, information counselor of the Soviet embassy, called this evening. I'm not sure what motivated his call except the hope that he could get wired in regarding American developments. Ambassador Dobrynin is still in Moscow.

He was convinced the *Pueblo* was seized inside North Korean territorial waters. He said his government had so informed the State Department. He pointed to the admission of Rusk and McNamara as confirming this. When I said that Arthur Goldberg, an honorable man, had shown conclusive evidence regarding the location of the *Pueblo*, Sedov replied that the navy had not told the State Department where the ship was located and that Goldberg undoubtedly thought that he was telling the truth.

When I suggested that the way to improve U.S.-USSR relations was for Russia to give us some support regarding the *Pueblo*, Sedov replied: "What do you want us to do? Take them by the collar and shake them?"

**WEDNESDAY, FEBRUARY 7** | The war news has continued bad, and there is still some fighting in pockets of Saigon, with the ancient capital of Hue still almost entirely in the hands of the Vietcong. Averell gave the official line that the local South Vietnamese population had not been won over to the Vietcong and did not rise up to join in a revolution. He regarded this as a victory for us.

Averell admitted that Westmoreland was no great shakes as a military commander and that it might be wise to dump him. He described Westmoreland as a good staff officer but no genius as a strategist, who, he felt, made a mistake by putting American marines in an exposed position at Khe Sanh—real estate not worth the expenditure of life.

**SUNDAY, FEBRUARY 11** | PALM BEACH FL—Back when I had a radio program which brought in $4,000 a week and I didn't have to make so many lectures to balance the budget, Luvie and I used to come to Palm Beach for two weeks every winter. Palm Beach was full of hate-Roosevelt businessmen and society dowagers, but we had a good time swimming at the Bath and Tennis Club. I haven't been back there for probably twenty years but suspect it hasn't changed much, except that people are now hating Johnson instead of Roosevelt.

We watched British prime minister Harold Wilson on *Face the Nation*, a program taped when he was in Washington last week for the White House dinner. He came off well and took a firm stand against the use of atomic weapons in Vietnam.

Later Gene McCarthy was on *Meet the Press*. He did well, though he was put on the spot for having become alarmed over a "rumor" regarding the use of atomic tactical weapons. The question was, why did he circulate rumors? Of course, there is no doubt that the Joint Chiefs of Staff considered these weapons for some time. They have developed tactical weapons by which artillery can fire nuclear shells, and they have been itching to try them in battle.

**WEDNESDAY, FEBRUARY 14** | As a valentine, I have been notified by Simon & Schuster that the Putnam Company is threatening suit to prevent publication of our book *Congress on Trial*. Jack and I had signed a contract with them some seven years ago. Marian checked my records and believes that I never returned to Putnam the $2,200 paid in advance. This is no time for me to pay it.

Marian gave me another valentine—a memo that I was $4,200 overdrawn at the bank if I gave Luvie all the checks I owe her. Milk sales are down, Felicia's tuition is to be paid, and the dairyman wants repairs on the milking parlor. I bat my head on the lecture circuit to get caught up, but I never seem to succeed.

John Donovan came in this morning with word that the Liberty Lobby would drop their suit. John thinks the best thing to do is accept it without asking costs, which, if paid, would give me about $500.

*Time* has purchased the *Newark Evening News* and part of MGM. There seems to be a working relationship between Seagrams and *Time* to control MGM. If *Time* extends its control much further, it will be as powerful as *Pravda* in the Soviet Union.

Talked briefly with Hubert Humphrey. I sounded him out on Vance Hartke's peace proposal. He said he would help. He agreed that the administration was in a difficult position and that the war news was bad despite optimistic propaganda. One interesting development was that former Premier Ky, now vice president, had turned out to be a real hero during the recent Saigon shooting. He was out on the streets, under fire, urging men into battle.

FRIDAY, FEBRUARY 16 | PHOENIX—LBJ had a press conference today and staged a slashing attack on the critics of General Westmoreland. He left me out, claiming that the attack originated abroad. He also swore that atomic weapons had not been considered for use in Vietnam. I have transcribed a radio program in which I say they were considered by the Joint Chiefs but vetoed by Johnson.

SUNDAY, FEBRUARY 18 | The Vietcong have staged an attack on forty cities in South Vietnam. It occurred just as most of the fighting had quieted down, except in Hue. The military announced that the attacks were expected, but this sounds like baloney. Even General Westmoreland's headquarters were attacked.

Listened to Ramsey Clark on *Meet the Press*. He was asked whether it was true that J. Edgar Hoover had been independent of all recent attorneys general and refused to take orders from them. Ramsey blinked, then said that Hoover was doing a very important job, that he needed a certain amount of independence, that he was very cooperative and had "never failed to carry out a request." Of course, he'd told me just a few weeks ago that Hoover had refused to give him the names of the cases in which the FBI had tapped wires.

Took Agnes across the street for tea with Mrs. Preston Davie, a Republican and one of the social powers in this Goldwater stronghold. She complained that we had seen no great presidents in recent years.

Agnes reminisced about the days when Eugene [Meyer] fixed copper prices during World War I. In those days, she said, all you had to do was to talk to Bernard Baruch, and the two of them talked to the Guggenheims, who controlled copper, and they agreed that the price was getting too high and should be kept down. Today it isn't that simple.

Agnes said Baruch had quite an affair with Clare Booth Luce and was the one who persuaded her to develop as a magazine editor. I remember when she was editor of *Vanity Fair*, she ordered a story from me on Washington DC, which was not too good. Her pointers on improving it were excellent. I adopted them, and the piece was published.

**SATURDAY, FEBRUARY 24** | Talked with Pat Brown on the telephone. He is upset over the war and says he would like to withdraw from the California delegation supporting Johnson for reelection. "I'd rather be with my son, Jerry," Pat said. Jerry is now battling for Gene McCarthy. Pat is doing his best to patch up the California Democratic feuds and even ate crow by going to lunch with Sam Yorty. I know how much he must have hated this because Yorty cut his political throat by helping Reagan in the 1966 election.

Pat kept coming back to the war while talking politics. He wondered why Johnson couldn't say that since U Thant has recommended an end to the bombing, we were going to take his advice. Pat thinks Reagan is not doing well and has rolled up a lot of opposition; however, Harry Lerner, with whom I also talked, feels just the opposite. The voters still are fooled by that toothy television smile, he feels. Reagan says just the right thing. He is no political fool, and Harry thinks he is going to end up as the Republican nominee for president. [Henry] Salvatori and the right-wingers have all the money in the world to spend, and they're doling it out quietly for Republican delegates in various states.

**MONDAY, FEBRUARY 26** | (Dined at the Yugoslav embassy with U.S. ambassador George Allen, Leonard Marks, and several former members of the American embassy in Belgrade.) The [Yugoslav] ambassador made an interesting remark about the Czechs, who had taken a strong stand lately for new intellectual freedom and against the hard line of Moscow. If Czechoslovakia improved its independent position and the right of professors and the intelligentsia to speak out, he said, this would be very wholesome. He added, "The Czechs are not backward like us in the Balkans, so this would have considerable impact around the world."

The ambassador wanted to know more about Radio Free Europe. Most Communist leaders have considered this an enemy, but the ambassador remarked that it had done some very effective work. He did not elaborate, but since Radio Free Europe urges independence from Moscow, apparently he agreed with this objective.

The ambassador wanted to know what I thought about the American presidential race. I said that Rockefeller could get the nomination if the Rockefeller financial empire really threw its weight into the battle. Otherwise, Nixon would get it and probably lose.

The ambassador remarked that the Russians were fully aware of Nixon's position *vis-à-vis* them and that they would much prefer Johnson. Rockefeller, I suggested, was just as much for the war as Johnson, though probably open-minded regarding coexistence.

MONDAY, MARCH 4 | The Senate was finally able to get cloture on the civil rights bill. Dirksen, at the last minute, had come around for the bill and drummed up a few extra Republican votes. Frank Carlson of Kansas finally voted for it. He's retiring from the Senate this year. Sen. Bourke Hickenlooper of Iowa, also retiring from the Senate, voted the other way.

TUESDAY, MARCH 5 | Today Nixon made a proposal to end the war in Vietnam. He said he would talk to the Russians and get them to exert their influence. How little does he seem to realize his standing with the Russians.

Eddie Weisl Jr. phoned me, noting that Sen. Eugene McCarthy failed to vote for cloture on the civil rights bill. He got to the Senate floor too late to vote—didn't seem to care enough about it to be on time.

WEDNESDAY, MARCH 6 | I talked on the phone with Charles Evers in Jackson, Mississippi. He is running for Congress and thinks he has a chance to win next Tuesday. He said he talked to a white college audience last week and didn't get a boo. He has also talked to other white groups, chiefly on the steps of the courthouse. He's won some white votes. If all the Negroes turn out to vote for him who have registered, he could win.

"The trouble is that when people haven't voted for a hundred years, they don't realize the importance of it," said Evers. I have written a column about him for tomorrow, and he thinks the *Jackson Clarion-Ledger* will probably use it. "They haven't attacked me yet," he said.

SUNDAY, MARCH 10 | Up about 4:00 a.m. to draft a letter to Lyndon. I have written him a couple of letters lately which I haven't sent, but this one I shall send and follow up with some columns diagnosing the war. This morning it was reported that Westmoreland had asked for 200,000 additional troops.

Leonard Marks came to lunch. I read him the letter to Lyndon, which he thought was good. Even before I mentioned it, he said I should write some columns trying to influence the president. He feels the president is more dug in, getting ever firmer on the war. He sees only three advisors, Walt Rostow, Rusk, and the secretary of defense. Leonard thinks Clark Clifford may be a good influence. He thinks I should see Clark and talk to him about peace overtures. We discussed the plan which I previously talked over with Vance Hartke and the Yugoslav ambassador. Leonard thinks the chief problem is that the Russians fear that if they curtail arms to North Vietnam, the Chinese will step in. I said the Chinese couldn't replace the Russians in a hurry.

Leonard thought the president might listen to me more than some around the White House, especially since not many of them are able to talk to him on the subject of the war. I doubt it, but I'll try. Leonard says that all the leaders in the administration are worried. He agrees with me that the country is torn asunder and that bitterness is increasing. I have seldom seen Leonard so disturbed.

We went to dinner at the Don Edwardses' in honor of Margaret and Andreas Papandreou. When we got there, Justice William O. Douglas and Judge Dave Bazelon were already there, and we hung around an hour and forty minutes before dinner was served. Even then it probably wouldn't have been served had not Bill gone up to Clyda Edwards and said he and Cathy had to leave.

At dinner I sat through a lugubrious briefing by Andreas, during which I went to sleep; however, I had a couple of fruitful private talks with him. He said he had been tortured under the Patakos dictatorship. They had him in solitary confinement with thirteen guards. They followed him wherever he went, even into the shower.

Every one of his father's cabinet has been confined and questioned, and his father still has his house surrounded by agents. At first there were guards in front of the house who put down the names of every visitor. "The test of your friendship is who comes to see you after you are released from jail and can receive visitors," he said. "I was there thirty days before I left, and I had a hundred visitors. They will all be cross-examined."

The most important thing, he said, was that Papadopoulos, the new prime minister, had long been the contact man between the army and the Greek Central Intelligence, which is called KYP [Kentriki Ypiresia Pliroforion]. When Papandreou had been in the cabinet, he discovered that the CIA had been sending funds direct to KYP, and he protested to Papadopoulos. He is convinced the CIA knew all about the revolution, if it did not actually plan it.

There is no question, says Andreas, regarding the influence of the American military with the present regime, also with the Turkish army officers. He says that Tom Pappas, who is now the economic king of Greece, in effect has rewritten his contract and is making more money than ever—at the expense of the Greek people. The Litton Industries contract is all in their favor, with hefty commissions to them if they attract new capital. Andreas thinks this is because Tex Thornton, head of Litton Industries, is a pal of the president. He also suspects that the [diplomatic] recognition of the junta took place partly as a result of the contract signed with Litton Industries.

**TUESDAY, MARCH 12** | In Austin I had lunch with Creekmore Fath and his wife and later attended a cocktail party held by the Foreign Policy Association, where I met a lot of Texas U. professors and some of the Texas liberals. It's claimed that Texas U. ranks next to the University of California as a hotbed of dissent. Certainly, there are a few real liberals left in Texas. They are not happy with Lyndon, but in the pinch they'll vote for him.

Spent part of the afternoon and evening watching the televised hearing between Rusk and the Foreign Relations Committee over the Gulf of Tonkin. Rusk did not come off well, though the sympathy down here in Texas seems to be generally with him. It seemed to me that the senators made a monkey out of his efforts to fool them with the facts on the Gulf of Tonkin, which obviously were rigged.

Significantly, Jack had the story of how the American commander of the USS *Maddox* was not at all sure he had been attacked, and we published it August 16, 1964, at the same time that the Senate was rushing hell-bent to pass a resolution supporting the president. It was one of the phoniest deals ever put across on Congress and by Congress.

Charles Evers lost in Mississippi, but he put up a good fight and immediately went around to congratulate his white victor, the former assistant to racist John Bell Williams.

Late in the evening the returns began coming in from New Hampshire, showing that Gene McCarthy in effect won. He got the majority of the delegates and came very close to Johnson's total vote. This is the same kind of setback which Kefauver delivered to Harry Truman in 1952 and which undoubtedly helped Truman decide not to run.

**WEDNESDAY, MARCH 13** | Late in the day Bobby Kennedy made the amazing announcement that he was reconsidering his statement of only two days ago that under no circumstances would he run against Johnson. Obviously, he was impressed with what Gene McCarthy had done in New Hampshire. His willingness to let somebody else do the pioneering is going to strike a sour note with some people. It certainly did with me.

The gold drain has reached massive proportions, with frantic trading on the Paris, London, and other European gold markets. Lyndon has been hit by the New Hampshire defeat, the drain on the dollar, and the setback in Vietnam all at once. I sometimes wonder how this is going to affect his heart condition and his general health. The doctors say that a man who is riding the crest of the wave is not bothered but a man who experiences setbacks in his work is likely to have a recurrent heart condition. This was one reason they kept Eisenhower touring Europe, so that he could get the plaudits of the crowds. Lyndon has been making quick flights to military bases, where the security is good. He hasn't gone out to brave a real crowd for a long time.

**THURSDAY, MARCH 14** | The gold drain is continuing so fast that for the first time I think in perhaps the last fifty years the dollar is in some jeopardy.

Kennedy is making moves as if he would announce for president. Here is a young man who looks younger than he is and whose only real asset is the fact the he's the brother of a dead president yet who is determined to become president. Another candidate is in the race who has exactly his viewpoint on the war, yet Bobby, having seen McCarthy's success in New Hampshire, is determined to make him move over.

Talked with Leonard Marks on the telephone. He said he had discussed my letter with the president. Lyndon was upset by it, and Leonard said that he particularly didn't like my suggestion that Bobby Kennedy be one who might go to Russia and have some influence as a negotiator. "How could he make a suggestion like that?" the president asked.

I concede that coming now, at a time when Bobby's about to challenge him, the suggestion was not good; however, I wrote the letter some days ago, and my prediction apparatus regarding Bobby was obviously not in working gear.

At any rate the president has written me a letter in which he says he is continuing to champion the cause of the underdog, as I have done in past years, and is continuing to work for peace. Under the circumstances it was a good letter, and I felt sorry I had added to all his woes and troubles by writing him.

SATURDAY, MARCH 16 | (Hosted Earle and Sarah Clements.) Earle, who handled Johnson's campaign in 1960, said there was no doubt that when a man was not able to get out and meet people in the hustings, he lost votes. They don't understand it if a candidate is tied up with the problems of war, as Johnson is today.

Bobby's announcement for president came at a ten o'clock press conference in Washington, during which he was subjected to a lot of questions as to why he let Senator McCarthy break the ice in New Hampshire. He handled these questions rather well, though he didn't look too good on TV. His haircut was abominable. Earlier Gene McCarthy had said he would be glad to give Bobby a job licking stamps provided he would cut his hair. NBC played back the Kennedy press conference three times, which made us wonder what Bobby had on NBC.

We speculated with Earle as to whether Johnson would conceivably accept Bobby Kennedy as his running mate. Earle recalled that when he was governor of Kentucky, he had attended the governors' conference at Plymouth, New Hampshire, in 1948, when Tom Dewey, then governor of New York, had lashed out against the teachers' lobby. This had caused Gov. Earl Warren of California to take vigorous exception.

"You don't know what a lobby is," Earle quoted Warren as saying. "You never had to deal with the power lobby, the water lobby, the liquor lobby. When it comes to teachers, I'm on their side. They represent children. And the children are the future of this country. Some of them will be sitting around this table in the future."

Earle said that Warren became quite indignant. All the Democrats listened, not saying a word. They had to go dress for dinner, or the argument might have continued longer. Walking up the corridor with Warren later, Earle told him that he was with him. "That kind of philosophy," said Warren, "is why the Republicans don't win."

"About two weeks later," added Earle, "Warren was running for vice president on the Dewey ticket."

SUNDAY, MARCH 17 | McCarthy was on *Face the Nation* and Bobby on *Meet the Press* this morning. Bobby did better than he did yesterday and looked pretty good. He still looks very young to be a candidate for president, however, and on the whole McCarthy comes off much better on television. Bobby's chief following, the kids, have now gone over in large part to Gene. I suspect that the split between them is really going to help Lyndon and may renominate him; however, it's also going to split the Democratic Party and probably lead to Nixon's election.

Last night I confessed that if Bobby were nominated, I might well vote for Nixon.

Mrs. Peter Strauss, whose husband owns WMCA in New York and who is now with African Aid in Washington, told me that Bobby was already putting the heat on Tammany, Bronx, and Brooklyn leaders to line up for him. Tom Rees and Don Edwards of California talked as if they would go for Bobby if Gene McCarthy doesn't get up enough steam.

MONDAY, MARCH 18 | Bobby Kennedy flew to Kansas to speak before Kansas State College in Manhattan. He got an enthusiastic response. It's a lively audience, as I found out some time ago when I spoke there. Almost anyone can get a big response. The president, who went to Texas over the weekend, flew home via Minneapolis, where he spoke before the farmers' union. I saw him on television, and it didn't seem to me that he made much impact. He kept repeating the importance of winning the war.

Hubert Humphrey telephoned from Minneapolis to say he wanted to give me the correct version of the dispute between Lyndon and Bobby over a plan by Bobby to appoint a commission to study the war. Bobby claims the White House leaked a cockeyed version of the story. The White House isn't saying anything.

Actually, Bobby's reported plan to have a commission study the war and whether it should be dropped or escalated was based upon the idea that if Johnson accepted it, he, Bobby, would not run for president. The general impression I got was that this was political blackmail, and while the commission idea wasn't too bad, I don't blame Lyndon for refusing it.

Spent the morning talking to various Democratic leaders about the manner in which Bobby is putting the heat on delegates to switch to him. It's the same tactic he used for his brother eight years ago. The story of Bobby's ruthlessness at that time has never really been told.

TUESDAY, MARCH 19 | (Lunched with attorney Hobart Taylor to discuss possible representation of me in various libel suits.) Hobart is retained by Chrysler and some other big corporations to handle their problems with Negroes. He said he was going to Atlanta with two Chrysler vice presidents tomorrow to talk to dealers about the Chrysler program of hiring and training Negroes. In Detroit, Chrysler has done an amazing job of breaking in

Negroes on technical work without the usual written examination. In oral exams the Negroes have done well. Many of the southern Negroes cannot read or write; nevertheless, they can take up mechanics fairly quickly.

We talked about the coming summer and the likelihood that violence would set Johnson back politically. Hobart didn't think there was much that could be done. He said Johnson had done more for the Negro than any other ten presidents put together—apparently including Lincoln. He'd failed, however, to appoint politically minded Negroes and, according to Hobart, had listened too much to John Macy of the Civil Service Commission. Macy had picked Negroes who were well trained but didn't have political influence.

When I asked about the idea of having some congressmen sit down with Martin Luther King to impress upon him the fact that violence during the spring march on Washington would cause congressmen to become even more anti-Negro, Hobart replied: "It's no good. King can't control his followers. Today, if I tell 'em to stop, they will, but how long I can do this, I don't know. We're Americans. We're not going to listen to the white man who says look what we've done for you lately, just be patient."

I talked to Governor Docking in Kansas, who entertained Bobby and Ethel Kennedy Sunday night and was with him when he had meetings at Kansas State and KU [the University of Kansas]. The students poured out in unprecedented numbers and nearly tore his clothes off. Docking, however, though impressed and rather shaken by Bobby's popularity, still intends to stick with Johnson.

I talked to Jim Scheuer and his political assistant, who say that Bobby is conducting a blitzkrieg with New York politicians. He doesn't even have to threaten them or twist an arm. A call from a Kennedy henchman throws the fear of God into New York assemblymen or district leaders. They are switching to Kennedy.

We held a Big Brothers awards dinner. About two-thirds of the Big Brothers were Negroes. This is quite a triumph. I had been trying for many years to get more Negro Big Brothers, and we haven't really begun to succeed until the last two years. Dr. C. Randolph Taylor of the Medical School of Howard University gave a talk, telling how he grew up in Harlem and got into trouble with the law but was helped by a Big Brother. He said he had been grateful to Big Brothers ever since. It was a satisfying evening, and in many respects I shall be sorry to bow out. Ten years of directing Big Brothers, however, is a long time.

**WEDNESDAY, MARCH 20** | David Berger asked me to call him in Monaco, which I did. He wanted me to call Princess Grace Rainier in Monaco, which I did, and interviewed her over the telephone. I felt awkward, partly because it's difficult over the transatlantic telephone to talk to a young princess about what she does for humanity. Then, too, I used to know her father. We were contemporaries when he was rowing for Penn and I was at Swarthmore. Jack Kelly was one of the great oarsmen of his day. Anyway, Princess Grace seemed to be a dedicated young lady, especially compared with her friend Jackie, who has been gallivanting all over the social world.

George Christian telephoned to say that the president was happy to get my second letter and George wanted me to come see him soon.

Lunched with the Soviet ambassador. I told him I thought Johnson would win the nomination and that previous to Bobby's getting into the race, I'd had doubts as to whether LBJ would run again. Now I was sure he would. The enmity between Bobby and the president is deeper and more vindictive than most people realize.

Dobrynin said he was convinced the president was definitely trying to follow a policy of better relations with the USSR. He pointed out in turn that the Soviet government had never been critical of Johnson—this despite the fact that the president had ordered the bombing of North Vietnam one day after Kosygin arrived in Hanoi.

From this I got to the question of peace and the fact that if Johnson could get a peace agreement in Vietnam before the election, he would be sure to win. The ambassador had been following the Rusk-Fulbright debate carefully and asked me why Rusk had not answered Fulbright when the latter demanded to know whether the State Department or the White House would consult with the Senate before taking further steps to escalate the war.

I said I thought it was because Rusk was not too good on his feet and didn't handle himself [well] before the Senate committee.

I tried some ideas on him, such as a UN police force to prevent bloodshed when American troops withdrew and the idea of the United States paying for the reconstruction of North and South Vietnam. He thought that a police force might be a good idea, but he emphasized first that American troops must withdraw and that we should stop fighting; also he poured cold water on the idea of paying for the reconstruction of the two countries.

"Some of your senators have talked about rebuilding the bombed areas," Dobrynin said. "This doesn't ring a responsive note in Asia. Just because you put up the money to rebuild is no reason why you should bomb. It sounds mercenary. You bomb, and then you rebuild."

Dobrynin didn't hold out much hope that the Soviet Union would help Johnson win the peace. When the chips are down and Nixon is nominated, they might be more helpful.

I suggested there were other areas where Russia could cooperate and that the Soviet Union had been causing trouble in the Near East by rearming the Egyptians and Syrians. Dobrynin argued the opposite. He said: "We did not start the war there. It was a surprise attack by Israel. When it was over and Israel refused to leave the territories she had taken, the Arabs asked us for arms. They said they were in danger of being attacked again. It was only at this point that we sent arms to Egypt and Syria."

I said that Russian intelligence forces had stoked Nasser by telling him the Israelis were about to attack. Dobrynin didn't deny this. He did say, "All the friendly Arab countries—Morocco, Lebanon, Algeria, Libya, Kuwait—tell us they have been to the State Department and expressed the desire to straighten out the regional problem, but [the] State Department says they can't do anything until after the election."

"It seems to me," said Dobrynin, "the Arabs have come a long way in stating that they would recognize the existence of Israel as a nation. In return they want their property back."

**SATURDAY, MARCH 23** | I saw Ronnie Dugger at the White House wearing a press badge. I wonder whether the White House knew he was working on a devastating book against Lyndon, which will be out in June. The publishers have already sold twenty-five thousand copies. Ronnie remarked he had been looking into my early columns on Brown & Root and the income tax job which Lyndon did for them. This is something I have kept in my files for years.

I suspect that the White House knows all about Ronnie and figures the best thing to do is to let him have the run of the White House.

Despite the fairly good money I have been earning this winter, Miss Canty tells me that I'm $6,000 overdrawn if she mails out the checks I have just signed. One reason was the lawyers' fees. John's is modest, but the others aren't. Another reason is the heavy farm expenses. I have gone in for too many cows, and the dairy personnel have let production drop. Finally, I suppose that writers are just never too efficient. Perhaps it's a good thing to keep us spurred on; otherwise, I would take things easy, and now I'll have to go to work in earnest on the Warren book.

**SUNDAY, MARCH 24** | Yesterday the Communist bloc called an emergency meeting in Dresden to chide the Czechs on their democratic movement. The East Germans are particularly worried, also the Russians. The smaller Communist countries, I suspect, are sympathetic. The new Czech secretary of the Communist Party, Alexander Dubček, went there to give them reassurances.

**MONDAY, MARCH 25** | Bobby Kennedy toured Southern California, including Watts, where he got a tremendous ovation. While he has been good on civil rights, he actually hasn't been anywhere near as effective as Johnson. The older Negro leaders remember this but not the young ones.

In Washington, McCarthy has refused to team with Bobby, which was wise. He isn't going to profit from any cooperation. The young people are still irked at Bobby coming in at the last minute, and it's much better for Gene to be independent.

Lyndon gave a rip-roaring speech at the AFL building trades meeting [Conference of the Building and Construction Trades Department, AFL-CIO], defending the war. I talked to Representative Tiernan of Rhode Island and Max McCarthy of Buffalo, who is sticking with Lyndon despite pressure from Bobby.

**TUESDAY, MARCH 26** | King Hussein has been boiling regarding the Israeli attack on Jordan a few days ago. He had been a moderating factor in the Arab world but now isn't. The Israeli military obviously inspired the raid. It was to put down saboteurs and Jordanians along the border who have been raiding Israelis at night. The fact is the Israelis are going to have trouble of this kind for a long time unless they give up some of the territory. They will never give up Jerusalem, however.

**WEDNESDAY, MARCH 27** | Gen. Creighton Abrams, the deputy chief of staff, is here for talks with LBJ. Jack reports he wants permission to cross into Laos and Cambodia for major battle. It's impossible to operate effectively against the North Vietnamese when they retreat across the border and cannot be pursued. Khe Sanh is only seven miles from the demilitarized zone and fourteen miles from Laos, and artillery in the Laotian mountains are pounding the fort at Khe Sanh. I can see Abrams's point; however, if the president authorizes him to do battle across the borders, we will be immediately accused of escalating the war.

Bobby Kennedy has toned down his attacks on the president. In Pittsburgh a couple of days ago he was bitter, blaming the president for the dope addicts among youth, draft card burnings, and the general hippie movement. Yet speaking before San Fernando College in Los Angeles two days ago, he said American troops could not be withdrawn from South Vietnam even if there was peace and that draft dodgers should go to jail.

Significantly, Bobby has hired as one of his speechwriters Pete Hamill, who wrote probably the most seditious column I have ever seen, accusing Johnson of murdering Jack Kennedy. It was published by the *New York Post* about two years ago; however, Hamill is so erratic that he can't keep up a regular column and was dropped, only to be taken up by Bill Moyers for syndication. This is the tip-off that Moyers really had an all-out break with Johnson and went over to Bobby. I couldn't quite believe it when I heard the reports at the time Moyers left, but there's evidence since then that Bill got his job with *Newsweek* through Bobby Kennedy.

**THURSDAY, MARCH 28** | Talked with Orville Freeman, who has been in Wisconsin campaigning for Lyndon against both Bobby Kennedy and McCarthy. Most people have forgotten that nearly all the members of the present cabinet are Kennedy men. Orville reminded me that he had campaigned so hard for Kennedy in 1960 that he lost out in his bid for reelection as governor of Minnesota.

"People wonder about Lyndon Johnson. He comes off on the air as a politician, but he isn't," he said. "When you work with him, he has lived up to every challenge. He's been so far ahead on most of these difficult political questions that it's hurt him. For instance, why would he be for home rule in the District of Columbia? It hasn't helped him politically. It's actually hurt him. He's for it because he thinks it's right. When you see a guy like that go down the line for what's best for the United States, you can't desert him."

Orville recalled how he and Hubert and Gene McCarthy had grown up together in Minnesota and helped organize the Democratic-Farmer-Labor Party. He said he and Hubert had picked Walter Mondale to be the new senator from Minnesota when Hubert retired from the Senate, and he went on to compare Mondale's record with McCarthy's.

"The trouble with Gene is that he's lazy. He hasn't put his name on one piece of legislation. Meanwhile, Mondale has authored the meat inspection bill, helped put the Civil Rights Bill through the House, and he's the author of the [National] Farmer Bargaining act [National Farm Act].

**FRIDAY, MARCH 29** | Dr. Martin Luther King was in Memphis yesterday, staging a protest march which got out of hand and caused a lot of destruction. You could see the Negroes, particularly, waving their clubs when they got before the TV cameras. I have contended that television is one reason for these riots. First, because the rioters want to get on television; second, because the television commercials give the impression that the white world is based on wealth.

As a result of the Memphis riot, I recorded a prediction for WTOP that King would call off his march on Washington. It was a long shot. It invoked a lot of comment from the TV technicians and cameramen. Their remarks regarding Negroes probably were a pretty good cross-section of American sentiment and indicate that the more violence there is in this country, the less sympathy the Negroes win. This is particularly true in Congress.

This was what the Civil Disorders Commission emphasized—namely, that the Negro problem was in part due to race prejudice. Yet Wilbur Cohen, the new secretary of HEW, made a speech this week pooh-poohing the commission's report. Obviously, he did it on instructions from the White House.

Bobby Kennedy has been getting a cool reception in New Mexico and Arizona. They like Goldwater there more than they like Bobby. Part of his campaign is built on smart public relations. He's now enlisted Lally and Yann Weymouth, who are moving to Washington. This will have an effect on the policies of the *Washington Post*.

**SUNDAY, MARCH 31** | I turned the president on at 9:00 p.m. He started talking about the war and announced a bombing pause, apparently with no strings attached. He also announced a small call-up of reserves and an increase in the war budget by about $2.5 billion. He also made a pitch—a fairly effective one—for higher taxes and said he would go along with cutting the budget.

At the very end he departed from the transcript which he had handed out to newspapermen in advance and began to talk about the need for unity in the country. He mentioned his long years—thirty-seven—of public service. At the very end he announced that he would not be a candidate for the Democratic nomination, nor would he accept it.

The commentators were left flustered and completely off base. The immediate reaction was that the president had bowed to his own unpopularity and was withdrawing because he couldn't win. I recall, however, several hints he had given me, dating back about two years, that he might not run. I wish I had stuck to those hints and my own hunch, rather than listening to others.

I thought the president handled it sincerely. Congress will now have to listen to him on key matters, or the public reaction will be against them. His moves for peace may now get somewhere. I strongly suspect that the Russians will put the heat on Hanoi. After all, they don't want Nixon, and Nixon is probably the logical beneficiary from Johnson's withdrawal.

WEDNESDAY, APRIL 3 | After the White House session I flew to Boston for a speech at MIT; very small audience. I urged them that if they had any influence with the administration of MIT to use it to get Walt Rostow returned. He's a disaster in Washington.

THURSDAY, APRIL 4 | Leonard Marks phoned to say members of the cabinet were almost in tears yesterday when the president thanked them for their loyalty. He repeated some of the things he'd told us yesterday but in more detail.

"You are not my original appointees," he said, "but down in Texas we believe in partnership. When the partner dies, you don't throw out the farmhands. You don't throw the widow out of the house. You settle up the accounts and take care of the farmhands' families.

"When John F. Kennedy died, I tried to continue his program with his personnel. If he were sitting here today, I think he would approve of what we have done."

Arthur Goldberg replied, "I'm the senior member here in years, if not in service. It's been a privilege to serve with you, Mr. President. We've all admired your courage, and we believe that while your present achievements may not be entirely appreciated at this time, history will show how great they have been."

The president said if anyone wanted to leave, he would understand it. Leonard said there were no moves in this direction. He also said Humphrey was going to wait awhile to see if he could get some powerful forces behind himself for president. George Meany had announced Governor Hughes of New Jersey was going to hold back and support him later. The president had talked to Dick Daley of Chicago, who promised to be in Hubert's corner, even though Bobby is now claiming him. Leonard thought there had been a welling of support for Hubert.

I told Leonard about my talk at the White House and the president's reference to my letter. "He needed nudging," Leonard said, "and your letter may have been the factor which nudged him into action."

George Christian telephoned with a message from the president saying he had received a wonderful letter from the chief justice and wanted me to know about it. He described the chief justice as the "best man" in the United States, and he was grateful to me for bringing them closer together. I don't think I was responsible, but I didn't argue. George said the president was leaving late tonight, after a Democratic fund-raising dinner, for Marshfield, California, where he'll confer with Eisenhower, and then on to Honolulu to confer with General Westmoreland.

Later in the afternoon I attended a State Department reception for visiting journalists. Jean Baube told me the French had just received word that the Iron Curtain was being taken down around Czechoslovakia that day—that is, the barbed wire entanglements and the strict guards along the frontier between Czechoslovakia and West Germany. This really is a change.

I was standing outside the George Washington University Hospital, waiting for Luvie to come down from a visit with Agnes Meyer, when I heard over the radio that Martin Luther King had been shot in Memphis. There were no details. Later we dined with Ernest Cuneo at the Gangplank, Tyler's new restaurant, [on] a barge anchored to the shore of the Potomac. We speculated as to what the shooting would do to the already uneasy Negro world.

Later we got the news that King was dead. It was a sniper's bullet, and the presumption, of course, is that it must have been a white man. The governor of Tennessee has called out the National Guard. I suspect all hell will break loose in the major cities.

FRIDAY, APRIL 5 | Rioting and burning broke out almost immediately in Washington today. It continued in the Negro shopping areas of Seventh Street and Fourteenth Street all day. I have never seen Washington in such turmoil.

I remember vividly the 1932 Bonus Army march, when General MacArthur used tanks and cavalry to push about 20,000 straggling, poverty-stricken veterans out of town. The threat of the Bonus Army was peanuts compared with what happened when the students of Howard University and a lot of other young Negroes started burning and looting today. After all, there were only 20,000 Bonus Marchers, as against a Negro population of 55 percent in a city of 800,000 today.

As I drove home from WTOP along Wisconsin Avenue at 2:30 p.m., the schools were closing, and streams of young Negroes were huddling at the bus stops or running along the streets. They didn't know what it was about except that there was excitement and burning downtown. I am sure that most of the Negro population which is participating in the violence has no idea what Martin Luther King stood for or what the issues are. They are just like a young college crowd after a football game at Swarthmore, which wants to do something, and the recognized way of doing it is to loot. The tragedy is that this is taking place under a southerner president who has done more for the Negro than any man since Lincoln.

For a while this afternoon it was difficult to telephone and impossible to reach the Capitol. There was no looting in Georgetown or any disorder, but fire engine sirens could be heard screaming through the streets, and I remembered what Dick Gregory told me in 1964, that if the Negro population ever turned loose, the big cities would be unable to handle the fires. The Negroes would simply open the fire hydrants and lower the water pressure. That was not done at this time, but there were so many fires that volunteer fire engine crews had to be called in from nearby Maryland and Virginia.

President Johnson called a meeting of civil rights leaders at the White House—the most prominent Negroes, together with Thurgood Marshall of the Supreme Court and Chief Justice Warren. He also called a joint session of Congress for Monday at 9:00 p.m. and canceled his trip to Honolulu.

At around six thirty Mayor Washington clamped a curfew on everyone, and the streets of Georgetown became as empty as at six thirty on a Sunday morning. It was eerie silence, as if the city had gone dead. As we left the house to go to dinner at Sheldon Cohen's, however, we could see a huge red glow over the inner city.

Things were peaceful in the Maryland suburbs, where we dined. It illustrated the justice of the open housing provision in order to permit Negroes to live in the suburbs. Hitherto they have been, for all practical purposes, barred.

At the dinner was Gen. Yitzhak Rabin, the former Israeli chief of staff, now ambassador in Washington. I had not seen him since I interviewed him in Tel Aviv in December 1965. We talked about Nasser, whom he said had gotten rid of three of the men closest to him, one having committed suicide. Nasser resigned in a tactic to let the Egyptian Socialist Party demand that he remain. It worked. Rabin didn't put much credence to the State Department story that Nasser was in poor health nor the CIA report that communism would come to Egypt in a couple of years.

Sheldon confirmed the reports that Bobby Kennedy used income tax returns ruthlessly when he was attorney general in order to retaliate against his critics and enemies. He even permitted Carmine Bellino, a private detective and pet of the Kennedy family, to pick out some of the tax returns of people whom Bellino was investigating. On the other hand, Johnson has been very strict about not permitting tax returns to get into anyone's hands except in major criminal cases.

**SATURDAY, APRIL 6** | Looting continued during the night. Bands of young Negroes did not pay too much attention to the curfew. A total of seven hundred were arrested, but it was impossible to arrest more than the ringleaders.

This morning Woodrow Mossberg Jr. did not turn up for work [at the farm]. He had been up all night with the Rockville Volunteer Fire Department helping in downtown Washington. He came in around about nine thirty or ten to say he had never been through such an experience in his life. Young Negroes broke into stores to ransack the places and carry out the loot. Then a second band would come in, see that the loot had been removed, and broke up the furniture. Then a third gang would come in and set fire to the place. Woodrow said that the police stood by, not interfering. They arrested a few of the ringleaders but apparently figured that if they fired any shots, the whole city would become immersed in civil war.

And all this for a man who, while he did much for the Negro cause, was nothing compared with the great job done by Roy Wilkins, Whitney Young, and some of the others and whose private life would never bear scrutiny. He had a yen for white women, and when J. Edgar Hoover once called him a liar and Martin Luther King went to see Hoover for a showdown, he came out as mild as a lamb. Hoover had shown him the FBI record—or part of it—on his sex activities. Apparently, the record of the march to Selma was included.

Last night Jackie Kennedy made a statement of sympathy for Mrs. King. It was a good statement, obviously written for her by the Bobby Kennedy PR people. It will help the Kennedy image.

Albert Chambers, one of the Negroes who works on the farm, remarked as I drove him home, "Ain't it a shame about that man." He didn't know Martin Luther King's name.

Yesterday Stokely Carmichael urged Negroes to arm themselves. It seemed to me close to sedition, but he has not been locked up. A list of stores and finance companies to be burned and looted has now been secured by the police. It shows also the gasoline stations where gas can be secured for Molotov cocktails. Instructions are to burn the lists of Negro indebtedness at the pawnshops and finance companies.

In the afternoon I went to see Ed Morgan, who lives in Kenwood. It was a fairyland of cherry blossoms, with the branches drooping out to form tunnels of white over the streets. What a contrast to the burning and looting and bedlam of downtown Washington. Ed confided that the community of Kenwood was armed to the teeth. Today, incidentally, the Senate Judiciary Committee reversed its previous vote in favor of a gun control bill.

By prearrangement I met at Ed's house with Quinn Tamm, former assistant director of the FBI and now head of the International Association of Police Chiefs, together with his public relations man, Charlie Moore, also an ex–FBI agent.

Tamm said that Herb Jenkins, the Atlanta police chief, was considered one of the most liberal in the nation. He did not permit the looting which was taking place in Washington. If a store window was broken open, Jenkins put one of his officers in front with a shotgun with orders to shoot in the legs if there was any looting.

Significantly, there has been no trouble in Baltimore, where Police Chief Donald Pomerleau has been working hard at community relations. He has hired more Negro cops and has been able to increase his force to [about] 12 percent high school graduates and about 20 percent Negroes. In contrast, Bob Murray, the former chief of police in Washington, simply would not employ a single Negro. Now there are many Negroes on the force, but it has taken time to get enough. There is a big demand for young Negroes who are educated, and it's hard to get enough for the police force.

In contrast to Pomerleau's methods in Baltimore, Tamm said, were the methods of Chief Rizzo in Philadelphia, who was tough but also operated a quiet city. Tamm said he felt sorry for Ramsey Clark, who had done an excellent job for law enforcement; nevertheless, [he] was getting the brunt of the criticism, together with Johnson.

Hoover has managed to get all police training put in his hands as far as federal funds are concerned. Tamm said this training constituted a one-hour lecture on the jurisdiction of the FBI.

Hoover gets gifts from his agents on his birthday, January 1, on the anniversary of his joining the FBI, and at Christmas. This spring he received flowers for his garden. The agents gripe about this but contribute. He has received air cooling and a porch for his house, built by the agents.

Hoover was for Nixon in 1960; nevertheless, JFK reappointed him on the morning after his election. Obviously, the file on Kennedy was thick. Hoover is a consistent Republican and during the Nixon-Kennedy campaign conferred in Florida with Bill Rogers, Nixon's close friend.

Tamm had previously refused to talk to me about the FBI, but we agreed today that we would talk further. After he left, Ed told me about his client, the Mafia member who was in on the plot to assassinate Fidel Castro on the instructions of Bobby Kennedy. The client has been indicted, and Ed, in order to defend him, has asked the Justice Department for the record of the electronic eavesdropping. The department has acknowledged that it does have such a record.

Ed has received a call from the counsel of Central Intelligence, whom he had known in the FBI. The counsel pleaded with Ed not to handle the defense of his client in such a manner as to reveal the transcript of the electronic bugging. He confirmed that it would go up to the attorney general, Bobby Kennedy, who had ordered the assassination of Castro. Ed refused to cooperate. He said his first duty was to his client.

The client, incidentally, has a Mafia record so bad that Ed said it would shock even me.

We talked about Bobby. At one time Ed did him a great favor, which Bobby obviously did not appreciate. A friend of Ed's lived on one side of Bobby Kennedy's mistress. He used to park his Justice Department car, with a cabinet tag, in front of her house in Georgetown while he went in and laid her. He was so indiscreet that he never pulled down the blinds. On the other side of the house lived Harold Gibbons, a vice president of the Teamsters. I had heard this story previously from Gibbons. Ed said that he tipped off Bobby and he discontinued his noonday visits.

Late today the White House announced that the United States had proposed to Hanoi that peace talks be held in Geneva. There has been no reply from Hanoi, and the news of peace has been drowned out by the death of Martin Luther King and its aftermath.

SUNDAY, APRIL 7 | Rioting continued Saturday night. A total of twelve thousand troops have now been brought into the District of Columbia. This is probably a good many more troops than the British brought in to burn the city in 1812. Certainly, it is far more than General MacArthur used to evict the 1932 Bonus Army.

We spent the day at the farm, where my only problems are animals, machinery, and soil, which has been too wet to disk.

In the evening Mayor Washington held a meeting with a citizens' group to report on the effort being made to help the homeless. This is a "plus" feature of the riots. Though the Negroes brought shame on the city, the white population is turning around—or at least the more intelligent members—to help those who caused the chaos. Committees have been formed to feed, house, and even contribute cash to the homeless. On the Committee for Food are representatives of the chain stores, despite the fact that some of the chain stores were gutted. The *Post* this morning carried pictures of Safeway, the interior of which is a shambles.

A total of about four thousand people have been arrested. The police did a good job of avoiding bloodshed and arresting the ringleaders instead.

MONDAY, APRIL 8 | As we drove in from the farm this morning, troops were stationed along Wisconsin Avenue. There was at least one soldier to every block, in some cases two soldiers walking in pairs. Never did I expect to see this in Washington.

A Harold Monat telephoned me from McLean, Virginia, to say that a Negro woman working for him had been in Stokely Carmichael's suite and discovered that the original date for the riots in Washington were to be June 18 and 19, but they had been shoved forward following King's assassination. It was planned that the riots would start in Washington, and then as the troops entered here, the riots would move on to Baltimore, thus forcing the troops to spread themselves thin. This was close to what happened.

Tonight army searchlights played up and down Rock Creek Valley between Georgetown and the Negro section on the other side. It gave one an eerie feeling. The burning has stopped, and the city is much more quiet.

WEDNESDAY, APRIL 10 | The president telephoned this afternoon, much to the speculation of the town, which immediately heard about the call. I am not sure why he called. He said he wanted to thank me for putting the civil rights bill through. "Two years ago, no one would have said we could pass open housing," the president said, "but I've got the bill right here now, and I wanted to thank you for what you did. You kept plugging away on this bill, and if it hadn't been for you, we wouldn't have passed it."

This was a considerable exaggeration, but I accepted the compliment without argument. After all, it was his time on the telephone. He said, incidentally, that two of the leaders were in the room, but he did not specify who they were. I assumed they were Speaker McCormack, who would be a little surprised at Lyndon's call to me, and maybe Hale Boggs, who wouldn't be.

"I've got a problem I want to ask you about," the president said. "Larry O'Brien is leaving. He's going out to Indiana to help Bobby Kennedy. Bobby put the pressure on him. We heard about it through the papers. I want to appoint Marvin Watson to replace him in the Post Office. What do you think of him?"

I replied that I thought he was a fine man. "I'd go ahead with the appointment," I said, knowing full well that he would do it anyway. "Marvin deserves recognition. He's been very loyal to you."

"Don't say anything about this," LBJ said, and we rang off.

I telephoned George Arnold in Los Angeles to ask him if he would like to become a member of the FCC. I figured now was the time to get something for my friends and family and that this would have all the grandchildren in Washington. George is thinking it over.

FRIDAY, APRIL 12 | Hubert Humphrey flew off, supposedly for the Virgin Islands, which seemed strange in view of the fact that now's the time to corral delegates and political leaders. Hubert has not yet announced; however, he's been working behind the scenes and had a couple of sessions with Larry O'Brien to persuade Larry not to work for Kennedy. Larry said he considered Humphrey the most qualified candidate, but apparently the Kennedys had a hold on him.

I talked to Hubert in Florida, where he stayed for the weekend instead of going to the Virgin Islands. There has been a lot of jockeying over where to hold the talks with North Vietnam. I told Hubert I thought the president was in a bad light as a result of turning down both Cambodia and Warsaw as sites, since he'd said repeatedly, "I'll go anywhere, at any time, to talk peace." Hubert said the president wanted the talks to be held in Asia because we have some problems with our allies there. He was hoping the talks could be held in Rangoon or New Delhi. He agreed that foot-dragging put the president in a bad light but seemed confident the talks would be held. Hubert said he would be back in Washington on Tuesday. We did not discuss his campaign.

Later I talked to Arthur Goldberg and expressed the same misgiving to him about the haggling over where the talks should be held. Arthur said Hanoi wanted Warsaw because the Chinese were already meeting there with the United States, and the North Vietnamese could then argue to the Chinese that since they were meeting there, there was no reason why the North Vietnamese should not also meet with the United States there.

"Hanoi's getting a lot of pressure from the Chinese," Arthur explained. I said I had seen two memos from Rostow and Rusk to the president in which Rostow raised a red flag about the talks.

"Obviously, there's going to be foot-dragging by some of the people who have been overruled," Arthur said.

(Lunch with Israeli ambassador Yitzhak Rabin.) At luncheon I'd asked Rabin how he liked being a diplomat after being head of the Israeli army. I meant the question rather humorously, but he took it seriously. "I served four years as chief of staff," he said, "and under the Israeli custom I serve wherever I am directed."

We had a long, frank discussion about the Near East and the war in Vietnam. He summarized all the losses we were taking as a result of the latter. "You are using up your resources," he said. "You have let the Russians become supreme in the Near East. You have lost many of your Asian friends. You are losing some of your European friends. And there's no question but that the racial problems here at home are in part the result of the war in Vietnam. You are bogged down so you can't move, and there's nothing that delights the Russians more than this."

"If we opened up the Suez Canal," Rabin said, "the Russian fleet would be the first to move through it, and their control of the Near East would be complete. They doubtless would move to Yemen."

I noted that tactics by the Israeli military were alienating the moderate Arabs and making it difficult for such Arab leaders as Bourguiba. I said that, when in Egypt, I had the impression that the Egyptian people were reconciled to Israel and wanted to cooperate at least to the point of having no war. The ambassador replied that the Arab peoples carried no influence or weight with their governments. They did what Radio Cairo or the propaganda agencies told them to do. He argued that the most essential move for the United States was to get together all the Arab leaders who were friendly and warn them that unless they did something to pressure Nasser, the region would end up in the hands of the Soviet Union.

"Why do you think he's warming up to Russia and taking trips to Moscow?" Rabin asked. "Why are the Turks getting friendly? The reason is they see you weakening.

"If we are armed, we can get along as far as the Arab world is concerned, unless the Russians actively intervene. We have been the best asset you have in the Near East. We've kept the Russians out of the Suez Canal, but right now there's a Russian bomber squadron visiting Syria and Egypt. If the Egyptians should bomb our canal positions while the Russian bombers are in Cairo, it would be very difficult for us to retaliate without hitting the Russians. We couldn't ascertain which planes were which."

Rabin argued that Israel's first need was more bombers to offset the Russian bombers which have been sent to Egypt and the French bombers which are being sold to Iraq.

I told Rabin how the president, out of a clear blue sky, had mentioned the fact that he had no treaty with Israel but had to do something about "little Israel." Rabin said that two or three weeks ago he had talked to Rostow about aid for Israel in case of crisis and that Rostow had replied there was no treaty. We suspected that probably it was a result of Rostow's memo to the president that he had made this observation to me.

SUNDAY, APRIL 14 | Luvie and I dined with Agnes Meyer, the first dinner she's had since she returned from the hospital. The chief justice and Nina were there. Politics was the chief subject of conversation. The chief thought Humphrey would be saddled with LBJ's policies on the war, and because the southern delegates would be supporting him, it would look as if he had sold out on his old courageous stand for civil rights. There was general agreement that Bobby was a menace, that he had peaked and was leveling off.

There was discussion of the riots and why Stokely Carmichael was not arrested. The chief pointed out that they couldn't convict him for urging Negroes to get arms since this was what the Minutemen had done and a lot of white men had done. He pointed to the difference between Carmichael and Rap Brown, who actually was at the scene of the riot and started it.

Luvie had talked to Abigail McCarthy earlier in the day and told her that Bobby had bought off McCarthy's leader at Notre Dame by offering him free college expenses. Dick Goodwin jumped to Bobby because his speeches were not being used by McCarthy. He wrote one speech which was used. Mrs. McCarthy had advised her husband to let Dick go earlier since he was sure to jump anyway. Gene's writing his own speeches.

I mentioned that a former state governor had told me about the argument between Tom Dewey and Earl Warren during the summer of 1948 and that it was even hotter than I had reported. The chief confirmed this. He said that Tom Dewey had wanted the governors to raise a fund of $250,000 to investigate the teachers' lobby.

"I get along with the lobbies," Dewey had said. "I talk with them and get them to work with me."

"If they cooperate with you, then there must be something wrong with you," the chief had replied. "A year or so later Dewey called me up. 'You remember what I told you about being able to work with the lobbies?' he said. 'Well, I was a liar. I took a good licking from them upstairs right now.'

"Your column was right as far as it went," the chief remarked. "But you didn't go far enough."

SUNDAY, APRIL 21 | Averell arrived late last night. This morning after breakfast we had a long talk about the Vietnamese peace negotiations. He disagreed with me that Warsaw could have been a suitable negotiation city. It has been supplying arms to North Vietnam and therefore is resented by South Vietnam, ranking after Russia, China, [and] Czechoslovakia as the fourth largest supplier of arms.

He feels that the jockeying over a site for the truce talks should have been done in private, not public, and particularly that the White House should not have gotten involved. The president should be aloof, he said, so that he could yield or make concessions at the proper time.

He described Phnom Penh, the capital of Cambodia, as an insult to us and said that there had been debate inside the State Department as to whether to include Kuala Lumpur, Malaysia, on the list of possible cities because it was known in advance that this would be considered an insult to North Vietnam. The State Department thought it was a good idea to put Malaysia on the list so as to give North Vietnam a chance to raise a rumpus over it.

Averell then told me how he had been sent to eight Latin American capitals, immediately after the Dominican crisis, to explain our situation. "I had no instructions," he said. "I simply had to use my own judgment. Five of the countries lined up with us publicly, and three agreed to go along privately.

"Whenever I have taken a trip for the president, I have asked him in advance what his instructions were. He has always told me: 'You know how to do it. Go ahead and do it your way.'"

Averell read my column of Friday on Rostow. "The trouble with Rostow is that he doesn't give the president the other side of the picture. It's his job to sort out the position papers and the reports from abroad. He sorts them out in such a way as to give the president a one-sided picture.

"Harry Hopkins did just the opposite for FDR. I remember taking reports into Hopkins. Roosevelt always wanted them typed on one page. If they were longer than one page, he wouldn't read them. Frequently, the president was about to initial the page, when Hopkins would say: 'Don't do that. You better call Stimson, or you better call Hull.' He knew that the president's initials on the sheet of paper didn't mean too much unless the cabinet officer concerned agreed. Morganthau used to come in early in the morning and get Roosevelt's okay without anyone interfering."

Averell felt the trouble with Rostow was that he was an economist and an economist should not advise on political matters.

"Is there any way we can get peace this year?" Averell asked. "If Nixon is the nominee," I replied. In that case the Russians would bring pressure for peace if they thought Nixon had a chance to win.

Averell asked for my advice on how to handle the negotiations. I suggested first that the public be prepared for long negotiations; second, that U Thant be entrusted with picking the site; and third, that Paris should be the city for the conference.

I also suggested that the United States get some of the neutral and smaller Communist nations to bring pressure on Ho Chi Minh. "I don't think much of U Thant," Averell said, "but the American people do, so it might be a good idea to have him pick the site.

"The Russians and the French have the greatest influence. We're told that the Russians did not talk to Ho Chi Minh regarding the president's first peace proposal. They attacked the proposal. Then, after Hanoi had accepted it, Moscow praised it. They never want to be out front of North Vietnam. They particularly dislike being called the imperialist stooge of the United States.

"It's unfortunate that Johnson is so sensitive about de Gaulle. It would be better to use him. If de Gaulle wants a Nobel peace prize for settling the war in Vietnam, let him have it. We should use him."

The United States now has eight thousand North Vietnamese prisoners, and North Vietnam only has about three hundred U.S. pilots. Thus, Averell thought that exchange would be fairly simple. The North Vietnamese prisoners are being held by South Vietnam, but they are subject to inspection by the International Red Cross and have been well treated.

Averell had some revealing things to say about what happened in North Vietnam when the Communists took over and what might happen again if they dominated the South. There was a lot of murder and bloodshed.

"I don't agree with Schlesinger and Galbraith that the Communist danger is over," he said. "It is less but not over. The Russian bear has become conservative. We can get along with him, but Castro is out to cause us trouble wherever he can. We have reached an accommodation with Russia on India and Pakistan, and we can do it on Vietnam. Russia wants an independent Vietnam as a buffer against China.

"We must keep our Asian allies informed. Our word is at stake in Southeast Asia, just as it was over Berlin with our European allies. Europe has confidence in us now. They know we will not go back on our word. We have to do the same with our Asian allies. That's one reason we must have President Park of South Korea and the Saigon government in on the truce talks. These talks are going to be difficult, but I believe peace can be accomplished."

**MONDAY, APRIL 22** | I called Liz Carpenter to ask for an appointment with Lady Bird to talk to her about the president's big decision. Liz sidestepped. She said that Lady Bird wasn't talking about it. She didn't want to get identified with the decision and later have her husband say, "Yeah, yeah, now see what you made me do." Lady Bird is smart.

**TUESDAY, APRIL 23** | READING PA—Sat around for two hours with members of the host committee. They were dedicated, prosperous businessmen, worried about their community, which has a small minority of Negroes, some of them quite militant. Race relations have been fairly good on the whole, and the Jewish employers seem to be going out of their way to employ Negroes.

I asked them their advice on publishing the column on Martin Luther King and his affair with Mrs. Evans. With the exception of one man, they all voted no. They felt it would disrupt the Negro world and for no real cause. I have held up the column for several days trying to make up my mind. Jack had telephoned me in Florida suggesting immediate publication but was glad to go along with a delay.

The column is a reflection on the FBI and is important. It's also a fact that King was something of a phony in some ways, but the good far outweighs the phoniness, and he has now become a hero.

I flew back to Washington late at night, tired. I think I'm going to have to give up these late-night trips.

**WEDNESDAY, APRIL 24** | Talked to Ben Bradlee of the *Post* about the column on King. He was opposed to it though thought there was some merit in using it in an exposé of the FBI, provided we could nail down the statement by Mrs. Evans that J. Edgar Hoover had written a letter to Mrs. King.

**THURSDAY, APRIL 25** | Arthur Goldberg has resigned from the UN. The last time I saw him he had been reconciled to remaining, and when I talked to him over the phone about a week ago, he expressed no great problems.

We watched Arthur on television, and he did not seem happy. I suspect the decision came suddenly and was not to his liking.

**FRIDAY, APRIL 26** | Hubert Humphrey telephoned this morning to report on his trip to Mississippi. He was bubbling with enthusiasm over his reception there. Six or seven thousand people were in the Coliseum to hear him, and he also had an important integrated breakfast with about four hundred Mississippi leaders, ranging from Charles Evers to the lieutenant governor, who is white.

I talked with Horace Busby, LBJ's former speechwriter. I'd heard that he had more to do with the president's decision not to run again than almost anyone else. After the talk I concluded this was true.

Horace talked about the Bobby Kennedy campaign and the fact that Bobby was using a lot of second-string staff who were trying to undercut the men at the top, such as Ted Sorensen, an excellent man. Most of Bobby's staff are has-beens and leftovers who didn't get along well with the Kennedy administration.

Horace told how the newspapermen traveling with Bobby were getting fed up with him and had coined a description: "The Ruthless Rabbit." Riding on the Wabash Cannonball, the special whistle-stop campaign train, David Breasted of the *New York Daily News* got up a song to the tune of "Casey Jones" about the train and the Ruthless Rabbit. Bobby, walking through the train, heard part of the music and asked that they play it for him. Breasted, taken by surprise, had to comply but changed the Ruthless Rabbit to Ruthless Robert.

Jack Valenti, whom I saw late in the day, was also vehement about Bobby's staff. One of them he was sore about was Dick Goodwin, whom he and Bill Moyers had recommended to Johnson and whom Johnson had hired against his own better judgment. "The president has a sixth sense as to who's loyal to him and who isn't," Jack said. "He knew Goodwin was not loyal. Later Goodwin left him—no loss—then went with McCarthy, then deserted McCarthy for Bobby."

SATURDAY, APRIL 27 | The dogwood is still in bloom; azaleas are budding. The creeping phlox is all over the front embankment in purple, lavender, and pink. The river is fairly high. The laurel has never been so luxurious. The iris are beginning to bud. The cows are producing four thousand pounds of milk a day. The grass is luxuriant. There is a slight rain, but it's good for the grass, if not for the children.

Humphrey announced at noon at a big luncheon at the Shoreham. He was forceful but a little old-fashioned in his approach. Of course, he was hamstrung because he's harnessed with the Johnson administration's position—which I think history will prove has been excellent, aside from Vietnam. There was a little too much atmosphere of the old-time politician. Perhaps I'm oversensitive about this.

MONDAY, APRIL 29 | Luvie left for Indianapolis to campaign for McCarthy. Franklin Roosevelt Jr. stopped to pick her up. He, too, is flying to Indianapolis but to campaign for Bobby. This is interesting. In the New York gubernatorial race last year Bobby turned his back on Franklin for the Democratic nomination. If he had supported Franklin, Frank would have won. I wonder what Bobby has offered Frank for his support now.

WEDNESDAY, MAY 1 | The *Chicago Daily News* telephoned Jack to object to my column critical of Bobby Kennedy, linking him to the McCarthy committee. I suppose this is the first of the political gripes during this election year.

I had a cocktail party for Sinatra and HHH. We spent most of the time in the garden. I finally yielded to the demands of the *Washington Post* that they send a reporter. They sent Maxine Cheshire, whom everybody hates but I have defended when Liz Carpenter tried to get her fired.

Only one member of the cabinet, Bob Weaver (he is strong for Humphrey) [came to the party]. I don't know whether the other cabinet members stayed away because of the president's recent ban on political activity.

Saw the president in order to get his version of how he arrived at the decision to not seek reelection. He was surprisingly prompt. I told him that I'd felt for about two years that he wasn't going to run again but that my wife thought differently. "You follow your wife's advice, and I followed mine, but my wife was wrong," he replied.

I added that I'd presumed one of the factors in his decision was the fact that as a representative and senator, he had watched the eroding influence of Roosevelt, Truman, Eisenhower, and Kennedy and knew that his influence must necessarily erode likewise. He said it wasn't quite that way.

"Even before 1964, Lady Bird and I talked over whether I should run. When you've had a heart attack, as I did, when you've been down in the valley of the shadow of death, you have to think carefully about these things. I came out of that heart attack not remembering anything. I didn't want to be another Woodrow Wilson.

"My grandmother had a stroke when she was about sixty and had to spend her life in a wheelchair. I remember it as a boy. My father had a stroke at the age of fifty, and my uncle had one at fifty-eight.

"God has been good to me. I've made a remarkable recovery from my heart attack, but these are some of the things I had to consider in 1964.

"So Lady Bird said, 'We'll count every day.' And she began counting fourteen hundred–odd days.

"Last fall, I talked to a lot of friends as to whether I should run. I talked to Abe Fortas, Clark Clifford, Dean Rusk, McNamara, and Westmoreland. I talked to Marvin Watson and some of the secretaries. I even wrote out a statement of withdrawal last fall and carried it around in my pocket, together with Truman's statement that he was not going to run again. At that time I thought of April 1 as the deadline.

"John Connally looked it over. He was interested because he did not want to run again, and he figured if I wasn't going to run, he wouldn't either. He telephoned here the day before the State of the Union speech to see whether I had changed my mind. He didn't talk to me, but he left word to call back if I had changed. We did not call him back.

"McNamara knew I wasn't going to be here next year. This was one reason he left when he did. Bobby got out that statement that I had fired McNamara, and McNamara couldn't reply without giving away my future plans.

"Before the State of the Union I had the statement we had drafted earlier and had halfway memorized it. I could say it without the teleprompter. We cut out the word *seek* and the word *accept*, then we put them back again. That morning I gave it to Lady Bird, and she tinkered with it a bit and put brackets around one or two words. She had to dress early to go up to the Capitol to be with the wives. I had given her the excerpt for the speech.

"John Connally called that day and told me I should go ahead. 'You'll never have a better forum,' he said. But I thought I should get my messages to Congress up to Capitol Hill before I made any announcement. After the announcement I would never get my legislation passed. So, again, I set up an April 1 deadline.

"When I got up on the rostrum before Congress and reached into my pocket to get the excerpt for the speech, it wasn't there. When I got back home, I raised hell with Lady Bird. 'What in the hell did you do with that message?' I asked her. Then we went into the bedroom and found it by my telephone. I don't know how it got there. Maybe Lady Bird put it down by the telephone, or maybe I did. In any case by that time we didn't care.

"There were several personal factors that made me reach my decision. One was you. Your letter really affected me. You've helped me, and your family's helped me, and when I got a letter from you saying you were going along with me on most of my program but you had to leave me on the war, I began to think. You never did go along with the war, but I could feel you bear down a little harder on it.

"And I noticed that *Life* magazine changed its policy, and *Time* changed a bit. So did the *Washington Post*. All these things had their effect.

"Then there was Walter Reuther. I'd worked with him on education and antipoverty and a lot of other things, but I heard he was flirting with Bobby. I called him in Detroit to ask him how things were out there. He said he supposed they were fine. I asked him what the UAW was going to do, and he supposed they'd be all right. I said, 'What do you mean "suppose"? You know perfectly well you run the United Auto Workers.'

"He said they had to leave it to the Executive Council. I told him, 'You are the Executive Council.' I could tell that he was weakening. After all we'd been through together, working on legislation together, this hit me.

"Then I got to talking to my daughters. They're fine girls, married to fine boys. Pat Nugent had been down in Austin trying to get into the war, but his outfit wasn't going to be called, and he finally came back here to his old outfit near Washington. Chuck Robb has been in the marine corps eight years. He could be mustered out any time. Seven of those eight years he's been trying to go to Vietnam. He didn't have to go, but he maneuvered around trying to get there. He didn't appeal to the president. He's a bright boy, the best marine we had to handle things around the White House.

"Finally, he and Lynda Bird went out to the West Coast. When they went to the airport, she got there in thirty minutes, and he could have gone with her by private car, but he chose to go with his men by bus. It took them an hour. She waited for him, and then the television cameras came in trying to take pictures of them. They trampled one lady with a small child and pushed some children out of the way. You know how photographers are. They're pretty rough, but television cameramen are even rougher. And if you belong to a network, you think you own the world. It got so that nobody could say good-bye, and Chuck and Lynda couldn't say anything to each other. Finally, he went into the plane thirty minutes early and sat down so the TV cameramen would let the other people alone.

"The next morning Lynda Bird was due to come back at about six thirty. She flew the "red-eye" all night. Lady Bird and I decided that we wanted to meet her. We didn't want her coming into the White House that early all alone. So, we left word with the Secret Service to notify us thirty minutes in advance. We were awake and lying in bed before the Secret Service called. Then we went out to the South Gate to meet her.

"She talked to me about what a fine boy Chuck was, as if he was never coming back. And she said: 'Daddy, I want to ask you a question. Why do we have to fight over there when the people don't want us? Why do we have to send two hundred boys over there in Chuck's company, whether they want to go or not, when the people don't want us?' Her questions made an impression.

"That morning I had Horace Busby come over, and he wrote the first draft of my statement." The president went over to his desk and picked up a statement and brought it back to me. He read part of it aloud. It was too long, and he remarked, "If we had used all of it, I wouldn't have had any time left for the rest of my speech. So, we cut it down.

"Here, you can keep this. You're the only one I have given it to."

During our conversation LBJ called either George Christian or Tom Johnson to come in and take notes and bring me a pad. Christian finally came in toward the end of our conversation. Among other things Juanita Roberts brought in a copy of the letter which the chief justice had written to the president after he withdrew. It was a beautiful letter, giving Johnson credit for pioneering for better race relations. The chief justice said that the end of discrimination would not come in Johnson's lifetime but that he had paved the way for it.

"I think he's done more for this country than any other man of this era," the president told me. "He's got the courage of a Daniel Boone or a Davey Crockett, and yet he's as kindly as a grandmother. He's wise, and he doesn't say anything unless it's worth saying."

Toward the end of our conversation we talked about peace negotiations and the president's fear they were not getting anywhere. He got out the map and showed me the number of troops and supplies that were infiltrating south—a total of seventy thousand men in April and about thirty-three thousand men in the last week. He said that men who had been used for repair work had now donned uniforms and were fighting. The whole of North Vietnam had been taking advantage of the bombing pause to rehabilitate itself. Supplies were all over the streets of Haiphong, and a new base had been established at Thanh Hoa. He suggested that I write a column warning North Vietnam that the bombing might be resurrected, and he also said: "You get around among some of these Eastern Europeans. You might tip them off that the bombing pause will be over if they don't bring pressure on their friends in North Vietnam."

He talked about negotiations with Ho Chi Minh and said he had written Ho a letter for peace and that frequently you could get more done by these quiet appeals. "Every day or so," he said, "I write a private letter to somebody. I wrote several to Khrushchev in the old days.

"When I said I was going to go anywhere at any time to talk peace, a formal conference—I was referring to private talks. I still am willing to go anywhere, but you can't hold a state conference in some little town or in a Communist capital.

"The Poles tap our wires all the time. And the Jews would never understand it if we went to Warsaw, where Jews are no longer safe on the streets. We're willing to meet in Romania, a capitalist country, Algiers, or Austria. I don't want to meet in Paris. De Gaulle has been trying to embarrass us, and he's not willing to do anything unless he brings about the peace himself. I would even meet in Moscow, though I'm not anxious to."

I asked him about meeting in Yugoslavia. He was agreeable, though he said that North Vietnam had no embassy there. He discussed the idea of meeting on a boat, which was the proposal of General Ridgeway.

It was obvious the president was convinced that the North Vietnamese did not really want to talk peace. He said, "I'm under steady pressure from people who say I'm causing loss of life by not bombing.

"Why don't you write a story reminding people that there are 120 nations in the world, outside of Warsaw and Cambodia, where we would be delighted to meet, but write it carefully. Don't get me in the position of causing loss of life from all these supplies and men that are infiltrating. Just point out that the president's job is a tough one."

**FRIDAY, MAY 3** | At 1:00 a.m. last night the president received word from Hanoi that Paris would be acceptable for the truce talks. This must have been about thirty minutes after we left the White House.

On Wednesday the president said emphatically he would not accept Paris. I had tried to argue with him that de Gaulle could be an asset in helping to bring about peace, but the president was down on de Gaulle. He said de Gaulle was determined to show that he was right about peace in Vietnam. I had hoped to persuade the president that he could use de Gaulle for the betterment of mankind and the reestablishment of cordial Franco-American relations, but I'm not a very convincing talker, and the president had already made up his mind.

Apparently, he changed his mind in a hurry. I would be interested in knowing who helped him change it. Certainly, Arthur Goldberg did not. Jack had a story for the radio broadcast saying that this was the real reason for the break between the two men. Goldberg had asked U Thant to mediate the question of the truce talk site, and U Thant had come up with Paris, but the president brushed this aside, thereby putting Arthur in a difficult position. He resigned.

**THURSDAY, MAY 9** | Deke DeLoach, J. Edgar Hoover's liaison with the White House, called to see me. He came to lunch with Jack and showed me some amazing documents involving Bobby Kennedy and wiretaps. Bobby had telephoned me some months ago claiming he had nothing to do with wiretapping and putting the blame on Hoover. These documents show quite the contrary. His name is signed to one authorization. I suspect Deke was prompted by the president to talk to me.

We discussed the Martin Luther King assassination and the elusive murderer, James Ray. Deke thinks he's probably in Mexico in some remote mountain village. The Negro world is claiming that the FBI is remiss in not tracking

Ray down because Hoover was a critic of King. Deke says all investigations are in his hands, not Hoover's, and that he has been doing his darnedest. I am sure he is telling the truth.

Marvin Watson suggests that now is the time for J. Edgar Hoover to step down. He has wondered whether a discreet suggestion from the president might induce Hoover to do so. I doubt it. The interesting point is that LBJ is thinking of a "discreet suggestion" rather than merely refusing to extend Hoover's exemption from mandatory retirement at the age of seventy.

THURSDAY, MAY 16 | Dean Rusk has issued a denial of a story by Chalmers Roberts yesterday that the United States would be willing to accept members of the Communist National Liberation Front in the South Vietnamese government. Rusk came out with a ringing denial, issued personally, which he doesn't often do.

I suspect Roberts jumped the gun on something Averell was planning to spring later at the Paris truce talks. Harriman has been conducting the talks in a dignified manner—no forensics, no political speeches. On the other hand, the North Vietnamese have been playing to the gallery. Meanwhile, de Gaulle is having real problems. The student strike at the Sorbonne has spread to the factories, not merely in Paris but Lyon. It's never been this bad since de Gaulle came to power. When he first did, there was opposition from the right, so the Communist Party sent word that they would support him in any showdown. Now, however, it's the left wing (with some Communist support) causing the trouble.

THURSDAY, MAY 23 | De Gaulle was endorsed by the chamber of deputies today by a margin of about ten votes. The Communist Party voted against him, though David Karr claims the Communist emergency squads in the streets have worked for him.

We are beginning to get kickbacks from the column on Bobby Kennedy tapping the wires of Martin Luther King. It's due to be published tomorrow, and various papers, which have it in advance, are raising the red flag. Ben Bradlee of the *Post* telephoned Deke DeLoach today, which worried DeLoach. We had hoped to get more of the confidential FBI memos before publication, but it looks as if we won't. The FBI is running scared. In fact, they demanded we modify the column I have written for today for release Monday.

Leonard advised that now was the time to put across some good TV interviews with the president for ABC, such as what happened between him and

Kosygin. "He's saving some of these for his book, but he could talk to you about some of them. Remember, they won't be much good after he leaves the White House."

We went to Agnes Meyer's for dinner in honor of Dobrynin. John Gardner was there, also Kay Graham, Marquis Childs, and the Phil Geyelin. I had a nice talk with Phil, who was quite complimentary about my Big Brothers dinner. I have not known him well. He is a strong Bobby Kennedy man but agreed that the story on Bobby's wiretapping of Martin Luther King should be published.

Gardner had a talk with Reagan and rubbed his eyes in bewilderment over the idea of having him as president. "It would be like turning the clock back fifty years," Gardner said. "He has no understanding of what the world is all about." John was rather concerned over the Rockefeller-Reagan meeting in New Orleans. It looks as if Rockefeller was trimming his sails in order to get delegates.

Ambassador Dobrynin is amazing. He manages to keep up a lighthearted repartée with everyone, even when they rib him a bit. He understands American politics better than most of our politicians. He has done an excellent job; so has his wife. She sticks to such nonpolitical topics as the weather, the architecture and art of Moscow, and her dacha in the country. She has just come back from spending the winter there.

Kay Graham asked Dobrynin about the present UN and the difficulty of getting real work accomplished with Tanzania, as it did today, blasting the nonproliferation pact. Dobrynin remarked that the UN was not turning out as it was originally conceived by the founders in San Francisco. He observed that the two nations which know best the dangers of nuclear war are now united in trying to prevent the danger of nuclear war but are getting no support from the others. "I must say that we do a little better than you in controlling our friends and allies," he said.

FRIDAY, MAY 24 | The *Washington Post* published the King–Bobby Kennedy column, deleting the sex references. It made a pretty good column even the way they edited it. Today I got calls from Portland, Oregon, wanting to reprint the column, and from Gene Wyman in Los Angeles, wanting to do likewise. The *New York Times* also called to report that Larry O'Brien in Portland remarked that they expected a last-minute smear story which couldn't be answered. I told the *Times* that perhaps the best part of the Bobby Kennedy wiretap story was coming out after the Oregon primary.

Jack reports the FBI is increasingly jittery and is holding back on the important memo of July 16, 1963, in which Courtney Evans reported on his conversation with Bobby Kennedy, dissuading him from the first wiretap on King. Jack asked me to reach Hubert Humphrey, which I finally managed to do. He was in Missouri, having traveled through South Dakota and parts of Kansas en route to a dedication ceremony in St. Louis. I told him we needed the July 16 memo.

De Gaulle announced he would submit a referendum to the people in June whereby they could vote on a new program. If they rejected it, he would resign. The speech was met with derision on the part of many. The students rioted further and even set fires to the Bourse. They hoisted the black flag over the Bourse building. I still don't see how things got out of hand so suddenly in Paris. They are experiencing real anarchy.

We dined at the Venezuelan embassy. Joan Gardner reminded me that she had told me a long time ago that Bobby Kennedy had put a wiretap on the telephone of Martin Luther King. I'd forgotten that at the Franklin Roosevelt, Jr. dinner she and I had talked about Bobby, and she did tell me about the King wiretap. I must have been a lousy newspaperman to let this go over my head for so long. "I was sworn to secrecy," said Joan. "I was told not to tell anyone. And I didn't, except to Drew Pearson, who has 638 newspapers." She was rather delighted with the whole thing.

THURSDAY, MAY 30 | The president held a press conference at the LBJ Ranch, exhibiting General Westmoreland once again to the public. Westmoreland is statuesque but repeated that the enemy was on the run and getting desperate, while he has shown conclusively that the U.S. Army cannot keep order. To some extent Saigon has become the Dien Bien Phu of our war.

The most important part of the president's press conference was a planted question whether he would accept the $6 billion cut in the budget, voted by the House Ways and Means Committee, in return for the 10 percent surtax increase. On May 3 Johnson held a press conference in which he scolded Congress and told them to "bite the bullet" and pass the surtax. This time it was he who bit the bullet and accepted a $6 billion cutback, instead of $4 billion. That extra $2 billion will be taken out of anti-poverty, big city redevelopment, or education. What it means is that the Great Society program has been severely bitten into and partially put on the shelf.

Jack called Senator McCarthy to get him prepared. McCarthy told him he had found a bug in his hotel conference room that night. Also, that Sen. Mark Hatfield had tipped him off that Pierre Salinger was paying waitresses at the Benson Hotel twenty dollars apiece to listen in on the conversations of the McCarthy entourage. They were coached before they went on duty and then reported when they went off duty and given twenty dollars. Jack called Senator Hatfield, who confirmed the story. Jack cut a special insert in our radio program for this evening.

**SUNDAY, JUNE 2** | I didn't get a chance to listen to the [Kennedy-McCarthy] debate last night, but I gathered from Luvie and Jack it was a dud. Neither man got off any fireworks, and McCarthy failed to bring out the Pierre Salinger eavesdropping and to push home the Dr. King wiretapping against Bobby. Jack telephoned McCarthy three times on Saturday, and when they talked the third time, McCarthy was all set to punch, and punch hard—but didn't.

Bill Lawrence did ask Bobby about [the] King wiretap and got an evasive answer; however, he didn't deny anything. It would have been great if he had called me a liar, but he didn't. He said that as attorney general he had been required to sign various wiretap orders and that he wasn't going to discuss any individual wiretaps. He added that he had nothing to do with it.

**MONDAY, JUNE 3** | I found that Jack had substituted for the column I left behind a story on Pierre Salinger tipping waitresses twenty dollars each in the Benson Hotel in Portland to spy on luncheon and dinner customers, including McCarthy people. He included in the story the fact that McCarthy had found an electronic bug in his conference room when meeting with the Malcolm X people in Los Angeles. It looked like a continued pattern of eavesdropping by Bobby Kennedy.

**TUESDAY, JUNE 4** | Senator Hatfield of Oregon telephoned that he'd had a call from Salinger, raising Cain because we quoted Hatfield regarding the eavesdropping incident in the 121 Benson Hotel. Salinger asked that Hatfield send him a telegram denying the whole business. Hatfield refused.

Subsequently, Ben Bradlee of the *Post* called to say he'd had several phone calls from Salinger and his lawyer demanding that the story be killed. Jack did some checking and found that, contrary to Salinger's statement that he had never been in the Benson Hotel, he had actually stayed there for two weeks in May and had not yet paid his bill. The people whom Jack talked to in Portland and who, in turn, had talked to the waitresses found that the management had called in the waitresses and raised Cain. The waitresses had clammed up; however, Ben is convinced the story is accurate and is standing by us, except that he is rather pained by the frequent columns we have had criticizing Bobby Kennedy. "Why don't you dig up some stuff on Hubert Humphrey or McCarthy?" he said.

There just isn't anything to be dug up on Humphrey. His life is pretty much an open book, and I have been following it carefully for twenty years. We have also written a lot about McCarthy and his voting record for the oil depletion allowance and for higher-priced drugs. We can't go on repeating this. On the other hand, Bobby has led a fairly unscathed life as far as press criticism is concerned. Now unreported events seem to be turning up from all sorts of sources. Perhaps the most damning is a deposition which has turned up in the General Aniline and Film [Corp.] case showing that Bobby, as attorney general, turned the company back to its Swiss stockholders for a very small amount of money compared with the real value, and the reason was that his brother-in-law, Prince Radziwill, had been hired by the Swiss firm. I hinted at this in an early column when Bobby was attorney general, but the whole thing is a shocker, and it's all spelled out in a sworn deposition.

In the afternoon Lloyd Shearer of *Parade* magazine called from Los Angeles to say that the voting trend looked as if Bobby was going to lose. He credited Jack's and my stories on Martin Luther King's wiretapping with the loss of the Negro vote.

[Pages missing, including Pearson's reaction to Robert F. Kennedy's assassination.]

. . . I wrote a special column, the second in two days. Yesterday we sent out by telegraph a special column replacing the one on Salinger's eavesdropping. The substitution was made not because of Salinger's threats but because of the attack on Bobby. We devoted most of the broadcast to Bobby, including an editorial over the question of crime on television.

Ellen called late in the evening to say that a news program had named me, the *New York Times*, and Mayor Sam Yorty as the three chief enemies of Bobby Kennedy. Later I learned it was Sandy Vanocur who had been traveling on the plane with Bobby's body and was talking to Teddy Kennedy, who was quite bitter. I imagine I'll hear more of this.

FRIDAY, JUNE 7 | Ernest Cuneo came to breakfast, and we talked about Bobby. He was a strange person: able, dynamic, dedicated, sensitive in a way, but ruthless. He could be extremely kind and thoughtful. I remember when he took the trouble to come to the Russian baseball game at the University of Maryland when we were trying to raise money for Big Brothers. And I remember the money he raised for a swimming pool for one of the playgrounds in the Cardoza District and the halfway houses he helped to build for boys who were getting out of reformatories. Yet he was also ruthless as a Joe McCarthy investigator and almost as flagrant as his brother in his infidelity. There was no question that he did have an affair with Marilyn Monroe before she committed suicide, though the book about this was highly exaggerated. And he also had that famous case in Paris with Candy Bergen, about which Dave Karr claims to have a monitored tape.

"They were beautiful people," said Ernest, "but it was so expensive. People around them went broke trying to keep up with the standard. And everyone around John F. Kennedy who tried to emulate him got a divorce: Salinger, Sorensen, Schlesinger. All their marriages broke up. His father financed his presidential campaign, and it's reported that he got his money back within one year."

It's a tragic family—three sons dead and one daughter and one in a mental institution. Maybe this is because they pushed too hard, were too ruthless in overcoming all obstacles, and used money as their God. Maybe it was retribution. Old Joe was a man who'd do anything for power and for the achievement of his ambition to put his sons in the White House.

Kennedy's body was flown to New York today and is lying in state in St. Patrick's Cathedral. Crowds are flocking through. Luvie remarked it must be comforting to have a strong religion, something you can cling to in time of death. I wonder, however, whether Kennedy's religion was not more of a form than a fact. The body is to come by special train to Washington tomorrow, to be interred next to his brother in Arlington Cemetery.

It was only in March that Bobby announced he was running for president. Three fast and furious months of campaigning, and now he is dead.

SATURDAY, JUNE 8 | Bobby's funeral began at ten this morning at St. Patrick's Cathedral and lasted until about ten thirty tonight in Arlington Cemetery. It was an Old World pageant such as we seldom see anymore. It was a great tribute and also a political masterpiece. About seventy thousand people streamed through St. Patrick's during the night to view the casket. Finally, the police had to stop the line and clear the church for the funeral. The highlight was

Teddy Kennedy's eulogy to his brother, which had all the earmarks of being a political declaration that he was going to run. He emphasized youth—the fact that Alexander the Great was thirty-two years old when he conquered the East; that Thomas Jefferson was about the same age when he declared that all men are free and equal; and he brought in Christopher Columbus and his youth and Joan of Arc and her youth. It was a moving speech, and it also had important political overtones.

The train was three hours late reaching Washington, due to a late start and the fact that two spectators were killed at Elizabeth and that the train slowed down at every city where there was a crowd.

I thought about the advantages of youth in world leadership. I was never a great admirer of Dwight Eisenhower as president, and I admired John F. Kennedy much more, but Kennedy got us into the Bay of Pigs fiasco, where Eisenhower had that decision to make in November 1960 and decided against it. Kennedy rolled up two divisions to go into Laos, got himself into a crisis over Berlin by calling for a showdown with Khrushchev, then sent the first real troops into South Vietnam. Eisenhower did none of these things. He was slow and vacillated at times, but after John Foster Dulles died, he did a fairly good job in foreign affairs.

The Eisenhower years were dreary years. We didn't have glamour in the White House. We had dull stag parties, with Mamie seldom present, but we didn't get into any major wars. There wasn't as much to write about as there was under Kennedy, but the international boat was not rocked.

In 1960, before Kennedy was nominated, I wrote that he was inexperienced in the field of foreign affairs. Kennedy approached Jack with a lot of argument that I was unfair, and I agreed that if I had the facts wrong regarding his foreign affairs experience, I would correct them. Jack came up with an interesting set of facts, supplied him by Kennedy, which consisted chiefly of trips taken abroad in the summertime to the French Riviera, plus living in England when his father was ambassador. He was very young then, however, and the trips to Europe were superficial. I couldn't see that he had any real foreign affairs background.

He picked Dean Rusk as secretary of state, a man who knew Asia well but did not know the rest of the world. Rusk has turned out to be reasonably good on the rest of the world but poor on Asia. And at the start Kennedy spurned the advice of Adlai Stevenson, Fulbright, Senator Cooper, and others to take the initiative with Khrushchev regarding Berlin. He waited and waited to discuss Berlin until he was in exactly the wrong position. By spring 1961 Khrushchev was sore at having been spurned earlier, and Kennedy was bargaining from a position of weakness following the Bay of Pigs fiasco.

Kennedy did learn, but he learned at the expense of the United States, and when you're president, you cannot afford that kind of an education.

Johnson, of course, didn't do much better in regard to Asia and, at first, Latin America. Regarding Europe, however, and later Latin America, he has done well.

Foreign affairs depend on experience. Youth is an advantage when it comes to political revolution and domestic change, but you need some wisdom and experience to guide you in both. What we need in running the country is a mixture of youth, energy, age, and wisdom.

President Johnson flew up to St. Patrick's Cathedral, along with Lady Bird. He looked ill at ease when he commiserated with the Kennedy family. I suspect that most people knew how bitter had been their relationship.

The president was also on hand at Union Station in Washington to receive the funeral train, and he drove in the funeral procession to Arlington, where again he shook hands with the Kennedy family before the casket was lowered. He was in a sort of damned-if-you-do, damned-if-you-don't position. Some people probably will criticize him for shedding crocodile tears. If he hadn't gone, he would have been criticized even more.

What might Teddy Kennedy do during the next few days? McCarthy and Bobby Kennedy had managed to create an impression in the minds of the American people that Hubert Humphrey is old and out-of-date and a run-of-the-mill politician not to be trusted. Unfortunately, Hubert's face on television comes off as if he were an old-fashioned politician. It's a bad contrast to the young, handsome visage of Teddy Kennedy. Hubert talked about happiness, and today we are steeped in tragedy.

I suspect that if Teddy Kennedy makes an all-out drive for the Democratic nomination, he could probably get it. Such is the power of television. Such is the compulsion of pity.

There have been some other developments in the world today, though you'd never know it. James Earl Ray was picked up in London as the assassin of Martin Luther King. He was traveling on a Canadian passport.

More trouble has developed in the Poor People's March. Bayard Rustin, who organized the successful 1963 civil rights march on Washington, has pulled out of the proposed demonstration [to be held] June 19. Membership in

Resurrection City has dropped from three thousand to about seven hundred. There is internal dissension, plus rape and robberies among the members.

**SUNDAY, JUNE 9** | Was I too hard on Bobby Kennedy? Tyler doesn't think so. Regarding the assassination, he says that Bobby asked for it. When you permit a crowd to come as close as he did, to steal a dozen or so pairs of cufflinks and even take off your shoes, you are courting disaster. This is something that feeds on itself. When people see television shots of crowds doing this or read in the newspapers about it, they also do it.

Tyler also thinks Bobby came into the race in a deliberate attempt to defeat LBJ this year and knowing he himself could not get the nomination. He had figured that if Johnson was elected president again and served another four years, the Democratic Party was bound to go out of office in 1972 and the Republicans would enjoy eight years. This total of twelve years would take history beyond the point where he could run. So, he figured his best bet was to let the Republicans win in 1968 and get their eight years over with. Then he, Bobby, could win in 1976.

Of course, Bobby got into the race in early March, well before the president announced he was not going to run, on March 31. And knowing how carefully he calculates in advance and recalling how quickly he jumped in after McCarthy scored his victory in New Hampshire, Tyler's reasoning may well be correct.

The Kennedys do think years in advance, as taught them by their father, who had planned many years ago that his son Joseph P. Kennedy Jr. would be the first Catholic president of the United States.

It will take a long time, however, for the public to catch up with the real Bobby Kennedy. He was a man who kept his goals for the common man. He was thoughtful of other people though ruthless toward his enemies. He was a young man of great wealth, who was not afraid to use his wealth for better things, though its chief use was the fulfillment of personal ambition. There's nothing wrong with ambition. Certainly, the Rockefeller family has had it, but they have used their wealth and their ambition in a more kindly, constructive manner. Nelson Rockefeller has not ridden roughshod over everyone around him. Perhaps if he'd had a little more of the Bobby Kennedy in him, he would be top man in the Republican race for president today. If Rockefeller had used his fortune, for instance, in the same way the Republican Eastern establishment used it to nominate Eisenhower in 1952, Rockefeller would easily be the front-running Republican candidate.

The real hero of these tragic days has been Ethel Kennedy. I suppose the secret of her heroism is that she has faith. She has faith in her family, faith in herself, and most of all, faith in her religion. She has borne herself nobly.

Lally Graham Weymouth, who, with her husband, worked hard for Bobby, was out at the farm today, indignant that her mother rode on the funeral train and is now visiting at Hickory Hill, whereas she, Lally, and Yann did not enjoy either. She does not realize that with the Kennedys privileges go to the rich and the powerful, and the *Washington Post* is a powerful newspaper. "Mother," says Lally, "didn't even like Bobby."

Dobrynin was also at the dinner. He came late, apparently delayed by the crisis over Berlin. George McGhee, former ambassador to West Germany, and Ambassador Knappstein told me that the situation was serious. They have been expecting the East Germans to crack down for some time, in view of the fact that the United States is involved in South Vietnam. East Germany is now requiring trucks, passengers, and vehicles crossing it between West Germany and Berlin to have passport visas and pay a transit tax. Seventy percent of the traffic between West Germany and Berlin is overland or by barge. Thirty percent is by air.

Ulbricht, the hard-boiled Stalinist who heads East Germany, has been chafing at the new developments in the Communist world. Apparently, the Russians have had to appease him by going along with this latest move.

**TUESDAY, JUNE 18** | The Supreme Court yesterday handed down a historic decision on housing, finding that the law of 1866 was still valid. The law gives a Negro the same right as a white man in getting housing and permits him to sue anyone who denies it. It puts into effect immediately the open housing provision of the Civil Rights Bill, which otherwise was not going into effect until the end of the year and applied then only to apartment houses of more than five units. This is a more sweeping decision and the interesting thing is that Potter Stewart, the conservative Republican member of the Court, wrote the opinion. I can see the hand of the chief justice here.

**SATURDAY, JUNE 22** | Had an appointment with the president at 1:00 p.m. to talk over the FCC vacancy. In the morning Leonard Marks called to say the president had some opposition to Joe Borkin and he had several other candidates, including Rex Lee, the former governor of Samoa, whom Leonard considered to be an excellent man.

I came in through the diplomatic entrance and saw that the limousine of the secretary of defense was parked there. I waited in the Fish Room.

I saw the president at one forty. He was dressed in a brown summer suit and said that Averell Harriman had come in this morning to report on the truce talks.

I asked whether Averell was optimistic. He replied: "He is not as optimistic as Clark Clifford, nor as pessimistic as I am. I don't think anything will come of it, though Clark thinks we're making some progress. At any rate we're winning the support and respect of some of the European countries. The Swedish press, the Dutch press, the Western European press generally, has called attention to the attacks on Saigon while these talks are continuing. I think sentiment has turned in our favor.

"I've just come from a weeping daughter who received a letter from her husband." He pulled a letter out of a side pocket from Chuck Robb and leaned over so I could read it as he read it aloud. It was addressed to "My darling Lynda" and went on to tell how they had been fighting almost every day. One detachment went out in advance and got booby-trapped, losing three men, with many others seriously wounded. Chuck concluded the letter by saying he was going forward into the mountains and would not be able to write to her for a good many days. It was a hurried letter, written by a man who sees death all around him, and I can understand why Lynda was worried.

The president told me Chuck had started out with about 160 men and was now down to around 120 or 130.

"We are losing 500 men a week, while they are losing 5,000. These are kamikaze attacks, where the men can't possibly survive—only they're worse than the Japanese kamikaze attacks because a good many men are involved. They're fighting for the effect on the Paris truce talks. They seem to want to drive a wedge between us. We don't know, but they may be succeeding between Vice President Ky and President Thieu. Ky disappears from time to time, and we don't know what he's up to. This new premier, Huong, is a pretty tough cookie and doesn't always get along with Ky."

I reminded the president that he'd asked me to talk to some of the Eastern European leaders about pressuring the North Vietnamese and that I had done so with the Soviet and Yugoslav ambassadors without tangible success. I told him I had talked also with the Romanian, who was reasonably receptive and told me Romania had excellent relations with the North Vietnamese, probably better than any other country.

I told the president that I had argued with the Romanian ambassador there was grave danger of a right-wing swing in this country if the war was not settled. I had pointed to the defeat of Senator Kuchel in California and some of the other right-wing moves and reminded the Romanian that he did not want Nixon.

The president interrupted to say he'd talked to about twenty-five Democratic leaders and that all of them privately said it looked as if Nixon would get the nomination on the Republican ticket and would win. "The best thing to do when you're in an election," the president said, "is to show an air of confidence—that you're going to win, but privately almost every Democratic leader I talk to thinks the opposite."

I said that when I talked to the Romanian, I talked merely as a newspaperman and that I thought if there was some official spokesman who could talk to the Romanians, it might have some impact. I suggested: "Now that the chief justice is going to be a private citizen, you might consider sending him on a mission to Romania. He has been over there, and the Romanians like him and respect him, and he might be able to do some good."

I said the foreign minister of Romania was now president of the UN General Assembly. President Johnson said he had met and talked with him and that the vice premier of Romania was coming here soon. He was hoping to see him. He mentioned that he had great confidence in the chief justice and would be willing to send him on a mission anyplace.

He went on to say he was going to try to persuade the chief justice to remain on. "I may not accept his resignation," the president said. "I'm going to have great difficulty getting anyone confirmed to take his place. The chief justice recommended Abe Fortas, and my inclination would be to appoint him; however, the Republicans will probably vote against him, and so will the southern Democrats. Eastland will simply sit on the appointment in the Judiciary Committee."

"They'll just bottle up the appointment . . . I wish some crusading newspaper would wage a campaign against all these congressional vacations. They've just been home for Memorial Day, and they're going to take a week off in advance of the Fourth of July. Then they'll leave a week before the first of August in order to get home for the Republican convention; then they'll go away before the Democratic convention. Then they'll take another week off at Labor Day. I figure I'm going to have all sorts of trouble getting anything through the remainder of this Congress."

We went over the names of prospective Court appointees. The president had obviously been thinking about this carefully. I told him the chief justice had discussed his retirement with me before the word leaked out and that he was fearful Nixon was going to be elected. The president said Warren's letter had mentioned health only, that obviously he didn't want to have the word get out that he was fearful of Nixon's being elected and appointing his successor.

The president named Senator Muskie of Maine as a good man. I concurred. Also Fred Harris of Oklahoma, whom he said, however, was tied up as Humphrey's campaign manager.

"How about Senator Kuchel of California?" I asked.

"The [American] Bar Association [ABA] won't recommend him. He's a lawyer, hardly practiced. Warren appointed him as his controller," the president replied. "I'm having a hard time now getting him appointed as a member of the circuit court of appeals. I think I'll get it across, but the Senate doesn't want to confirm anyone that the Bar Association doesn't recommend."

I suggested Ken Keating, the former senator from New York, and Johnson thought this was an excellent idea. Keating is sixty-eight.

"He's already on the court in New York and would be an excellent appointment," the president said. I said I'd seen Keating a few days before and that he was looking fit and healthy.

"I've already mentioned Rusk," he continued. "Poor Rusk. He agreed to see a delegation of Mexican Americans and told them to bring about six. He said he wanted a quiet session without any cameras. They came with over a hundred people and television cameras. All these people are doing is to cost their friends votes. Their best friend was Hubert Humphrey, and they're hurting him every day they demonstrate."

Resuming to the Supreme Court vacancy, I expressed some surprise that the chief justice had recommended Abe Fortas. I said I thought some of Abe's opinions had not gone down well.

"The job of chief justice is partly to maneuver and administrate," the president replied. "He has to make sure that the right man writes the right opinions. He tells me that Abe is a very good maneuverer. I also gather that Hugo Black has gone right around the circle and is now a conservative. They've made some hints that he ought to get off, but he doesn't move.

The chief actually announced in Court that he was going to retire because of his age, but Hugo didn't take the hint. Then there's John Harlan, who's seventy-seven and has to hold a paper right up to his eyes in order to see it. Bill Douglas has a bad heart. They tried to persuade him not to come to Court last Monday to read his dissent. And Byron White, who they thought would be a liberal, has turned out to be a conservative.

I mentioned Arthur Goldberg, pointing out that I had probably been responsible for a certain amount of ill will between the two men because I had written the story in December that Arthur was going to resign, which probably shouldn't have been written.

"You weren't responsible," the president said. "He told that to five or six people. I didn't draft Arthur to get off the Court, though most people thought I had. Ken Galbraith came in to tell me Arthur was unhappy, didn't like all the routine legal work, and that he would like to get back in the cabinet. He turned down the secretary of HEW, but he did say he'd like to be UN ambassador, so I appointed him. Then I began to hear rumors that Arthur was unhappy and thinking about resigning.

"Finally, last December, he came to me and said he was thinking about resigning. All right, I said, when? He fixed a date of about January 18 but then said he'd have to talk it over with Dorothy.

"Well, January 18 came, and I didn't hear from him. Then another month, then another month. Finally, he said he wanted to resign this June, so I'm giving a reception for him on Monday, as I do for every member of the cabinet who leaves."

"You're going to be awfully bored when you leave here," I said. "No, I don't think so," he replied. "I like young people and I've got a lot of plans to work with them. I'm going to make talks, perhaps ten or so a year, about the problems of government. The International Institute at Princeton had eight hundred applications last year, of which four hundred were from top students. They could only take in thirty or forty. We'll take some of them down at my new institute.

"We're going to teach government. We're going to train people to run for Congress or mayor or president. Hitherto they've taken ex-newspapermen or lawyers or ex-politicians, and they've run for Congress. I think I can teach government. I have held positions in almost every branch of it. I began with the National Youth Administration, then Congress. I was never defeated. I was elected to the Senate, and within one year I had become minority leader and later majority leader. I was chairman of five different committees, from Space to Preparedness. Then I became vice president and served for a year and a half for the balance of the Kennedy term and another four years now. I think I know government and can help to train these young people.

"Our building is going to open next September. That should have been a tipoff as to whether I was going to run. I think the best way to educate young people is through bull sessions, and that's what we're going to do."

In the course of this discussion I mentioned the fact that my grandsons, Lyndon and Danny Abell, were down at the ranch. The president said: "Bess Abell is the most efficient woman I have ever known. She can get things done without any commotion, get her own way without you realizing it. She'll ask you how many people for a party and you say 150. She says why not 200 and you say no. Then she says: 'Well, you forgot Drew Pearson. He hasn't been around to the White House this year.' Then she'll add, 'What about the lawyers?' and she'll remember someone else, and pretty soon you're back up to 200, and she's done it all without you realizing that she was opposed to you.

"Lady Bird says that if she could afford it, she would hire Bess to stay on after she leaves. She'd hire Bess and Liz Carpenter. As it is, she's going to have them reserve every April to come down there to the ranch to put on some pageants."

When I first came in, the president picked up a sheaf of papers and put them on his side table. I suspected they were reports on the candidates for the FCC, and he now picked them up and said: "I can't appoint your friend. I've had some complaints about him." He then read from a Civil Service Commission report on six or eight candidates.

Joe Borkin's record showed he was pushed by me but did not mention such backers as Thurman Arnold and Magnuson. I asked him about this, and he said he had not read the Thurman Arnold letter. The report on Joe said he was engaged in antitrust activities, was controversial and not a team player. It also mentioned the fact that there had been some publicity regarding his appointment.

I said the FBI had leaked that story through the *Washington Star*, and the president replied that wouldn't make any difference. I am sure the FBI leaked it deliberately, knowing the president's fondness for crossing up any newspaperman who scoops him.

I argued that the FCC was half-asleep and needed shaking up. "You've had a lot of criticism over the FCC," I said. He interrupted: "I read your column.

I haven't done a damn thing with the FCC. I put those properties down in Austin under a trust to my children and wife, and I don't even see the balance sheet. I'm not permitted to. The only thing the FCC can do would be to remove the licenses of those stations."

The president got rather het up over this, and I concluded that I shouldn't have mentioned it. I said, however: "Criticism isn't always fair. You've been unfairly criticized on a lot of things, and this criticism of you does persist and is vigorous. I have counteracted it, have talked to Leonard about it. I know what the facts are; nevertheless, the criticism is there. What you need is someone who will really shake up the FCC, and Borkin would do it."

I didn't get very far. I'm sure some of the networks registered their squawk immediately after the premature publication in the *Washington Star*. I had to confess that Rex Lee and Weisl were good men. As I left, the president said, "You talk this over with Leonard some more, particularly Lee, Weisl, and Borkin.

As I went out the door, I came away feeling I had lost the battle over Borkin. With this president you have to be tough in trading. I had written him a letter in which I said I wouldn't be irked with him, and he obviously remembered this because during the course of our conversation he said, "You said in your letter I have a lot of headaches, and you are so right."

I telephoned Joe Borkin afterward and gave him the report. He said he was not too unhappy, though I think he was.

P.S. Toward the end of our conversation I suggested he might consider persuading J. Edgar Hoover to retire so that a successor could be appointed rather than leaving it to Nixon. "I've considered that," Lyndon replied. "But unless you got an agreement from Hoover and the appointment of somebody he wanted, there would be hell to pay on Capitol Hill. Hoover has fellows like Dirksen and Mundt eating out of his hand. I don't know what the reaction would be to a young fellow such as Deke DeLoach."

I suggested that the job did not require Senate confirmation, but he corrected me. "It does under the new crime bill. I had a hard time deciding whether to sign it. That was one of the things I objected to. The chief justice dated his letter of retirement before the date when I signed the bill so it wouldn't look as if he was protesting."

THURSDAY, JUNE 27 | This morning I was confronted with a page 1 story that Abe Fortas had been appointed chief justice, with Judge Homer Thornberry taking his place as associate justice. I wasn't surprised about Fortas but [was] surprised at the latter because the president told me he did not know that he wanted to bring Homer up from Texas. In retrospect I suspect he was trying to throw me off for fear I would write the story.

FRIDAY, JUNE 28 | (En route to Washington, from Bemidji, Minnesota.) I wrote a column on Minnesota politics. When I got to the office, I had a call from Walt Rostow—a surprise since he has not called since I took some side-swipes at his hawkish advice to LBJ. He called this time to suggest a story on the president's persistence in plugging for better relations with Soviet Russia.

Rostow's point is legitimate. Foreign Minister Gromyko yesterday made an important speech before the Supreme Soviet, welcoming disarmament talks with the United States. This was an important switch because only a couple of weeks ago, when Johnson made a favorable statement about improving relations with Russia, TASS came back with a blunt rebuff. Walt pointed out that the president had accomplished something more important than the test ban treaty, which had a limited objective, and that if he hadn't been dogged, both at Glassboro, before Glassboro, and since, he wouldn't have gotten anywhere.

"People miss the fact that despite the war in Vietnam he has kept his eye on the relationship with the Soviet Union," Walt said. "It would have been easy for him to be distracted, to say, 'Let's wait.' But he didn't. These negotiations have been personally managed by him. In my opinion it's one of the great personal achievements since World War II.

"We are at a stage in Vietnam, and also in the Near East, where things could break either way. We could get a break for peace or not. I think it's important that the president get some recognition regarding this and also that people abroad realize that he's not losing power but is in a position to put across these important moves.

"*Time* last week carried an unfortunate story that things were slowing down at the White House and that he was a lame-duck president with nothing more to do. The fact is that he has never been working harder. He has taken himself out of politics in order to try to accomplish something important on the peace front. If the world regards him as impotent and a lame duck, then he won't have a chance to end the war in Vietnam. He has a chance to do big things simply because he's taken himself out of politics."

Remembering the Russian reaction to his March 31 speech and the fact that the Vietnamese were then willing to talk peace, I think Rostow was right. Rostow said that Secretary Rusk and Bill Foster were great soldiers on the disarmament front but it had been the president who pushed ahead. He emphasized three speeches that LBJ had made—at the anniversary of the Glassboro conference, at the UN regarding nonproliferation, and at the recent signing of the consular convention. TASS panned him. Nevertheless, he pushed ahead.

He had written a series of letters to Kosygin in which the theme was "this is the time" for us to move, "this is the way our two countries must go."

I called George Christian to tell him I was writing the story about the negotiations and suggested that the story would be stronger if I had a little straw with which to build the bricks—namely, the text of one of the letters to Kosygin or some good quotes. George replied that this would make the Russians very nervous and might spoil the results of the talks.

The president has been good on the subject of Soviet-American relations. He has seen the goal exactly as it is, but I recall some hectic arguments I've had with him in the past, particularly on one occasion when he was about to blast the Russians and I urged him not to. Bill Moyers sided with me, and we finally toned him down. I remember telling him that someday he would need the Russians and, for God's sake, not to alienate them.

**WEDNESDAY, JULY 10** | Johnson has broadened his drive to improve relations in Latin America by indirectly approaching Fidel Castro about a resumption of diplomatic relations. This is real pioneering though somewhat overdone.

Also, he has received word from Premier Kosygin, who would like to discuss the Near East. I don't know when Kosygin's letter arrived, but right now President Nasser of Egypt is in Moscow and, according to reports, getting a cool reception. The Russians apparently have got him to agree to permit Israeli ships to transit the Suez Canal, and obviously they want it opened for the use of Soviet ships. Nasser has also agreed on recognizing Israel as a state. The Russians, I gather, have held back on any further shipments of arms to Egypt and are using this as a club.

All this fits into a possible opening for LBJ to weld a new peace in the Near East. It will be difficult but can be done.

**FRIDAY, JULY 12** | The Abe Fortas hearings have gone into their second day. I suspect LBJ will batter down the opposition. Larry Temple called me from the White House to give me a precedent for Earl Warren's resignation, subject to a replacement. It was an exchange of letters between Teddy Roosevelt and Justice Gray in which Gray resigned subject to his replacement.

Congress is rushing toward a close, and as usual, the lobbyists are getting in their final licks. I've written a column on the trucking lobby and the manner in which it has ridden over the beautification program, the protection of historic sites, and wildlife refuges. What the lobby has done is scandalous. It's more powerful than any other in the country and for years got its way with Congress under Eisenhower, whereas the teachers got nothing. Today it is still powerful but has to operate more behind the scenes than before.

MONDAY, JULY 22 | LBJ has flown back to the ranch from Honolulu. The general reaction to his statement that there would be no coalition government [in South Vietnam] and no de-escalation of the war has been sour. He knocked peace hopes sky high. I had broadcast only yesterday evening that there was great optimism regarding a cease-fire.

Nelson Poynter, publisher of the *St. Petersburg Times*, came to lunch, and we speculated as to why Lyndon reversed himself. Obviously, there had been optimism around the White House prior to his trip to Honolulu. Our only conclusion was that he got carried away by the military or that he bowed to the persuasiveness of President Thieu. I recalled the atmosphere of efficiency and persuasion when I was in Pearl Harbor last summer. It's easy to go along with that atmosphere. "In other words, he got brainwashed," said Nelson.

WEDNESDAY, JULY 24 | Last night, after Mayor Stokes got back to Cleveland, shooting started in the Negro section. Some Negro snipers took potshots at the police towing a car. The incident was unprovoked. Three policemen were killed, and afterward a Negro named Ahmed Evans boasted to the police that he would have killed more if his gun had not jammed.

Jack, with whom I talked in Miami, says the FBI has definite word of a black nationalist conspiracy to stir up trouble in the big cities this summer and eventually take over Washington.

We staged our Latin American panel at the IPA. I'm afraid it was a little dull as far as the audience was concerned because they don't understand Latin American problems. As far as Latin America was concerned, it was quite stimulating. Enrique Tejera París brought up the problem of Haiti and what we were going to do about it if it exploded. Covey Oliver was asked some pointed questions from the floor about Cuba and what we were going to do about Castro. He did not mention my report that we had begun talks with Castro through third parties to resume diplomatic relations. I tried to inveigle this out of him, but he didn't rise.

After the discussion most of the panel participants had luncheon with me. The luncheon had to be a little rushed because Gene McCarthy finally consented to speak at one o'clock today. He arrived right on time. Dan and I met him at the front entrance of the hotel, and Luvie introduced him. She did it beautifully.

I thought McCarthy did not speak well. He addressed himself to the problems of government and the presidency but wandered around. His thoughts were not organized, and in some respects he talked down to his audience. Since I sat behind him, I could see that he had no well-organized notes; however, he answered questions well.

I took the privilege of introducing Luvie myself. Dan had expected to do so, but I usurped the privilege. My introduction was also brief: "I now present a lady whose birthday coincides with that of Simón Bolívar and who will introduce the next speaker—Mrs. Drew Pearson."

We had our big Latin American dinner in the evening, with Hubert Humphrey as the honored guest. I had some misgivings about this because so many Latin American ambassadors were out of town, but it went well.

There was . . . hardly a vacant seat. I had only one minor complication. The dean of the diplomatic corps, Sevilla-Secasa, the Nicaraguan ambassador, wanted to speak in tribute to Bolívar. Obviously, I couldn't very well say no.

When we got word that Hubert was on his way, I told him that I would introduce him while I went out to meet the vice president. He replied, "No, I want to speak after the vice president arrives." That ended that. I told Hubert, and he was very cooperative. Actually, Sevilla-Secasa did not speak long and made a nice tribute to Bolívar.

Enrique, who was supposed to introduce the vice president, gave an adroit and diplomatic presentation in which he emphasized the fact that he was a good friend of all the candidates, and in the end he let me make the final introduction. Hubert rose to the occasion by twitting Enrique regarding his diplomatic finesse. "I was expecting, and hoping, to get an endorsement," he said.

Hubert was at his best. He held the crowd with him every minute and was far superior to McCarthy. He also answered questions eloquently and to the point.

As I escorted Hubert to his car, he told me he was really crushed by

Johnson's speech in Honolulu. "He pulled the rug right out from under me," said Hubert. "It gave me an awful wallop."

I asked, "What happened?"

"I don't know," Hubert replied. "I'm going to come out with some policies of my own next week. If you're going to be around, I'll talk to you."

What a handicap Hubert labors under. He has been so far ahead of this and other administrations on almost everything. He has been a pioneer on Latin America even before JFK. He introduced the first disarmament resolution in the Senate during Eisenhower's administration, when nobody thought disarmament could ever get anywhere. Now it's achieving some success. And he's been against war, but he has been stuck with Johnson's policies. If it weren't for the war in Vietnam, they would be good policies, but this is the one overriding issue.

THURSDAY, JULY 25 | The talk of the IPA Convention today was the terrific job Hubert Humphrey did and his contrast with Gene McCarthy. Yet I suspect that Gene would have come out better on television if the two men's performance were compared not by a live audience but a TV audience. McCarthy looks taller, more statuesque, has a better face. Hubert's face is small and round, a bit puckish.

The European panel, which had caused so many headaches, went off on schedule and well. The Yugoslav and Romanian ambassadors are not always lucid, due chiefly to the language handicap, but they were courageous. They made it clear that the European satellite countries wanted to be independent from Russia though friendly with Russia. They said that they were standing by Czechoslovakia.

It was an important panel discussion which could never have taken place a couple of years ago. The ambassadors of the Communist world would never have gone for it. The Dutch and Swiss ambassadors were wonderful. They gave the right touch and balance. The Dutch ambassador was particularly good in standing up for NATO. The consensus was that Europe had pulled together. The nations could, and should, be individualistic as far as their cultures were concerned, but there must be cooperation, not only between the Western nations but between the East and the West.

SATURDAY, AUGUST 3 | (Departed for Republican National Convention in Miami.)

**SUNDAY, AUGUST 4** | The psychological buildup has started. Nixon is using the same techniques John F. Kennedy used in Los Angeles. Today he announced that Oklahoma had come out for Nixon. Actually, Oklahoma had been for Nixon all along. The announcement made it appear that the bandwagon rush was on; however, the Reagan and Rockefeller forces are busy trying to chip away at Nixon's strength. He needs 667 votes to win on the first ballot, and at present he apparently has 631.

The big question marks remain the Ohio and Michigan delegations. Romney wants to be vice president and is waiting to get some pledge from Nixon before he springs over to him. Representative Rhodes of Ohio is waiting.

**THURSDAY, AUGUST 6** | Nixon arrived last night and held a press conference this morning. He did well. He looked better than before. His jaw did not protrude as much as usual, and he did not look as if he had nuts in his cheeks.

Reagan announced today that he was definitely running. Hitherto, he has been only a favorite son. In talking to Eugene Wyman in Los Angeles, I got what may be a clue for the announcement. One of the California delegates reported to Gene that Governor Rhodes of Ohio had told Reagan to announce in order to solidify votes in the South. If he did announce, Rhodes promised to back him on the third ballot. The jockeying to get Reagan delegates in the South has become animated. Most of the South is solid for Nixon. Nixon has enlisted as his chief emissary in the South none other than Strom Thurmond, the most disagreeable Dixiecrat of them all, in his attempts to discredit Abe Fortas in the chief justice confirmation hearings. There is no senator more impossible in his political point of view than Strom Thurmond: anti-Negro, probably anti-Semitic, pro–Liberty Lobby. Yet he is Nixon's right-hand man.

Among other things Strom Thurmond took the Mississippi delegation out on a yacht yesterday to keep them in line for Nixon. They were veering toward Reagan.

I have not been to the convention yet. Television does such a good job that the temptation is to sit in the comfort of the hotel room. There was only one session today, in the evening, at which Everett Dirksen tried to get a bored audience to listen to the platform being read. He succeeded reasonably well.

Tom Dewey is here and, of course, Harold Stassen. I wrote a column about running for office too young, how Dewey, Stassen, Nixon, would all have done better had they waited. I threw in the mistakes of John F. Kennedy when he was first elected, mistakes now largely forgotten but which set the United States and world peace back some years.

**WEDNESDAY, AUGUST 7** | This is the big night. The balloting began. It was preceded, however, by eight hours of nominating speeches. In addition to the three main candidates, the delegates had to listen to nominating and seconding speeches for Romney of Michigan, Case of New Jersey, Carlson of Kansas, Rhodes of Ohio, Hatfield of Oregon, and Stassen of Minnesota.

Stassen's nephew made the outstanding remark of the evening when, upon concluding, he said, "Thank you for your inattention."

Thurmond made a sixty-second speech, in which he bowed out as a favorite son from South Carolina and threw his delegation to Nixon. This was the tip-off that the South was going to stand firm behind Nixon.

I got to the convention about eight thirty. It was a maze of confusion on the perimeter and oratory in the center. Crowds milled around the hot dog stands, and paid workers carried printed placards, boosting their candidate as part of floor demonstrations. Each candidate was allotted fifteen to twenty minutes for a demonstration. It became boring after the first two. Nevertheless, each candidate seemed to think he must have one.

It became apparent as the balloting progressed after midnight that southern delegates were not deserting to Reagan. In addition, Nixon's forces had been working hard on such key states as New Jersey, which split about fifty-fifty between him and Sen. Clifford Case. The result was that Nixon won by the time the voting got to Wisconsin; however, his margin at the end of the balloting was only twenty-five—not very impressive.

**THURSDAY, AUGUST 8** | Luvie and I stayed up until almost 3:00 a.m. last night, watching the interviews after Nixon's victory. Nixon was calm, suave, confident. He announced with some cockiness that after the Oregon primary, he had "never made a mistake." He knew the nomination at that time was in the bag.

Rockefeller and his family appeared on television at about 2:00 a.m. He looked tired and disappointed but managed to smile. He was a good sport and gave his best wishes to Nixon—just the opposite of Nixon's sour performance after he lost to Pat Brown in California in '62 and scolded the press.

Happy Rockefeller looked sad. She smiled, though she looked as if she had been crying a few minutes before. Nelson's best line was when he said: "Little Nelson will be happy. 'Now, Daddy,' he says, 'we can play more together.'"

I spent the morning swimming, packing up, and writing a column. About noon I went down to send the column. On the elevator several people were talking about Nixon's announcement that Maryland governor Spiro Agnew would be his vice presidential running mate.

The general viewpoint of the newspapermen was that Nixon, having announced early this morning that he had made no mistake, had now made his first—and a lulu. I was able to pick up a few details of the choice. Nixon had met most of the early morning after his nomination with a group of twenty advisors, most of them from the South. The moderates from the North were not present. Nixon had given a promise to the southern delegates that he would pick a vice president acceptable to them, and Strom Thurmond had vetoed Mayor Lindsay of New York, Senators Percy of Illinois, Hatfield of Oregon, and Ed Brooke from Massachusetts.

Agnew was acceptable. He is the son of a Greek restaurant keeper who started out courageously in Maryland but has now swung over to the more moderate conservatives. He is honest, handsome, and can deliver a good speech. Almost no one in the nation knows him. He will not help the ticket, and Nixon really needs some help.

We flew home in the afternoon in time to watch the closing session on television. Northern Republicans staged a revolt over Agnew, and while they lost, they managed to put a little life in the Republican convention. First, they tried to persuade Mayor Lindsay to run for vice president. He declined. I think he could have won; however, there was an agreement between Rockefeller and Reagan and the top leaders to stick with Nixon. So, Lindsay made his nominating speech for Agnew and then got in a limousine and left the convention.

Good old George Romney was finally nominated for vice president to try to defeat Agnew. The drive, however, was not well organized. If they'd had a little time, they might have rolled up some impressive opposition; however, in the end, Agnew won about three to one.

FRIDAY, AUGUST 9 | LBJ dropped something of a political bombshell late yesterday when he called Nixon on the telephone and invited him to lunch at the ranch on Saturday. This is going a bit beyond the call of bipartisanship. Of course, Lyndon has the No. 1 objective of keeping the Republicans away from attacking his Vietnam policy. Here he is the most vulnerable. I suspect he would throw Hubert Humphrey on the rocks if he could get the Republicans to go along. Nixon originally was for getting into Vietnam almost before anyone else, so he will probably be tranquilized by Lyndon.

The general reaction among Democrats, however, was that LBJ was almost throwing Hubert to the wolves.

I talked to Hubert on the telephone in Waverly, Minnesota, on Wednesday. He had four vice presidential candidates lined up as possibilities: Shriver, Muskie of Maine, Governor Hughes of New Jersey, and Mayor Alioto of San Francisco.

He remarked that Shriver wanted the job. He also said he was impressed with Alioto, whom, apparently, he had met for the first time at the Democratic fund-raising dinner. Tyler had come away from that dinner with the same opinion of Alioto.

SUNDAY, AUGUST 11 | Called Hubert Humphrey. He had just come back to Washington from Minnesota. George McGovern has just announced that he is running for president.

I asked Hubert about this and how he felt toward McGovern. "I have sort of a sweet feeling toward George. I can't help it. I respect him on the war issue. His children and mine used to have rabbits and guinea pigs together, and I helped him get elected to the House the first time—I think it was 1960. We had one of those receptions that you have for candidates to raise money, and I asked my friend Mary Lasker to raise some. Later he was defeated for the Senate and was planning to run again in 1962, after Francis Case died. The lieutenant governor of South Dakota, Frank Linley, announced that he was going to run too. I finally persuaded him to get out of the race. George was elected that year.

"It seems to be my luck that the two men I have grown up with are running against me. George seems to have been sold a bill of goods—probably by the Kennedys—that he could be of service, but he's not being of service to himself.

"George was taken out to California two weeks ago, where he conferred with Jesse Unruh and where he was quoted as saying that he could not support me. Later he came back and told me that he had been misquoted. He never made such a statement, he said. Then in Chicago about a week ago, where Unruh was present, there was another meeting. I think Sorensen and Schlesinger were there. All the Kennedys are sore at McCarthy, so they boosted George into running.

"You work with a fellow for years, and then, bingo, you find him running against you. But I'm not going to get angry about it," Hubert said.

Hubert said he didn't think there would be any problem on the Democratic platform. I asked him about his plan to make a statement different from the president's regarding Vietnam. He didn't quite answer me about this, though he seemed optimistic. "Things have started to move," he said, "regarding Vietnam. There's been a lull in the fighting, and the question is whether this is a signal from Hanoi. One top negotiator is coming back to Paris via Moscow. The Russians have reduced their supplies to North Vietnam, which is significant.

"I confess I'm concerned and disappointed that I don't get any help from the administration. Not one member of the cabinet is speaking up, even for the administration, let alone for me.

"The biggest achievement of the president is what he's doing with Russia, but no one is talking about it." Hubert said he thought the president recognized he went too far in Honolulu when he made the statement supporting President Thieu. "In his March 31 telecast he said that almost any act would be viewed as a reasonable response," Hubert said. "But he dropped that afterward when he went out to Honolulu."

**WEDNESDAY, AUGUST 14** | Lunched with Liz Carpenter. We discussed the interview with Lady Bird that I'm trying to get for the German magazine *Jasmine.*

Liz was interested in the candidacy for vice president of Governor Hughes of New Jersey. She said Mrs. Hughes had gone on a rice diet and reduced her weight by eighty pounds. "There's a fat women's vote in this country," said Liz, who is a bit on the plump side herself.

Hubert Humphrey had a session with some students yesterday where he frankly referred to the students as "escapists." Afterward he discovered that two newspapermen were present, and there was quite a scene about asking them not to report what Hubert had said. They refused.

**SATURDAY, AUGUST 17** | I have written a column and sent it to New York on Eisenhower. In it I call the shots as they are, which probably is not wise. Too much emphasis on Ike's cautious outlook on life for most Republican editors.

**SUNDAY, AUGUST 18** | We had a small swimming-supper party at the farm, though nobody swam except the West German ambassador and I. He was a former editor of the *Frankfurt Zeitung*, before it was suppressed by Hitler, and a strong battler against Nazism. The Israeli ambassador also came but didn't swim. He and the West German have very cordial relations.

I had a talk with Justice Bill Brennan, who was afraid the chief justice will hurt his place on the Supreme Court if he remains on, now that he's announced his retirement. The conversation was inspired by the fact I predicted over the weekend that Abe Fortas would not be confirmed. Bill thinks that even if Nixon is elected, the chief will have to resign in order to protect his place in history. Otherwise, it makes him appear to be part of a petty political feud.

I recalled the bitter statements Nixon had made in Miami Beach about the Court. Bill was familiar with them. He still thinks the chief's position in history is more important than the future course of the Court. On the other hand, the appointment of one or two conservative judges would mean that all the wonderful work the Court has done in the last fifteen years could be reversed in a short time.

The Israeli ambassador, Yitzhak Rabin, was eloquent at dinner. He said the Israeli army could easily sweep on to Cairo and take it even today. The desert between the Suez Canal and Cairo is flat and unimpeded. There is nothing to stop a tank invasion. The Egyptians have begun building up their defenses but still haven't done much.

He said: "The only thing that could happen, probably would happen, is that Russia would intervene. If some mad commander in Tel Aviv should give an order to advance on Cairo, I hope that others with more common sense would countermand it."

He pointed out that Brezhnev in Belgrade last February said the American Sixth Fleet must leave the Mediterranean. "You have no idea what impact this had all over the Mediterranean, from Italy to France, chiefly because no one in the United States answered it and pointed out that the Sixth Fleet was there to stay."

The ambassador went on to say the Russians were delighted with the Vietnam War and it was poppycock to think they would use their influence to help end it. "It is costing them only a billion and a half dollars a year," he said. "It's costing you over $30 billion a year. It is affecting your economy, endangering your dollar, causing you ill will all over the world. It has permitted them to negotiate new deals with Pakistan, once your firm ally. The Russian fleet is now in the Indian Ocean for the first time in history. They have a new deal with Iran and with Turkey, once your strong allies. They are spreading out with their influence in Western Europe and Latin America. They have nuclear submarines in the Mediterranean.

"Why should they want to help you end the war in Vietnam? I am convinced," he said, "they will let the war continue for another three or four years. They are finding their empire disintegrating with Czechoslovakia and Romania. They will watch your empire of interest also disintegrate."

The ambassador was asked what would have happened if Israel had not launched the Six-Day War last June. He replied that, among other things, Egypt would have taken over the entire Near East. King Hussein and King Faisal would have disappeared. Indirectly, they consider Israel an asset in the Near East, but they can't sell it to the Jordanian and Saudi Arabian people.

"We have been careful not to make three mistakes that you have made. First, we are leaving all local government to the Jordanians. We have told the mayors and the city councils, you are responsible for governing your city. We are not going to intervene. We are merely protecting the entire area, but you are responsible for internal order and government. In this way we have managed to govern a million people with only 326 Israeli administrators.

"Second, we have not punished any community for terror. We have sought those who were directly responsible and punished them, not the others. In the old capital of Hue in South Vietnam, you destroyed an entire city to get at a small handful of Vietcong. This means that many who did not want to become terrorists had no alternative. It didn't make any difference to them whether they became terrorists or not. They were punished anyway.

"Third, we have not permitted any unemployment in Palestine. We have spent a lot of money on public works, keeping people busy. This means that they don't easily become terrorists."

WEDNESDAY, AUGUST 21 | Up early to drive into Washington. En route heard on radio that the Red Army had marched into Czechoslovakia at midnight last night. The Russian ambassador had called at the White House to notify the president about 9:00 p.m. local time. Armies from Poland, East Germany, Hungary, and Bulgaria also participated.

This knocks out my prediction that the Red Army would not invade Czechoslovakia. I had just finished writing a letter to editors giving some of my views on the situation. I didn't think the Russians would make such a foolish mistake.

I telephoned West German ambassador Knappstein. He said he thought that Walter Ulbricht of East Germany had turned the tide. Ulbrecht was in Bratislava last week and was booed by the Czechs. He flew to Moscow immediately thereafter and probably pushed for action. The ambassador thinks Ulbrecht fears the spread of intellectual independence in East Germany, such as that which has taken over in Czechoslovakia.

Jack and I autographed books at Woodward & Lothrop, quite a contrast to the days when I published the first book, *Washington Merry-Go-Round*. Then W&L refused to carry it at first. At Brentano's it was carried but kept under the counter and sold only on request. *The Case against Congress* is a more revealing book than *Washington Merry-Go-Round*, but times have changed, and muckraking is much more popular.

FRIDAY, AUGUST 23 | Van says that he has seen something in the *New York Times* to the effect that Dubček of Czechoslovakia was in the process of investigating Jan Masaryk's death, which probably involved his murder by Brezhnev. It's suspected that this was why Dubček was arrested and Czechoslovakia invaded.

Sol Linowitz yesterday said Hubert Humphrey was very down over the treatment given him by LBJ and wonders whether the president doesn't really want the Republicans to follow him in office. Nixon has now adopted the president's war policy, while Hubert questions it. Therefore, the president may want a Republican to succeed him, first to carry out his war policy and second to show the country the contrast between his regime and Nixon's.

Leonard says Humphrey has approximately fifteen hundred delegates pledged at Chicago but may hold some back on the first ballot in order to make the convention more competitive.

All the intelligence reports, which Jack has seen from FBI and military headquarters, suggest real turmoil in Chicago. They have already uncovered plots against Humphrey's and McCarthy's lives.

Leonard says Hubert is livid over the so-called neutrality of the Johnson administration. Not one cabinet member has spoken out for him. They met after the National Security Council meeting on Czechoslovakia, but this was the first time they had seen each other in weeks.

Meanwhile, Nixon appears to be going like a house afire. He has had conferences with various GOP leaders who were against him prior to Miami Beach. They appear to have patched up differences.

The Russians are trying to install a new government in Czechoslovakia—favorable to them. President Svoboda has flown to Moscow. He is seventy-three years old, a famous Czech commander during the war, and friendly with the Russian military leaders; however, all indications are he is not bowing. First Party Secretary Dubček has disappeared, under arrest. There are reports he has been executed.

SATURDAY, AUGUST 24 | (Departed for the Democratic National Convention in Chicago.) Went to the Conrad Hilton Hotel to mingle with the delegates. There's an air of defeatism that Humphrey can't win. Everybody's saying that Humphrey will get the nomination but lose to Nixon.

I have a cubbyhole of a room in the Hilton, where it took me forty minutes to register. I have never seen such inefficiency. The room was quite a contrast to the palatial suite I had in 1956, when I had a beautiful picture window looking out on the lake.

In 1956 I spent most of my time finishing a series for the *Saturday Evening Post*, "Confessions of a SOB," and left almost immediately thereafter for Israel. Adlai Stevenson's nomination was a foregone conclusion, though there was a bitter battle later over the vice presidency between John F. Kennedy and Kefauver.

We went to dinner with Ernest Cuneo in the Pump Room at the Hotel Ambassador East. Liz and Les Carpenter joined us. Everyone and his brother was in the Pump Room, including Chet Huntley and family and Kay Graham with her family.

During dinner we reminisced about past conventions. Liz Carpenter remembered in 1956 Sam Rayburn had received the edict that Adlai Stevenson was going to throw the contest for vice president open to the convention. "Sam," according to Liz, "had come back to his hotel suite with his eyes blazing to remark, 'I like smoke-filled rooms.'"

MONDAY, AUGUST 26 | A Ted Kennedy blitz has begun. It's based upon the idea that Hubert, though he can be nominated, can't win and they need a young, new face to lead the party. It's based in part also on the fact that John Connally of Texas has not come out for Hubert nor some of the other favorite son delegates, such as George Smathers of Florida.

I tried to call LBJ at the ranch in Texas. The White House operator kept me on the phone, for he was talking. I then suggested that she call me back. I'm sure she was being very conscientious and truthful. Later she called back to say that he was tied up in a conference, and about an hour or so later I got a call from Leonard Marks, who had been instructed by the president to find out what I wanted. I told him there was a move on to nominate Ted Kennedy and that I thought the president ought to get word to some of the delegations where his friends were in charge, such as Connally of Texas and Smathers of Florida, along with Buford Ellington of Tennessee. Otherwise, the convention might well be stampeded for Kennedy. Leonard said he would get word to the president and call me back. After lunch he called to say he had talked to Jim Jones, the president being out on the ranch relaxing for the day. Jim said the president had received several messages along this line and was familiar with the situation. The president was of the opinion that if Humphrey came out for a strong Vietnam War plank, the southern delegations would fall in line.

Leonard also said that Jones reported that the president had asked Gen. Creighton Abrams what would happen if they stopped bombing North Vietnam. General Abrams had replied that when the United States had stopped bombing, trucks had come from North Vietnam at the rate of 1,000 a week. They were curtailed to 150 a week after the bombing was resumed. He felt strongly there would be danger to American lives were the bombing to stop.

I suspect the president is using the big southern delegations he controls to hold over Hubert's head to make sure he gets a strong war plank. Hubert has been trying to patch up a compromise which will satisfy both the McGovern-McCarthy forces and the hawks.

The Teddy Kennedy boomlet, we agreed, is being engineered chiefly by the men around him. Power is sweet. Twice they have tasted power, and now they are frustrated by lack of it.

Cuneo, the expert on Joe Kennedy, says that Gloria Swanson, Joe's mistress, is bitter at Rose. Gloria is now about eighty. She has a letter from John F. Kennedy, written to her when he was twelve, telling about his youthful achievements. Apparently, she was a sort of a halfway mother to the Kennedy boys while she slept with their father. She snarls, "I was closer to Joe Kennedy than Rose Kennedy ever was."

**WEDNESDAY, AUGUST 28** | Earlier I had dinner with Ernest Cuneo at the Blackstone Hotel. When we came out, we got a whiff of tear gas in the street between the Blackstone and the Conrad Hilton. The hippies outside the Hilton had started a showdown with the police.

Jack pointed out that the advance intelligence he read showed that the hippies were going to seek a confrontation with the police on Tuesday in Lincoln Park and another on Wednesday in seeking to march to the convention. This was what happened.

Calm was restored in front of the Hilton in about fifteen minutes. I could hear the chanting from the hippie meeting in the park across the way, but there was no more violence.

The convention voted for president tonight. Texas, Tennessee, and Florida voted for Hubert. Jack earlier got an indication that Buford Ellington of Tennessee had been discussed as secretary of agriculture, with Farris Bryant of Florida as a possible member of the cabinet. I have a hunch also that John Connally will be considered for secretary of defense. It was a foregone conclusion that with this backing Hubert would win.

During the debate the New York and California delegations threatened to walk out because of the rioting. Carl Albert refused to entertain a motion that the convention be suspended because, he said, such a motion was not entertainable during balloting. I am sure he was right, but this gave the protestors more of an excuse. The California delegation, under Jesse Unruh, was looking for trouble anyway.

**FRIDAY, AUGUST 30** | I have been trying to get the Czech ambassador all week. He is evasive. I gather he doesn't want to talk to newspapermen; however, I saw the Yugoslav ambassador late this afternoon as reports circulated that Russian troops were on the Romanian border and might enter both Romania and Yugoslavia.

"We shall fight," said the ambassador. "We will not get very far, but we shall fight. The Romanians will also fight. In 1951 Russian troops were along our border, but they never invaded. I don't know what is happening in the Soviet Union. They are going to live to regret this."

**MONDAY, SEPTEMBER 2** | BERLIN—We were met by a young man from the mayor's office, Lutz-Erich Worch, with a bouquet of tiger lilies for Luvie. He seemed disappointed Luvie wasn't there and had to carry the flowers, by this time a bit wilted. Our baggage, as I suspected, did not arrive, despite talking to two Air France functionaries in Paris.

We were received almost immediately by the governing mayor of Berlin, Herr Klaus Schutz, an earnest-looking middle-aged man, much different from the ebullient Ernst Reuter, who was mayor during the Berlin airlift.

John [Donovan] and I have a nice Roman sitting room in the Berlin Hilton looking out over the zoo. It is stacked with flowers and fruit, and everything would be fine if we just had our baggage.

At four thirty I visited the Free Berlin broadcasting station. They use a few feature films from the United States, such as *Flipper* and *Lassie*, and avoid crime and violence. Both this station and the other radio and television stations are government owned.

Tonight we went to a late supper at the home of Axel Springer, the publisher. It is in the trees in a suburban section of Berlin—in an old country residence once owned by a nobleman. Springer is a big, genial man who speaks English fairly well and who had as his guests several leading businessmen and newspaper associates. We had a supper of caviar, fruit, and raspberries. There was also champagne and vodka.

The conversation dealt mainly with the Czech crisis and the psychological impact on Berlin. It has slowed business. People feel they have a better future elsewhere. Springer says that he moved to Berlin because it is the most important city in Germany and he felt it was symbolic of the importance of Germany. It is still the biggest city in Germany, 2.5 million people, but is standing still compared with Hamburg and Munich, which have pushed ahead. Russia is trying to make Germany the villain and the reason for the Czechoslovakia invasion, claims that Germany has troops on the Czech border. Actually, this comes at a time when Germany has been more pacific than ever.

"Could the invasion of Czechoslovakia be another Sarajevo?" I asked. "It could be. We have excellent military intelligence," they said. "We even have some inside the Kremlin. And we are worried."

"Hitler invaded Poland when he was at his lowest ebb," said Springer. "Today Russia is at a low ebb, and this is what worries me."

Having been up nearly all night, we went to our hotel early. The baggage still hasn't arrived.

**TUESDAY, SEPTEMBER 3** | We took a tour through East Berlin. John had never been there and was fascinated with the formalities going through Checkpoint Charlie. In the past I have driven through the entrance to East Berlin with no passport problems at all. Then, you simply drove through even without showing your passport. This time it took us thirty minutes. Our chauffeur is a young Bolivian student, and since he is a non-German, he had no problem getting in and out.

East Berlin hasn't changed much from the days when Luvie and I were here in 1963. The shops look prosperous, and there are flowers in the middle of the street. The people look fairly well fed. We visited a museum which featured some of the ancient statues and temples brought from Pergamon on the Turkish coast. I did not realize when I was there how many of the buildings had been removed to East Berlin.

We went back through the Berlin Wall to the Axel Springer Building, which is built right alongside the wall, and lunched on the nineteenth floor. From Springer's office you can see down on the wall guards in their towers and the dogs on leashes, barking and snapping between the barbed wire entanglement and the wall. The wall is now a series of fortifications about one hundred feet wide. I don't see how anyone could possibly cross over; however, five hundred East German guards have crossed over in the last couple of years. Since they are supposed to guard the wall, they have an advantage.

Springer has become the unofficial champion of Israel and the Jews. When I asked him why, he pointed to some pictures on the wall of his editors and said that one-third of them were Jewish. "I owe it to them, and to the Jews of Germany, to make up for the horrible crime we committed against them," he said.

Springer has been to Israel several times and once undertook a confidential mission to the Vatican on behalf of Israel.

After lunch Springer took me on a tour of the wall—on his side. "Over there are two German guards, watching me through binoculars, and wondering what I am doing," he said. "Here is my wall, and there is Mr. Ulbricht's wall. And in some places we share the same wall."

Springer is the man against whom the Berlin students rioted last spring. It seemed to me, however, he is doing a good job for better human relations. He is a staunch friend of the United States as well as of Israel.

We went to the Berlin opera. I am not much of an opera fan, though on the whole I enjoyed it. John was even able to translate the title of the opera, *The Magic Flute*, from the program.

Before going to the opera we took a helicopter ride over Berlin to see the army and its commander, Maj. Gen. Wilber G. Fergusson. [He] briefed us at military headquarters, which was more interesting than the average military briefing, which usually puts me to sleep.

Berlin, we were told, is surrounded by 470,000 Russian and East German troops, and there are about 6,000 American troops in West Berlin, plus some French and British. The British commander is General Bowes-Lyon, a cousin of the queen.

Every four months General Fergusson goes to see the one remaining prisoner in Spandau Prison, Rudolph Hess. The Americans and British have proposed that Hess be released since he is now seventy-four years old and has been confined since 1941, when he parachuted into Lord Hamilton's estate to propose an alliance between Germany and England. Fergusson says he looks about the way he did then, except his hair is gray. It requires six hundred men to guard Spandau Prison just for Rudolph Hess.

**WEDNESDAY, SEPTEMBER 4** | VIENNA—[Ambassador] Sullivan believes the Russian move into Czechoslovakia was hurried, a decision made at the spur of the moment. They didn't know what to do, so they did something.

The Russian haste was shown by the fact that the radio and TV stations remained unoccupied for several days. Also, the Czech Politburo held a meeting, with occupation forces swirling all around it. The occupation had no political direction.

Sullivan says the Austrian Communists have been bitter in their denunciation of the Russian action. He believes the Russians will not feel the effects of their occupation for some time, but they will feel it in time in Czechoslovakia's role in foreign aid, which has been major in the Communist world. Czechoslovakia has sent arms to Egypt and Africa. The Russians told them to sell arms and let them collect the bill. The Czechs even bought Cuban sugar, produced Skoda cars, steel, and other important exports. The Czechoslovakian exhibit at the Montreal Expo '67 was one of the best. Czech music and culture were excellent exports. Now much of this will end.

Browsing through Vienna made me think of the various times I have been here in the past.

Luvie and I stopped briefly in Vienna in 1958, en route home from Romania and Italy. The opera house had just been built, and we attended an opera. It was in 1955 that Khrushchev gave Austria independence and neutrality by removing Russian troops. I remember he told us about it in some detail and made the point that it was foolish to have troops on the soil of small countries. I wonder what he would do about Czechoslovakia were he in power today.

**THURSDAY, SEPTEMBER 5** | (Breakfasted with Czech editor and refugee Stanislav Boutin.) "When the Russians dominated Czechoslovakia in 1948," Boutin said, "they insisted that a secret room be set up in every Communist

Party headquarters. This was to guard against an American invasion, which they said was threatening. We laughed at the idea, but they insisted. Each room had its code for transmitting messages, its weapons, and a small supply of food. Although we laughed, we had to go ahead with the idea. In the end we used these secret rooms against the Russians. It was from these rooms that we operated our newspapers for many days after the Russian invasion. The Russians had forgotten all about the rooms.

"And we were able to keep television and radio going for about ten days by shifting the location of the signal every fifteen minutes. The Russians had no idea where the signal was coming from."

Boutin said he had talked to Dubček's assistant after the meetings at Bratislava and Cierna, where the Russians and Czechs tried to reconcile their differences before the invasion. At these meetings Kosygin was just as tough as the others, and so was Brezhnev. Shelest, the Ukrainian prime minister, was shaking his fists. He was the toughest of all. Suslov, supposed to be the Stalinist and the toughest member, was not. He had charge of the European Communist parties and what their reaction would be to any Czech invasion.

"After the invasion four top leaders of the country were taken to Moscow in handcuffs—Dubček; Smrkovsky, president of the assembly; Kriegel, president of the national front; and Cronik, the prime minister. President Svoboda was also taken to Moscow, though not in handcuffs. The other four were kept in the dungeon while the leaders talked to Svoboda, or tried to. He, however, refused to talk until his compatriots were released and brought up to join him in the discussions. He even threatened to commit suicide if they were not released. They were kept a total of four days in jail with bread and water and scanty toilet facilities. Finally, they were released and brought up to participate in the discussions.

"Svoboda emerges as the hero of this crisis. He was the military leader who fought for Czechoslovakia's liberation against the Nazis in 1945, when he came to know Marshal Zhukov and Marshal Koniev. He held a position of great importance in the early days of Czechoslovakia, but around 1950 or '51 President Gottwald's son-in-law, Pensky, wanted to be secretary of defense, replacing Svoboda. Gottwald talked to Stalin, said he had no confidence in Svoboda, and thus Svoboda was purged and relegated to the job of an accountant on a farm co-op.

"In 1958, Khrushchev came to Czechoslovakia and asked, 'Where is my old friend Svoboda?' At this point Svoboda was brought back from the farm co-op to see Khrushchev and later elevated back to a position of power. When President Novotny, a hard-line Stalinist, was kicked out in January, Svoboda was put in his place. As president, and as an old friend of the Russian military, Svoboda was able to negotiate from a position of prestige.

"When the Russians invaded," said Boutin, "they expected a quisling to rise up to help them take over the country. There was none. There was almost unanimous resistance by the Czech people. When the Russians invaded Hungary in 1956, they took János Kádár with them. Kádár has given Hungary a moderate regime. There has been no criticism of Russia. Hungarians can travel, and one-third of them do. They enjoy a sort of loose Communist system. The Russians were hoping that a Kádár would emerge in Czechoslovakia, but none has.

"Kádár made a secret visit to Czechoslovakia as an envoy for the Russians before the final showdown. He tried to persuade them to go slow and compromise. Otherwise, they would have trouble. Dubček refused.

Boutin said the Russians tolerated the independence of Romania on foreign policy as long as Romania did not stray far from pure communism. They also tolerated Yugoslav independence as long as Yugoslavia did not criticize Russia and also because the Yugoslavs were pretty tough to get along with anyway, and a military invasion would mean guerrilla warfare for years. [Hc] thought that Czechoslovakia could follow two courses under the Russians: either the Russians would look for some excuse to take over completely, such as an assassination of one of their leaders; or the Czechs would cooperate in a sort of Hungarian compromise, and the troops would then be withdrawn.

In order to bring about a compromise, Czech leaders in Prague have requested the exiles in Vienna to make no statements regarding the Russians which might rock the boat.

**WEDNESDAY, SEPTEMBER 18** | NEW YORK—(Advised Humphrey that he was handicapped by his proximity to LBJ and should resign.) Hubert said he'd considered this; however, there were three reasons he could not step down. First, there were the material reasons that he wouldn't have an office, telephone service, etc., and because of the scarcity of campaign funds, he really needed these. Second, if he did resign, the Senate would elect a successor, probably paying tribute to Dick Russell by making him vice president. Then, if anything should happen to the president and Dick Russell should succeed him, Hubert said, "I could never forgive myself."

Finally, he said that a break with the president would cause turmoil inside the administration and bitter resentment by the president. "The president would be like a woman scorned," he said. "He doesn't help you much, but he can hurt you."

Before he left, he said that the telegram which President Johnson sent to Governor Connally in Texas was unsolicited. It gave Hubert the first real endorsement from the president. He said he had been meeting with the president to thank him for it, which was why he was late.

SUNDAY, SEPTEMBER 22 | The chief justice and Nina came for supper at the farm. Betty and Dan [Moore] were there, but after supper the chief and I had a private talk. I reported to him regarding my conversations in Paris with Averell Harriman about a Vietnam truce and my report later to Hubert.

"Poor fellow," said the chief, referring to Hubert's dilemma and the fact that he couldn't bolt the president. "I can't conceive that the president wants Nixon to win. Yet he's acting that way. I think I could write a speech which would win a lot of praise for the president and which might elect Hubert."

The chief had a good idea on how Nixon's $18,000 expense fund could be revived—namely, by referring to the $15,000 paid to Abe Fortas in lecture fees, drawing a comparison between that and the Nixon fund, in which Nixon was running errands for the contributors to his fund.

MONDAY, SEPTEMBER 23 | Talked with Larry O'Brien about getting a senator to make a comparison between the Nixon $18,000 personal expense fund and the $15,000 paid to Abe Fortas; also to get someone to go after Nixon on his conflicts of interest. Larry was interested and suggested that Dan Inouye of Hawaii might do it. I countered that Teddy Kennedy, Pastore, or Lister Hill would be better. Larry didn't think there was a chance of Kennedy doing it.

Talked with Senator Muskie about going after Nixon's record. He had no ideas. He mentioned that Margaret Chase Smith was in the hospital, having had an operation for arthritis of the hips. "Margaret and I have gotten along pretty well in recent years," Muskie observed, which is quite a tribute to him. Margaret has never gotten along with any other senator from Maine.

THURSDAY, SEPTEMBER 26 | Tyler's appointment as chief of protocol was announced by the White House yesterday. The newspapers featured the man-and-wife team which would now be running social affairs at the State Department. One headline said something about "The Abells are in."

Danny and Lyndon were in school yesterday when they got a phone call to come home. A White House chauffeur picked them up and took them to the White House after a rapid change of clothes, and they had their pictures taken with the president, Mrs. Johnson, and their own father and mother.

Tyler took time out today to come to the Big Brothers' luncheon and was an important contributor to plans for the fall dinner.

Late this evening George Ball suddenly resigned, and Russ Wiggins, editor of the *Washington Post*, who was retiring in December, was appointed to take his place. Russ is a wonderful man, but I can't quite see him with the quickness on his feet and the skill at repartee which is necessary to make a showing in public at UN Security [Council] meetings. It was announced that Ball would now campaign for Hubert Humphrey. This is important, and George passed out a statement on the importance of a stable foreign policy and the fear of what would happen if Nixon took over. Nevertheless, there must be something else behind his sudden resignation. Ball was only confirmed by the Senate as ambassador to the United Nations this week. The next day he resigned.

SATURDAY, SEPTEMBER 28 | This is [grandson] Drew's wedding day and should be a joyous one; however, I have never felt so blue. Part of it, I suppose, is the fact that he is getting married when he's not really old enough to know what he's doing. Then this morning the papers carried a story on the crushing blow to school integration delivered by the House and Senate conferees on money for HEW. They really cut the ground out from under the government's ability to deny funds to schools which do not integrate. It will set the clock back fifty years or so in the South and undo everything the Supreme Court has tried to accomplish. It has now been fourteen years since the Supreme Court's decision of 1954, and still the South is not really integrated.

On top of this the Senate Foreign Relations Committee voted to delay ratification of the multi-nuclear proliferation treaty. If the United States doesn't ratify it, no other country will. The negotiators had a tough enough time getting an agreement between the United States and the Soviet Union.

Both of these moves result from Nixon's leadership. He has publicly urged a delay on the nuclear pact, and his Republican friends in the committee voted to follow his lead. He's also come out against withholding federal funds to nonintegrated schools, and this was exactly what the House and Senate conferees voted to do.

**TUESDAY, OCTOBER 1** | There are few Negroes either in this part of Missouri or in northeastern Arkansas, where I was last night. There are no racial problems. The schools in Fayetteville were integrated in 1948, six years before the Supreme Court desegregation decision. School authorities in Arkansas told me the schools of Little Rock were now a model of integration, and they probably would have been integrated very peacefully in 1956 had not [Governor] Faubus wanted to make political hay at the expense of the schools.

**THURSDAY, OCTOBER 3** | DENVER—There is much sentiment for Wallace in Colorado, and the more racial disturbances there are and the more crime in the streets, the stronger he becomes.

My trail has been crossing Ed Muskie's. He was in Denver today, Pueblo this afternoon, and back up to Boulder tomorrow. He is making an excellent impression. I spoke before a middle-class Republican audience, and I doubt if a Democrat was present. This is a heavily Democratic community, where the steelworkers are strong, but you wouldn't know it from my audience.

Being in Pueblo reminded me of the same balmy autumn weather in 1948 when I traveled with Harry Truman through southern Colorado. There were pitifully small crowds, little enthusiasm, and everybody thought Truman was going to lose. Yet he won. I doubt, however, whether Humphrey can repeat this political miracle.

**SATURDAY, OCTOBER 5** | ODESSA TX—Harold Young met me. He has now married Mary Louise, once the secretary to then-representative Lyndon Johnson of Texas. Harold himself was secretary to Henry Wallace when [Wallace was] vice president. Charlie Marsh, who had taken both Wallace and Lyndon Johnson under his wing, wanted a practical politician who could guide Wallace and brought Harold up from Texas. Harold is looking older but still has his liberal point of view.

"I suppose Wallace will be just a footnote to history," he said. "We had great hopes for him, but Truman and the bosses were determined to put him on the sidelines.

"If it wasn't for Charlie Marsh, Lyndon would be back in Texas as a backwoods ex-congressman. It's too bad Charlie hadn't lived to see Lyndon in the White House."

"Lyndon invites us up to dinner every so often," Harold said, "and when we come, he always invites us to stay in the White House. It's a pretty expensive dinner trip for us to take, and we can't afford to go too often."

Johnson came out officially for Hubert Humphrey today.

**MONDAY, OCTOBER 7** | WASHINGTON DC—Talked to Dave Karr in Paris, who tells me he learned through Sargent Shriver that Hubert Humphrey had been cut off from getting the cables on Vietnam since January 1966. Prior to that, whenever a difficult situation arose and the president wanted someone to champion his Vietnamese policy, Humphrey was given a spoon-fed briefing and told to go out and do his stuff. This, of course, was what got Humphrey on the wrong side with so many doves.

**THURSDAY, OCTOBER 10** | DETROIT—My suitcase was lost en route, and I arrived without clothes, without breakfast, in time to speak before a women's forum in Grosse Pointe. The ladies I talked to are about 90 percent for Nixon.

Humphrey has been touring New York. He still has almost no money, and today Arthur Goldberg, who is supposed to be managing his campaign, made the statement that "a few years of Nixon wouldn't be so bad."

**SATURDAY, OCTOBER 12** | Hale Boggs says the attorney general of Louisiana, Grimillion, has been indicted in a scandal involving the Mafia and that Governor McKeithen is on the way to being indicted.

**TUESDAY, OCTOBER 15** | Kay Raley called me in Denver to say the newspapers had reported on the murder in Annapolis. Later, in Dallas, I bought the paper while waiting for the midnight plane and found that even the *Dallas News* had played up the fact that "Drew Pearson's Niece Was Charged with Murder." It made it look as if [somehow] I was involved. [The niece, Ann Pearson, claimed she held a knife to protect herself from her boyfriend's lunge at her. The knife pierced his heart. She was acquitted.]

**WEDNESDAY, OCTOBER 16** | There have been rumors regarding a Vietnam truce, and Jack [was] briefed. He reported that Gen. Creighton Abrams, the new commander in South Vietnam, had been doing an excellent job and that the North Vietnamese were on the run. Lyndon had even stopped telling Abrams how to run the war, as he did with General Westmoreland. Westmoreland was a better political front but not a good commander. Second, there seemed to be trouble among the North Vietnamese population. They were getting tired of the war. Third, the Russians were more on our side. They want us off their backs in Czechoslovakia and Romania. They don't want Nixon to deal with it later [regarding a truce].

There continue to be some differences between the White House and the negotiators in Paris, Harriman and Vance. LBJ has made some concessions in their direction; however, judging by the speeches in Hanoi, the North Vietnamese government is just as adamant against a truce as ever.

THURSDAY, OCTOBER 17 | Telephone call with Leonard Marks. He gives credit to Nixon for behaving like a statesman regarding the truce talks. Nixon issued a statement that he had confidence in the president. Ball told me one trouble with the truce talks were the leaks. Prime Minister [John] Gorton of Australia has been spouting like a fountain, and there have been leaks from Saigon, where the government is not anxious for a truce. These make it hard for the North Vietnamese to save face.

I had arranged with Bill Helis in New Orleans to do some sleuthing regarding a reported campaign fund of about half a million dollars, which the American Greeks are raising to back Nixon and Agnew, their fellow Greek. Bill had a session yesterday with Tom Pappas of Boston, who is raising money for Nixon-Agnew and said that the Republican goal was $21 million. This makes Hubert's loan of $5 million look puny. Pappas denied that any Greeks outside the United States were raising money, particularly Onassis. The story has just broken that Jackie Kennedy is going to marry Onassis, and people can hardly believe it; however, her mother, Mrs. Hugh Auchincloss, announced it this afternoon.

Nick Katzenbach has just flown to Yugoslavia for an interview with Tito as a gesture of support for Yugoslavia. Jack has written a column for release tomorrow which says the United States cannot give any support to Romania if it is attacked—for geographical reasons. Jack reported that the Red Armies were on the Romanian border and could sweep over Romania in a short time. When I showed the column to the ambassador, he admitted the military situation might be difficult but predicted that Romania could put up a battle for a long time.

He said the United States could probably stop the invasion of Romania by warning the Russians in advance. He also thought the United States could have avoided the Czech crisis by putting the screws to the West Germans regarding their borders.

"The West Germans say they accept the Oder-Neisse line," the ambassador said, "and they say they believe the Munich Pact was a mistake, but then they say that for political reasons they can't do anything about these things. If the United States was firm with West Germany, it could remove any Russian excuse."

**FRIDAY, OCTOBER 18** | The president had a warm talk with Foreign Minister Debré of France, Leonard says, in which they patched up some old problems. French radio and television are going all out to warm up relations with the United States. Leonard reports that an agreement is just about reached to release the crew of the *Pueblo*. He also says the Russians are being helpful regarding a truce in Vietnam. They want to get Southeast Asia settled so they can concentrate on the problems of China.

Later in the morning Leonard called to say he'd talked to the president and that while LBJ appreciated my solicitude regarding the truce, things were not jelled, and he wasn't ready to talk.

The truce talks have been obscured by the furor over Jackie's marriage. She left today for Greece on a special Olympic Airlines plane owned by Onassis, taking with her the children, her mother, and stepfather. Mrs. Peter Lawford and Mrs. Steve Smith, two of her sisters-in-law, also went along. Rose Kennedy has been silent and refuses to make any comment.

Onassis has about as a high rating in Europe as I have with the Liberty Lobby. He's made millions by dodging taxes and trampling on other people. His wife, Tina Livanos, once said of him, "How would you like to look 'round the room at a dinner party and know that your husband had slept with every woman in the room?"

Of course, Jackie was a something of a tart back in the days when she was a photographer for the *Times-Herald*, but the American public doesn't know this. She has been on a pedestal, especially since the assassination.

**SATURDAY, OCTOBER 19** | (To the home of Sen. Ernest Gruening for dinner.) Much of the evening was devoted to talking about Jackie Kennedy and Onassis. One guest, who had been in the State Department, told how, when the State Department wanted Jackie's help when she was in the White House by entertaining important diplomatic ladies from Latin America, she refused. She was a lousy first lady when it came to real help, though she had glamour and publicity. I remember how well she did when she spoke in Venezuela in Spanish and how proud Jack was of her.

The reaction in the foreign press to the marriage is very sour. Europeans know Onassis for what he is—an international philanderer. He makes a specialty of wooing internationally famous women, and now he has reached the top.

Of course, Jackie had a hard time in the White House. Her husband treated her abominably in many respects. She is reported to have worked out a deal that if he was going to philander, she would have the right to go abroad every summer and do some stepping out on her own. This was what she did.

Just before the assassination in Dallas, the veil was beginning to come down on some of the scandals of the Kennedy administration. The assassination stopped everything. Kennedy has been a martyr ever since and his wife a saint. By this one move—marrying Onassis—Jackie has destroyed the veil of martyrdom.

FRIDAY, OCTOBER 25 | Saw the president at 6:30 p.m. Leonard had tipped me off to ask for an interview, and the president had a folder all set with some material in it for me, including various messages he had sent to Congress pertaining to certain bills which he felt should be emphasized.

He didn't get around to this until very late. He was in a good mood because of the birth of a granddaughter around midnight.

He then read me a speech he was going to deliver about nine this evening on the radio. "The radio costs only $16,000," he said, "as against $125,000 for a TV hookup. And you get about three minutes of time from the television shots they take of you free. We can't afford all this radio and TV time that Nixon is throwing around. We have to watch our money."

The speech was a hearty endorsement of Hubert Humphrey. It was couched in nonpartisan language. Johnson called it "a presidential type of speech." He had Tom Johnson, who was with us, take out several uses of the word *trust* because he said he didn't want to imply too often that Nixon couldn't be trusted, though he did want to get that general idea across. I suppose the speech went about as far as the president could go and still be reasonably nonpartisan, which he wants to be in view of the war.

Earlier that day Nixon let off a blast in New York accusing the Humphrey forces of playing politics by pulling a cheap trick to get a truce. Nixon said he was sure that Johnson was not a party to this and went on to say some nice things about Lyndon, but Lyndon was not fooled.

I tried to find out whether there were any real developments on the war front. I asked him to give me the background. He reiterated that there was actually no more news than he had given to the press yesterday or, as a matter of fact, a couple of days before.

"We've made a proposal to North Vietnam, and we haven't heard from them. We hear they're considering it, but we don't know how serious they are about it. As a matter of courtesy, we had to keep some of our allies informed. We told the Australian prime minister, Gorton, what we were doing, and he made a statement as if he were behind the whole thing.

"Actually, this upsets the North Vietnamese. Everything was supposed to be a secret. So they say, 'Screw you'—and we have to try to get the show back on the road.

"Then we tell Souvanna Phouma in Laos that there may be a time when we will stop bombing the North. We do this because we don't want him to be surprised. After all, he's got some enemy troops on his soil. So, he goes out and makes a statement just as if we had an agreement.

"I suppose it's because everybody is so anxious for peace. I know I am. I have been pushing at this thing for months. The reason I made my statement of March 31 was so I could stay out of politics and work more effectively toward peace. Now Nixon says I'm playing a cheap trick.

"It's like a baby's fever. It goes up to 106 and then down to 98. Everything was all tension around here the day before yesterday. We were expecting Lynda to have her baby. Lady Bird was supposed to go down to Austin to make a speech for Hubert. Luci was supposed to be at the Democratic Women's Club to raise money for Hubert, where Little Lyn Nugent was to be the star performer. At the same time, Luci wanted to be around with her sister because she'd had a baby, and she wanted to tell Lynda how to have one.

"That morning Lyn woke up with a fever. It was up to 102. Everybody said that Luci ought not to take Lyn to the Democratic reception, but she said, 'He's one of the performers and can't go back on his act.' So, she led him across the stage. I don't know what's in his head, but I can tell you what's in his legs. They're just as sturdy as his Lithuanian ancestors. He walked right out there, waving his flag, and waved when they told him to wave and waved good-bye, and then the band struck up, and he did a little Humphrey dance."

At this point the president got up and did a little Humphrey dance himself.

"Then, when they got Lyn back home, they found that his fever had gone down to 98.6. There was nothing wrong with him. That's just like the war. These peace overtures blow hot and cold. You never can tell where they are, but I can tell you, we're trying.

"You wrote a column from Paris saying that two peace proposals had been made that I'd turned down. I took that column of yours and cabled it right across to Paris and asked them where are the two proposals. They had nothing to say. They said they never talked to you. They didn't know where you got that stuff. Of course, I know that you can talk to them through other people. Vance was especially upset. He sent back a long cable denying everything. He said he'd never talked to you."

"That's right," I said. "I never talked to him."

"I suppose that column was written by Jack Anderson," said the president. "Whenever you write a column that's critical of me, you claim Jack writes it. You've been writing columns and blaming it on Jack for thirty years."

"No," I corrected, "thirty-seven years. I've been writing a column for thirty-seven years."

I asked whether the Russians had been helping. The president replied: "Yes, I think they have. I think they've always been helping. I have always thought the Chinese were against us and the Russians were for us. They come in to see me and tell me they don't have much influence.

"I thought I had things all worked out with Kosygin for peace in Vietnam. He was agreeable at Glassboro. Then he went back and apparently couldn't move his other people."

By this time the president had sent his speech out to the teleprompter to have it copied. He also showed me a poll from an Indian reservation in Washington State, showing Nixon and Humphrey running almost neck and neck—thirty-seven to thirty-six. He also said Wilbur Cohen, the secretary of HEW, had come in this morning to congratulate him on his granddaughter and had brought with him a Nobel Prize winner, Dr. Nirenberg. Wilbur had handed him a $25,000 Social Security policy for his new granddaughter. The president didn't know that these things existed. "I thought Social Security was for old duffers like you and me. But this insurance policy is good for $25,000 until you're twenty-one. During that time, if your father dies or if Chuck Robb doesn't come back from Vietnam, this baby gets an income of about eighty dollars a month. So, Social Security begins at the cradle."

We talked about politics. I told him I'd been at Temple, Texas, where he had some friends, and at Odessa, where he had very few friends except for Harold Young and Mary Louise. The president's face lit up at this. He doesn't forget Texas or politics. I told him I had spoken in Harrisburg, Pennsylvania, last night to a Republican audience, and although I put in a hard pitch against Nixon, I said, "I don't think I changed a vote."

He wanted to know why I thought Jackie had married Onassis. I said I thought it was money. The president said Cardinal Cushing, who had defended Jackie, had resigned this afternoon in a huff, irked at the Vatican for opposing his statement on Jackie. "He's an arrogant old fellow," said LBJ.

He said NBC was going to be indicted shortly for tapping the wires of the Democratic Platform Committee. He also made some vigorous statements about the probability that Nixon would be tapping everybody's wire if he got into office. "You ought to write that up," he said. "Tell about NBC being indicted, then tell about Nixon going in for wiretapping."

The president had a lot to say about the way television programming was ruining young minds and causing crime. "The Violence Commission," he said, "is looking into it, and the network presidents are scared to death. You ought to keep their feet to the fire. And bring Nixon in and ask him what he's going to do about it."

We went over to the desk, and while he looked at some pictures of Abba Eban, I told him I had a picture taken at the ranch that I wanted him to autograph. "I want you and the chief justice and Mrs. Meyer to come down to the ranch sometime if you're not too busy going out on that Onassis yacht," the president said.

He showed me a note, written by Joe Califano, in reply to a story leaked by Rep. Melvin Laird of Wisconsin, that four men on the president's staff were pressing for a politically motivated truce: Clark Clifford, Joe Califano, George Ball, and Cy Vance. Joe wrote that he could not conceivably understand why he was so quoted since he had not talked to anyone. The effect of Laird's leak and a statement by Nixon's press relations man, Klein, was to launch a smear that there was a politically motivated peace and then let Nixon knock it down.

In talking about the fact that NBC was going to let a woman producer take the rap for bugging, the president said, "That's like you blaming things on Jack Anderson."

The president said he was going to get me down to his school at the University of Texas, only wasn't going to pay anything but my expenses. "I'm going to invite Stokely Carmichael and Rap Brown and some of those other radicals, and I'm going to have the darnedest debate you ever heard."

Toward the end of the interview I gave LBJ a copy of a letter which Douglass

Campbell wants written in the president's own handwriting. I explained that Doug had handwritten letters from almost every president beginning with George Washington. Doug had drafted a letter for the president to send him regarding the Supreme Court vacancy, in which he said he was not going to appoint any replacement to the chief justice.

The president handed the note over to Tom Johnson with an instruction to revise it. "Leave out that part about my not appointing another chief justice. I may do it."

SATURDAY, OCTOBER 26 | Last night Harry Lerner called from Los Angeles to say Pat Brown was giving speeches in Ohio, Pennsylvania, and New York and that he, Harry, had tried to persuade Pat to give the real story on Nixon's past, including the Howard Hughes $205,000 loan. Pat was reluctant.

This morning I called Pat in Akron and told him I heard he was chickening out. He protested and said he was willing to deliver a really tough series of speeches on Nixon. Accordingly, I went through my file and discovered a letter from Richard Rogan, who at my request had interviewed Mickey Cohen in Alcatraz some years ago about Nixon's money-raising activities and how the underworld had contributed heavily to him in '48 or '50.

I spent the afternoon and evening writing a speech for Pat, first having called Bob Martin of the Democratic National Committee, who was delighted that Brown was willing to go to town. Bob came out to the farm about nine thirty and read over the speech. He almost hit the ceiling with delight and predicted that Pat Brown would not deliver it. I also discovered in my files a letter from an official of Union Oil to Frank Waltman of Sun Oil disclosing that a $52,000 fund had been raised for Nixon when he was in the House of Representatives in 1950. Frank Waltman used to work for the *Baltimore Sun* in the Washington Bureau when I was with the *Sun*. He was an excellent reporter. Bob thought this letter was even better than the Mickey Cohen document. We tried to telephone Pat Brown in Downingtown, Pennsylvania, but he was busy speaking. We adjourned for the evening with no decisions.

SUNDAY, OCTOBER 27 | I tried all morning to get Pat Brown on the telephone but gave him too much time to wake up, and he slipped on to New York. Meanwhile, Harry Lerner, whom I woke up early in the morning in California, recommended that George Ball was the man to deliver the Mickey Cohen and Union Oil Company speeches. Harry predicted that Pat would never move. I got George in New York and told him the stories.

He seemed interested but said he would have to consult with Hubert and Larry O'Brien.

At lunch Jack Vaughn, head of the Peace Corps, sat beside Pepita and entertained us with stories on Bobby Kennedy, who had come to see him when, as a senator, he was going to Latin America. Vaughn's function was to brief Bobby. During the course of the conversation the Bay of Pigs incident came up. Vaughn warned Bobby that he would get some critical questions as to his part in that tragic event. Whereupon Bobby threatened to punch him in the nose. Vaughn offered to go out in the hall. Bobby cooled off.

In Rio de Janeiro on that trip, Bobby attended a formal dinner given by the American embassy and delivered one of his usual speeches that the leaders of Brazil had to get with the young people. The rich and the establishment must reform. They must divide up the wealth.

Roberto Campos, minister of economy, got to his feet, white in the face. "We Brazilians can run our own affairs," he said. "We don't go up to the United States and tell you how to run your country. You don't come down here and tell us how to run ours."

Lincoln Gordon, the ambassador, sat sipping his wine. Vaughn said that the reactions to Bobby in Chile had been bad; also in Peru, when he made a speech boasting about his nine children. This was at a time when the United States was trying to teach birth control.

Bob Martin came to the farm shortly after lunch. Hubert Humphrey had given a directive that there are to be no rough statements during the closing days of the campaign, and Bob argued that no one connected with Humphrey should deliver the speeches that I had outlined yesterday. He wanted to leave it all to me. Tyler argued that I had done enough and my columns were already so vigorously in favor of Humphrey that I would be in trouble.

I have had no reply from George Ball and have been unable still to get Brown on the phone. Harry Lerner, who talked at length to both Bob Martin and me again, predicted that Brown would not deliver the speech. He felt that the Humphrey crowd would have to come up with someone in order to get real play, that most editors would leave my stories out and the whole thing would be ignored.

Nixon went on the air with *Face the Nation*—the first time he's been on a news panel for two years. He looked very sour. He handled the questions pretty well, however, even though they were tough ones. Actually, he didn't say anything, but he gave the appearance of doing so.

Pat Brown finally called back. I told him what I had in mind for him, and he shied away. He asked that I send him the speech but said, "I've just built up a pretty good law practice, and I sure wouldn't like to be sued." I told him the chances of a suit were almost nil, but he was still worried.

Nixon, when asked about the *New York Times* editorial critical of Agnew, made his usual counterattack by calling the *Times* guilty of gutter politics. When David Broder called his attention to the fact that in two days he hadn't even mentioned Agnew's name, Nixon replied that he had been naturally concentrating on his own campaign.

The Gallup poll shows Humphrey up but still a long way from winning.

TUESDAY, OCTOBER 29 | Flew from Fort Lauderdale to Boston. In the Miami airport Marian called me to say that I had a letter from an architectural editor named Blake stating that Nixon had been under psychiatric treatment and giving me the name of Dr. Arnold Hutschnecker, who had treated Nixon.

When I got to Atlanta, I telephoned Blake, who said he had known Hutschnecker well, and Hutschnecker had talked about Nixon as a man who ought not to have his finger on the nuclear trigger. The doctor said he was concerned as to whether he ought to speak out about a former patient. Blake said he thought if I worked on Hutschnecker enough, I could get him to talk.

I did not have time to call Hutschnecker from the Atlanta airport but called him immediately after I got to my hotel in Boston. Hutschnecker said he'd had Nixon as a patient when he was vice president, that it was a delicate matter and he did not know whether he should talk about it. I pointed out that this was a matter of vital concern to the American people since the president must have his finger on the nuclear trigger. The doctor said for me to call back at 4:00 p.m., that he had patients with him.

I immediately asked Jack to telephone Herb Klein in California to get comment on the fact that we had a statement from Dr. Hutschnecker confirming that Nixon was his patient.

I called Hutschnecker back at 4:00 p.m., but he had changed his story. He said quite blandly that Nixon had been his patient for matters involving internal medicine, not psychiatry. I asked why Nixon had come all the way to New York. Hutschnecker didn't have any answer to this but said that the press had eventually become suspicious and he had advised Nixon to get a doctor in Washington.

I had written a story and dictated it over the phone to the office but had to kill it. I wasn't sure Hutschnecker was telling me the truth, and I have had such hell from editors already that I decided to play it safe. If I had more time I could probably develop the facts, but the time before [the] election is getting very short.

Already, several papers have bellyached about my Nixon columns and notified me they were not using them.

**SUNDAY, NOVEMBER 3** | Spent the morning in my motel, working on a magazine story for *Redbook* on "First Ladies I Have Known." Joe Borkin says I should write a second article on "Second Ladies I Have Known." That is, presidential mistresses. Woodrow Wilson had quite a stable, and, of course, there was Nan Britton, the famous mistress of Warren Harding, and Luci Rutherford of FDR's day, and finally, so many mistresses of John F. Kennedy that you couldn't count them.

The *Detroit Free Press* this morning has a front-page story predicting that Michigan will go for Humphrey.

**MONDAY, NOVEMBER 4** | Bob Martin telephoned to say that Nixon had not filed his contributions by Sunday night. They were due under the Corrupt Practices Act on October 31 and previously due on the fifteenth of October. He was in violation of the law. Dean Acheson issued a press statement calling attention to this fact, but the Associated Press didn't even move it. Yet Nixon is supposed to be the great champion of law and order.

**TUESDAY, NOVEMBER 5** | This is the big day. Everything is calm.

I voted at Christ Church in Georgetown, then had lunch with two men representing Four Star Television from New York. They proposed a three-minute filmed TV program five times a week to be syndicated to independent stations.

We went to dinner at Joan Gardner's and were so fascinated watching the election returns that we hardly ate any dinner, which, fortunately, was buffet. The evening started off badly. Humphrey looked far behind. Then, just before midnight, he took a spurt. For a while it looked as if he could win. We went home and to bed but still kept the television on until 3:00 a.m. By that time I figured that Nixon probably had it and went to sleep.

**WEDNESDAY, NOVEMBER 6** | Awoke at six. The election is still undecided. Humphrey seems to be ahead in the popular vote and is running strong in some of the states where he was not expected to do so, such as New Jersey and California, even Illinois; however, I don't see how he could possibly overtake Nixon in the Electoral College.

At about 11:00 a.m. Hubert conceded. He telephoned Nixon and made a statement on television in a choked voice which bordered on tears. It was somewhat like his concession to Kennedy after the West Virginia defeat. Hubert lost to Kennedy in West Virginia because the Kennedy family simply swamped the state with money, including $200 each to every Baptist preacher. Hubert lost to Nixon yesterday partly because of a large amount of money, partly because of a better "advance" organization, and partly because of disunity in the Democratic Party. If McCarthy had come out two weeks earlier for Hubert instead of the night before the election, I think he would have won.

A big jinx, of course, was the early Gallup Poll, which showed him way behind. It made money raising difficult. Big contributors don't like to bet on a sure loser.

It seems inconceivable that a man of Nixon's background, who was ruthless, unfair, and cowardly regarding such people as Helen Gahagan Douglas and Jerry Voorhees and who was defeated not only by Kennedy but by Pat Brown, has now been elected president of the United States. He was a kid-glove McCarthyite, using Joe McCarthy's tactics for political purposes.

Basically, however, the country has not changed. The closeness of the vote shows this.

The worst part of the election was the defeat of some noble senators who had stood up for honesty and liberalism, such as Wayne Morse in Oregon and Joe Clark in Pennsylvania. Mike Monroney, an old southern liberal who was a member of the Senate Ethics Committee, lost in Oklahoma. Wayne Morse is only a little behind his opponent and has a chance to win, but the others are hopelessly defeated. Wayne had been too courageous. He had taken on too many enemies.

(Attended formal dinner at the Dutch embassy.) I sat beside Mrs. Bill Blair, the wife of the former law partner of Adlai Stevenson, who latterly has been ambassador to the Philippines and to Denmark. She told me how Nixon had come to Copenhagen around 1962, when he was running for governor of California, to participate in the Fourth of July ceremony. Ambassador Blair met him at the airport and told him about the reception which had been arranged for him at the American embassy and cautioned him that the Danes were very punctual and that he should be on time. The Danes did get there on time, some of them sitting in their automobiles outside the embassy until the stroke of the hour when the reception was to begin. Nixon, however, arrived forty-five minutes late. He had an audience with the king, whom he also kept waiting. Subsequently, he didn't bother to address even a note to the ambassador or his wife, thanking them for their entertainment.

Sometime later, when Nixon came through Manila, when Bill was ambassador there, the Blairs carefully left town and let him be entertained by the chargé d'affaires.

I had an interesting talk with Bill Brennan, who said there had been a stream of Court justices come into his room that morning. Bill Douglas had come in to announce that even if he had to go around in a wheelchair, he was going to stick it out for another eight years and not let Nixon appoint his successor. Byron White had been in to moan [about] the results of the election, and so had the chief justice. The chief apparently feels that he must let his resignation stand subject to acceptance by the president, whether the president is Johnson or Nixon.

We discussed the fact that Strom Thurmond is going to have veto power on new Supreme Court appointees and the terrible effect this will have on the Court. Bill is convinced there will be three vacancies fairly soon for Nixon to fill. Justice Harlan is having trouble with his eyes. He had cataracts, now wears very thick glasses and can scarcely see unless he holds the print close to his eyes. Bill described him as a sweet man but one always at odds with the Court liberals.

Hugo Black, now eighty-three, is not what he was. He sometimes finds himself opposed to his old liberal friends.

Bill thought, however, that if there was a liberal chief justice appointed, that the present Court majority could continue. He described Potter Stewart, the one-time conservative, as a man you could live with. He wrote the strongest decision in the obscenity case. He said he didn't know how to define obscenity but he knew it when he saw it. Stewart has written some of the other major liberal decisions.

We discussed the probability that the Senate could not refuse to confirm Goldberg because it would put it in the position of turning down two Jews in succession. Even Senator Griffin of Michigan and Bill Fulbright have said publicly they would have voted for Goldberg had he been appointed. Bill thought that the president would have to reconvene Congress in order to confirm any appointment he made now. He could use the excuse of ratifying the nonproliferation nuclear pact to bring the Senate back into session.

**THURSDAY, NOVEMBER 7** | Washington is still numb. My telephone has hardly been ringing. A lot of people are recovering their lost sleep. Others are too bruised at the defeat. The popular vote is still seesawing back and forth, sometimes with Nixon in the lead, sometimes with Humphrey in the lead.

**SATURDAY, NOVEMBER 9** | Hubert Humphrey has flown to Florida to see Nixon en route to the Virgin Islands. Ed Muskie went along. Hubert gushed over the president-elect.

Joe Fowler has resigned as secretary of the treasury, and so has Nick Katzenbach, as undersecretary of state. Nick will become vice president of IBM.

The Saigon government, which has been kicking over the traces against the truce talks in Paris, now indicates that it will be the chief negotiator in Paris, with the United States playing second fiddle. Jack has turned up some good stuff regarding the deliberate moves by President Thieu and Vice President Ky to sabotage the peace efforts in order to swing the election to Nixon. Nixon, of course, was the advocate of war in Southeast Asia for a long period of time, but I suspect he'll be a dove as president. He can profit from all the mistakes of the Democrats and come out as Eisenhower did, as a man of peace, even though it's a compromised peace.

**SUNDAY, NOVEMBER 10** | We had dinner with Bess and Tyler. The boys were models of behavior. Bess told an interesting story of election night in Texas. The president was supposed to dine with neighbors, the [A. W.] Mursuns, but kept watching the election returns to see if Hubert was coming out on top. Lady Bird kept reminding him that they were due at dinner, but he kept watching. Finally, they left.

Tyler had gone to Minneapolis to watch Hubert and hold his hand on the last crucial night.

He says Hubert could have won New Jersey (and probably California) if he had played his cards differently. The Humphrey forces spent $175,000 in New Jersey to get out the vote, but the bosses put it in their pockets. Governor Hughes moaned over the failure, but he did little to prevent it.

Mayor Hugh Addonizio of Newark was afraid the Negroes would vote against him for reelection and did nothing to register them. If the Negroes had voted, it would have made the difference between victory and defeat for Humphrey.

In California, Jesse Unruh came out against the president in a tough, critical speech two weeks before Election Day. Unruh, of course, is a strong Kennedy man and never was for Johnson or his friends.

**TUESDAY, NOVEMBER 12** | Yesterday LBJ entertained the Nixons at lunch, which lasted until 5:00 p.m. From the newspaper photos of LBJ shepherding the Nixon family into the White House, it looked as if he was more for Dick than for Hubert; however, I suspect that this is chiefly because Lyndon wants his Vietnam and Russian policies approved by the new administration.

**WEDNESDAY, NOVEMBER 13** | (Comments on speech at the National Press Club.) I had prepared rough notes, including the decision I had to make about publishing a column about Nixon's psychiatric treatment. At the last minute I decided not to use it. During the question-and-answer period, when I was asked a question as to what kind of a criterion I used as between the inane, the spectacular, and the unsubstantiated, I replied that, naturally, I used the inane and the spectacular and then went on to describe how I had not used the story on Nixon's treatment. This ended the speech and the Q&A period. Things began to pop this afternoon, and I know they will be popping more later.

Gloria Steinem of *New York* magazine has been doing research on Nixon's psychiatric treatment and tells me that Nixon's chief treatment came after he was defeated for governor in 1962, at which time he lost his appetite and was supposed to go to a sanitarium in Connecticut. In the end he did not go, though all preparations were made to receive him there. Instead, he took psychotherapeutic treatments from an analyst in New York, two hours a day, five days a week. Miss Steinem has talked to Dr. Hutschnecker, who has admitted that he received a call from the Nixon office between my conversation with him in the morning and my subsequent conversation at 4:00 p.m. He confirmed to her that he had changed his story between phone calls.

**THURSDAY, NOVEMBER 14** | My phone has been ringing about Nixon's psychiatric treatments. The *New York Post* is running a tough story in my favor. The *New York Times* has an objective story. The *Washington Post* has a prejudiced story against me. Mrs. Levitt, whose brother had treatments under Dr. Hutschnecker, called me to say that Hutschnecker had come to Washington as late as 1959 and 1960 to telephone her that Nixon had asked him to come down. Her brother-in-law, Norman Levitt, was taking treatments from Hutschnecker at the same time, and there is no question but that it was psychosomatic medicine, she says. I got in touch with Norman, who confirmed this but did not want to be quoted. On the other hand, one of Hutschnecker's former patients, William Block, says he can be quoted.

**FRIDAY, NOVEMBER 15** | Had an appointment with the president at 1:00 p.m. I was ushered into the president's office at about one minute after one—the most prompt appointment I've had with him. He wore a light-gray flannel suit and a red necktie. When I entered, he said, "Here comes Rudolph Valentino Pearson." I complimented him on his good-looking outfit. Actually, he looked very well, far better than his TV appearances. During the course of our talk I remarked on this. He said he had quit worrying about it, that he didn't bother to put makeup on, and there was always a lot of turmoil during his TV appearances.

I'm not sure why the president wanted to see me. He was in a jovial mood. He said that late last summer he got an intimation from the North Vietnamese, through their negotiator in Paris, that they might be open to peace talks. The negotiator said: "You've been wanting us to sit down with the South Vietnamese representative. What else do you want?"

"We told them the only other thing we wanted was what we'd already talked about, namely that the demilitarized zone should be free of military activity," the president said. "We talked back and forth for some weeks. We could see that they were interested in a truce but had been debating whether they could get better terms out of Nixon.

"Then somebody over here makes a speech and says we should halt the bombing. Then Hubert made a speech saying we should halt the bombing. With no ifs or ands. And the next day the North Vietnamese diplomat leaves Paris for Hanoi. That does it. The whole thing is off. I was so sad I could cry. I got the three candidates together on the telephone and told them what had happened."

I asked the president who had made the speech that touched off the problems. He said it was McGeorge Bundy. "He called us up and said he was going to make the speech, and we asked him not to, but he made it anyway.

"For the last few weeks we have been talking to South Vietnam, trying to get things back on track. We haven't told them they've got to come to Paris. We haven't told them they have to have a coalition government. We've been very careful not to do this, but we have told them we think this is the best way to get peace.

"Long ago I learned that you can't put a gun to a man's head and get results. I remember, when I was a young representative, I made a speech before the REA [Rural Electrification Administration] and told the electric power company to go to hell. All the farmers clapped, and I thought I'd done pretty good. Then I went over to see Alvin Wirtz (undersecretary of the interior) in Harold Ickes's office, and he told me that I had spoiled everything. 'We just about had the power company ready to go along with the REA people,' Al said, 'when you come along with that speech.'

"'You told the power company to go to hell. Well, you can tell 'em to do it all right, but if they don't want to go, they're not going to go.'

"That's when I learned not to tell people to go to hell. I used to sit opposite Bob Taft in the Senate. He was the stubbornest man I knew, except for maybe Bill Knowland, and I never could get anything out of them by telling them to go to hell."

The president said he still thought he could get a truce in Vietnam. He said he had talked to Nixon fully and hoped that he had policy steered in the right direction.

When I congratulated him on the statement he made this morning that American foreign policy would be run by this president, not by Nixon, until January 20, Lyndon explained that he'd asked Nixon to okay inviting the NATO leaders to Washington next September to commemorate the twentieth anniversary of NATO and that he wanted Rusk to do the inviting this week at Brussels. Since Nixon would then be president, he had to clear it with Nixon. Nixon agreed. The president said he thought this was probably what started Nixon off on the wrong tack in making the statement he did yesterday about helping to decide foreign policy.

I had the feeling that the president was making a swan song. He sent out for a speech he'd made at Gettysburg when he was vice president in '63. It was a great speech, and I commented on it at the time, noting that Johnson had done more for Negroes than any man since Abraham Lincoln. He inscribed on the side of the speech, "To Drew Pearson, who has helped to keep the races together." He also scribbled on the side of his Negro voting rights speech, "To Drew Pearson, who has helped me every step of the way."

MONDAY, NOVEMBER 18 | I wrote a letter to the president early this morning emphasizing the importance of getting a chief justice who would carry on the Great Society; otherwise, Nixon is certain to sabotage it. I called

Hubert in Miami Beach, telling him in guarded language about the chief justice situation and my talk with the president. I urged him to emphasize to the president that the appointment should be made now, not after January 3, when only seventeen days would be left for confirmation.

Later I called Arthur in New York. He said there had been some developments in the American Bar Association, which had supported Fortas for confirmation. [Lawyer] Bernie Siegel of Philadelphia has asked William Gosset, attorney for the Ford Motor Company, to do some checking regarding future Supreme Court vacancies. Gosset is a friend of Arthur. The two men got to know each other when Arthur was negotiating for the United Auto Workers with Ford. Arthur said he'd learned that Gosset would be very friendly to having him appointed interim to the Court.

**THURSDAY, NOVEMBER 21** | FORT DODGE IA—The Vietcong have renewed hostilities. I'm sure this development will impede the truce talks. Meanwhile, the United States is waiting for Saigon to sit at the peace table. I suspect there's never been a case in the history of the nation when we have been so abject in letting a small nation call the tune regarding our foreign policy.

On the plane I read Bobby Kennedy's "Thirteen Days" in *McCall's* magazine. It's a fascinating story of the Cuban missile crisis, though some important parts are left out.

I spoke before a staunch Republican dinner group, but they were friendly, and we had a good time.

**WEDNESDAY, NOVEMBER 27** | The South Vietnam government has finally yielded to our pressure and is sending a delegation to the Paris truce talks. It's headed by Vice President Ky. This is not going to be good. Ky is a grandstander, originally from Hanoi, who is hated there, and it's mutual. He'll use Paris as a sounding board for propaganda.

Rockefeller had a session with Nixon yesterday; so did Sen. Ed Brooke. Both have turned down places in the cabinet. I'm not surprised at Brooke, who was disillusioned with Nixon during the campaign; however, I am surprised at Nelson. He was much too loyal to Nixon during the campaign, even though he disliked him personally. I thought he would probably serve. Nelson has told Arthur Goldberg something of his feelings over losing out for president. He would have been a great leader of the nation. Sometimes, however, sex puts a crimp in a man's political ambition.

**THURSDAY, NOVEMBER 28—THANKSGIVING DAY** | Tyler, Bess, Ellen, Felicia, the Clementses, the Vournases, and John Donovan all came to dinner. We had a good time. Bess tells me that son Lyndon was so upset [about] Hubert Humphrey's election loss that he would hardly speak for two days. The teacher telephoned from school to find out what the trouble was. He's over it now, however, and is his usual sunny, self-sufficient self.

I had an interesting talk with Earle [Clements] about John Foster Dulles and South Vietnam. He reminded me of a story I had written in 1954 about a conference Dulles had with the Democratic leaders of the House and Senate, including Speaker McCormack and Sen. Dick Russell of Georgia. Dulles proposed that the United States send troops into what was then French Indochina and wanted to get the Senate reaction in advance.

Russell was vigorous in opposing it. "That means war," he said. Dulles denied this. He had a rather weak excuse that we would merely send in a police force. "When you commit the flag, you commit the country," said Russell.

Earle said he had asked Admiral Radford, chairman of the Joint Chiefs of Staff, whether his colleagues agreed with him. "No," replied the admiral. "How many of them disagree?" asked Earle. "I am the only one who favors this," confessed Radford, "but I am the only one familiar with Southeast Asia. The others are not experienced in this area."

This, together with the opposition of Dick Russell, killed the Dulles proposal. I asked whether Lyndon Johnson was present, and Earle didn't think so. It was at about this time that Nixon made his speech before the American Society of Newspaper Editors, announcing that troops would be landed in French Indochina to rescue the French at Dien Bien Phu.

**FRIDAY, NOVEMBER 29** | Talked with Hubert Humphrey on the phone regarding Goldberg. He said he had two talks with the president, one very brief on the telephone, the other lengthy, in which he said he was hoping to delay paying back all the money borrowed for his campaign so that some of it might be used to reelect the congressional class of 1970 and '72, because upon them will depend the continuance of the Johnson program.

"Even more important," he told the president, "is the Supreme Court. If Nixon appoints a chief justice and a couple of other justices, all that you have done . . . could go down the drain. This will be a lot more serious than electing some congressman because we can rectify our loss in the next election."

He said the president listened carefully and expressed general agreement, though he didn't say what he would do.

When I asked Hubert whether he thought the president would meet with Kosygin, he said he thought so.

"You've been taking a lot of beatings," he told LBJ, "which are not deserved. If you can get a peace in South Vietnam and then talk with Kosygin, you can really leave behind some monuments that nobody can destroy."

Hubert referred to the South Vietnamese government as "phony sons of bitches" who were intent on sabotaging the peace. I told him I thought his statement the night before the election was one of the best he had made on the subject.

**SATURDAY, NOVEMBER 30** | Jim Rowe and I had an interesting talk about Lyndon and Hubert. He described both as lousy political organizers. Since Jim was campaign manager for Lyndon in 1958, he should know. And in 1960 he was one of the campaign managers for Hubert.

Clayton Fritchey, who is just back from Czechoslovakia and Eastern Europe, gave the best description of Nixon I've heard: "We have had dumb presidents, screwballs as president, but never one like Nixon—mean, scheming, ruthless, and venal," says Clayton. "Anyone else but Humphrey could have defeated Nixon."

Clayton says my columns on Nixon's psychiatric treatments had a real impact. They were quoted all over Europe.

**SUNDAY, DECEMBER 1** | Agnes Meyer says the president and Mrs. Johnson dropped in to see her last week. They called and asked if they could come at seven fifteen. "Knowing Lyndon, I got ready and downstairs at six forty-five," Agnes said. "And he came before seven.

"He wanted to know when I was going to take him on one of those trips that I had taken with the chief justice and the Drew Pearsons. I told him this winter I was going to the Arizona Inn. So he said: 'That sounds just right for me. Lady Bird would like to get away from some housekeeping.'

"So," said Agnes, "I have reserved a house for him in February. He wants the chief and you and Luvie invited too."

I told her I was supposed to go to the inauguration of the president of Venezuela. I want to get the chief justice and Luvie made special ambassadors for the inauguration.

**WEDNESDAY, DECEMBER 4** | Talked with C. R. Smith, secretary of commerce and former head of American Airlines. He is a big, easygoing Texan, as homey as an old shoe, who, when I complimented him on being the outstanding man in Kappa Sigma, replied that I was. He remarked that he had read over my record in *Who's Who* and was impressed with the number of foreign assignments I had covered. I reminded him that sketches in *Who's Who* were written by the parties concerned. Smith illustrates the type of cabinet member Johnson has been appointing: highly qualified but so quiet that you hardly know they're in Washington.

We dined with Agnes Meyer and tried to talk her into switching from Arizona to Jamaica or Barbados for the winter, but she remained adamantly for Tucson. I know that Lyndon Johnson, if he does go to Arizona, will hate being around with all those Goldwater people and Birchites.

Nixon has been interviewing many people but is slow about appointing a cabinet. Apparently, he's being supercautious.

The president is packing up every scrap of paper connected with his administration and sending it to Texas for his library. He is gutting the files even more than the Kennedy family did.

**THURSDAY, DECEMBER 5** | We went to dinner at the White House, undoubtedly the last dinner I shall go to. Nixon will not be inviting me, and he may be there for eight years. Eight years from now I will be almost eighty.

It was very gay yet somewhat sad. As we danced on the marble floor of the hallway near the front door, I could see outside the grandstands being built, every day a little higher.

The crowd inside was carefree despite the construction, which would be finished on January 20, at which time a limousine bringing Richard Nixon would drive up to the front door and carry LBJ up to the Capitol, the Capitol where he worked so long and which he ruled for years—for the last time.

Hubert was in an ebullient mood. As we sat down, he reached for the nuts.

"Let's get fat," he said. "By the end of this campaign I had lost six pounds, so when I went down to the Virgin Islands, I never ate so many desserts in my life."

Hubert was in a mood which made you think he'd never lost the election. When I told him I was predicting he would teach at the University of Minnesota and spend some time on politics, he said, "You never made a righter prediction."

"I won all my home precincts," he said. "I carried Huron, South Dakota, where I lived. I carried the place where I was born. I carried Wright County, Minnesota, and it's so reactionary that any Democrat who carries it ought to be convicted for vote stealing. I carried the state of Minnesota. In fact, I should have won.

"When is the president going to get some of this good French wine," said Hubert, taking a drink of American wine.

As I came through the receiving line, the president stopped me to express his ire at Nixon for calling the chief justice without clearing it with him. "Who does he think he is?" said the president. "He's not president of the United States yet."

After dinner he got hold of me a second time and expressed more indignation.

"I thought you were going to put on a campaign for Arthur," he said. "I thought you were going to get some Senate support for him."

The president, of course, has a habit of blaming things on other people when he's been slow himself. In this case I didn't mind taking the blame. He talked as if there was still time to do something about Arthur's appointment.

"Who does he think he is?" said LBJ, referring to Nixon. "He may get run over on December 20. He may get sick. He may not be president. Yet he's stepping in to appoint the chief justice. You ought to get hold of Arthur. Get hold of some of the senators and take a nose count. See if we can get him confirmed."

The president talks fast, and there was more. A lot of people were milling around, but they kept somewhat aloof long enough for him to finish his lecture to me.

I asked him whether he was aiming at an appointment after January 3 or interim. "Either one," he said. I told him I'd talked to Arthur that morning and Arthur was all set for a fight. I should have suggested that he call Arthur himself but didn't think fast enough.

Afterward I talked to Hubert and relayed the conversation to him. He suggested I call Senators Frank Church, Fulbright, and Phil Hart. The president had mentioned Fulbright and Bob Griffin of Michigan, both of whom had been against Abe Fortas but both of whom had said publicly they would have been for Goldberg if appointed.

During my forty-four years in Washington I have been invited to the White House for dinner only in the Kennedy and Johnson administrations. Roosevelt used to invite me to a regular press reception every year, but I never went. With Truman I was in the doghouse, also with Eisenhower. With your daughter-in-law serving as social secretary, however, things change.

**FRIDAY, DECEMBER 6** | At the suggestion of Pare Lorentz, I called on Dr. Harrison Brown of the National Academy of Sciences to ask him about Dr. Kissinger, whom Pare reported was a terrible hawk. Dr. Brown reported just the contrary. Kissinger is against the war in Vietnam and for a missile agreement with Soviet Russia. Brown said he had attended the Pugwash Conference with Kissinger in Czechoslovakia, where his reactions were dovish. He said he felt encouraged over the appointments of Kissinger and [Dr. Alvin] DuBridge, the president of Caltech, who is Brown's boss. Prior to that he had been down in the dumps over Nixon's election.

This morning I called Arthur Goldberg to report my conversation with the president. We concluded that, unquestionably, Nixon had pulled another fast one, inasmuch as Herbert Brownell had talked to Nixon about Arthur's appointment, and so had Max Fisher of Detroit. Nixon didn't want to be faced with the problem of opposing Goldberg, so he adroitly telephoned the chief justice to get him to stay on until June. I did not speak to the chief about this at the White House last night. I figured it was not the time and place. Besides, he was sucked in by wanting to be too polite to Nixon. Arthur and the president are both slightly peeved at him.

I told Arthur I was going to go ahead with a poll of some of the senators and asked him whether he was still ready for a fight. He was hesitant but finally decided that he was. He hoped, however, that Johnson would call a special session, which I don't think he will do. He made the stipulation that the president, if he was going to make an interim appointment, do it right away. Arthur thought it would have to be done by Monday.

Last night Arthur answered Tom Dewey's proposal to junk the Fifth Amendment. He said he was surprised that the [American] Bar Association [ABA] had not risen to the defense of the Fifth Amendment. There was a concerted action by Henry Friendly of the Second Circuit and Dewey and the Republicans to kill the Fifth Amendment.

I called Senator Hart of Michigan, Senator Church in Idaho, and Senator Mansfield down in Florida regarding the battle over Goldberg. They all expressed support for him but felt the president had waited too long. There were varying opinions for and against an interim appointment and a special session. Most of them were opposed to a special session as merely getting senators sore by disrupting their Christmas vacation plans. Mike said he recommended a special session only if Nixon would go along with ratification of the nonproliferation pact, but apparently Nixon had not done so.

I typed a brief memo, summarizing the phone calls, and went to the Iranian reception, where I knew the president was going to be, and handed it to him. He said, "Keep this very close." I had already written a story about it for the *Washington Post* at the suggestion of Arthur. He felt that someone had to leak the story and get it out in the open if we were going to get any action. It's a long shot, and I don't think it will work, but the future of social legislation in the United States for the next ten or twenty years is at stake. The president reviewed to me what I had been telling him in the past—namely, that Nixon wanted to gut the whole Court and reverse his programs, which of course is all too true. If they overturn the Fifth Amendment, they will overturn not only Johnson's program but the basic freedoms of the United States.

**SATURDAY, DECEMBER 7** | This is twenty-seven years after the attack on Pearl Harbor, a day that started out humdrum and ended in tragedy. We had prepared a routine broadcast, which we junked completely after news of the attack came in shortly after lunch. Those were the days, fortunately, when we were doing a live broadcast. In the quarter century that has passed since then, the United States has become the aggressor in the eyes of the Asian world, in an area which Japan once wanted to take over. We have jeopardized most of our gains in Asia. The Japanese would like to get us out of Okinawa. The Filipinos are critical. The Japanese, who once were dominated by the warlords, are now dominated by smart businessmen. They have gained where we have lost. The moral, I suppose, is that victory in war doesn't pay. Therefore, why fight wars anymore?

**SUNDAY, DECEMBER 8** | PENNSYLVANIA—Up early to meet Ellen and Lockwood at seven thirty for breakfast and a drive out to Embryville to the old Friends meeting[house], where Mother is buried. It was a bleak, cold Sunday, but the sun was shining, and the wind in the pine trees moaned ever so softly, as if reminding us of the woes of the world. Mother used to love the wind in the pine trees. She said they were always talking. She is buried just below them. Her birth and death dates are inscribed: 1874 and 1942. (Father's were 1871 and 1938.)

**TUESDAY, DECEMBER 10** | WASHINGTON DC—Sen. Strom Thurmond of South Carolina made a statement which helped me mobilize some support for Goldberg. He said Johnson had taken a poll of the Senate and found that sentiment was against Goldberg for chief justice and this was why he dropped plans to call a special session of the Senate to get confirmation.

I used this as a lever to get a statement from Mike Mansfield and Ed Muskie. They were willing to come to Goldberg's defense against Strom. Before that they were reluctant.

It's the Senate's battle and Johnson's battle and the nation's battle. If Nixon appoints a chief justice in June, it will certainly set the "Great Society" program back for five or ten years. The Court will then reverse all the Warren policies, just as the Supreme Court in the early days of FDR reversed his policies on child labor, the Wagner Act, the NRA [National Recovery Administration], and the Agricultural Adjustment Act.

Yet fellows like Mansfield and Muskie are loath to get in and pitch for a chief justice who will preserve the social program they voted for during the last eight years.

I talked with Humphrey. He said he had been at the White House dinner last night and that Johnson had mentioned the Goldberg matter to him. "I saw you conspiring with Drew Pearson at dinner the other night," LBJ said, as if it was Hubert's and my problem, not his.

**WEDNESDAY, DECEMBER 11** | Nixon's "TV extravaganza," in which he announced his new cabinet. Instead of announcing the cabinet day by day, as Kennedy and other presidents have done, he saved them all for one big televised performance. It went off well. He started the show by announcing that Walter Washington would continue as mayor. This was the only Negro he appointed.

Aside from this the cabinet might well have been the governing body of the Chevy Chase Club, which bans both Negroes and Jews and doesn't have too many Catholics. Scotty Reston commented afterward that it was the "bland leading the bland," and the *London Times* commented that it was a team of gray men in gray flannel suits.

Actually, it was a better cabinet than I had expected, even though there were no Democrats, no women, no Jews, and no Rockefellers. I think there was one Catholic, John Volpe of Massachusetts, who will be secretary of transportation.

Nixon was relaxed and did fairly well—not half as well, however, if it had been Hubert Humphrey, who would have put a lot of humor and human interest into the announcement.

**THURSDAY, DECEMBER 12** | The European press has been more caustic than the American press regarding the Nixon cabinet. The *London Mirror* said, "It was a white, middle-class America who put Nixon into power, and the men he has chosen to back him represent white, middle-class America.

"They paraded in front of the TV cameras, with their families, all big strong men—far removed from the students, far removed from black power calling out in the ghettos."

The *Guardian* called the cabinet "competent, able and humdrum." The Rotterdam *Algemeen-Dagblad* said that "great vision is lacking," while the Dutch Socialist paper, *Het Vrije Volk*, called the cabinet "sheer disappointment."

**TUESDAY, DECEMBER 17** | Arthur Goldberg telephoned from New York. He wanted to know whether there were any new developments about the Supreme Court. I told him I had stopped working as of last Saturday, at which time I had expected to hear from him but hadn't.

When Arthur talked to the chief, it was obvious the chief was upset over the whole business. The chief had a talk with the president, and apparently the president was irked at him, felt that the chief had no business promising Nixon to remain on until June since he, Johnson, was still president and could accept the chief's resignation at any time.

**FRIDAY, DECEMBER 20** | Went to the Senate, attending a newspaper luncheon given by Sen. Tom Kuchel of California, who is retiring. I got a phone call from Liz Carpenter that Lady Bird would see me at about 2:00 p.m. She has not been feeling very well, and in addition, the president is still in the hospital.

I was ushered into the upstairs living room overlooking the old State Department, the one which the Kennedys used so much. The last time I was there, Lynda Bird, seven months pregnant, had come out in her bare feet and nightie to greet Frank Sinatra and me and the vice president at about 12:30 midnight.

There was half a banana left on a saucer on a table beside the window, and the room, while orderly, had the appearance of being lived in.

Lady Bird, when she appeared, looked well and, as usual, quite pretty. She said the president was not feeling well, still suffering from a sore throat, and the doctors would give her no idea of when he was coming back—three to five days, they had said originally, and he's now been in the hospital two.

I told her that my German editors wanted me to interview her regarding the most joyous and saddest moments in the White House. She winced a little bit at the latter but said in regard to the former:

"I suppose the most joyous time of all was last Christmas. We like to think that we came into the White House four and we're going out eight. Of course, we were only seven then. My two handsome sons-in-law were here. Of course, we knew they would be in Vietnam later, but we tried not to let it be too much of a shadow.

"My husband had been flying around the world. He was on a sad mission, to attend the funeral of a good friend, the prime minister of Australia. He visited our troops, Ayub Khan in Pakistan, and the pope to get his very important views on peace. We did not know when to expect him home. Then suddenly he returned on Christmas morning.

"It was the most joyful Christmas. Little Lyn was so cute. He reacted to everything edible and some things that were not, especially the bright lights.

"This year, Christmas will be a little sad because the two boys are away. And we never can tell what may happen to them, but we're happy because Lucinda is here now."

Turning to the other joyous occasions, Lady Bird said, "I enjoyed both weddings. They were just a delight. Lynda's wedding here at the White House was a wonderful mixture of people: her baby doctor from Texas, people she had known at the Cathedral School, from the University of Texas, some of the Johnson City home folks, and our Alabama cousins. It was the story of her life.

"Luci's wedding was the same. I was so proud of my two girls. They were calm, easy, assured, just as if they were saying, 'This is exactly what I always planned to do.'"

I had a hard time getting Lady Bird to talk about the sadder moments in the White House.

"I like to forget the sad moments," she said. "I only like to remember the joyful moments."

I prompted her by saying that I assumed the saddest moment was after the assassination in Dallas. At this point Luci came into the room, looking more beautiful than ever. Her jet-black hair was drawn up into a sort of a straight fountain, making her look taller than she is. She resembles her mother, both in height and in looks, though she talks with the volubility of her father. With her mother present, however, she did not do much talking, refers to her mother as "ma'am" and to me as "sir." Luci promptly picked up the half a banana and whisked it out of the room, explaining that Lyn had finished his lunch there before napping.

"We were talking about the events after November 22," Lady Bird explained to her daughter. "Drew wanted me to recall some of the sad moments in the White House. I like to forget about those things, but I do remember that chandeliers were draped in black, and wherever you looked outside the White House windows, the flags were at half-mast. It was a sad and awesome moment, when we felt like intruders."

"I remember it was December 7," volunteered Luci, as her mother hesitated. "It was Pearl Harbor Day, and I, being a war baby, had never realized what Pearl Harbor Day meant before. That made it extra sad."

"But Mrs. Kennedy had picked the day," Lady Bird reminded her. "We had lived at The Elms until that time, not wishing to intrude. A great burden had fallen on my husband. I realized his awesome responsibility. We had done everything we could think of to lighten the terrible shock to Mrs. Kennedy, and the least we could do was to make the moving easier for her. We felt so sad."

I asked whether Jackie Kennedy's failure to show up for the dedication of the Rose Garden [had] been another sad moment, but Mrs. Johnson denied this.

"We understood perfectly her not wanting to come. There were too many sad memories to be revived. We had picked a date, hoping that she could be there, but she had made no definite promises, and she did send her mother instead. Her mother was most gracious. She didn't know me before, but I knew her.

"On one of those rare occasions when I was really sick and in the hospital, the doctor was trying to get me a nurse, but there were no nurses available. Finally, he said that another patient had pretty well recovered and he would try to get her to spare her nurse. She did so, and I was always grateful for having her nurse. Later I asked the doctor who it was who had been so generous, and he told me that it was Mrs. Auchincloss."

At about this time we were interrupted by a very young man in red rompers who came walking, with considerable dexterity, into the room holding a large orange in his hand. A nurse was discreetly in the background. Little Lyn was asked to shake hands, and when I got up to greet him, he promptly threw the orange at me. I was not too dexterous in catching it. Lyn made the rounds of his grandmother and mother, ruffling up his grandmother's dress and handing her an ashtray with a TV remote in it. The remote appeared to be his personal property, but the ashtray was not and was rescued. Also rescued was a box of White House matches. His mother admonished that matches were not to be his, and he surrendered them. Having pleasantly interrupted the interview for a few minutes, he waddled out.

We talked about what the president would do after he left the White House. [She said,] "I hope Lyndon will not undertake a regular teaching course at the Lyndon B. Johnson School in Texas. I want him just to be free to relax and to do what he pleases, just unwind." Luci said she would love to take a course on government under her father.

I recalled that I had once told him he was going to be bored when he left the White House. Then he had told me about his plans and said he wanted me to come to Texas to speak at the school. Only, he said, he was not going to pay me my regular fee. He said I charged too much.

"Oh, that would be wonderful if you would come down," said Lady Bird. "You must come."

I asked about the president's decision not to run again and the statement that he was planning to insert in his State of the Union message. "He blamed you for misplacing that statement," I said.

"I don't think that I was responsible for that," Lady Bird said. "I think Lyndon finally found the statement just where he had left it, by the telephone."

I recalled an item in her diary about a special message to Congress in April 1965, when the president was in his pajamas, writing his speech, and Jack Valenti was white as a ghost for fear the speech would not be ready in time for delivery.

"All moments are tense when Lyndon's about to make a speech," said his wife. "He has to write in the final lines, and nobody ever knows whether he'll finish on time. Everyone is tense, except him. He's the only one who is calm. I've never seen him flustered."

I recalled that no other president in my memory—and I have been here since Coolidge—had been part of the city of Washington for so long: thirty-four years. "Won't you miss Washington?" I asked.

"Yes, we have been here a long time, and we'll miss Washington," Lady Bird said, "but we've been careful to keep our roots back in Texas. Texas has always been home. We'll want to come back to Washington but not to live here. We won't want to be has-beens in a city of so many other has-beens."

As I rose to excuse myself, Lady Bird offered to show me the family Christmas tree. It was in the upstairs center living room, which looks out on the Harry Truman porch. There was the smell of evergreen in the air. On the top of the tree Mrs. Johnson pointed to a star which they had resurrected from Mrs. Roosevelt's tree ornaments.

Most interesting of all was the array of stockings over the mantelpiece. They were red with white trimmings at the top and rather voluminous stockings, with the name of the owner embroidered in gold on each. There was Lucinda, the latest arrival, Lyn, Charles (Chuck Robb), and finally there was a stocking in the very center which was inscribed "President of the United States." Mrs. Johnson explained that a friend of theirs had prepared the stockings.

Luci then took me downstairs to see the big official tree. We talked by the tree for perhaps ten minutes. I had never really talked with Luci before. She talked of the great experience she'd been through living in the White House and seeing history made.

"It's something I'll never forget," she said. "Being here, watching my father. If people could only know how hard he works, how much he gives for them. He really doesn't care what happens to him; he just has to get things done. If he has to be sacrificed, if his health suffers, he really doesn't care. People so misunderstand.

"Coming from his part of the country, no one could understand how he has worked so hard for civil rights. And they don't know how much it has cost him with his own people—how many friends he has lost."

[Mrs. Johnson's diary was published in 1970, after Pearson died. Pages of her diary may have been shared with friends prior to its publication.]

SATURDAY, DECEMBER 21 | The Apollo flight to the moon was launched at eight thirty this morning. Its goal is to orbit the moon and return, carrying three astronauts. It has now been nine years since Soviet Russia hit the moon. I remember Nikita Khrushchev arriving in Washington in the summer of 1959 and carrying a duplicate of the Soviet satellite which had hit the moon and presenting it to Eisenhower with some exultation and pride. I have lost track of the various flights to the moon and around it since then. I had thought that people were not much interested anymore, but I guess I am wrong, for there is a tremendous interest in the Apollo flight today.

It's leaked out that Nixon has bought two houses on Key Biscayne. Houses in this fashionable area are not cheap, and Nixon has certainly come a long way from when he used part of the $20,000 secret fund to acquire a house in Wesley Heights. He has done a lot of financial finessing, each time buying a more expensive house. One of the rawest deals he pulled was when he got the Teamsters to finance a big house in Beverly Hills. Of course, the public is not going into all this now, and I will be crucified with some of my editors if I did so.

SUNDAY, DECEMBER 22 | Finished typing out the Lady Bird Johnson interview for *Jasmine* magazine in Munich. The president is still in the hospital.

MONDAY, DECEMBER 23 | The *Pueblo* crew has been released under a peculiar arrangement whereby the United States signed a confession but denounced the confession before it was actually given to the North Koreans.

Vice President Ky has returned to Saigon from Paris. Clark Clifford's tough statements, coupled with Senator McGovern's description of Ky as a tinhorn dictator, have undermined morale in Saigon. When Ky got home, however, he reversed himself about the question of negotiating with the National Liberation Front.

THURSDAY, DECEMBER 26 | The astronauts have swung around the moon and started their descent home. The big question was whether their engines would be strong enough to break away from the pull of the moon's gravity so as to leave that area and return. This was accomplished.

SATURDAY, DECEMBER 28 | Dined at George Baker's. Elizabeth Hennings, widow of the late senator from Missouri, was there, together with Paul Kramer. We speculated about the role Pat Nixon would play in Washington. Elizabeth said that when Pat was the wife of the vice president, she was as timid as a schoolgirl at White House parties. She used to go around timidly shaking hands, saying, "Mrs. Eisenhower told me to speak to all of you."

Paul Kramer thought that she would now pay back those who had ignored her. She had already been ruthless in crossing off guests to David and Julie's wedding, Paul said, including the first doctor (Dr. Hull), who had treated Ike.

There was disagreement on this point. Personally, I doubt if she will be vindictive. We agreed that a great story could be written about the women who have dominated history because they were ignored. The most notable case was that of Mrs. Edith Galt, the Virginia divorcée who was snubbed in Washington because she was so obviously on the make.

She wanted to go to Paris; he didn't. She hadn't been to Paris, and she prevailed. It was Mrs. Galt who ruled the United States after Wilson's stroke, permitting him to see no one.

SUNDAY, DECEMBER 29 | [Clark] Clifford was definitely at loggerheads with Dean Rusk and had taken over the conduct of foreign affairs as far as the peace talks are concerned. The generals have been told they are not going to get any more troops. General Abrams had now settled down to winning the war with South Vietnamese troops. I was surprised the army was turning out such intelligent young officers.

Kay Halle reminded me of a conversation we had in 1952 which pertained to Dr. Hutschnecker, Nixon's psychiatrist. Dr. Hutschnecker had been consulted by a member of the Rosenwald family, who was a friend of Adlai Stevenson, and during the course of getting to know Dr. Hutschnecker, he had remarked that he was thinking of moving down to Washington. "One of my patients is young Congressman Nixon."

Kay said that I was going to file it away for possible future use. "I see that you looked it up in the file at the end of the elections this year," Kay said. I confessed that my filing system wasn't that good and that I had stumbled on the information elsewhere.

Kay said that Dr. Hutschnecker had diagnosed Nixon's problem as being cold with his wife. Nixon had read an article, written by Hutschnecker in *Reader's Digest*, so looked him up. "A frozen butterfly," was how Kay described Pat Nixon. "She'll be tough and vindictive."

I argued that she would be relaxed, but Kay disagreed. She felt Pat was afraid of the big job ahead. Kay, who understands the nuances of the male and female better than I do, pointed out that Nixon had been going around a lot with Bebe Rebozo, a suspicious character. Nixon, she said, had been drinking heavily around 1965 and after the defeat in California. Pat also took the California defeat very hard. She went into seclusion for one month afterward.

TUESDAY, DECEMBER 31 | I telephoned the president early this morning in Texas. Apparently, he was asleep but called me back in about thirty minutes to wish me a happy new year. I suggested that as an aftermath to the bombing of the Beirut airport by Israel, he might withhold the sale of the fifty Phantom jets. I said he was in a better position to take this action than anyone else because he had long been a staunch friend of Israel. I recalled how Mrs. Golda Meir told me in 1957 how then-senator Johnson had been the chief defender of Israel regarding the transit of ships through the Suez Canal after the 1956 Sinai War. The president listened carefully, then said he was not going to cancel the sale of the Phantom jets.

"I held up that contract hoping that the Russians would agree not to sell any planes to Egypt; however, we couldn't get them to go along. Israel needs those jets. We have made strong representations in Tel Aviv through Barbour. We have registered our disapproval at the United Nations. Wiggins is making a strong statement there. We have moved to censure Israel at the Security Council."

I congratulated the president on handing so many stable matters to Nixon. The president ticked off some, such as very low unemployment, a stable dollar, better balance of payments. And he put special emphasis on the Paris talks for peace in Vietnam. It was obvious he had been hoping very much to get a formal start toward peace in Paris before he left office.

I told him what a charming visit I'd had with his youngest daughter and his wife. He did not argue with me. "She's a nice girl," he said, referring to Luci.

# 1969

## ANNALS

On July 20 Apollo 11 landed lunar module *Eagle* on the moon. Neil Armstrong and Edwin "Buzz" Aldrin became the first humans to set foot on its surface. They stayed on the lunar surface for twenty-one hours. The mission fulfilled the late President Kennedy's goal of landing a man on the moon before the decade was completed. The crew and craft returned safely on July 24.

Militarily, the United States and the Soviet Union were at near parity. The two were the only nations equipped with intercontinental ballistic missiles and long-range bombers.

The public wanted President Nixon to end the war in Vietnam and "win the peace." He and his national security advisor, Henry Kissinger, set out to forge a new structure for peace favorable to the United States.

Nixon shared the world stage with Soviet general secretary Leonid Brezhnev. After losing a referendum, French president Charles de Gaulle resigned from office. Former President Eisenhower died. Nixon's daughter Julie married Eisenhower's grandson David. (It was Eisenhower who renamed the presidential retreat in Maryland "Camp David," after both his father and grandson.)

Yasser Arafat took over as chairman of the Palestine Liberation Organization (PLO). In Israel, Golda Meir became prime minister.

West Germany's Willy Brandt became chancellor. He set out to pursue his *ostpolitik* (Eastern) policy. He later was awarded the Nobel Peace Prize for his efforts to improve West Germany's relations with East Germany, Poland, and the Soviet Union.

The USSR's seven-month border conflict with China was finally resolved when Soviet premier Alexei Kosygin flew to Beijing and met with Chinese premier Chou En-lai.

Nixon had written in 1967 that the United States needed to improve its relations with China. China's border clashes with the Soviet Union helped convince Mao that he, too, needed a Sino-American relationship.

U.S. Senate minority leader Everett Dirksen (R-IL) died. He was a strong anti-Communist and advocate for civil rights.

Sen. Edward "Ted" Kennedy became the body's majority whip.

In Libya, Col. Muammar Gaddafi seized power.

On September 1 Drew Pearson died of a heart attack. He was not quite seventy-two and was by far the most widely syndicated newspaper columnist in the nation.

Some basic facts in 1969:

World population: 3,637,281,889

U.S. population: 202,676,946

U.S. gross domestic product: $984.4 billion

Makeup of U.S. Congress (based on 1968 election):

Senate: Democrat 57, Republican 43

House of Representatives: Democrat 243, Republican 192

Number of women in the Senate 1 (1%), House 10 (2.3%)

—Ed.

# THE DIARY

SATURDAY, JANUARY 4 | Spent the day trying to finish the *Playboy* piece on Congress. George Christian telephoned during the afternoon to say: "I'm calling on instructions to say that your column today is incorrect. The president had a very friendly talk with Allon, and there was no such conversation as you describe."

At first I didn't understand what George was talking about. Then I remembered that the column for today had told how deputy prime minister of Israel Allon had called to see the president in September and had reminded him that both Nixon and Humphrey had favored the sale of the Phantom jets to Israel; therefore, there was no reason why the president should not complete this sale; however, the president became irritated and reminded Allon that he was still the president.

"The source of the story," I said, "was the Drew Pearson broadcast back in September. I just looked up something we had written before and rehashed it."

I ascertained later that the story had come from Mike Feldman, who is the attorney for the Israeli embassy and who should know what he was talking about. I am sure the story is correct but that LBJ has just suffered a lapse of memory. Sometimes he likes to forget things.

**WEDNESDAY, JANUARY 8** | PHILADELPHIA—Lunch with Harold Stassen, whom I had not seen to any great extent since he and I launched balloons over the German-Czech border in the summer of 1951. He has aged a bit, though his toupée makes him look younger than he is. I wanted to get some material for my Khrushchev book, which someday I hope to finish. Stassen, during the Eisenhower administration, was in charge of disarmament and actually tried to pioneer some of the moves which were made later by Kennedy and Johnson, including the test ban treaty.

I asked him first about the 1955 Geneva Summit Conference.

"Dulles was determined that the unification of Germany should be the chief topic at Geneva," Stassen said. "He didn't want any discussion of people-to-people friendship or disarmament. Nelson Rockefeller and I were the chief advocates of the latter two. We felt that in order to get peace, you had to get the Russian and American people speaking to each other.

"There were some strong contenders inside the administration who said if you let the Russians into this country, you also left the country open to spies. We argued that, unquestionably, some spies would come in, but what little they could find would be far outweighed by the good which returning Russians could do in promoting American-Russian friendship. Furthermore, when they saw what was happening in this country, they would become liberalizing agents for change in Russia.

"Just before the Geneva conference, Ike called me in and said: 'Foster feels very strongly we should not discuss these broad ideas that you have in mind. Would you mind staying in Paris during the first part of the conference?'

"On Tuesday evening, when the conference was about half over, Colonel Goodpaster, now General Goodpaster, called us in Paris and asked us to come to Geneva. We had worked on the Open Skies agreement, which has now been pretty well carried out by satellite inspection, and people-to-people friendship.

"Dulles was joined by Admiral Radford, chief of Naval Operations, and Admiral Strauss, head of the Atomic Energy Commission, in being flatly opposed to relaxing the Cold War. Dulles argued that Chancellor Adenauer didn't want any relaxation, didn't want any close relations between Russia and the United States. His objections were so emphatic that you couldn't help wonder whether he was talking for himself or for Adenauer.

"Toward the end, as Foster knew he didn't have much time to live, he said to me, 'I wish I had come around to your way earlier and been able to build up a permanent monument for myself.'

"Foster was a strict authoritarian, and when the president once gave his orders, that was that. Thus, after Ike changed policy at Geneva, Foster went along with him. Ike had always wanted to open things up with the Soviet but was troubled by the dissension within his ranks. There were men with such strong views as Dulles, Radford, and Strauss. Obviously, Ike listened to them.

"At Geneva, Eisenhower emphasized how much each country would suffer if there was another atomic war. At one reception Khrushchev elbowed his way up to Ike with an interpreter and said, 'Do I understand you to mean that another war would wipe out all civilization?'

"'Mr. Khrushchev,' replied Ike, 'your generals and scientists must be telling you the same things that ours are. Not only would civilization be wiped out, but since the wind blows from West to East, after the next war all civilization would be destroyed north of the equator. The future of the world would be south of the equator.'"

"During the London disarmament talks in 1957, Dulles took over the meeting. He sent me home. That just about ended my part in the disarmament talks, in fact ended my participation in the Eisenhower administration."

I flew back to Washington right after lunch and had a talk with Sen. Teddy Kennedy. He had telephoned me on Monday, suggesting we get together, and he came by the house at 6:00 p.m. Jack, who heard about the session, said he wanted to come too, though it seemed to me that this might give the appearance of ganging up on Teddy. On the whole it didn't work out that way, in fact was very pleasant.

Teddy didn't mention the past or any of the criticism of his brother Bobby. Nor did we mention his alleged ambitions to be president. He did pay tribute to Hubert Humphrey, saying he hoped to follow the fine precedents Hubert had set when he was Democratic whip.

Jack had written a story, which I spiked, to the effect that the real battle within the Democratic Party would come between Humphrey and Teddy, when Humphrey was reelected to the Senate and Mike Mansfield stepped down.

Teddy said he hoped to cooperate with Nixon and the Republicans as long as Nixon followed a reasonably liberal program. I suggested that it might be possible for him to work out an alliance between the moderate Republicans, led by Hugh Scott, and the liberal Democrats. Teddy thought this would be difficult.

Teddy . . . indicated he would give us some support on the confirmation fight over Hickel. He didn't have to be steamed up on this. I asked his advice regarding a story which I was thinking about writing which brought up Nixon's McCarthyism—namely, the job Nixon did in undercutting Dr. Edward U. Condon, then director of the Bureau of Standards, because his wife had attended a Yugoslav cocktail party. Condon was not only forced to leave government, but Nixon called to have his security clearance canceled with the navy so that he couldn't hold a job with Corning Glass.

Teddy hesitated to give advice, though Jack was quite ready to volunteer his, namely not to write the story.

**THURSDAY, JANUARY 9** | (Attended dinner the previous evening hosted by the George Vournases in honor of Bill Helis.)

Bill told me that at our cocktail party he had talked with Spiro Agnew, who had complained that the press was down on him. Even his speech at New Orleans to the mayors, Agnew said, had been criticized. Bill suggested that the best man to give Agnew advice on the press was me.

**FRIDAY, JANUARY 10** | The Israeli ambassador, Yitzhak Rabin, lunched with me at the Cosmos Club. He has . . . a contagious smile and a frank way of talking. The Israeli government was smart in sending him over here, even though part of the motivation was his differences with General Dayan. He had just come back from consultations in Jerusalem, he said.

Russia delivered notes to the United States, Britain, and France on December 31, proposing terms for peace. Their plan is for Israel to withdraw to its former borders, and afterward—the ambassador stressed *afterward*—Israel would get promises from Egypt for passage through the Straits of Aqaba. Nothing is said about the Suez Canal. There would be recognition of Israel's borders, however. The ambassador said these terms were unacceptable to Israel.

He said that Russia was pushing peace talks now, probably for two reasons: (1) because it's hopeful of doing something with this administration more than with Nixon; (2) it fears another outbreak of war.

In the latter case Israel was certain to win again, and Russia would have a hard time alibiing with its Arab allies another refusal to stay out of the war. It has remained aloof through two wars when its arms were involved, and the pressure would be considerable to intervene in the third war.

"How do you know Israel is certain to win?" I asked.

"Because the situations have changed materially in our favor since June 1967. We are now in a very strong position along the Suez Canal. The canal is deep there, and it would be impossible for opposing forces to cross the canal and come up on the other side. We have fortifications on our side, and the bank is very steep.

"In addition," the ambassador continued, "the flying time between Egypt and Tel Aviv is now twenty minutes instead of nine minutes. We have extended the borders all the way south through the Sinai Peninsula. Thus, the element of surprise is not so important."

"You told me in Tel Aviv it was seven minutes, not nine," I said. The ambassador smiled. "Well, seven minutes or nine minutes," he said, "either way, we now have twenty minutes."

I suggested that the chief result of the Beirut raid was to further alienate the moderate Arabs and that I did not think there would be peace in Israel until the moderate Arabs were strengthened.

The ambassador gave me a lengthy explanation as to why El Al, the Israeli airline, was so important and how it had to be protected against sabotage, and retaliation at Beirut was the only way. Regarding the moderate Arabs, he didn't think that Israel had lost anything with the moderate Arab leaders. He said conversations were still taking place with leaders in Lebanon and Jordan.

"We cannot give their names," he said, "because we have sworn not to, but they are important people." Then he added: "It will take ten to fifteen years to get peace in the Near East. We must demonstrate that Israel is there to stay and, in due course, peace will come. It will not come soon."

This was the most realistic prediction I have ever heard from a responsible Israeli official about the future.

SUNDAY, JANUARY 12 | Nephew Drew Pearson came to Sunday night supper. I had not really had a visit with him since he returned from Vietnam. He had a very interesting report on the main problem in South Vietnam—namely, the will to fight. When the local people see American troops virtually occupying their country, when they see the great affluence, the great amounts of money spent, they simply say, "Why should we fight?" They even see

American troops guarding ARVN [Army of the Republic of Vietnam] troops as if they were prisoners of war. In the villages ARVN troops will occupy them sporadically but leave if there's much resistance.

Drew thought Americans should stay out of the limelight. He said one of the great assets of the Vietcong was the Russian-Chinese-built rifles, the AK-47 and AK-50, which fire about thirty rounds and are sort of small machine guns. In comparison, the American M-16 fires about a dozen rounds. Furthermore, the M-16 is constantly getting stuck. Unless it's kept extremely clean, the heat and jungle dust cause it to jam. No grease and no ramrod are sent with the rifle. The Communists' AK-47 and 50 are built with chrome barrels, so they don't corrode and get stuck. The M-16 is not chrome lined. The Pentagon says it would cost too much.

The AK-47/50 began to appear with the Vietcong in 1964. The United States had plenty of time to mobilize and supply the M-16 but didn't get it into the hands of South Vietnamese troops until this year. This has been a sad reflection on the great efficiency of the capitalist system—namely, that we could not produce weapons any faster than the Communists did.

Dave [Karr] had a report the Russians were concerned about Nixon and had information that he was going to go back to the old hard line. As a result, the Russians want to get the decks cleared as far as possible with Johnson. Nixon, he feels, wants to get France back in NATO and rev up the Japanese to a stronger position.

Jack Valenti, coming through Paris, remarked: "Nixon will look back on January as the happiest days of his life. He's having all the fun of being president without the responsibilities."

**WEDNESDAY, JANUARY 15** | This administration is slowly, almost painfully, grinding to a close. Much of its time is given over to farewell parties. There is at least one a day. Today Luvie and I attended the reception at the Pan-American Union given by the heads of diplomatic missions in honor of Dean Rusk. As we passed through the reception line, Rusk said, "Well, you'll have some new men to go after next week."

Whereupon Mrs. Rusk quickly intervened. "Oh, he hasn't been so hard on you." Mrs. Rusk has been a mousy, dedicated woman, whom I have seen faithfully attending all diplomatic receptions for eight years. She even goes to the Communist receptions as a substitute for her husband. She seldom says anything, but she's always there.

The diplomats really staged a gorgeous reception for Rusk. It was like the old days when I was a young newspaperman and attended the diplomatic reception on New Year's morning given by the secretary of state. I remember buying a cutaway coat and gray striped trousers to attend. I had an inferiority complex in those days, and dress was important.

Most of my old friends were at the reception, ranging from the Czech ambassador to Galo Plaza and Sol Linowitz. I told Galo that I had talked to Bill Rogers about having the president-elect call on him as secretary-general of the OAS and that Rogers thought it was a good idea, though he didn't see how he could get Nixon down to Washington from New York before the inauguration. Galo says that the general reaction to the new administration in Latin America is skeptical or sour.

We left the reception early, before the president arrived and went on to the Dale Millers' reception, chiefly because it was held in 15 Dupont Circle and brought back a lot of memories of old days when we used to dine there with Cissy [Patterson] once or twice a week. The furniture has not changed much. There was an orchestra playing in the ballroom where Cissy once gave a dance in Ellen's honor. The place was packed.

The Senate Interior Committee has been holding a hearing on Wally Hickel, the secretary of the interior [nominee], whom I have been exposing in a series of columns. I don't see how Nixon could have found a less qualified man. Obviously, the oil interests put him up to Nixon at the last minute. Despite his terrible qualifications, Frank Church of Idaho, whom I had asked specifically to do some cross-questioning, did just the opposite. At one point he smilingly told Hickel, "They haven't laid a glove on you, Governor."

I wrote a story for publication tomorrow regarding Elliot Richardson, the new undersecretary of state, and his drinking record. He was arrested three times for driving under the influence of alcohol. Richardson is a good man, and I knew him slightly when he was in HEW under Eisenhower. He was one of the better men of the Eisenhower administration, and I hated to write this; however, the rules are firm at the State Department that an alcoholic is a security risk.

The *Washington Post* phoned to say they were not running the column, and I suspect they gave it to Bill Rogers. At any rate Fulbright staged a quick hearing for Richardson in which he denounced the column.

FRIDAY, JANUARY 17 | Early this week Bill Douglas asked me to come see him at the Supreme Court. He gave me a letter from a Vietnamese in Geneva showing that the No. 2 South Vietnamese on the Paris negotiating team was a paid agent for the CIA. Bill feels that the CIA permeates almost everything in the South Vietnamese government.

The Senate Interior Committee has done such a slipshod job in investigating Hickel that they're letting him pull the wool over their eyes regarding his oil speculations. Finally, working through the Sierra Club, I got a list of some of the oil leases for which Hickel had applied in past years. It showed that he was a heavy oil speculator. I did a special column for the *Post* for publication tomorrow. Supposedly, the last hearings on Hickel will be tomorrow morning, and this may throw a monkey wrench into the final debate.

Went to the White House to say good-bye to the president. He has had a long series of callers saying good-bye and new Nixon cabinet members to welcome. My interview was scheduled for 6:45 p.m., and while waiting I had a talk with Sergeant Mascio at the desk downstairs. Stenographers and various personnel were leaving for the evening, some to come back on Monday, some not. Mascio said the new administration had been interviewing personnel to see if anyone would stay, but some of the girls were quite emotional about working only for Democrats. They could not possibly work for Republicans, they said. On the other hand, the regular White House staff—servants, guards, messengers, communications personnel—will remain.

The sergeant said that work seemed to get later and later at the White House. Truman closed the office promptly at 5:00 p.m. Eisenhower didn't get to work until late in the morning and sometimes worked until seven. The Kennedy administration worked to all hours of the night, and Johnson has been the worst of all.

The president, when I finally saw him at about seven forty-five, was in a mellow mood. He was autographing photographs at the long table behind his desk. For the first time since he's been president, we talked while he was sitting at his big desk. Usually, we sit by the fireplace, where he uses his rocking chair.

I told him I'd come in to say good-bye and that I had just signed a contract that afternoon to write a book about him.

"Well, you'll have to come down to the ranch and spend a week later on," he said. "I've got a library there which is going to look out over the countryside which is going to be the greatest thing for historical research in the country. The University of Texas has already raised $25 million for the library and the Johnson school. I haven't raised any money while in office. Truman and Eisenhower raised some for their libraries, but I didn't want to be under obligation to anyone."

He showed me the desk blotter the cabinet had given him, which was really not a blotter but a glass-encased list of all the bills passed during his five years in the White House. It was entitled "Landmark Legislation of Lyndon B. Johnson," and it was quite impressive. He went over it in some detail. I can't remember all the bills, but he pointed to the Voting Rights Bill and said: "That's the one I'm proudest of. It's because it liberated about 20 percent of our population and made them equal. I tried to pass it in 1957 when I was in the Senate, but we couldn't make it.

"And here's open housing. I never did think we'd pass that, and you didn't either. Of course, the assassination of Martin Luther King helped."

He pointed to Social Security as helping more people than any bill on the statute books and said that Social Security would increase in 1972 by a considerable amount. He emphasized the education bills, both public school and higher education.

"And here is oil for beautification." He pointed to a bill passed in 1968. "We cut down on Lady Bird's beautification bill over here, pointing to a bill passed in '64, but they didn't realize until later that they were giving us $2 billion from Tidelands oil. We can pay for all the beautification the country needs through this bill."

I did not remind him that when he was a senator he and I had a terrible row over Tidelands Oil and his battle to give the oil offshore to the states of Texas, California, Louisiana, etc. Of course, the way it worked out was much better than I expected, inasmuch as the first three miles off the coast has not been very productive of oil. The areas beyond the three-mile limit have been, and these are reserved for the federal government.

"Here is the Model Cities Bill," he said, pointing to a bill passed (I think) in 1967. "At first we called it the Demonstration Cities Bill, but when all the demonstrations began to take place, we figured we could never pass it under that name. It's one of the best things Bob Weaver has done.

"George Romney came down to see me yesterday, and I told him the most important thing in housing was mass housing. He went up to the Senate committee that afternoon and gave them a big pitch for mass housing."

I asked how he had gotten along with the new cabinet. He said he had seen every one of them. We talked briefly about his press relations and today's luncheon at the National Press Club. "The place was packed," he said, "and they kept me for about an hour answering questions. They asked me what I was going to do when I got back to Texas.

"I told them, 'I'm going to take my hat and put it on my head and sit in the rocker on the front porch. That's what Sam Rayburn used to like to do. And I'm going to sit there for about fifteen minutes. Then I'm going to get up and look for Walter Lippmann." This sally at Walter, who has been absent from Washington for about three years, apparently provoked a terrific reaction.

"We totaled up our press conferences and found that I had given more than Kennedy or Eisenhower. Kennedy used to have these televised press conferences. I don't think they amounted to much, but they got a lot of public attention. I have had conferences right here in my office where they could ask me any question under the sun and got a transcript of the record afterward. And I find that George Christian and my press staff have given twenty-three hundred press briefings. And I've had occasional newspapermen come in to see me privately, as you are, but I notice that Evans and Novak, who write as if they knew what was going on, actually don't know a damn thing. They have not been in here at all, nor have some of the other woolly heads, like Joe Kraft, who write as if they know everything.

"Now you may cut up on me. And you can be mean, but you usually do have the facts."

I told the president that I understood he was going to take some time off at Palm Springs. He said yes, that they were going to take advantage of an invitation from Mrs. Winthrop Rockefeller. "She's been doing a lot of work on mental health," he added. "You know these Rockefellers. They may have more money than you and I, but you wouldn't know it by the way they work. Each one of them is doing something for their country. David Rockefeller's working on Latin America; Laurance Rockefeller has done more for the national parks than any other private citizen. John handles the Rockefeller charities, and Nelson is in politics.

The president showed me two snapshots of his two sons-in-law at a French Catholic orphanage in Da Nang, giving Christmas presents to Vietnamese children. I complimented him on his family.

"I think I've been awfully lucky," he said. "I've got two great girls. I've appreciated what you have written about them (which was not always true because I scolded Lynda Bird for her trip to Spain). Of course, Bess and Liz have helped."

I told him I understood he's asked each of his cabinet members to prepare a list of outstanding problems for the new person succeeding them and that Ramsey Clark has prepared a list of cases which were pending and that Rusk has prepared six volumes on foreign affairs for Bill Rogers. I suggested that if I could get some copies of these, I could check up on the new administration and see if they were carrying things out.

"I didn't know that," the president said. "I wish I'd known it earlier. I could have taken it up at the cabinet meeting today." He said he would see what he could do, but I am sure he won't.

"Have you seen the latest poll?" he said. He rang for his secretary to bring in the polls to show it to me. "I think we sent it to the files after you read it," she said.

On this happy note my last session with LBJ ended. The first time I saw him in his office in 1963, he had shown me a poll. This time he wasn't able to show it to me, but he said that his rating had gone up 50 percent in the Middle West.

He said good-bye and then, following me to the door, called out as I was in the next room: "You come down and spend a weekend with Luvie at the ranch. We'll have you speak at Southwest College and the university. I'm not going to pay you any of those high fees."

As I said good night to Sergeant Mascio downstairs, I remarked that I probably wouldn't be seeing him again. He said he thought I would, but I suspect it will be at least four years before I enter the private downstairs office of the White House.

SATURDAY, JANUARY 18 | The town is beginning to fill up with inauguration visitors. Several thousand hippies and yippies have also arrived for the counter-inauguration. Nixon is staying in New York and will not come down for the big gala.

The Hickel hearings were held most of Saturday, which is unusual. Scoop Jackson was trying to rush approval through. My revelations that Hickel had been an oil speculator gummed up the works. They finally put the whole matter over until Monday morning at eight thirty.

Westerners on the committee seem so anxious to get along with Hickel that they are taking anything he says without investigation. Believe it or not, my old friend Ernest Gruening testified for him today. What a sellout.

**MONDAY, JANUARY 20** | This is the big day. I hated to see it come. I never could have imagined that Richard Nixon would become president.

I was dictating a speech against Wally Hickel, to be delivered by Senator Tydings, and forgot to turn on the television to watch Nixon until after most of the prayers had been given. I was just in time to see the chief justice swear in Nixon as president. The chief was calm, impressive, and master of the occasion. He looked like a chief justice, and he was a chief justice. No one would have dreamed how much he despised Nixon. No one would have remembered—if they knew—how Nixon had double-crossed the chief in 1952 to block his nomination for president.

Hubert Humphrey stood alongside, a good sport to the end.

Lyndon looked blank. It was not his day. He was bowing out. And he looked completely neutral. I suspect that he was glad Nixon—rather than Hubert—was taking his place.

Nixon's speech was very good. It was well written and well delivered and emphasized, more than anything else, peace. If he lives up to these words, he'll be a great president. It may be that he will. I certainly hope so.

In the afternoon I watched Lyndon take off from Andrews Air Force Base for Texas. He played his role right to the end, going to the crowds along the barrier to shake hands and say good-bye. We could see Bess in the crowd but not Tyler. We heard later that she was quite shaken up. I can understand it. After all, she has been with Lady Bird now for approximately eight years. And life will certainly change.

At the White House this morning Nixon was waiting to drive up to the Capitol with Johnson, and he suggested to Hubert that he, Hubert, deliver his inaugural speech.

Hubert was equal to the occasion. "How long is it?" he asked. Nixon replied it was 225 words and would take about twenty minutes to deliver. "I think it will take more than that," Hubert said. "You know, Mr. President, I was thinking of delivering such a speech, but you got in my way." No one would ever know from talking to Hubert that his heart was almost breaking.

**TUESDAY, JANUARY 21** | Nixon went to the balls in his honor last night, and Bill Neel and Marian tell me that, toward the end, he appeared to be a little tipsy.

Yesterday Teddy Kennedy was true to his word and objected to a vote on confirming Hickel. The vote will now go over to Wednesday and could be on Thursday. They are waiting to print the record of the hearings. I talked to Senator Muskie this morning, and he intends to come out against Hickel. I tried to persuade Sen. Margaret Chase Smith to do likewise but doubt I succeeded. The Sierra Club has dug up more details regarding Hickel's oil leases. It all adds up to the fact he was actively an oil speculator.

We won't be able to block Hickel's confirmation, but at least he will know he's been in a good fight. The mail and the editorial reaction has been overwhelmingly anti-Hickel. Significantly, the *Anchorage Times* has dropped all of my recent Hickel columns.

Johnson yesterday awarded the Medal of Freedom to his great columnist friend Bill White, who never said an unkind thing about him; and to Merriman Smith of the UPI. Luvie is sore that my work for the Friendship Train, Big Brothers, etc., is overlooked. The trouble was that on occasion I could be critical of Lyndon, not as much as he deserved but more than he liked.

WEDNESDAY, JANUARY 22 | Something has happened between Udall and LBJ. Udall was going to announce the setting aside of 7.5 million acres of national parks. Then, on Monday, Johnson cut it down to 400,000 acres. The rumor is that Johnson was sore because Udall insisted on naming the Washington Stadium the "Robert F. Kennedy Memorial Stadium."

Johnson parted on bad terms with Ramsey Clark and Bill Wirtz also. He was sore at Wirtz over Vietnam and indicated to me that he was peeved with Ramsey Clark on several things. I suspect the last was regarding the antitrust suit against the Ford Motor Company and other auto manufacturers. Henry Ford II gave a farewell party to LBJ and was on very close terms with him.

THURSDAY, JANUARY 23 | Ernest Gruening called this morning, asking me to lunch with Wally Hickel, the new secretary of the interior, tomorrow. He said that Hickel was sure to be confirmed and that I could help guide him. I must leave for North Carolina tomorrow at noon so couldn't make it, but we finally hit upon next Monday for breakfast.

Dorothy Gruening told me that last night Hickel had been tight and, dining at the Georgetown Inn, was bragging about what he was going to do to me. He was confirmed this afternoon by a vote of seventy-three to sixteen. Significantly, however, the really important senators voted against him: Teddy Kennedy, Muskie, Mansfield, Fred Harris, the Democratic National chairman, John Pastore, et al. I guess my call to Fred Harris must have done the trick. My call to Margaret Chase Smith did not work. She voted for him.

Later in the afternoon Teddy Kennedy telephoned me to report on the vote. He has the efficiency of his two brothers, who never forgot to follow through on a commitment. Teddy said he didn't use my speech but that he thought the vote, while we lost, was helpful.

**FRIDAY, JANUARY 24** | Nixon has rescinded the air routes which Johnson awarded to various lines across the Pacific in December. Johnson favored his friends. His friends were stacked for American, and American got nothing.

Alan Boyd, former secretary of transportation, has turned up as president of the Illinois Central Railroad, simultaneous with a federal grant given to Illinois Central for $25 million. Boyd is an ethical man, and I doubt if he had anything to do with this, but it looks bad just the same.

Arrived at my motel room this afternoon, and immediately the phone rang. A voice said: "This is the LBJ Ranch. The president wants to speak to you."

It sounded familiar. I waited. Finally, what must have been Johnson's voice came on the line. I answered, in fact shouted, but the voice faded away. Finally, the operator's voice came on, saying that the president "had taken another call" and they would call back if they needed me. They never did call back, and I suspect Lyndon changed his mind. Probably he wanted to squawk about the piece Jack wrote in the column today that the safety equipment at the LBJ Ranch, belonging to the air force, was being kept there despite the air force's request to get it back.

If the president had gotten through to me and complained, I could not have given the old alibi that Jack wrote the story—even though true. He has heard that too many times. Anyway, he didn't call back, and I feel rather sorry for him because of all the stories that are breaking now about his feuds with the cabinet, the favoring of his friends with air routes, and Alan Boyd's job with the Illinois Central. He left Washington in a blaze of glory. Now the last thirty days don't look so glorious.

**SUNDAY, JANUARY 26** | Averell and Marie Harriman came to dinner. He has been back from Paris exactly a week. Averell was frank on the subject of President Thieu of South Vietnam. He called him "devious, two-faced, the worst possible excuse for an executive," who feels that American troops are in South Vietnam for the purpose of supporting him. He and Vice President

Ky got only 30 percent of the vote in an area representing 67 percent of the population.

Averell was also critical of Ellsworth Bunker, the American ambassador, who supported Thieu. "I don't know what's happened to Bunker," he said.

"Nixon now has three hawks running his peace negotiations: Cabot Lodge in Paris, Ellsworth Bunker in Saigon, and Alexis Johnson" (the new undersecretary of state).

Rogers, Averell said, was fine, but there's no one around him who's experienced. Welch in Paris and Elliot Richardson are inexperienced.

Of course, Averell has never loved Dean Rusk, so I should not have been surprised when I asked why in Bobby Kennedy's book *Thirteen Days*, on the Cuban missile crisis, Bobby referred to the fact that Rusk had other duties and was not around very much. "You don't know Rusk," Averell noted. "He never accepts any responsibility." Averell wondered whether newspapermen really understood the basic difference between Rusk and Clark Clifford over the peace talks in Paris, when Clifford made it clear that the South Vietnamese would have to get off the pot and attend the talks. I remarked that there must have been a clash at the weekly White House luncheons between Rusk and Clifford and asked whether the negotiators in Paris got any of this.

"We could tell afterward what happened," Averell said, "but we couldn't tell who argued about what. The weekly luncheons," he said, "were a poor way to decide policy," yet he didn't particularly like the comments on National Security Council meetings.

Averell said he was going to give Nixon a hundred days; then, if there were no results in Vietnam, "I'll move on."

He's been asked to consult with the new administration, though so far there hasn't been much consultation. "I'll keep quiet for two years," he said.

"There was no question that Bunker gave assurances to the White House on October 29 that President Thieu would participate in the peace talks the next Monday," Averell said. "Then Thieu brazenly went back on his word."

Averell thought it was a mistake for Nixon to wait three months while they read up on the record regarding disarmament talks.

At dinner Marie sat on my right, and I never have known her to be so critical of LBJ. "All this time I have kept quiet," she said, "but all this time I have hated Johnson. You never heard me breathe a word against him, but I think he's grotesque, crude, obscene. I think the way he treated Walter

Jenkins and some of the others around him was shameful. He called Walter language which can't repeat." And then she went ahead and repeated it.

FRIDAY, JANUARY 31 | Early in the day Nixon turned up in the Washington slums, burned last April, and in company with Mayor Washington and George Romney of HUD. He announced a $30 million urban renewal project. He also announced this morning a crime program for the District of Columbia which included hiring one thousand extra policemen, ten more judges, forty more prosecutors, and a tightening of the bail system regarding dangerous criminals. All of this had been advocated by local authorities and the DC Crime Commission. It made favorable headlines, and Nixon was smart enough to call in the editors of the local newspapers to announce the scheme.

Luvie sat beside Stewart Udall at dinner. He was quite critical of his old boss during the final days of the Johnson administration. LBJ, in the end, refused to authorize about six million acres of national parks which Stewart wanted. Stewart said that Johnson was impossible to deal with and that Lady Bird had thrown up her hands in despair and given him up. The only reason he, Stewart, stayed on was Lady Bird.

I am sure there was some truth in this, but it was not all true. I remember Lyndon praising Udall to the skies.

I had an interesting talk with Jane Thompson, who has just come back from Moscow. Tommy told me later that he had retired as ambassador chiefly because he had a warning that he might have cancer. There were two spots on his X-ray which indicated this; however, when he got home, he came through all right. He is now going to spend halftime advising the State Department.

Jane said Moscow was not what it was in the days under Khrushchev, when she and Tommy were invited down to the palace and out to Khrushchev's dacha for weekends. The present regime is playing everything close to the chest, and you don't see them as in the free-and-easy days of Mr. K. Tommy tried his best to see Mr. K. but got the brush-off.

I met the new secretary of the navy, former Gov. John Chafee of Rhode Island. He is a nice guy and has been out looking at the old Thrift House in Travilah with a view to renting it. I can see that some pretty good personnel have been brought into the administration.

Later, at the dance, I bumped into Elliot Richardson, the undersecretary of state, whom I had "maligned" for driving under the influence of liquor. We shook hands before either one of us really knew who the other was, and he gave me some rather vigorous, though quiet, sarcasm about digging up his past, which, he said, was inaccurate.

Richardson had just come from the White House, where Nixon had his first reception, a white-tie affair with decorations for the ambassadors and the chargé d'affaires. Apparently, it went well and was something of a contrast to the black-tie affairs of LBJ. There was no bar for hard liquor, only champagne and a fruit punch. This was like getting back to the days of Herbert Hoover, and I think on the whole made a good impression. Incidentally, French champagne was served, which LBJ used to boycott. I bumped into Ambassador Charles Lucet, resplendent with his French Legion of Honor and other ambassadorial decorations. I told him I understood de Gaulle took a little pride in the fact that he had predicted Nixon's comeback and thus was leaning over backward to improve Franco-American relations. The ambassador said that he was always the last to know about these things.

Poor Averell, now seventy-seven, seemed to think he had to stay to the bitter end of the dance given in his honor. Luvie and I left at one thirty.

[From February 5 through February 22 the Pearsons joined Agnes Meyer and Chief Justice and Nina Warren in Arizona. While there, they stayed closely attuned to actions of the new Nixon administration.]

**WEDNESDAY, FEBRUARY 5** | The chief and I had a good talk after the swim and later at dinner. He wondered how soon Nixon could coast without coming up with a program. "He has sent no message to Congress outlining his plans, and I noted that Carl Albert was quoted the other day as saying that Congress would have to go ahead with the Johnson program."

I suggested that perhaps Nixon didn't want to be in the same position of supporting the Johnson program yet at the same time didn't want to be in the position of opposing it. Of necessity Nixon was going to have to adopt public housing, education, school integration, and similar Johnson measures and that perhaps it was smart politics for him to say nothing about his domestic program but concentrate on foreign affairs.

"How long will he be able to postpone doing anything for Negroes?" the chief asked. "They've been very patient. How long will they continue to be so? Sooner or later Nixon will have to face up. He'll have to choose between Strom Thurmond and the Negroes."

The chief said that while he was worried about the students, he was more worried that repressive measures might drive them underground. This would result in sabotage, which could be easy in this country and terrible in its consequences. Therefore, he felt the students ought to be given a chance to blow off steam to some extent.

We discussed the new secretary for HEW, Bob Finch, the former lieutenant governor of California. "He was almost untried in California," the chief said.

I pointed out that Finch had just delayed cutting off school funds from five southern districts which have not integrated. He was giving them sixty days' grace. "And after fifteen years' delay," the chief remarked, referring to the fifteen years since the Supreme Court's school desegregation decision.

**THURSDAY, FEBRUARY 6** | Nixon had his second press conference this morning. We watched it on television. I thought he did very well. One of the most interesting questions was to the effect that the Liberty Lobby had been critical of Ambassador Yost because of Yost's former connections with Alger Hiss. "In view of your more than passing interest in Alger Hiss, what is your reaction to this criticism?" was the question. Nixon answered by saying he was not interested in Yost's activities twenty years ago, that he was familiar with Yost's record. He considered him a loyal American, a valuable asset at the UN, and had contributed materially to the problems of the Near East solution at the last Security Council conference.

Afterward the chief and I took a long walk. He thought Nixon had done well too. "It will be a great thing," he said, "if he should turn out to be a good president." I thought this was rather sporting of him in view of Nixon's sabotage of him when Warren aspired to be president in 1952.

"Of course, he's had a lot of experience at press conferences and in figuring out his policies," the chief added. "The important thing is how he'll be as an administrator. In the House of Representatives he had no administrative experience at all, and as vice president, he had none. Now he faces the toughest administrative job in the world."

The chief thought he might have trouble with Moynihan, who had very positive views regarding housing for the big cities, and perhaps with fellows like Strom Thurmond, who was opposed to aid for the big cities and the Negroes. I suggested there might be trouble between Moynihan and George Romney, secretary of HUD. Both are strong-willed men, though Romney seems to be winning the confidence of the bureaucrats inherited from Bob Weaver. Romney has come out for massive housing.

The situation between Henry Kissinger and Secretary of State Bill Rogers also may cause trouble. Both have duplicate jobs dealing with foreign policy. The chief expressed confidence in Bill and thought he was an admirable choice. He expressed misgivings about John Mitchell, the attorney general. "I don't see how his experience as an attorney for the floaters of municipal bonds is going to help him much," the chief said.

We speculated whether it would be possible to turn the clock back again on the remarkable progress made toward civil rights since 1954. The chief thought not. "It's no longer a matter of interpreting the Constitution," he said. "It's now written into the law by Congress. Congress has specifically provided that Negroes shall have access to parks, swimming pools, and restaurants which deal in interstate commerce, and almost every restaurant buys food that comes through interstate commerce. No longer do civil rights depend upon an interpretation of the Fourteenth Amendment. Congress has gone a long way toward making the advances of the Negro impossible to scale down."

I recalled that I had gone in to say good-bye to Lyndon Johnson and he had shown me the glass blotter, given him by the cabinet, outlining all of the bills he had passed and that he had pointed to the Negro voting rights bill as the most important.

"LBJ spoke out loud and clear in his message to Congress," the chief said. "He never hesitated. He is responsible for the great progress we have made. When he was a senator, his two civil rights bills were not as courageous, but probably that was as far as he could go at that time."

We met with Supreme Court justice Bill Douglas and his wife for lunch; lamented the departure of Wayne Morse from the Senate. The two Supreme Court justices discussed with some alarm the Nixon administration proposal of having private citizens engage in crime prevention. They concluded it would likely lead to vigilante groups, private spies, and even a revival of Ku Klux Klanism.

Bill remarked that the State Department had been handicapped not only by the loss of its China experts, as a result of the McCarthy purge, but also the loss of its one expert on French Indochina, Gene Gregory, who was purged from the State Department because he argued that the French could not win and should get out of Vietnam. Bill had given me a letter from Gregory giving the lowdown on the South Vietnamese delegates in Paris, which I have been slow about using. John P. Davies, one of the China experts who was purged, had been cleared nine times. Even so, [he] was kicked out of the State Department by John Foster Dulles. Two days before Nixon was inaugurated, Dean Rusk reinstated him—I suspect because he figured it would never get done after Nixon took over.

We went swimming this afternoon, even though it was chilly. The chief remarked how well Bill Douglas was looking and expressed the hope that he could remain on the bench for another eight years. "We're going to need him," he said.

"I was hoping that you might change your mind," I said. "No, I made up my mind some time ago," the chief replied. "I considered it very carefully and I'm not going to change it. Bill Douglas is eight years younger than I am and he should be able to stay for eight years."

**FRIDAY, FEBRUARY 7** | The news broadcasts from Washington this evening showed Roy Wilkins after he visited President Nixon. "I told him," Wilkins said, "that he had very little time left. By that I don't mean a week or a month but soon."

The chief thinks Wilkins is right, that the Negro population will not wait long for Nixon to move. I asked the chief what he would do if he were president, and he replied that he would send a State of the Union message to Congress, followed by subsequent specific messages outlining housing measures, education, and so on, aimed at the alleviation of poverty and the problems of the big cities.

Nixon met with a group of students who had been studying in Senate offices. They were assembled in the East Room of the White House, where Nixon spoke to them and came out flatly for the right of eighteen-year-olds to vote.

The chief disagreed. He felt that ten million new voters aged between eighteen and twenty-one would have no real concept of what their voting obligations and citizenship were all about. He recalled that the issue first came up when he was governor of California, when Ellis Arnall put across eighteen-year-old voting in Georgia. California, however, did not adopt it, and only four states have done so since.

I may be getting conservative, but I think the chief is right.

**SATURDAY, FEBRUARY 8** | The chief does not think Nixon is wise in going abroad so soon in his first term. He has too many domestic problems to iron out. The trip will make a big splash and favorable publicity, but this will wear off.

I suggested that Nixon was anxious to talk to de Gaulle and try to secure his cooperation. The chief said he had met de Gaulle when he attended Winston Churchill's funeral in London. "He was gracious and charming. 'And how is your great President? Please give him my regards and profound admiration,' he said, referring to President Johnson. He was just as humble as he could be. I am sure he will be the same way with Nixon, but I doubt whether he gives him any concessions.

"The leaders of Western Europe have been considering their problems for years. They know what they want. They know their own problems in detail. It seems doubtful that any important problems can be settled by visiting seven countries in eight days. There will be dinners and luncheons and official receptions, and about the only time remaining for talks will be about an hour here and there. I do not see how the trip can possibly come to any great result."

Agnes isn't feeling well. We had dinner by ourselves. The conversation drifted around to Nixon and the Eisenhowers. Eisenhower, it developed, had never invited the Nixons to the Gettysburg farm.

"Ike had the military attitude toward a subordinate," the chief said. "And Nixon was a subordinate. He admired George Humphrey, the secretary of the treasury, because he had money, but Nixon had no money and was inferior in rank."

I suggested that young David Eisenhower and his bride, Julie, probably won the election for Nixon because they put Ike in a position where he had to endorse Nixon for president.

The chief figures that Nixon must give Vice President Agnew some kind of a buildup, but it won't be easy. He's been put in charge of municipal problems, but there's bound to be some friction between Agnew, George Romney, and Moynihan.

SUNDAY, FEBRUARY 9 | The first really warm day. We had a walk and a swim this morning.

I mentioned that four cabinet members had been on the outs with Johnson toward the end: Udall, Cohen, Ramsey Clark, and Bill Wirtz. The chief said he suspected that the president was irked at him also because he didn't withdraw his resignation as chief justice.

"He didn't say anything to me, but word was sent that he would like to have me withdraw my letter of resignation after Fortas failed confirmation. I just couldn't do that. It would have made it appear that it was a purely political move. I had to think of the Court and its prestige and my colleagues. I had made up my mind that now was the time for me to retire, and I didn't discuss it with anyone except Nina. I called up the White House and asked to see the president and got word back that the president would see me that morning. It was the last day of Court, the last conference we were to have.

"I told the president I had put in almost fifty years of government service and almost fifteen years on the Supreme Court and that I wanted to retire during his administration, during the administration of a president who was a friend of the Court and who could appoint my successor.

"I had written him a letter stating that under section so-and-so of the law I wanted to avail myself of the opportunity to retire and that I submitted my resignation subject to his acceptance. I did not resign, as the press reported, subject to the appointment of my successor. It was purely subject to his decision as to when he would accept the resignation."

The chief was disturbed that the press reported he was to remain until a successor was appointed. I recall that the White House had called me and read me a letter—I think it was by Oliver Wendell Holmes—[about] resigning subject to the appointment of a successor. In other words, the White House was apparently deliberately putting out the idea that the chief was to serve until a successor was appointed.

"When I came back to the Court, I told the conference of my decision that same morning. I knew it would leak because those things have a habit of doing so, but those were the only people who knew about it: the president, my colleagues on the Court, and Nina.

"After Abe failed of confirmation and after the election, I received a letter from Senator Dirksen as chairman of the Inaugural Committee, asking me to swear in the new president. I wrote back that I would be delighted to do so. There was nothing else I could do. It would have looked terrible if I had refused. About a day or two later Nixon called me. He was in Washington. He thanked me for my letter agreeing to swear him in and then said he'd been thinking about the Court, and changes on the Court, and he thought it would be wise if there were complete continuity on the Court during the present term. Therefore, he asked me if I would remain until the end of the present session. I told him that I had submitted my resignation subject to the decision of the president, that I didn't know what President Johnson's decision would be but that if he did not act, I would be happy to remain until the term was over in June.

"After this was announced by Nixon, I got a telephone call the next day from Abe Fortas, who was in Puerto Rico, who said President Johnson was unhappy and suggested I telephone him. I asked him why. Abe said that presidents like to be consulted, and the president was taken by surprise at the Nixon announcement that I was going to remain on the Court for the balance of the term. I said that if it would do any good, I would be glad to call the president, and I did. I told him exactly what had happened.

"He told me that he had some idea of appointing Arthur Goldberg as my successor as an interim appointee. I did not tell him that, in view of his strong stand against interim appointments when he was in the Senate, I had felt it highly unlikely that he would make an appointment between the adjournment of Congress and the convening of the new Congress. I told l him I had always thought Arthur would be an admirable appointment and that he had my letter and was free to act on it at any time."

I told the chief that on December 8 I had dined at the White House and that the president had cornered me privately to chide me about my alleged failure to build up Arthur Goldberg for the Court and that he had been obviously irked at Nixon. He said: "Nixon is not the president yet. He has no right to ask the chief to continue. Who does he think he is, already stepping in to take over the power of the president?" I said that the president had asked me to sound out some of the Senate leaders about an interim appointment and also talk to Arthur about it, which I'd done.

"I made a report to the president and handed it to him personally," I said. "And I also reported that Arthur would accept an interim appointment. I heard nothing further, and obviously, the president changed his mind."

"I don't like to say this," the chief said, "but I am quite sure the president never had any intention of appointing Goldberg. He talked about it, but if he'd really wanted to do it, he would have gone ahead. He was irritated with Arthur and told me so, but he just didn't like Arthur and wasn't going to make the appointment. Of course, he could have appointed Arthur to the Court and Abe Fortas as chief justice, and the Senate would have confirmed both."

I agreed. "Sometimes," I said, "the president will spoil some of the great things he has been doing by his own personal likes and dislikes. At stake was something much more than a personal friend. At stake was his whole program and the Court decisions for the next ten years. The next chief justice can erode all of the Court decisions."

"He's been a great president," the chief added. "He got this country moving on certain vital issues where it had been stymied for a hundred years. The things he started may be eroded somewhat in the next few years, but they can't be stopped. No other president has been able to move them as he has. And we can forgive him his personal likes and dislikes."

**MONDAY, FEBRUARY 10** | LBJ telephoned this morning. The operator did not announce him as "President Johnson" as he did when the call came through four days after the inauguration.

Lyndon called to say no regarding my request that Axel Springer Jr. come down to take some photographs, but he said it so nicely that I couldn't get sore. He said he had about 150 requests, including the *Times* (which in the past he has never loved) wanting interviews and photographs.

"I've never had so much trouble as I did over that *Stern* interview," he said, not realizing that *Stern* is the mortal enemy of Springer and that the trouble he had was not with the *Stern* interview but with the *Quick* interview. I did not take the time to set him straight. I did point out that this morning, featured on the front page, was an interview with Peter Lisagor published in *True* magazine.

"That was done before we came down here," LBJ said. "I've had twelve hundred letters a day and am having a hard time answering them. I want to get squared away with all the problems here. What do you think I should do?"

"Putting myself in your position," I said weakly, "I suppose I would say no."

I suppose I could have argued him into it, but I didn't try. I asked if he was going to Palm Springs. "Not unless it gets too cold here, in which case we might go to Florida. The weather is wonderful here. We've got our daughters here with their children, and we're enjoying them. Laurance Rockefeller wanted me to come to Palm Springs, but I don't think I'll go now. Lady Bird says she can't get me to stand still. You and Luvie have got to come down here in the spring."

In the interview in *True* he admitted that he had made a mistake in not trying to win over the youth of the nation, especially regarding the importance of entering into the war in Vietnam. He also said that the Chicago convention had alienated youth from Hubert Humphrey. I don't see how he could have gotten the youth of the nation with him over the war in Vietnam no matter what he did or how hard he tried.

**TUESDAY, FEBRUARY 11** | At lunch we talked about Winston Churchill's funeral. The chief had been appointed official American representative by

Johnson to the funeral, along with Eisenhower. Nina said that she and the chief were attending an Indian dinner in New York when the White House telephoned to say that Eisenhower had insisted on going early the next morning to London instead of a day later, as originally planned. As a result, they had to fly back to Washington that night, and Nina finally got the chief's clothes ready during the night, including his top hat, cutaway coat, etc. She was so busy getting him ready that she didn't have time to get ready and go herself.

"Eisenhower is probably the most selfish man I know," the chief remarked. "He had no concern whatsoever for other people."

At any rate the chief sat right behind the queen of England in Westminster Abbey. I asked whether the funeral had been overdone, recalling that Churchill had planned it all himself. The chief said it had not, that it was a respectful and inspiring ceremony.

**THURSDAY, FEBRUARY 13** | This morning the chief handed me a clipping from the Tucson paper regarding banking conflicts of interest. It told how Wright Patman of Texas was trying to plug the loophole in the Bank Holding Corporation Act and how the administration was not in favor of this; also how the administration had appointed more big bankers than ever before, ranging from Douglas Kennedy of Illinois Continental of Chicago, now secretary of the treasury, to the director of the budget, whom I think is from Chase Manhattan. The chief was indignant. "Imagine," he said, "owning a bank and also a couple of business firms and being able to loan money to your business enterprise at cheaper rates than its competitor. A lot of firms can't always get loans, but if they are owned by a bank, they could."

Nixon is going to Florida over the weekend, and Pat is remaining in Washington. Her excuse is that she has a van load of furniture from New York to unload and get straightened out in the White House. Luvie says she has refrained from giving me a message from Kay Halle to the effect that Nixon is a pansy. She told Kay I had enough problems without writing this. I don't believe the thing about Nixon. It's true that Nixon has been palling around . . . with Bebe Rebozo, and it's interesting also that Pat has not been with him at any time during the recent campaign. She stayed at home. I suspect this is a Madison Avenue gimmick to get away from the fact that she was constantly beside him in the old days, especially during that famous Checkers-the-dog broadcast when he alibied for his personal expense fund.

**FRIDAY, FEBRUARY 14** | Yesterday the Peruvian navy fired on an American fishing boat fifty miles out to sea and captured a second boat, thus bringing the whole Peruvian crisis to public attention. I have been warning about this for some time. Sol [Linowitz] thinks that what is needed is a special ambassador, such as Averell Harriman, to go to Lima and try to straighten out the crisis. While Nixon is engrossed in European affairs, the Peruvian crisis drifts. Sol has talked to the Argentine ambassador about the possibility of having the Argentine foreign minister act as mediator to prevent a showdown. He has also discussed the matter with Galo Plaza, who unfortunately cannot act because he is an Ecuadorian, and Ecuador has no relations with Peru.

Nelson Rockefeller has discussed his impending mission to Latin America with Sol and wanted to know whom he should take on the trip. I suggested Wayne Morse, former chairman of the Foreign Affairs Subcommittee on Latin America. Sol had suggested Frank Church.

Viron Vaki, the acting assistant secretary of state for Latin American affairs, has been taken by Kissinger to the White House, which means that Kissinger is rapidly building up his own little State Department across the street. He has been reaching into the State Department for various other experts. Unfortunately, Bill Rogers doesn't understand foreign affairs at all so that Nixon leans on Kissinger for expert advice. Elliot Richardson also doesn't understand foreign affairs.

The *Wall Street Journal* this morning carried a story regarding overtures between the United States and Castro to resume relations with Cuba. Sol said that Bob McCloskey, the State Department's spokesman, had denied this but that there had been some underground discussions, and Castro was being cooperative regarding the return of hijacked planes. The USSR wants to trade with Latin America, Sol said, and the Latin American countries have been telling them to get Castro to pipe down. The next move may be to take Cuba into the OAS. "If Cuba applied for membership," Sol said, "it would be very difficult to turn her down."

**TUESDAY, FEBRUARY 18** | An Israeli airplane was attacked by Arab commandos at Zurich, Switzerland. No passengers were killed, and all the Arabs were arrested or killed. Nixon is going to have to move fast on the situation, or it will blow up in his face. If you look below the surface, it seems to me that Nixon has really not moved fast on anything except his trip abroad.

**THURSDAY, FEBRUARY 20** | I wrote a column on Ambassador Annenberg, leaving out some of the lurid stuff about him; even so, I am sure that some of my publishers, including the *Washington Post*, will not use it.

Senator Hatfield of Oregon telephoned me regarding Walter Hickel, whom he thinks is loading up the Interior Department with oil and public utilities men. I gathered that progressive Republicans were going to exert their independence behind the scenes at last, even though they had to vote with Nixon.

Nixon is leaving early Sunday morning for Europe. I had written a column for release Saturday regarding the possibility of spoiling favorable Communist reaction to his general policies by going to NATO first. The *New York Times* this morning published a front-page story, obviously leaked by the White House, telling how he was being careful to discuss everything with the Russians and probably would go to Russia later. He and Dobrynin had a talk earlier in the week.

**MONDAY, FEBRUARY 24** | WASHINGTON DC—The Court of Appeals this morning handed down a unanimous decision in our favor in Senator Dodd's suit against us for taking and using his papers. I hope this will end the Dodd litigation. It's dragged out for almost three years and has cost me around $25,000, even though we have won almost every move.

Judge Holtzoff in the lower court had held that we were guilty of using stolen property. Judge Skelly Wright, writing the opinion for the U.S. Court of Appeals [for the District of Columbia Circuit], held that though you could argue no one should use information they received when given to them illicitly, it was hardly practical to take this position.

**TUESDAY, FEBRUARY 25** | I had an early appointment with Dobrynin, who had just returned from Moscow. When I asked how the Kremlin viewed Nixon's trip, he replied: "We are waiting. We have told president Nixon that we are ready to talk any time. He has said he has a new administration and it will take a little time for him to get settled. We understand this. We are waiting to talk whenever he is ready."

I said I'd had lunch with Yuri Zhukov recently and he seemed to be more friendly toward the United States. The ambassador remarked that Zhukov didn't necessarily represent the Soviet government. He had received an invitation to visit in the United States, first the Dartmouth conference, then a trip to California as the guest of the *Los Angeles Times*, and he had asked his boss whether he could take the trip. There was nothing official about it, the ambassador said.

This was interesting in view of the fact that Zhukov and his tough editorials in *Pravda* have always been considered representative of the Soviet point of view.

**THURSDAY, FEBRUARY 27** | LBJ called from the ranch shortly after breakfast. We chatted pleasantly. He said he'd been to Houston to hear Van Cliburn play. "We both had trouble with the autograph seekers," he said. A student group in Houston had staged a Van Cliburn concert, and he, the ex-president, wanted to go down to participate.

"Hoover has a nice little library up in Iowa," Lyndon said when I asked him about his trip up there. Most of his documents, however, were sent to Stanford University and never came back. "I've got the finest cartoon collection in the United States for my library," Lyndon added, "three thousand of them, and most of them mean. They give me a long nose and make me look like what the younger generation wants to think of me."

Lyndon said he'd been relaxing and philosophizing and that the real "readin' and writin'" would start in June.

I told him we missed him in Washington, and I also said I had spent a nice vacation in Arizona with the chief justice and Agnes Meyer. "The chief thinks you're probably a little miffed at him," I said.

"I'm not miffed at anyone," LBJ replied. "I just thought that Nixon took advantage of a man who wanted to be nice when he said he would stay on until June."

"I've got so few real friends that I never would be miffed at him," the president added. "Of course, he could have said, 'I've got a letter on the president's desk giving him my resignation, and it's up to him to act on it,' but Nixon had intervened with the chief and then Nixon took advantage of his good nature.

"I let two or three balls go by me every day when I was in office, and this was one of them. I'm sorry about it, but it was of no great moment."

I am afraid that it was. I am afraid that when Nixon appoints the successor to the chief justice, all of the chief's liberal policies on the Supreme Court will be reversed.

**FRIDAY, FEBRUARY 28** | Frank Waldrop, together with Borkin and Levin, came to lunch. Borkin and Waldrop recounted the days when President

Sukarno of Indonesia visited the United States and they were approached by the Indonesian embassy that what would really make Sukarno happy was a couple of white women. They approached the State Department regarding this, and the State Department was horrified. Finally, they delegated the responsibility to the representative of Shell Oil, who performed efficiently and added the cost of the women to the Indonesian government account.

Nixon experienced riots in Italy last night. As a result, I had to kill one paragraph of the story released for Monday. I had thought there would be no riots, that the Communist Party would be reasonably friendly and would have things under control. As far as I could tell, the riots were sparked by left-wing students, with the Communist Party not participating.

**SATURDAY, MARCH 1** | Last night Clay Shaw was acquitted in New Orleans—a vote of confidence for the Warren Commission. The chief justice has never budged from his position. I am sure he was right in the first place.

**SUNDAY, MARCH 2** | It snowed all yesterday afternoon and night and again today. This has given me a chance to get caught up. I have written three columns on Ambassador Walter Annenberg, publisher of the *Philadelphia Inquirer*, whom Nixon is appointing to the Court of St. James. It's a pure political payoff. I helped to convict Annenberg's father of income tax evasion, and Walter has been sore at me ever since.

Actually, he didn't have to be convicted. He pled guilty. Henry Morganthau had told me that Annenberg Sr. had been keeping a mistress, who was camouflaged as his secretary and whom he charged off as a business expense on the ground that she was a secretary. Internal Revenue gave her a typing test and found she couldn't type. Therefore, all her expenses were declared nondeductible, and this was one ground for the tax case against him. Rather than face the charge on the witness stand that he had deducted the cost of his mistress and have his wife and family humiliated, Annenberg pleaded guilty. I wrote the story about the mistress, for which the Annenberg family never forgave me.

**MONDAY, MARCH 3** | HOBE SOUND FL—We arrived about 1:00 a.m., driving from Palm Beach in a rented car. It is peaceful and quiet but a little chilly. Marie [Harriman] and Mary Russell were playing cards when we arrived. This is supposed to be the really exclusive haven of the rich. The island is a long, narrow strip along the ocean, with mansions along the waterfront, a golf course in the middle of two roads, with shade trees on each side.

I got up at eight o'clock and found everyone else asleep; however, Averell came down a bit later, and we had breakfast together and a long talk during most of the day.

He is pleased with Nixon's intelligence regarding Russia though disappointed over his failure to push the peace talks regarding Vietnam. After Averell came back from Paris, he asked to see the new secretary of state and was given an appointment almost immediately. They spent forty-five minutes together, and subsequently, Rogers had him see Nixon.

"Nixon showed the greatest intelligence of any president I have talked to regarding peace with Russia," Averell said. "He asked intelligent questions. He wants to know. Kennedy wouldn't listen. It took Johnson some time, though he eventually came around to firmly realizing that the peace of the world depended upon Russia and the United States. Nixon grasped this immediately."

Averell refers to Dean Rusk as "Field Marshal Rusk" and says he took us back to the Dulles age. "You never knew what motivated him, but I think Abe Fortas was the evil genius. He told Johnson that his place in history depended upon victory in Southeast Asia. And since he saw the president more frequently than anyone else, his advice counted heavily. What he knew about the war or Southeast Asia, I have no idea.

"It took Clark Clifford only about three days after he became secretary of defense to discover that Bob McNamara was right. At first McNamara was taken in by the military and believed we could win in Vietnam. He said so back in 1963—though he was not taken in as badly as Maxwell Taylor. In September 1965 he changed and persuaded Johnson to stop the bombing for thirty-seven days.

"This was during the last week in 1965, and I got a call from the president: 'Averell, are your bags packed? McNamara's got a plane waiting for you. I want you to go to Hungary and other countries to see if we can extend the peace in Vietnam. Dean thinks Hungary is important.'

"I saw Dean Rusk that night. He was not for it. I saw McNamara, who was. I got back to the president the next morning and pushed off for Poland first. I got there at 3:00 a.m. Washington time. [Ambassador] Gronousky met me at the airport to say that he had arranged a meeting with Foreign Minister Rapocki in one hour. I asked him to make it an hour and a half while I shaved and bathed. I spent the day talking to Rapocki, then Gomułka, who gave us hell for being in Vietnam at all. Within twenty-four hours the Poles had sent Michalowski, now ambassador in Washington, to Moscow, Peking, and Hanoi. The Poles spent a week working on North Vietnam, trying to pressure them for us.

"I saw Tito, Shastri, Ayub [Khan], the latter being on the way to see Kosygin at Tashkent. I also stopped off in Romania. All the Communist nations wanted better understanding between the United States and the Soviet Union. They were afraid of war between them."

Averell said that Clark Clifford, after he became secretary of defense, had persuaded Lyndon to make his March 31 speech, stopping the bombing of most of North Vietnam, and had tried to make him stop altogether. Lyndon was irked at Clifford at times, and their old friendship was strained a bit when he found that Clark had taken exactly the same position as McNamara. The fact that the two men agreed and the further fact that Lyndon had enjoyed a close personal relationship with Clifford, which he didn't have with McNamara, tipped the balance of the scales and brought about the partial bombing halt in March.

Again, it was Clifford who put across the complete bombing halt in October. Averell said the announcement for this halt was ready on October 29 but that Johnson, supercautious and always bowing to the military, held it up until October 31 in order to have a further conference with General Abrams. President Thieu had agreed in advance with Ambassador Bunker to go along with this but then pulled back.

"There is no question that the South Vietnamese were stalling in order to let Nixon win," Averell said. "Some of Nixon's associates probably encouraged them, but they didn't really need any encouragement. From November 5 to January 20 it has been one continual stall, with the South Vietnamese waiting for Nixon to take over. Meanwhile, two hundred American boys have been killed every day. During that period we did accomplish a little. We decided on the type of table, but this could have been done long before. The United States suggested it early, and the Russians finally pushed the North Vietnamese into agreement. The Russians were helpful, especially in October, in getting the North Vietnamese to agree to meet with South Vietnam."

Averell said Clark Clifford was a man who got most disgusted with the South Vietnamese stalling and finally sounded off at his very vigorous press conference in December. "The reason he had this press conference," Averell said, "was that in December Johnson said, 'You haven't held a press conference lately.' This was Clark's cue, and he let loose with his statement about Vice President Ky and the manner in which the South Vietnamese were stalling."

"Cabot Lodge is a good man," Averell said. "Cy Vance speaks highly of him. He is a little dumb at times; however, everything is waiting on Nixon. He is giving the orders to Lodge. There was an agreement between us and the North Vietnamese before I left Paris that there should be private talks. This is where you really can accomplish things; however, Nixon hasn't given Lodge the green light, and all orders are coming from Washington."

Averell said Vance had just returned from Paris and telephoned him this morning. Vance, he said, had done a great job during the very tense period around October 31, when he slept in his office. This was because phone calls from Washington would start coming in to Paris at about 3:00 a.m. Washington would not start work on serious business until after 6:00 p.m., which was midnight, Paris time. Averell said Johnson could probably have had a peace, or a real start toward it, last July. At that time a bombing pause was all arranged, but Hubert Humphrey spoke out and promised it. At this point Johnson cut his throat.

Averell said there had been twenty or thirty coffee breaks in Paris during which American and North Vietnamese delegates talked. The North Vietnamese were frank and reasonably friendly in discussing the future. They looked to the United States for miracle rice, also technical aid and help with their irrigation and reclamation problems. They are very proud and feel that they have won the war. They base this on the fact that they withstood the bombing of their interior, which is true. They don't want to be under either Russia or China.

"The only peace that can come in Vietnam," Averell said, "is to take over the South. You don't like to say that your country is wrong, but there is no question in my mind that we have made a serious mistake by waiting so long before beginning private talks. The United States had an agreement with North Vietnam six weeks ago to talk secretly, and Nixon has not gone ahead."

Averell has probably seen more diplomacy and played a vital part in it than any other living human being. He began when he was fairly young as an observer for FDR. He is now approaching seventy-eight.

Averell said when he got back from Paris this winter, he sent word to the new secretary of state, Bill Rogers, that he would like to see him. "He asked me for advice on the peace talks. I told him the president has got to get rid of

Bunker, Alexis Johnson, and Lodge. Rogers replied, 'Don't you think Lodge is a little better than the others?' I agreed."

I was surprised that Kennedy had never called Averell regarding Russia. Averell was in Paris when Kennedy was en route to Vienna and attended a dinner at the American embassy, where he sat beside Eunice Shriver. She asked him, "Would you like to talk to my brother about his trip to Vienna?"

Averell replied in the affirmative, whereupon she leaned over across the table and said, "Jack, Governor Harriman would like to talk to you about your trip to Vienna."

"What would you do?" the president shot back.

"Well, I would not be serious with Khrushchev," Averell said. "I'd deal with him in a very light vein."

Averell explained that he had been surprised by Eunice's action and this was the best answer he could think of on the spur of the moment. This was the extent of Kennedy's consultation with a man who had served in Moscow as an ambassador and knew the Russians probably better than almost any other American diplomat.

We speculated as to why Kennedy started on such a tough policy with Khrushchev, when Khrushchev obviously wanted to conciliate. Averell thought it had to do with the narrow margin by which Kennedy was elected and the fact that he felt he had to appease the right-wing Republicans.

Averell noted that Nixon has abandoned "linkage"—that is, linking foreign policy with talks on missile limitation and the antiballistic missile system. Originally, Nixon had thought it was necessary to discuss all these at one conference as a sort of a bargaining move with the Russians. Now he has changed his mind. The subjects are too complicated and have to be taken up separately.

Nixon has revived the old National Security Council System of paper shuffling. General Goodpaster is in charge. Nixon wants reports on all the alternatives in each move in the field of foreign affairs. He is very cautious. The position papers are written chiefly by third echelon government experts, and nobody really reads them. As a result, there are terrible delays in making decisions.

"Kissinger is a good man," Averell said, "but he's swamped with paperwork. There should be some tactical moves by those in command. You cannot postpone these decisions indefinitely."

**TUESDAY, MARCH 4** | Averell told me this morning, before the Thayers arrived, that one of John Foster Dulles's greatest mistakes was being in awe of the Senate. He once told Averell, "I'm not going to make the same mistake as Dean Acheson of not getting along with the Senate."

This was why he fired Thayer, also men like John P. Davies and Jack Service, whom McCarthy criticized; and why he put a McCarthy man, Scott McLeod, in as his security officer at the State Department.

Averell and Charlie Thayer speculated regarding the changes in Russia and how soon this system would break up. Would it come slowly or suddenly? They were convinced the system could not last indefinitely. In general people are accustomed to the economic phases of the system. They don't object to the manner in which consumers' goods are handled by the government. The trains and air schedules are run almost like that in any other country, even though by the government. What they object to is the loss of their personal freedoms, the right to speak out. The present government, being conservative, has been tougher regarding these than Khrushchev was. And they are resurrecting Stalin somewhat, chiefly because he represents the opposite of Khrushchev, and they have to show that Khrushchev and his liberal ideas were wrong.

The *New York Times* today carries an interesting story from Paris, where the North Vietnamese delegate says that the current shelling of Saigon is to counteract the military pressure of the United States. Averell pointed out that we are always talking about negotiating from strength, which means after we have achieved some military victories. The North Vietnamese are now also moving to negotiate from strength.

I had asked him yesterday how we could really get out of Vietnam without a disastrous retreat, and Averell said he thought there were two ways. "We can either make an orderly withdrawal after obtaining our objectives," he said, "or if the South Vietnamese refuse to support us, if they stage another coup, if they become too unreasonable, then we can simply get out on our own."

"What about our Asian allies?" I asked.

"They would understand this," Averell said. "They understand the South Vietnamese situation completely."

Tonight Nixon gave a one-hour press conference report on his trip abroad. Averell pointed out there was one very important news item in the report—namely, that Israel and the Arab States would be entitled to a guarantee of the peace terms once peace was adopted. Nixon said that the four powers could not "impose" peace, which, in my opinion, is surrendering a very important bargaining weapon. He should know full well that he can impose peace simply by cutting off the shipment of Phantom jets to Israel, and Russia can impose peace on the Egyptians by cutting off their arms supply.

Nixon said he had discussed the Near East rather fully with all four powers involved. He was fairly moderate regarding South Vietnam and the Vietcong attacks, saying that most of them had been on military targets. This was quite a concession to make, even though true.

**WEDNESDAY, MARCH 5** | Yesterday Jack telephoned from Washington to say that Senator McClellan of Arkansas, chairman of the Senate Operations Committee, who is investigating left-wingism among the antipoverty program personnel, had secured from Margaret Lauren McSurely some diaries or love letters of mine. Margaret was arrested in Kentucky and is due to testify with her husband this week. McClellan, who hates me, was planning to use the papers, or whatever she has, and a staff member reported that he was gleeful over the opportunity.

I can't remember writing Margaret any love letters, though she did keep my diary, and she may have retained carbons. She also kept a diary of her own. There was one letter I wrote to her from Sioux Falls, South Dakota, paraphrasing John Steinbeck about the importance of keeping present-day society on tenterhooks, or something like that. This was when she was in Mississippi doing what I thought was an important job for civil rights during that very difficult summer of 1964, when they were blowing up about twenty churches in Mississippi.

Senator Ribicoff of Connecticut told me today that the papers had been seized when the McSurelys' home was raided in Kentucky and that the Sixth Circuit Court of Appeals had ordered them returned. Therefore, McClellan would probably have to obey the court order. I also talked to Warren Magnuson, who said he would talk to Scoop Jackson, who is on the committee. He reported back late last night that Scoop thought the papers would be restrained by the court order.

I have now been accused by Senator Dodd of being a homosexual. Now it looks as if Senator McClellan was trying to accuse me of being the opposite.

Averell thinks change in Russia will come without force or revolution. Thayer does not. He thinks the military will eventually take over and from that will come a democratic government. Already, the military has great power and very few political convictions.

The reason Khrushchev was kicked out, Charlie says, was that he had permitted too much liberalization. Brezhnev told him it had gone too far. And they invaded Czechoslovakia for the same reason. Czechoslovakia had gone too far toward a democracy. They had committed the cardinal sin of permitting an opposition party to form. This cannot be done under the Communist system. This was also why Kosygin was so careful not to stray away from his home base when he talked to Lyndon at Glassboro. He appeared to agree with LBJ on a lot of things but would go back to headquarters afterward to issue his own tough communiqué, repeating the line of the Kremlin. He didn't want to make the mistake that Khrushchev did.

**THURSDAY, MARCH 6** | The North Vietnamese bombarded Saigon again yesterday. While Averell notes that this is a definite violation of their agreement with us, nevertheless they're only doing what the American military previously did—namely, escalating the war in order to negotiate from strength. He is concerned over the delays and fears that Nixon may have lost the peace momentum previously achieved in Paris by himself and Cy Vance.

Nixon is now out on a limb as a result of his press conference Monday night. He has scolded the North Vietnamese for bombarding, yet he hasn't begun secret peace talks. If he now goes ahead with the secret talks, he may be accused by right-wing critics of . . . appeasement.

The *New York Times* today published a detailed account of how Clark Clifford reversed his military men and persuaded Johnson to put across the first bombing halt of March 31. The *Times* has more details, but they scooped me on an important story I have been nursing for too long.

Averell said that Clifford first got discouraged about the future of the war when he visited Australia, the Philippines, and other allies in order to get more troops. None would provide troops, except the Koreans, and they set a very big price.

**FRIDAY, MARCH 7** | The UPI and the AP have been calling Averell from Washington regarding a column by Jimmy Wechsler in the *New York Post* quoting Averell as saying that the Saigon bombing is retaliation for American escalation. Averell refused to comment, standing by his previous television statement of about a week ago which was largely to this effect.

The *New York Times* carried the second detailed report of how Johnson came to his big decision curtailing the bombing on March 31. The story continues to make Clark Clifford the hero and Dean Rusk finally going along, reluctantly at first. Toward the end of today's story the *Times* states that in July last year Harriman and Vance "tried to talk the President into a total bombing halt . . . It was strictly a ploy. They accepted the military estimate that the lull was not deliberate and that the enemy was merely regrouping and refitting his forces, but they suggested that President Johnson treat it as a deliberate restraint anyway."

Averell emphatically denies this, in fact had told me earlier that the North Vietnamese had definitely withdrawn from the South as a gesture toward peace. It was not a ploy.

This morning's papers carried the story that Charles Meyer, former vice president of Sears and in charge of their stores in Bogotá, had been made assistant secretary of state for Latin American affairs. It's about time. I called Sol Linowitz in Washington later in the day, and he says that Meyer is a good man, though he has the handicap of being a director of United Fruit, which had a terribly bad name throughout Latin America. Several other people turned down the job.

Secretary Laird arrived in Saigon yesterday, probably to be brainwashed. Averell thinks the North Vietnamese know that Nixon is a hawk and figured he would be more difficult to negotiate with, so they are now showing their military strength.

There are several stories, obviously inspired by or coming out of the White House and the Pentagon that Nixon will go ahead with the thin antiballistic missile system, though perhaps delay building it for one year.

Rep. Frank Thompson of New Jersey telephoned today with a suggestion that we compromise the libel suit with Bob Burkhardt, secretary of state of New Jersey. I said I would be delighted, in fact that Vice President Humphrey had acted as intermediary for me previously—without success.

**SATURDAY, MARCH 8** | The *Miami Herald* this morning carried a front-page story from Paris to the effect that the North Vietnamese have broken the terms of the truce in that it had been agreed there should be no shelling of civilians in the cities and no enemy troops in the demilitarized zone. The story said that various minutes had been made of twenty or thirty private talks, all of which confirmed this.

Averell, at the breakfast table, said this was true but went further to explain that the United States had insisted on, first, "prompt and produc-tive" talks, later changing this to "prompt and sincere" talks; however, the South Vietnamese had not been prompt. At first there was stalling because North Vietnam did not want to sit with South Vietnamese representatives. Later, in October, when this was agreed to, the South Vietnamese balked at sitting. One way or the other "prompt" talks were delayed by the shape-of-the-table controversy until January 18, two days before Nixon took office.

Averell elaborated on the delay of last July, which occurred when LBJ was upset over intelligence reports that the North Vietnamese were regrouping for an attack and also at Hubert, who was eager for peace and kept jumping the gun. This made LBJ so sore that the progress made in Paris was thrown out the window. Averell and Vance kept telling Washington that the North Vietnamese were sincere in their pullback and were not grouping for a big offensive; however, Lyndon wouldn't believe it. He also blew his top when Hubert made a speech which he interpreted as mixing peace with politics.

Averell gave an interesting diagnosis of Sargent Shriver, who now appears to have been a rather poor executive in charge of the antipoverty program.

"Chip Bohlen had given up," Averell said, "when he was ambassador to France. He went out on the golf course every day. He did nothing about French-American relations. Shriver came in like a ball of fire. He had about thirty ideas per day, about two of them good. He spoke French with an atro-cious American accent, but at least he tried. When he came to a place where he couldn't find the right word, he substituted an English word and put an accent on the end. The French loved it and loved him."

SUNDAY, MARCH 9 | The Russians have reacted to the anti-Russian Chinese demonstrations in Peking by staging massive counterdemonstrations in front of the Chinese embassy in Moscow. It looks as if bitterness has reached an all-time high. Averell says the United States is not doing enough to take advantage of this split.

For the first time we have heard Marie [Harriman] criticize Jackie Ken-nedy. She never liked moving out of her house for Jackie's occupancy in the winter of 1963–64, but she kept very quiet about it. Today she let drop the fact that Jackie never once invited her around for tea. The Secret Service men did when Jackie was away. Marie made some interesting, though sad, comparisons between Ethel Kennedy, who was terribly upset over the assas-sinations but held her tears back, and Jackie, who was hard-boiled.

Ethel used to go up to the Kennedy graves two or three times a week, taking along her younger children. They used to push each other around and play in the grass, asking their mother such questions as "Is Daddy really up there?" "Do you think Daddy is happy up there?" "Is Daddy seeing Uncle Jack up there?" Ethel would answer them patiently and straight-faced in the affirmative each time.

Teddy Kennedy, according to Marie, doesn't go out to small dinners because some reference to his brothers might come up and melt him into tears. He has learned to go out in bigger groups and speak without dissolving. We all thought that Teddy probably has more potential than either of his two brothers. Marie brought out the fact that when Teddy suffered an airplane accident and almost broke his back, he spent his time studying Spanish and American history.

Dean and Alice Acheson and Franklin and Sue Roosevelt came for dinner. Sue is looking prettier than ever. Dean has kept his weight down and doesn't show the fact that he is around seventy-seven, though he doesn't look as young as Averell. I can understand why a lot of people mistake him for me, and when I kidded him about it, he said that he was asked to sign autographs frequently in my name and that he always obliged.

Dean and Alice have been in Antigua and Barbados, where they saw Anthony Eden. Dean is finishing a book of memoirs, and Eden is writing another. Eden was one of the last remaining public figures who resigned when he disagreed with his government, having bowed out when Eisenhower raised hell with him over the British invasion of Suez in 1956.

Franklin Roosevelt Jr. told how Johnson had called him in when he was undersecretary of commerce and bawled him out in almost abusive language and fired him. I believe it was when Franklin was running for governor of New York and at the same time keeping his job as undersecretary.

Dean told Luvie and the other women how Johnson had called him in for advice and became so abusive that Dean got up and walked out. Later Johnson telephoned him to apologize and asked him to come back, which Dean did but walked out again when Johnson became abusive.

Someone asked whether Johnson had ever been abusive with me. He had not.

At dinner Alice asked Averell how Ellsworth Bunker was getting along in Saigon, and the sparks immediately flew. Bunker was Dean's classmate at Yale, I believe. At any rate Dean brought him into the government as ambassador to Italy and then Argentina, where he did a great job. Now Averell thinks he has kowtowed too much to the military in Saigon and should be fired. He said so in very blunt terms.

FDR Jr. has upped the sales of Fiat cars and is moving from Washington to New York because he has so much business. He also represents Jaguar and had a talk with Prime Minister Harold Wilson some time ago to warn him that the British economy would continue to be bad if labor continued its wildcat strikes. Production has been down in the British auto plants to the point where they can't fill orders. British labor is defeating the British Labour government. Meanwhile, the production of Volkswagens and Fiats goes steadily ahead in Germany and Italy.

**TUESDAY, MARCH 11** | This is our last day at Hobe Sound. Time has gone by quickly. We'll be leaving early tomorrow. I marvel at [Averell's] youth, not merely physical but mentally. This morning he is still grousing over Dean's backwardness and asked me whether it was because Dean had retrogressed or he, Averell, had progressed. I told him it was a little bit of both. He summarized Dean's speech as being in favor of three things: (1) a reasonable settlement in Vietnam; (2) preserving the "towers of NATO in Europe"; and (3) the support of our friends, namely the white Africans in Rhodesia, South Africa, and Portuguese Africa. He also proposed that we forget about foreign aid, and Averell quickly made the point that Europe didn't need any more foreign aid while Africa, Asia, the areas Dean wanted to forget, did.

"This means that we concentrate on an area which has about six hundred million people—namely, Western Europe, Canada, and the United States, the Atlantic Community. And we forget the rest of the world with three and a half billion people," he said.

The morning paper carries hints that Nixon has awakened to the importance of private talks in Paris and authorized them. There was another significant story that Russia was losing its influence in Paris because of the rift between China and Russia over the Ussuri River border incident. Some of the Vietcong are siding strongly with the Chinese. This could further hamper the peace talks.

"I think Nixon was counting rather heavily on Russian influence in Paris," Averell said. "He indicated this when I talked to him. I told him not to count on it too much."

Averell and I reminisced about different campaigns for president. Averell also recalled the dedication of the Truman Library in Independence, when Herbert Hoover sat in the sun on a very hot day in a rather thick suit with a vest, perspiring. Averell had asked him to share a seat with him in the shade, but Hoover indicated that Truman had invited him and he was going to stay put. "He was so grateful over Truman's having resurrected him from the dead. He delivered a flowery tribute to Truman, a sincere one."

"The Senate and House leaders of both parties were there and delivered tributes to Truman," Averell said, "but then they read a telegram from Eisenhower, who was not there. It said, 'It has come to my attention that a number of private citizens have raised funds for a library in which will be deposited the documents and papers of former President Truman. This is to inform you that, as of this day, I have instructed the Archivist of the United States to take all due care of these documents.'"

Eisenhower never could forgive Truman his opposition to him in the 1952 election, Averell said.

"For a long time he didn't forgive me either. I saw him during a trip to London for Churchill's funeral. I was probably the closest American to Churchill but was not invited by the White House to attend as an official representative. It was poor staff work on Johnson's part, and I don't blame him. There was a furor over the fact that Hubert was not appointed as a representative. I think there was a certain amount of jealousy on the part of the president toward Hubert. He was always downgrading him; however, I called and hooked a ride to London in Ike's special plane."

FRIDAY, MARCH 14 | WASHINGTON DC—[Hosted a dinner in honor of newly elected California senator Alan Cranston.]

Gaylord Nelson said the Democrats would filibuster against the ABM and persuaded Cranston, in my presence, to go along with it.

"We tried to defeat the filibuster," Nelson said, "but they wouldn't give it up. So we'll use it against them. My grandfather always said, 'If they are throwing stones at you, don't throw back crabapples.'"

Leonard Marks, also at the dinner, had been down to the [LBJ] ranch, where he said Lyndon was calm and serene. He's building a library as big as a shipyard, is quite pleased with the fact that he's getting two thousand letters a day. And when he went up to Rochester, Minnesota, for a physical exam, two hundred people were out in the cold to meet him, which also pleased him.

Senator Nelson said he had served in the Wisconsin Senate with Melvin Laird and found him to be intelligent and likable.

"I was minority leader of the Senate," Nelson said, "when Laird was majority leader. In the evening Laird used to come to my house, where we'd have a drink and talk out our problems together until late. You can't help but like Laird. He knows the defense budget from A to Z. It will be difficult for the generals to fault him."

After everyone had gone and I was almost ready for bed, Averell Harriman came by. He had attended a Georgetown forum of some kind. He reminded me that the military had admitted in the *New York Times* of Thursday or Wednesday that they had given the wrong advice to the Executive Branch of the government. Averell felt that Nixon, in his press conference announcing the ABM, was too pat and too rehearsed in his answers. We both had the feeling that Nixon was getting boxed in regarding Vietnam and there was a danger he might escalate.

**MONDAY, MARCH 17** | GRAND FORKS ND—[This] is where the Sentinel, part of the antiballistic missile system, will be placed, and I was interested in the local reaction. It is good. Grand Forks figures three thousand new people will come in to build the Sentinel, which will mean more employment. They already have 150 Minutemen [Minuteman missiles] around North Dakota and have gotten used to living with nuclear death.

The people here are more concerned with the floods which are rising on the Red River, which flows north into Canada and Lake Winnipeg. Because it flows north, the northern end of the river does not thaw until after the southern end of the river, and the ice in the water piles up. It's predicted that Grand Forks will be under water in another couple of weeks.

**TUESDAY, MARCH 18** | SPOKANE WA— Senator Dill met me at the airport. He's a phenomenal character, a young Northwest progressive elected to the House of Representatives around 1914 or 1915, who broke with Woodrow Wilson over the war, later was defeated, and came back to the Senate to pioneer Grand Coulee Dam, which was the father of the many public power projects built by FDR; and also authored the Federal Communications Act. Dill lives in a mansion atop a hill, which looks down over the city of Spokane, brightly lit at night from the hydroelectric power which he planned and made possible. The hillside is covered with spruce trees and snow.

"General Electric never realized it," Dill told me, "but they were partly responsible for Grand Coulee Dam. I was chairman of the Senate Commerce Committee, working on the Federal Communications Act, and they had a TV process they wanted me to see in Schenectady. I thought, while I was there, I would talk to Governor Roosevelt in Albany, so I wrote him a letter. I really didn't have much idea that Roosevelt, a cripple, could become president; however, you can't discount any man who has been two times governor of New York. I got word from Roosevelt that the Mrs. was away and for me to come in and have dinner with him.

"He bought the Grand Coulee Dam idea immediately. And that was how it began. I never dreamed at the time that there would be ten other dams on the Columbia River, but now there are."

The senator had been to Russia during the summer to attend a world power conference and to visit the Bradsk Dam on Lake Baikal, which he said was the biggest freshwater lake in the world, bigger than all the Great Lakes put together. It was having some pollution problems as the result of wood pulp factories along the shore which have been dumping their waste into the river. This is a shame because the lake is probably one of the clearest in the world. The senator was quite impressed with the friendliness of the Russian people. The Russian government was not out to hide anything and made everything available to the power delegates. Some Czech engineers were there but did not go home when the invasion of Czechoslovakia took place. They said they were more interested in power than in politics.

Bill Bennett of San Francisco telephoned the office, and subsequently, I got hold of him regarding the Nixon administration's killing of the case against El Paso Natural Gas, the biggest gas monopoly in the United States. The new attorney general, John Mitchell, dropped the latest antitrust phase of the case five days after assuming office, despite the fact the Nixon law firm, of which he was a senior partner, had received about $771,000 in law fees from El Paso. I wired a story back to Washington this afternoon. It could be the first real toe stubbing of the Nixon administration. I can't imagine why any attorney general would be so dumb, or else venal, as to dismiss an important case of this kind immediately after assuming office.

**THURSDAY, MARCH 20** | SAN FRANCISCO—Bill Bennett, who is steamed up over the El Paso Natural Gas dismissal, drove me to San Francisco State College, where I had lunch with President Hayakawa and George Outland, a liberal member of Congress who is teaching there. George was defeated by a congressman named Bramblett on the slogan "Turn out Outland and substitute integrity." Before Bramblett's term was up, I had managed to expose his kickback operations, for which he was subsequently convicted and which helped to defeat him. He sued me for $100,000, but the suit evaporated after his indictment.

This was a historic day at San Francisco State. The strike by students appears to be settled. Hayakawa told me they had accepted his terms with no amnesty, though later they tried to renege on this.

The violence at San Francisco State cannot be exaggerated. Several offices were burned out completely. There were a total of fifty fires or explosions in one day. Most of the damage was done by black militants, though there was some by Spanish Americans.

The college started out as a very up-to-date institution, founded by Pat Brown. Its location is excellent, the buildings modern, the neighborhood much cleaner than the grimy locations of Brooklyn Polytechnic, Temple in Philadelphia, or even Yale. The institution suffered, however, from having eight presidents in eight years, some of them inexperienced and apparently all of them weak. A young faculty ran away with the place.

Hayakawa told me that some of the older members of the faculty had been persecuted by the right wing in the Joe McCarthy era and had built up a protective attitude that all things liberal were right, even when backed by violence. I'm not sure that the public would understand this, but it is true that intense persecution in McCarthy's day did bring about a reaction, just as the activities of the extreme left wing today are reacting in favor of the conservatives.

I suggested to Hayakawa the idea that students today had no great cause. In my day they were hepped up over World War I. Twenty-five years later they had a cause in World War II. The issues there were clearly defined in that Hitler was a tyrant and the Japanese had committed aggression at Pearl Harbor. Today there was a miserable war in Vietnam which most people opposed but the students had to fight in. As a result, they had no cause, they couldn't achieve, and they saw wealth and corruption all around them.

Hayakawa didn't entirely buy this. "The students of history," he said, "have not struck. They know that mankind achieves his goals in an uphill battle. The history student knows the setbacks as well as the victories. It's been the students of English and art who have been striking. They don't realize that the world progresses slowly, but it does progress."

**FRIDAY, MARCH 21** | Senator Fulbright gave Laird a rough going over today before the Foreign Affairs Committee. Stuart Symington, I thought, did a particularly good job by bringing out the fact that the ABM system probably won't work. This hearing was in contrast to the sweetheart deal given Laird by the Armed Services Committee. Stennis and Fulbright come from neighboring states, but they're as different as a Holstein and a Black Angus. It's generally conceded that the ABM will pass the Senate, but Fulbright certainly scored some votes against it.

**SATURDAY, MARCH 22** | Yesterday Vice President Agnew issued a scorching denial of Jack's column, saying that the oilmen had contributed money to Nixon in return for a promise that the Nixon administration would veto the free point of entry at Machiasport, Maine. I did not see the story beforehand but frankly am a little skeptical about it. I distrust anything Armand Hammer is putting across, and he is head of the Occidental Oil Company. Also, I distrust Mike Feldman, his lawyer and Jack's source.

Today the Justice Department telephoned, trying to slap down my story for Monday's release on the dismissal of the El Paso Natural Gas case. The Justice spokesman claims that the decision to dismiss was made January 17. The actual motion to dismiss was made January 25, and one of the lawyers whom I got on the phone in Salt Lake City said that when he was in Washington on January 21, they were still debating it.

**MONDAY, MARCH 24** | The *Washington Post* did not use the El Paso Natural Gas column this morning regarding the $771,000 paid to the Nixon law firm by El Paso. Apparently, they were subjected to Justice Department pressure over the weekend. Later one of the editors called me and indicated they would run the story if there were some further clarification, which I gave them.

I wrote a speech for Sen. Birch Bayh of Indiana to deliver on the El Paso monopoly subject; also called Stuart Symington, who wasn't too helpful, together with Gaylord Nelson of Wisconsin and Phil Hart of Michigan, who were more helpful. They promised to ask some cooperative questions of Bayh. Finally got hold of Sen. Fred Harris of Oklahoma, the chairman of the Democratic National Committee, who is almost inaccessible on the telephone. He promised to help. At the end of the day, however, Bayh telephoned to say that he had not got off the ground today, was going to New York tomorrow, and would speak on Wednesday.

Nixon has come back from California after conferring with Ambassador

Ellsworth Bunker and some others, who flew in from Saigon. He issued a statement over the weekend condemning the student tumult but offering no real solutions. His pattern seems to be one of statement making, caution, but no action. The capital is still stewing over the ABM debate. Senator Fulbright is accusing the Nixon administration of planning to go ahead and deploy the missiles even before Congress votes, thus presenting Congress with a fait accompli.

Lunched with Leonard Marks, who reports that LBJ is still sending him memos with items he wants passed along to me. LBJ hasn't gotten over his extravagant ways, even though he pays for everything now himself. Recently, he wanted a special head on a shower and couldn't get it locally. They telephoned all over the United States. Finally, the showerhead was shipped in by plane a day or two later.

Hubert Humphrey has made a study of the manner in which the newspapers treated his trip abroad and the few student demonstrations, with the way in which they played down Nixon's demonstrations. Leonard figures that Hubert can't make it, that Muskie doesn't have the money, and that Teddy is the man. He is going to get aboard the Teddy Kennedy bandwagon. He thinks I should have [a] luncheon with Bob Ellsworth of the White House staff to talk to him about some of the problems facing Nixon. I pointed out that I was pretty well stamped as an anti-Nixon man but would follow his advice.

The White House has sent word to the State Department that there are to be no Democratic ambassadors. Some will be allowed to stay on, but the resignations of all will be accepted before long. Leonard points out that this is in direct contrast to Johnson, who picked a lot of Republicans.

TUESDAY, MARCH 25 | Bill Bennett of San Francisco lunched with me and Joe Borkin, then held a press conference to promote his views on El Paso Natural Gas and the new Justice Department. The conference was poorly attended. I am afraid we are crying in the dark at a time when the Democrats are too shortsighted, too impotent, and too complacent to do anything about what I think is a scandalous conflict of interest. Birch Bayh telephoned yesterday to say that he would make his speech on Wednesday. So far I have been unable to drum up any real support for him.

Meanwhile, the veneer on the new Nixon is wearing thin. Last weekend he appointed Otepka, the right-wing State Department official who was fired for giving documents to Sen. Tom Dodd, to the Subversive Activities Control

Board. This is a $36,000 job and quite a promotion for Otepka, compared with the firing he got from Dean Rusk, which had just been upheld both by Civil Service and by Bill Rogers, the new secretary of state, who refused to take him back.

Today Nixon follows this by appointing Otepka's lawyer, Roger Robb, to the U.S. Court of Appeals. Roger has been trying to get this job for years. I have managed to block it with Johnson and others. Roger has represented Fred Howser against me when Bill Rogers was my attorney. He has represented Fulton Lewis, also against me, and was the attorney for Bernard Goldfine and Sherman Adams at the time they caught Jack [Anderson] bugging a room at the Carlton Hotel.

Robb's father, who is on the court of appeals, managed to kill the Child Labor Act for ten or fifteen years, and Robb's voting will be just the same. Tom Dodd and Jim Eastland have been pushing him for years, and now they have succeeded. The old Nixon is coming through.

**THURSDAY, MARCH 27** | The *Washington Post*'s reaction to Bill Bennett's efforts this morning was negative. They had a story which really played up the Justice Department's denials more than his position; however, he telephoned me later in the day to say that the press reaction in California was excellent.

Bill Rogers testified before the Fulbright committee this morning and did pretty well. He didn't really answer many detailed questions, but he did promise that there would be no escalation of the war and pledged peace negotiations. I would say that Bill is going to exert a healthy and important influence in the Nixon administration, though it's reported he will be chief justice in June. I would much rather see him in that position than some of the other sour apple conservatives around Nixon.

**FRIDAY, MARCH 28** | Eisenhower died this morning. He has been in the hospital for ten months fighting off a succession of heart attacks. Finally, he became too weak, too tired, and too old. He was seventy-eight.

Teddy Kennedy today took on Strom Thurmond and Everett Dirksen regarding the South Carolina textile mills and the flagrant manner in which the Pentagon ignored segregation in those mills. Dirksen and Strom Thurmond were all set to defend the Nixon administration and the companies involved. They did a pretty good job too; however, Teddy [Kennedy] was courageous, effective, and right. As time passes, he looks to me as if he is the man for 1972. This is too bad in a way because Hubert Humphrey is really a great human being, and so is Muskie; however, the waves of politics and popularity must be taken as they come, and I am afraid the wave has passed Hubert and Muskie by.

SATURDAY, MARCH 29 | Luvie wanted me to go to WTOP to do a piece on Eisenhower as per their request because, she said, I had been a little mean to him in the column this morning. It was a column written last summer in contemplation of his possible death when he suffered a heart attack. It was different from the heaps of praise which he's getting now.

Later in the day, at the farm, we had a discussion about Ike. Ches, who is spending the weekend, shared Luvie's view that I had been too critical. Luvie felt that history would make Ike the great man of peace, a man who had stopped the war in the Near East, who had kept us out of war in Vietnam. She was impressed with the speeches that had been played over on the radio during the day, speeches addressed to peace.

Later in the evening CBS staged a roundtable discussion on Eisenhower, in which Omar Bradley, Bob Anderson of Texas, Al Gruenther, his bridge-playing partner and staff officer, and finally Kevin McCann, his ghostwriter, participated. It was interesting that Bradley, who knew Ike's defects as a combat commander better than anyone else, did not mention the manner in which Eisenhower had cut off Bradley's gasoline and supplies when he could have crossed the Rhine before Christmas in 1944. Bradley had been quite critical personally, and there are hints of criticism in his book. Nor did he mention the trip he, Bradley, had made to Washington in 1948, when some of the Democrats were thinking of running Eisenhower for president as a Democrat. At that time Bradley warned Truman and others not to push Eisenhower because he could not make decisions.

I think history will show Ike more or less as I have shown him to be, a kindhearted man of goodwill who wanted to do right but had so much trouble making up his mind that he set the United States and the world back for about eight years. If he had rallied behind Earl Warren on the school desegregation decision in 1954, we would be years ahead with the racial problem today. And if he had overruled John Foster Dulles's boycott of the Soviet Union early in his administration, we would not be experiencing the difficult and dangerous competition we are in today.

Ike did make one great statement three days before he left office, warning of the military-industrial complex. It was Kevin McCann who wrote it into his speech, and Ike didn't really know it was there. He has said privately that he didn't know why he made it. Nevertheless, this will be one of the great things history will record in his favor, and I personally intend to use it for all it's worth.

MONDAY, MARCH 31 | Luvie and I watched on television Ike's funeral services at the National Cathedral. The last time we were there for a funeral was when Adlai Stevenson lay in state, and the time before that was when Fred Vinson died. I remember after that service President Eisenhower kissed Mrs. Vinson. Now he is gone, and Mrs. Vinson is retired from social life, so much so that no one knows she exists. And in the fifteen years since, how much the world has changed.

Watching the ceremony brought back a flood of memories. Margaret [Brown] remarked this morning that Ike should not have a church funeral because he had never been baptized. I remember in Paris, when he was at SHAPE [Supreme Headquarters Allied Powers Europe] and I visited him, he appeared a bit sensitive about his lack of church affiliation because suddenly he pulled a coin out of his pocket and, out of a clear blue, said: "That's my religion. I believe a man's church is where he is. It's what his life is." He was right in his philosophy. The coin he handed me was a silver piece, about the size of a half-dollar, with a cross on it. It meant nothing, but he had kept it in his pocket as a symbol.

Watching the funeral and Mamie Eisenhower sitting in the front row bearing up bravely, I remembered the first time I had seen her. It was at Davenport, Iowa, where a platform had been built out alongside a courthouse under a big tree from which Ike made a speech. There was quite a crowd around. Mamie was sitting on the platform, and when Ike gave the signal, "Now I want you to meet my Mamie," she tripped out looking very pretty, dressed in a gay cotton print dress, and waved to the crowd.

I suspect this was one of Mamie's biggest moments. Before then she had been ignored, sometimes forgotten, left lonely in the Wardman Park Hotel while Ike was abroad for almost four years. She had become addicted to alcohol, but who wouldn't under those circumstances? She had heard rumors of Ike's [British uniformed driver] girlfriend, and he may have even written her about a divorce. Certainly he considered it. Now, at this Iowa event, Mamie was essential to Ike's winning the election. She knew it. And she reacted to it.

I remember that I had warned Rosser Reeves of the Ted Bates advertising agency, which was masterminding Ike's campaign, about Kay Summersby, the British WAC. He thanked me for it, and I noted that shortly thereafter it was announced that Kay Summersby had married a good-looking stockbroker. I am sure this was no accident. Later they were divorced.

Nixon sat in the front row at the funeral, the same row as General de Gaulle, the Shah of Iran, and President Bourguiba of Tunisia. LBJ sat about five rows back with Lady Bird. She looked very pretty, and he looked younger and rested. Some of the lines had gone out of his face. He played everything very low-key and obviously did not want to be the center of interest. I learned later that Liz Carpenter had urged him to hold a press conference, but he refused. He was right.

Watching Nixon there on the front row recalled the time when Ike had almost dropped him from the Republican ticket in 1952, after the $18,000 expense fund scandal. Nixon had flown across the United States, from California to Wheeling, West Virginia, after his famous little dog telecast, and as his plane landed, Clint Mosher, formerly of the *Brooklyn Eagle*, had overheard Nixon curse. He said something like, "God damn him, making me come clear across the United States for this."

A moment later Nixon was out of the plane's door, walking up the runway, where Ike embraced him as if nothing at all had happened.

Under the surface Ike was never too happy about Nixon, and it was not an accident when, in 1960, Nixon was running for president, Ike told newspapermen at a press conference, when asked what Nixon's major contribution had been, "Give me a week or so, and I'll give you an answer."

I lunched at the F Street Club with Sol Linowitz, who is retiring the first of May. I talked to him about possibly taking Tyler into his law firm. At an adjacent table were Jack McCloy, former ambassador to Germany and assistant secretary of war, together with Bob Lovett, former secretary of state. They had come down for the funeral. They were good public servants.

THURSDAY, APRIL 3 | Ike was buried yesterday in Abilene, Kansas, where he grew up. His friends had built a special chapel with three crypts in the floor, all planned in advance for his burial, that of Mamie, and their son, who died at the age of two. Harry Darby, now a great breeder of Charolais cattle, raised the money and planned it, though Ike had worked out all the details of his funeral.

There has been a bad reaction to my special column on Ike, a lot of protest mail. I figured there would be.

**FRIDAY, APRIL 4** | Nixon has flown to Florida again. He was in California last weekend. He is almost never in Washington on weekends, in contrast to LBJ, who, when he first took office, worked every Saturday and Sunday here in Washington.

Nixon now, apparently, has picked an island retreat in the Bahamas where there is a huge estate. We speculated as to how his home would be financed. The obvious answer is the publicity which real estate interests get from his residing there.

Meanwhile, the federal education budget is being cut 10 percent, and the Job Corps is being sliced by $100 million. The big city ghettos are getting restless. This is the anniversary of Martin Luther King's assassination, and troops had to be called out in Chicago.

**SATURDAY, APRIL 5** | Nixon has appointed his brother to a $30,000 job in Alaska. If Lyndon had appointed his brother, Sam Houston Johnson, to any job, even a two-bit clerical post, it would have raised Cain.

**MONDAY, APRIL 7** | We have been receiving a barrage of letters, very critical of my column on Eisenhower, particularly the reference to his love affair with Kay Summersby during the war. The paper in Winona, Minnesota, canceled. John Osenenko called from New York to say that the *New York Post* had received a barrage also.

In retrospect I suppose I was too frank in writing that column. It was written last August, and if the syndicate had given me a chance to revise it before sending it out a second time, I would have done so.

**THURSDAY, APRIL 10** | King Hussein was at the Press Club today and outlined what I thought was a forward and conciliatory outline for peace, including the transit of Israeli ships through the Suez Canal; however, he called for the return of all property seized by Israel in the Six-Day War, which the Israelis will never consent to as far as the old city of Jerusalem is concerned.

**SATURDAY, APRIL 12** | Nixon has reversed Johnson's awards of transpacific air routes, giving Pan American Airways [new routes]. Pan Am has been a heavy contributor to the Republicans for years. It's now paying off.

[This is the last entry Drew Pearson made in his diary. He was beginning to have health problems. His daily syndicated newspaper column continued but was more often jointly written with his associate, Jack Anderson. From April 12 through September 1 Pearson had twenty-four solo bylines and one hundred with Anderson. Most of the solo bylined columns appeared in June and early July.

Pearson spent most of August in hospital. Late that month his doctors thought it might be helpful to let him recuperate out of the hospital, and he spent a few days at his beloved farm. On Labor Day, Monday, September 1, he expressed to his stepson, Tyler Abell, a wish to be driven around the farm to see how things were going. He talked with some of the farmworkers, then said he was tired and would like to go back to bed. He retired to his bedroom to take a nap but did not awaken. His heart had given out. He was three months and ten days short of his seventy-second birthday.

Anderson wrote a memorable column on September 3 commemorating Drew Pearson's life. He wrote: "Of all the names he was called during four decades as Washington's top investigative reporter, 'muckraker' was the one he liked best . . . Even while pursuing scoundrels in high places, he remained a gentle, compassionate man, never callous, never jaded . . . Above all else, however, he was a crusader. He passionately believed that public office was a public trust."

Anderson continued Pearson's column but wrote under his own byline (sometimes sharing it with one of his staff writers). In July 2004, having been diagnosed with Parkinson's disease, he retired. Anderson died the following year, at age eighty-two.]

# PEARSON FAMILY TREE

Paul Martin Pearson (1877–1938) m. Edna Wolfe (Pearson)

(1) Andrew "Drew" Russell Pearson (1897–1969)
  m. (1925–28) Felicia Gizycka (Pearson, Magruder) (1905–99)

  Ellen Cameron Pearson (Arnold) (1926–2010)
    m. (1946) George Longan Arnold (1921–93)

  — Drew Pearson Arnold (b. 1948)
  — George Longan Arnold Jr. (b. 1952)
  — Joseph Patterson Arnold (b. 1954)
  — Felicia Cameron (b. 1960)

(2) Andrew "Drew" Russell Pearson (1897–1969)
  m. (1936) Luvie Butler Moore (Abell, Pearson) (1909–92)

  Tyler Abell (stepson, b. 1932)
    m. (1955) Bess Clements

  — Dan Tyler Abell (b. 1958)
  — Lyndon Abell (b. 1960)

— Leon Morris Pearson (1899–1963)
— Barbara Wolfe Pearson (Lange, Godfrey) (1910–2003)
— Ellen Cameron Pearson (Fogg) (1913–73)

# GLOSSARY OF NAMES

**Abell, Elizabeth "Bess"** White House social secretary, 1963–69; wife of Tyler Abell; daughter of former Kentucky governor and U.S. senator Earle Clements

**Abell, Tyler** U.S. chief of protocol; assistant postmaster general in the Johnson administration; stepson of Drew Pearson

**Abrams, Creighton** U.S. Army general (four stars); commanded U.S. military operations in Vietnam, 1968–72

**Acheson, Dean** Secretary of state, 1949–53

**Adair, Edwin Ross** R-IN, member of the House of Representatives (hereafter abbreviated as HR), 1951–71

**Adams, Sherman** R-NH, White House chief of staff, 1953–58 (resigned); governor, 1949–53

**Addonizio, Hugh** D-NJ, Mayor of Newark, 1962–70; HR, 1949–62

**Adenauer, Konrad** Chancellor of West Germany, 1949–63; leader of the Christian Democratic Union

**Adzhubei, Aleksei** Journalist, son-in-law of Nikita Khrushchev, member of the USSR Central Committee, 1961–64; editor of *Izvestia*, 1959–64; chief editor, *Komsomolskaya Pravda*, 1957–59

**Agnew, Spiro** R-MD, Vice president of the United States, 1969–73 (resigned); governor, 1967–69

**Aiken, George** R-VT, Senator, 1941–75; governor, 1937–41

**Albert, Carl** D-OK, HR, 1947–77; speaker of the House, 1971–77; House majority leader, 1962–71

**Alioto, Joseph** Mayor of San Francisco, 1968–76

**Allen, George E.** Friend of Dwight D. Eisenhower; director, Reconstruction Finance Corporation, 1946–47; author

**Allen, George V.** Director, Foreign Service Corporation, 1966–68; earlier assignments: ambassador to Greece, India and Nepal, Yugoslavia, and Iran

**Allen, Robert** Journalist; with Pearson, wrote anonymous 1931 book *Washington Merry-Go-Round* and in 1933 started a syndicated column of the same name

**Alliluyeva, Svetlana Iosifovna** Daughter of Joseph Stalin; Soviet defector, 1967; author

**Allon, Yigal** Deputy prime minister of Israel, 1968–77

**Alphand, Hervé** French ambassador to the United States, 1956–65

**Alphand, Nicole** Wife of Hervé Alphand

**Alsop, Joseph W.** Journalist and author; syndicated columnist (with Robert Kintner, 1937–40; with brother, Stewart, 1946–58); continued own column through 1974

**Alsop, Stewart** Journalist and author; *Newsweek* columnist, 1968–74; editor, *Saturday Evening Post*, 1958–68; syndicated columnist (with brother, Joseph), 1946–58

**Anderson, Clinton P.** D-NM, Senator, 1949–73; secretary of agriculture, 1945–48

**Anderson, Jack** Investigative reporter working for Drew Pearson; later successor to Pearson's Washington Merry-Go-Round newspaper column and 1972 Pulitzer Prize winner

**Anderson, Martin** Publisher/owner of the *Orlando* (FL) *Sentinel* and *Evening Star*, 1931–65

**Anderson, Robert B.** Secretary of the treasury, 1957–61; secretary of the navy, 1953–54

**Anfuso, Victor L'Episcopo** D-NY, New York State supreme court judge, 1963–66; HR, 1955–63 and 1951–53

**Annenberg, Walter** Publisher and philanthropist; U.S. ambassador to the United Kingdom, 1969–74

**Arnold, George** Son-in-law to Drew Pearson and former husband to Ellen Pearson, 1947–59

**Arnold, Thurman** Associate judge for Court of Appeals of the DC Circuit, 1943–45; U.S. assistant attorney general, 1938–43; cofounder of Washington law firm Arnold, Fortas and Porter; his son, George, was Drew Pearson's son-in-law

**Attlee, Clement** Prime minister of the United Kingdom, 1945–51; leader of the Labour Party, 1935–55

**Attwood, Simone** Wife of William Attwood

**Attwood, William** U.S. ambassador to Kenya, 1964–66; U.S. ambassador to Guinea, 1961–63; journalist; speechwriter for John F. Kennedy, 1960

**Auchincloss, Hugh** Lawyer, stockbroker, author, stepfather of both Jacqueline Kennedy and Gore Vidal

**Baker, George** Neighbor and friend of Pearson, former foreign service officer

**Baker, Howard** R-TN, Senator, 1967–85; later White House chief of staff; U.S. ambassador to Japan

**Baker, Robert "Bobby"** Former Senate page from South Carolina and protégé of Sen. Lyndon Johnson; Senate's secretary to the majority, 1955–63 (resigned after allegations of misconduct and a scandal involving government contracts)

**Ball, George W.** Lawyer, economist; undersecretary of state, 1961–66; U.S. permanent representative to the United Nations, 1968

**Barbour, Walworth** U.S. ambassador to Israel, 1961–73

**Barnet, Richard J.** Founder of the LEF Institute for Policy Studies, 1963; State Department aide in the U.S. Arms Control and Disarmament Agency, 1961–63

**Baron, Sydney S.** Public relations executive and friend of Drew Pearson

**Barron, William W.** D-WV, Governor, 1961–65

**Bartlett, Charles** Pulitzer Prize–winning journalist; syndicated columnist; Washington correspondent, *Chattanooga Times*, 1948–63; longtime friend of John F. Kennedy

**Bartlett, Edward Lewis** D-AK, Senator, 1959–68; delegate, 1945–59

**Bass, Perry R.** Texas oilman and philanthropist, nephew of Sid Richardson

**Bates, William H.** D-MA, HR, 1950–69

**Baube, Jean** French journalist; longtime press relations counselor at the French embassy in Washington DC

**Bayh, Birch** D-IN, Senator, 1963–81

**Bazelon, David** Chief judge, U.S. Court of Appeals for the District of Columbia Circuit, 1962–78

**Beame, Abraham "Abe"** D-NY, Mayor of New York City, 1974–77; Democratic nominee for mayor, 1965

**Belli, Melvin** San Francisco attorney, known as the King of Torts; represented many celebrity clients

**Bellino, Carmine** Senior congressional investigator whose work led to the convictions of Teamster leaders James R. Hoffa and Dave Beck

**Ben-Gurion, David (b. David Gruen)** Zionist leader; Israel's first prime minister and defense minister, 1955–63 and 1948–53

**Benitez, Jose** Deputy high commissioner, U.S. Trust Territory of the Pacific, 1961–64; friend of Bobby Baker, he resigned in 1964 (was later exonerated)

**Bennett, Wallace F.** R-UT, Senator, 1951–74

**Bennett, William Tapley, Jr.** U.S. ambassador to Portugal, 1966–69; U.S. ambassador to the Dominican Republic, 1964–66

**Benson, Ezra Taft** Secretary of agriculture, 1953–61

**Benton, William** D-CT, founder, with Chester Bowles, of the Benton & Bowles advertising agency; U.S. ambassador to UNESCO, 1963–68; Senator, 1949–53

**Betancourt, Rómulo** President of Venezuela, 1959–64 and 1945–48

**Bible, Alan** D-NV, Senator, 1954–74

**Bicks, Robert** Assistant attorney general and head of the Antitrust Division of the U.S. Justice Department, 1959–61

**Bingham, Jonathan** D-NY, HR, 1965–83

**Black, Elizabeth** Wife of Associate Justice Hugo Black

**Black, Hugo** D-AL, Associate justice of the U.S. Supreme Court, 1937–71; senator, 1927–37

**Black, Shirley Temple** American child film actress; U.S. ambassador to Czechoslovakia, 1989–92; chief U.S. protocol officer, 1976–77; U.S. ambassador to Ghana, 1974–76

**Blair, William McCormick, Jr.** U.S. ambassador to the Philippines 1964–67; U.S. ambassador to Denmark, 1961–64

**Blake, Peter** Editor, *Architectural Forum*, 1950–72

**Blatnik, John** D-MN, HR, 1947–74

**Block, Herbert** Pulitzer Prize–winning editorial cartoonist and author (known as Herblock)

**Blough, Roger** Chairman and chief executive officer, U.S. Steel, 1955–69

**Boggs, James Caleb** R-DE, Senator, 1961–73; governor, 1953–60; HR, 1947–53

**Boggs, Linda** D-LA, HR, 1973–91; widow of Thomas Hale Boggs

**Boggs, Thomas Hale** D-LA, HR, 1941–43 and 1947–73

**Bohlen, Charles "Chip"** U.S. ambassador to France, 1962–68; U.S. ambassador to the USSR, 1953–57

**Bolton, Frances** R-OH, HR, 1940–69

**Borkin, Joseph** Washington DC lawyer and friend of Drew Pearson

**Bosch, Juan** President of the Dominican Republic, 1963

**Bourguiba, Habib** President of Tunisia, 1957–87

**Boutin, Bernie** Director, U.S. General Services Administration, 1961–64; Democratic candidate for governor, 1958 and 1960; mayor of Laconia, New Hampshire, 1955–59

**Bowles, Chester** D-CT, U.S. ambassador to India, 1963–69 and 1951–53; HR, 1959–61; governor, 1949–51

**Boyd, Alan** Chairman, Civil Aeronautics Board, 1961–65; U.S. secretary of transportation, 1967–69; founder, with William Benton, of the Benton & Bowles advertising agency

**Boykin, Frank** D-AL, HR, 1935–63

**Brademas, John** D-IN, President, New York University, 1981–91; HR, 1959–81

**Bradlee, Benjamin** Executive editor, *Washington Post*, 1968–91

**Bradley, Omar** U.S. Army general (five stars); chairman, Bulova Watch Company, 1953–73; chairman, Joint Chiefs of Staff, 1949–53

**Bramblett, Ernest K.** R-CA, HR, 1947–55

**Brandt, Willy** Chancellor of West Germany, 1969–74; leader of the Social Democratic Party of Germany, 1964–87; Nobel Peace Prize winner, 1971

**Brennan, Marjorie** Wife of Associate Justice William Brennan

**Brennan, William, Jr.** Associate justice of the U.S. Supreme Court, 1956–90

**Brewster, Ralph Owen** R-ME, Senator, 1941–53; HR, 1935–41; governor, 1925–29

**Brezhnev, Leonid** General secretary of the Soviet Union, 1964–82

**Bridges, Styles** R-NH, Senator, 1937–61

**Brooke, Edward** R-MA, Senator, 1967–79 (first popularly elected African American senator)

**Brooks, Jack** D-TX, HR, 1953–95

**Brown, Constantine** Coauthor, with Pearson, of *The American Diplomatic Game* (1935); correspondent during and after World War I; columnist and later foreign news editor, *Washington Star*

**Brown, Edmund G. "Pat"** D-CA, Governor, 1959–67

**Brown, George** Deputy leader of the British Labour Party, 1960–70

**Brown, Harrison** Physicist and geochemist; professor at the California Institute of Technology, 1951–77

**Brown, Margaret** The Pearsons' cook for many years

**Brucan, Silviu** Romanian ambassador to the United Nations, 1959–62

**Bryan, William Jennings** D-NE, Secretary of state, 1913–15; Democratic Party presidential nominee, 1896, 1900, and 1908; HR, 1891–95

**Bryant, C. Farris** D-FL, Governor, 1961–65

**Buchwald, Arthur** Writer, humorist, and syndicated columnist

**Buckley, William F., Jr.** Conservative intellectual; founder of the *National Review*; host of *Firing Line*, 1966–99

**Bull, Odd** Norwegian lieutenant general; chief of staff, United Nations Truce Supervision Organization in Palestine, 1963–70

**Bullitt, William, Jr.** U.S. ambassador to France, 1936–40; U.S. ambassador to the USSR, 1933–36

**Bundy, McGeorge** President, Ford Foundation, 1966–79; assistant to the president for National Security Affairs, 1961–66

**Bundy, William F.** Assistant secretary of state for Far Eastern affairs, 1964–69; brother of McGeorge Bundy

**Bunker, Ellsworth** U.S. ambassador to South Vietnam, 1967–73; U.S. ambassador to India, 1956–61; U.S. ambassador to Italy, 1952–53; U.S. ambassador to Argentina, 1951–52

**Burchett, Wilfred** Australian journalist who, from the 1950s, developed close relationships with Communist leaders in Vietnam, Cambodia, and China

**Burdin, Betsy** Friend of Luvie Pearson

**Burns, William Haydon** D-FL, Governor, 1965–67; mayor of Jacksonville, 1949–65

**Busby, Horace** Special assistant to President Johnson, speechwriter, 1963–68

**Bush, George Herbert Walker** R-TX, President of the United States, 1989–93; vice president of the United States 1981–89; director of Central Intelligence, 1976–77; chief, U.S. Liaison Office in the People's Republic of China, 1974–76; chairman, Republican National Committee, 1973; U.S. ambassador to United Nations, 1971–73; HR, 1967–70

**Bush, Prescott** R-CT, Senator, 1952–63; father of George H. W. Bush

**Byrd, Harry** D-VA, Senator, 1933–65; governor, 1926–30

**Byrd, Harry, Jr.** D/I-VA, Senator, 1965–83

**Byrnes, James** D-SC, Governor, 1951–55; secretary of state, 1945–47; associate justice of the U.S. Supreme Court, 1941–42; senator, 1931–41; HR, 1911–25

**Byroade, Henry A. "Hank"** U.S. ambassador to Burma, 1963–68; U.S. ambassador to Afghanistan, 1959–62; U.S. ambassador to South Africa, 1956–59; U.S. ambassador to Egypt, 1955–56; U.S. Army brigadier general, 1946–55

**Caamaño, Francisco** Constitutionalist president of the Dominican Republic, 1965

**Cabot, John** U.S. ambassador to Poland, 1962–65; U.S. ambassador to Brazil, 1959–61; U.S. ambassador to Colombia, 1957–59; U.S. ambassador to Sweden, 1954–57

**Cafritz, Gwendolyn** President, Morris and Gwendolyn Cafritz Foundation, 1964–88; Washington socialite

**Cain, James C.** Longtime personal physician to Lyndon Johnson and his family, including during the presidential years

**Calhoun, Chad** Vice president, Kaiser Aluminum; advisor to President Osagyefo Dr. Kwame Nkrumah of Ghana on the Akosombo Dam project

**Califano, Joseph** Special assistant to President Johnson, 1965–69

**Cannon, Howard Walter** D-NV, Senator, 1959–83

**Canty, Marian** Pearson's chief secretary and bookkeeper for more than twenty years

**Capehart, Homer** R-IN, Senator, 1945–63

**Carey, James B.** First president of the International Union of Electrical Workers

**Carlson, Eric** Expert on economic development in Latin America

**Carlson, Frank** R-KS, Senator, 1950–69; governor, 1947–50; HR, 1935–47

**Carmichael, Stokely** Chairman, Student Nonviolent Coordinating Committee, 1966–67; author; activist

**Carpenter, Mary Elizabeth "Liz"** Journalist; press secretary to Lady Bird Johnson, 1963–69; administrative assistant to Vice President Johnson, 1961–63

**Carroll, John Albert** D-CO, Senator, 1957–63; HR, 1947–51

**Carthy, Albert** Secretary-general of the Socialist International, 1957–69

**Case, Clifford, Jr.** R-NJ, Senator, 1955–79; HR, 1945–53

**Case, Francis Higbee** R-SD, Senator, 1951–62; HR, 1937–51

**Castro, Fidel** President of Cuba, 1976–2008; commander in chief of the Cuban Revolutionary Armed Forces, 1959–2008; prime minister of Cuba, 1959–76

**Cater, S. Douglass** Special assistant to President Johnson, 1964–68

**Caudle, T. Lamar** Head of the Tax Division of the U.S. Department of Justice, 1947–51

**Cavanagh, Jerome** Mayor of Detroit, 1962–70

**Celebrezze, Anthony Joseph** D-OH, Secretary of health, education, and welfare, 1962–65; mayor of Cleveland, 1954–62

**Celler, Emmanuel** D-OH, HR, 1923–73

**Chafee, John** R-RI, Senator, 1976–99; secretary of the navy, 1969–72; governor, 1963–69

**Chalk, O. (Oscar) Roy** Washington DC entrepreneur

**Chandler, Albert "Happy"** D-KY, Governor, 1955–59 and 1935–39; commissioner, Major League Baseball, 1945–51; senator, 1939–45

**Chandler, Harry** Early twentieth-century real estate developer in Los Angeles; president, Times Mirror Company; publisher of the *Los Angeles Times*, 1917–41 (succeeded by his son, Norman)

**Chapman, Oscar** Secretary of the interior, 1950–53

**Charney, David B.** Former newspaperman; public relations executive who did work on behalf of the Chinese nationalists and the International Teamsters Union in the 1950s

**Chernoff, Howard** Advisor to Sen. Harley Kilgore of West Virginia

**Cheshire, Maxine** *Washington Post* society reporter/columnist during the Kennedy and Johnson years

**Chiang Kai-shek** Leader of the Republic of China, 1930s–1975

**Childs, Marquis** Journalist and winner of the 1970 Pulitzer Prize for Commentary

**Christian, George, Jr.** Journalist; White House press secretary, 1966–69; press secretary to Texas governor John B. Connally, 1963–66

**Christopher, George** Mayor of San Francisco, 1956–64

**Church, Frank** D-ID, Senator, 1957–81

**Churchill, Randolph** Member of the UK House of Commons, 1940–45; son of Winston Churchill

**Churchill, Winston** Prime minister of the United Kingdom, 1951–55 and 1940–45

**Clark, Charles Patrick** Lobbyist and lawyer involved in a libel suit against Drew Pearson

**Clark, S. Joseph, Jr.** D-PA, Senator, 1957–69; mayor of Philadelphia, 1952–56

**Clark, Thomas** Associate justice of the Supreme Court, 1949–67; U.S. attorney general, 1945–49

**Clark, William Ramsey** U.S. attorney general, 1967–69; son of Thomas Clark

**Clay, Lucius** U.S. general (four stars); commander, U.S. Forces in Europe and military governor of the U.S. Zone, Germany, 1947–49 (during the Berlin blockade)

**Clements, Earle** D-KY, Senator, 1950–57; governor, 1947–50; father of Bess Abell, Drew Pearson's daughter-in-law

**Clements, Sarah** Wife of Earl Clements and mother of Bess Abell

**Cleveland, Harlan** U.S. ambassador to NATO, 1965–69

**Clifford, Clark** Secretary of defense, 1968–69; White House counsel, 1946–50; Washington DC lawyer

**Cobey, Herbert** Ohio manufacturer of farm equipment; friend of Drew Pearson

**Coffin, Tristram "Tris"** Journalist and author; one-time reporter for Drew Pearson's column

**Cohen, Benjamin** Worked as an aide in the administrations of Roosevelt and Truman

**Cohen, Mickey** Organized crime figure

**Cohen, Sheldon S.** Commissioner of the Internal Revenue Service, 1965–69

**Cohen, Wilbur** Secretary of health, education, and welfare, 1968–69

**Cohn, Marcus** Attorney who formed firm of Cohn & Marks in 1946 with Leonard Marks, who became President Johnson's director of U.S. Information Agency

**Coleman, James** D-MS, Judge of the U.S. Court of Appeals for the Fifth Circuit, 1965–81 (on Senior status, 1981–84); governor, 1956–60

**Condon, Edward U.** Physics professor, University of Colorado at Boulder, 1963–70; Washington University, St. Louis, 1956–63

**Connally, John** D-TX, Secretary of the treasury, 1971–72; governor, 1963–69

**Connelly, Matthew** Appointments secretary to President Truman, 1945–53

**Connole, William** Consumer advocate; served on Federal Power Commission, 1955–60

**Constantine II** King of Greece, 1964–73; brother-in-law to King Juan Carlos of Spain

**Cook, William Mercer** U.S. ambassador to Gambia, 1965–66; U.S. ambassador to Senegal, 1964–66; U.S. ambassador to Niger, 1961–64

**Coolidge, Calvin** R-MA, President of the United States, 1923–29; vice president of the United States, 1921–23; governor, 1919–21

**Cooper, John Sherman** R-KY, Senator, 1956–73, 1952–55, and 1946–49

**Corcoran, Thomas E.** R-IL, HR, 1977–84

**Corcoran, Thomas G.** Lobbyist; member of Franklin Roosevelt's "Brain Trust"; counsel, Reconstruction Finance Corporation, 1932, 1934–40; clerk for Justice Oliver Wendell Holmes, 1926–27

**Cordiner, Ralph** Chairman and CEO, General Electric, 1958–63; president, General Electric, 1950–58

**Corman, James** D-CA, HR, 1961–81

**Costello, Harry** One-time investigator for Drew Pearson

**Cotton, Norris** R-NH, Senator, 1975 and 1954–74; HR, 1947–54

**Cousins, Norman** Author; journalist; editor of *Saturday Review*, 1942–72; activist for nuclear disarmament; peace activist

**Coughlin, Charles** Controversial Roman Catholic priest and radio program host

**Cranston, Alan** D-CA, Senator, 1969–93; California state controller, 1959–67

**Cromwell, James "Jimmy"** Author; former husband of Doris Duke

**Culver, John Chester** D-IA, Senator, 1975–81; HR, 1965–75

**Cuneo, Ernest** Friend and source of Drew Pearson; liaison officer at the Office of Strategic Services during World War II

**Cuneo, Margaret** Wife of Ernest Cuneo

**Curtis, Carl** R-NE, Senator, 1955–79; HR, 1939–54

**Cushing, Richard** Roman Catholic prelate; named as a cardinal, 1958; archbishop of Boston, 1944–70

**Cutler, Lloyd** Washington DC attorney; White House counsel, 1994 and 1979–81

**D'Alesandro Thomas J., Jr.** D-MD, Mayor of Baltimore, 1947–59; HR, 1939–47

**Daley, Richard J.** D-IL, Mayor of Chicago, 1955–76

**D'Amato, Constantine "Cus"** Boxing trainer and manager of Floyd Patterson, Mike Tyson, and others

**Daniel, Price** Member of National Security Council; head of Office of Emergency Preparedness; assistant to the president for federal-state relations, 1967–69; governor of Texas, 1958–63

**Davies, John, Jr.** Diplomat; expert on China; target of Senator Joseph McCarthy

**Davies, Joseph** U.S. ambassador to Belgium, 1938–39; U.S. envoy to Luxembourg, 1938–39; U.S. ambassador to the Soviet Union, 1936–38

**Dawson, William** D-IL, HR, 1943–70

**Dayan, Moshe** Israeli foreign minister, 1967–74; previously career military officer

**Dean, Arthur** New York lawyer and diplomat; advisor to Presidents Eisenhower, Kennedy, and Johnson; helped draft the Nuclear Test Ban Treaty (1963)

**de Gaulle, Charles** President of France, 1959–69

**DeLoach, C. "Deke"** Deputy director of Federal Bureau of Investigation, 1965–70 (career spanned 1942–70)

**Dennison, Robert** Commander in chief of the U.S. Atlantic Fleet and Atlantic Command, 1960–63

**Denny, Ludwell** Journalist and writer

**Derounian, Steven** R-NY, HR, 1953–65

**DeSapio, Carmine** New York secretary of state, 1955–59; head of Tammany Hall, 1949–61

**Dewey, Thomas** R-NY, Governor, 1943–55; Republican Party presidential nominee, 1944 and 1948

**Dienar, Baruch** Israeli film producer

**Dill, Clarence** D-WA, Senator, 1923–35; HR, 1915–19

**Dillon, C. Douglas** Secretary of the treasury, 1961–65; U.S. ambassador to France, 1953–58; financier

**Dilworth, Richardson** D-PA, Mayor of Philadelphia, 1956–62

**Dirksen, Everett** R-IL, Senator, 1951–69; HR, 1933–49

**DiSalle, Michael** D-OH, Governor, 1959–63

**Di Silva, Joseph T.** Union leader; head of AFL-CIO Retail Clerks Local 770, 1937–73

**Dix, Albert** Publisher of the *Frankfort (KY) State Journal*, 1962–96

**Dixon, George** Journalist and friend of Drew Pearson

**Dixon, Paul Rand** Chairman and commissioner, Federal Trade Commission, 1961–69

**Dixon, Ymelda** Society columnist for the *Washington Evening Star*; daughter of Sen. Dennis Chávez (D-NM); wife of George Dixon

**Dobrynin, Anatoly** Soviet ambassador to the United States, 1962–86

**Docking, George** D-KS, Governor, 1957–61

**Dodd, Thomas** D-CT, Senator, 1959–71; HR, 1953–57

**Donohue, F. Joseph "Jiggs"** President, DC Board of Commissioners, 1952–53; Washington DC lawyer

**Donovan, Robert John** Washington DC libel lawyer, retained by Pearson beginning in 1947

**Douglas, Helen Gahagan** D-CA, Democratic nominee for U.S. Senate, 1950 (lost to Richard Nixon); HR, 1945–51

**Douglas, Lewis "Lou"** D-AZ, U.S. ambassador to the United Kingdom, 1947–50; director of Bureau and Budget, 1933–34; HR, 1927–32

**Douglas, Paul** D-IL, Senator, 1949–67

**Douglas, William O.** Associate justice of the Supreme Court, 1939–75

**Douglas-Home, Alec** Prime minister of the United Kingdom, 1963–64

**Dubinsky, David** President, International Ladies' Garment Workers' Union, 1932–66

**Duff, James** R-PA, Senator, 1951–57; governor, 1947–51

**Dugger, Ronnie** Freelance journalist; founding editor, *Texas Observer*, 1954–61

**Duke, Angier Biddle** U.S. ambassador to Denmark, 1968–69; U.S. ambassador to Spain, 1965–67; U.S. chief of protocol, 1961–65; U.S. ambassador to El Salvador, 1952–53

**Duke, Doris** Heiress, horticulturalist, art collector, philanthropist

**Dulles, Allen** Director of Central Intelligence, 1953–61

**Dulles, Eleanor** State Department official, 1942–62; sister of John Foster and Allen Dulles

**Dulles, John Foster** Secretary of state, 1953–59

**Dungan, Ralph** U.S. ambassador to Chile, 1964–67; special assistant to the president, 1961–64

**Duong Van Minh** President of the Republic of Vietnam, 1975 and 1963–64

**Dwyer, Florence "Flo"** R-NJ, HR, 1957–73

**Eastland, James** D-MS, Senator, 1943–78 and June–September 1941

**Eaton, Cyrus** Investment banker and peace activist during the Cold War

**Eban, Abba** Israeli foreign minister, 1966–74; Israeli deputy prime minister, 1963–66; Israeli education minister, 1960–63; Israeli ambassador to the United States, 1950–59; Israeli ambassador to the United Nations, 1949–59

**Eden, Anthony** Prime minister of the United Kingdom, 1955–57

**Edwards, William Donlonn** D-CA, HR, 1963–95

**Eichmann, Adolf** Nazi death camp officer, apprehended in Argentina, tried and executed in Israel

**Eisenhower, Dwight D.** R-KS, President of the United States, 1953–61

**Ellender, Allen Joseph** D-LA, Senator, 1937–72

**Ellington, Buford** Governor of Tennessee, 1967–71

**Ellsworth, Robert E.** R-KS, Permanent Representative to NATO, 1969–71; assistant to President Nixon, 1969; HR, 1961–67

**Engelhard, Charles** D-NJ, American businessman and major fund-raiser for the Democratic Party

**Engle, Clair** D-CA, Senator, 1959–64

**Erhard, Ludwig** Chancellor of Germany, 1963–66; minister of economics, 1949–63

**Eshkol, Levi** Prime minister of Israel, 1963–69

**Estes, Billy Sol** Texas businessman; tried and convicted in 1963 in a scheme involving fraudulent loans, kickbacks, and bribes on nonexistent ammonia storage tanks; served six years in prison

**Evans, Rowland** Columnist, author, commentator

**Evans, Siliman, Jr.** Publisher of the *Nashville Tennessean*

**Evers, Charles** D/R-MS, Mayor of Fayette, 1985–89 and 1969–81; brother of Medgar Evers

**Evers, Medgar** Slain civil rights leader

**Falcón Briceño, Marcos** Foreign minister of Venezuela, 1961

**Fanfani, Amintore** Prime minister of Italy, 1960–63

**Fannin, Paul** R-AZ, Senator, 1965–77; governor, 1959–65

**Farley, James** Early key supporter of Franklin D. Roosevelt; postmaster general, 1933–40; chairman, Democratic National Committee, 1932–40

**Farrell, Ray** Commissioner of U.S. Immigration Service, 1961–67

**Fascell, Dante** D-FL, HR, 1955–83

**Fath, Creekmore** Counsel to the Freedom of Information subcommittee of the Senate Commerce Committee in the 1960s; held several positions in the Franklin D. Roosevelt administration; lawyer; Democratic activist from Texas

**Federenko, Nicolai T.** Soviet diplomat; ambassador to the United Nations, 1963–68

**Feldman, Myer "Mike"** White House (legal) counsel to President Johnson, 1963–65, and President Kennedy, 1961–63

**Fentress, Ephraim S.** Co-purchased two Waco, Texas, newspapers in 1927 to form the *Waco Tribune-Herald*

**Ferguson, Homer** R-MI, Senator, 1943–55

**Ferrer, José María Hipólito Figueres** President of Costa Rica, 1970–74, 1953–58, and 1948–49

**Finch, Robert** R-CA, Counselor to the president, 1970–72; secretary of health, education, and welfare, 1969–70

**Findley, Paul** R-IL, HR, 1961–83

**Finletter, Thomas** U.S. permanent representative to NATO, 1961–65

**Fisher, Max** Philanthropist and activist in Jewish causes

**Foley, Edward** Washington DC attorney and friend of Drew Pearson; chairman, 1961 Presidential Inaugural Committee; a founder of Big Brothers of the National Capital Area

**Ford, Gerald R. "Jerry"** R-MI, President of the United States, 1974–77; vice president of the United States, 1973–74; HR, 1949–73

**Ford, Henry, II** CEO, Ford Motor Company, 1960–79 (grandson of founder Henry Ford)

**Forman, James** Civil rights activist

**Forrestal, James** Secretary of defense, 1947–49; secretary of the navy, 1944–47

**Fortas, Abraham "Abe"** Associate justice of the Supreme Court, 1965–69; cofounder of Washington DC law firm, Arnold, Fortas and Porter

**Foster, William C.** Director, U.S. Arms Control and Disarmament Agency, 1961–69

**Fowler, Henry "Joe"** Secretary of the treasury, 1965–68; undersecretary, 1961–64

**Franco, Francisco** Caudillo of Spain, 1939–75

**Frankel, Max** Journalist

**Frankfurter, Felix** Associate justice of the U.S. Supreme Court, 1939–62

**Freeman, Orville** D-MN, Secretary of agriculture, 1961–69; governor, 1955–61

**Friendly, Alfred** Journalist; managing editor, *Washington Post*, 1955–65; 1968 Pulitzer Prize winner for International Reporting

**Friendly, Henry** Judge on the U.S. Court of Appeals for the Second Circuit, 1959–74 (chief judge, 1971–73)

**Fritchey, Clayton** Journalist, syndicated columnist; director of public affairs,

United States Mission to the UN, 1961–65; assistant secretary of defense, 1950–52; assistant to the president (Truman), 1952; deputy chairman, Democratic National Committee, 1953–57

**Fulbright, J. William** D-AR, Senator, 1945–74

**Furtseva, Yekaterina Alexeyevna** Soviet minister of culture, 1960–74

**Galbraith, John Kenneth** U.S. ambassador to India, 1961–63; economist, author, intellectual

**Gandhi, Indira** Prime minister of India, 1980–84 and 1966–77

**Gardner, Joan** Friend of the Pearsons; wife of Arthur Gardner Jr.

**Gardner, John William** Secretary of health, education, and welfare, 1965–68

**Garrison, Jim** District attorney of Orleans Parish, Louisiana (1961–73); began investigating the assassination of President Kennedy in 1966

**Gavin, James M.** U.S. ambassador to France, 1961–62; much-decorated U.S. Army lieutenant general, 1924–58 (led paratroops in Europe in World War II)

**George, Walter** D-GA, Senator, 1922–57

**Geyelin, Philip** Editorial page editor, *Washington Post*, 1968–79; Pulitzer Prize winner, 1970

**Gheorghiu-Dej, Gheorghe** President of the State Council, Romania, 1961–65; secretary-general of Romanian Communist Party, 1955–65 and 1944–54

**Gibbons, Harold** Executive assistant to Teamsters president James R. Hoffa, 1957–63

**Giraud, Henri** French army general; captured by the Nazis, later escaped; head of the French Free Forces in North Africa

**Godwin, Mills Edwin, Jr.** D/R-VA, Governor, 1974–78 and 1966–70

**Goelet, Jane Monroe** Wife of U.S. ambassador Llewellyn Thompson

**Goldberg, Arthur** U.S. ambassador to the UN, 1965–68; associate justice of the U.S. Supreme Court, 1962–65; U.S. secretary of labor, 1961–62; general counsel, United Steel Workers of American, 1955–60

**Goldberg, Dorothy** Wife of Arthur Goldberg

**Goldfine, Bernard** Boston textile manufacturer whose infamous association with Sherman Adams forced Adams to resign as White House chief of staff in 1958

**Goldwater, Barry** R-AZ, Senator, 1969–87 and 1953–65; Republican Party nominee for president, 1964

**Goldwater, Barry, Jr.** R-CA, HR, 1969–83

**Gomułka, Władysław** First secretary of the Polish United Workers' Party, 1956–70 and 1945–48

**Goodell, Charles** R-NY, Senator, 1968–71; HR, 1959–68

**Goodman, Julian** President, NBC, 1966–74

**Goodpaster, Andrew** Supreme commander of NATO Forces, 1969–74; assistant to the chairman, Joint Chiefs of Staff, 1963–67; White House staff secretary, 1954–61

**Goodwin, Richard** Speechwriter for Robert Kennedy and Eugene McCarthy, 1968, and for President Johnson, 1965; secretary-general of the International Peace Corps, 1962–65; deputy assistant secretary of state for Latin America, 1961–62

**Gordon, John "Jack"** Consultant to Kennedy administration on the 1961 Seattle World's Fair

**Gordon, Lincoln** U.S. ambassador to Brazil, 1961–66

**Gore, Albert, Sr.** D-TN, Senator, 1953–71

**Gosset, William T.** Longtime general counsel of Ford Motor Company; elected president, American Bar Association, 1998

**Graham, Donald** Executive vice president, Washington Post Company, publisher and CEO/chairman; reporter, *Washington Post*, 1971–75; patrolman, Washington Metropolitan Police Department, 1969–70; information specialist, First Cavalry Division in Vietnam, 1967–68; son of Philip and Katherine Graham

**Graham, Frank** D-NC, Senator, 1949–50

**Graham, Katherine** Chairwoman of the board, Washington Post Company, 1963–91; publisher, 1969–79; first woman CEO of a Fortune 500 company

**Graham, Philip** Publisher of the *Washington Post*, 1946–63; husband of Katherine Graham

**Graham, William "Billy"** Leading evangelical pastor of the twentieth century

**Green, William J., Jr.** D-PA, 1949–63, 1945–47

**Green, William J., III** D-PA, HR, 1964–77

**Gregory, Richard "Dick"** African American activist, social critic, entrepreneur, comedian

**Griffin, Robert** R-MI, Senator, 1966–79; HR, 1957–66

**Grimillion, Jack P. F.** Louisiana state attorney general, 1956–72

**Gromyko, Andrei** Chairman, Presidium of the Supreme Soviet, 1985–88; foreign minister of the USSR, 1957–85

**Gruening, Ernest** D-AK, Senator, 1959–69

**Gruenther, Alfred M.** General (four stars); Supreme Allied Commander in Europe, 1953–58

**Guevara, Ernesto "Che"** Marxist revolutionary, born in Argentina; commander of La Cubaña fortress, 1959 following Fidel Castro's assumption of power in Cuba; killed by the Bolivian army, 1967

**Guy, William** D-ND, Governor, 1961–73

**Guylay, L. Richard "Lou"** Public relations director, Republican National Committee, 1960, 1955–57

**Haddad, William F.** Former investigative reporter for *New York Herald Tribune*

**Hagerty, James** White House press secretary (Eisenhower administration), 1953–61

**Halle, Kay** Cleveland journalist, author, radio broadcaster, department store heiress

**Halleck, Charles** R-IN, HR, 1935–69

**Hamill, Pete** Journalist, novelist; columnist and editor, *New York Post*, *New York Daily News*

**Hammarskjöld, Dag** Secretary of the United Nations, 1953–61; posthumously awarded the Nobel Peace Prize, 1961

**Hannegan, Robert** Chairman, Democratic National Committee, 1944–47; postmaster general, 1945–47; commissioner of Internal Revenue, 1943–45

**Harding, Warren** R-OH, President of the United States, 1921–23; senator, 1915–21

**Harlan, John** Associate justice of the U.S. Supreme Court, 1955–71

**Harman, Avraham** Israeli ambassador to the United States, 1959–68

**Harriman, Marie** Wife of Averell Harriman, 1929–70

**Harriman, W. Averell** D-NY, Governor, 1955–59; ambassador at-large in Kennedy and Johnson administrations; U.S. ambassador to the United Kingdom, 1946; secretary of commerce, 1946–48; U.S. ambassador to the Soviet Union, 1943–46

**Harris, Fred** D-OK, Senator, 1964–73

**Harris, Oren** D-AR, HR, 1941–66

**Hart, Phillip** D-MI, Senator, 1959–76

**Hartke, Vance** D-IN, Senator, 1959–77

**Hatfield, Mark** R-OR, Senator, 1967–97; governor, 1959–67

**Hay, John Milton** Secretary of state, 1898–1905

**Hayakawa, Samuel I.** R-CA, Senator, 1977–83; president, San Francisco State College, 1968–73; academic scholar

**Hayden, Carl** D-AZ, Senator, 1927–69; HR, 1912–27

**Hayward, Pamela** U.S. ambassador to France, 1993–97; wife of Averell Harriman, 1971–86

**Hébert, Felix Edward "Eddie"** D-LA, HR, 1941–77

**Helis, William G., Jr.** Louisiana oil producer; represented President Johnson at the 1964 wedding in Athens of Greek king Constantine to Princess Anne-Marie of Denmark

**Heller, Walter** Chairman, White House Council of Economic Advisors, 1961–64

**Hennings, Thomas, Jr.** D-MO, Senator, 1951–60; HR, 1935–40

**Herter, Christian** R-MA, Secretary of state 1959–61; governor, 1953–57

**Heston, Charlton** Film actor

**Hickel, Walter "Wally"** R/I-AK, Governor, 1990–94, 1966–69; secretary of the interior, 1969–70

**Hickenlooper, Bourke B.** R-IA, Senator, 1945–69; governor, 1943–45

**Hill, Joseph Lister** D-AL, Senator, 1938–69; HR, 1923–38

**Hill, Robert C.** U.S. ambassador to Mexico, 1957–60

**Hillings, Patrick** R-CA, HR, 1951–59

**Hinckley, Robert H.** Assisted Edward Noble in founding the America Broadcasting Company (ABC); founder, Hinckley Institute of Politics

**Hobby, Oveta Culp** Member, National Advisory Commission on Selective Service, 1963–69; secretary of health, education, and welfare, 1953–55; coeditor and publisher, *Houston Post*; co-owner and director, radio station KPRC; director, Women's Army Corps in World War II, 1942–45

**Ho Chi Minh** President of the Democratic Republic of [North] Vietnam, 1945–69

**Hodges, Luther** D-NC, Secretary of commerce, 1961–65; governor 1954–61

**Hoff, Phillip** D-VT, Governor, 1963–69

**Hoffa, James** President, International Brotherhood of Teamsters, 1958–71

**Hohenlohe, Stephanie Julianne von** Austro-Hungarian princess and confidant to Adolf Hitler and other top Nazi officials; interrogated by the U.S. Office of Strategic Services (OSS) during World War II

**Holifield, Chester** D-CA, HR, 1943–74

**Hollings, Ernest "Fritz"** D-SC, Senator, 1966–2005; governor, 1959–63

**Hollis, Dr. Ernest** Expert on education

**Holmes, Oliver Wendell, Jr.** Associate justice of the U.S. Supreme Court, 1902–32

**Holt, Harold** Prime minister of Australia, 1966–67

**Holt, Henry** Founder of Henry Holt and Company, publishers

**Holtzoff, Alexander** Judge, U.S. District Court for the District of Columbia, 1945–67

**Hooker, Sally** Classmate of Elizabeth "Lally" Graham at Radcliffe College

**Hoover, Herbert** R-CA, President of the United States, 1929–33

**Hoover, J. Edgar** Director of Federal Bureau of Investigation, 1924–72

**Hopkins, Harry** Secretary of commerce, 1938–40; aide and confidant to President Roosevelt during the New Deal and World War II

**Horan, Hume** Diplomat, Department of State Libyan desk office, 1966–70

**Hosmer, Craig** R-CA, HR, 1953–74

**Houphouet-Boigny, Felix** President of Côte d'Ivoire, 1960–93

**Howser, Frederick N.** R-CA, Attorney general of California, 1947–51

**Hruska, Roman Lee** R-NE, Senator, 1954–76; HR, 1953–54

**Hughes, Howard** Reclusive and wealthy aviator, manufacturer, and film producer

**Hughes, Richard** D-NJ, Chief justice of New Jersey Supreme Court, 1973–79; Governor, 1962–70

**Hull, Cordell** Secretary of state, 1933–44; senator, 1931–33; HR, 1923–31; winner of the Nobel Peace Prize, 1954, for his role in establishing the United Nations

**Humphrey, George** Secretary of the treasury, 1953–57

**Humphrey, Hubert** D-MN, Senator, 1971–78 and 1949–64; vice president of the United States, 1965–69; presidential nominee, 1968

**Humphrey, Muriel** D-MN, wife of Hubert Humphrey; senator (appointed on her husband's death), 1978

**Huntley, Chet** Co-anchor, with David Brinkley, of NBC's evening news program, 1956–70

**Huntschnecker, Arnold** Psychotherapist and friend to Richard Nixon

**Hussein bin Talal** King of Jordan, 1952–99

**Ibn Saud, Abdul Aziz** King of Saudi Arabia, 1932–53

**Ickes, Harold** Secretary of the interior, 1933–46

**Imbert, Antonio** Dominican Republic army major general; involved in assassination of dictator Rafael Trujillo; president of the republic for four months in 1965

**Jackson, Gardner Pat** New Deal activist, best known for his work in the Southern Tenant Farmers' Union

**Jackson, Henry "Scoop"** D-WA, Senator, 1953–83; HR, 1941–53

**Jackson, Robert** Associate justice of the U.S. Supreme Court, 1941–54; U.S. chief counsel for prosecution in the Nuremberg Trials, 1945–46; U.S. attorney general, 1940–41

**Jackson, Sam** D-IN, Senator, January–November 1944

**Jacobson, Jake** Figure in the Sen. Thomas Dodd controversy

**Javits, Jacob** R-NY, Senator, 1957–81; state attorney general, 1955–57; HR, 1947–54

**Jenkins, Walter** Lyndon Johnson aide, 1939–64

**Jensen, Robert C.** Hubert Humphrey's press secretary; fired in late 1965

**Jessel, George** American comedian, actor, writer, movie producer

**Johnson, Claudia Alta "Lady Bird" Taylor** Wife of Lyndon Johnson and first lady of the United States, 1963–69

**Johnson, George E.** Fund-raiser for San Francisco mayor George Christopher

**Johnson, Hiram** R-CA, Senator, 1917–45; governor, 1911–17

**Johnson, John H.** Chairman and CEO, Johnson Publishing Company

**Johnson, Louis** Secretary of defense, 1949–50

**Johnson, Luci Baines** Daughter of President Lyndon Johnson

**Johnson, Lynda Bird** Eldest daughter of Lyndon and Lady Bird Johnson; married to Charles Robb, former governor of Virginia

**Johnson, Lyndon** D-TX, President of the United States, 1963–69; vice president, 1961–63; senator, 1949–61; HR, 1937–49

**Johnson, Tom** Journalist; White House fellow in the Johnson administration; later aide to the president

**Johnson, U. Alexis** U.S. ambassador to Japan, 1966–69; U.S. ambassador to Thailand, 1958–61; U.S. ambassador to Czechoslovakia, 1953–58

**Johnston, Eric** Chairman, Motion Picture Association of America, 1945–63

**Jones, James R.** Appointments secretary to President Johnson, 1965–69

**Jones, Jesse Holman** Democrat politician; Texas entrepreneur; U.S. secretary of commerce, 1940–45

**Jones, Robert** D-AL, HR, 1947–77

**Jordan, Benjamin Everett** D-NC, Senator, 1958–73

**Kádár, János** General secretary of the Hungarian Socialist Workers' Party, 1956–88

**Kaiser, Henry** American industrialist

**Karamanlis, Konstantinos** President of Greece, 1980–85 and 1990–95; prime minister of Greece, 1974–80, 1961–63, 1958–61, and 1955–58

**Karr, David** Journalist; businessman; one-time Pearson staff member; accused of being a Communist by Sen. Joseph McCarthy in 1950; in later years a frequent liaison between USSR and American business interests.

**Katzenbach, Nicholas** Undersecretary of state, 1966–69; attorney general, 1965–66; acting attorney general, 1964–65; deputy attorney general, 1962–64; assistant attorney general, 1961–62; joined IBM as general counsel and vice president, 1969

**Kaufman, Irving** Judge, U.S. Court of Appeals for the Second Circuit, 1961–87

**Keating, Kenneth** R-NY, U.S. ambassador to India, 1969–72; senator, 1959–65

**Kefauver, Estes** D-TN, Senator, 1949–63; unsuccessful candidate for the Democratic presidential nomination, 1952, 1956; unsuccessful candidate for vice president of the United States on the Adlai Stevenson ticket, 1956

**Kellis, James** CIA operative and NATO officer

**Kelly, Grace** Princess consort of Monaco, 1956–82; Academy Award–winning film actress

**Kennan, George** U.S. ambassador to Yugoslavia, 1961–63; U.S. ambassador to the Soviet Union, 1952; director of policy planning, U.S. State Department, 1947–49

**Kennedy, Edward** D-MA, Senator, 1963–2009; brother of John F. and Robert F. Kennedy

**Kennedy, Ethel** Wife of Robert F. Kennedy

**Kennedy, Jacqueline** Wife of President Kennedy and first lady of the United States, 1961–63

**Kennedy, John F.** D-MA, President of the United States, 1961–63; senator, 1953–61

**Kennedy, Joseph** Father of President Kennedy; U.S. ambassador to United Kingdom, 1938–40; chairman, Securities and Exchange Commission, 1934–35

**Kennedy, Robert** D-NY, Senator, 1965–68; U.S. attorney general, 1961–64

**Kennedy, Rose** Wife of Joseph Kennedy and mother of President Kennedy and Senators Robert F. and Edward M. Kennedy

**Kenyatta, Jomo** President of Kenya, 1964–78; prime minister, 1963–64

**Keogh, Eugene J.** D-NY, HR, 1937–67

**Kernahan, Galal** Southern California–based Hispanic activist

**Kerr, Robert** D-OK, Senator, 1949–63; governor, 1943–47

**Kerr, Walter** Journalist; general manager, *New York Times* International edition, 1962–65; Washington bureau chief, *New York Herald Tribune*, 1954–56

**Khan, Ayub** President of Pakistan, 1958–69

**Khrushchev, Nikita** First secretary of the Communist Party of the Soviet Union, 1953–64

**Kiesinger, Kurt Georg** Chancellor of West Germany, 1966–69

**Killion, George** Chairman of the board, Metro-Goldwyn-Mayer, 1957–77; president, American Shipping Lines, 1947–66; leading figure in the Democratic Party

**Kim Il Sung** Supreme leader of North Korea, 1948–94

**King, Larry** Author, including a book about Bobby Baker; Miami radio and television interviewer in the 1960s (not to be confused with the later radio/television personality)

**King, Martin Luther, Jr.** Civil rights leader, clergyman

**Kintner, Robert E.** Special assistant to President Johnson and cabinet secretary, 1966–67; president, NBC, 1956–66; president, ABC, 1949–56

**Kissinger, Henry** Secretary of state, 1973–77; national security advisor, 1969–75

**Klein, Herb** Communications director in the Nixon White House; press secretary in three Nixon campaigns

**Klein, Julius** U.S. Army major general (ret.); publicist; key figure in 1966 Senate investigation into whether Sen. Thomas Dodd used his influence for Klein's benefit

**Knappstein, Karl Heinrich** West German ambassador to the United States, 1962–68

**Knight, Goodwin** D-CA, Governor, 1953–59

**Knight, John "Jack"** Newspaper publisher, 1933–69; merged his company with the Ridder Company in 1969 to form Knight-Ridder Company, a national chain

**Knowland, William "Bill"** R-CA, Senator, 1945–59

**Kohler, Foy** U.S. ambassador to the Soviet Union, 1962–66

**Kollek, Theodor "Teddy"** Mayor of Jerusalem, 1965–93

**Komer, Robert W.** Deputy national security advisor, 1965–68; headed "pacification" program in Vietnam

**Kosygin, Alexei** Chairman, Council of Ministers for the Soviet Union, 1964–80

**Kraft, Joseph** Columnist; journalist; speechwriter for John Kennedy's 1960 presidential campaign

**Kramer, Paul** Friend and neighbor of Pearson; worked at the CIA

**Krock, Arthur** Pulitzer Prize-winning journalist; columnist, *New York Times*, 1933–66

**Kuchel, Thomas** R-CA, Senator, 1953–69

**Kung, Louie** Nephew of Chiang Kai-shek; contributor to Nixon's 1950 Senate campaign

**Kuznetzov, Vasili** First deputy chairman, Presidium of the Supreme Soviet, 1977–86; deputy foreign minister of the Soviet Union, 1955–77

**Ky, Nguyên Kao** Vice president of South Vietnam, 1967–71; prime minister, 1965–67

**LaBouisse, Henry** Executive director, UNICEF, 1965–79; U.S. ambassador to Greece, 1962–65

**Lacy, William** Career diplomat at the State Department; U.S. ambassador to South Korea, May–October 1955

**Laird, Melvin** R-WI, secretary of defense, 1969–73; HR, 1953–69

**Lamb, Charles** English essayist, 1775–1834

**Lanahan, Frances "Scottie"** Daughter of F. Scott and Zelda Fitzgerald; writer for the *Washington Post* and *New York Times* in the 1960s

**Langer, William "Wild Bill"** R-ND, Senator, 1941–59; governor, 1933–34 and 1937–39

**Lasker, Mary** Health advocate and philanthropist

**Lasky, Victor** Conservative columnist; author of *JFK: The Man and the Myth* (1963)

**Lausche, Frank** D-OH, Senator, 1957–69; governor, 1945–47 and 1949–57

**Laval, Pierre** French politician; official in the Vichy regime after the fall of France, 1940, and its head of state, 1942–44; prime minister of France, 1935–36 and 1931–32

**Lawrence, David** Founder of *U.S. News and World Report*

**Lawrence, David L.** D-PA, Governor, 1959–63

**Lawrence, William "Bill"** ABC News political affairs editor, 1961–71

**Leader, George** D-PA, Governor, 1955–59

**Leche, Richard** D-LA, Governor, 1936–39

**Lee, H. Rex** Last appointed governor of American Samoa, 1961–67

**LeHand, Marguerite "Missy"** Private secretary to Franklin Roosevelt, 1920–41

**Lehman, Herbert** D-NY, Senator, 1950–57; governor, 1933–42

**Leighter, Jackson** Washington DC public relations man; represented Pearson

**LeMay, Curtis** U.S. Air Force general (four stars); air force chief of staff, 1961–65

**Lerner, Harry** Campaign advisor to Governor Pat Brown and source to Pearson regarding California politics

**Lewis, Fulton, Jr.** Conservative radio news network commentator, 1936–66

**Lewis, John** D-GA, HR, 1987–present; chairman, Student Nonviolent Coordinating Committee, 1963–66

**Lindsay, John** R-NY, Mayor of New York City, 1966–73; HR, 1959–65

**Linowitz, Sol M.** U.S. ambassador to the Organization of American States, 1966–69; chairman, Xerox Corporation, 1961–66; lawyer

**Lippmann, Walter** Pulitzer Prize–winning journalist and author; founder of the *New Republic* (1914); his syndicated column, Today and Tomorrow, ran 1931–67

**Lodge, Henry Cabot, Jr.** R-MA, U.S. ambassador to West Germany, 1968–69; U.S. ambassador to South Vietnam, 1965–67 and 1963–64; Republican nominee for vice president, 1960; U.S. ambassador to the United Nations, 1953–60; Senator, 1947–53 and 1937–44

**Long, Edward** D-MO, Senator, 1960–68

**Long, Huey** D-LA, Senator, 1932–35; governor, 1928–32

**Long, Russell** D-LA, Senator, 1948–87

**Longworth, Alice Roosevelt** Eldest daughter of Theodore Roosevelt; wife to Speaker of the House Nicholas Longworth; first cousin to Eleanor Roosevelt

**Lorentz, Pare** Filmmaker; made influential documentaries of the Great Depression

**Lovett, Robert A.** Secretary of defense, 1951–53; deputy secretary of defense, 1950–51; undersecretary of state, 1947–49; financier

**Lübke, Heinrich** President, West Germany, 1959–69 (resigned)

**Lucas, Scott** D-IL, Senator, 1939–51; HR, 1935–39

**Luce, Clare Boothe** R-CT, HR, 1943–47; author, playwright, war correspondent, editor; head of *Time*, *Life*, and other magazines; wife of Henry Luce

**Luce, Henry** Founder of *Time* magazine; CEO of Time-Life Co.; husband of Clare Booth Luce

**Lucet, Charles** French ambassador to the United States, 1965–72

**Lumumba, Patrice** Prime minister of the Democratic Republic of Congo [Zaire], June–September 1960

**Lundeen, Ernest** D-MN, Senator 1937–40; HR, 1933–37 and 1917–19

**Lytton, Bart** Financier, Democratic fund-raiser

**MacArthur, Douglas** American general; supreme commander, Allied Powers in the Pacific, 1945–51

**Macmillan, Harold** Prime minister of the United Kingdom, 1957–63

**Macomber, William B.** Assistant secretary of state for legislative affairs, for management, 1969–73; assistant secretary of state for legislative affairs, 1967–69

**MacRae, Sheila** Actress and singer

**Maddox, Lester** D-GA, Governor, 1967–71

**Magnuson, Warren** D-WA, Senator, 1944–81

**Mahoney, Florence** Advocate for liberal policies and driving force on health issues

**Mankiewicz, Frank** Journalist and lawyer; press secretary to Sen. Robert Kennedy, 1966–69; Peace Corps regional director, Latin America, 1964–66

**Mann, Thomas** Undersecretary of state for economic affairs, 1965–66; assistant secretary of state for Inter-American affairs, 1964–65 and 1960–61; U.S. ambassador to Mexico, 1961–63; U.S. ambassador to El Salvador, 1955–57

**Mansfield, Michael** D-MT, Senator, 1953–77; Senate majority leader, 1961–77; Democratic whip, 1957–61; HR, 1943–53

**Mantle, Mickey** Major League baseball player (New York Yankees), 1951–68

**Mao Tse-tung** Paramount leader of the People's Republic of China, 1949–76

**March, Frederic** American film and stage actor

**Marcus, Stanley** President, Neiman Marcus department store, 1950–72

**Marcus, Wendy** Lawyer and daughter of Stanley Marcus

**Marín, Luis Muñoz** Governor of Puerto Rico, 1949–65

**Marks, Leonard** Director, U.S. Information Agency, 1965–68

**Marsh, Charles** Newspaper publisher, philanthropist, Democratic Party activist, and advisor to Lyndon Johnson

**Marshall, George C.** Secretary of defense, 1950–51; U.S. Army chief of staff, 1939–45

**Marshall, Thurgood** Associate justice of the U.S. Supreme Court, 1967–91; U.S. solicitor general, 1965–67

**Martin, Edwin** U.S. ambassador to Argentina, 1964–68; assistant secretary of state for Inter-American affairs, 1960–64

**Martin, William McChesney, Jr.** Chairman, Federal Reserve Bank, 1951–70

**Masaryk, Jan** Patriot; foreign minister of Czechoslovakia; died in 1968 under mysterious circumstances after assumption of power by Communist government

**Mathias, Charles "Mac," Jr.** R-MD, Senator, 1969–87; HR, 1961–69

**Maverick, F. Maury** D-TX, Mayor of San Antonio, 1939–41; HR, 1935–39

**May, Herbert** Wealthy Pittsburgh businessman and husband of Marjorie Merriweather Post

**McCarthy, Abigail** Catholic author and educator; wife of Eugene McCarthy

**McCarthy, Eugene** D-MN, Senator, 1959–71

**McCarthy, Joseph** R-WI, Senator, 1947–57

**McCarthy, Richard "Max"** D-NY, HR, 1965–71

**McClellan, John** D-AR, Senator, 1943–77

**McClendon, Sarah** Freelance White House reporter, 1946–97

**McClintock, Robert** U.S. ambassador to Argentina, 1962–64

**McCloy, John J.** Member of the Warren Commission; American high commissioner for Occupied Germany, 1949–52; president, World Bank Group, 1947–49; U.S. assistant secretary of war, 1941–45

**McCone, John A.** Director of Central Intelligence, 1961–65

**McCormack, Edward "Ed"** D-MA, State attorney general, 1959–63; lost to Ted Kennedy in 1962 Democratic Primary for the U.S. Senate; nephew of Speaker John McCormack

**McCormack, John** D-MA, HR, 1928–71; speaker of the House of Representatives, 1962–71; majority leader, 1955–62, 1949–53, and 1939–47

**McDonald, David** President, United Steelworkers of America, 1952–65

**McGee, Gale** D-WY, Senator, 1959–77

**McGovern, George** D-SD, Senator, 1963–81; HR, 1957–61; Democratic Party nominee for president, 1972

**McGrory, Mary** Journalist; columnist, *Washington Star*, 1947–81, then *Washington Post*; winner of the Pulitzer Prize, 1975

**McInerney, James** Assistant attorney general, 1950–53

**McIntyre, Thomas** D-NH, Senator, 1962–79

**McKeithen, John J.** D-LA, Governor, 1964–72

**McLeod, Iain** British Conservative politician, credited with coining the phrase *nanny state*

**McLeod, R. W. Scott** U.S. ambassador to Ireland, 1957–61; head of Department of State's Bureau of Security and Consular Affairs, 1953–57

**McMahon, Brien (b. James O'Brien McMahon)** D-CT, Senator, 1945–52

**McMillan, John** D-SC, HR, 1939–73

**McNamara, Patrick Vincent** D-MI, Senator, 1955–66

**McNamara, Robert** President, World Bank, 1968–81; secretary of defense, 1961–68

**McPherson, Harry** Counsel and special counsel to President Lyndon Johnson, also speechwriter, 1965–69; assistant secretary of state for educational and cultural affairs, 1964–65; deputy undersecretary of the army for international affairs, 1963–64; general counsel, Senate Democratic Policy Committee, 1961–63

**McRae, Gordon** Singer, film actor

**Means, Marianne** Columnist with Hearst Newspapers' Washington Bureau, 1958–2008

**Meany, George** President, AFL-CIO, 1955–79; president, AFL, 1952–55

**Meir, Golda** Prime minister of Israel, 1969–74; foreign minister, 1956–66; labor minister, 1949–56

**Mellon, Andrew** Donated his extensive art collection and cash to establish the National Gallery of Art in Washington DC, 1937; secretary of the treasury, 1921–32

**Menshikov, Mikhail** Soviet ambassador to the United States, 1958–62

**Meriwether, Charles** Director, Export-Import Bank of Washington, 1961–65

**Merrill, Fred** Director, East-West Exchanges Staff, Office of Public Affairs, Department of State

**Mesta, Perle** Socialite; U.S. ambassador to Luxembourg, 1949–53

**Metcalf, Lee** D-MT, Senator, 1961–78; HR, 1953–61

**Meyer, Agnes** Eugene Meyer's widow and influential philanthropist and political activist; mother of Katherine Graham

**Meyer, Eugene** Owner/chairman, *Washington Post*, 1933–59; chairman, Federal Reserve Bank, 1930–33; first president of the World Bank, 1946; father of Katherine Graham

**Meyner, Robert** D-NJ, Governor, 1954–62

**Mikoyan, Anastas** Chairman, Presidium of the Supreme Soviet, 1964–65; first deputy chairman, Council of Ministers, 1955–64; minister of foreign trade, 1938–49 and 1953–55; full member of the Politburo, 1935–66; candidate member of the Politburo, 1926–35

**Miller, Joseph "Bill"** Campaign consultant who worked for both John F. Kennedy and Lyndon Johnson

**Miller, William** R-NY, HR, 1951–65; Republican Party nominee for vice president, 1964

**Mills, Wilbur** D-AR, HR, 1939–77

**Mitchell, John** U.S. attorney general, 1969–72

**Moley, Raymond** Columnist for *Newsweek*, 1937–68; advisor to President Franklin Roosevelt, 1932–36

**Molotov, Vyacheslav** Minister of foreign affairs for the Soviet Union, 1953–56 and 1939–49

**Monroney, Almer Stillwell "Mike"** D-OK, Senator, 1951–69

**Morgan, Edward** Counsel, Senate Foreign Relations Committee, 1950–51; former FBI agent, retiring as chief inspector, 1947; attorney

**Morgan, Edward P.** Journalist; co-anchor of ABC television news in the 1960s

**Morgenthau, Henry, Jr.** Secretary of the treasury, 1934–45

**Morgenthau, Robert** New York County district attorney, 1975–2009; U.S. attorney for the Southern District of New York, 1962–70 and 1961–62; son of Henry Morgenthau Jr.

**Moro, Aldo** Prime minister of Italy, 1963–68

**Morse, Wayne** R/D-OR, Senator, 1945–69

**Morton, Thruston** R-KY, Senator, 1957–68

**Mosk, Stanley** Associate justice, California supreme court, 1964–2001; California attorney general, 1958–64

**Moss, Frank** D-UT, Senator, 1959–77

**Moss, John E.** D-CA, HR, 1953–79

**Mowrer, Richard** Journalist

**Moyers, Bill** White House press secretary, 1965–67

**Moynihan, Daniel Patrick** D-NY, Senator, 1977–2001; U.S. ambassador to the UN, 1975–76; assistant secretary of labor, 1961–64

**Multer, Abraham J.** D-NY, HR, 1947–67

**Murphy, Charles** White House counsel, 1950–53

**Murphy, Frank** D-MI, Associate justice of the U.S. Supreme Court, 1940–49; U.S. attorney general, 1939–40; governor, 1937–39

**Murphy, George** R-CA, Senator, 1965–71; vice president, Desilu Studios, 1958–61; Technicolor Corporation, 1961–64; former film actor

**Murray, Philip** President, United Steelworkers of America, 1942–52; president, Congress of Industrial Organizations (CIO), 1940–52

**Muskie, Edmund** D–ME, Secretary of state, 1980–81; senator, 1959–80; governor, 1955–59

**Nader, Ralph** Activist; attorney; author; Green Party presidential nominee, 2000 and 1996

**Nannen, Henri** Founder and head of German magazine *Der Stern*, 1948–80

**Nasser, Gamal Abdel** President of Egypt, 1956–70

**Neal, Fred Warner** Author; journalist; foreign policy specialist; professor of political science, Claremont Graduate School (CA), 1957–83

**Neel, William** Worked for Drew Pearson, 1946–69, managing his syndicated radio program and business newsletter

**Nehru, Jawaharlal** Prime minister of India, 1947–64

**Nelson, Gaylord** D-WI, Senator, 1963–81; governor, 1959–63

**Nenni, Pietro** Foreign minister of Italy, 1968–69; secretary-general of the Italian Socialist Party

**Neuberger, Maurine** D-OR, Senator, 1960–67

**Niarchos, Stavros** Greek shipping tycoon

**Nirenberg, Marshall W.** Nobel laureate in medicine, 1968

**Nixon, Richard** R-CA, President of the United States, 1969–74; vice president, 1953–61; senator, 1951–53; HR, 1946–50

**Nkrumah, Kwame** President of Ghana, 1960–66

**Noble, Edward J.** Founder, American Broadcasting Company (ABC)

**Noe, James Albert "Jimmy"** D-LA, Governor, January–May 1936

**Nofziger, Franklyn "Lyn"** Press secretary to Governor Reagan, 1966–68; assistant to President Reagan, 1982–84; Republican campaign consultant; author

**Norris, George** R-NE, Senator, 1913–43; HR, 1903–13

**Novak, Robert** Columnist, author, commentator

**Noyes, David** Journalist; assistant to President Truman, 1953–72; consultant to President Truman, 1948–53

**Nugent, Patrick** Son-in-law of Lyndon Johnson and husband of Luci Baines Johnson, 1966–79

**Nugent, Patrick Lyndon** Grandson of Lyndon Johnson; son of Patrick and Luci Baines Johnson Nugent

**Nye, Gerald** R-ND, Senator, 1925–45

**O'Brien, Lawrence F. "Larry"** Chairman, Democratic National Committee, 1968, 1970–72; U.S. postmaster general, 1965–68; special assistant to the president for congressional relations, 1961–65

**O'Connor, Cassie** Alleged mistress of Barry Goldwater

**O'Daniel, Wilbert Lee "Pappy"** D-TX, Senator, 1941–49; governor, 1939–41

**O'Donnell, Kenneth** White House appointments secretary, 1961–63

**O'Dwyer, William** D-NY, Mayor of New York City, 1946–50

**Oliver, Covey T.** Assistant secretary of state, Inter-American Affairs, 1967–68; ambassador to Colombia, 1964–66

**Osenenko, John** Newspaper syndicate executive, 1951–71

**Oswald, Lee Harvey** Assassin of President Kennedy

**Oswald, Marina** Wife of Lee Harvey Oswald

**Otepka, Otto** Member, U.S. Subversive Activities Control Board, 1969–71

**Outland, George E.** D-CA, HR, 1943–47

**Palmer, Dwight** President, General Cable Corporation; active in the National Urban League; member of President Truman's committee to enforce desegregation in the armed forces

**Papandreou, Andreas** Prime minister of Greece, 1993–96 and 1981–89; son of Prime Minister George Papandreou

**Papandreou, George** Prime minister of Greece, 1964–65, 1963, and 1944–45

**Pappas, Thomas** Prominent Boston Republican; U.S. ambassador to Greece during the Eisenhower administration; friend of Richard Nixon and Spiro Agnew

**Paris, Enrique Tejera** Ambassador of Venezuela to the United States, 1963–68

**Parker, Mack Charles** Lynching victim in Mississippi, April 24, 1959

**Parker, William** Chief of the Los Angeles Police Department, 1950–66

**Pastore, John** D-RI, Senator, 1950–76; governor, 1945–50

**Patman, John William Wright** D-TX, HR, 1929–76

**Patterson, Alicia** Founder of *Newsday*, Long Island newspaper, 1939; her cousin Felicia Patterson Gizycka was Drew Pearson's former wife

**Patterson, Floyd** Two-time world heavyweight boxing champion; Olympic gold medalist, 1952

**Patterson, John** D-AL, Governor, 1959–63

**Patterson, Paul** R-OR, Governor, 1952–56

**Patton, Thomas** President, chief executive, and chairman, Republic Steel, late 1960s

**Paul VI** Pope, head of the Catholic Church, and sovereign of the Vatican State, 1963–78

**Pauley, Edwin** California oilman and Democratic Party fund-raiser

**Peabody, Endicott "Chubb"** D-MA, Assistant director, Office of Emergency Planning, 1967–68; governor, 1963–65; brother of Marietta Tree

**Peale, Norman Vincent** Author, commentator, Protestant pastor

**Pearson, James** R-KS, Senator, 1962–78

**Pearson, Lester** Prime minister of Canada, 1963–68; winner of Nobel Peace Prize, 1957

**Pearson, Luvie Butler Moore** Wife of Drew Pearson

**Pell, Claiborne** D-RI, Senator, 1961–97

**Penkovsky, Oleg** Colonel in the Soviet military intelligence unit (GRU) who gave American and British agents intelligence about USSR's emplacement of missiles in Cuba

**Pepper, Claude** D-FL, HR, 1963–89; senator, 1936–51

**Pepper, Mildred** Wife of Claude Pepper

**Pepper, William** Head of *Newsweek*'s Rome Bureau, 1962

**Perrone, Nicola Carlo** Italian historian and journalist

**Peurifoy, John** American diplomat; U.S. ambassador to Thailand (1954–55), Guatemala (1953), and Greece (1950–53)

**Philby, Harold "Kim"** British intelligence agent and a double agent for the USSR

**Phouma, Souvanna** Prime minister of Laos, 1962–75, 1960, 1956–58, and 1951–54

**Pilcher, John Leonard** D-GA, HR, 1953–65

**Pillion, John R.** R-NY, HR, 1953–63

**Pius XII** Pope, head of the Catholic Church, and sovereign of the Vatican State, 1939–58

**Post, Marjorie Merriweather** American socialite; owner of General Foods; wife of U.S. ambassador Joseph Davies, 1935–55

**Potter, Charles** R-MI, Senator, 1952–59; HR, 1947–52

**Potter, Philip** Chief, Washington Bureau, *Baltimore Sun*, 1964–72

**Powell, Adam Clayton** D-NY, HR, 1945–71

**Powers, Francis Gary** U-2 pilot shot down over USSR, 1960

**Pritchard, Edward F., Jr.** Kentucky lawyer, Democratic Party activist in New Deal years

**Proskauer, Joseph** New York attorney, 1930–70; New York State appellate judge, 1927–30; New York State supreme court judge, 1923–27

**Proxmire, William** D-WI, Senator, 1957–89

**Rabin, Yitzhak** Prime minister of Israel, 1992–95 and 1974–77; ambassador to the United States, 1968–73; chief of staff of the Israel Defense Forces, 1964–68

**Radford, Arthur** Admiral, U.S. Navy; chairman, Joint Chiefs of Staff, 1953–57

**Rainier III** Prince of Monaco, 1949–2005; husband of American actress Grace Kelly, 1956–82

**Raley, Kay** One of Pearson's secretaries

**Rankin, James** Solicitor general of the United States, 1956–61

**Raskin, Marcus "Hal"** Assistant to National Security Advisor McGeorge Bundy, 1961–63; cofounder, Institute for Policy Studies

**Ray, James Earl** Assassin of Martin Luther King Jr., 1968

**Rayburn, Sam** D-TX, HR, 1913–61; speaker of the House of Representatives, 1955–61, 1949–53, and 1940–47

**Reagan, Ronald** R-CA, President of the United States, 1981–89; governor, 1967–75; film actor

**Rebozo, Charles "Bebe"** Florida banker and close friend to Richard Nixon for over forty years

**Reed, Stanley** Associate justice of the U.S. Supreme Court, 1938–57; U.S. solicitor general, 1935–38

**Reed, Winifred** Wife of Stanley Reed

**Reedy, George** White House press secretary, 1964–65

**Rees, Thomas** D-CA, HR, 1965–77

**Reeves, Rosser** Head of the Ted Bates advertising agency, in charge of television for Dwight Eisenhower's 1952 presidential campaign

**Reid, Ed** Head of the Alabama League of Municipalities, 1935–65

**Reid, Ogden** R/D-NY, HR, 1963–75; U.S. ambassador to Israel, 1959–61; president and editor, *New York Herald Tribune*, 1955–59

**Reinhardt, George Frederick "Fred"** U.S. ambassador to Italy, 1961–68

**Reischauer, Edwin O.** U.S. ambassador to Japan, 1961–65

**Resnick, Joseph** D-NY, HR, 1965–69

**Reston, James "Scotty"** Pulitzer Prize–winning journalist, *New York Times*; Washington bureau chief, 1953–64; associate editor, executive editor, vice president

**Reuss, Henry** D-WI, HR, 1955–83

**Reuther, Walter** President, United Automobile Workers, 1946–70

**Reynolds, James** Undersecretary of labor, 1967–69; assistant secretary for labor-management relations, 1961–65

**Rhodes, James Allen** R-OH, Governor, 1975–83 and 1963–71

**Ribicoff, Abraham** D-CT, Senator, 1963–81; secretary of health, education, and welfare, 1961–62; governor, 1955–61

**Richardson, Elliot** Secretary of commerce, 1976–77; U.S. ambassador to the United Kingdom, 1975–76; U.S. attorney general, May–October 1973; secretary of health, education, and welfare, 1970–73; undersecretary of state, 1969–70

**Richardson, Sid** Texas oilman, cattleman, philanthropist

**Rickover, Hyman G.** Admiral, U.S. Navy; "father" of the Nuclear Navy; director, Nuclear Propulsion Program, 1955–61; longest-serving naval officer in U.S. history (63 years)

**Ridder, Marie** Journalist; married to Walter Ridder; deputy to director, Project Head Start, and liaison to Lady Bird Johnson, 1964–68

**Ridder, Walter** Chief, Washington Bureau, Knight-Ridder newspapers, 1956–67

**Rivers, Lucius Mendel** D-SC, HR, 1941–70

**Robb, Roger** Judge, U.S. Court of Appeals for the District of Columbia Circuit, 1969–82

**Roberts, Chalmers** Columnist for the *Washington Post*

**Robertson, Absalom Willis** D-VA, Senator, 1946–66; HR, 1933–46

**Rockefeller, David** Chairman and CEO of Chase Manhattan Corp., one of the nation's largest banks during the years of this book

**Rockefeller, John Davison "Jay," IV** D-WV, West Virginia house of delegates, 1966–68; VISTA volunteer, Emmons, West Virginia, 1964–66; desk officer, Peace Corps, 1962–63; great-grandson of oil tycoon John D. Rockefeller

**Rockefeller, Laurance S.** Brother of David, Nelson, Winthrop, and Abby Rockefeller; prominent venture capitalist and philanthropist

**Rockefeller, Mary** First wife of Nelson Rockefeller

**Rockefeller, Nelson** R-NY, Vice president of the United States, 1974–77; governor, 1959–73

**Rockefeller, Winthrop** R-AR, Governor, 1967–71

**Rockwell, George Lincoln** Leader of the American Nazi Party, 1958–67

**Rogers, Paul** D-FL, HR, 1955–79

**Rogers, William P.** Secretary of state, 1969–73; U.S. attorney general, 1957–61

**Rolvaag, Karl** D-MN, Governor, 1963–67

**Rometsch, Ellen** East German spy, rumored to have been mistress of President Kennedy

**Romney, George W.** R-MI, Secretary of housing and urban development, 1969–73; governor, 1963–69

**Rooney, John J.** D-NY, HR, 1944–74

**Roosevelt, Anna** Daughter of Franklin and Eleanor Roosevelt

**Roosevelt, Eleanor** First lady of the United States, 1933–45

**Roosevelt, Elliot** Son of Franklin and Eleanor Roosevelt

**Roosevelt, Franklin D., Jr.** D-NY, chairman, Equal Employment Opportunity Commission, 1965–66; Liberal Party nominee for governor, 1966; Democratic Party nominee for New York State attorney general, 1954; HR, 1949–55

**Roosevelt, Franklin Delano** D-NY, President of the United States, 1933–45; governor, 1929–32

**Roosevelt, James** D-CA, HR, 1955–65; son of Franklin and Eleanor Roosevelt

**Rose, Alex** Labor leader in the American Hatters' Union; cofounder of the American Labor Party; and vice chairman, Liberal Party of New York

**Rostow, Walt** National security advisor, 1966–69

**Ruby, Jack** Night club operator, Dallas; assassinated Lee Harvey Oswald on November 24, 1963, two days after the Kennedy assassination

**Rusk, Dean** Secretary of state, 1961–69; president, Rockefeller Foundation, 1952–61

**Russell, Donald S.** D-SC, Governor, 1963–65

**Russell, Richard** D-GA, Senator, 1933–71; governor, 1931–33

**Rustin, Bayard** Leading strategist of the civil rights movement, 1955–68

**Ryan, Clendenin, Jr.** American businessman, owner of the *American Mercury* magazine, staunch anti-Communist

**Salinger, Pierre** D-CA, Senator, August–December 1964; White House press secretary, 1961–64

**Saltonstall, Leverett** R-MA, Senator, 1945–67; governor, 1939–45

**Salvatori, Henry** Geophysicist, California businessman, philanthropist, active in Republican politics

**Sandburg, Carl** Writer and Pulitzer Prize winner

**Sanger, Richard** Public affairs officer, Bureau of Near Eastern, South Asian, and African Affairs, State Department; author

**Sarnoff, David** Chairman, Radio Corporation of America (RCA), 1919–70

**Sato, Eisaku** Prime minister of Japan, 1964–72

**Satukov, Pavel A.** Editor of Soviet newspaper *Pravda* in the early 1960s

**Sayre, Francis, Jr.** Episcopal dean of the National Cathedral, 1951–78

**Scheuer, James** D-NY, HR, 1975–93 and 1965–73

**Schlesinger, Arthur, Jr.** Historian, author, prominent liberal Democrat

**Schröder, Gerhard** West German minister of defense, 1966–69; West German minister of foreign affairs, 1961–66; West German minister of defense, 1953–61

**Scott, Hugh** R-PA, Senator, 1959–77; HR, 1947–59 and 1941–45

**Scranton, William** R-PA, U.S. ambassador to the United Nations, 1976–77; Governor, 1963–67; HR, 1961–63

**Sculz, Tad** *New York Times* foreign correspondent

**Segal, Bernard** President, American Bar Association, 1969–70; Philadelphia civil rights attorney

**Selassie, Haile** Emperor of Ethiopia, 1930–74; Ethiopia's regent, 1916–30

**Selden, Armistead** D-AL, HR, 1953–69

**Service, John** Diplomat; expert on China; target of Sen. Joseph McCarthy

**Sevareid, Eric** CBS television news commentator, 1963–77

**Shapiro, Ludmilla** Russian-born journalist/photographer; wife of Henry Shapiro, who reported from Moscow for United Press International (UPI), 1934–73

**Shapp, Milton** D-PA, Governor, 1971–79

**Shaw, Clay** New Orleans businessman tried in 1969 for conspiracy in the assassination of President Kennedy and acquitted

**Shelepin, Alexander** Member of the Soviet Politburo, 1964–65; Central Committee of the USSR Communist Party, 1961–65; head of the KGB, 1958–61

**Shelley, John "Jack"** D-CA, Mayor of San Francisco, 1964–68; HR, 1949–64

**Shriver, Eunice Kennedy** Wife of Sargent Shriver; sister of John, Robert, and Ted Kennedy; founder of the Special Olympics, 1968

**Shriver, Sargent** D-MD, Democratic Party nominee for vice president, 1972; U.S. ambassador to France, 1968–70; director, Office of Economic Opportunity, 1965–68; director, Peace Corps, 1961–66

**Sihanouk, Norodom** King of Cambodia, 1993–2005 and 1941–55 (effectively the country's ruler from 1953 to 1970)

**Simpson, Andy** Pearson friend from his work in the Balkans just after World War I

**Smathers, George** D-FL, Senator, 1951–69

**Smith, Alfred** D-NY, Democratic Party nominee for president, 1928; governor, 1919–20 and 1923–28

**Smith, Cyrus Rowlett** Secretary of commerce, 1968–69; CEO, American Airlines, 1934–68 and 1973–74

**Smith, Earl** U.S. ambassador to Cuba, 1957–59

**Smith, Howard K.** Chief correspondent and general manager, *CBS News*, Washington DC, 1961; reporter and anchor, ABC television/radio networks, 1961–75

**Smith, Margaret Chase** R-ME, Senator, 1949–73; first woman to be nominated for the presidency at a national party convention (Republican, 1964)

**Smoot, Reed** R-UT, Senator, 1903–33

**Soames, Christopher** Son-in-law of Winston Churchill; Conservative politician; UK ambassador to France, 1966–72

**Solzhenitsyn, Aleksandr** Author and Soviet dissident

**Sommer, Theo** German newspaperman; deputy editor of the weekly *Die Zeit*, 1968–73; foreign editor, 1958–68

**Sontag, Fred** Author; public affairs/research consultant; special consultant to Rep. Thomas B. Curtiss, 1957–69

**Sorensen, Theodore "Ted"** D-NE, White House counsel, 1961–64

**Spaatz, Carl "Tooey"** Chief of staff of the U.S. Air Force, 1947–48; commanding general, U.S. Army Air Forces, 1946–47

**Sparkman, John** D-AL, Senator, 1946–79

**Spellman, Francis** Roman Catholic cardinal, 1946–67; archbishop of New York, 1939–67

**Spong, William** D-VA, Senator, 1966–73

**Springer, Axel** Owner of several German newspapers and magazines, including *Die Welt* and the tabloid *Bild*

**Staggers, Harley** D-WV, HR, 1949–81

**Stalin, Joseph** General secretary of the Communist Party of the Soviet Union, 1922–53

**Stanton, Frank** Vice chairman, CBS, 1971–73; president, CBS, 1946–71

**Stassen, Harold** R-MN, Governor, 1939–43; from 1948 frequent seeker of presidential nomination

**Steinem, Gloria** Feminist, journalist, founder of *Ms.* magazine

**Steinhardt, Laurence** U.S. ambassador to Canada, 1948–50; U.S. ambassador to Czechoslovakia, 1945–48; U.S. ambassador to Turkey, 1942–45; U.S. ambassador to the Soviet Union, 1939–41; U.S. ambassador to Peru, 1937–39; U.S. ambassador to Sweden, 1933–37

**Stennis, John** D-MS, Senator, 1947–89

**Stevenson, Adlai** D-IL, U.S. ambassador to the UN, 1961–65; Democratic Party nominee for president, 1952 and 1956; governor, 1949–53

**Stevenson, Coke Robert** D-TX, Governor, 1941–47; lost to Lyndon Johnson in the 1948 Democratic primary for Senate

**Stewart, Potter** Associate justice of the U.S. Supreme Court, 1958–81

**Stewart, Robert** British foreign affairs secretary, 1968–70 and 1965–66

**Stimson, Henry** Secretary of war, 1940–45; secretary of state, 1929–33

**Stoessel, Walter John, Jr.** U.S. ambassador to Poland, 1968–72; deputy assistant secretary of state for European Affairs, 1965–68

**Stokes, Carl** Mayor of Cleveland, 1968–71

**Strauss, Robert** D-TX, Attorney, founder of Akin, Gump, Strauss, Hauer & Feld in Dallas; active in Democratic politics and longtime associate of Lyndon Johnson; chairman, Democratic National Committee, 1972–77

**Sukarno** President of Indonesia, 1945–67

**Sullivan, William H.** Career foreign service officer; U.S. ambassador to Laos, 1964–69

**Summersby, Kay** Member of the British Mechanized Transport Corps in World War II, assigned as General Eisenhower's driver

**Suslov, Mikhail** Second secretary of the Communist Party of the Soviet Union, 1965–82

**Svoboda, Ludvík** President of Czechoslovakia, 1968–75

**Swainson, John** D-MI, Governor, 1961–63

**Sylvester, Arthur** Assistant secretary of defense for public affairs, 1961

**Symington, Evelyn** Wife of Stuart Symington, daughter of New York senator James Wolcott Wadsworth Jr., and granddaughter of Secretary of State John Hay

**Symington, Stuart** D-MO, Senator, 1953–76; first secretary of the U.S. Air Force, 1947–50

**Taft, Robert** R-OH, Senator, 1939–53

**Talbot, Philip** U.S. ambassador to Greece, 1965–69

**Tamm, Quinn** Executive director, International Association of Chief of Police, 1961–75; former assistant director of Federal Bureau of Investigation, 1954–61

**Tankersley, Ruth "Bazy"** Friend of the Pearsons; Arabian horse breeder; newspaper publisher; niece of Robert R. McCormick; owner of the *Chicago Tribune*

**Taper, S. Mark** Southern California real estate developer, financier, philanthropist

**Tapp, Jessie** Chairman, Bank of America, 1955–65

**Tate, James** Mayor of Philadelphia, 1962–72

**Taylor, Hobart, Jr.** Director, U.S. Export-Import Bank, 1965–68; Washington DC attorney

**Taylor, Maxwell** U.S. ambassador to South Vietnam, 1964–65; chairman, Joint Chiefs of Staff, 1962–64

**Temple, Larry** Special counsel to President Johnson, 1967–69

**Thayer, Charles** American diplomat and author; expert on the Soviet Union; brother-in-law of Charles Bohlen; target of Sen. Joseph McCarthy

**Thieu, Nguyên Văn** President of the Republic of Vietnam, 1965–75

**Thomas, Elmer** D-OK, Senator, 1927–51; HR, 1923–27

**Thomas, John Parnell** R-NJ, HR, 1937–50

**Thomas, Norman** Presidential nominee for the Socialist Party of America, 1928, 1932, 1936, 1940, 1944, and 1948

**Thompson, Jane** Wife of diplomat Llewellyn Thompson

**Thompson, Lawn** The Pearsons' physician and friend

**Thompson, Llewellyn "Tommy"** U.S. ambassador to the Soviet Union, 1967–69 and 1957–62; U.S. ambassador to Austria, 1955–57

**Thompson, Theo Ashton** D-LA, HR, 1953–65

**Thornberry, William Homer** D-TX, Nominated to U.S. Supreme Court, 1968; circuit judge, U.S. Court of Appeals, 1965–95; U.S. district judge, 1963–65; HR, 1949–63

**Thurmond, Strom** D/R-SC, Senator, 1956–2003 and 1954–56; governor, 1947–51; Dixiecrat Party nominee for president, 1948

**Tiernan, Robert O.** D-RI, HR, 1967–75

**Tito, Josip Broz** President of Yugoslavia, 1953–80; general of the League of Communists of Yugoslavia, 1939–80; prime minister of Yugoslavia, 1943–63

**Tolson, Clyde** Associate director of Federal Bureau of Investigation, 1930–72

**Tower, John** R-TX, Senator, 1961–85

**Tree, Marietta** U.S. representative to the Trusteeship Council, 1964–65; U.S. representative to UN Commission on Human Rights, 1961–64; wife of Ronald Tree

**Tree, Ronald** American-born British journalist; member of the British Parliament, 1933–45; husband of Marietta Tree

**Trippe, Juan** Founder of Pan American World Airways

**Trotsky, Leon** Marxist revolutionary; member of the Politburo, 1919–26 and 1917; people's commissioner for army and navy affairs, 1918–25; people's commissioner for foreign affairs, 1917–18; founder of Red Army

**Troyanovsky, Oleg** Advisor to Khrushchev; diplomat; Soviet ambassador to Japan, 1967–76

**Trudeau, Arthur** Lieutenant general, U.S. Army; chief of U.S. Army Intelligence, 1953–55

**Trujillo, Rafael** Dictator of the Dominican Republic, 1930–61

**Truman, Harry S.** D-MO, President of the United States, 1945–53; vice president January–April 1945; senator, 1935–45

**Tshombe, Moise** Prime minister of Congo, 1964–65; president of Katanga Province, 1960–63

**Tully, Andrew** Syndicated newspaper columnist and author of sixteen books

**Tuttle, Elbert** Judge of the U.S. Court of Appeals for the Fifth Circuit, 1954–81 (chief judge, 1960–67)

**Tydings, Millard** D-MD, Senator, 1927–51; HR, 1923–27

**Udall, Stewart** D-AZ, Secretary of interior, 1961–69; HR, 1955–61

**Ulbricht, Walter** Chairman, State Council of the German Democratic Republic, 1960–73; general secretary of the Central Committee of the Socialist Unity Party of the German Democratic Republic, 1950–71

**Unruh, Jesse** D-CA, State treasurer, 1975–87; speaker of the California Assembly, 1961–69

**U Thant** Secretary-general of the United Nations, 1961–71

**Valenti, Jack** Special assistant to President Johnson, 1963–66; president of the Motion Picture Association of America, 1966–2004

**Vance, Cyrus** Secretary of state, 1977–80; deputy secretary of defense, 1964–67

**Vandenberg, Arthur** R-MI, Senator, 1928–51

**Vandenberg, Arthur, Jr.** Son of Sen. Arthur Vandenberg

**Vanden Heuvel, William** Aide to Robert Kennedy at the Justice Department and during his campaigns for U.S. Senate and president; U.S. deputy ambassador to the United Nations, 1979–81

**Vanocur, Sander** NBC News White House correspondent in the 1960s and early 1970s

**Vaughan, Harry** Military aide to President Harry Truman, 1945–53

**Vaughn, Jack** Director, Peace Corps, 1966–69; assistant secretary of state for Inter-American affairs, 1965–66

**Vidal, Gore** Essayist, novelist, playwright

**Vinson, Carl** D-GA, HR, 1914–65; chairman, Committee on Armed Services, 1949–53 and 1955–65

**Vinson, Fred** Chief justice of the Supreme Court, 1946–53; secretary of the treasury, 1945–46

**Volpe, John** R-MA, Secretary of transportation, 1969–73; governor, 1965–69 and 1961–63

**Vournas, George "Vasso"** Washington DC lawyer; president of the American Hellenic Educational Progressive Association; close friend of Pearson

**Vournas, Helen** Wife of George Vournas

**Wadsworth, James Wolcott, Jr.** R-NY, HR, 1933–51; senator, 1915–27

**Wagner, Robert F., Jr.** D-NY, U.S. ambassador to Spain, 1968–69; mayor of New York City, 1954–65; son of U.S. senator Robert F. Wagner Sr.

**Waldo, Thayer** Journalist

**Waldrop, Frank** Journalist and author; managing editor, *Washington Times-Herald*, 1948–53

**Walker, John "Johnny," III** Art historian; director, National Gallery of Art, 1956–69; married to Margaret Gwendolyn Mart "Margie" Drummond

**Wallace, George** D-AL, Governor, 1983–87, 1971–79, and 1963–67; presidential nominee for the American Independent Party, 1968

**Wallace, Henry** D-IA, Progressive Party presidential nominee, 1948; secretary of commerce, 1945–46; vice president of the United States, 1941–45; secretary of agriculture, 1933–40

**Wallace, Lurleen** D-AL, Governor, 1967–68 (succeeding her husband, George, who under state law could not serve consecutive terms)

**Wallenberg, Leo** American journalist

**Walter, Francis Eugene** D-PA, HR, 1933–63

**Walton, William** Painter and friend of John F. Kennedy; chairman, U.S. Commission of Fine Arts, 1963–71

**Ward, Barbara** Economist and writer

**Warren, Earl** R-CA, Chief justice of the U.S. Supreme Court, 1953–69; governor, 1943–53

**Warren, Nina** Wife of Chief Justice Earl Warren

**Washington, Walter** D-DC, Mayor, 1975–79 (first elected mayor since 1871); member, Washington DC Commission, 1967–74 (appointed); first African American chief executive of a major U.S. city

**Watson, Thomas, Jr.** CEO, IBM Corporation, 1956–71; president, Boy Scouts of America, 1964–68

**Watson, W. Marvin** U.S. postmaster general, 1968–69; White House appointments secretary, 1963–68

**Weaver, Robert C.** Secretary of housing and urban development, 1966–68

**Weisl, Edwin L., Jr.** Assistant attorney general, 1967–69 (Civil Division) and 1965–67 (Lands Division)

**Weisl, Edwin L., Sr.** Longtime unofficial advisor to Lyndon Johnson; senior partner in New York law firm Simpson, Thacher & Bartlett

**Welles, Benjamin** Journalist and son of B. Summer Welles and his first wife, Esther "Hope" Slater

**Welles, B. Sumner** Undersecretary of state, 1937–43

**Welles, Harriett** Wife of B. Sumner Welles

**Welsh, Edward** Executive secretary, National Aeronautics and Space Council

**Wessin y Wessin, Elías** Dominican Republic air force general who led coup to oust the Juan Bosch government in 1963

**Westmoreland, William** U.S. Army general (four stars); head of U.S. Military Assistance Command, Vietnam, 1964–June 1968, then U.S. Army chief of staff through 1972

**Weymouth, Elizabeth "Lally"** Daughter of Philip and Katherine Graham

**Wheeler, Burton K.** D-MT, Senator, 1923–47; 1924 nominee for vice president on Robert LaFollette's Progressive Party ticket

**Wheeler, Earle Gilmore "Bus"** U.S. Army general; chairman, Joint Chiefs of Staff, 1964–70; U.S. Army chief of staff, 1962–64

**Wheeler, John N. "Jack"** Journalist, author; headed the North American Newspaper Alliance, 1930–66 (syndicate that distributed Pearson's column)

**White, Byron "Whizzer"** Associate justice of the U.S. Supreme Court, 1962–93; U.S. deputy attorney general, 1961–62; professional football player, 1938, 1940–41

**White, Lee C.** Chairman, Federal Power Commission, 1966–69; special counsel to President Johnson, 1965–66 (associate, 1963–65); assistant special counsel to President Kennedy, 1961–63

**White, Walter** Head of the NAACP, 1931–55

**Whitney, John Hay "Jock"** Publisher, *New York Herald Tribune*, 1961–66; U.S. ambassador to the United Kingdom, 1957–61; prominent Republican

**Whittaker, Charles Evans** Associate justice of the U.S. Supreme Court, 1957–62

**Wicker, Thomas "Tom"** Journalist; *New York Times* columnist, 1966–92; author

**Wiggins, James Russell** U.S. ambassador to the United Nations, 1968–69; editorial page editor, *Washington Post*, 1955–68

**Wiley, Mary Margaret** Wife of Jack Valenti, 1962–2007; secretary to Lyndon Johnson

**Wilkins, Roy** Executive secretary of the NAACP, 1955–77

**Williams, Edward Bennett** Founder of the Williams and Connolly law firm

**Williams, Gerhard Mennen "Soapy"** D-MI, U.S. ambassador to the Philippines, 1968–69; assistant secretary of state for African affairs, 1961–66; governor, 1949–61

**Williams, John James** D-DE, Senator, 1947–70

**Willis, Edwin** D-LA, HR, 1949–69

**Willkie, Wendell** Republican Party nominee for president, 1940

**Wilson, Charles** Secretary of defense, 1953–57

**Wilson, Edith Galt** Second wife of widower President Wilson (m. 1915)

**Wilson, James Harold** Prime minister of the United Kingdom, 1964–70 and 1974–76

**Winchell, Walter** Syndicated newspaper columnist and radio/television commentator

**Windsor, Margaret** Younger sister of Queen Elizabeth II

**Wirtz, Alvin** Texas attorney; early supporter of Lyndon Johnson; undersecretary of the interior, 1940–41

**Wirtz, William Willard** Secretary of labor, 1962–69

**Witwer, Allan** Manager La Jolla Beach Hotel, La Jolla, California

**Wolff, Lester** D-NY, HR, 1965–81

**Woodring, Henry Hines** Secretary of war, 1936–40

**Wrightsman, Charles Bierer** Oil executive, patron of the arts, and friend of President Kennedy

**Wyman, Eugene "Gene"** Los Angeles attorney who was active in Democratic politics

**Yarborough, Ralph** D-TX, Senator, 1957–71

**Yorty, Samuel "Sam"** D-CA, Mayor of Los Angeles, 1961–73; HR, 1951–55

**Yost, Charles W.** U.S. ambassador to the United Nations, 1969–71; career diplomat

**Young, Stephen** D-OH, Senator, 1959–71

**Young, Whitney, Jr.** President, National Urban League, 1961–71

**Zhukov, Georgy** Minister of defense of the Soviet Union, 1955–57; deputy commander in chief, 1942–45

**Zhukov, Yuri** Columnist and editor at *Pravda*; chairman, USSR State Committee for Cultural Relations with Foreign Countries, 1957–67

# INDEX

*Throughout the index, "DP" is used to signify Drew Pearson.*

African Americans (*cont.*)
appointed as justice, 455; Meredith's university enrollment, 120; and poverty in California, 350; training programs for, 376, 552–53; voting power of, 395, 547; voting rights, 9, 222. *See also* civil rights movement; desegregation; race relations
African national independence movements, 2
Agnew, Spiro, 438, 602, 620, 656, 673, 697
Agriculture Department, 283–84
aid-to-education bill, 325
Aiken, George, 288, 472–73
airline strike, 419–20
air routes, 666, 704
AK-47/50, 658
Alabama: civil rights movement in, 81, 295, 297, 470; Meriwether in, 67–68; race riots in, 81, 181
Alaska, 249
Albania, 55, 108
Albert, Carl, 610, 669
Aldrin, Edwin "Buzz," 652
Alexander, Henry, 131
Alfonso, Perez, 85, 133
*Algemeen-Dagblad* (newspaper), 644
Algeria, 120, 480, 486–87, 510, 555
Alioto, Joseph, 603
Allen, George E., 43
Allen, Robert, 132
Alliluyeva, Svetlana, 455
Allon, Yigal, 653–54
Alphand, Hervé, 236
Alphand, Nicole, 235
Alsop, Joseph W., 334, 394
Alsop, Stewart, 36, 151
aluminum strike, 326
amendments (constitutional): Fifteenth Amendment, 4–5; Fifth Amendment, 641; Fourteenth Amendment, 249; Twenty-Fifth Amendment, 456; Twenty-Fourth Amendment, 222

American Friends Service Committee, xviii, 351
American Jewish Committee dinner, 396–97
Ames, Bill, 507
Anderson, Clinton, 37, 68, 106, 123
Anderson, Eugenie, 347
Anderson, Jack, 108; April 1960 interview with HHH, 11; on attempted Castro assassination, 470; Billie Sol Estes story, 135; Bob Kintner story, 479; Carlton Hotel room bug, 699; *The Case against Congress*, 607; *Congress on Trial* suit, 544; and the Dodd case, 370, 376, 380, 389–90, 394, 395, 397; and the Don Reynolds story, 231; on DP and Khrushchev, 128; on DP's impact, 704; on the Goldwater affair, 266–67; and Howard Smith, 226; interviewing Javits, 408; JFK assassination conspiracy theories, 470–72; JFK's funeral procession story, 215; on JFK's inexperience, 585; on *The Joe Pyne Show*, 490; on John McCormack, 459; and LBJ, 297, 420, 624; and LBJ's crime report, 269; on the MacArthur documents, 241; McNamara-Westmoreland story, 516; on the McSurely love letters, 687; on Nixon contributions, 697; on RFK's peace feeler attempts, 461; on Romney, 438; and Russell, 486; Salinger-McCarthy eavesdropping story, 581–82; on Soviet-Cuban relations, 214; steel strike tip, 2; taking over the column, 704; and Ted Kennedy, 655–56; on the Valenti-Moyers feud, 393; Vietnam stories, 343–44, 364, 405, 432; on the Walter Jenkins story, 266
Anderson, Martin, 263–64
Anderson, Robert B., 48, 49–50, 700

Andrade, Victor, 465
Anfuso, Victor L'Episcopo, 133–34
Annenberg, Walter, Jr., 679, 681
Annenberg, Walter, Sr., 681
anti-ballistic missile (ABM) system, 483, 496, 693–94, 697–98
antipoverty program, 534–35, 541, 581
Apollo 8, 648
Apollo 11, 649, 652
Apple, R. W. "Johnny," 516
Arab-Israeli relations: 1969 El Al hijacking, 678; Nixon on, 686–87; popular opinion of, 567–68; Six-Day War, 455, 480–81, 482, 484, 606, 703; Soviet Union and, 519, 555, 657; United Nations and, 519–20
Arafat, Yasser, 652
Argentina, 26, 27, 502
Argyll, 11th Duke of (Ian Campbell), 189–90
Arlington Zoning Board ruling, 133
Armistice Day (1963), 204
Armstrong, Neil, 652
Arnall, Ellis, 672
Arnold, Drew Pearson (DP's grandson), 505–6, 617
Arnold, Ellen Pearson (DP's daughter), 583
Arnold, Frances, 83, 85
Arnold, George (DP's son-in-law), 349–50, 566
Arnold, Thurman, 83, 85, 127, 398
Arnold, Thurman, Jr., 593
Arnon, Michael, 23
Artukovic, Andrija, 269
Arvid, Inga, 52
Ashdod, Israel, 367
Ashmore, Harry, 500
Asian Development Bank, 414
Atomic International Committee, 39
atomic weapons. *See* nuclear weapons
Attlee, Clement, 505
AT&T satellite giveaway bill, 134

Attwood, Simone, 142–43
Attwood, William, 142–43, 232, 247, 272–73
Auchincloss, Hugh, 133
Auchincloss, Janet, 620, 646
Australia, 528–29
Austria, 613
*autobahn* incident (1963), 199–200, 202
automotive industry, 125–26
Ayers, Bill, 163
Ayub Khan, 88, 111, 530

B-52 bomber, 328
Baggs, Bill, 500
Baikal, Lake, 695
Baker, George, 143, 163, 165, 209, 511, 649
Baker, Howard, 510
Baker, Robert "Bobby": and campaign contributions, 368–70; and Earle Clements, 368; investigation of, 230; and JFK, 293–94; and LBJ, 216, 226–27, 460; political ambitions, 311; sex scandal, 203; trial of, 231, 234, 441, 460
Baker, Wilson, 395
*Baker v. Carr*, 120, 477–78
Balaguer, Joaquín, 366
Ball, George W., 291, 312, 399, 409, 625; advising LBJ, 379, 513; and the Dominican crisis, 316–17; on Katanga, 118; and the Paris truce talks, 620; resignation of, 617; on Union Oil story, 626–27; on Vietnam riots, 389; on the Vietnam War, 341, 393–94, 424
*Baltimore Sun* (newspaper), xix
Bandaranaike, Sirimavo, 366
Bank Holding Corporation Act, 677
Barbados (West Indies), 291
Barnet, Richard J., 275, 337–38
Barnett, Ross, 120
Barrientos Ortuño, René, 417–18, 466

Cavanagh, Jerome, 381
CBS network, 700
Celebrezze, Anthony Joseph, 42, 128
Celeste, Frank P., 128
censorship (U.S. military), 123
Central Intelligence Agency (CIA). *See* CIA (Central Intelligence Agency)
Chafee, John, 668
Chalk, O. (Oscar) Roy, 213
Chambers, Albert, 562
Chandler, Dorothy Buffum, 448
Chandler, Norman, 448
Chandler, Otis, 448
Chapman, Oscar, 44
Charnay, David, 42–43
Chase National Bank, 16, 205
Chautauqua circuit, xviii
Chernoff, Howard, 132
Cheshire, Maxine, 517, 573
Chiang Kai-shek, 42, 81, 142, 383–84, 469
Chiari, Roberto, 225
Chicago, 421
Childs, Marquis, 89, 580
China: American perceptions of, 48; Cultural Revolution in, 366; in East Africa, 273; and India, 120, 149, 150, 151, 154, 156–57, 378; and Indonesia, 427–28; nuclear power of, 254, 259; and Pakistan, 352; relations with Poland, 356; relations with the U.S., 398, 399, 408, 425–26, 436, 499, 653; relations with USSR, 91, 183, 184, 214, 215, 293, 344, 381–82, 382–83, 432–33, 690, 692; six-month truce with USSR, 50; and Taiwan, 142; tensions with USSR, 11–12, 39, 55, 108, 109, 127, 137, 148, 150, 652; and the UN, 273–74, 364, 419, 437, 443–44; use of bribery by, 165–66; U.S. surplus food to, 132, 137–38; during the Vietnam War, 292, 327–28, 341, 344, 567, 569

China lobby, 42–43
Chotiner, Murray, 45
Chou En-lai. *See* Zhou Enlai
Christian, George, Jr., 528; as LBJ's press secretary, 450, 486, 492–93, 496, 554, 560, 576, 653–54; press briefings of, 514, 662; on the Reagan story, 508; on U.S.-Soviet relations, 596; on the USS *Pueblo* crisis, 540; during Vietnam, 526
Christopher, George, 377
Chrysler corporation, 552–53
Church, Frank, 291, 309, 344, 503–4, 641–42, 659
church-and-state separation, 72
Churchill, Randolph, 189, 389
Churchill, Winston, 178–79, 189, 286, 354, 409, 476, 676–77, 693
CIA (Central Intelligence Agency): and the AFL, 538; and Arabian Oil, 123; in Bolivia, 502; Castro assassination plot, 470–71; and the Cuban crisis, 79; DP on, 77; DP's briefing on Khrushchev, 103; Dry Tortugas Islands operation, 232; and the Freedom Fighter prisoners, 158; General Trudeau at, 123; and the Greek KYP, 548–49; and McCone, 132; in South Vietnam, 660
City Club (Cleveland) speech (1962), 128
Civil Aeronautics Board (CAB), 44
Civil Rights Act, 9, 279, 286, 336–37, 363, 547, 565–66, 588
civil rights movement: boycotts during, 284; and COFO, 264–65, 275–76; economic pressure used, 271–72; and education, 433; Eisenhower's impact on, 700; and fair housing, 588; Governor Wallace's opposition to, 161, 297; under JFK, 54; Justice Department in, 56, 249; LBJ's role in, 69–70, 209, 216; in McComb, 262; and NAACP,

civil rights movement (*cont.*)
275–76; under Nixon, 669–70, 671,
672; opposition to, 286; political
effects of, 184, 196, 202; political
office bonding issues, 528; race-
based marriage restrictions, 455;
riots during, 81, 280–81; San Francisco riots, 429; in Selma, 294–95;
and SNCC, 401; training programs,
214; violence during, 252, 280–81.
*See also* desegregation; King, Martin Luther, Jr.; race relations
Clark, Jim, 219
Clark, S. Joseph "Joe," 4, 5, 310, 501,
630
Clark, Thomas "Tom," 107
Clark, William Ramsey, 290, 508, 515,
545, 563, 663, 665
clean elections bill, 139
Clements, Earle, 32, 46, 66, 68, 146,
215–16, 368, 551, 637
Cleveland (OH), 597
Clifford, Clark, 536; affairs of, 47;
confirmation hearings, 539; diet
of, 538; and the DuPont tax deal,
311; on JFK's oil trust, 324; and LBJ,
510, 574; possible political appointments, 399, 524; as secretary of
defense, 682; during Vietnam, 358,
513–14, 589, 625, 649, 650, 667,
683, 688
coal miners' strike (1919), 351
COFO (Council of Federated Organizations), 264, 275–76, 280, 295
Cohen, Mickey, 626
Cohen, Sheldon S., 394, 561–62
Cohen, Wilbur, 558, 624
Cohn, Marcus, 527
college construction bill (1963), 214
Columbia, 115–16
communications satellite debate, 195
communism: American fear of, 141;
changes in, 237; in the Dominican
Republic, 316; and the domino

theory, 331–32; as JFK foreign
affairs issue, 88; labor propaganda
of, 55–56; in North Vietnam, 255; in
Venezuela, 113
Communist Party Congress, 108, 109,
110
*Concord Monitor* (newspaper), 451
Condon, Edward U., 656
Congo, Republic of, 37, 38, 118–19, 122,
272–73, 276–77
Congress (U.S.): and civil rights, 671;
Gulf of Tonkin Resolution, 223,
374–75, 417; influence of lob-
bies on, 597; LBJ on vacations of,
590–91; seniority system in, 535;
Urban Coalition project, 541. *See
also* amendments (constitutional);
*senate committees*
*Congress on Trial* (Pearson and Ander-
son), 544
Connally, John, 57, 59–60, 84, 213, 227,
442, 574–75, 608–9, 610
Connole, William, 9–10
consular treaty (U.S.-Soviet), 199, 382,
460, 467, 475, 483, 495–96, 503–4
Cook, William Mercer, 429
Cooke, Alistair, 328, 333
Cooper, Glenn, 410
Cooper, John Sherman, 197, 235, 396,
406, 502
Corcoran, Thomas G., 38, 82, 452
Cordela, Garcia, 61
Corman, James "Jim," 508
*Corpus Christi Caller-Times* (newspa-
per), 241
Corrupt Practices Act, 227, 629
cortisone, JFK's use of, 66
Costa Rica, 118–19
Council of Federated Organizations
(COFO), 264, 275–76, 280, 295
Courshon, Arthur, 368
Cowans, Byron, 204
Cowles, Mike, 167
Cox, Wendell, 421

Cranston, Alan, 236, 693
Creole Oil Company, 112
Crnobrnja, Bogdan, 501–2
Cronkite, Walter, 532
Cuba: and Che Guevara, 455–56; DP travels through (1961), 65; Guantanamo, 5–6, 232, 233; missile crisis, 120–21, 147–48, 150–54, 169, 174–75, 667; relations with USSR, 184, 214; Russian arms in, 143, 146, 168, 268; U.S. ambassadors to, 35; U.S. relations with, 29, 158, 160, 224, 678; and U.S.-Soviet relations, 206–7, 234–35. *See also* Bay of Pigs invasion
Cuneo, Ernest "Ernie," 66–67, 188, 509, 608; at the 1964 Democratic convention, 250; and the Dodd case, 395, 411; on the Geneva summit conference, 9; on the Kennedy family, 583–84, 609; on LBJ and the press, 430; on MLK Jr.'s assassination, 560
Cuneo, Margaret, 9, 66–67
Cushing, Richard, 58, 625
Czechoslovakia: 1968 Soviet invasion of, 532, 606–7, 611, 613–15, 620–21, 688; as arms supplier to North Vietnam, 569; democratic movement, 546, 556; improving U.S. relations, 4, 295–96; materials exchange with Poland, 127; removal of the Iron Curtain, 560

D'Alesandro, Thomas J. "Tommy," Jr., 32
Daley, Richard J. "Dick," 421, 559–60
Daniel, Price, 508
Darby, Harry, 702
D'Arze, Guevara, 502
Davie, Eugenie Mary (Mrs. Preston), 545
Davies, John P., Jr., 671–72, 686
Davis, Sammy, Jr., 276

Dawson, William "Bill," 456–57
Dayan, Moshe, 481
*The Day the Earth Stood Still* (film), ix
Dean, Arthur, 134, 177–78, 513
Dean, Russell, 131
Debré, Michel, 621
defense contractors, 69–70, 99, 101–2
de Gaulle, Charles, 331–32; at the 1960 Paris conference, 21; on the Berlin crisis, 82; and DP, 12; in Germany, 176; and NATO, 366; political career of, 236, 579, 581; resignation of, 652; security issues, 34; during the student strikes, 579; and Vietnam peace talks, 570, 578; and Warren, 672–73; in World War II, 354, 409–10, 476
DeLoach, C. "Deke," 380, 429–30, 578–79
Delta Ministry (National Council of Churches), 377
demilitarized zone (DMZ), 420
Democratic National Convention (1960), 30–31, 31–32
Democratic National Convention (1964), 250–51
Democratic National Convention (1968), 533, 608–10
Denmark, 630–31
desegregation: of Alabama schools, 470; Big Brothers' January 1962 dinner, 122–23; in Birmingham, 127; Congress's role in, 671; Eisenhower's impact on, 700; federal funding setbacks to, 617–18; Governor Wallace on, 161; in McCombs, 272; and Meredith's university enrollment, 120; South Carolina textile mills case, 699; as unconstitutional, 54; of the White House Photographers Association, 73. *See also* civil rights movement; race relations
Detroit race riots, 455

Dewey, Thomas "Tom," 2–3, 551, 569, 600, 641
Diem, Ngo Dinh, 81, 202, 489–90
Dill, Clarence, 418, 694–95
Dillon, Clarence Douglas, 16, 49–50, 51, 70, 86, 131, 177, 305–6, 513
Dirksen, Everett: at the 1968 Republican National Convention, 600; and the civil rights bill, 547; cloture petition of, 251; death of, 653; and desegregation, 699; and the Dominican crisis, 317; and LBJ, 234, 468; McCone vote, 124; on a Senate code of ethics, 490; and Vietnam election observers, 498; and Warren, 674
DiSalle, Michael, 42, 47, 128
disarmament: and China, 361, 364; Geneva conference (1955), 654–55; Geneva conference (1960), 28; Geneva conference (1962), 132; importance to Khrushchev, 17; obstacles to, 127, 275; and U.S. munitions production, 35. *See also* nuclear weapons
District of Columbia (DC). *See* Washington DC
Dobrynin, Anatoly: Agnes Meyer's dinner for, 169; on the consular treaty, 503–4; and the Cuban missile crisis, 121; "Dobrynin pause," 432; doing the Twist, 131; on improving U.S.-Soviet relations, 239; on Khrushchev's removal, 267–68; and LBJ, 260, 335; meetings with DP, 137–39, 140; and Nixon, 679–80; showing opposition to U.S., 304; skills of, 580; on U.S.-German relations, 224–25, 244; on U.S.-Soviet relations, 177–78, 234–35, 435–36, 554–55; and the Vietnam War, 289, 296–97, 328–30, 335, 356, 435–36, 458–59
Dobrynin, Irina, 169, 224–25, 580

Docking, George, 553
dockworkers strike, 326
Dodd, Grace Murphy, 411
Dodd, Thomas: in 1964 election, 250; investigation of, 376, 389–91, 394, 402, 419, 430, 477; and Katanga, 169, 401; and Klein, 370, 444; libel suit against DP, 380, 395, 397, 410–11, 452, 679; questioning Gen. Wheeler, 542; Senate Ethics hearings, 395–96, 406, 408–9, 467–68, 482, 485–86
dollar crisis, 49–50, 550
Dominican Republic, 82–83, 179, 313–18, 319–22, 324–25, 340, 366
Donohue, F. Joseph "Jiggs," 74–76
Donovan, John, 544–45, 610–13
Douglas, Donald, 370
Douglas, Emily, 294
Douglas, Helen Gahagan, 630
Douglas, Mercedes, 176
Douglas, Paul, 57, 68, 251, 438
Douglas, William O. "Bill": Chinese visa, 399; on the CIA in South Vietnam, 660; and the civil rights movement, 249; divorce of, 163, 176; health of, 592; on JFK's cabinet, 51; as justice, 154, 155, 185–86, 631; on the State Department, 671–72
Douglas Aircraft, 10, 157
Dowling, Walter, 17–18
draft (military), 342–43, 356, 404, 512
Dry Tortugas Islands operation, 232
*Dr. Zhivago* (film), 460
Dubček, Alexander, 532, 556, 607, 608, 614, 615
Dubinsky, David, 292, 337
DuBridge, Alvin, 641
Duda, Karel, 245, 281
Dugger, Ronnie, 555
Duke, Angier Biddle, 143
Duke, Doris, 387–88, 390
Duke, Robin, 172
Dulles, Allen, 51, 103

Dulles, John Foster, 42, 159, 238, 342, 499, 637, 654–55, 672, 686
Duncan, John, 122, 136
Dungan, Ralph, 216
DuPont-GM tax deal, 293, 311
Duvalier, François, 179

Early, Steve, 148
East Germany: access restrictions in, 89, 588; and the Berlin Wall, 54; and Czechoslovakia's democratic movement, 556; increased sentiment for unification of, 338; international recognition of, 17–18; and the invasion of Czechoslovakia, 606–7; Oder-Neisse line, 192, 305; push of farm collectivization, 14; Soviet position on, 89, 91–92, 358. *See also* Berlin crisis (1961)
Eastland, James, 37, 130, 699
Eastman, James, 9
Eaton, Cyrus, 300
Eaton, Frederick, 28
Eban, Abba, 248, 480
Eden, Anthony, 354, 409, 479, 691
Ed Foley Big Brothers dinner (1961), 74–76
*The Ed Sullivan Show*, 223
Edwards, Clyda, 548
Edwards, William Donlonn "Don," 548, 552
Egbert, Sherwood, 125
Egypt: food aid to, 400, 407; Nasser in, 561–62; relations with Israel, 478–79, 510, 567–68, 605, 656–57; relations with USSR, 555, 596, 687; in the Six-Day War, 480–84, 486; U.S. relations under LBJ, 276–77
Eichmann, Adolf, 23, 24–25, 26, 120
Eisenhower, David, 652, 673
Eisenhower, Dwight D. "Ike": at the 1955 Geneva conference, 654–55; during the 1960 election, 33, 44;

at the 1960 Paris conference, 2, 19, 20–23, 21–23; on the Bay of Pigs invasion, 78–79; cancellation of Japan trip (1960), 25–26; at Churchill's funeral, 677; death of, 652, 699; and de Gaulle, 354; DP's characterization of, 240; extramarital affairs of, 701–2, 703; funeral of, 701–2; impact on space exploration, 73; and JFK, 51, 58, 121; legacy of, 585, 700–701; on military censorship, 123; and Nixon, 332, 673, 702; religious beliefs of, 701; and Rockefeller, 3, 23; and Truman's library, 693; UN speech (1960), 41; and the Vietnam War, 430, 499, 513; work habits of, 660. *See also* Eisenhower administration
Eisenhower, Julie Nixon, 652, 673
Eisenhower, Mamie, 701
Eisenhower administration: defense funding, 35; and the dollar crisis, 47–48, 49–50; do-nothing program of, 4; role in Bay of Pigs invasion, 54; scandals of, 7; U.S.-Soviet relations during, 654–55; Wiental on lying of the, 28. *See also* Eisenhower, Dwight D. "Ike"
El Al Airline, 657, 678
election of 1950, 42–43
election of 1952, 332
election of 1960: Democratic convention, 30–32; Democratic strategies, 3, 5, 7; Hughes loan story, 43–44, 45; Humphrey in, 5, 11, 29; JFK in, 36–37, 45; possible vote fraud, 48; Republican convention, 32–34; results of, 1, 46–47; role of religion on, 6; role of television in, 1; televised debates in, 1, 42
election of 1964, 202, 222, 250–54, 256, 259, 263–67, 269–71
election of 1966, 438

election of 1968, 546, 551–52, 553,
556, 557, 602–3, 607, 616; African
American votes in, 547; debates in,
582; Democratic National Conven-
tion, 608–10; Greek fundraising
during, 620; Humphrey announcing
candidacy, 573; LBJ's withdrawal
from, 558–60; Little Lyn campaign-
ing in, 623; Republican National
Convention, 600–602; results of, 533,
629–30, 632–33, 640; RFK's announc-
ing candidacy, 549–50, 551, 587
Ellender, Allen Joseph, 37, 130, 131
Ellington, Buford, 610
Ellston, Dean, 203
El Paso Natural Gas, 695, 697, 698
Emmerich, Oliver, 271–72
Engelhard, Charles, 31
*Engel v. Vitale*, 120
Engle, Clair, 50
*Enterprise* (ship), 512
Erdman, Robert, 183–84, 472
Erhard, Ludwig, 207, 221, 439
Erickson, Alfred, 110
espionage, 17, 192–93. *See also* U-2
incident
Estensorro, Paz, 465
Estes, Billy Sol, 6–7, 34, 135–36
Ethiopia, 246
Evans, Ahmed, 597
Evans, Courtney, 581
Evans, Rowland, 507, 521, 662
Evers, Charles, 275–76, 280, 547, 549
extramarital affairs: of Bill Douglas,
176; Bobby Baker's role in, 203;
effect of JFK's, 163; of Eisenhower,
701–2, 703; of Harriman, 189; of
JFK, 36, 45, 47, 51–53, 66–67, 80,
163, 176, 198, 203–4, 451, 622, 629;
of the Kennedy family, 423, 453,
524, 564, 584, 609; of LBJ, 136, 147,
203, 238–39; of MLK Jr., 562, 571–
72; of Phil Graham, 167–68, 178; of
Rockefeller, 527

*Face the Nation*, 544, 627
Factor, Jake "The Barber," 158
Fairbanks, Douglas, Jr., 189, 190
Fairless, Ben, 64
Falcón Briceño, Marcos, 61–62, 113–
14, 172
Fanfani, Amintore, 85, 133–34, 487
Fannin, Paul, 391
farm bill, 130, 141
farm price supports, 283–84
Farrell, Ray, 515
Fascell, Dante, 129, 432
Fath, Creekmore, 43, 51–52, 549
Faubus, Orval, 618
FBI. *See* Federal Bureau of Investiga-
tion (FBI)
FCC. *See* Federal Communications
Commission (FCC)
Federal Bureau of Investigation (FBI):
and Borkin's record, 593; and the
Dodd case, 391, 394, 430; espio-
nage cases, 193; investigation of
DP and Anderson, 380; and MLK
Jr.'s affair, 572; MLK Jr.'s assassina-
tion, 578–79; and Oswald, 470–71;
and the Warren Commission, 442;
wiretapping of, 203, 441–42, 579,
581. *See also* Hoover, J. Edgar
Federal Communications Commis-
sion (FCC), 101–2, 288, 527, 588–89,
593–94
Federal Power Commission (FPC),
288–89, 460
Federenko, Nicolai T., 347, 437, 479,
480, 484, 519
Fejos, Paul, 52
Feldman, Myer "Mike," 71, 654, 697
Fergusson, Wilber G., 612–13
Fern, Ben, 418, 467
Ferrer, José María Hipólito Figueres,
315–16, 321
Ferrie, David, 470–72
Fielding, Roman, 220
Fifteenth Amendment, 4–5

Fifth Amendment, 641
Finca Vigia (Lookout Farm), 54
Finch, Robert "Bob," 670
Findlay, Paul, 336
fish conservation, 503
Florida, 265–66, 368
Foley, Edward, 75
food programs, 137, 142, 207, 388, 400, 407
Ford, Gerald R. "Jerry," 163, 336, 449, 515
Ford, Henry II, 336, 540, 541, 665
Ford Foundation investigation, 445
Foreign Affairs Committee, 180, 697
Foreman, Clark, 89
Forman, James, 401
Forrestal, James "Jim," x, 107, 392, 498–99, 517
Fortas, Abraham "Abe," 69, 357, 675; advisor to LBJ during Vietnam, 510, 513; appointment hearings, 596, 674; and the Baker case, 216, 230; chief justice appointment, 594–95; and the Dominican crisis, 315; as justice, 398; as possible Court appointee, 590, 591–92, 605; vote on the A-bomb secret, 106–7
Foster, William C. "Bill," 149, 654–55
Fourteenth Amendment, 249
Fowler, Henry "Joe," 312, 440, 441, 632
Fox, Yolanda, 376
FPC. See Federal Power Commission (FPC)
France: 1968 student strikes in, 579; and disarmament, 28; DP's trip to (1965), 353–54; Merci Train, 535–36; and NATO, 404; protests in, 532; relations with U.S., 621, 690; student riots in, 581
Franco, Francisco, 38
Frankel, Max, 324
Frankfurter, Felix, 52, 127–28, 144, 155, 375, 478

Frasier, George, 453–54
Frear, Allen, 311
Frederica (queen of Greece), 228–30, 230–31
Free Berlin broadcasting station, 611
Freedom Fighters (Cuban), 157–58, 160
Freeman, Janet, 130
Freeman, Orville, 29, 130, 135–36, 217–18, 287, 377, 378, 388, 557–58
Free Speech movement, 279
Frelinghuysen, Marian, 163
Friedan, Betty, 366
Friedman, Milton "Milt," 26, 27, 484–85
Friedmann, Mrs. Tuvia, 24–25
Friedmann, Tuvia, 23, 24–25, 26, 27
Friendly, Alfred, 6, 211, 220, 233, 269
Friendly, Henry, 641
Friendship Train, xix, 5, 88, 353, 536, 665
Fritchey, Clayton, 109, 428, 499; and Adlai Stevenson, 137, 151, 339; Adriatic coast tour (1962), 142–43; on the Cuban Freedom Fighter situation, 158; on the Dodd case, 396; on Nixon, 638; and Phil Graham, 179; on the Vietnam War, 273, 451
Fulbright, J. William "Bill": ABM hearings, 697; on the Bay of Pigs, 79; criticism of de Gaulle, 331; debate with Rusk, 554; DP's characterization of, 237–38; on the foreign aid bill, 278; on Goldberg, 631, 640; on JFK's leadership, 99–100; and LBJ, 48, 374, 385; on LBJ's Philippines trip, 427; on the McCone vote, 123, 124; as potential secretary of state, 53; on quality of U.S. ambassadors, 121; and Richardson, 659; on troops in Germany, 496; on the Vietnam War, 305–7, 328, 374–75, 414, 416–17, 510–11, 512
Furtseva, Yekaterina Alexeyevna, 107, 178, 303

Gabaldon, Arnoldo, 112
Gaddafi, Muammar, 653
Gagarin, Yuri, 73
Gaitskell, Hugh, 126
Galbraith, John Kenneth "Ken,"
    156–57, 159, 196–97, 209, 392, 421,
    425–26, 592
Galt, Edith, 650
Gandhi, Indira, 157, 366, 379–80, 419
Gardner, Joan, 235, 236, 536, 581, 629
Gardner, John William, 580
Garrigues, Antonio, 192
Garrison, Jim, 470–72
Gates, Tom, 403
Gavin, James M., 374, 413
Gemini, 351
General Aniline and Film Corpora-
    tion, 583
General Dynamics, 369–70
General Electric, 101–2, 432, 694–95
General Motors, 53, 534
General Motors–DuPont tax deal,
    293, 311
Geneva Summit Conference, 9,
    654–55
genocide convention, 397, 398
Germany: Acheson's policy on, 217;
    DP on post-war Germany, 14–18;
    increased sentiment for unifica-
    tion of, 338; LBJ on reunification
    of, 243; military bases in Spain, 18;
    Oder-Neisse line, 192, 305; U.S.
    policy toward, 16; U.S. relations
    with, 176, 242–43, 244, 338; and
    U.S.-Soviet relations, 200, 207;
    U.S. troops in, 224–25; U.S. troop
    withdrawals, 241–42, 496. See also
    Berlin crisis (1961)
germ warfare, 338
Geyelin, Philip, 580
Gibbons, Harold, 213, 564
Gibson, George, 276
Gilpatrick, Ross, 186
Giraud, Henri, 476

Gizycka, Felicia Patterson (DP's first
    wife), xix, 181
Glass, Andy, 485
Glassboro conferences, 488, 491–95
Goa (India), 117–18
Goldberg, Arthur, 70; American Jew-
    ish Committee dinner honoring,
    396–97; and Bill Douglas, 185–86;
    on China in the UN, 443–44; on
    the civil rights movement, 249;
    and disarmament, 364; and
    Humphrey's 1968 campaign, 619;
    on JFK administration, 86–87,
    136; on JFK's conflicts with DP,
    145–46; on JFK's foreign policy,
    86, 126–27; on the Kennedy
    family, 464; in the Labor Depart-
    ment, 55–56, 125–26, 143, 145; and
    LBJ, 384–86, 559; on McNamara's
    resignation, 520–21; on Near East
    issues, 441, 479, 482, 519–20;
    and the pope on Vietnam, 413; as
    possible interim Court appointee,
    478, 631, 636, 640, 641–42, 643,
    644, 675; and the *Pueblo* crisis,
    540, 543; resignation from UN,
    572, 578, 592; on Rusk, 108–9;
    during the Six-Day War, 480; and
    the steel strike, 2, 131, 133; on the
    Supreme Court, 154–55; Supreme
    Court appointment, 143, 144–45;
    on Vietnam, 341–42, 343, 345–47,
    367, 373–74, 436–37, 468–69, 567;
    wanting to resign, 518–19, 524–25;
    work with the UN, 344–47, 355–57,
    397–400, 519
Goldberg, Dorothy, 86, 125, 143, 185,
    519
gold drain, 550
Golden, Harry, 14–15
Goldfine, Bernard, 699
Goldsborough, Arthur, 32
Goldwater, Barry, 33, 99, 222, 233, 253,
    255, 257, 270

Gomez, Juan Vicente, 61

Gomułka, Władysław, 261–62, 373, 682

Goodpaster, Andrew, 413, 654, 685

Goodwin, Richard "Dick," 143, 371, 421, 440, 568–69, 573

Gordon, John "Jack," 110, 128–29, 368, 414

Gordon, Kermit, 283

Gordon, Lincoln, 627

Gore, Albert, Sr., 56–57, 172

Gorton, John, 620, 623

Gosset, William T., 636

Gottlieb, Sandy, 275

Gottwald, Klement, 614

Graham, Donald "Donny," 330

Graham, Katherine "Kay," 193, 229, 427; assassination plots ad, 219; and the Baker scandal, 216; at Bobby Kennedy's funeral, 588; on the California credibility gap, 507; conflict with Marie Ridder, 143; health of, 71–72; and Jackie Kennedy, 198–99; on LBJ and the press, 360, 377, 502; on the Luci Johnson story, 371; marital troubles of, 166, 179; marriage of, 127, 452; and the *Post*, 347–48; on the UN, 580; on the Vietnam War, 330–31

Graham, Philip: on Connally column, 57; death of, 193; extramarital affairs of, 163, 167–68, 178; health problems of, 164–65, 175, 452; on the Hughes loan story, 45, 52–53; and Jackie Kennedy, 198; marital troubles of, 179–80; marriage of, 127; and *Newsweek*, 108; on the *Post*, 44; purchase of *Newsweek* magazine, 72; on RFK as attorney general, 52; wife's TB scare, 71–72

Grand Coulee Dam, 694–95

Grand Forks (ND), 694

Gray, Horace, 597

Great Britain: British embassy garden party, 139–40; declining power of, 9; labor strikes in, 692; Near East resolution proposed by, 519–20; political sex scandals in, 187, 189–90; relations with U.S., 187–88; during the Vietnam War, 330

Greece, 476, 548–49

Green, Dan, 518

Green, William J. "Bill," Jr., 213, 219

Greenspun, Hank, 69

Gregory, Gene, 671–72

Gregory, Richard "Dick," 276, 280–81, 282, 292, 348–50, 401, 429, 561

Griffin, Robert "Bob," 631, 640

Grimillion, Jack P. F., 619

Gromyko, Andrei: at the 1961 Communist Congress, 109; on Cold War tensions, 198; on disarmament talks, 197, 595; impact on U.S. elections, 206; and LBJ, 431, 432–33, 434; meetings with JFK, 72, 107; relations with U.S., 182, 303, 439; on trouble in Europe, 426–27; on U.S. troop reductions, 199–200, 224; on Vietnam, 356, 364, 446, 474–75

Gruening, Dorothy, 665

Gruening, Ernest, 4, 8, 130, 344, 531, 664, 665

Gruenther, Alfred M., 700

Grumman (contractor), 370

Guantanamo naval base, 232, 233

*Guardian* (newspaper), 644

Guerrero, Perez, 112–13

Guest, Lilly, 443

Guevara, Ernesto "Che," 455–56, 502

Guggenheim, Harry, 151

Gulf of Tonkin incident, 223, 549

Gulf of Tonkin Resolution, 223, 374–75, 417

Gunther, John, 443

Guthman, Ed, 215

Gutierrez, Felix, 79

Guy, George, 252, 262, 272

Humphrey, Hubert H. (*cont.*)
of, 622; and McCone, 124; on
McNamara's resignation, 520–21;
in Minnesota, 557; negative press,
361–62, 698; at Nixon's inauguration, 664; political achievements
of, 599; political organization of,
638; on post-VP plans, 639–40;
on problems with staff, 371–72;
public perception of, 586; on the
*Pueblo* crisis, 539–40; RFK-MLK Jr.
wiretapping story, 581; on Supreme
Court vacancy, 637–38, 643; on
U.S.-Soviet relations, 434–35;
as vice president, 433–34; vice
presidential nomination, 250; and
Vietnam peace talks, 545, 566–67;
and the Vietnam War, 305–6, 329,
331–32, 462–63, 500, 619, 634;
White House dinner honoring,
537–39
Hungary, 204–5, 233, 606–7, 615
Hunt, Lois, 229
Huntley, Bill, 269
Huong, Tran van, 589
Hussein bin Talal (king of Jordan), 11,
248–49, 480, 482, 510, 556, 703
Hutschnecker, Arnold, 628–29, 633–
34, 650

Ickes, Harold, 130, 319, 448
Ickes, Jane, 294
Illinois Central Railroad, 666
Imbert, Antonio, 322
Imbrie, Katherine (Mrs. Robert), 3
Immigration Service scandals, 515
*Independence* (ship), 506, 507–8, 509,
517
India: conflicts with China, 120,
149, 150, 151, 154, 156–57; Indira
Gandhi as PM, 366, 379–80; as a
neutral nation, 159; recognition
of East Germany, 18; U.S. aid to,
352, 378–79, 383–84, 388; and the

Vietnam War, 327–28, 379; Voice of
America treaty, 196–97
Indonesia, 277, 282, 375, 427–28, 463,
680–81
Inozemisey, Nikolai, 205–8, 301
integration. *See* desegregation
international fishing limit, 503
International Platform Association
(IPA), 344, 418–19, 597–99
Iran, 2, 111–12
Iraq, 2
Ireland, 190
Irene, Princess of Greece, 228–29
iron ore industry, 63–64
Israel: 1968 El Al hijacking, 678; Axel
Springer's work for, 612; bombing
of Beirut's airport, 650–51; con-
flicts with Jordan, 439, 441, 556;
DP's 1964 trip to, 247–49; DP's
1965-1966 trip to, 364–65, 367; and
Egypt, 407; and Eichmann, 24–25,
120; Meir as PM, 652; relations
with Arab nations, 510, 519–20,
555, 567–68, 605, 656–57, 686–87,
703; Six-Day War, 455, 478–79,
480–85, 486, 493, 606; Suez
conflict, 506; Syrian–Sea of Galilee
incident, 137
Italy, 133–34, 191–92, 530, 681
Ivory Coast, 352–53

Jackson (MS), 528
Jackson, Henry "Scoop," 663, 687
Jacobson, Jake, 377–78
Janeway, Eliot, 524
Japan: and Douglas Aircraft, 10;
Eisenhower's cancelled trip to,
25–26; impact of Vietnam War on,
463; Mansfield's popularity in, 472;
Nehru on power of, 378; role in
Asia, 642; Tokyo riots, 24, 26
Javits, Jacob "Jake," 68, 89–90, 124,
172, 408, 418
Javits, Marian, 89–90

Jenkins, Herb, 563

Jenkins, Walter, x–xi, 227, 230, 241, 256, 257, 259, 264, 266, 667–68

Jensen, Robert C. "Bob," 371

Jewish Americans, 325, 396–97, 457

*The Joe Pyne Show*, 490

Johnson, Claudia Alta "Lady Bird" (LBJ's wife), 60, 164, 239; 1962 Near East tour, 147; 1964 dinner for queen of Greece, 228–30; alleged speeding of, 241; beautification program of, 287–88, 661; on Bess's efficiency, 593; at Eisenhower's funeral, 702; and LBJ's 1964 campaign, 253–54; and LBJ's election withdrawal, 571, 574–75; on LBJ's health, 644–45; on Lynda Bird, 396; on Lyndon's affair, 136; memory of, 285; and Mme Chiang Kai-shek, 81; plans after office, 647–48; TV wealth of, 263–64; on White House experiences, 645–46

Johnson, Louis, 391–92

Johnson, Luci Baines (LBJ's daughter), 228, 323, 386; campaigning for Humphrey, 623; DP's interview with, 645–48; family of, 497; fiancé's transfer, 371, 374; *Life* story on, 253; religion of, 335–36; wedding of, 412, 645

Johnson, Lynda Bird. *See* Robb, Lynda Bird (LBJ's daughter)

Johnson, Lyndon B. (LBJ): abusive behavior of, 691; achievements of, 279–80, 648, 661, 675–76; and Adlai Stevenson, 232; after leaving office, 592–93, 647, 660–61, 662, 676, 680, 693, 698; and Agnes Meyer, 638; air route awards, 666; American Jewish Committee dinner (1966), 396–97; Asia-Pacific tour (1966), 430–31; assuming presidency, 209; awarding the Medal of Freedom, 665; Big

Brothers' dinner (1962), 123; and Bill Green, 219; on Bill Moyers, 444–45; and Bobby Baker, 216, 227, 231, 234, 293–94, 460; and Brown & Root, 135, 237; and Charlie Marsh, 618; and civil rights, 69–70, 209, 294–95, 297, 336–37, 455, 553, 565–66, 671; on congressional vacations, 590–91; criticism of, 234, 236–37, 667–68; on the Cuban crisis, 77; daily routine of, 308, 318–19; and Dean Rusk, 342; and de Gaulle, 331, 476; and the Dodd case, 394; DP's relationship with, 58, 66, 71, 277–78, 285, 290, 310, 312, 315, 342, 385–86, 506, 635, 691; on draft protests, 356; and Dubinsky, 337; and Eisenhower, 23, 26; at Eisenhower's funeral, 702; election of 1960, 6, 24, 32, 46; election of 1964, 222, 250–54, 256, 259, 263–67, 269–71; election of 1966, 438; election of 1968, 517, 551–52, 556–57, 607–9, 616, 619, 632; election of 1968 withdrawal, 532, 558–60, 574–77; extramarital affairs of, 136, 147, 203, 238–39; family of, 335–36, 412, 648; and FDR Jr.'s resignation, 536; on Fulbright, 48, 53; Glassboro conference, 491–95; as "guest chairman" of Democratic caucus, 56–57; health of, 69, 286, 354–55, 360–61, 362, 439, 440–41, 550, 574, 644–45; and the Hoffa case, 213–14; human side of, 312–13; and Humphrey, 282–83, 284, 362–64, 433–35, 462–64, 521, 622, 693; inauguration of, 284–85; and Indira Gandhi, 379; and J. Edgar Hoover, 402; and JFK, 35, 70, 186; JFK assassination commission, 212; Justice Department investigations of, 7–8; on Katzenbach, 290; on the MacArthur documents,

Johnson, Lyndon B. (LBJ) (*cont.*)
240–41; and McNamara, 520, 521–23; memory of, 241; Mora luncheon (1967), 487–88; on NBC's wiretapping, 625; Near East tour (1962), 146–47; and Nixon, 437–38, 602–3, 633, 635, 640, 664; on oil industry, 319, 323–24; and Phil Graham, 164–65; political organization of, 638; popularity of, 243, 295, 327, 366, 419, 441, 472–73, 501, 532; presidential library, 639, 661, 680; press relations, 328, 332–34, 360, 416, 430, 448, 502, 514–15, 662; and the *Pueblo* crisis, 540; and RFK, 186, 215–16, 550, 554, 557, 586; and riots following MLK Jr.'s death, 561; Rostow as advisor to, 570; round-the-world trip (1967), 528–31; Salinger's defense of, 421; Southeast Asia trip (1961), 84; and the space race, 73–74; speaking abilities of, 240, 431–32, 461; and Stanton, 3; State of the Union address (1965), 281; televised press conferences of, 240–41; Texas ranch of, 490–91, 496–98; TFX contract, 186, 369–70; on tourism, 287–88; trip to Panama (1964), 223; on TV and crime, 625; and Tyler Abell, 34, 218–19; and Udall, 665, 668; and the UN, 334–35; and Valenti, 412–13; as vice president, 86, 250; and Walter Jenkins, 257, 259, 264; and Warren, 377, 381, 644, 673–75; White House dinners, 172, 228–30, 537–39. *See also* Johnson administration; Vietnam War
Johnson, Owen, 130
Johnson, Tom, 622, 626
Johnson, U. Alexis, 84, 330
Johnson administration: ambassadors in, 414–15; budget proposals of, 515, 542; China-Pakistan conflict,
352; civil rights legislation, 69–70, 214, 671; criticism of policies of, 234, 237; domestic programs and policies, 214, 298, 310, 325–26, 346, 534–35, 581; and the Dominican crisis, 313–15, 316–17, 319–22, 324–25; economic retaliation against press, 517; farewell receptions for, 658–59; farm price supports, 283–84; FCC vacancy, 588–89, 593–94; food aid to India, 388; foreign policies, 277, 346, 459; FPC appointees, 288–89; Goldberg's resignation, 525; Goodwin in, 573; on Guantanamo water cutoff, 233; Immigration Service scandal, 515; international opinion of, 503; JFK's cabinet and staff in, 70, 215–16, 324; legislative achievements, 279–80, 661; and McNamara, 522–23; NATO policies under, 47; Near East policies, 596; nuclear policies, 243–44; parochial school aid, 226; preparations for Nixon, 660, 661, 663; during the Six-Day War, 480–81, 484; staff of, 448–49, 673; Supreme Court vacancy, 590–91, 626, 637–38, 642, 644, 675; tax increases, 502; unemployment under, 326, 449; U.S.-Chinese relations under, 398, 443; U.S.-German relations under, 241–43, 439; U.S.-Israeli relations under, 415–16, 568, 650–51, 653–54; U.S.-Latin American relations under, 391, 473–74, 596; U.S.-Panama relations under, 225, 226, 320; U.S.-Soviet consular pact, 467; U.S.-Soviet relations under, 224–25, 239–40, 242, 260, 278, 322–23, 382–83, 415, 432–33, 439, 446–47, 450, 488–89, 495–96, 510, 595–96. *See also* Johnson, Lyndon B. (LBJ); Vietnam War
Johnston, Eric, 11–12, 33, 107

Kennedy, Joan Bennett (Ted Kennedy's wife), 165

Kennedy, Joe, Jr., 453

Kennedy, John F. "Jack" (JFK): assassination investigation, 212–13, 252, 254, 442; assassination of, 208, 209–10; assassination theories, 219, 292, 457–58, 459–60, 471–72, 518; Big Brothers' dinner, 74–76; blackmail politics, 10; and civil rights, 184, 202; conflicts with DP, 143–44, 145–46; courage of, 7; criticism of, 195–96, 202–3; and Dean Rusk, 342; DiSalle's reelection bid, 128; and Eisenhower, 51; election of 1956, 134; election of 1960, 1, 29, 30, 31–32, 42, 46–48; European trip (1961), 83; extramarital affairs of, 36, 45, 47, 51–53, 66–67, 80, 163, 176, 198, 203–4, 451, 622, 629; family tragedies, 584; first press conference, 60; Freedom Fighters rally, 160; funeral of, 210–11, 212; funeral procession, 215; General MacArthur on, 29; and Gloria Swanson, 609; health problems, 66, 85; inauguration of, 54, 58; Ireland trip (1963), 190; Italy tour (1963), 191–92; and Jackie, 80, 143–44, 621–22; and J. Edgar Hoover, 402, 564; and LBJ, 70, 186; losing liberal support, 129; oil properties of, 324; and Phil Graham, 164–65, 166; political career of, 585–86; popularity of, 37, 158, 198, 234, 254, 518; press conferences of, 662; and the race riots, 181; religion of, 38; and RFK, 464; Southern supporters of, 80–81; speaking abilities of, 240; on the steel strike, 131; talks with Adzhubei, 124; Venezuela trip (1961), 114–15; Vienna summit with Khrushchev, 55; vote buying of, 28–29; White House dinners, 172–73. *See also* Kennedy administration

Kennedy, Joseph "Joe" (JFK's father), 97, 122, 587; on the 1960 election results, 46–47; character of, 453, 584; and DP, 180–81; extramarital affairs of, 453, 609; health problems, 117, 125; helping with Jewish migrations, 44; and JFK's affairs, 52, 53, 67, 204; on Kennedy oil properties, 324

Kennedy, Robert F. "Bobby" (RFK): assassination of, 533, 583, 587; as attorney general, 70; Big Brothers' dinner, 122–23; blackmail tactics, 566; and Bolshakov, 155; and Boykin, 457; and Bridges, 294; and Castro, 457–58, 564; confirming Meriwether, 81; and the Cuban missile crisis, 120–21, 152; and the Dodd case, 380; on DP, 180–81; DP's 1961 meeting with, 101–2; DP's 1964 story on, 269; DP's characterization of, 583–84, 587–88; election of 1960, 30, 36, 46; election of 1964, 222, 251; election of 1968 announcing candidacy, 541–42, 550, 551; election of 1968 campaign, 532, 550–53, 556–58, 568–69, 572–73, 587; election of 1968 McCarthy debate, 582; extramarital affairs of, 423, 524, 564, 584; family horseback rides, 140; and FDR Jr., 573; funeral of, 584–85, 586; on Goldberg's appointment, 144; Gore Vidal's conflict with, 142; Harriman's birthday party, 439–41; and the Hoffa case, 150, 222; house hunting in DC, 107; and JFK, 86; and JFK's affairs, 176, 203; at JFK's funeral, 212, 215; and Keogh, 111, 184, 190; in Latin America, 627; and LBJ, 186, 511, 554; and McCone, 132; oil properties of, 324; political power of, 327; as possible attorney general, 52; and the President's Club funds, 449; press coverage of, 334, 361–62, 583; proposed nuclear treaty, 330; relations with Soviets, 97, 122; ruthlessness of, 134, 562, 584; steel industry investigations, 464; and Sukarno, 228; swimming pool party, 141; "Thirteen Days" article, 636, 667; during the Vietnam War, 461–63, 512–13; and wiretapping, 578, 579–81

Kennedy, Rose (JFK's mother), 212, 453, 609, 621

Kennedy administration: advisors in, 87–88, 99–100; Bay of Pigs invasion, 54, 76–79, 84, 100, 158; and the Berlin crisis, 50, 82, 84–85, 97–99, 107, 131–32, 358; blackmail politics in, 294; budget of, 167; cabinet member appointments, 48–53, 51, 70; cabinet members relationships, 86, 145; China-India conflict, 156; civil rights issues, 54, 120; consulting Harriman on Soviets, 685; criticism of, 84, 86–87, 159–60, 195–96; Cuban missile crisis, 147–48, 150–51, 152–53, 174; Cuba relations, 158; domestic policies, 80; in East Africa, 159–60; foreign policies of, 86, 126–27, 340; GM-DuPont tax deal, 293; Goldberg's Court appointment, 144–45; impact of right wing on, 91, 144; influence of sex in, 163; Iran relations, 111–12; on Laos, 72–73, 138; Latin America relations, 173; LBJ's reappointment of members of, 236, 324; and Meriwether, 68, 69, 71; military censorship, 123; and NATO's surface nuclear fleet, 187–88; on nuclear testing, 85, 101, 168, 174, 177–78, 181–82, 186, 188, 192; Pakistan relations, 111–12; recognition of Mongolia, 384; Skybolt

missile, 157; space exploration, 54, 73; space weapons ban, 197; Supreme Court appointees, 136; tax program, 168; TFX contract, 293; trade bill approval, 142; UN bond issue, 130; U.S.-Soviet relations, 72–73, 92–93, 96–99, 126–27, 193, 202–3, 206; and Vietnam, 424, 426; wheat for Poland, 127; wheat to USSR, 199; work habits of, 660. *See also* Kennedy, John F. "Jack" (JFK)

Kenney, John, 410
Kenworthy, Ed, 452
Kenya, 246–47, 272–73
Kenyatta, Jomo, 247, 272–73
Keogh, Eugene "Gene," 111, 183–84, 190, 191, 254
Keogh, Vincent, 111, 183–84, 190
Kerr, Robert "Bob," 11, 134, 293, 311, 369, 370, 460
Kerr, Walter, 19
Ketcham, Anne, 410–11
Khanh, Nguyen, 276
Khrushchev, Nikita: 1960 summit meeting collapse, 2, 20–22; and Albania, 108; alleged affair of, 178; and the *autobahn* incident, 199–200, 202; and the Berlin crisis, 84–85, 97–98, 358; on China-India conflict, 149; Cuban missile crisis, 147–48, 150–51, 152–53, 169, 174–75; defense spending under, 90, 183; de-Stalinization program of, 55; on disarmament, 132; DP's CIA briefing regarding, 103; DP's interviews of, 93, 94–96, 102, 193–95; and East Germany, 89, 358; and Eisenhower, 19, 26, 41, 655; ideas for improved U.S. relations, 206–8; and JFK, 46, 685; on Laos, 72, 138, 179, 407; and LBJ, 224; Menshikov on opposition to, 104; and Molotov, 110; New York

Ky, Nguyen Cao, 387–88, 395, 425, 463, 489, 521, 545, 589, 632, 636, 649, 666–67
KYP (Kentriki Ypiresia Pliroforion), 548–49

labor unions, 86–87, 116–17, 125–26, 155, 366, 422–24. *See also* strikes
Laird, Melvin, 625, 689, 694, 697
Lake Maracaibo, 64
Lamb, Charles, 495
La Morita (Venezuela), 114–15
Lanahan, Frances "Scottie," 143
Landauer, David, 248
Landon, Alf, 132
land reforms (South Vietnam), 533
Landrum-Griffin Act, 116–17
Lane, Mark, 442
Laos, 72–73, 98, 104, 138, 179, 407, 463, 499, 556–57
Latin America: Humphrey's policies in, 361–62; July 1968 panel at the IPA, 597–99; Rockefeller's 1969 mission to, 678; summit conference, 466, 473–74; U.S. relations with, 37, 314, 320, 325, 391, 473–74, 596, 689; and the Vietnam War, 569–70
Lausche, Frank, 42
Laval, Pierre, 354
Lavrov, Vladimir, 247
Lawford, Lady May, 154
Lawford, Peter, 154
Lawrence, David, 218
Lawrence, David L., 6
Lawrence, William "Bill," 582
Leader, Henry, 30
Lebanon, 555
Lechin, Juan, 465
Lee, H. Rex, 589
Lehmann, Arno, 100–101
Leighter, Jackson, 332
LeMay, Curtis, 196
Lemnitzer, Lyman, 70, 187–88
Leoni, Raúl, 235, 474

Lerner, Harry, 437, 516, 526, 546, 626, 627
Levin, Alex, 438
Levitt, Norman, 633–34
Lewis, Don, 65
Lewis, Fulton, Jr., 699
Lewis, John, 87, 401
libel suits: against DP, 380, 395, 397, 410–11, 452, 679; against Reagan, 526
*Liberty* (ship), 483–84, 485
Liberty Lobby, 531, 544–45, 670
Libya, 480, 555
Linares, Briceño, 316
Lincoln, Abraham, 326
Lindsay, John, 418, 602
Linowitz, Sol M., 477, 607, 678, 689, 702
Lippmann, Walter, 122, 291, 309, 327, 333, 360, 518, 662
Lisagor, Peter "Pete," 27
Livanos, Tina, 621
Lodge, George, 128, 347
Lodge, Henry Cabot, Jr.: on Argentine-Israeli conflict, 27; election of 1964, 256; and Nixon, 34, 684; opposition to LBJ's negotiation policy, 356; during Vietnam, 347, 357, 372, 387, 388, 399, 469, 513, 684
*London Mirror* (newspaper), 644
*London Times* (newspaper), 643
Long, Earl, 280
Long, Huey, 280
Long, Russell, 280, 317, 375, 485, 486
Longworth, Alice Roosevelt, 185, 273, 443
Lopez Mateos, Adolpho, 39
Lorentz, Pare, 641
Los Angeles riots, 348–50
Louis, Victor E., 435
Lovett, Robert A. "Bob," 702
Lovett, Sidney, 444
*Loving v. Virginia*, 455

Meyer, Charles, 689
Meyer, Eugene, 133, 545–46
Meyner, Robert, 31
Miami (FL), 110
*Miami Herald* (newspaper), 690
Michalowski, Jerzy, 683
Mikoyan, Anastas, 300, 302, 304, 344
military censorship, 123
Miller, Joseph, 249–50
Miller, Ray, 42
Miller, William, 150, 238, 253, 255
Millimet, Joe, 451
Mills, Wilbur, 502, 515
milo, 378, 388
Minh, Duong Van "Big," 202
minimum wage act (Puerto Rico), 55
mining industry, 63–64
*Miranda v. Arizona*, 366
Mississippi, 271–72, 284, 286
Mississippi Freedom Democrats, 535
Mitchell, John, 671, 695
MLF (multi-lateral force), 187–88, 189, 224–25, 243, 275, 617
Model Cities Bill, 661
Molotov, Vyacheslav, 39, 108, 110
*Mona Lisa* (painting), 158, 163
Monat, Harold, 565
Mondale, Walter, 557–58
Mongolia, 384
Monroe, Marilyn, 584
Monroney, Almer Stillwell "Mike," 8, 83, 369, 406–7, 472, 630
Monroney, Mary Ellen, 83
Montana State College, 141
Montgomery (AL), 81, 295
moon project, 201–2, 652
Moore, Charlie, 563
Moore, Tom, 186
Morales, Angel, 82
Morales Carrion, Arturo, 160
Morgan, Edward, 178, 203, 457–58, 459–60, 470, 563, 564
Morgan, Howard, 340–41
Morgan, Wendy, 133

Morganthau, Henry, Jr., 525, 681
Moro, Aldo, 487, 530
Morocco, 480, 555
Morse, Wayne, 171, 503, 678; in the 1960 election, 3; in the 1968 election, 630; and the Bay of Pigs invasion, 78, 79; during the Cuban missile crisis, 168; and the Dodd case, 390, 391, 411; DP's Cuban investigation request, 35; at the IPA conference, 418, 419; and JFK, 50; July 1961 dinner with DP, 88–89; and Kefauver's death, 195; on marines in the Dominican Republic, 313, 314–15; and Meriwether's nomination, 67–68; on Rhodesia, 399; and the Vietnam War, 328–29, 341, 372, 374–75, 419; vote on McCone, 123
Morton, Thruston, 502
Mosher, Clint, 702
Mosk, Stanley, 236
Moss, John E., 44, 389
Mossberg, Woodrow, Jr., 562
Mostovatz, Nikolai, 206–8
Moyers, Bill, 323, 325, 344, 377–78, 596; on the Dominican crisis, 315; feud with Valenti, 393; and the genocide convention, 398; LBJ on resignation of, 444–45; on LBJ's health, 355; on the Reynolds case, 232; and RFK, 557
Moynihan, Daniel Patrick, 279, 670
Multer, Abraham J. "Abe," 190, 213
multi-lateral force (MLF), 187–88, 189, 224–25, 243, 275, 617
Mundelein, George, 38
Mundt, Karl, 205
Muñoz Marín, Luis, 315–16, 321
Murchison, Clint, Sr., 401–2
Murphy, Bob, 513
Murphy, Charles, 135
Murray, Bob, 563
Murray, Philip, 87

Murrow, Edward R., 414
Muskie, Edmund, 591, 616, 618, 632, 643, 665, 700

NAACP (National Association for the Advancement of Colored People), 275–76, 295
El Nación (newspaper), 113
Nader, Ralph, 279, 534
Nannen, Henri, 492
Nasser, Gamal Abdel, 40, 276–77, 407, 455, 478–79, 480–84, 510, 561–62, 596
National Association for the Advancement of Colored People (NAACP), 275–76, 295
National Council of Churches, 377
National Press Club speech, 633
NATO (North Atlantic Treaty Organization), 47, 50, 152, 187–88, 322, 351, 354, 366, 404
natural gas legislation, 57
natural gas lobby, 59
NBC network, 479, 551, 625
Nedzi, Lucien, 403
Neel, William "Bill," 128, 664
Nehru, B. K., 298, 378–80
Nehru, Jawaharlal, 40, 117, 118, 149, 157, 196–97, 222
Nelson, Gaylord, 472, 693–94, 697
Neuberger, Maurine, 4, 134, 228
Newark Evening News, 545
newspaper industry: DP on monopolies in, 128; labor issues in, 125; newspaper strike (1962), 155
Newton, Huey, 366
New York (state), 534–35
New York City blackout (1965), 359–60
New York Mirror (newspaper), 155
New York Post (newspaper), 125, 155, 633, 688
New York Times (newspaper), 233, 580, 633, 679, 686, 688–89

Ngo Dinh Diem, 81, 202, 489–90
Nichols, Lou, 391
Nirenberg, Marshall W., 624
Nixon, Don, 43, 44, 528, 703
Nixon, Pat, 649, 650, 677
Nixon, Richard: on Ambassador Yost, 670; on Argentine-Israeli resolution, 27; assassination attempt (1958), 62; on the Bay of Pigs invasion, 79; and the Captive Nations Week resolution, 83; China lobby campaign contributions, 42–43; on civil rights, 617–18; criticism of, 630–31, 638; and Dr. Condon, 656; and Eisenhower, 332, 673, 702; election of 1960 campaign, 23, 32, 33, 34, 44, 45, 48; election of 1960 debates, 42; election of 1960 results, 1, 46; election of 1968 campaign, 547, 552, 600–602, 607, 622, 627, 628; election of 1968 campaign funds, 616, 620, 626, 629, 697; election of 1968 results, 533, 629–30, 632–33; first tour abroad, 672–73; inauguration of, 663–64; January 1969 White House reception, 669; and JFK's assassination, 456; at JFK's inauguration speech, 58; and LBJ, 234, 437–38, 602–3, 633, 635, 640; loan scandals, 44, 45; on McCarthy, x; mental health treatments of, 628–29, 633–34, 650; on the multi-nuclear proliferation treaty, 617–18; on race relations, 526; and riots in Italy, 681; ruthlessness of, 630; spending habits, 649, 703; steel industry strike settlement, 2; on the U-2 spy flights, 23; and Vietnam peace talks, 652, 688, 692; on the Vietnam War, 437–38, 547, 620, 632; and Warren, 674–75, 680

Nixon administration: ABM systems, 698; cabinet and staff of, 660, 668–69, 670–71; cabinet appointments, 636, 639, 643–44, 659, 698–99; civil rights under, 669–71; conflicts of interest in, 677; domestic programs of, 668, 669–70; El Paso Natural Gas case, 695; Harriman on members of, 667; Israeli-Arab peace talks, 686–87; method of operation, 698; rescinding air routes, 666, 704; Supreme Court vacancy, 605, 637, 641; U.S.-Chinese relations under, 653; U.S.-Soviet relations under, 679–80, 682, 685; on voting age changes, 672

Nobel Prize, 1, 652

Noble, Edward J., 517

Noe, Jimmy, 535

Nofziger, Franklyn "Lyn," 506, 507, 509

North Dakota, 694

North Korea, 536, 538–40, 543, 649

North Vietnam: arms suppliers to, 569; attacks on Americans, 330–31; bombing by, 686, 688; and China, 292, 364; connections with South Vietnam, 521; crossing borders during war, 556; and India, 379; refusal to cooperate with the UN, 327–28; relations with Soviet Union, 88, 289, 364, 435–36; religious conflicts in, 254–55; request for peace talks, 405; and the SEATO pact, 499; superior weapons of, 658; Tet Offensive, 532, 542, 543–45. See also Vietnam War

Novak, Robert, 507, 521, 662

Novotny, Antonin, 615

NOW (National Organization of Women), 366

Noyes, David, 507

nuclear testing: inspections issue,

134, 149, 177, 224–25; JFK's proposed ban on, 195–96, 197; JFK's resumption of, 101; JFK's suspension of, 149, 168; Khrushchev's proposed ban on, 192; LBJ's proposed ban on, 255, 278; role of politics in, 174, 188; role of trust in, 88–89, 92; Soviet resumption of, 97, 99–100, 105–6

nuclear weapons: China's development of, 254; and the Cuban missile crisis, 120–21; in Israel, 364–65; knowledge to build, 101, 225; LBJ's policies on, 243; U.S. cutback of raw materials, 243–44. See also disarmament; MLF (multilateral force)

Nugent, Patrick (LBJ's son-in-law), 367, 371, 374, 497, 575–76, 662

Nugent, Patrick Lyndon (LBJ's grandson), 497–98, 623

Nutting, Anthony, 479

OAS (Organization of American States). See Organization of American States (OAS)

O'Brien, Lawrence F. "Larry," 83, 191, 196, 566, 580, 616

Occidental Oil Company, 697

Ochs, John, 309

O'Connor, Cassie, 266–67, 438

O'Daniel, Wilbert Lee "Pappy," 367

Oder-Neisse line, 189, 192

O'Donnell, Kenneth, 196, 216

O'Hare, Michael, 410, 467–68, 485, 486

oil industry: campaign contributions by, 227, 697; and Connally, 57, 59; and Hickel, 660, 665; and LBJ, 319, 323–24, 460, 661; in the Near East, 2; in Venezuela, 85, 133

Olds, Leland, 460

Oliver, Covey T., 597–98

Onassis, Aristotle, 620, 621–22
Onassis, Jacqueline. *See* Kennedy, Jacqueline "Jackie" (JFK's wife)
OPEC (Organization of Petroleum Exporting Countries), 2
open housing bill, 661
Oppenheimer, J. Robert, 169
Oppenheimer, Katherine, 169–70
Organization of American States (OAS): Cuba in, 124, 678; during the Cuban missile crisis, 152, 153; in the Dominican crisis, 314, 315–16, 317, 319–22, 325, 366
Organization of Petroleum Exporting Countries (OPEC), 2
Orinoco Mining Company, 64
Ormsby-Gore, William, 139–40
Osenenko, John, 703
Oswald, Lee Harvey, 208–10, 209, 212–13, 218, 252, 254, 458, 459–60, 470–72
Otepka, Otto, 698–99
Otero Silva, Miguel, 113
Outland, George E., 695–96
Oval Office, 74–75
Oxner, Alton, 472, 535

pacification program (Vietnam), 533
Pakistan, 111–12, 352
Palestine Liberation Organization (PLO), 652
Paley, William "Bill," 189
Palmer, Bruce, 514
Palmer, Dean, 507
Palmer, Dwight, 10
Panama, 223, 225, 226, 228, 236, 320
Panama Canal, 226
Panama Canal Treaty, 225
Panama Treaty (1903), 230
Pan American Airways, 43, 704
*Pandora* (sailing yacht), 235
Papadopoulos, Georgios, 548–49
Papandreou, Andreas, 476, 535, 548–49

Papandreou, Margaret, 548
Pappas, Thomas, 32–33, 549, 620
Paraguay, 325
Paris: Pearsons's 1965 trip to, 353–54; Vietnam truce talks, 578, 589–90, 604, 620, 623–24, 632, 634–35, 636, 666–67, 689–90, 692
Paris summit conference (1960), 18–23
Parker, Mack Charles, 56
Parker, William, 348, 350
Pastore, John, 666
Patman, John William Wright, 445, 677
Patterson, Alicia, 79–80, 142–43, 151, 340
Patterson, Eleanor "Cissy," xix, 185
Patterson, Floyd, 122
Patton, Thomas, 464
Paul VI (pope), 413, 530
peace movement (Vietnam), 505–6
Peale, Norman Vincent, 38
pea patch (DP's), 139, 140, 428
Pearl Harbor, 642
Pearson, Andrew Russell "Drew" (DP): biographical background, xviii–xix; death of, xix, 653, 704; family tree, 705; farm of, 355, 573; finances of, 544–45, 555–56; health problems of, 354, 475–76, 531, 534, 703–4; influence of, xvii, 704; as a journalist, ix, xi–xii, xvii–xviii; libel suits against, 380, 395, 397, 410–11, 452, 679, 689; marriage and family life, 511; popularity of column, ix, xvii, xix, 653; reflections on war, 204; Veterans' Day (1963) recollections, 204; on youth in world leadership, 585–86
Pearson, Ann (DP's niece), 619
Pearson, Drew (DP's nephew), 122, 425, 533–34, 542, 657–58

Putnam Company, 544

Quaison-Sackey, Alex, 274
Quemoy Island, 42, 50, 499
Quinn, Eileen., 252

Rabin, Yitzhak, 365, 561–62, 567–68, 605–6, 656–57
race relations: equality in government positions, 69–70; impact of violence on, 558; improvements in, 136, 473; and job discrimination, 528; during Los Angeles riots, 348–50; MLK Jr.'s role in, 571–72; during San Francisco riots, 429; and *Star Trek*, 366–67; tension in the South over, 111, 618. *See also* civil rights movement; desegregation
Radford, Arthur, 637, 654–55
Radio Free Europe, 546–47
Radziwill, Prince Stanislaw, 583
Rafferty, Max, 201
Raley, Kay, 540, 619
Raskin, Marcus "Hal," 275, 337–38
Rather, Dan, 445
Ratiani, Georgi, 428–29
Ray, James Earl, 578–79, 586
Rayburn, Sam, 23, 82, 127, 450, 608
RB-47 incident, 41, 47, 60
REA (Rural Electrification Administration), 635
Reagan, Ronald, 377, 432; as California governor, 456, 505; DP's possible suit against, 526; homosexual scandal, 506, 507–9, 511, 516–17; Pat Brown on, 406; as potential presidential candidate, 546, 580; at the Republican National Convention, 600–602
Reber, Ben, 354
Rebozo, Charles "Bebe," 650, 677
*Redbook* (magazine), 629
redistricting bill, 510
Redwood National Park, 387–88, 390

Reed, Winifred, 127–28
Reedy, George, 334
Rees, Thomas, 552
Reeves, Rosser, 702
Reid, Ed, 67, 68, 180–81, 295
Reiner, Phillip, 44
Reinhardt, George Frederick "Freddie," 131
Rembrandt painting, 110
Renee, Dr., 141
Republican National Convention (1960), 32, 33–34
Republican National Convention (1968), 599–602, 600–602
Resnick, Joseph, 378, 449, 517
Reston, James "Scotty," 219, 328, 333, 334–35, 521–22, 643
Resurrection City, 587
Reuss, Henry, 44
Reuther, Walter, 32, 125–26, 237, 422, 488, 575
Reynolds, Don, 227, 230, 231, 232, 233
*Reynolds v. Sims*, 120
Rheinmetal, 400
Rhodes, James Allen, 600
Rhodesia, 399
Ribicoff, Abraham "Abe," 49, 50, 86, 121–22, 160, 687
Richardson, Elliot, 659, 668–69, 678
Richardson, Sid, 59, 402
Ridder, Marie, 143
Ridder, Walter, 133, 143
Ridgeway, Matt, 131, 413
riots: during the 1968 Democratic convention, 609–10; anti-police shootings in Cleveland, 597; during the civil rights movement, 81, 280–81, 558; following MLK Jr.'s assassination, 532, 560–61, 562–65, 568; in France, 581; in Italy, 681; in Los Angeles, 348–50; race riots of 1967, 455; in San Francisco, 429, 696; in South Vietnam, 388; in Tokyo, 24
Rivers, Lucius Mendel, 403, 522, 537

Rizzo, Frank, 563
Robb, Chuck (LBJ's son-in-law), 576, 589, 662
Robb, Lynda Bird (LBJ's daughter), 228–29, 253–54, 396, 400, 412, 576, 589, 623, 644, 645, 662–63
Robb, Roger, 699
Roberts, Chalmers, 151, 480–81, 526, 579
Roberts, Juanita, 576–77
Robertson, Absalom Willis, 68
Rockefeller, David, 85, 112, 133, 662
Rockefeller, Jeannette, 662
Rockefeller, John Davison "Jay," IV, 169, 662
Rockefeller, Laurance S., 662
Rockefeller, Margaretta "Happy," 601
Rockefeller, Mary, 33, 124, 130, 392
Rockefeller, Nelson, 172; at the 1955 Geneva Summit Conference, 654; in the 1960 election, 24, 32, 33, 46; in the 1964 election, 202, 222; in the 1966 election, 375, 438; in the 1968 election, 547, 600–602; and the Baker scandal, 203; and Bob Weaver, 124–25; cutting poverty studies, 535; divorce of, 119, 124; and Eisenhower, 23; on Eisenhower's do-nothing program, 4; extramarital affairs of, 527; in Latin America, 678; and Nixon, 636; use of wealth, 587–88; and the wheat deal, 205
Rodgers, Buck, 333
Rogan, Richard, 626
Rogers, William P. "Bill," 56, 332, 659, 670–71, 678, 682, 684–85, 699
Romania, 293, 589–90, 610, 615, 620
Romney, George W., 126, 168, 202, 424, 438, 501, 600–602, 661, 668, 670
Rooney, John J., 384, 414
Roosevelt, Eleanor, 120, 136, 148
Roosevelt, Elliott, 255–56

Roosevelt, Franklin, Jr., 53, 235–36, 327, 375, 536, 573, 691–92
Roosevelt, Franklin D. (FDR): compared to LBJ, 236; and de Gaulle, 409–10, 476; and DP, x; and the Grand Coulee Dam, 695; Harriman on, 348; health of, 475; Hopkins as advisor to, 570; influence of Catholic Church over, 38; on Joe Kennedy, 453; mistresses of, 629; and Sumner Welles, 351
Roosevelt, James "Jimmy," 148, 189, 226, 235–36, 347
Roosevelt, Sue, 691
Roosevelt, Theodore "Teddy," 417, 597
Rosenhaus, Matty, 368
Rosensteel, Lou, 391
Rosenthal, Jack, 380
Ross, Charles, 288–89
Rostow, Elspeth, 217–18
Rostow, Walt: as advisor to LBJ, 217–18, 416, 510, 570; DP on, 126, 559; and the Glassboro conference, 493; on JFK's administration, 84–85, 87–88; on LBJ's relations with Soviet Union, 595–96; and Papandreou, 476; and the *Pueblo* crisis, 540–41; on U.S.-Israeli relations, 568; on U.S.-Soviet relations, 492; on Vietnam, 426, 461
Roudebaugh, Charles, 507
Rowe, Jim, 638
Roy, Alphonse, 451
Ruby, Jack, 209, 470–72
Rural Electrification Administration (REA), 635
Rusk, Dean, 70, 83, 148, 172, 178, 285, 409, 434, 460, 591, 650, 663; on American honor, 350–51; and the Bay of Pigs invasion, 76, 84; and China, 254, 398, 426, 443–44; criticism of, 175, 196, 384, 682; and the Cuban missile crisis, 152, 667;

and de Gaulle, 366; and the Dodd case, 401; and the Dominican crisis, 316–17; farewell receptions for, 658–59; firing Otepka, 699; on foreign policy, 203; and Fulbright, 238, 554; and the Glassboro conference, 493; and Goldberg, 108–9, 398, 399; at the IPA conference, 418–19; and JFK, 86; and John P. Davies, 672; and LBJ, 313, 379, 520, 574; and the *Pueblo* incident, 543; reported resignation of, 235, 539; as secretary of state, 342, 585; staff of, 355; on the Straits of Tiran, 480–81; and U.S.-Soviet relations, 199–200, 224, 275, 382–83, 407–8, 492; and the Vietnam War, 303, 307, 330, 346, 374, 407–8, 462, 513, 526, 549, 579, 689; and Walter Judd, 160; on Yugoslavia, 180

Rusk, Virginia, 658

Russell, Donald S., 250, 311

Russell, Mary, 178, 681

Russell, Richard "Dick," 60, 196, 236, 270, 345–46, 482, 512, 637

Russia. *See* Soviet Union (USSR)

Rustin, Bayard, 586

Ruth, Babe, 55

Rutherford, Luci, 629

Ryan, Ed, 211, 403

Sabin, Albert, 120

Sagan, Carl, 366–67

Salinger, Pierre, 51, 115, 116, 125, 163, 177, 401; during 1960 election, 36; on the Cuban crisis, 78; on desegregation, 73; and the Dodd case, 420–21; eavesdropping of, 582; on Khrushchev, 139; political ambitions of, 235–36; as press secretary for LBJ, 214, 215; resignation of, 235; on the Secret Service story, 211; on visit with Adzhubei, 124

Salisbury, Harrison, 452

Saltonstall, Leverett, 123, 195

Salvatori, Henry, 546

Sammons, Herbert, 505

Sandys, Duncan, 159

SANE (National Committee for a Sane Nuclear Policy), 275

San Francisco, 255, 429

San Francisco State College, 695–96

Sanger, Richard "Dick," 37

Santaella, Hector, 63

Santora, Doris, 176

Sapir, Pinhas, 367

Satukov, Pavel A., 259

Saudi Arabia, 2, 222

Sayre, Dean Francis, Jr., 336

Schenley Industries Liquor Company, 391

Scheuer, James "Jim," 484, 553

Schlesinger, Arthur, Jr., 100, 143–44, 342, 348, 421

Schlesinger, Elmer, 185

Schröder, Gerhard, 338

Schultz, Henry, 368

Schutz, Klaus, 610

Schwallenbach, Law, 106

Schwirkmann, Horst, 260

Scott, Hugh, 81, 99–100

Scranton, William "Bill," 253

Seale, Bobby, 366

seat belt laws, 279

SEATO (Southeast Asia Treaty Organization), 159, 499

SEC (Securities and Exchange Commission), 90

Secret Service, 211, 241, 252

Sedita, Frank, 375

Sedov, Boris, 543

Selassie, Haile (emperor of Ethiopia), 246

Selden, Armistead, 171, 173

Selma (AL), 294–95, 297, 395

Seltzer, Louis, 128, 129

Senghor, Leopold, 429

seniority system (U.S. Congress), 535

Stevenson, John, 347
Stewart, Patrick, 364
Stewart, Potter, 588, 631
Stewart, Tom, 171
Stimson, Henry L., 101, 106–7
Stoessel, Walter John, Jr., 302
*Story of a Small Planet* (play), 142
St. Paul's Chapel (England) dedication, 45
Strauss, Franz Josef, 18, 240
Strauss, Lewis, 101
Strauss, Peter, 552
Strauss, Robert "Bob," 45, 654–55
strikes: airline strike, 419–20; aluminum strike, 326; in the auto industry, 117, 125–26; coal miners' strike, 351; in France, 579; in Great Britain, 692; maritime strike, 86–87; newspaper strike, 155; steel strike, 2, 131, 133
Studebaker strike, 125–26
subway bill (1963), 213
Suez Canal, 479, 481, 482, 506, 596, 657, 703
Sukarno, 40, 277, 282, 375, 427, 681
Sullivan, Charles, 498–99
Sullivan, Ed, 485
Sullivan, Tom, 400
Sullivan, William H. "Bill," 254–55, 613
"Summer of Love" (1967), 455
Summersby, Kay, 702
Supreme Court (U.S.): assigning of opinions, 154–55; ban of public prayer, 120, 142; changing role of, 477–78; chief justice vacancy, 590, 591–92, 635–36, 640–41; during the Cuban missile crisis, 154; expansion of civil liberties, 366; Goldberg's appointment to, 144–45; importance of, 251; JFK's appointees to, 136; Marshall as first African American on, 455; members of, 185–86; and Nixon, 631; open housing provision, 588; on race-based marriage restrictions, 455; on reapportioning seats, 120; on segregation, 54; Warren's resignation from, 673–75, 680
Suslov, Mikhail, 258, 299, 304, 614
Svoboda, Ludvik, 608, 614–15
Swanson, Gloria, 67, 453, 609
Sylvester, Arthur, 291, 389, 403
Symington, Evelyn, 230
Symington, Stuart, 28, 32, 123, 195, 230, 375, 473, 697
Syria, 137, 248, 437, 439, 480–84, 555
Szilard, Leo, 169–70, 174

Taft, Robert "Bob," 635
Taiwan, 131, 142, 436, 469
Talbot, Philip, 476
Tamm, Quinn, 563–64
Tana, Lake (Ethiopia), 246
Tankersley, Ruth "Bazy," 201
Taper, S. Mark, 369
Tapp, Jessie, 51
Tate, James, 202
Taylor, C. Randolph, 553
Taylor, Harold, 330
Taylor, Hobart, Jr., 552–53
Taylor, Maxwell, 276, 306, 307, 325–26, 330, 426, 513
Taylor, Tip, 6
Teamsters, 213, 422
Tejera Paris, Enrique, 62, 234–35, 314, 474, 489, 523, 597–98
television, 1, 120
television networks, 8
Temple, Larry, 596–97
Tenure, Pamela, 176, 203–4
Tet Offensive, 532, 542, 543–44, 545
Texas, 82
Texas University, 549
TFX (Tactical Fighter Experimental) contract, 186, 293, 369–70
Thatcher, Herbert, 18
Thayer, Charles, 686, 687–88

Thiêu, Nguyen Van, 527–28, 529, 589, 632, 666–67, 683
"Thirteen Days" (Kennedy), 636, 667
Thomas, Albert, 135
Thompson, Frank, 689
Thompson, Jane, 270, 447, 668
Thompson, Lawn, 476, 531
Thompson, Llewellyn "Tommy": appointment to Moscow, 430; on the *autobahn* incident, 199–200; Cuban missile crisis, 153; Dobrynin's praise for, 138; Glassboro conference, 492, 493; on Khrushchev, 149–50; LBJ on, 447; and *Pueblo* crisis, 539; retirement of, 668; during Six-Day War, 482–83; on Soviet-Chinese split, 182–83, 382–83; on Soviet politics, 182–83, 260–61, 274; U-2 incident, 358–59; on U.S.-Soviet relations, 442; and the Vietnam War, 289, 292–93, 356
Thornberry, William Homer, 594–95
Thornton, Charles Bates "Tex," 549
Thurmond, Strom, 99, 197, 311, 600, 601, 602, 631, 643, 670, 699
*Ticonderoga* (ship), 223
Tidelands Oil, 661
Timberlake, Clare H., 37
*Time* (magazine), 1, 545
Tito, Josip Broz, 40, 105, 180, 198, 296, 373, 381
Tokyo (Japan) riots, 24
tourism industry, 287–88
Tower, John G., 82, 125
Townsend, Kathleen Kennedy (RFK's daughter), 101, 102, 140
trade bill (1962), 142
training programs, 540, 541, 552–53
Trapnell, Ed, 100–101
Travell, Janet, 229
Tree, Marietta, 330, 338, 340
Trippe, Juan, 136
Trout, Damon, 176
Troyanovsky, Oleg, 259

truck lobby, 597
Trudeau, Arthur, 123, 124
*True* (magazine), 676
Trujillo, Rafael, 37, 60–61, 82–83
Truman, Harry S., 129, 197, 354, 450; in the 1960 campaign, 28, 29, 41–42; health of, 256, 507; and Louis Johnson, 391–92; on the Panama Canal, 223; praise for, 351; and staff members, 525; work habits of, 660
Truman Library, 693
Tshombe, Moise, 118, 159–60
tularemic fever, 338
Tully, Andrew, 374
Tumulty, Joe, 119
*Turner Joy* (ship), 223
Tuttle, Elbert, 184
Twenty-Fifth Amendment, 456
Twenty-Fourth Amendment, 222
Tydings, Millard, 457

U-2 incident, 2, 12–13, 20–23, 26, 41, 358–59
Udall, Stewart, 78, 168–69, 201–2, 319, 324, 665, 668
Ulbricht, Walter, 588, 607
UN (United Nations). *See* United Nations (UN)
unemployment: effects on crime, 400; under LBJ, 326, 449; programs to counter, 376–77, 540, 541
Union Oil, 626–27
unions. *See* labor unions
United Nations (UN): Adlai Stevenson's role in, 339; and China, 364, 419, 437, 443–44; and the Cuban missile crisis, 152–53; disarmament talks, 364; Dobrynin on, 580; and the Dominican crisis, 315–16; Eisenhower's September 1960 speech at, 41; Goldberg's work in, 519, 572; Indonesia's removal from, 282; JFK's bond issue, 130; and the Katanga crisis, 159–60;

ban talks, 149, 177–78, 181–82, 278; observers proposal, 206; and proposed elections in Vietnam, 306–7; and the *Pueblo* crisis, 539–40, 543; respective arms budget cuts, 281; role of parity in, 442; Soviet missile unveiling (1967), 510; Soviet planes over Alaska, 174–75; Soviet weapons in Vietnam, 322–23, 658; and space exploration, 197; and spying, 415; suggestions for improving, 155, 206–8, 239–40; and Vietnam peace efforts, 330, 344, 346–47, 474–75, 624; Vietnam War's impact on, 356–57, 428–29, 554–55, 605–6; visiting Soviet students on, 404–5

U.S. Steel, 43, 63–64, 131

U Thant: during Arab-Israeli conflicts, 478, 484; during the Cuban missile crisis, 147; and Goldberg, 374; at JFK's funeral, 232; and Khrushchev, 262; Vietnam peace negotiations, 343, 346, 360, 405–6, 407, 570, 578

Vaki, Viron, 678

Valenti, Jack, 263, 307, 319, 332, 440; on Bobby Kennedy's staff, 573; and LBJ, 412–13; on LBJ and Dirksen, 468; leaving the White House, 393; and the Lincoln Memorial ceremony, 216; on the McCarthy race, 524; on McNamara's resignation, 523; on Nixon, 658; on Nugent's transfer, 371

Valenti, Mary Margaret, 136, 147, 468

Vance, Cyrus, 186, 625, 684, 690

Vanocur, Sander "Sandy," 583

Vaughn, Jack, 322, 627

Venezuela: Betancourt government, 133; Communism in, 113; and Cuba, 234–35; during the Dominican crisis, 314, 325; DP's 1961 trips to, 60–65, 112–15; JFK's 1961 trip to, 114–15; oil industry in, 85, 133; in OPEC, 2

Veterans' Day (1963) recollections, 204

Vichnevski, Sergei, 245

Victor (Russian interpreter), 95

Vidal, Gore, 141–42

Vienna, 613–15

Vietnam War: attempts at peace during, 360, 367, 461–63, 500, 526–28, 530, 545, 564, 566–67, 569–71, 577–78, 597, 619–20, 636, 682–84; attempts at peace talks by Hanoi, 405–6, 407, 533–34; B-52 bombing mission, 328; bombing by North Vietnam, 393–94, 686, 688; bombing during, 286–87, 373–74, 420, 431, 446–47, 500, 609, 682; bombing halts, 496, 688–89; bombing strategy during, 500; casualties in, 360, 589; China in, 292–93; connection to Bay of Pigs, 393, 424; credibility gap, 452; demilitarized zone, 420; Eisenhower on U.S. need to win, 430; events leading up to, 499; fake SAM site, 342–44; Fulbright proposal, 328; Galbraith on escalation of, 426; Gulf of Tonkin incident, 223; Gulf of Tonkin Resolution, 374–75; Humphrey on chances for peace, 521; impact of bombing on peace talks, 462; impact on U.S. politics, 632; India's position on, 378–79; international opinion on, 295–97, 532; JCS's recommendation of germ warfare in, 338; LBJ's advisors during, 325–26, 335–36, 372, 388, 510–14, 548; LBJ's defense of, 308–10, 589; LBJ's policy in, 312, 351–52, 413–17, 496; LBJ's role in peace talks, 595–96; Nixon's policy in, 652; North Vietnam tactics in,

Vietnam War (*cont.*)
556–57; number of U.S. troops in,
517; obstacles in peace talks, 689–
90; Paris peace talks, 589–90, 604,
620, 621, 622–24, 634–35, 666–67,
689–90, 692; peace movement,
505–6; Premier Ky in, 387, 489;
prisoners of war, 419, 571; public
opinion of, 330–31, 364, 455, 532;
role of American honor in, 350–51;
role of the UN in, 327–28, 340–41,
342, 345–47, 436–37; South Vietnamese troops in, 650; Soviet role
in peace talks, 435–36, 439; student
protests of, 279; Tet Offensive, 532,
542, 543–44, 545; use of gas in, 303;
U.S. foreign relations impacted by,
501; U.S. justifications for, 331–32,
384–85; and U.S. role in Germany,
427; U.S.-Soviet relations during,
289, 328–30, 435, 458–59; U.S.-
Soviet relations impacted by, 300,
301–2, 305–6, 356–57, 428–29, 474–
75, 490, 554–55, 605–6; view of
Americans in Vietnam, 425; weap-
ons comparisons, 657–58. *See also*
North Vietnam; South Vietnam
Vinson, Carl, 522
Vinson, Fred, 106, 380, 508, 701
Vishnevski, Sergei, 428, 474–75
vocational training bill (1963), 214
Voice of America treaty, 196–97
Volpe, John, 643
Voorhees, Douglas, 110
Voroshilov, Kliment, 108
voting age, 672
Voting Rights Bill, 661
Vournas, George, 211–12
Vournas, Helen, 211–12
Vournas, Vasso, 88
*Het Vrije Volk* (newspaper), 644

Wabash Cannonball, 572–73
Wagner, Robert F. "Bob," Jr., 327

Waldman, Jules, 113
Waldo, Thayer, 143
Waldrop, Frank, 680–81
Walker, John "Johnny," III, 110
Wallace, George, 161, 181, 295, 297,
526
Wallace, Henry, 106–7, 618
Wallace, Lurleen, 395, 618
Wallenberg, Leo, 134
*Wall Street Journal* (newspaper), 678
Waltman, Frank, 626
Walton, William "Bill," 46–47, 131,
158–59, 195–96, 220, 227–28, 254,
292, 392
Ward, Stephen, 187
Warren, Charles, 505
Warren, Earl: 1967 trip to Bolivia,
465–66; on the 1968 election, 577,
616; American Jewish Committee dinner, 396–97; Black Sea
trip, 178, 193–94; at Churchill's
funeral, 676–77; criticism of,
469; and the Dodd case, 400;
on Goldberg's resignation, 525;
health of, 251; on JFK assassination theories, 459–60; and LBJ,
498, 560; on lobbies, 551; on making speeches, 128–29; and Nixon,
641, 644, 664, 674–75; on the
Nixon administration, 669–70,
670–71, 677; on Nixon's first foreign tour, 672–73; and Pat Brown,
200–201; picketing of, 231; on the
race riots, 568; resignation of,
590, 591, 605, 631, 644, 673–75,
680; on role of the Supreme
Court, 477–78; and Tom Dewey,
569; White House birthday party
for, 381; White House dinner
honoring, 537–39
Warren, Nina, 193, 251, 538, 677
Warren Commission, 252, 254, 292,
442, 471, 518, 681
Washington, George, 530

## Other works by Peter Hannaford

*Presidential Retreats*

*Reagan's Roots*

*Ronald Reagan and His Ranch: The
Western White House, 1981–89*

*The Quotable Calvin Coolidge*

*The Essential George Washington*

*The Quotable Ronald Reagan*

*My Heart Goes Home: A Hudson
Valley Memoir (editor)*

*Recollections of Reagan*

*Remembering Reagan (coauthor)*

*Talking Back to the Media*

*The Reagans: A Political Portrait*